ISBN 978-1-332-93654-0
PIBN 10440061

1 MONTH OF
FREE
READING

at
www.ForgottenBooks.com

By purchasing this book you are eligible for one month membership to ForgottenBooks.com, giving you unlimited access to our entire collection of over 700,000 titles via our web site and mobile apps.

To claim your free month visit:
www.forgottenbooks.com/free440061

THE
MARROW
OF
MODERN DIVINITY,
In Two PARTS.

PART I.

Touching both the COVENANT OF WORKS, and the COVENANT OF GRACE: With their Use and End, both in the Time of the Old Testament, and in the Time of the New. Clearly describing the WAY to eternal Life by JESUS CHRIST.

In a DIALOGUE betwixt

EVANGELISTA, a Minister of the Gospel,
NOMISTA, a Legalist,
ANTINOMISTA, an Antinomian, and
NEOPHITUS, a young Christian.

By EDWARD FISHER, A. M.
THE EIGHTH EDITION,
With NOTES,

By that eminent and faithful Servant of JESUS CHRIST,

Mr THOMAS BOSTON,

Late Minister of the Gospel at ETTRICK.

To which is added,

The TWELVE QUERIES, which were proposed to the *Twelve Marrow-men*, by the COMMISSION of the GENERAL ASSEMBLY of the CHURCH of SCOTLAND, 1721. With the *Marrow-men's Answers* to said *Queries*.

2 COR. xiii. 8. *For we can do nothing against the Truth, but for the Truth.*

FALKIRK:
Printed and sold by PATRICK MAIR.
M,DCC.LXXXIX.

Mr CARYL's Recommendation and Imprimatur.

I HAVE perused this ensuing Dialogue, and find it tending to peace and holiness; the author endeavouring to reconcile and heal those unhappy differences, which have lately broken out afresh amongst us, about the points therein handled and cleared: for which cause, I allow it to be printed, and recommend it to the reader, as a discourse stored with many necessary and seasonable truths, confirmed by scripture, and avowed by many approved writers: all composed in a familiar, plain, moderate stile, without bitterness against, or uncomely reflections upon, others: which flies have lately corrupted many boxes of (otherwise precious) oinment.

May 1. 1645.

JOSEPH CARYL.

THE

PREFACE.

WHOSOEVER thou art, to whose hands this book
shall come, I presume to put thee in mind of the
divine command, binding on thy conscience, Deut. i. 17.
" Ye shall not respect persons in judgment, but you shall
" hear the small as well as the great." Reject not the
book with contempt, nor with indignation neither, when
thou findest it intituled, *The Marrow of Modern Divinity*,
left thou do it to thine own hurt. Remember, that our
blessed Lord himself was accounted " a friend of publicans and sinners," Mat. xi. 19. " Many said of him,
He hath a devil, and is mad; why hear ye him?" John
x. 20. The apostle Paul was slanderously reported to be
an Antinomian; one who, by his doctrine, encouraged
men to do evil, Rom. iii. 8. and made void the law,
verse 31. And the first martyr, in the days of the
gospel, was stoned for pretended " blasphemous words
against Moses, and against the law," Acts vi. 11, 13.

The gospel method of sanctification, as well as of
justification, lies so far out of the ken of natural reason,
that if all the rationalists in the world, philosophers and
divines, had consulted together to lay down a plan, for
repairing the lost image of God, in man, they had never
hit on that which the divine wisdom hath pitched upon,
viz. That sinners should be sanctified in Christ Jesus,
1 Cor. i. 2. by faith in him, Acts xxvi. 18. Nay, being
laid before them, they would have rejected it with dis-
dain, as foolishness, 1 Cor. i. 23.

In all views, which fallen man hath, towards the
means of his own recovery, the natural bent is to the
way of the covenant of works. This is evident in the
case of the vast multitudes throughout the world embracing Judaism, Paganism, Mahometanism, and Popery.
All this agree in this one principle, " That it is by doing
men

men muft live," tho' they hugely differ as to the things to be done for life.

The Jews, in the time of Julian the apoftate, attempted to rebuild their temple, after it had lain many years in ruins, by the decree of heaven never to be built again; and ceafed not, till, by an earthquake, which fhook the old foundation, and turned all down to the ground, they were forced to forbear, as Socrates the hiftorian tells us, *lib.* 3. *cap* 20. But the Jews were never more addicted to that temple, than mankind naturally is, to be building on the firft covenant; and Adam's children will by no means quit it, until mount Sinai, where they defire to work what they do work, be all on a fire about them. O that thefe, who have been frighted from it, were not fo ready to go back towards it.

Howbeit, that can never be the channel of fanctification, what way foever men prepare it, and fit it out for that purpofe; becaufe it is not, by divine appointment, the miniftration of righteoufnefs and life, 2 Cor. iii.

And hence it is always to be obferved, that as the doctrine of the gofpel is corrupted, to introduce a more rational fort of religion, the flood of loofenefs and licentioufnefs fwells proportionably; infomuch that mortality brought in for doctrine, in room and ftead of the gofpel of the grace of God, never fails to be, in effect, a fignal for an inundation of immorality in practice. A plain inftance hereof, is to be feen in the grand apoftafy from the truth and holinefs of the gofpel, *viz.* Popery: and on the other hand, real and thorow reformation in churches is always the effect of gofpel-light breaking forth again from under the cloud which had gone over it; and hereof the church of Scotland among others, hath oftener than once had comfortable experience.

The real friends of true holinefs do then exceedingly miftake their meafures, in affording a handle, on any occafion whatfoever, for advancing the principles of

Legal-

Legalism; for bringing under contempt the good old way, in which our fathers found reft to their fouls, and for removing the ancient land-marks which they fet.

It is now about fourfcore years fince this book made its firft entrance into the world, under the title of *The Marrow of Modern Divinity*, at that time, not unfitly prefixed to it: but it is too evident, it hath outlived the fitnefs of that title. The truth is, the divinity therein taught, is no more the *modern*, but the *ancient* divinity, as it was recovered from underneath the antichriftian darknefs; and as it ftood, before the tools of the late refiners on the Proteftant doctrine were lifted up upon it; a doctrine which, being from God, muft needs be according to godlinefs

It was to contribute towards the preferving of this doctrine, and the withftanding of its being run down, under the odious name of Antinomianifm, in the difadvantageous fituation it hath in this book, whofe undeferved lot it is to be every-where fpoken againft, that the following notes were written.

And herein two things chiefly, have had weight. One is, Left that doctrine, being put into fuch an ill name, fhould become the object of the fettled averfion of fober perfons; and they be thereby betrayed into Legalifm. The other is, Left in thefe days of God's indignation, fo much appearing in fpiritual judgments, fome taking up the principles of it, from the hand of this author and ancient divines, for truth; fhould take the fenfe, fcope, and defign of them, from (now) common fame; and fo be betrayed into real Antinomianifm.

Reader, Lay afide prejudices, look and fee with thine own eyes, call things by their own names, and do not reckon Anti-Baxterianifm, or Anti-Neonomianifm to be Antinomianifm; and thou fhalt find no Antinomianifm taught here; but thou wilt perhaps be furprized to find, that that tale is told of Luther, and other famous Pro.

teftant

teſtant divines, under the borrowed name of the deſpiſed *E. F.* the author of the *Marrow of Modern Divinity.*

For thy eaſe and benefit in this edition, the book is divided into Chapters and Sections, greater and leſſer, according to the ſubject-matter, with running Titles, not uſed in any addition of it heretofore : Typographical errors, not a few, are by comparing of copies of ſeveral impreſſions, here corrected : the periods, which in many places were ſomewhat indiſtinct, are, thro' the whole, more carefully diſtinguiſhed, to the rendering of the ſenſe of the author more clear : the letters of reference, brought into the Edinburgh edition 1718, for avoiding of the ſide margin, which preceding editions had, are here retained for the ſame reaſon ; and ſo are the ſcripture texts in the body of the book, which were there brought from the ſide margin of fore-going im-preſſions ; the proper places being aſſigned to ſuch of them as were found to be miſplaced. The appendix is reſerved for the ſecond part, where the author himſelf placed it.

As for the notes, in them, words, phraſes, and things are explained ; truth cleared, confirmed and vindicated : the annotator making no bones of declaring his diſſent from the author, where he ſaw juſt ground for it.

I make no queſtion but he will be thought by ſome to have conſtructed too favourably of ſeveral paſſages : but, as it is nothing ſtrange, that he incline to the charitable ſide, the book having been many years ago bleſſed of God to his own ſoul ; ſo, if he hath erred on that ſide, it is the ſafeſt of the two, for thee and me, judging of the words of another man, whoſe ends, I be-lieve with Mr Burroughs, to have been *very ſincere for God, and the reader's good.* However, I am ſatisfied he has dealt candidly in that matter, according to his light.

Be adviſed always to read over a leſſer ſection of the book, before reading any of the notes thereupon, that you may have the more clear underſtanding of the whole.

I

I conclude this preface, in, the, words of, two eminent
profeſſors of theology, deſerving our ſerious regard.

"I dread mightily that a rational ſort of religion is
"coming in among us: I mean by it, a religion that
"conſiſts in a bare attendance on outward duties and
"ordinances, without the power of godlineſs; and thence
"people ſhall fall into a way of ſerving God, which is
"mere deiſm, having no relation to Chriſt Jeſus, and
"the Spirit of God." Memoirs of Mr Haliburton's
Life, page 199.

"*Admoneo igitur vos*, &c. *i. e.* Therefore I warn
"you, and each one of you, eſpecially ſuch as are to
"be directors of the conſcience, that you exerciſe your-
"ſelves in ſtudy, reading, meditation and prayer, ſo as
"you may be able to inſtruct and comfort both your
"own and others conſciences in the time of temptation;
"and to bring them back from the law to grace; from
"the active (or working) righteouſneſs to the paſſive
"(or received) righteouſneſs: in a word, from Moſes
"to Chriſt." *Luth. comment. in epiſt. ad Gal.* p. 27.
April, 1726.

To the R E A D E R.

IF thou wilt pleaſe to peruſe this little book, thou ſhalt
find great worth in it.   There is a line of a gracious
ſpirit drawn through it, which hath faſtened many precious truths together, and preſented them to thy view:
according to the variety of mens ſpirits. the various ways
of preſenting known truths are profitable.   The grace
of God hath helped this author in making his works; if
it in like manner help thee in reading, thou ſhalt have
cauſe to bleſs God for theſe truths thus brought to thee,
and for the labours of this good man, whoſe ends, I
believe, are very ſincere for God and thy good.

JER. BURROUGHS.

ADVERTISEMENT.

WHEREAS it hath been handed about, and by some publifhed, to diminifh the credit of the enfuing book, That the author Edward Fifher, was a poor illiterate barber, without any authority to vouch it; it is thought proper to prefix the following account of him, from Wood's *Athenæ Oxonienfis*, Vol. II. p 198.

" Edward Fifher, the eldeft fon of a knight, became
" a gentleman-commoner of Brazen-nofe college, Aug. 25.
" 1627 took on his degree in Arts, and foon after left
" that houfe. Afterwards, being called home by his
" relations, who were then, as I have been informed,
" much in debt; he improved that learning, which he
" had obtained in the univerfity, fo much, that he be-
" came a noted perfon among the learned, for his great
" reading in ecclefiaftical hiftory, and in the fathers, and
" for his admirable fkill in the Greek and Hebrew
" languages. His works are,

" I. An appeal to the confcience, as thou wilt an-
" fwer it at the great and dreadful day of Jefus Chrift.
" Oxford, 1644. Quarto.

" II. The Marrow of Modern Divinity. 1646.
" Octavo.

" III. A Chriftian caveat to old and new Sabbata-
" rians. 1650.

" IV. An anfwer to fixteen queries, touching the
" rife and obfervation of Chriftmas."

OCcafionally, lighting upon this dialogue, under the approbation of a learned and judicious divine ; I was thereby induced to read it, and afterwards, on a ferious confideration of the ufefulnefs of it, to commend it to the people in my public miniftry.

Two things in it efpecially took with me : Firft, The matter, the main fubftance being diftinctly to difcover the nature of the two covenants, upon which all the myfteries, both of the law and gofpel, depend. To fee the firft Adam to be *primus fœderatus* in the one ; and the fecond Adam in the other : to diftinguifh rightly betwixt the law ftanding alone as a covenant, and ftanding in fubordination to the gofpel as a fervant ; this I affure myfelf to be the key, which opens the hidden treafure of the gofpel. As foon as God had given Luther but a glimfe hereof, he profeffed that he feemed to be brought into Paradife again ; and the whole face of the fcripture to be changed to him * : and he looked upon every truth with another eye.

Secondly, the manner ; becaufe it is an *irenicum,* and tends to an accommodation and a right underftanding. Times of reformation have always been times of divifion : Satan will caft out a flood after the woman, as knowing that more die by the difagreement of the humours of their own bodies, than by the fword ; and that, if men be once engaged, they will contend, if not for truth, yet for victory.

Now, if the defference be in things of leffer confequence, the beft way to quench it, were filence. This was Luther's counfel, given in an epiftle written to the divines affembled in a fynod at Nuremberg : *Meum confilium fuerit (cum nullum fit ecclefiæ periculum) ut hanc caufam finatis, vel ad tempus fpitam (utinam extinctam) jacere, donec tutiore et meliore tempore, animis in pace firmatis, et charitate adunatis, eam difputetis.* I think it were good counfel concerning many of the difputes of our times. But

---

* Portis apertis Paradifum intraffe. Tom. i.

But if the difference be of greater concernment than this is, the beſt way to decide it, is to bring in more light; which this author hath done, with much evidence of ſcripture, backed with the authority of moſt modern divines: ſo that whoſoever deſires to have his judgment cleared in the main controverſy between us and the Antinomians, with a ſmall expence, either of money, or time, he may here receive ample ſatisfaction. This I teſtify upon requeſt, profeſſing myſelf a friend both to truth and peace.

November 12.   **W. STRONG.**

✳✳✳✳✳✳✳✳✳✳✳✳✳✳✳✳✳

To the R E A D E R.

THIS book, at firſt well accommodated with ſo valuable a teſtimony as Mr. Caryl's; beſides its better approving itſelf to the choice ſpirits every where, by the ſpeedy diſtribution of the whole impreſſion; it might ſeem a needleſs or ſuperfluous thing, to add any more to the praiſe thereof: yet meeting with detracting language from ſome few, (by reaſon of ſome phraſes, by them either not duly pondered, or not rightly underſtood) it is thought meet, in this ſecond impreſſion, to relieve that worthy teſtimony, which ſtill ſtands to it, with freſh ſupplies; not for any need the truth, therein contained, hath thereof, but becauſe either the prejudice or darkneſs of ſome mens judgments doth require it: I therefore, having thoroughly peruſed it, cannot but teſtify, that, if I have any the leaſt judgment, or reliſh of truth, " he that finds this book, finds a good thing," and not unworthy of its title; and may account the ſaints to have obtained favour with the Lord in the miniſtration of it; as that, which, with great plainneſs and evidence of truth, compriſes the chief (if not all the) differences that have been lately ingendered about the law. It hath, I muſt confeſs, not only fortified my judgment, but alſo warmed my heart, in the reading of

it;

it; as indeed inculcating throughout the whole dialogue, the clear and familiar notion of thofe things, by which we live, (as Ezek. xvi. fpeaks in another cafe) and it appeareth to me, to be written from much experimental knowledge of Cnrift, and teaching of the Spirit. Let all men, that tafte the fruit of it, confefs, to the glory of God, "He is no refpecter of perfons; and endeavour to "know no man henceforth after the flefh," nor envy the compiler thereof the honour to be accounted, as God hath made him in this point, a healer of breaches, and a reftorer of the overgrown paths of the gofpel. As for my own part, I am fo fatisfied in this teftimony I lend, that I reckon whatever credit is thus pawned will be a glory to the name that ftands by, and avows this truth, fo long as the book fhall endure to record it.

JOSHUA SPRIGGE.

X X X X X X X X X X X X X X X X X

Grace and peace to you in Chrift Jefus.

My loving Friend in Chrift,

I Have, according to your defire, read over your book, and find it full of evangelical light and life; and I doubt not, but the oftener I read it, the more true comfort I fhall find in the knowledge of Chrift thereby; the matter is pure, the method is apoftolical; wherein the works of love, in the right place, after the life of faith, be effectually required. God hath endowed his *Fifher*, with the net of a trying underftanding, and difcerning judgment and difcretion; whereby, out of the cryftaline ftreams of the well of life, you have taken a mefs of the fweeteft and wholefomeft fifh that the world can afford; which if I could daily have enough of, I fhould not care for the flefh, or the works thereof.

SAMUEL PRITTIE.

THIS book came to my hand by a merciful and moſt unexpected diſpoſure of providence, and I read it with great and ſweet complacence. It is now entierly out of print, tho' much deſired, and highly prized by many exerciſed to godlineſs, who had the happineſs to ſee and peruſe it. But, in regard one copy could not ſerve many, and the demands for it are ſtrong by ſundry excellent ones of the earth, and ſome perſons of a clear diſcerning in theſe moſt neceſſary and weighty matters; the motion of a new impreſſion fell in, as a native reſult from deſires of more light, excited by the ſpirit of truth in the hearts of wiſdom's chi'dren, and ſome of theſe endowed with learning, as well as piety. It contains a great deal of the marrow of revealed and goſpel truth, ſelected from authors of great note, clearly enlightened, and of moſt digeſted experience; and ſome of them were honoured to do eminent and heroical ſervices in their day. Thus the Chriſtian reader hath the flower of their labours communicated to him very briefly, yet clearly and powerfully. And the manner of conveyance, being by way of amicable conference, is not only fitted to afford delight to the judicious reader, but layeth him alſo at the advantage of trying, thro' grace, his own heart the more exactly, according to what echo it gives, or how it reliſheth or is diſpleaſed with the ſeveral ſpeeches of the communers. Touching the matter, it is of the greateſt concernment, *viz.* The ſtating aright both law and goſpel, and giving true and clear narrations of the courſe of the cloud of witneſſes, in the following of which, many have arrived at a glorious reſt. The excellent accounts are managed in ſuch a manner, as to detect the rocks on either hand, upon which the danger of ſplitting is exceedingly great. Here we have the greateſt depths, and moſt painted deluſions of hell, in oppoſition to the only way of ſalvation, diſcovered with marvellous brevity and evidence, and that by the concurring ſufferages of burning and ſhining lights, men of the cleareſt experience, and honoured of God to do eminent ſervice in their day, for advancing the intereſts of our Lord's kingdom and goſpel.

The relucence of gofpel-light has been the choice mean, bleffed by the Lord, for the effectuating of great things, in the feveral periods of the church, fince that light brake up in Paradife, after our firft fin and fall : and ever fince the balance hath fwayed, and will fway, according to the better or worfe ftate of matters in that important regard. When gofpel-light is clear, and attended with power, Satan's kingdom cannot ftand before it ; the prince and powers of darknefs muft fall as lightening from heaven. And, upon the contrary, according to receffions from thence, Chriftian churches went off, by degrees, from the only foundation, even from the rock Chrift, until the man of fin, the great Antichrift, did mount the throne. Neverthelefs, while the world is wondering after the beaft, behold ! evangelical light breaks forth in the midft of Papal darknefs ; and hereupon Antichrift's throne fhakes, and is at the point of falling ; yet his wounds are cured, and he recovers new ftrength and fpirits, thro' a darkening of the glorious gofpel, and perverfion thereof, by anti-evangelical errors and herefies.

That the tares of fuch errors are fown in the reformed churches, and by men who profefs reformed faith, is beyond debate ; and thefe, who lay to heart the purity of the gofpel doctrine. Such dregs of Antichriftianifm do yet remain, or are brought in amongft us. Herein the words of the apoftle are verified, *viz.* " Of your " own felves fhall men arife, fpeaking perverfe things, " to draw away difciples after them :" and as this renders the effays for a further diffufion of evangelical light the more neceffary and feafonable ; fo there is ground to hope, that, in thefe ways the churches of Chrift will gradually get the afcendant over their enemies, until the great Antichrift fhall fall, as a trophy before a gofpel-difpenfation. For the Lord will " deftroy him by the " breath of his mouth, and with the brightnefs of his " coming." That this excellent and fpiritual piece may be bleffed to the reader, is the prayer of, &c.

Their fincere wellwifher, and fervant in the work of the gofpel. CHARNOCK, DEC. 3. 1717. JA. HOG.

To the HONOURABLE

Colonel JOHN DOWNES, Efq;

One of the Members of the Honourable
Houfe of Commons in Parliament,
Juftice of Peace, and one of the
Deputy-Lietenants of the County of
Suffex, and Auditor to the Prince his
highnefs of the Dutchy of Cornwall,
E. F. wifheth the true knowledge of
GOD in JESUS CHRIST.

Moft Honoured Sir,

ALTHO' I do obferve that new editions,
accompanied with new additions, are
fometimes publifhed with new dedications;
yet fo long as he, who formerly owned the
fubject, doth yet live, and hath the fame affections towards it, I conceive there is no need
of a new patron, but of a new epiftle.

Be pleafed then, moft honoured Sir, to give
me leave to tell you, that your clemency of
place did fomewhat induce me, both now and
before, to make choice of you for its patron;
but your endowments with grace did invite
me to it, God having beftowed upon you fpecial fpiritual bleffings in heavenly things in
Chrift; for it hath been declared unto me by
them that knew you, when you were but a
youth, how Chrift met with you then; and,
by fending his Spirit into your heart; Firft,
Convinced you of fin; as was manifeft by thofe
conflicts, which your foul then had, both with

Satan and itſelf, whilſt you did not believe in Chriſt. 2dly, Of righeouſneſs ; as was manifeſt by the peace and comfort, which you afterwards had, by believing that Chriſt was gone to the Father, and appeared in his preſence, as your advocate and ſurety, that had undertaken for you. Thirdly, Of judgment; as hath been manifeſt ever ſince, in that you have been careful, with the truly godly man, Pſal. cxii. 5. to guide your affairs with judgment, in walking according to the mind of Chriſt.

I have not forgotten what deſires you have expreſſed to know the true difference between the *covenant of works*, and the *covenant of grace ;* and experimentally to be acquainted with the doctrine of free grace, the myſteries of Chriſt, and the life of faith. Witneſs not only your high approving of ſome heads of a ſermon, which I once heard a godly miniſter preach, and repeated in your hearing, of the life of faith ; but alſo your earneſt requeſt to me, to write them out fair, and ſend them to you into the country ; yea, witneſs your highly approving of this Dialogue, when I firſt acquainted you with the Contents thereof, encouraging me to expedite it to the preſs ; and your kind acceptance, together with your cordial thanks for my love, manifeſted in dedicating it to your honoured name.

Sith, then, worthy Sir, it hath pleaſed the Lord to enable me both to amend it, and to enlarge it, I hope your affection will alſo be enlarged towards the matter therein contained, confidering that it tends to the clearing of thofe forenamed truths, and thro' the blefling of God, may be a means to root them more deeply in your heart. And truly, Sir, I am confident, the more they grow and flourifh in any man's heart, the more will all heart-corruptions wither and decay. Oh! Sir, if the truths, contained in this Dialogue, were but as much in my heart, as they are in my head, I were a happy man; for then fhould I be more free from pride, vain-glory, wrath, anger, felf-love, and love of the world, than I am: and then fhould I have more humility, meeknefs, and love both to God and man, than I have: O! then fhould I be content with Chrift alone, and live above all things in the world; then fhould I experimentally know, both how to abound, and how to want; and then fhould I be fit for any condition, nothing could come amifs unto me. Oh that the Lord would be pleafed to write them in our hearts by his blefled Spirit!

And fo, moft humbly befeeching you ftill to pardon my boldnefs, and to vouchfafe to take it into your patronage and protection; I humbly take my leave of you, and remain,

Your obliged Servant,

to be commanded,

E. F.

TO ALL SUCH

Humble-hearted R E A D E R S,

As fee any need to learn, either to know themfelves,
or God in Christ.

Loving Christians,

COnfider, I pray you, that as the firft Adam did, as
a common perfon, enter into covenant with God
for all mankind, and brake it, whereby they became
finful and guilty of everlafting death and damnation:
even fo Jefus Chrift, the fecond Adam, did, as a common perfon, enter into covenant with God his Father,
for all the elect *, that is to fay, all thofe that have, or
fhall believe on his name †, and for them kept it ‡: whereby they become righteous, and heirs of everlafting life
and falvation‖: and therefore it is our greateft wifdom,
and ought to be our greateft care and endeavour, to
come out §, and from the firft Adam, unto, and into, the
fecond Adam ¶; that fo we may have life through his
name, John xx. 31.   And

---

* The covenant (viz. of
works) being made with Adam
not only for himfelf, but for
his pofterity, all mankind,
defcending from him by ordinary generation, finned in him
and fell with him in his firft
tranfgreffion.   Shorter Catechifm.   Queft. 16.
  The covenant of grace was
made with Chrift, as the fecond
Adam; and, in him, with all
the elect, as his feed.   Larger
Catechifm, Queft 31.

† See Chap. II. Sect. 2.
‡ Namely, by doing and
dying for them, viz. the elect.
‖ Thus the impetration or
purchafe of redemption, and
the application of it are taught
to be of the fame extent; even
as Adam's reprefentation, and
the ruins by his fall, are: the
former extending to the elect,
as the latter unto all mankind.
§ Of.
¶ Uniting with Chrift by
faith.

B 3.

'And yet alas! there is no point in all practical divinity, that we are naturally so much averse and backward unto, as unto this; neither doth Satan strive to hinder us, so much from doing any thing else as this: and hence it is, that we are all of us naturally apt to abide and continue in that sinful and miserable estate that the first Adam plunged us-into; without-either taking any notice of it, or being at all affected with it; so far are we from coming out of it. And if the Lord be pleased by any means to open our eyes, to see our misery, and we do thereupon begin to step out of it; yet alas! we are prone rather to go backwards towards the first Adam's pure estate *, in striving and struggling to leave sin, and perform duties, and do good works, hoping thereby to make ourselves so righteous and holy, that God will let us into Paradise again to eat of the tree of life, and live for ever; and this we do, until we see the flaming sword at Eden's gate, turning every way to keep the way of the tree of life †, Gen. iii. 24. Is it not ordinary, when the Lord convinceth a man of his sin (either by means of his word or his rod) to cry after this manner: O I am a sinful man! for I have lived a very wicked life; and therefore surely the Lord is angry with me, will damn me in hell: O what shall I do to save my soul? And is there not at hand some ignorant, miserable comforter, ready to say, Yet, do not despair, man, but-repent of thy sins, and ask God forgivenness, and reform your life; and doubt not but he will be merciful unto you ‡; for he hath promised (you

---

* *i. e.* To the way of the covenant of works, which innocent Adam was set upon.

† *i. e.* Till we be brought to despair of obtaining salvation in the way of the covenant of works. Mark here, the spring of Legalism, namely, the natural bias of man's heart towards the way of the law, as a covenant of works;

and ignorance of the law, in its spirituality and vast extent, Rom. vii. 9. and x. 2, 3.

‡ There is not one word of Jesus Christ the glorious Mediator, nor of faith in his blood, in all the advice given by this Casuist to the afflicted; and agreeable thereto is the effect, it hath upon the

know) that at what time foever a finner repenteth him of his fins, he will forgive him *.

And doth he not hereupon comfort himfelf, and fay, in his heart at leaft, O if the Lord will but fpare my life, and lengthen out my days, I will become a new man! I am very forry, that I have lived fuch a finful life ; but I will never do as I have done for all the world: O, you fhall fee a great change in me! believe it.

And hereupon he betakes himfelf to a new courfe of life ; and, it may be, becomes a zealous profeffor of religion, performing all Chriftian exercifes both public

----

afflicted; who takes comfort unto himfelf, without looking unto the Lord Jefus Chrift at all; as appears from the next paragraph.

Behold the fcripture pattern in fuch a cafe, Acts ii. 37, 38. " Men and brethren, ' what fhall we do? Then ' Peter faid unto them, Re- ' pent, and be baptized every ' one of you in the name of ' Jefus Chrift, for the remif- ' fion of fins.' Chap. xvi. 30. 31. ' Sirs, what muft I do to ' be faved? And they faid, ' Believe on the Lord Jefus ' Chrift, and thou fhalt be ' faved.' And thus the directory, title, concerning the vifitation of the fick, paragraph 8. " If it appear that ' he hath not a due fenfe of ' his fins, endeavours ought ' to be ufed to convince him ' of his fins, to make known ' the danger of deferring re- ' pentance, and of falvation ' at any time offered, to awa- ' ken the confcience, and to ' rouze him out of a ftupid

' and fecure condition, to ap- ' prehend the juftice, and wrath ' of God.' [Here this miferable comforter finds the afflicted, and fhould have taught him concerning an offended God, as there immediately follows] ' before whom, none ' can ftand, but he that, being ' loft in himfelf, layeth hold ' upon Chrift by faith.'

* This fentence, taken from the English fervice book is in the practice of piety, edit. Edin. 1672. p. 122. cited from Ezek. xxxiii. 14, 16. and reckoned amongft thefe fcriptures, an ignorant miftake of which keeps back a finner from the practice of piety. But the truth is, it is not to be found in the Old or New Teftament; and therefore it was objected againft, as ftanding in the fervice-book, under the name of a fentence of fcripture, pretended to be cited from Ezek. xviii. 21, 22. Reafons fhewing the neceffity of reformation, &c Lon. 1660. p. 26.

and private, and leaves off his old companions, and keeps company with religious men ; and so, it may be, goes on till his dying day, and thinks himself sure of heaven and eternal happiness : and yet, it may be, all this while is ignorant of Chrift and his righteousness, and therefore establisheth his own.

Where is the man, or where is the woman, that is truly come to Chrift, that hath not had some experience, in themselves, of such a disposition as this ? If there be any that have reformed their lives, and are become pro-fessors of religion, and have not taken notice of this in themselves more or less, I wish they have gone beyond a legal professor, or one still under the covenant of works.

Nay, where is the man or woman, that is truly in Chrift, that findeth not in themselves an aptness to with-draw their hearts from Chrift, and to put some confi-dence in their own works and doings ? If there be any that do not find it, I wish their hearts deceive them not.

Let me confess ingenuously. I was a professor of religi-on, at least a dozen of years, before I knew any other way of eternal life, than to be sorry for my sins, and ask forgivenness, and strive and endeavour to fulfil the law, and keep the commandments, according as Mr Dod, and other godly men had expounded them : and truly, I remember, I was in hope, I should at last attain to the perfect fulfilling of them ; and, in the mean time, I conceived, that God would accept the will for the deed, or what I could not do, Chrift had done for me.

And tho' at last, by means of conferring with Mr Thomas Hooker in private, the Lord was pleased to convince me, that I was yet but a proud Pharisee; and to shew me the way of faith and salvation by Chrift alone ; and to give me (as I hope) a heart in some mea-sure to embrace it ; yet alas ! thro' the weakness of my faith, I have been, and am still apt to turn aside to the covenant of works ; and therefore have not attained to that joy and peace in believing, nor that measure of

love

love to Chrift, and man for Chrift's fake, as I am confident many of God's faints do attain unto in the time of of this life. The Lord be merciful unto me, and increafe my faith.

And are there not others (though I hope but few) who being enlightened to fee their mifery, by reafon of the guilt of fin, tho' not by reafon of the filth of fin; and hearing of juftification freely by grace, thro' the redemption which is in Jefus Chrift, do applaud and magnify that doctrine, following them that do moft preach and prefs the fame, feeming to be (as it were) ravifhed with the hearing thereof, out of a conceit that they are by Chrift, freely juftified from the guilt of fin, tho' ftill they retain the filth of fin *. Thefe are they that content themfelves with a gofpel knowledge, with mere notions in the head, but not in the heart; glorying and rejoicing in free grace and juftification by faith alone; profeffing faith in Chrift, and yet are not poffeffed of Chrift: thefe are they that can talk like believers, and yet do not walk like believers: thefe are they that have language like faints, and yet have converfations like devils; thefe are they that are not obedient to the law of Chrift, and therefore are juftly called Antinomians.

Now both thefe paths † leading from Chrift, have been juftly judged as erroneous; and, to my knowledge, not only a matter of eighteen or twenty years ago, but alfo within thefe three or four years, there hath been much ado, both by preaching, writing, and difputing, both to reduce men out of them, and to keep them from them;

---

* Mark here the fpring of Antinomianifm; namely, the want of a found conviction of the odioufnefs and filthinefs of fin, rendering the foul lothfome and abominable in the fight of a holy God. Hence as the finner fees not his need of, fo neither will he receive and reft on Chrift for all his falvation; but will go about to halve it, grafping at his juftifying blood, neglecting his fanctifying Spirit; and fo falls fhort of all part or lot in that matter.

† Viz. Legalifm and Antinomianifm.

and hot contentions have been on both fides, and all, I fear, to little purpofe : for, hath not the ftrict profeffor accord-ing to the law, whilft he hath ftriven to reduce the loofe profeffor according to the gofpel, out of the Anti-nomian path, intangled both himfelf and others the fafter in the yoke of bondage ? Gal. v. 1. And hath not the loofe profeffor according to the gofpel, whilft he hath ftriven to reduce the ftrict profeffor according to the law, out of the legal path, by promifing liberty from the law, taught others, and been himfelf the fervant of corruption ? 2 Pet. ii. 19.

For this caufe I, tho' I be nothing, have, by the grace of God, endeavoured in this dialogue, to walk as a middle man betwixt them both ; in fhewing to each of them his erroneous path, with the middle path (which is Jefus Chrift received truly, and walked in anfwerably) * as a means to bring them both unto him, and make them both one in him : and oh ! that the Lord would be pleafed fo to blefs it to them, that it might be a means to produce that effect.

L

---

* A fhort and pithy defcrip-tion of the middle path, the only path-way to heaven; Jefus Chrift (the way, John xiv. 6) received truly by faith, John i. 12. this is overlooked by the Legalift) and walked in anfwerably, by holinefs of heart and life, Col. ii. 6. this is neglected by the Antinomi-an. The Antinomian's faith is but pretended, and not true faith; fince he walks not in Chrift anfwerably: The Lega-lift's holinefs is but pretended, and not true, holinefs; fince he hath not received Chrift truly, and therefore is incapable of walking in Chrift, which is the only true holinefs com-petent to fallen mankind.— Thus both the Legalift and Antinomian are, each of them, deftitute of true faith, and true holinefs: forafmuch as there can be no walking in Chrift, without a true receiv-ing of him ; and there can-not be a true receiving of him, without walking in him. So both of them are off the only way of falvation; and continuing fo, muft needs pe-rifh. Wherefore it concerns every one, who has a value for his own foul, to take heed that he be found in the mid-dle-path.

I have (as you may fee) gathered much of it, out of known and approved authors; and yet have therein wronged no man; for I have reftored it to the right owner again in notes. Some part of it my manufcripts have afforded me; and of the reft I hope I may fay, as Jacob did of his venifon, Gen. xxvii 20. The Lord hath brought it unto me. Let me fpeak it without vain glory, I endeavoured herein to imitate the laborious bee *, who out of divers flowers gathers honey and wax, and thereof makes one comb; if any foul feels any fweetnefs in it, let them praife God, and pray for me, who am weak in faith, and cold in love.

　　　　　　　　　　　　　　　　　　　　　E. F.

* Burt. Mel. p. 8.

Mr BELFRAGE's *Recommendation to this* EDITION.

I HAVE frequently perufed, with great fatisfaction, The *Marrow of Modern Divinity,* Firft and Second Parts: and as far as I can judge, it will be found by thofe who carefully read it, very ufeful for illuftrating the Difference between the Law and the Gofpel, and preventing them from fplitting either on the rock of Legality on the one hand, or the rock of Antinomianifm on the other. And accordingly recommend it (by defire) as a Book filled with precious, feafonable and neceffary Truths, clearly founded upon the Sacred Oracles.

FALKIRK, *Dec.*9th, 1788.　　　JOHN BELFRAGE.

A CATALOGUE of the Writers Names, out of whom I have collected much of the matter contained in this enfuing dialogue.

A

Mr Ainfworth
Dr Ames

B

Bp Babington
Mr Ball
Mr Baftingius
Mr Beza
Mr Robert Bolton
Mr Samuel Bolton
Mr Bradford
Mr Bullinger

C

Mr Calvin
Mr Carelefs
Mr Caryl
Mr Cornwall
Mr Cotton
Mr Culverwell

D

Mr Dent
Dr Diodati
Mr D. Dixon
Mr Downham
Mr Du Pleffe
Mr Dyke

E

Mr Elton

F

Mr Forbes
Mr Fox
Mr Frith

G

Mr Gibbons
Mr Thos. Goodwin
Mr Gray, *junr.*
Mr Greenham
Mr Grotius

H

Bp Hall
Mr T. Hooker

L

Mr Laeftanno
Mr Lightfoot
Dr Luther

M

Mr Marbeck
Mr Marfhall
Peter Martyr
Dr Mayer
Wolfangius Mufculus

O

Bernardin Ochine

P

Dr Pemble
Mr Perkins
Mr Polanus
Dr Prefton

R

Mr Reynolds
Mr Rollock
Mr Roufe

S

Dr Sibbs
Mr Slater
Dr Smith
Mr Stock

T

Mr Tindal
Mr Robert Town

V

Mr Vauchan
Mr Vaumeth
Dr Urban Regius
Dr Urfinus

W

Mr Walker
Mr Ward
Dr Willet
Dr Williams
Mr Wilfon.

THE

MARROW

OF

MODERN DIVINITY,

WITH NOTES.

INTERLOCUTORS.

Evangelista, a Minister of the Gospel.
Nomista, a Legalist.
Antinomista, an Antinomian. And,
Neophitus, a young Christian.

The INTRODUCTION.

§ 1. *Differences about the Law.* § 2. *A threefold Law.*

Nom. SIR, my neighbour Neophitus and I, having lately had some conference with this our friend and acquaintance Antinomista, about some points of religion, wherein he differing from us both, at last said, he would be contented to be judged by you our minister; therefore have we made bold to come unto you, all three of us, to pray you to hear us, and judge of our differences.

C

Evan. You are all of you very welcome to me : and if you pleafe to let me hear what your differences are, I will tell you what I think.

§ 1. *Nom.* The truth is, Sir, he and I differ in very many things; but more efpecially *about the law :* for I fay, The law ought to be a rule of life to a believer ; and he faith, It ought not.

Neo. And furely, Sir, the greateft difference betwixt him and I, is this : He would perfuade me to believe in Chrift ; and bids me rejoice in the Lord, and live merrily, tho' I feel never fo many corruptions in my heart, yea, tho' I be never fo finful in my life : the which I cannot do, nor, I think, ought not to do ; but rather to fear, and forrow, and lament for my fins.

Ant. The truth is, Sir, the greateft difference betwixt my friend Nomifta, and I, is about the law ; and therefore, that is the greateft matter we come unto you about.

Evan. I remember, the apoftle Paul willeth Titus, to " avoid contentions and ftrivings about the law, becaufe they are unprofitable and vain," Tit. iii. 9. And fo I fear, yours have been.

Nom. Sir, for my own part, I hold it very meet, that every true Chriftian fhould be very zealous for the holy law of God ; efpecially now, when a company of thefe Antinomians do fet themfelves againft it, and do what they can quite to abolifh it, and utterly to root it out of the church : furely, Sir, I think it not meet they fhould live in a Chriftian commonwealth.

Evan. I pray you, neighbour, Nomifta, be not fo hot, neither let us have fuch unchriftian-like expreffions amongft us ; but let us reafon together in love, and with the fpirit of meeknefs, 1 Cor. iv. 21. as Chriftians ought to do. I confefs with the apoftle, " It is good to be zealoufly affected always in a good thing," Gal. iv. 18. But yet, as the fame apoftle faid of the Jews, fo I fear, I may fay of fome Chriftians,

that " they are zealous of the law," Acts xxi. 20.
yea, fome would be doctors of the law ; and yet neither
underftand " what they fay, nor whereof they affirm,"
1 Tim. i. 7.

Nom. Sir, I make no doubt, but that I both know
what I fay, and whereof I affirm ; when I fay and
affirm, that the holy law of God ought to be a rule of
life to a believer : for I dare pawn my foul of the
truth of it.

Evan. But what law do you mean ?

Nom. Why, Sir, what law do you think I mean ?
Is there any more laws than one ?

§ 2. *Evan.* Yea, in the fcriptures there is mention
made of divers laws, but they may all be comprifed
under thefe three, *viz.* The law of works, the law of
faith, and the law of Chrift * ; Rom. iii. 27. Gal. vi. 2.

* Thefe terms are fcriptural, as appears from the texts
quoted by our author, namely, Rom. iii. 27. " Where is
" boafting then? it is excluded : by what law? of works?
" nay; but by the law of faith," Gal. vi. 2. " Bear ye one
" another's burdens, and fo fulfil the law of Chrift." By the
law of works is meant the law of the ten commands as the
covenant of works; by the law of faith, the gofpel, or covenant
of grace : for, juftification being the point upon which the
apoftle there ftates the oppofition betwixt thefe two laws, it
is evident that the former only is the law that doth not exclude
boafting; and that the latter only is it, by which a finner is
juftified, in a way that doth exclude boafting. By the law of
Chrift is meant the fame law of the ten commands, as a rule of
life in the hand of a Mediator, to believers already juftified, and
not any one command of the law only; for bearing one another's burdens is a fulfilling of the law of Chrift, as it is a
loving one another : but, according to the fcripture, that love
is not a fulfilling of one command only, but of the whole law of
the ten commands, Rom. xiii. 8, 9, 10. " He that loveth ano-
" ther hath fulfilled the law. For this, Thou fhalt not com-
" mit adultery, Thou fhalt not kill, Thou fhalt not fteal, Thou
" fhalt not bear falfe witnefs, Thou fhalt not covet : and if
" there be any other commandment, it is briefly comprehended
" in this faying, namely, Thou fhalt love thy neighbour as
" thyfelf." Therefore love is the fulfilling of the law : It is a
fulfilling of the fecond table directly, and of the firft table in-

and therefore I pray you tell me, when you say, the law ought to be a rule of life to a believer, which of thefe three laws you mean?

---

directly and confequentially; therefore by the law of Chrift is meant, not one command only, but the whole law.

The law of works is the law to be done, that one may be faved; the law of faith is the law to be believed, that one may be faved; the law of Chrift, is the law of the Saviour, binding his faved people to all the duties of obedience, Gal. iii. 12. Acts xvi. 31.

The term *law* is not ·here ufed unnivocally; for the law of faith is, neither in the fcripture fenfe, nor in the fenfe of our author, a law properly fo called. The apoftle ufeth that phrafe only in imitation of the Jews manner of fpeaking, who had the law continually in their mouths. But fince the promife of the gofpel, propofed to faith, is called in fcripture, " the law of " faith;" our author was fufficiently warranted to call it fo too. See Chap. I. § 3. fo the law of faith is not a proper preceptive law.

The law of works, and the law of Chrift, are in fubftance but one law; even the law of the ten commandments, the moral law, that law which was from the beginning, (Chap·II. Sect 3.) continuing ftill the fame in its own nature, but vefted with different forms. And fince that law is perfect, and fin is any want of conformity unto, or tranfgreffion of it; whatever form it be vefted with, whether as the law of works, or as the law of Chrift; all commands of God, unto men, muft needs be comprehended under it; and particularly, the command to repent, common to all mankind, Pagans not excepted, who doubtlefs are obliged, as well as others, to turn from fin unto God; as alfo the command to believe in Chrift, binding all, to whom the gofpel-revelation comes; tho' in the mean fime this law ftands under different forms, to thefe who are in a ftate of union with Chrift by faith, and to thefe, who are not. So the law of Chrift is not a new proper preceptive law, but the old proper preceptive law, which was from the beginning under a new accidental form.

The diftinction between the law of works, and the law of faith, cannot be controverted, fince the apoftle doth fo clearly diftinguifh them, Rom. iii. 27.

The diftinction betwixt the law of works, and the law of Chrift, as above explained, according to the fcripture, and the mind of our author, is the fame in effect with that of the law, as a covenant of works, and as a rule of life to believers. Weftm. Confef. chap. 19 art. 6. and ought to be admitted. For (1.) Believers are not under, but dead to the law of works,

Nom. Sir, I know not the difference betwixt them; but this I know, that the law of the ten commandments,

---

Rom. vi. 14. " For ye are not under the law, but under grace." Chap. vii. 4. " Wherefore, my brethren, ye also are become " dead to the law." But they are under the law to Chrift: " Ye alfo are become dead to the law,—That ye fhould be " married to another, even to him who is raifed from the " dead." *ib.* 1 Cor. ix. 21. " Being not without law to God, " but under the law to Chrift." Some copies read here, " Of " God, and of Chrift;" the which I mention, not out of any regard to that different reading, but that upon the occafion thereof the fenfe is owned by the learned, to be the fame, either way. To be under the law to God, is, without queftion, to be under the law of God; whatever it may be judged to import more, it can import no lefs. Therefore to be under the law of Chrift, is to be under the law of God. This text gives a plain and decifive anfwer to the queftion, How the believer is under the law of God? namely, as he is under the law to Chrift. (2.) The law of Chrift is an eafy yoke, and a light burthen, Matth. xi. 30. But the law of works to a finner is an unfupportable burthen, requiring works as the condition of juftification and acceptance with God, as is clear from the whole of the Apoftle's reafoning, Rom. iii. (And therefore is called the law of works, for otherwife the law of Chrift requires works too) and " curfing every one that continues not in all things written " in it to do them," Gal. iii. 10. And the Apoftle affures us, that " what things foever the law faith, it faith to them, who " are under the law," Rom. iii 19. The duties of the law of works, as fuch, are, as I conceive, called by our Lord himfelf, " heavy burthens, and grievous to be born," Mat. xxiii. 4. " For they (*viz.* the Scribes and Pharifees) bind heavy burthens " and grievous to be born, and lay them on men's fhoulders; " but they themfelves will not move them with one of their " fingers " Thefe heavy burthens were not human traditions, and rites devifed by men, (for Chrift would not have commanded the obferving and doing of thefe, as in this cafe he did. ver. 3. " Whatfoever they bid you obferve, that obferve and do,") neither were they the Mofaic rites and ceremonies, which were not then abrogated; for the Scribes and Pharifees were fo far from not moving thefe burthens with one of their own fingers, that the whole of their religion was confined to them, namely, to the rites and ceremonies of Mofes's law, and thofe of their own devifing. But the duties of the moral law, they laid on others, binding them on with the tie of the law of works; yet

commonly called the moral law, ought to be a rule of life to a believer.

———————————————————

made no conscience of them in their own practice. The which duties nevertheless our Lord Jesus commanded to be observed and done.

" He who hath believed on Jesus Christ, (tho' he be freed from the curse of the law) is not freed from the command and obedience of the law, but tied thereunto by a new obligation, and a new command from Christ. Which new command from Christ, importeth help to obey the command." Practical use of saving Knowledge, Title, the third Warrant to believe, Fig. 5.

What this distinction amounts to is, that thereby a difference is constitute, betwixt the ten commands, as coming from an absolute God out of Christ unto sinners; and the same ten commands, as coming from God in Christ, unto them; a difference, which the children of God, sisting their consciences before him, to receive the law at his mouth, will value as their life; however they disagree about it, in words, and manner of expression. But that the original indispensible obligation of the law of the ten commands, is in any measure weakened, by the believer's taking it, as the law of Christ, and not as the law of works; or that the sovereign authority of God the Creator, which is inseparable from it for the ages of eternity, (in which channel soever it be conveyed unto men) is thereby laid aside; will appear utterly groundless, upon an impartial consideration of the matter. For is not our Lord Jesus Christ, equally with the Father and the Holy Spirit, JEHOVAH, the sovereign, supreme, most high God, Creator of the world? Isa. xlvii. 4. Jerem. xxiii. 6. with Psal. lxxxiii. 18. John i. 3. Rev. iii. 14. Is not the name (or sovereign authority) of God in Christ? Exod. xxiii. 21. Is not he in the Father, and the Father in him? John xiv. 11. Nay, doth not " all the fulness of the Godhead dwell in him?" Col. ii. 9. How then can the original obligation of the law of the ten commands, arising from the authority of the Creator, Father, Son and Holy Ghost, be weakened by its being issued unto the believer, from and by that blessed channel, the Lord Jesus Christ?

As for the distinction betwixt the law of faith and the law of Christ; the latter is subordinated unto the former. All men by nature are under the law of works; but taking the benefit of the law of faith, by believing in the Lord Jesus Christ, they are set free from the law of works, and brought under the law of Christ, Matth. xi. 28, 29. " Come unto me, all ye that labour " and are heavy laden——take my yoke upon you."

Evan. But the law of the ten commandments, or moral law, may be either faid to be the matter of the law of works, or the matter of the law of Chrift: And therefore I pray you tell me, in whether of thefe fenfes, you conceive it ought to be a rule of life to a believer?

Nom. Sir, I muft confefs, I do not know what you mean by this diftinction; but this I know, that God requires that every Chriftian fhould frame and lead his life, according to the rule of the ten commandments: the which if he do, then may he expect the blefling of God both upon his foul and body; and if he do not, then can he expect nothing elfe, but his wrath and curfe upon them both.

Evan. The truth is, neighbour Nomifta, the law of the ten commandments, as it is the matter of the law of works, ought not to be a rule of life to a believer *. But in thus faying, you have affirmed that it ought; and therefore, therein you have erred from the truth. And now, friend Antinomifta, that I may alfo know your judgment, when you fay the law ought not to be the rule of life to a believer, I pray, tell me what law you mean?

Ant. Why, I mean, the law of the ten command-ments.

Evan. But whether do you mean that law, as it is the matter of the law of works, or as it is the matter of the law of Chrift?

Ant. Surely, Sir, I do conceive, that the ten com-mandments are no way to be a rule of life to a believer; for Chrift hath delivered him from them.

Evan. But the truth is, the law of the ten command-ments, as it is the matter of the law of Chrift, ought to be a rule of life to a believer †; and therefore, you

---

* See the following note.

† The law of the ten commands, being the natural law, was written on Adam's heart in his creation; while as yet it

having affirmed to the contrary, have therein alfo erred from the truth.

---

was neither the law of works, nor the law of Chrift, in the fenfe wherein thefe terms are ufed in fcripture, and by our Author. But after man was created, and put into the garden, this natural law, having, unto man liable to fall away from God, a threatening of eternal death in cafe of difobedience; had alfo a promife of eternal life annexed to it, in cafe of obedience, in virtue of which, he having done his work, might thereupon plead and demand the reward of eternal life. Thus it became the law of works, whereof the ten commands were, and are ftill the matter. All mankind being ruin'd by the breach of this law, Jefus Chrift obeys and dies in the room of the elect, that they might be faved. They being united to him by faith, are, thro' his obedience and fatisfaction imputed to them, freed from eternal death, and become heirs of everlafting life: So that the law of works, being fully fatisfied, expires as to them, as it would have done of courfe, in the cafe of Adam's having ftood the time of his trial (fee Chap. 2' Sect. 2) howbeit it remains in full force, as to unbelievers But the natural law of the ten commands (which can never expire or determine, but obligeth in all poffible ftates of the creature, in earth, heaven and hell) is, from that moment the law of works expires as to believers, iffued forth to them (ftill liable to infirmities, though not falling away like Adam) in the channel of the covenant of grace, bearing a promife of help to obey, (Ezek. xxxvi. 27.) and, agreeable to their ftate before the Lord, having annexed to it a promife of the tokens of God's fatherly love, for the fake of Chrift, in cafe of that obedience; and a threatning of God's fatherly difpleafure, in cafe of their difobedience. John xiv. 21. " He that hath my commandments, and keepeth " them, he it is that loveth me; and he that loveth me, fhall " be loved of my Father; and I will love him, and will manifeft " myfelf to him." Pfal. lxxxix. 31, 32, 33. " If they break my " ftatutes, and keep not my commandments; Then will I vifit " their tranfgreffions with the rod, and their iniquity with " ftripes. Neverthelefs, my loving kindnefs will I not utterly " take from him, nor fuffer my faithfulnefs to fail." Thus it becomes the law of Chrift to them; of which law alfo the fame ten commands are likewife the matter In the threatnings of this law, there is no revenging wrath: and in the promifes of it, no proper conditionality of works: But here is the order in the covenant of grace, to which the law of Chrift belongs; a beautiful order, of grace, obedience, particular favours, and chaftifements for difobedience. Thus the ten commands ftand,

Nom. The truth is, Sir, I muſt confeſs, I never took any notice of this treefold law; which, it ſeems, is mentioned in the New Teſtament.

Ant. And I muſt confeſs, if I took any notice of them, I never underſtood them.

Evan. Well give me leave to tell you, that ſo far forth as any man comes ſhort of the true knowledge of this threefold law *; ſo far forth he comes ſhort, both of the true knowledge of God, and of himſelf: and therefore, I wiſh you both to conſider of it.

Nom. Sir, if it be ſo, you may do well to be a means to inform us, and help us to the true knowledge of this threefold law: and therefore, I pray you, firſt tell us what is meant by the law of works.

---

both in the law of works, and in the law of Chriſt, at the ſame time; being the common matter of both. But as they are the matter of (*i. e.* ſtand in) the law of works, they are actually a part of the law of works; howbeit, as they are the matter of, or ſtand in, the law of Chriſt, they are actually a part, not of the law of works, but of the law of Chriſt. And as they ſtand in the law of Chriſt, our author expreſsly aſſerts againſt the Antinomian, that they ought to be a rule of life to a believer; as they ſtand in the law of works, he juſtly denies againſt the Legaliſt. Even as when one and the ſame crime ſtands forbidden in the laws of different independent kingdoms; it is manifeſt, that the rule of life to the ſubjects, in that particular, is the prohibition, as it ſtands in the law of that kingdom whereof they are ſubjects reſpectively, and not as it ſtands in the law of that kingdom of which they are not ſubjects.

* Not of the terms, here uſed to expreſs it by; but of the things thereby meant, to wit, the covenant of works, the covenant of grace, and the law as a rule of life to believers; in whatever terms theſe things be expreſt.

CHAP. I.

Of the Law of Works,

OR,

Covenant of Works.

§ 1. *The nature of the covenant of works.* § 2. *Adam's fall.* § 3. *The sinfulness and misery of mankind by the fall.* § 4. *No recovery by the law or covenant of works.* § 5. *The covenant of works binding, tho' broken.*

§ 1. *Evan.* THE law of works, opposed to the law of faith *, Rom iii. 27. holds forth as much as the covenant of works: for it is manifest, saith Musculus, that the word, which signifieth covenant or bargain, is put for law: so that you see, the law of works is as much to say as the covenant of works. The which covenant the Lord made with all mankind, in Adam, before his fall: The sum whereof was, "Do this, and thou shalt live; and if thou do it not, thou shalt die the death †." In which covenant there was first contained a precept, Do this; Secondly, a promise joined unto it, If thou do it, thou shalt live; Thirdly, A like threatning, If thou do it not, thou shalt die the death. Imagine, saith Musculus, That God had said to Adam, Lo, to the intent that thou mayest live, I have given thee liberty to eat, and have given thee abundantly to eat ‡: Let all the fruits of paradise be in thy power, one tree except, which see thou touch not, for that I keep to mine own authority: the same is the tree of knowledge of good and evil; if thou touch it, the meat thereof shall not be life, but death.

---

* Ball on the covenant of grace, p. 9. Com. Pla. Eng. p. 118.
† Lev. xviii. 5. Gen. ii. 17. Ames. Med. Eng p. 48.
‡ Com. Pla. p. 31.

Nom. But, Sir, you said that the law of the ten commandments, or moral law, may be said, to be the matter of the law of works; and you have also said, that the law of works, is as much to say, as the covenant of works: whereby it seems to me, you hold that the law of the ten commandments, was the matter of the covenant of works; which God made with all mankind, in Adam before his fall.

Evan. That's a truth agreed upon by all authors and interpreters, that I know. And indeed the law of works (as a learned author * faith) signifies the moral law; and the moral law, strictly and properly taken, signifies the covenant of works †.

Nom. But, Sir, what is the reason you call it but the matter of the covenant of works?

Evan. The reason why, I rather chuse to call the law of the ten commandments, the matter of the covenant

---

* Downham on Juftif. p. 443. 465.

† The moral law is an ambiguous term among divines. (1.) The moral law is taken for the decalogue or ten commands simply. So the law in ten commandments, is owned to be commonly called the moral law, Weftm. Conf. Chap. 19. Art. 2, 3. And thus our author hath hitherto used that term, reckoning the moral law not the covenant of works itself, but only the matter of it. (2.) The moral law is taken for the ten commands, having the promise of life, and threatening of death annexed to them; that is, for the law (or covenant) of works. Thus the moral law is described to be, " The declaration of " the will of God to mankind, directing and binding every one " to personal, perfect, and perpetual conformity and obedience " thereunto, in the frame and difposition of the whole man, " foul and body, and in performance of all these duties of " holiness and righteousness which he oweth to God and man; " promifing life upon the fulfilling, and threatening death upon " the breach of it." Larg. Cat. Queft. 93. That this is the covenant of works, is clear from Weftm. Conf. Chap. 19. Art. 1. " God gave to Adam a law, as a covenant of works, by which " he bound him, and all his pofterity, to perfonal, entire, exact, " and perpetual obedience; promifed life upon the fulfilling, " and threatened death upon the breach of it." And this our author owns to be the fenfe of that term, ftrictly and properly

of works, than the covenant itself, is, becaufe I conceive that the matter of it cannot properly be called the covenant of works, except the form be put upon it; that is to fay, except the Lord require; and man un- dertake to yield perfect obedience thereunto, upon con- dition of eternal life and death.

And therefore till then, it was not a covenant of works, betwixt God and all mankind in Adam. As for example, you know, that although a fervant * have an ability to do a mafter's work; and though a mafter have wages to beftow upon him for it: yet is there not a covenant betwixt them, till they have thereupon agreed. Even fo, tho' man at the firft had power to yield perfect and perpetual obedience to all the ten-commandments; and God had an eternal life to beftow upon him: yet was there not a covenant betwixt them, till they were thereupon agreed.

Nom. But, Sir, you know there is no mention made in the book of Genefis, of this covenant of works; which, you fay was made with man at firft.

Evan. Though we read not the word Covenant be- twixt God and man, yet have we there recorded what

---

taken; the reafon whereof I conceive to be, that the moral law properly fignifying the law of manners, anfwers to the fcripture term the law of works, by which is meant the covenant of works. And if he had added, that, in this fenfe, believers are delivered from it, he had faid no more, than the Larger Cate- chifm doth, in thefe words, '' They that are regenerate, and '' believe in Chrift, be delivered from the moral law, as a cove- '' nant of works.'' Queft. 97. But in the mean time, 'tis evident, he does not here ufe that term in this fenfe; and in the next paragraph, fave one, he gives a reafon why he doth not fo ufe it.

* Not a hired fervant, for there is a covenant betwixt fuch an one and the mafter; but a bond fervant, bought with money, of another perfon, or born in the mafter's houfe; who is obliged to ferve his mafter, and is liable to punifhment in cafe he do not, but cannot demand wages, fince there is no covenant between them.

This was the cafe of mankind, with relation to the Creator, before the covenant of works was made.

may amount to as much *; For God provided, and promifed to Adam, eternal happinefs, and called for perfect obedience; which appears from God's threatening, Gen. xi. 17. For if man muſt die if he difobeyed, it implies ftrongly, that God's covenant was with him, for life, if he obeyed.

Nom. But, Sir, you know the word covenant fignifies a mutual promife, bargain, and obligation, betwixt two parties †. Now tho' it is implied, that God promifed man, to give him life, if he obeyed; yet we read not, that man promifed to be obedient.

Evan. I pray take notice, that God doth not always tie man to verbal expreffions ‡ : but doth often contract the covenant in real impreffions, in the heart and frame of the creature ‖ ; and this was the manner of covenanting with man at the firſt § : for God had furnifhed his foul with an underſtanding mind ¶, whereby he might difcern good from evil, and right from wrong ; and not only fo, but alfo in his will was moſt great uprightnefs **, and his inſtrumental parts ††, were orderly framed to obedience. The truth is, God did engrave in man's foul,

---

* Ball on the Covenant, p. 6.
† Walker on the Covenant, p. 39.
‡ Ball on the Covenant, p. 5.
‖ The foul approving, embracing, and confenting to, the covenant; which, without any more, is plain language; though not to men, yet unto God, who knoweth the heart.
§ The covenant being revealed to man created after God's own image, he could not but perceive the equity and benefit of it ; and fo heartily approve, embrace, accept, and confent to it. And this accepting is plainly intimate, in Eve's words to the ferpent, Gen. iii. 2, 3. " We may eat of the fruit of the trees of the garden : but of the fruit of the tree which is in the midſt of the garden, God hath faid, Ye ſhall not eat of it ; neither ſhall ye touch it, left ye die."
¶ Calv. Inſt. fol. Eng. p. 8.
** Eccl. vii. 29.
†† Executive faculties and powers, whereby the good known and willed was to be done.

D

wifdom and knowledge of his will and works, and integrity in the whole. foul, and fuch a fitnefs in all the powers. thereof; that neither the mind did conceive, nor the heart defire *, nor the body put in execution, any thing, but that which was acceptable to God : fo that man, endued with thefe qualities, was able to ferve God perfectly.

Nom But, Sir, how could the law of the ten commandments be the matter of this covenant of works; when they were not written, as you know, till the time of Mofes?

Evan. Though they were not written in tables of ftone, until the time of Mofes †; yet were they writ in the tables of man's heart in the time of Adam : for we read that man was created in the image, or likenefs, of God, Gen. i. 27. And the ten commandments are a doctrine, agreeing with the eternal wifdom and juftice that is in God; wherein he hath fo pointed out his own nature, that it doth, in a manner, exprefs the very image of God. And, doth not the apoftle fay, that the image of God confifts in knowledge, righteoufnefs, and true holinefs? And is not knowledge, righteoufnefs, and true holinefs, the perfection of both the tables of the law ‡? And indeed, faith Mr Rollock, it could not well ftand with the juftice of God, to make a covenant with man, under the condition of holy and good works, and perfect obedience to his law; except he had firft created man holy and pure, and ingraven his law in his heart, whence thofe good works fhould proceed.

Nom. But, yet I cannot but marvel, that God, in making the covenant with man, did make mention of no other commandment, than that of the forbidden fruit.

Evan. Do not marvel at it : for by that one fpecies

---

* Bafting, Cat. p. 8.
† Urfin. Cat. p. 517.   Calv. Inft. p. 190.   Col. iii. 10. Eph. iv. 24.
‡ Treat. of Effect. Call. p. 20. or thereabouts.

of fin, the whole genus, or kind is fhewn; as the fame law, being more clearly unfolded *, Deut. xxvii. 26. Gal. iii. 10. doth exprefs. And indeed, in that one commandment the whole worfhip of God did confift; as obedience, honour, love, confidence, and religious fear; together with the outward abftinence from fin, and reverend refpeft to the voice of God: yea, herein alfo confifted his love, and fo his whole duty, to his neighbour. † So that, as a learned writer faith, Adam heard as much ‡ in the garden, as Ifrael did at Sinai; but only in fewer words, and without thunder ‖.

Nom. But, Sir, ought not man to have yielded perfeft obedience to God, tho' this covenant had not been made betwixt them?

Evan. Yea, indeed, perfeft and perpetual obedience was due from man unto God; tho' God had made no promife to man: for when God created man at firft, he put forth an excellency from himfelf into him; and therefore it was the bond and tie that lay up n man, to return that again unto God §: fo that man being God's creature, by the law of creation, he owed all obedience and fubjeftion to God his Creator ¶.

Nom. Why then was it needful, that the Lord fhould make a covenant with him, by promifing him life, and threatening him with death?

---

* Hugo Grot Defenf. Fid. p. 7. 1.

† That one commandment was, in effeft, a fummary of the whole duty of man: the which clearly appears, if one confiders, that the breach of it, was a tranfgreffing of all the ten commands at once, as our author afterwards diftinftly fheweth.

‡ Of the law.　　‖ Lightfoot Mifcel. p. 282.

§ God having given man a being after his own image, a glorious excellency, it was his natural duty, to make fuitable returns thereof, unto the Giver, in a way of duty, being and afting for him: even as the waters, which originally are from the fea, do, in brooks and rivers, return to the fea again. Man, being of God as his firft caufe, behoved to be to him a this chief and ultimate end, Rom. xi. 36.

¶ Reynolds on Pfal. cx. p. 403.

Evan. For anſwer hereunto, in the firſt place, I pray you underſtand, that man was a reaſonable creature; and ſo, out of judgment, diſcretion and. election, able to make choice of his way : and therefore, it was meet there ſhould be ſuch a covenant made with him; that he might, according to God's appointment, ſerve him after a reaſonable manner *. Secondly, it was meet there ſhould be ſuch a covenant made with him, to ſhew that he was not ſuch a prince on earth, but that he had a ſovereign Lord † : therefore God ſet a puniſhment upon the breach of his commandment ‡ ; that man might know his inferiority, and that things betwixt him and God, were not as betwixt equals. Thirdly, It was meet there ſhould be ſuch a covenant made with him, to ſhew that he had nothing by perſonal, immediate, and underived right ; but all by gift and gentleneſs ‖. So that, you ſee, it was an equal covenant §, which God, out of his prerogative royal, made with mankind in Adam, before his fall.

Nom. Well, Sir, I do perceive that Adam, and all mankind in him, were created moſt holy.

Evan. Yes, and moſt happy too : for God placed him in paradiſe, in the midſt of all delightful pleaſures and contents ; wherein he did enjoy moſt near and ſweet communion with his Creator, in whoſe preſence is " fulneſs of joy, and at whoſe right hand are pleaſures for evermore," Pſal. xvi. 11. So that if Adam had received of the tree of life ¶, by taking and eating of it, while he ſtood in the ſtate of innocency, before his fall ; he had certainly been eſtabliſhed in a happy ſtate for ever, and

---

* Reynolds on Pſal. cx. p. 405.
† Gibbons on Gen. p. 97. Ball on the Cov. p. 11.
‡ *Viz.* The puniſhment of death, upon the breach of his commandment, touching the forbidden fruit.
‖ Reynolds on Pſal cx. p. 406.
§ *i. e.* An equitable covenant, fair and reaſonable.
¶ Walker on the Cov. p. 89.

could not have been feduced and fupplanted by Satan; as fome learned men do think, and as God's own words feem to imply, Gen. iii. 22. *

§ 2. *Nom.* But it feemeth that Adam did not continue in that holy and happy eftate.

Evan. No indeed; for he difobeyed God's exprefs command, in eating the forbidden fruit; and fo became guilty of the breach of the covenant †.

---

* The author faith, that fome learned men think fo; and that the words, Gen. iii 22. feem to imply fo much: but all this amounts not to a pofitive determination of the point. The words are thefe, " Behold, the man is become as one of us, to " know good and evil: and now, left he put forth his hand, " and take alfo of the tree of life and eat, and live for ever."— Whether or not thefe words feem to imply fome fuch thing, I leave to the judgment of the reader. whom I incline not to entertain with mine own, or others conjectures, upon the head. But three things I take to be plain, and beyond conjecture, in this text. 1. That there is no irony nor fcoff here, as many think there is; but, on the contrary, a moft pathetic lamentation over fallen man. The literal verfion and fenfe of the former part of the text, run thus; " Behold the man that was as one " of us," &c. Compare, for the verfion, Lam. iii 1. Pfal. lii. 7. and for the fenfe, Gen. i. 26, 27. " And God faid, Let us make " man in OUR image "——" So God created man in his own " image," &c. The latter part of the text I would read thus; " And eat, that he may live for ever:" Compare, for this verfi- on, Exod. iv. 23. 1 Sam. vi 8. 'tis evident the fentence is broke off abruptly, the words, " I will drive him out," being fup- prefs'd; even as in the cafe of a father, with fighs, fobs and tears, putting his fon out of doors. 2. That it was God's defign, to prevent Adam's eating of the tree of life, as he had eaten of the forbidden tree; " Left he——take alfo of the tree " of life:" Thereby mercifully taking care, that our fallen father, to whom the covenant of grace was now proclaimed, might not, according to the corrupt natural inclination of fallen mankind, run back to the covenant of works for life and falva- tion, by partaking of the tree of life, a facrament of that cove- nant; and fo reject the covenant of grace, by eating of that tree now, as he had before broken the covenant of works, by eating of the tree of knowledge of good and evil. 3. That at this time Adam did think, that by eating of the tree of life he might live for ever. Further I dip not here, in this matter.

† Mr Slater on the 2 Cov.   D 3

Nom. But, Sir, how could Adam, who had his under-standing so sound, and his will so free to chufe good, be so difobedient to God's exprefs command?

Evan. Tho' he and his will were both good, yet were they mutably good; so that he might stand or fall, at his own election or choice *.

Nom. But why then did not the Lord create him immutable? or, why did he not so over-rule him in that action, that he might not have eaten the forbidden fruit † ?

Evan. The reafon why the Lord did not create him immutable ‡, was, becaufe he would be obeyed out of judgment and free choice; and not by fatal neceffity, and abfolute determination ‖; and withal let me tell you, it was not reafonable to reftrain God to this point; to make man fuch a one as would not, or could not fin at all § ; for it was at his choice to create him how he pleafed. But why he did not uphold him with ftrength of ftedfaft continuance; that refteth hidden in God's fecret counfel ¶. Howbeit, this we may certainly conclude; that Adam's

---

* Dent. Pathway, p. 304.

† Thefe are two diftinct queftions, both of them natively arifing from a legal temper of fpirit: and I doubt, if ever the heart of a finner fhall receive a fatisfying anfwer, as to either of them, until it come to embrace the gofpel way of falvation, taking up its everlafting reft in Chrift, for wifdom, righteoufnefs, fanctification and redemption.

‡ Reynolds on Pfal. cx. p. 405.

‖ See the following note.   § Calv. Inft. p. 81.

¶ Immutability, properly fo called, or abfolute unchange-ablenefs, is an incommunicable attribute of God, Mal. iii. 6. Jam. i. 17. And mutability, or changeablenefs, is fo of the nature of a creature, that it fhould ceafe to be a creature, or a dependent being, if it fhould ceafe to be mutable. But there is an immutability, improperly fo called, which is competent to the creature; whereby it is free from being actually liable to change, in fome refpect: the which, in reference to man, may be confidered two ways. 1 As putting him beyond the hazard of change by another hand than his own. 2. As putting him beyond the hazard of change by himfelf. In the former fenfe,

ftate was fuch, as ferved to take away from him all excufe ; for he received fo much, that of his own will he wrought his own deftruction * : becaufe this act of his was a wilful tranfgreffion of a law, under the precepts whereof, he was moft juftly created † ; and unto the malediction whereof, he was as neceffarily and righteoufly fubject, if he tranfgreffed : for, as being God's creature, he was to be fubject to his will ; fo, by being God's prifoner, he was as juflly fubject to his wrath ; and that fo much the more, by how much the precept was moft juft, the obedience more eafy, the tranfgreffion more unreafonable, and the punifhment more certain.

§ 3. *Nom.* And was Adam's fin and punifhment imputed unto his whole offspring?

Evan. Yea indeed ; for faith the apoftle, " Death paffed upon all men, for that all have finned ;" Rom. v. 12 or, in whom all have finned, that is in Adam. The very truth is, Adam, by his fall, threw down our

---

man was indeed made immutable in point of moral goodnefs; for he could only be made finful or evil by himfelf, and not by any other. If he had been made immutable in the latter fenfe, that immutability behoved either to have been woven into his very nature; or elfe to have rifen from confirming grace. Now God did not create man thus immutable in his nature, which is it that the firft queftion aims at: and that for this very good reafon, *viz.* That at that rate, man would have obeyed by fatal neceffity and abfolute determination, as one not having fo much as a remote power in his nature to change himfelf. And neither glorified faints, nor angels, are thus immutable ; their immutability in goodnefs entirely depending on confirming grace. As for immutability by confirming grace, which is it that the fecond queftion aims at ; it is conferred on glorified faints and angels: but why it was not afforded to Adam at his creation, our author wifely declines to give any reafon. " The reafon," faith he, " why the Lord did not create him immutable, was, Be-" caufe, &c. But why he did not uphold him with ftrength " of ftedfaft continuance, that refteth hidden in God's fecret " counfel."

* *i. e.* He received fo much ftrength, that it was not of weaknefs, but wilfulnefs, that he deftroyed himfelf.
† Reynolds on Pfal. cx. p. 406.

whole nature * headlong into the fame deftruction †, and drowned his whole offspring in the fame gulph of mifery ‡. And the reafon is, becaufe, by God's appointment, he was not to ftand, or fall, as a fingle perfon only ; but as a common public perfon, reprefenting all mankind to come of him ‖, § : Therefore as all that happinefs, all thofe gifts and endowments, which were beftowed upon him, were not beftowed upon him alone, but alfo upon the whole nature of man ¶ ; and as that covenant which was made with him, was made with whole mankind ; even fo he, by breaking covenant, loft all, as well for us as for himfelf. As he received all for himfelf and us ; fo he loft all, both for himfelf and us * *.

Nom. Then, Sir, it feemeth, by Adam's breach of covenant, all mankind were brought into a miferable condition.

Evan. All mankind by the fall of Adam received a twofold damage ††. 1*ft* A deprivation of all original goodnefs. 2*dly*, An habitual natural pronenefs to all kind of wickednefs ‡‡ : For the image of God, after which they were created, was forthwith blotted out ; and in place of wifdom, righteoufnefs and true holinefs, came blindnefs, uncleannefs, falfehood and injuftice.— The very truth is, our whole nature ‖‖ was thereby corrupted, defiled, deformed, depraved, infected, made infirm, frail, malignant, full of venom, contrary to God ; yea enemies and rebels unto him §§. So that, faith Luther ¶¶, this is the title we have received from

---

* *i e.* All mankind.
† Calv. Inft. p. 106, 107. ‡ With himfelf.
‖ Goodwin's triumph of Faith, p. 85.
§ *Viz.* By virtue of the bleffing of fruitfulnefs, given before the fall.
¶ *i. e.* All mankind. * * Pemble Vind. Fid. p. 99.
†† Seven Golden Candlefticks, p. 3.
‡‡ Baften. Cat. p. 10. ‖‖ *i. e.* All mankind.
§§ Urban Reg. in Chr. Scr. to Emaus, p. 12.
¶¶ Chof. Scr. p. 9.

Adam, in this one thing we may glory, and in nothing elfe at all; namely, that every infant that is born into this world, is wholly in the power of fin, death, Satan, hell and everlafting damnation. Nay, faith Mufculus *, the whirlpool of man's fin in Paradife, is bottomlefs and unfearchable.

Nom. But, Sir, methinks, it is a ftrange thing, that fo fmall an offence, as eating the forbidden fruit feems to be, fhould plunge whole mankind into fuch a gulph of mifery.

Evan. Though at the firft glance it feems to be a fmall offence; yet if we look more wiftly † upon the matter, it will appear to be an exceeding great offence ‡: for thereby intolerable injury was done unto God; as 1ft, His dominion and authority, in his holy command was violated. 2dly, His juftice, truth and power, in his moft righteous threatenings, were defpifed. 3dly, His moft pure and perfect image, wherein man was created in righteoufnefs and true holinefs, was uttery defaced. 4thly, His glory, which by an active fervice the creature fhould have brought to him, was loft and defpoiled. Nay, how could there be a greater fin committed, than that when Adam at that one clap broke all the ten commandments. ‖.

Nom. Did he break all the ten commandments, fay you? Sir, I befeech you fhew me wherein?

Evan. 1. He chofe himfelf another God, when he followed the devil §.

2. He idolized and deified his own belly ¶; as the apoftle's phrafe is " he made his belly his God."

3. He took the name of God in vain, when he believed him not.

4 He kept not the reft and eftate wherein God had fet him **.

---

* Com. Pla. p. 14.   † *i. e.* Earneftly.
‡ Reynolds on Pfal. cx. p. 407.
‖ Lightfoot Mifcel. p. 183.   § Ibid.
¶ That is.   * * See the note * page 49.

5. He diſhonoured his Father which was in heaven; and therefore his days were not prolonged in that land, which the Lord his God had given him.

6. He maſſacred himſelf and all his poſterity.

7. From Eve he was a virgin, but in eyes and mind he commited ſpiritual fornication.

8. He ſtole (like Achan) that which God had ſet aſide not to be medled with; and this his ſtealth is that which troubles all Iſrael, the whole world.

9. He bare witneſs againſt God, when he believed the witneſs of the devil, above him.

10. He coveted an evil covetouſneſs, like Amon, which coſt him his life *, and all his progeny. Now whoſo-ever conſiders, what a neſt of evils here were committed at one blow, muſt needs, with Muſculus †, ſee our caſe to be ſuch, that we be compelled every way to commend the juſtice of God ‡; and to condemn the ſin of our firſt parents; ſaying concerning all mankind, as the prohpet Hoſea doth, concerning Iſrael, "O Iſrael, thou haſt deſtroyed thyſelf." Hoſ. xiii. 9.

§ 4. *Nom.* But, Sir; had it not been poſſible for Adam, both to have helped himſelf and his poſterity, out of this miſery; by renewing the ſame covenant with God, and keeping it for afterwards?

Even. No, by no means; for the covenant of works, was a covenant no way capable of renovation ‖, ſ. When he had once broke it, he was gone for ever: be-

---

* 2 Sam. xiii.   † Com. Pla. p. 13.

‡ *i. e.* To juſtify God.

‖ Bolton's true Bounds, p. 13. 5.

ſ The covenant of works could by no means be renewed by fallen Adam, ſo as thereby to help himſelf and his poſterity out of this miſery; the which is the only thing in queſtion here. Otherwiſe indeed it might have been renewed; which is evident by this ſad token, that many do actually renew it, in their covenanting with God, being prompted thereto, by their ignorance of the high demands of the law, their own utter inability, and the way of ſalvation by Jeſus Chriſt. And from the ſame principle our Legaliſt here makes no queſtion, but Adam might have renewed it, and kept it too, for the after-time: only he

caufe it was a covenant between two friends; but now fallen man was become an enemy. And befides, it was an impoffible thing for Adam to have performed the conditions, which now the juftice of God did neceffarily require at his hands: for he was now become liable to the payment of a double debt; to wit, the debt of fatisfaction for his fin committed in time paft, and the debt of perfect and perpetual obedience, for the time to come; and he was utterly unable to pay either of them.

Nom. Why was he unable to pay the debt of fatisfaction for his fin committed in time paft?

Evan. Becaufe his fin in eating the forbidden fruit (for that is the fin I mean*) was committed againft an infinite and eternal good †; and therefore merited an infinite and eternal fatisfaction; which was to be either fome temporal punifhment equivalent to eternal damnation, or eternal damnation itfelf. Now Adam was a finite creature, therefore between finite and infinite there could be no proportion: fo that it was impoffible for Adam to have made fatisfaction, by any temporal punifhment; and if he had undertaken to have fatisfied by an eternal punifhment, he fhould always have been fatisfying, and never have fatisfied, as is the cafe of the damned in hell.

Nom. And why was he unable to pay the debt of perfect and perpetual obedience for the time to come?

Evan. Becaufe his precedent power to obey, was by his fall utterly impaired: for thereby his underftanding was both feebled and drowned in darknefs ‡; and his will made perverfe and utterly deprived of all power to will well; and his affections were quite fet out of order;

---

queftions, whether or not Adam might thereby have helped himfelf and his pofterity toe, out of the mifery they were brought into by his fin?

* That being the fin in which all mankind fell with him, Rom. v. 15. † Urfin Cat. p. 112. ‡ Ibid. Cat. p. 112.

and all things belonging to the bleſſed life of the ſoul were extinguiſhed both in him and us*: So that he was become impotent, yea dead, and therefore not able to ſtand in the loweſt terms to perform the meaneſt condition. The very truth is, our father Adam falling from God, did, by his fall, ſo daſh him and us all in pieces; that there was no whole part left, either in him or us, fit to ground ſuch a covenant upon. And this the apoſtle witneſſeth, both when he ſaith, "We are of no ſtrength;" and, "The law was made weak becauſe of the fleſh," Rom. v. 6. and viii. 3.

Nom. But, Sir, might not the Lord have pardoned Adam's ſin without ſatisfaction?

Evan. O no, for juſtice is eſſential in God; and it is a righteous thing with God, that every tranſgreſſion receive a juſt recompenſe †: And if recompenſe be juſt, it is unjuſt to pardon ſin without ſatisfaction. And tho' the Lord had pardoned and forgiven his former tranſgreſſion; and ſo ſet him in his former condition of amity and friendſhip: yet having no power to keep the law perfectly, he could not have continued therein ‡.

Nom. And is it alſo impoſſible for any of his poſterity to keep the law perfectly?

Evan. Yea, indeed, it is impoſſible for any meer man, in the time of this life, to keep it perfectly; yea, though he be a regenerate man; for the law requireth of man, that he "love the Lord with all his heart, ſoul and might;" and there is not the holieſt man that lives, but he is fleſh as well as ſpirit, in all parts and faculties of

---

* Calv. Inſt. p. 117. Bolton's true Bonds, p. 133.

† 2 Theſſ. i. 6. "Seeing it is a righteous thing with God, to recompenſe tribulation to them that trouble you." Heb. ii. 2. "Every tranſgreſſion and diſobedience received a juſt "recompenſe."

‡ But would have ſinned again, and ſo fallen under the curſe anew.

his foul; and therefore cannot love the Lord perfectly. Yea, and the law forbiddeth all habitual concupiscence, not only saying, " Thou fhalt not confent to luft," but, " Thou fhalt not luft:" it doth not only command the binding of luft, but forbids alfo the being of luft; and and who in this cafe can fay, " My heart is clean?"

Ant. Then, friend Nomifta, take notice, I pray, that as it was altogether impoffible for Adam, to return into that holy and happy eftate, wherein he was created, by by the fame way he went from it * ; fo is it for any of his pofterity: and therefore I remember, one † faith very wittily, The law was Adam's leafe when God made him tenant of Eden; the conditions of which bond, when he kept not, he forfeited himfelf, and all us. God read a lecture of the law to him before he fell, to be a hedge to him to keep him in Paradife; but when Adam would not keep within compafs, this law is now become as the flaming fword at Eden's gate, to keep him and his pofterity out.

§ 5. *Nom.* But, Sir, you know, that when a covenant is broken, the parties that were bound, are freed and releafed from their engagements; and therefore, methinks, both Adam and his pofterity, fhould have been releafed from the covenant of works, when it was broken; efpecially confidering they have no ftrength to perform the condition of it.

---

* Walking back, by the way of the covenant of works, which he left by his finning.

Obj. " Do we not then make void the law," Rom. iii. 31. leaving an imputation of difhonour upon it, as a difregarded path, by pretending to return another way? *Anf.* Sinners, being united to Chrift by faith, return, being carried back the fame way they came; only their own feet never touch the ground; but the glorious Mediator, fuftaining the perfons of them all, walked every bit of the rod exactly, Gal. iv. 4, 5. Thus, in Chrift, the way of free grace, and of the law, fweetly meet together; and through faith we eftablifh the law, Ibid.

† Lightfoot Mifcel. p. 282.

E

Evan. Indeed it is true, in every covenant, if either party fail in his duty and perform not his condition; the other party is thereby freed, from his part; but the party failing is not freed, till the other releafe him: and therefore, tho' the Lord be freed from performing his condition, that is, from giving to man eternal life; yet fo is not man from his part: no, though ftrength to obey be loft, yet man having loft it by his own default, the obligation to obedience remains ftill; fo that Adam and his offspring are no more difcharged of their duties, becaufe they have no ftrength to do them, than a debitor is quitted of his bond, becaufe he wants money to pay it. And thus, neighbour Nomifta, I have, according to your defire, endeavoured to help you, to the true knowledge of the law of works.

C H A P. II.

Of the Law of Faith,

O R,

Covenant of Grace.

Sect. 1. *Of the Eternal Purpofe of Grace.* Sect. 2. *Of the Promife.* Sect. 3. *Of the Performance of the Promife.*

Ant. I Befeech you, Sir, proceed to help us to the true knowledge of the law of faith.

Evan. The law of faith is as much to fay as the covenant of grace, or the gofpel, which fignifieth good, merry, glad, and joyful tidings*; that is to fay, that God, to whofe eternal knowledge all things are prefent, and nothing paft or to come, forefeeing man's fall, before

---

* Tindal's path to holy fcripture, p. 378. 1 Tim. i. 9.
Eph. iii. 1. 3. Rom. i. 2. Gal. iv. 4.

all times purposed *, and in time promised †, and in the fulness of time performed ‡, the sending of his Son Jesus Christ into the world, to help and deliver fallen mankind ‖.

SECTION I.

Of the Eternal Purpose of Grace.

Ant. I Beseech you, Sir, let us hear more of these things; and first of all, shew how we are to conceive of God's eternal purpose, in sending of Jesus Christ.

Evan. Why, here the learned frame a kind of conflict in God's holy attributes §: and by a liberty, which the Holy Ghost, from the language of holy scripture, allow-

---

* 2 Tim. i. 9. " Who hath saved us, according to his own purpose and grace, which was given us in Christ Jesus, before the world began." Eph. iii. 11. " According to the eternal purpose, which he purposed in Christ Jesus our Lord."

† Rom. i. 1, 2. " The gospel of God, which he had promised, afore by his prophets in the holy scriptures."

‡ Gal. iv 4, 5. " But when the fulness of the time was come, God sent forth his Son, made of a woman, made under the law, to redeem them that were under the law."

‖ These are the good tidings, this is the law of faith, *i. e.* the law to be believed for salvation, which the apostle plainly teacheth, Rom. i. 16. " The gospel is the power of God unto salvation to every one that believeth." And ver. 17. " For therein is the righteousness of God revealed from faith to faith." In this last text, clouded with great variety of interpretations, I think there is a transposition of words to be admitted; and would read the whole verse thus ; " For therein is revealed the righteousness of God, by faith, unto faith ; as it is written, but, the just by faith shall live." The key to this construction and reading of the words in the former part of the verse, is the testimony adduced by the apostle in the latter part of it, from Hab. ii. 4. where the original text appears to me to determine the version of that testimony as here offered. The sense is, the righteousness which is by faith, namely, the righteousness of Christ, the only righteousness in which a sinner can stand before God, is in the gospel revealed unto faith, *i. e.* to be believed. See a like phrase, 1 Tim. iv. 3. translated after this manner.

§ Reynolds on Psal. cx. p 407, 408

E 2

eth them, they speak of God after the manner of men;
as if he were reduced to some straits and difficulties, by
the cross demands of his several attributes *†. For truth
and justice stood up, and said, that man had sinned; and
therefore man must die; and so called for the condemnation of a sinful, and therefore worthily a cursed creature;
or else they must be violated: for thou saidst (say they
to God) " In that day thou eatest of the tree of the
knowledge of good and evil, thou shalt die the death."
Mercy, on the other side, pleaded for favour, and appeals
to the great court in heaven: and there it pleads, saying,
wisdom and power, and goodness, have been all manifest
in the creation ‡ ; and anger and justice, they have been
magnified in man's misery, that he is now plunged into,
by his fall: but I have not yet been manifested ‖. O, let
favour and compassion be shewed towards man, wofully
seduced and overthrown by Satan ! O, said they § unto
God, It is a royal thing to relieve the distressed; and the
greater any one is, the more placable and gentle he
ought to be. But Justice replied, If I be offended, I must
be satisfied and have my right: and therefore I require,
that man, who hath lost himself by his disobedience,
should, for remedy, set obedience against it, and so satisfy the judgment of God. Therefore the wisdom of God
became an umpire, and devised a way to reconcile them ¶;
concluding, that before there could be reconciliation made,

---

* William's seven golden candlesticks, p 319.

† Hosea xi 8. " How shall I give thee up, Ephraim? How
shall I deliver thee, Israel? How shall I make thee as Admah?
How shall I set thee as Zeboim? Mine heart is turned within
me, my repentings are kindled together.

‡ Hooker's soul just, p 277

‖ Mercy requires an object in misery

§ *Viz.* Favour and Compassion

¶ Calv Instit, p. 117

there muſt be two things effected : 1*ſt*, A ſatisfaction of God's juſtice. 2*dly*, A reparation of man's nature *: which two things muſt needs be effected by ſuch a middle and common perſon † that had both zeal towards God, that he might be ſatisfied; and compaſſion, towards man, that he might be repaired : ſuch a perſon, as, having man's guilt and puniſhment tranſlated on him, might ſatisfy the juſtice of God, and as having a fulneſs of God's Spirit and holineſs in him, might ſanctify and repair the nature of man ‡. And this could be none other but Jeſus Chriſt, one of the three perſons of the bleſſed Trinity. And therefore he ||, by his Father's ordination, his own voluntary ſuſception, and the holy Spirit's ſanctification, was fitted for the buſineſs. Whereupon there was a ſpecial covenant §, or mutual agreement made between

---

* See the following note

† Reynolds on Pſal cx p 408

‡ As man lay in ruins by the fall, guilty and unclean, there ſtood in the way of his ſalvation by mercy deſigned, 1, The juſtice of God, which could not admit the guilty creature; and 2, The holineſs of God, which could not admit the unclean and unholy creature, to communion with him. Therefore, in the contrivance of his ſalvation, it was neceſſary, that proviſion ſhould be made for the ſatisfaction of God's juſtice, by payment of the double debt mentioned above; namely, the debt of puniſhment, and the debt of perfect obedience. It was alſo neceſſary, that proviſion ſhould be made for the ſanctification of the ſinner, the repairing of the loſt image of God in him. And man being as unable to ſanctify himſelf, as to ſatisfy juſtice (a truth which proud nature cannot digeſt) the Saviour behoved not only to obey and ſuffer in his ſtead; but alſo to have a fulneſs of the ſpirit of holineſs in him, to communicate to the ſinner, that his nature might be repaired, through ſanctification of the Spirit. Thus was the ground-work of man's ſalvation laid in the eternal counſel; the ſanctification of the ſinner, according to our author, being as neceſſary to his ſalvation, as the ſatisfaction of juſtice : for indeed the neceſſity of the former, as well as of the latter, ariſeth from the nature of God, and therefore is an abſolute neceſſity.

|| Reynolds on Pſal. cx. p. 408.

§ Ameſ. Med. p. 74.

God and Chrift, as is exprefled·Ifaiah liii. 10. that if Chrift would make· himfelf a facrifice for fin, then he fhould fee his feed, he. fhould prolong his days, and the " pleafure of the Lord fhould profper· by him.".— So in Pfal. lxxxix. 19. The mercies of this covenant between God and Chrift, under the type of God's covenant with David, are fet forth; " Thou fpakeft in vifion to thy holy One, and faidft, I have laid help upon One that is mighty," or as the Chaldee expoundeth, " One mighty in the law." As God had faid concerning his eleft *, I know that thefe will break, and never be able to fatisfy me; but thou art a mighty and fubftantial perfon, able to pay me; therefore I will look for my debt † off thee, (as Pareus well obferves) God did, as it were, fay to Chrift, What they owe me, I require it all at thy hands. Then faid Chrift, " Lo I come to do thy will! in the volume of thy book it is written of me, I delight to do they will, O my God, yea thy law is in my heart." Thus Chrift affented, and from everlefting ftruck hands with God ‡, to put upon him man's perfon, and to take upon him his name, and to enter in his ftead in obeying his Father, and to do all for man, that he fhould require, and to yield in man's flefh the price of the fatiffaction of the juft judgment of God, and in the fame flefh, to fuffer the punifhment that man had deferved: and this he undertook under the penalty that lay upon man to have undergone ‖. And thus was juftice fatisfied, and

---

* Ainfworth on the text. Goodwin Chrift fet forth, p. 75. ·

† *i. e.* The debt which the eleft owe to me. Thus was the covenant made betwixt the Father and the Son, for the eleft, that he fhould obey for them, and die for them.

‡ Pfal xl. 7, 8. Cal. Inftit. p. 117.

‖ The Son of God confented to put himfelf in man's ftead, in obeying his Father, and fo to do all for man that his Father fhould require; that fatisfaction fhould be made: farther, he, confented, in man's nature to fatisfy and·fuffer the deferved punifhment; that the fame nature that finned might fatisfy:

mercy magnified, by the Lord Jefus Chrift : and fo God took Chriſt's fingle bond; whence Chriſt is not only call-, ed, the " furety of the covenant" for us, Heb. vii 22. but the " covenant itfelf," Ifa. xlix. 8. And God laid all upon him, that he might be fure of fatisfaction; proteſting that he would not deal with us, nor fo much as expect any payment from us * ; fuch was his grace. And thus did our Lord Jefus Chriſt, enter into the fame covenant of works, that Adam did; to deliver believers from it † ‡ : he was contented to be under all that com-

---

and yet farther, he undertook to bear the very fame penalty, that lay upon man, by virtue of the covenant of works, to have undergone; fo fifting himfelf a proper furety for them, who, as the author obferves, muſt pay the fame fum of money that the debitor oweth. This I take to be the author's meaning : but the expreſſion of Chriſt's undertaking under the penalty, &c. is haiſh and unguarded.

* Hooker's foul juſt. p. 174.
† Goodwin's Chriſt fet forth, p. 83.
‡ Our Lord Jefus Chriſt became furety for the elect in the fecond covenant, Heb. vii. 22. And in virtue of that furetyſhip, whereby he put himfelf in the room of the principal debitors, he came under the fame covenant of works that Adam did; in fo far as the fulfilling of that covenant in their ſtead, was the very condition required of him as the fecond Adam in the fecond covenant, Gal. iv. 4, 5. " God fent forth his Son— made under the law, to redeem them that were under the law." Thus Chriſt put his neck under the yoke of the law, as a cove- nant of works, to redeem them who were under it as fuch. Hence he is faid to be the " end of the law for righteoufnefs to every one that believeth," Rom. x. 4. namely, the end for con- fumption, or perfect fulfilling of it by his obedience and death, which prefuppofeth his coming under it. And thus the law, as a covenant of works, was magnified and made honourable ; and it clearly appears how " by faith we eſtabliſh the law," Rom. iii. 31. *Queſt.* How then is the fecond covenant a covenant of grace ? *Anf.* In refpect of Chriſt, it was moſt properly and ſtrictly a covenant of works; in that he made a proper, real, and full fatisfaction, in behalf of the elect : but, in refpect of them, it is purely a covenant of richeſt grace, in as much as God accepted the fatisfaction from a furety, which he might have demanded of them ; provided the furety himfelf; and gives all to them freely, for his fake.

manding, revenging authority, which that covenant had over them; to free them from the penalty of it: and in that respect, Adam is said to be a type of Christ, as you have it, Rom. v. 14. " Who was the type of him that was to come." Unto which purpose, the titles which the apostle gives these two, Christ and Adam, are exceeding observable. He calls Adam the first man, and Christ our Lord the second man, 1 Cor. xv. 47. speaking of them as if there never had been any more men in the world, besides these two; thereby making them the head and root of all mankind, they having, as it were, the rest of the sons of men included in them. The first man is called the earthly man; the second man, Christ, is called the Lord from heaven, 1 Cor. xv. 47. The earthly man had all the sons of men born into the world, included in him; and is so called in conformity unto them, the first man * : the second man, Christ is called the Lord from heaven, who had all the elect included in him; who are said to be the first born, and to have their names written in heaven, Heb. xii. 23. and therefore are oppositely called heavnly men: so that these two, in God's account, stood for all the rest †. And thus you see, that the Lord, willing to shew mercy to the creature fallen ‡, and withal to maintain the authority of his law, took such a course as might best manifest his clemency and severity ||: Christ entered into covenant, and became suerty for man, and so became liable to man's engagements; for he that answers for a surety, must pay the same sum of money that the debtor oweth.

And thus have I endeavoured to shew you, how we are to conceive of God's eternal purpose, in sending of Jesus Christ to help and deliver fallen mankind.

---

* And so, in relation to them, is called the first man.
† Thus Adam represented all mankind in the first covenant: and Christ represented all the elect in the second covenant. See the first note on the preface.
‡ Ball on the Cov. p. 289. || Ibid. p. 207, 208.

SECTION II.

Of the PROMISE.

§ 1. *The Promise made to Adam.* § 2. *The Promise renewed to Abraham.* § 3. *The Law, as the Covenant of works, added to the Promise.* § 4. *The Promise and Covenant with Abraham, renewed with the Israelites.* § 5. *The Covenant of grace under the Mosaic dispensation.* § 6. *The natural Bias towards the Covenant of works.* § 7. *The Antinomian Faith rejected.* § 8. *The Evil of Legalism.*

§ 1. *Ant.* I Beseech you, Sir, proceed also to the second thing: and first tell us, when the Lord began to make a promise to help and deliver mankind.

Evan. Even the same day that he sinned *, which, as I suppose, was the very same day he was created † : for Adam, by his sin, being become the child of wrath, and

---

* This our author doth here positively assert, and afterward confirm. And there is plain evidence for it, from the holy scripture, which determines the time of the Lord's calling our guilty first parents before him, at the which time he gave them the promise, Gen. iii. 8. " And they heard the voice of the Lord God walking in the garden in the cool of the day." Heb. At the wind of that day, as Junius and Tremellius, Piscator and Picherellus read it; the which, as soon as it began to blow, might convince them, that their aprons of fig-leaves were no fit covers for their nakedness.

† Our author is far from being singular in this opinion. The learned Gataker (apud Pol. Synop. Crit. in Gen. iii. 23.) owns it to be the common opinion, tho' himself is of another mind, "§ That man fell, and was cast out of paradise, the same day in which he was created." And he tells us (ib. in Psal. xlix. 13.) that " Broughton doth most confidently assert, Adam not to have stood in his integrity so much as one day; and that he saith

both in body and in foul, fubject to the curfe, and feeing
nothing due to him but the wrath and vengeance of God;
he was " afraid, and, fought to hide himfelf from the
prefence of God," Gen. iii. 10. Whereupon the Lord
promifed Chrift unto him, faying to the ferpent, " I
will put enmity between thee and the woman, and between thy feed and her feed : He (that is to fay, the
feed of the woman ; for fo is the Hebrew text) fhall
break thy head, and thou fhalt bruife his heel.", ..This
promife of Chrift, the woman's feed, verfe 15. was the
gofpel * ; and the only comfort of Adam, Abel, Enoch,
Noah, and the reft of the godly fathers, until the time
of Abraham †.

---

out of Maimonides, " This is held by all the Jews, as alfo by
the Greek fathers." That this opinion is lefs received than
formerly, is, if I miftake not, not a little owing to the cavils of
the Deifts, who, to weaken the credit of the infpired hiftory,
alledge it to be incredible, that the events recorded Gen. i. 24,
25, 26. and ii. 7. and 18. to the end of the third chapter, could
all be crouded into one day. See Nicol's conference with a
Theift. The reafons to fupport it, take from the learned Sharp,
one of the fix minifters banifhed in the year 1696. Curf.
Theol. Loc. de Peccato. (1.) " Becaufe of the devil's envy,
who, 'tis likely, could not long endure to fee man in a happy
ftate. (2.) If man had ftood more days, the blefling of marriage
would have taken place, Adam would have known his wife,
and begot a child without original fin. (3.) The fabbath was
not fo much appointed for meditating on the works of creation,
as on the works of redemption. (4.) It appears from the words
of the ferpent, and of the woman, that fhe had not yet tafted
any fruit. (5.) When the Holy Ghoft fpeaks of the fixth day,
Gen. i. and of the day of the fall, 'tis with ה_א emphatic.
(Compare Gen. i. ult. and iii. 8) (6.) He fell fo foon that the
work of redemption might be the more illuftrious; fince man
could not ftand one day without the Mediator's help."——
How the fabbath was broken by Adam's fin, tho' committed
the day before, may be learned from Larg. Cat. on the 4th
command, which teacheth that " The fabbath is to be fanctified—and to that end, we are to prepare our hearts—that we
may be the more fit for the duties of that day;" and that
" The fins forbidden in the 4th commandment, are all omif-
fions of the duties required," &c.

* Urb. Reg. on Serm. to Emaus.
† In this promife was revealed; 1. Man's reftoration into the

Nom. I pray you, Sir, what ground have you to think that Adam fell the fame day he was created?

Evan. My ground for this opinion, is, Pſal. xlix. 12. which text Mr Ainſworth * makes to be the 13. verſe, and reads it thus; " But man in honour doth not lodge a night, he is likened unto beaſts that are ſilenced †.

---

favour of God, and his ſalvation; not to be effected by man himſelf, and his own works, but by another. For our firſt Parents, ſtanding condemn'd for breaking of the covenant of works, are not ſent back to it, to eſſay the mending of the matter, which they had marred before; but a new covenant is propoſed, a Saviour promiſed as their only hope. 2. That this Saviour was to be incarnate, to become man, the ſeed of the woman. 3. That he behoved to ſuffer; his heel, namely his humanity, to be bruiſed to death. 4. That by his death be ſhould make a full conqueſt over the devil, and deſtroy his works, who had now overcome and deſtroyed mankind; and ſo recover the captives out of his hand; " He ſhall bruiſe thy head," to wit, while thou bruiſeſt his heel. This encounter was on the croſs; there Chriſt treading on the ſerpent, it bruiſed his heel, but he bruiſed its head. 5. That HE ſhould not be held by death, but Satan's power ſhould be broken irrecoverably; the Saviour being bruiſed only in the heel, but the ſerpent in the head. 6. That the ſaving intereſt in him, and his ſalvation, is by faith alone, believing the promiſe with particular application to one's ſelf, and, ſo receiving him; for as much as theſe things are revealed by way of a ſimple promiſe.

* Ainſworth.

† " From this text, the Hebrew doctors, alſo, in Bereſhit Rabba, do gather, that the glory of the firſt man did not night with him; and that in the beginning of the ſabbath his ſplendor was taken away from him, and he was driven out of Eden." Cartwright apud Pol. Synopſ. Crit. in Loc. The learned Leigh, in his Crit. Sacr. in Voc. Lun, citing this text, faith, " Adam lodged not one night in honour; for ſo are the words, if they be properly tranſlated." He repeats the fame in his annotations on the book of Pſalms; and points his reader to Ainſworth, whoſe verſion does evidently favour this opinion, and is here faithfully cited by our author, though without the marks of compoſition, (lodge-a-night) there being no ſuch marks in my copy of Ainſworth's verſion or annotations, printed at London 1639. However the word Lun may ſignify to abide or continue, 'tis certain the proper and primary ſignification of it, is to night (at, in, or with;) I muſt be allowed the uſe of this word, to

That may be minded (faith he) both for the firſt man Adam, who continued not in his dignity, and for all his children.

Ant. But Sir, do you think that Adam and thoſe others, did underſtand that promiſed feed to be meant Chriſt?

Evan. Who can make any doubt, but that the Lord had acquainted Adam with Chriſt, betwixt the time of of his ſinning and the time of his ſacrificing, though both on a day?

Ant. But did Adam offer ſacrifice?

Evan. Can you make any queſton *, but that the bodies of thoſe beaſts, whoſe ſkins went for a covering for his body, were immeditely before offered in ſacrifice for his ſoul? ſurely thoſe ſkins could be none other but of beaſts ſlain †, and offered in ſacrifice ; for before Adam

---

expreſs the true import of the original one. Thus we have it rendered, Gen. xxviii. 11. tarried all night. Judg xix. 9. tarry all night. Ver. 10. tarry that night. Ver. 13. lodged all night. And ſince this is the proper and primary ſignification of the word, it is not to be receded from without neceſſity, the which I cannot diſcover here. The text ſeems to me to ſtand thus, word for word, the propriety of the tenſes alſo obſerved.— " Yet-Adam in-honour could not-night; he became-like as-the-beaſts, they were alike." Compare the Septuagint, and the vulgar Latin ; with which, according to Pool in Synopf. Crit. the Ethiopic, Syriac, and Arabic, do agree ; though unhappy in not obſerving the difference, between this and the laſt verſe of the Pſalm. Nothing can be more agreeable to the ſcope and context. Worldly men "boaſt themſelves in the multitude of their riches," ver. 6. as if their houſes ſhould continue for ever," ver. 11. And yet Adam as happy as he was in Paradiſe, continued not one night in his honour; it quickly left him; yea, he died, and in that reſpeft became like the beaſts; compare ver. 14. " Like ſheep they are laid in the grave, death ſhall feed on them." And after ſhewing that the worldly man ſhall die, notwithſtanding of his worldly wealth and honour; ver. 19. this ſuitable memorial for Adam's ſons, is repeated with a very ſmall variation; ver. 20, 21. " Adam was in-honour, but-could-not underſtand ; he became;" &c.

* Lightfoot Miſcel. p. 18. Vaughmeth on Bib. p. 15.

† Walker on the cov. p. 59.

fell, beasts were not subject to mortality, nor slaying. And
God's clothing of Adam and his wife with skins, signified,
that their sin and shame was covered with Christ's righteousness. And questionless the Lord had taught him, that
his sacrifice did signify his acknowledgement of his sin,
and that he looked for the seed of the woman *, promised to be slain in the evening of the world, thereby to
appease the wrath of God for his offence; the which,
undoubtedly, he acquainted his sons Cain and Abel with,
when he taught them also to offer sacrifice.

Ant. But how doth it appear that this his sacrificing
was the very same day that he sinned?

Evan. It is said, John vii. 3. concerning Christ, that
" They sought to take him, yet no man laid hands on
him, because his hour was not yet come;" but after that,
when the time of his suffering was at hand, he himself
said, John xii. 24. " The hour is come;" which day is
expressly set down by the evangelist Mark, Mark xv. 34,
42. to be the sixth day, and ninth hour of that day,
when " Christ, through the eternal spirit, offered up
himself without spot to God." Now, if you compare this
with Exodus xii. 6. you shall find that the paschal lamb,
a most lively type of Christ, was offered the very same
day and hour, even the sixth day, and ninth hour of the
day; which was at three of the clock in the afternoon † :
and the scripture testifieth, that Adam was created the
very same sixth day; and gives us ground to think that
he sinned the same day. And do not the fore-alledged
scripture afford us warrant to believe, that it was the
very same hour of that day; Gen. i. 26. when
Christ entered mystically and typically upon the work
of redemption, in being offered as a sacrifice for Adam's
sin ‡ : And surely we may suppose, that the covenant

---

* Gibbons on Gen.   † Ainsworth on the text.

‡ That the promise was given the same day that Adam

(as you heard) being broken between God and Adam, Juſtice would not have admitted of one hour's reſpite, before it had proceeded to execution to the deſtruction both of Adam and the whole creation; had not Chriſt, in the very nick of time, ſtood as the Ram (or rather the lamb) in the buſh, and ſtepped in to perform the work of the covenant. And hence I conceive it is, that St * John calls him " the lamb ſlain from the beginning of the world" † ‡. For as the firſt ſtate of creation was confirm-

---

ſinned, was evinced before: and from the hiſtory, Gen. iii. and the nature of the thing itſelf, one may reaſonably conclude, that the ſacrifices were annexed to the promiſe. And ſince the hour of Chriſt's death, was all along the time of the evening ſacrifice ; it is very natural to reckon, that it was alſo the hour of the firſt ſacrifice : even as the place on which the temple ſtood, was at firſt deſigned by an extraordinary ſacrifice on that ſpot, 1 Chron. xx. 18.—28. and xxii. 1. " At three o'clock in the afternoon Chriſt yieldeth up the ghoſt, Mark xv. 34. the very time when Adam had received the promiſe of this his paſſion for his redemption. Lightfoot on Acts ii 1.

* This word might well have been ſpared here ; notwith-ſtanding that we ſo read, in the title of the book of the Revelati-on, in our Engliſh Bibles ; and in like manner in the titles of other books of the New Teſtament, S. (*i. e* Saint) Mathew, S. Mark, S Luke, &c. It is evident, there is no ſuch word to be found in the titles of theſe books in the original Greek : and the Dutch tranſlators have juſtly diſcarded it, out of their tranſlation. If it is to be retained, becauſe John, Matthew, Mark, Luke, &c. were without controverſy ſaints ; why not on the ſame ground, Saint Moſes, Saint Aron, (expreſsly called the Saint of the Lord, Pſal. cvi. 16.) &c. no reaſon can be given of the difference made in this point, but that it pleaſed Antichriſt to cannonize theſe New Teſtament ſaints. but not the Old Teſtament ones. Cannonizing is an act or ſentence of the Pope, decerning religious worſhip and honours to ſuch men or women departed, as he ſees meet to confer the honour of ſaintſhip on. Theſe honours are ſeven. And the firſt of them is, That they are enrolled in the catalogue of ſaints, and muſt be accounted and called ſaints by all. Bellarmin. Diſp. tom. 1. Col. 1496.

† Rev. xiii. 8. Walker on the cov. p. 42.

‡ The benefits thereof (*viz.* of Chriſt's redemption) " Were

ed by the covenant which God made with man * ; and all creatures were to be upheld by means of obferving the law and condition of that covenant: fo that covenant being broken by man, the world fhould have come to ruin, had it not been as it were created anew, and upheld by the covenant of grace in Chrift.

Ant. Then, Sir, you think that Adam was faved:

Evan. The Hebrew doctors hold that Adam was a repentant finner † ; and fay, that he was by wifdom (that is to fay, by faith in Chrift) brought out of his fall; yea and the church of God doth hold, and that for necef-fary caufes ‡, that he was faved by the death of Chrift: yea, faith Mr Vaughan, it is certain he believed the promife concerning Chrift, in whofe commemoration he offered continual facrifice; and in the affurance thereof, he named his wife Hevah, that is to fay, life ‖ ; and he called his fon Seth, fettled or perfuaded in Chrift.

Ant. Well, now I am perfuaded that Adam did un-derftand this feed of the woman to be meant of Chrift.

Evan. Affure yourfelf, that not only Adam but all the reft of the godly fathers, did fo underftand it § ; as is manifeft in that the Thargum or Chaldee Bible, which is the antient tranflation of Jerufalm, hath it thus: Between thy fon and fon ¶ ; adding further by way of comment,

---

communicated unto the elect from the beginning of the world, in, and by thofe promifes, types and facrifices, wherein he was revealed, and fignified to be the feed of the woman which fhould bruife the ferpent's head, and the lamb flain from the beginning of the world." Weftm. Confeffion, chap. 8. art. 6.

* Ainfworth on Gen.   † Ibid.   ‡ Gibbons on Gen.

‖ So the Septuagint expound it. Others an Inlivener; not doubting, but Adam, in giving her this name, had the promifed life-giving feed, our Lord Jefus Chrift, particularly in view, amongft the all living, fhe was to be mother of.

§ Urb. Reg. on Chrift's ferm. to Emaus.

¶ Duplefs. Truenefs of Chrift. Relig. p. 226.

" So long, O ferpent, as the woman's childern keep the law, they kill thee; and when they ceafe do fo, thou ftingeft them in the heel, and haft power to to hurt them much; but whereas for their harm there is a fure remedy, for thee there is none : for in the laft days they fhall crufh thee all to pieces, by means of Chrift their King. And this was it which did fupport and uphold their faith until the time of Abraham.

§ 2. *Ant.* What followed then ?

Evan. Why then the promife was turned into a covenant with Adraham and his feed, and oftentimes repeated, that " in his feed all nations fhould be bleffed, Gen. xii. 3 and xviii. 18. and xxii. 18. * Which promife and covenant was the very voice itfelf of the gofpel, it being a true teftimony of Jefus Chrift; as the apoftle Paul beareth witnefs, faying, " The fcripture forefeeing that God,

---

* The antient promife given to Adam was the firft gofpel, the covenant of grace. " For man by his fall, having made himfelf uncapable of life by the covenant of works, the Lord was pleafed to make a fecond, commonly called the covenant of grace," Gen. iii. 15 Weftm. Conf. ff. chap 7 art 3. When that promife or covenant, in which the perfons it refpected were not exprefsly defigned, was renewed, Abraham and his feed were defigned exprefsly therein : and fo it became a covenant with Abraham and his feed. And the promife being ftill the fame, as to the fubftance of it, was often repeated; and in the repetition, more fully and clearly opened. So Jefus Chrift revealed to Adam, only as the feed of the woman, was thereafter revealed to Abraham, as Abraham's own feed : and thus was it believed and embraced, unto falvation, in the various revelation thereof. " God ——did feek Adam again, call upon him, rebuke his fin, convict him of the fame, and in the end made unto him a moft joyful promife, to w t, " That the feed of the woman fhould break down the ferpent's head," That is, he fuld deftroy the works of the devil ; quhilk promife, as it was repeated and made mair clear from time to time : fo was it imbraced with joy, and maift conftantly (*i. e.* moft ftedfaftly) received of all the faithful, from Adam to Noe, from Noe to Abraham, from Abraham to David, and fo furth to the incarnation of Chrift Jefus." Old Conf ff. art. 4.

would juſtify the Gentiles through faith, preached before the goſpel unto Abraham," Gal. iii. 8. ſaying, " In thee ſhall all the nations of the earth be bleſſed." And the better to confirm Abraham's faith in this promiſe of Chriſt, it is ſaid, Gen. xiv. 19. That Melchizedec came forth and met him, and bleſſed him. Now, ſaith the apoſtle, " This Melchiſedec was a prieſt of the moſt high God, and king of righteouſneſs, Heb. vii. 1, 2, 3. and vi. 20. and king of peace, without father and without mother, and ſo like unto the Son of God; who is a prieſt for ever, after the order of Melchiſedec:" and both king of righteouſneſs and king of peace, Jer. xxiii. 6. Iſa. ix 6. yea, and without father, as touching his manhood; and without mother, as touching his Godhead. Whereby we are given to underſtand, that it was the purpoſe of God, that Melchiſedec ſhould in theſe particulars reſemble the perſon and office of Jeſus Chriſt the Son of God *; and ſo, by God's own appointment, be a type of him to Abraham, to ratify and confirm the promiſe made to him and his ſeed, in reſpect of the eternal covenant †, to wit, that he and his believing ſeed ſhould be ſo bleſſed in Chriſt, as Melchiſedec had bleſſed him ‡. Nay, let me tell you more, ſome have thought it moſt probable, yea, and have ſaid, If we ſearch out this truth, without partiality, we ſhall find, that this Melchiſedec ||, which appeared unto Abraham, was none other than the Son of God, manifeſt by a ſpecial diſpenſation and privilege unto Abraham, in the fleſh, who is therefore ſaid, to

---

* Dickſon on the Heb.

† That paſt betwixt the Father and the Son, from everlaſting.

‡ Melchiſedec was unto Abraham, a type, to confirm him in the faith, that he and his believing ſeed ſhould be as really bleſſed in Chriſt, as he was bleſſed by Melchiſedec.

‖ William's ſeven golden candleſticks, p. 330, 331.

have " feen his day and rejoiced," John viii. 56. *
Moreover, in Gen. xv. we read that the Lord did again
confirm this covenant with Abraham : for when Abraham
had divided the beafts, God came between the parts like
a fmocking furnace and a burning lamp; which, † as
fome have thought, did primarily typify the torment and
rending of Chrift ‡; and the furnace and fiery lamp, did
typify the wrath of God running between, and yet did
not confume the rent and torn nature. And the blood
of circumcifion did typify the blood of Chrift ‖ : and the
refolved facrifice § of Ifaac on mount Moriah, by God's
appointment, did prefigure and forefhew, that by the
offering up of Chrift the promifed feed, in the very fame
place, all nations fhould be faved. Now this covenant
thus made and confirmed with Abraham, was renewed
with Ifaac, Gen. xxvi. 4. and made known unto Jacob, by
Jefus Chrift himfelf; for that man which wreftled with
Jacob, was none other but the man Chrift Jefus ¶; for
himfelf faid, that Jacob fhould be called Ifrael, a wreftler
and prevailer with God; and Jacob called the name of

---

* This feems to me to be a more than groundlefs opinion,
as being inconfiftent with the fcripture account of Melchifedec,
Gen. xiv. 18. Heb. vii. 1.—4. howbeit it wants not patrons
among the learned. The declaring of which is no juft ground
to fix it on our author: efpecially after his fpeaking fo plainly
of Chrift and Melchifedec, as two different perfons, a little
before. The text, John viii. 56. alledged by the patrons of that
opinion, makes nothing for their purpofe: " For all (we mean
the faithful fathers under the law) did fee (viz. by faith) the
joyful day of Chrift Jefus, and did rejoice."— Old Confeff. art. 4.

† Namely, the paffing of the furnace and burning lamp,
between the pieces.

‡ Ball on the cov. p. 49.

‖ Heb. ix. 22. " And almoft all things are by the law purged
with blood : and without fhedding of blood is no remiffion."
Compare Gen. xvii. 14. " The uncircumcifed man-child fhall
be cut off from his people; he hath broken my covenant."

§ Walker on the cov. p. 63.

¶ Gen. xxxii. 28. 30. Seven golden candlefticks, p. 322.

the place Peniel, becaufe he had feen God face to face. And Jacob left it by his laft will unto his childern, in thefe words, "The fcepter fhall not depart from Judah, nor a law-giver from between his feet, till Shiloh come," Gen. xlix. 10. That is to fay, Of Judah fhall kings come one after another, and many in number, till at laft the Lord Jefus come, who is King of kings, and Lord of lords: or, as the Targum of Jerufalm and Onkelos do trnflate it, until Chrift the anointed come *.

Nom. But, Sir, are you fure that this premifed feed was meant of Chrift?

Evan. The apoftle puts that out of doubt, Gal. iii. 16. faying, " Now unto Abraham and to his feed were the promife made †. He faith not, and to feeds, as of many, but as of one, and to thy feed, which is Chrift ‡." And fo no doubt, but thefe godly patriarchs did underftand it.

Ant. But, Sir, the great promife that was made unto them, as I conceive, and which they feemed to have moft regard unto, was the land of Canaan.

Evan. There is no doubt, but that thefe godly patri-archs did fee their heavenly inheritance (by Chrift) thro' the promife of the land of Canaan; as the apoftle teftifieth of Abraham, Heb. xi. 9, 10. faying, " He fojourned in a ftrange country, and looked for a city having a founda-tion, whofe builder and maker is God." Whereby it is evident, faith Calvin ||, that the height and eminency of

---

* Babbing on the text.

† To wit, the promifes of the everlafting inheritance, typified by the land of Canaan: the which promifes, fee Gen xii 7 and xiii. 15.

‡ *i e* Chrift myftical, Chrift and the church, the head and the members; yet fo as the dignity of the head being ftill re-ferved, he is to be underftood here primarily, which is fufficient for our author's purpofe; and his members fecondarily only.

|| Inftit. p. 204.

Abraham's faith, was, the looking. for an everlasting life
in heaven. The like testimony he gives of Sarah, Isaac,
and Jacob, saying, "all these died in the faith," Heb. xi. 13 *
implying, that they did not expect to receive the fruit of
of the promise till after death. And therefore in all their
travels, they had before their eyes, the blessedness of the
life to come: which caused old Jacob to say at his death,
Gen. xlix. 18. " Lord I have waited for thy salvation."
The which speech, the Chaldee paraphrase expounds thus,
Our father Jacob said not †, 1 expect the salvation of
Gideon, son of Joash, which is a temporal salvation; nor
the salvation of. Samson. son of Manoah, which is a
transitory salvation; but the salvation of Christ the son
of David, who shall come, and bring unto himself, the
sons of Israel; whose salvation my soul desireth. And
so you see, that this covenant made with Abraham in
Christ, was the comfort and support of these and the rest
of the godly fathers until their departure out of Egypt.

Ant. And what followed then?

Evan. Why then Christ Jesus was most clearly manifested unto them, in the passover lamb : for as that lamb
was to be without spot, or blemish, Exod. xii. 5. Even
so was Christ, 1 Pet i. 19 ·And as that lamb was taken
up the tenth day of the first new moon in March; even
so on the very same day of the same month came Christ
to Jerusalem ‡, to suffer his passion. And as that lamb

---

* That these three, together with Abraham, are here meant
by the apostle, and not these mentioned in the first seven verses
of the chapter, appears, if it is considered, that of them he spoke
last, ver. 9, 11. To none before them was the promise of Canaan
given; and they were the persons who had opportunity to have
returned to the country whence they came out, ver. 15.

† Ainsworth on the text.

‡ Tindal in his works, p. 430.

was killed on the fourteenth day at even ; juſt then, on the ſame day, and at the ſame hour *, did Chriſt give· up the Ghoſt : and as the blood of that lamb was to be ſprinkled on the Iſraelites doors, Exod. xii. 7. Even ſo is the blood of Chriſt ſprinkled on believers hearts by faith, 1 Pet. i. 2. And their deliverance out of Egypt, was a figure of their redemption by Chriſt †; their paſſing thro' the, red ſea, was a type of baptiſm ‡; when Chriſt ſhould come in the fleſh ; and their manna in the wilderneſs and water out of the rock, did reſemble the ſacrament of the Lord's ſupper, 1 Cor. x. 2. 3, 4. and hence it is that the apoſtle ſaith, " They did all eat the ſame ſpiritual meat, and did all drink the ſame ſpiritual dtink ; for they drank of that ſpiritual rock that followed them, and that rock was Chriſt." And when they were come ·to mount Sinai, the Lord delivered the ten command: ments unto them.

---

* Ainſworth on Exod. and Mark xv. 33, 34, 37·

† *i. e.* The deliverance of the Iſraelites out of Egypt, was a figure of the redemption by Chriſt.

‡ Not that it prefigured, or repreſented baptiſm as a proper and prophetical type thereof ; though ſome orthodox divines ſeem to be of that mind : but, that (as the author expreſſeth himſelf, in the caſe of the Manna and the Water out of the rock) it reſembled baptiſm ; being a like figure (or type) thereunto, as the apoſtle Peter determines, concerning Noah's ark with the waters of the deluge, 1 Pet. iii. 21. Even as the printer's irons are types of the letters impreſſed on the paper, both ſignifying one and the ſame word. For the antient church is expreſsly ſaid to have been baptized in the ſea, 1 Cor. x. 1, 2. And as the rock with the waters flowing from it, did not ſignify the Lord's ſupper ; but the thing ſignified by that New Teſta· ment ſacrament, namely Chriſt, ver. 4. So their baptiſm in the ſea did not ſignify our baptiſm itſelf ; but the thing repreſented thereby. And thus it was a type or figure anſwering to, and reſembling, the baptiſm of the New Teſtament church ; the one being an extraordinary ſacrament of the Old Teſtament, the other an ordinary ſacrament of the New, both repreſenting the ſame thing.

§ 3. *Ant.* But whether were the ten commandments, as they were delivered unto them on mount Sinai, the covenant of works, or no?

Evan. They were delivered to them as the covenant of works *.

---

* As to this point there are different sentiments among orthodox divines; though all of them do agree, that the way of salvation was the same under the Old and New Teſtament, and that the Sinai covenant, whatever it was, carried no prejudice to the promiſe made unto Abraham, and the way of ſalvation therein revealed, but ſerved to lead men to Jeſus Chriſt. Our author is far from being ſingular in this deciſion of this queſtion. I adduce only the teſtimonies of three late learned writers. " That God made ſuch a covenant (*viz.* the covenant of works) with our firſt parents—is confirmed by ſeveral places of ſcripture." Hoſ. vi. 7.——Gal. iv. 24. Williſon's ſacram. catech. p. 3. The words of the text laſt quoted, are theſe: " For theſe are the two covenants, the one from the mount Sinai, which gendereth to bondage." Hence it appears, that, in the judgment of this author, the covenant from mount Sinai was the covenant of works: otherwiſe there is no ſhadow of reaſon from this text, for what it is adduced to p ove.—— The Reverend Mr Flint, and Mr M'Claren, in their elaborate and ſeaſonable treatiſes againſt Profeſſor Simpſon's doctrine, (for which I make no queſtion, but their names will be in honour with poſterity) ſpeak to the ſame purpoſe. The former having adduced the foreceited text, Gal. iv. 24. ſaith, " Jam " duo fædera, &c." that is, " Now here are two covenants mentioned; the firſt the legal one, by ſin rendered ineffectual, entered into with Adam, and now again promulgate." Exam. Doctr. D. Joh. Simſ. p. 125. And afterwards, ſpeaking of the law of works, he adds. " Atque hoc eſt illud fædus, &c." that is, " And this is that covenant promulgate on mount Sinai, which is called one of the covenants, Gal iv. 24." Ibid. pag 131. The words of the latter, ſpeaking of the covenant of works are theſe; " Yea 'tis expreſsly called a covenant, Hoſ. vi. and Gal. iv." And Mr Gilleſpie proves ſtrongly, that Gal. iv. is underſtood of the covenant of works and grace; ſee his Ark of the Teſtament, Part 1. chap. 5 p. 180. The new Scheme examined, p. 176. The delivering of the ten commands on mount Sinai, as the covenant of works, neceſſarily includes in it the delivering of them as a perfect rule of righteouſneſs; foraſmuch as that covenant did always contain in it ſuch a rule, the true knowledge of which the Iſraelites were, at that time, in great want of, as our author afterwards teacheth.

Nom. But by your favour, Sir, you know that these people were the posterity of Abraham ; 'and therefore under that covenant of grace, which God made with their fathers: and therefore I do not think that they were delivered to them as the covenant of works; for, Sir, you know the Lord never delivers the covenant of works to any that are under the covenant of grace.

Evan. Indeed 'tis true, the Lord did manifest so much love to the body of this nation *, that all the natural seed of Abraham were externally, and by profession, under the covenant of grace made with their father Abraham; though 'tis to be feared many of them were still under the covenant of works made with their father Adam †.

Nom. But, Sir, you know, in the preface to the ten commandments, the Lord calls himself by the name of their God in general; and therefore it should seem, that they were all of them the people of God ‡.

———————————————————————

* Ball on the cov. p. 110.

† The strength of the objection in the preceeding paragraph lies here, namely, That at this rate, the same persons, at one and the same time, were both under the covenant of works, and under the covenant of grace; which is absurd. *Ans.* The unbelieving Israelites were under the covenant of grace made with their father Abraham, externally and by profession, in respect of their visible church state ; but under the covenant of works made with their father Adam, internally and really, in respect of the state of their souls before the Lord: herein there is no absurdity; for, to this day, many in the visible church are thus, in these different respects, under both covenants. Further, as to believers among them, they were internally and really, as well as externally, under the covenant of works, and that, not as a covenant co-ordinate with, but subordinate and subservient unto, the covenant of grace. And in this there is no more inconsistency, than in the former.

‡ *Viz.* As delivered from the covenant of works, by virtue of the covenant of grace.

Evan. That is nothing to the purpose *, for many

---

* That will not indeed prove them all to have been the people of God, in the sense before given ; for the reason here adduced by our author.

Howbeit, the preface to the ten commands, deserves a particular notice, in the matter of the Sinai transaction: Exod. xx. 2. " I am the Lord thy God, which have brought thee out of the land of Egypt, out of the house of bondage." Hence it is evident to me, that the covenant of grace was delivered to the Israelites on mount Sinia. For, the Son of God, the Messenger of the covenant of grace, spoke these words to a select people, the natural seed of Abraham, typical of his whole spiritual seed. He avoucheth himself to be their God; namely, in virtue of the promise, or covenant made with Abraham, Gen. xvii. 7. " I will establish my covenant—to be a God unto thee, and to thy seed after thee:" and their God, which brought them out of the land of Egypt; according to the promise made to Abraham, at the most solemn renewal of the covenant with him, Gen. xv. 14. " Afterward shall they come out with great substance." And he first declares himself their God, and then requires obedience; according to the manner of the covenant with Abraham, Gen. xvii. 1. " I am the Almighty God ; (*i e.* in the language of the covenant, The Almighty God TO THEE, to make THEE for ever blessed, through the promised SEED) walk thou before me, and be thou perfect."

But that the covenant of works was also, for special ends, repeated and delivered to the Israelites on mount Sinai; I cannot refuse, 1. Because of the apostle's testimony, Gal. iv. 24. " These are the two covenants; the one from the mount Sinai, which gendereth to bondage."—For the children of this Sinai-covenant, the apostle here treats of, are excluded from the eternal inheritance, as Ishmael was from Canaan, the type of it, ver. 30. " Cast out the bond woman and her son ; for the son of the bond woman shall not be heir with the son of the free woman." But this could never be said of the children of the covenant of grace, under any dispensation: tho' both the law covenant from Sinai, itself, and its children, were, even before the coming of Christ, under a sentence of exclusion, to be execute on them respectively in due time. 2. The nature of the covenant of works, is most expresly, in the New Testament, brought in, propounded and explained, from the Mosaical dispensation. The commands of it from Exod. xx. by our blessed Saviour, Matth. xix. 17, 18, 19. " If thou wilt enter into life, keep the commandments. He saith unto him, which ?

Jefus faid, Thou fhalt do no murder, Thou fhalt not commit adultery," &c.   The promife of it, Rom. x. 5. " Mofes de-fcribeth the righteoufnefs which is of the law, that the man which doth thofe things, fhall live by them."   The commands and promife of it together, fee Luke x. 25, 26, 27, 28.   The terrible fanction of it, Gal. iii. 10. " For it is written, (viz. Deut xxvii. 26) Curfed is every one that continueth not in all things which are written in the book of the law to do them."   3. To this may be added the oppofition betwixt the law and grace, fo frequently inculcated in the New Teftament, efpecially in Paul's epiftles.   See one text for all ; Gal. iii. 12. " And the law is not of faith, but the man that doth them fhall live in them." 4. The law from mount Sinai was a covenant, Gal iv. 24. " Thefe are the two covenants, the one from the mount Sinai:" and fuch a covenant as had a femblance of difannulling the covenant of grace, Gal. iii. 17. " The covenant that was confirmed before of God in Chrift, the law which was four hundred and thirty years after, cannot difannul :" Yea, fuch a one as did, in its own nature, bear a method of obtaining the inheritance, fo far different from that of the promife, that it was inconfiftent with it ; " For if the inheritance be of the law, it is no more of promife," Gal. iii. 18.   Wherefore, the covenant of the law from mount Sinai, could not be the covenant of grace ; unlefs one will make this laft not only a covenant feeming to deftroy itfelf, but really inconfiftent ; but it was the covenant of works, which indeed had fuch a femblance, and in its own nature did bear fuch a method, as before noted ; how-beit, as Ainfworth faith, " The covenant of the law now given could not difannul the covenant of grace," Gal. iii. 17. Annot. on Exod. xix. 1.

Wherefore, I conceive the two covenants to have been both delivered, on mount Sinai, to the Ifraelites.   1. The covenant of grace made with Abraham c ntained in the preface, repeated and promulgate there unto Ifrael, to be believed, and embraced by faith, that they might be faved ; To which were annexed the ten commands, given by the Mediator Chrift, the head of the covenant, as a rule of life to his covenant-people. 2. The covenant of works made with Adam, contained in the fame ten commands, delivered with thunderings and lightnings, the meaning of which was afterwards cleared, by Mofes defcribing the righteoufnels of the law, and fanction thereof ; repeated and promulgate to the Ifraelites there, as the original perfect rule, of rightnefs, to be obeyed, And yet were they no more bound hereby, to feek righteoufnefs by the law, than the young man was, by our Saviour's faying to him, Matth. xix. 17, 18. " If thou wilt enter into life, keep the commandments—Thou fhalt do no murder," &c. The later was a repetition of the former.

G

wicked and ungodly men *, being in the visible church,

Thus there is no confounding of the two covenants, of grace and works; but the later was ADDED to the former, as subservient unto it; to turn their eyes towards the promise, or covenant of grace, God gave it to Abraham by promise.— " Wherefore then serveth the law ? It was added, because of transgressions, till the feed should come," Gal. iii. 18, 19. So it was unto the promise given to Abraham, that this subservient covenant was added ; and that promise we have found in the preface to the ten commands To it, then, was the subservient covenant, according to the apostle, added, put or set to, as the word properly signifies. So it was no part of the covenant of grace, the which was entire to the fathers, before the time that it was set to it, and yet is, to the New Testament church, after that it is taken away from it; for, faith the Apostle, " It was added till the feed should come." Hence it appears, that the covenant of grace was, both in itself, and in God's intention, the principal part of the Sinai transaction; nevertheless the covenant of works was the most conspicuous part of it, and lay most open to the view of the people.

According to this account of the Sinai transaction, the ten commands, there delivered, must come under a twofold notion or consideration ; namely, as the law of Christ, and as the law of works ; and this is not strange, if it is considered, that they were twice written on tables of stone, by the Lord himself; the first tables, the work of God, Exod. xxxii. 16. which were broken in pieces, Ver. 19. called the tables of the covenant, Deut. ix. 11, 15. The second tables, the work of Moses, the typical mediator, Exod. xxxiv. 1. deposited at first, (it would seem) in the tabernacle, mentioned chap. xxxiii. 7. afterward, at the rearing of the tabernacle with all its furniture, laid up in the ark within the tabernacle, chap. xl. 20. according to the order thereanent, chap. xxv. 16. And whether or not some such thing is intimate, by the double accentuation of the decalogue, let the learned determine ; but to ocular inspection 'tis evident, that the preface to the ten commands, Exod xx. 2. and Deut. v. 6. stands in the original, both as a part of a sentence joined to the first command ; and also as an entire sentence, separated from it, and shut up by itself.

Upon the whole, one may compare, with this, the first promulgation of the covenant of grace, by the messenger of the covenant, in paradise, Gen. iii. 15. and the flaming sword placed there by the same hand, " turning every way, to keep the way of the tree of life."

* Ball on the cov. p. 213.

and under the eternal covenant, are called, the chosen of God, and the people of God, though they be not so; in like manner were many of these Israelites called the people of God, though indeed they were not so.

Nom. But, Sir, was the same covenant of works made with them, that was made with Adam?

Evan. * For the general substance of the duty, the law delivered on mount Sinai, and formerly engraven on man's heart, was one and the same: so that at mount Sinai, the Lord delivered no new thing; only it came more gently to Adam before his fall; but after his fall, came thunder with it.

Nom. I, but, Sir, as yourself said, the ten commandments, as they were written in Adam's heart, were but the matter of the covenant of works; and not the covenant itself till the form was annexed to them, that is to say, till God and man were thereupon agreed: now we do not find that God and these people did agree upon any such terms at mount Sinai.

Evan. No, † say you so? Do you not remember that

---

* Ball on the cov p. 113. Lightfoot Miscel. p. 186.

† Here there is a large addition in the 9th edition of this book, London 1699. It well deserves place, and is as follows; " I do not say, God made the covenaut of works with them, that they might obtain life and salvation thereby; no the law was become weak through the flesh, as to any such purpose, Rom. viii 3. But he repeated, or gave a new edition of the law, and that as a coveuant of works, for their humbling and conviction. And so do his ministers preach the law to unconverted finners still, that they, who " desire to be under the law, may hear what the law saith," Gal. iv. 21. And as to what you say of their not agreeing to this covenant, I pray take notice, that the covenant of works was made with Adam, not for himself only, but as he was a public person representing all his posterity; and so that covenant was made with the whole nature of man in him: as appears by Adam's sin and curse coming upon all, Rom. v. 12, &c. Gal. iii. 10. Hence all man are born under that covenant, whether they agree to it or no: tho' indeed, there is by nature such a proneness in all, to desire to be under that covenant, and to work for life, that if natural mens consent were asked, they would readily (tho' ignorantly) take upon them to do all that the Lord requireth: for do you not remember," &c.　　　G 2

the Lord confented and agreed, when he faid, Levit. xviii. 5. " Ye fhall therefore keep my ftatutes and my judgments, which if a man do, he fhall live in them." And in Deut. xxvii. 26. when he faid, " Curfed is he that confirmeth not all the words of this law to do them?" And do you not remember, that the people confented, Exod. xix. 8. and agreed when they faid, " All that the Lord hath fpoken, we will do?" and doth not the apoftle Paul give evidence, that thefe words were the form of the covenant of works, when he faith, Rom. x. 5. "Mofes defcribeth the righteoufnefs which is of the law, that the man that doth thefe things, fhall live in them :" And when he faith, Gal. iii. 10. " For it is written, curfed is every one that continueth not in all things, which are written in the book of the law to do them *". And in Deut. iv. 13 - Mofes doth in exprefs terms call it a covenant, faying, " And he declared unto you his covenant, which he commanded you to perform, even the ten commandments, and he wrote them upon tables of ftone." Now this was not the covenant of grace, for Mofes afterwords, Deut. v. 3 fpeaking of this covenant, faith, " God made not this covenant with your fathers, but with you:" And by fathers, all the patriarchs unto

---

* That the conditional promife, Lev. xviii. 5. (to which agrees Exod. xix 8.) and the dreadful threatening, Deut. xxvii 26. were both given to the Ifraelites, as well as the ten commands is bevond queftion: and that according to the apoftle, Rom. x. 5. Gal. iii. 10. they were the form of the covenant of works, is as evident as the repeating of the words, and expounding them fo, can make it. How then one can refufe the covenant of works to have been given to the Ifraelites, I cannot fee. Mark the Weftminfter Confef. upon the head, Of the covenant of works: " The firft covenant made with man, was a covenant of works, wherein life was promifed to Adam, and in him to his pofterity, upon condition of perfect and perfonal obedience." And this account of the being and nature of that covenant, is there proven, from thefe very texts among others, Rom. x. 5. Gal. iii. 10. chap. 7. art. 2.

Adam may be meant, faith Mr Ainfworth, who had the promife of the covenant of Chrift *. Therefore, if it had been the covenant of grace, he would have faid; God did make this covenant with them; rather than that he did not †.

Nom. And do any of our godly and Modern writers agree with you in this point?

Evan. Yea indeed, Polanus ‡ faith, The covenant of works is that, in which God promifeth everlafting life unto a man, that in all refpects performeth perfect obedience to the law of works, adding thereunto threatenings of eternal death, if he fhall not perform perfect obedience thereunto. God made this covenant in the beginning with the firft man Adam, whilft he was in the firft eftate of integrity; the fame covenant God did repeat and make again

---

* " But the covenant of the law, (adds he) came after, as the apoftle obferveth. Gal. iii. 17. ——They had a greater benefit than their fathers: for though the law could not give them life, yet it was a fchoolmafter unto (*i. e.* to bring them unto) Chrift, Gal. iii. 21, 24." Ainfworth on Deut. v. 3.

† The tranfaction at Sinai or Horeb (for they are but one mountain) was a mixed difpenfation: there was the promife or covenant of grace, and alfo the law; the one a covenant to be believed, the other a covenant to be done: and thus the apoftle ftates the difference betwixt thefe two, Gal. iii. 12. " And the law is not of faith, but the man that DOETH them fhall live in them." As to the former, viz. the covenant to be believed, it was given to their fathers, as well as to them. Of the latter, viz. the covenant to be done, Mofes fpeaks exprefsly, Deut. iv. 12, 13. " The Lord fpake unto you out of the midft of the fire—and he declared unto you his covenant, which he commanded you to PERFORM (or DO) even ten commandments." And chap. v. 3. he tells the people no lefs exprefsly, that " the Lord made not THIS COVENANT with their fathers."

‡ Subft. relig. octav. Eng. p. 184, 185.

by Mofes with the people of Ifrael. And * Dr Prefton faith, The covenant of works runs in thefe terms, "Do this and thou fhalt live, and I will be thy God." This was the covenant which was made with Adam, and the covenant that is expreffed by Mofes in the moral law. And Mr † Pemble faith, by the covenant of works we underftand, that we call in one word, the law, namely that means of bringing man to falvation, which is by perfect obedience unto the will of God : hereof there are alfo two feveral adminiftrations. The firft is, with Adam before his fall, when immortality and happinefs was promifed to man, and confirmed by an external fymbol of the tree of life, upon condition that he con-tinued obedient to God, as well in all other things, as in that particular commandment, of not eating of the tree of knowledge of good and evil. The fecond adminiftration of this covenant, was the renewing thereof with the Ifaelites at mount Sinai ; where, after the light of nature began to grow darker, and corruption had in time worn out the characters of religion and virtue firft graven in man's heart ‡ ; God revived the law by a compendious and full declaration of all duties required of man towards God, or his neighbour, expreffed in the decalogue : according to the tenor of which law, God entered into covenant with the Ifraelites ; promifing to be their God, in beftowing upon them, all bleffings of life and happinefs, upon condition that they would be his people, obeying all things that he had commanded ; which con-dition they accepted of, promifing an abfolute obedience, Exod. xix. 8. " All things which the Lord hath faid we will do ;" and alfo fubmitting themfelves to all punifh-ment, in cafe they difobeyed, faying Amen to the curfe of the law ; "Curfed be every one that confirmeth not all the words of the law to do them ; and all the people fhall fay, Amen."

---

* New cov. p. 317.　　　† Vind. Fid. p. 152.
‡ *i. e.* Had worn them out, in the fame meafure and degree, as the light of nature was darkened ; but neither the one, nor the other, was ever fully done, Rom. ii. 14, 15.

And Mr Walker * faith, that the firſt part o' the covenant, which God made with Iſrael at Horeb, was nothing elſe but a renewing of the old covenant of works † which God made with Adam in paradiſe ‡. And it is generally laid down by our divines, that we are by Chriſt delivered from the law, as it is a covenant ‖.

Nom. But, Sir, were the children of Iſrael, at this time, better able to perform the conditton of the covenant of works, than either Adam, or any of the old patriarchs were ; that God renewed it now with them, rather than before ?

Evan. No indeed, God did not renew it with them now, and not before, becauſe they were better able to keep it, but becauſe they had more need to be made acquainted, what the covenant of works is, than thoſe before. For though 'tis true. the ten commandments, which were at firſt perfectly written in Adam's heart, were much obliterated § by his fall, yet ſome impreſſions and reliqués thereof ſtill remained ¶ ; and Adam himſelf was very ſenſible of his fall, and the reſt of the fathers were helped by tradition ** †† ; and (ſaith Cameron) God did ſpeak to the patriarchs from heaven, yea and he ſpake unto them

---

* On covenant, p. 128.

† Wherein I differ from this learned author, as to this point ; and for what reaſons, may be ſeen, p. 58. note †

‡ Bolton's true bounds, p. 23.

‖ But not, as it is a rule of life ; which is the other member of that diſtinction.

§ Both in the heart of Adam himſelf, and of his deſcendents in the firſt ages of the world.

¶ Both with him and them.

** Rom. ii. 15. In Mr Bolt. p. 371.

†† The doctrine of the fall, with whatſoever other doctrine was neceſſary to ſalvation, was handed down from Adam ; the fathers communicating the ſame to their children, and children's children. There were but eleven patriarchs before the flood ;

by his angels. *†: but now by this time sin had almost obliterated and defaced the impressions of the law written in their hearts ‡; and by their being so long in Egypt, they were so corrupted, that the instructions and ordinances of their fatheas were almost all worn out of mind; and their fall in Adam was almost forgotten, as the apostle testifieth, Rom. v. 13, 14. saying, " Before the time of the law sin was in the world, but sin is not imputed when there is no law." Nay, in that long course of time betwixt Adam and Moses, men had forgotten what was sin: so although God had made a promise of blessing to Abraham and to all his seed, that would plead interest in it‖§; yet these people at this time were proud and secure, and

----

1. Adam, 2. Seth, 3 Enos, 4. Cainan, 5. Mahalaleel, 6. Jared, 7. Enoch, 8. Methuselah, 9. Lamech, 10. Noah, 11. Shem. Adam having lived 930 years, Gen. v. 5. was known to Lamech, Noah's father, with whom he lived 66 years, and much longer with the rest of the fathers before him; so that Lamech, and these before him, might have the doctrine from Adam's own mouth. Methuselah lived with Adam 243 years, and with Shem 98 years before the deluge. See Gen. v. And what Shem (who, after the deluge, lived 502 years, Gen. xi. 10, 11.) had learned from Methuselah, he had occasion to teach Arphaxad, Salah, Eber, Peleg, Reu, Serug, Nahor, Terah, Abraham, Isaac, Gen. xxi. 5. and Jacob, to whose fifty-first year he (viz. Shem) reached, Gen. xi. 10. and xxi. 25. and xxv. 26. compared, Vid. Bal. Op. Hist. Chron. p. 2, 3. Thus one may perceive, how the nature of the law and covenant of works, given to Adam, might be far better known to them, than to the Israelites after their long bondage in Egypt.

* Bullenger Com. Pla.
† *i. e.* And besides all this, God spake to the patriarchs, immediately, and by angels. But neither of these do we find, during the time of the bondage in Egypt; until the angel of the Lord appeared to Moses in the bush, and ordered him to go and bring the people out of Egypt, Exod. iii.
‡ The remaining impressions of the law, on the hearts of the Israelites.
‖ Reynolds on the use of the law, p. 584.
§ By faith, believing, embracing, and appropriating it to themselves, Heb. xi. 13. Jer. iii. 4.

and heedlefs of their eftate : and though fin was in them, and death reigned over them; yet they being without a law to evidence this fin and death, unto their confciences *, they did not impute it unto themfelves; they would not own it, nor charge themfelves with it, and fo by confe-quence found no need of pleading the promife made to Abraham, Rom v. 20. † ; therefore the law entered, that Adam's offence and their own actual tranfgreffion, might abound : fo that now the Lord faw it needful, that there fhould be a new edition and publication of the covenant of works ; the fooner to compel the elect-unbelivers to come to Chrift the promifed feed; and that the grace of God in Chrift to the elect believers, might appear the more exceeding glorious. So that you fee the Lord's intention therein was, that they, by looking upon this covenant, might be put in mind what was their duty of old, when they were in Adam's loins; yea, and what was their duty ftill, if they would ftand to that covenant, and fo go the old and natural way to work ‡ : yea, and hereby they were alfo to fee what was their prefent infirmity in not doing their duty ‖ ; that fo they feeing an impoffibility of obtaining life, by that way of works, firft appointed in paradife, they might be humbled and more heedfully mind the promife made to their father Abraham, and haften to lay hold on the Meffiah or promifed feed.

Nom. Then, Sir, it feemeth that the Lord did not

---

* Inafmuch as the remaining impreffions of the law, on their hearts, were fo weak, that they were not fufficient for the purpofe.

† By faith propoing it, as their only defence ; and opponing it to the demands of the law or covenant of works, as their only plea.

‡ Pemble, Vind. Fid. p. 155.

‖ How far they came fhort of, and could not reach unto, the obedience, they owed unto God, according to the perfection of the holy law.

renew the covenant of works with them, to the intent that they should obtain eternal life, by their yielding obedience to it.

Evan. No indeed, God never made the covenant of works with any man, since the fall, either with expectation that he should fulfil it * †, or to give him life by it; for God never appoints any thing to an end, to the which it is utterly unsuitable and improper. Now the law ‡, as it is the covenant of works, is become weak and improfitable to the purpose of salvation ||, and therefore God never appointed it to man since the fall to that end. And besides, it is manifest that the purpose of God, in the covenant made with Abraham, was to give life and salvation by grace and promise : and therefore his prupose in renewing the covenant of works, was not, neither could be, to give life and salvation by working; for then there would have been contradictions in the covenants, and instability in him that made them. Wherefore let no man imagine that God published the covenant of works on mount Sinai §, as though he had been mutable and so changed his determination in that covenant made with Abraham; neither yet let any man suppose, that God, now in process of time, had found out a better way for man's salvation, than he knew before : for as the covenant of grace made with Abraham ¶, had been needless, if the covenant of works made with Adam, would

---

* Bolton's true bounds, p. 132. 158.

† Nor before the fall neither, properly speaking; but the expression is agreeable to scripture stile, Isa. v. 4. " Wherefore when I looked it should bring forth grapes, brought it forth wild grapes ?"

‡ Reynolds on the use of the law.

|| Rom. viii. 3. " For what the law could not do, in that it was weak through the flesh ; God sending his own Son," &c.

§ Dr Willet on Exod. x.

¶ Pemble Vind. p. 154.

have given him, and his believing feed, life; fo after the
covenant of grace was once made, it was needlefs to
renew the covenant of works, to the end that righteoufnefs and life fhould be had by the obfervation of it. The
which will yet more evidenty appear, if we confider, that
the apoftle, fpeaking of the covenant of works as it was
given on mount Sinai, faith, " It was added becaufe of
tranfgreffion;" it was not fet up as a folid rule of
righteoufnefs, as it was given to Adam in paradife, but
was added or put to * : It was not fet up as a thing in
grofs, by itfelf †.

Nom. Then, Sir, it fhould feem that the covenant of
works was added to the covenant of grace, to make it
more complete.

Evan. O no, you are not fo to underftand the apoftle,
as though it were added by way of ingredieney, as a
part of the covenant of grace; as if that covenant had
been complete without the covenant of works ‡ : for then,
the fame covenant fhould have confifted of contradictory
materials, and fo it fhould have overthrown itfelf; for
faith the apoftle, " If it be by grace, then it is no more
of works; otherwife grace is no more grace : but if it be
of works, then it is no more of grace, otherwife work is
no more work, Rom. xi 6. But it was added by way
of fubferviency and attendance ; the better to advance

---

* It was not fet up by itfelf, as an entire rule of righteoufnefs,
to which alone they were to look, who defired righteoufnefs
and falvation; as it was in the cafe of upright Adam : for, no
man, fince the fall, can attain to righteoufnefs and life by the
moral law. Larg. Cat. Queft. 94. But it was added to the
covenant of grace, that by looking at it, men might fee, what
kind of righteoufnefs it is, by which they can be juftified in the
fight of God, and that by means thereof finding themfelves
deftitute of that righteoufnefs, they might be moved to embrace
the covenant of grace, in which that righteoufnefs is held forth
to be received by faith.

† Gal. iii. 19. Reynolds on the ufe of the law. ibid.

‡ Marfhall on infant baptifm.

and make effectual the covenant of grace *. So that although the fame covenant that was made with Adam, was renewed on Mount Sinai; yet I fay ftill, it was not for the fame purpofe. For this was it God aimed at, in making the covenant of works with man in innocency, to have that which was his due from man † : but God made it with the Ifraelites for no other end, than that man being thereby convinced of his, weaknefs, might. fly to Chrift. So that it was renewed only to help forward, and introduce another and a better covenant ; and fo to be a manuduction unto Chrift, *viz.* to difcover fin, to waken the confcience, and to convince them of their own impotency ; and fo to drive them out of themfelves to Chrift. Know it then, I befeech you, that all this while there was no other way of life given, either in whole, or in part, than the covenant of grace; all this while God did but-purfue the defign of his own grace : and therefore, was there no inconfiftency, either in God's will, or acts ; only fuch was his mercy, that he fubordinated the covenant of works, and made it fubfervient to the covenant of grace ; and fo to tend to evangelical purpofes ‡.

Nom. But yet, Sir, methinks it is fomewhat ftrange, that the Lord fhould put them upon doing the law, and alfo promife them life for doing, and yet never intend it.

Evan. Though he did fo, yet did he neither require of them that which was unjuft, nor yet diffemble with them in the promife ; for the Lord may juftly require perfect obedience at all mens hands, by virtue of that cove-

---

* Bolton's true bounds, p. 157.

† This was the end of the work, namely of making the covenant of works with Adam ; but not of the repealing of it at Sinai; it was alfo the end or defign of the worker, namely of God, who made the covenant with Adam, to have his due from man, and he got it, from the man Chrift Jefus.

‡ Reynolds on the ufe of the law.

nant which was made with them in Adam *: and if any
man could yield perfect obedience to the law, both in
doing and fuffering, he fhould have eternel life.; for we
may not deny (faith Calvin) but that the reward of eternal falvation belongeth to the upright obedience of the
law †‡. But God knew well enough, that the Ifraelites
were never able to yield fuch an obedience; and yet he
faw it meet ‖ to propound eternal life to them upon
thefe terms; that fo he might fpeak to them in their own
humour, as indeed it was meet: for they, fwelled with
mad affurance in themfelves, faying, "All that the Lord
commandeth we will do," and be obedient, Exod. xix. 8.
Well, faid the Lord, if you will needs be doing §, why,
here is a law to be kept; and if you can fully obferve
the righteoufnefs of it, you fhall be faved; fending them
of purpofe to the law, to awaken and convince them, to
fentence and humble them, and to make them fee their
own folly, in feeking for life that way ¶ : in fhort to
make them fee the terms under which they ftood, that fo
they might be brought out of themfelves, and expect
nothing from the law, in relation to life, but all from
Chrift. For how fhould a man fee his need of life by
Chrift, if he do not firft fee that he is fallen from the
way of life ** ? and how fhould he underftand, how far
he ftrayed from the way of life, unlefs he do firft find what
is that way of life : therefore it was needful that the
Lord fhould deal with them after fuch a manner, to drive
them out of themfelves, and from all confidence in the
works of the law; that fo by faith in Chrift they might

---

* Calv. Inftit. p. 157.

† *i. e* The perfect obedience of the law, as 'tis faid,
Eccl. vii. 29. " God made man upright."

‡ Pemble Vind. Fid. p. 164.   ‖ Calvin. ut fupra, p. 159.

§ Pen b e ibid.   ¶ Bolton's true bounds, p. 22.

** Calvin's inftit.

H

·obtain righteousnefs and life.   And juft so, did our Saviour alfo deal with that young expounder of the law, Matth. xix. 16. who it feemeth was fick of the fame difeafe, " Good mafter (faith he) what fhall I do that I may inherit eternal life." He doth not, faith Calvin *, fimply afk, which way or by what means he fhould come to eternal life, but what good he fhould do, to get it : whereby it appears, that he was a proud juftliciary, one that fwelled in flefhly opinion that he could keep the law, and be faved by it : therefore he is worthily fent to the law to work himfelf weary, and fo fee need to come to Chrift for reft †. And thus you fee that the Lord, to the former promifes made to the fathers, added a fiery law ; which he gave from mount Sinai, in thundring and lightning, and with a terrible voice, to the ftubborn and ftiff-necked Ifrael; whereby to break and tame them, and to make them figh and long for the promifed Redeemer.

§ 4. *Ant.* And, Sir, did the law produce this effect in them ?

Evan. Yea indeed did it ; as it will appear, if you confider, that although before the publifhing of this covenant, they were exceeding proud and confident of their own ftrength to do all that the Lord would have them do ‡ : yet when the Lord came to deal with them, as men under the covenant of works in fhewing himfelf a terrible Judge fitting on the throne of juftice like a mountain burning with fire, fummoning them to come before him by the found of a trumpet (yet not to touch Heb. xii. 19. 20. the mountain without a mediator) they were not able to endure the voice of words, nor yet to abide that which was commanded ‖, infomuch as Mofes himfelf did fear and quake ; and they did all of them fo fear and fright, fhake and fhiver, that their peacock feathers were

---

* Calv. Inftit. p. 402.   † Walker on the cov. p. 155.

‡ Dickfon on the Heb.   ‖ Babbing on Exod. xx.

now pulled down. This terrible fhew wherein God gave his law on mount Sinai, faith Luther *, did reprefent the ufe of the law : there was in the people of Ifrael that came out of Egypt a fingular holinefs; they gloried, and faid, " We are the people of God. We will do all that the Lord commandeth." Moreover, Mofes fanctified them, and bade them wafh their garments, refrain from their wives, and prepare themfelves againft the third day ; there was not one of them but he was full of holinefs; the third day Mofes bringeth the people out of their tents to the mountain in the fight of the Lord, that they might hear his voice ; what followed then ? why, when they beheld the horrible fight of the mount fmoking and burning, the black clouds, and the lightning flafhing up and down, in this horrible darknefs, and heard the found of the trumpet blowing long, and waxing louder and louder, they were afraid, and ftanding afar off, they faid not to Mofes as before, " All that the Lord commandeth we will do ; but, Talk thou with us, and we will hear ; but let not God talk with us, left we die." So that now they faw they were finners, and had offended God ; and therefore ftood in need of a mediator, to negotiate peace, and intreat for reconciliation between God and them : and the Lord highly approved of their words, as you may fee, Dut. v. 28 where Mofes repeating what they had faid, adds further, " The Lord heard the voice of your words, when ye fpake to me ; and the Lord faid unto me, I have heard the voice of the words of this people, which they have fpoken unto thee ; they have well faid, all that they have fpoken," to wit, in defiring a mediator †. Where I pray you take notice, that they were not commended for faying, " All that the Lord commandeth we will do. " No ‡, faith a

---

* On Gal. p. 154. † Walker on the cov. p. 70.
‡ The author of the benefit of Chrift's death.

H 2

godly writer, they were not praifed for any other thing,
than for defiring a mediator * † : whereupon the Lord
promifed Chrift unto them, even as Mofes teftifieth,
faying, " The Lord thy God fhall raife up unto thee,
a prophet like unto me ; from among you, even of your
brethren, unto him fhall you hearken, according to all
that thou defiredft of the Lord thy God in Horeb, in the
day of the affembly, when thou faidft, Let me hear the
voice of the Lord my God no more, nor ſ* this great
fire any more, that I die not : and the Lord faid unto
me, They have well fpoken, I will raife them up a
prophet from among their brethren like unto thee, and I
will put my words in his mouth, and he fhall fpeak unto
them all that I command him." And to affure us that
Chrift was the prophet here fpoken of, he himfelf faith
unto the Jews, John v. 46. " If ye had believed Mofes,
ye would have believed me ; for he wrote of me :" and
that this was it which he wrote of him, the apoftle Peter
witneffeth, Acts iii. 22. And fo doth the martyr Stephen,

---

* I fee no warrant for reftraining the ſ nfe of this text, to
their defiring of a mediator. The univerfal term, all that they
have fpoken, includes alfo their engaging to receive the law at
the mouth of the mediator, which is joined with that their
defire, ver. 27. " Go thou near, and hear all that the Lord our
God fhall fay ; and fpeak thou unto us all that the Lord our
God fhall fpeak unto thee, and we will hear and do." Ver. 28.
—" And the Lord faid,—They have well faid all that they have
fpoken." But there is a palpable difference between what they
fpoke. Exod. xix 8. and what they fpoke here, relative to their
own practice. The former runs thus, " All that the Lord
hath fpoken we will do." The latter thus, " And we will
hear and do:" the original text bears no more. The one
relates to obedience only ; the other to faith alfo, " We will
HEAR," i. e. believe. If. lv. 3. John ix. 27. Hence the object
of faith, that which is to be heard or believed, is called a report,
properly a hearing, Ifa liii. 1. Rom. x. 16. The former fpeaks
much blind felf-confidence ; the later a fenfe of duty, and a
willing mind; but withal, a fenfe of weaknefs, and fear of
mifmanagement.

† Ainfworth on Deut. xviii. 15, 16, 17, 18.

Acts vii. 37. Thus you fee, when the Lord had, by means of the covenant of works made with Adam, humbled them, and made them figh for Chrift the promifed feed, he renewed the promife with them, yea, and that covenant of grace made with Abraham *.

Ant. I pray Sir, how doth it appear, that the Lord renewed the covenant with them?

Evan. It doth plainly appear, in that the Lord gave them by Mofes the levitical laws, and ordained the tabernacle, the ark and the mercy-feat, which were all types of Chrift. Moreover, Lev. i. 1. " The Lord called unto Mofes, and fpake unto him out of the tabernacle †," and commanded him to write the levitical laws, and the tabernacle ordinances; telling him withal, Exod. xxxiv. 27. " That after the tenor of thefe words, he had made a covenant with him, and with Ifrael †." So Mofes wrote thofe laws, Exod. xxiv. 4. not in tables

---

* Making a promife of Chrift to them, not only as the feed of the woman, but as the feed of Abraham; and yet more particularly, as the feed of Ifrael: " The Lord thy God will raife up unto thee a prophet, from the midft of THEE, of THY BRETHREN," Deut. xviii. 15. And here it is to be obferved, that this renewing of the promife and covenant of grace with them, was immediately upon the back of the giving of the law on mount Sinai; for at that time was their fpeech, which the Lord commended as well fpoken; this appears from Exod. xx. 18, 19. compared with Deut. v. 23.——28. And upon that fpeech of theirs, was that renewal made; which is clear from Deut. xviii. 17, 18.

† From the mercy-feat, which was within the tabernacle. The tabernacle was an eminent type of Chrift, Heb. ix. 11. as the temple alfo was, John ii. 19. 21. So this reprefented God's fpeaking in a mediator, in Jefus Chrift. Here was a change, agreeable to the people's defire at mount Sinai; God fpeaks, not from a burning mountain, as before; but out of the taber- nacle; not with terrible thunderings, as at Sinai; but in a ftill fmall voice, intimated to us, and imitated by the extraordinary fmallnefs of one letter in the original word rendered *called*; as the Hebrew doctors do account for that irregularity of writing, in that word.

‡ Mofes exceedingly feared and quaked, (Heb. xii. 21.) while

H 3

of ftone, but in an authentical book *, faith Ainfworth †, called the book of the covenant, which book Mofes read in the audience of the people, Exod. xxiv. 7. and the people confented unto it. Then Mofes having before fent young men of the children of Ifrael, who were firft-born ‡, and therefore priefts until the time of the

---

he ftood among the reft of the Ifraelites, at mount Sinai, during the giving of the law, Exod. xix. 25. with chap. xx. 21. But here he is reprefented as Ifrael's federal head in this covenant, he being the typical mediator; which plainly intimates the covenant of grace to have been made with Chrift, and in him with all the elect; " I have made a covenant with thee, and with Ifrael," faith the text. See the firft note on the preface, from the Larger-Catechifm, Queft. 31.

* Mofes was twice on the mount with God, forty days; in the time of the fecond forty days, he received the order to write, mentioned Exod. xxxiv. 27. as appears, by comparing ver. 27. with 28. This comprehended his writing of the Levitical laws, but not of the decalogue or ten commands; for thefe laft God himfelf wrote on tables of ftone, ver. 28. compared with ver. 1. This peremptory divine order, Mofes, no doubt, did obey; underftanding it of writing in a book, fince he was not commanded to write another way. So, in a like cafe, before he went up into the mount for the firft forty days, he wrote Levitical laws in a book, called the book of the covenant; Exod. xxiv. 4. " And Mofes wrote all the words of the Lord." Ver. 7. " And he took the book of the covenant, and read." Compare ver. 18. This writing alfo comprehended Levitical laws, but not the ten commands. " For all the words of the Lord, which Mofes wrote, ver. 4. were all the words of the Lord, which Mofes told the people," ver. 3. And, what thefe were, appears from his commiffion, received for that effect, chap. xx. 21, 22. " And the people ftood afar off, and Mofes drew near unto the thick darknefs, where God was : and the Lord faid unto Mofes, Thus thou fhalt fay unto the children of Ifrael," &c. So all the words were thefe, which follow to the end of the 23d chapter.

† Ainfworth on the text.

‡ In the original text, ver. 5. they are called emphatically, The young men (or minifters, or fervants. 1 Sam. ii. 13, 15. Efth. ii. 2) of the children of Ifrael, to fignify that they were firft born. And fo Onkelos reads it, The firft-born of the children of Ifrael.

Levites *, to offer sacrifice of burnt-offerings, and peace-
offerings unto the Lord; " He took the blood and
sprinkled it on the people, and said, behold the blood of
the covenant, which the Lord hath made with you,
concerning these things :" whereby they were taught,
that by virtue of blood †, this covenant betwixt God
and them, was confirmed, and that Christ by his blood
shed should satisfy for their sins; for indeed the covenant
of grace was, before the coming of Christ, sealed by his
blood in types and figures ‡ ‖.

§ 5. *Ant.* But, Sir, was this every way the same
covenant, that was made with Abraham?

Evan. Surely I do believe, that reverend § Bullinger
spake very truly, when he said, that God gave unto
these people no other religion, in nature, substance, and
matter itself, differing from the laws of their fathers;
though, for same respects, he added thereunto many
ceremonies, and certain ordinances : the which he did to
keep their minds in expectation of the coming of Christ,
whom he had promised unto them ; and to confirm them
in looking for him, lest they should wax faint ¶, and as
the Lord did thus by the ceremonies, as it were, lead
them by the hand to Christ; so did he make them a
promise of the land of Canaan, and outward prosperity
in it, as a type of heaven, and eternal happiness ** : so
that the Lord dealt with them, as with children in their
infancy, and under age, leading them on by the help of
earthly things, to heavenly and spiritual ; because they
were but young and tender ††, and had not that measure

---

* Num. iii. 41.   † Dickson on the Heb.

‡ Walker on the cov. p. 13.

‖ The blood of the sacrifices representing the precious blood
of Christ.

§ Com. Pla. Eng.   ¶ Calv Inst. lib. 2.   ** Ibid. p. 157.

†† The church was in her minority under the law, Gal. iv.
1, 2, 3.

and abundance of the spirit, which he hath beftowed
upon his people, now under the gofpel *.

Ant. And, Sir, do you think that thefe Ifraelites at
this time did fee Chrift and falvation by him, in thefe
types and fhadows?

Evan. Yea, there is no doubt but Mofes and the reft
of the believers among the Jews. did fee Chrift in them:
for, faith godly † Tindal, though all the facrifices and
ceremonies had a ftar-light of Chrift, yet fome of them
had the light of the broad day a little before the fun-
rifing; and did exprefs him, with the circumftances and
virtue of his death, fo plainly, as if his paffion had been
acted upon a fcaffold; infomuch, faith he, that I am
fully perfuaded, and cannot but believe, that God had
fhewed Mofes the fecrets of Chrift, and the very manner
of his death aforehand. And therefore, no doubt, but
that they offered their facrifices, by faith in the Meffiah,
as the apoftle teftifieth of Abel, Heb. xi. 4. I fay, there
is no queftion, but every fpiritual believing Jew, when
he brought his facrifice to be offered, and, according to
the Lord's command, laid his hands upon it, Lev. i. 4.
whilft it was yet alive; he did from his heart acknowledge,
that he himfelf had deferved to die ‡, but by the mercy
of God he was faved ||, and his defert laid upon the
beaft §: and as that beaft was to die, and be offered in
facrifice for him; fo did he believe, that the Meffiah
fhould come and die for him; upon whom he put his
hands, that is, laid all his iniquities by the hand of faith ¶.

---

* Bolton's true bounds, p. 259.

† In his preface to Levit.   ‡ B. Babbing on the text.

|| From the death, he had deferved by his fin.
§ Typically.

¶ " The myftical fignification of the facrifices, and efpecially
this rite, fome think the opoftle means by the doctrine of laying
on of hands, Heb. vi. 2. which typified evangelical faith."
Henry on Lev. i. 4. 'Tis evident, that the offerer, by laying

So that, as Beza * faith, The facrifices were to them holy myfteries, in which, as in certain glaffes, they did both fee themfelves, to their own condemnation before God † ; and alfo beheld the mercy of God, in the promifed Meffiah, in time to be exhibited ; and therefore faith Calvin ‡, The facrifices and fatisfactory offerings, were called Afhemoth ||, which word properly fignifieth fin itfelf; to fhew that Jefus Chrift was to come and perform a perfect expiation, by giving his own foul to be an Afham, that is a fatisfactory oblation.

Wherefore you may affure yourfelf, that as Chrift was always fet before the fathers in the Old Teftament, to whom they might direct their faith; and as God never put them in hope of any grace, or mercy, nor never fhewed himfelf good unto them without Chrift, § : even fo the godly in the Old Teftament, knew Chrift, by whom they did enjoy thefe promifes of God ; and were joined to him ¶. And indeed, the promife of falvation never ftood firm, till it came to Chrift ** ; and there was their comfort, in all their trouble and diftreffes, according as it is faid of Mofes, Heb. xi. 26. 27. He endured

---

his hand on the head of the facrifice, did legally unite with it; laid his fin, or transferred his guilt upon it, in a typical and ceremonial way, Lev. xvi. 21. the fubftance and truth of which ceremonial action, plainly appears to be faith, or believing on Jefus Chrift ; which is the foul's affenting, for its own part, to, and acquiefcing in, the glorious device of " the Lord's laying on him the iniquities of us all," Ifa. liii. 6.

* On Job i.

† *i. e.* They faw themfelves, as in themfelves condemned by the holy law.

‡ Iuftit. p. 239. || Ibid. 152.

§ *i. e.* As an abfolute God out of Chrift, but always as a God in Chrift.

¶ To Chrift, by faith.

** It ftood, at firft, on man's own obedience ; which ground quickly failed; then it came to Chrift, where it ftood firm, Gen. iii. 15. " It (namely, the feed of the woman) fhall bruife thy head," to wit, the ferpent's head.

as feeing him who is invifible *, efteeming the reproach of Chrift greater riches than the treafuers of Egypt, for he had refpect to the recompenfe of reward.

And fo (as Ignatius faith) † the prophets were Chrift's fervants, who forefeeing him in fpirit, both waited for him as their mafter, and looked for him as their Lord and Saviour, faying, " He fhall come and fave us".

And fo faith Calvin ‡, So oft as the prophets fpeak of the bleffednefs of the faithful, the perfect image that they have painted thereof, was fuch as might ravifh mens' minds out of the earth, and of neceffity raife them up to the confideration of the felicity of the life to come : So that we may affuredly conclude with Luther ||, that all the fathers, prophets, and holy kings, were righteous and faved, by faith in Chrift, to come ; and fo indeed, as Calvin faith §, were partakers of all one falvation with us.

Ant. But, Sir, the Scripture feems to hold forth, as though they were faved one way, and we another way ; for you know the prophet Jeremiah makes mention of a twofold covenant : therefore it is fomewhat ftrange to me, that they fhould be partakers of one way, of falvation with us.

Evan. Indeed it is true, the Lord did bequeath unto the fathers righteoufnefs, life and eternal falvation, in and through Chrift the Mediator, being not yet come in the flefh, but promifed : and unto us in the New Tefta-ment, he gives and bequeaths them to us, in and through Chrift, being already come, and having actually purchafed them for us ¶ : and the covenant of grace was, before

---

* " Faith prefenting to his view at all times the great angel of the covenant, God the Son, the Redeemer of him and Ifrael." Suppl. Pool's Annot. on the text.

† Alledged by Dr Urb Reg.

‡ Calv. Inftit. p. 207. || On Gal. I am fure.
§ Inftit. p. 198. ¶ Walker on the cov.

the coming of Chrift, fealed by his blood in types and figures: and at his death in his flefh *, it was fealed, and ratified by his very blood, actually and in very deed fhed for our fins. And the old covenant in refpect of the outword form, and manner of fealing, was temporary and changeable; and therefore the types ceafed, and only the fubftance remains firm. But the feals of the new are unchangeable, being commemorative, and fhall "fhew the Lord's death until his coming again". And their covenant did firft and cheifly promife earthly bleffings †: and in and under thefe, it did fignify and promife all fpiritual bleffings and falvaton; but our covenant promifeth Chrift and his bleffings, in the firft place, and after them earthly bleffings.

Thefe and fome other circumftantial differences in regard of adminiftration, there was, betwixt their way of falvation or covenant of grace, and ours; which moved the author to the Hebrews, Heb. viii. 8. to call theirs old, and ours new: but in regard of fubftance they were all one, and the very fame ‡. For in all covenants, this is a certain rule; if the fubject matter, the fruit and the conditions be the fame, then is the covenant the fame ‖. But in thefe covenants Jefus Chrift

---

* Chrift—being put to death in the flefh, 1 Pet. iii. 18.

† Chiefly; in fo far as, in that difpenfation of the covenant of grace, the promifes of earthly bleffings were chiefly infifted on; and the promifes of fpiritual bleffings and falvation more fparingly.

‡ "There are not therefore two covenants of grace, differing in fubftance; but one and the fame, under various difpenfations." Weftm. Confeff. chap. 7. art. 6. And their covenant of grace, confirmed by the fprinkling of blood, Exod. xxiv. Heb. ix. 19, 20. (the which covenant they brake, by their unbelief fruftrating the manner in which it was adminiftred to them) was given to them, when the Lord had led them out of Egypt, and at Sinai too, as well as the ten commands delivered to them, as the covenant of works. This is evident from Exod. xx. 1—17. compared with Deut. v. 2.—22. and Exod. xx. 20, 21. compared with chap. xxiv. 3.—8. See page 75. note †.

‖ Urfin Cat. p. 129.

is the subject matter of both, salvation the fruit of both, and faith the condition * of both : therefore I say, tho' they be called two, yet they are but one ; the which is confirmed by two faithful witnesses. The one is the apostle Peter, who saith, Acts xv. 11. " We believe that thro' the grace of our Lord Jesus Christ, we shall be saved even as they ;" meaning the fathers in the Old Testament, as is evident in the verse next before. The other is the apostle Paul, who saith, Gal. iii. 6, 7. " Abraham believed God, and it was accounted to him for righteousness ; know ye therefore that they which are of faith, the same are the children of Abraham :" by which testimony, saith † Luther, we may see that the faith of our fathers in the Old Testament, and ours in the New, is all one in substance.

Ant. But could they, that lived so long before Christ, apprehend his righteousness by faith, for their justification and salvation ?

Evan. Yea indeed ; for as Mr Forbes ‡ truly saith, It is as easy for faith to apprehend righteousness to come, as it is to apprehend righteousness that is past : wherefore as Christ's birth, obedience and death were in the Old Testament, as effectual to save sinners, as now they are ‖ ;

---

* Not in a strict and proper sense, as that, upon the performance of which, the right and title to the benefits of the covenant are founded and pleadable ; as perfect obedience was the condition of the covenant of works ; Christ's fulfilling of the law, by his obedience and death, is the only condition of the covenant of grace, in that sense. But in a large and improper sense, as that whereby one accepts, and embraceth the covenant, and the proper condition thereof, and is savingly interested in Jesus Christ the head of the covenant. " The grace of God is manifested in the second covenant, in that he freely provideth, and offereth to sinners a Mediator, and life and salvation by him ; and requiring faith, as the condition to interest them in him," &c. Larg. Cat. Quest. 32.

{ † On Gal. p. 116. ‡ On Just. p. 90.

‖ Walker on the cov. p. 122.

so all the faithful forefathers, from the beginning, did partake of the same grace with us, by believing in the same Jesus Christ ; and so were justified by his righteousness, and saved eternally by faith in him. It was by virtue of the death of Christ *, that Enoch was translated, that he should not see death ; and Elias was taken up into heaven, by virtue of Christ's resurrection and ascention. So that from the world's beginning, to the end thereof, the salvation of sinners, is only by Jesus Christ ; as it is written, " Jesus Christ the same yesterday, and to day, and for ever," Heb. xiii. 8.

Ant. Why then, Sir, it seems that those who were saved amongst the Jews, were not saved by the works of the law.

Evan. No indeed, they were neither justified nor saved, either by the works of the moral law, or the ceremonial law. For, as you heard before, the moral law being delivered unto them, with great terror, and under most dreadful penailties, they did find in themselves an impossibility of keeping it ; and so were driven to seek help of a mediator, even Jesus Christ, of whom Moses was to them a typical mediator † ‡ : so that the moral law, did drive them to the ceremonial law, which was their gospel and their Christ in a figure ; for that the ceremonies did prefigure Christ, direct unto him, and require faith in him, is a thing acknowledged and confessed by all men ‖.

Nom. But, Sir, I suppose, though believers among the Jews were not justified and saved by the works of the law, yet was it a rule of their obedience.

Evan. It is very true indeed, the law of the ten com-

---

* Walker on the cov. p 29.

† *i.e.* A type, he being, to them, a typical mediator.

‡ Marshall on infants baptism.

‖ Ball on the cov. p. 119.

L

mandments was a rule for their obedience * ; yet not as
it came from mount Sinai †, but rather as it came from
mount Zion ; not as it was the law, or covenant of
works, but as it was the law of Chrift. The which
will appear, if you confider, that after the Lord had
renewed with them the covenant of grace, as you heard
before (Exod. xxiv. at the beginning) the Lord faid unto
Mofes, ver. 12. " Come up to me into the mount, and
be there, and I will give thee tables of ftone, and a law
that thou mayeft teach them." And after the Lord had
thus written them, the fecond time, with his own finger,
he delivered them to Mofes, commanding him to provide
an ark to put them into ; which was not only for the
fafe keeping of them, Dut. ix 10. and x. 5. but alfo to
cover the form of the covenant of works, that was formerly upon them, that believers might not perceive it ; for
the ark was a notable type of Chrift ; and therefore the
putting of them therein, did fhew that they were perfectly
fulfilled in him ‡, Chrift being " the end of the law for
righteoufnefs, to every one that believeth," Rom. x 4.
The which was yet more clearly manifeft, in that the book
of the law was placed between the cherubims ||, and upon
the mercy feat ; to affure believers, that the law now
came to them from the mercy-feat §; for there the Lord

---

* The obedience of the believing Jews.
† That is, in the fenfe of our author, not as the covenant of
works. But of the twofold notion or confideration, under
which the ten commands were delivered from mount Sinai,
fee page 58. note †.
‡ Reynolds on Pfal. 110. p. 35.
|| Bolton's true bounds, p. 52.
§ From an attoned God in Chrift, binding them to obedience,
with the ftrongeft ties, arifing from their creation and redemption jointly ; but not with the bond of the curfe, binding them
over to eternal death, in cafe of tranfgreffion, as the law, or
covenant, of works, doth with them who are under it, Gal. iii. 10.
The mercy-feat was the cover of the ark ; and both the one,
and the other, types of Chrift. Within the ark, under the cover
of it, were the tables of the law laid up ; thus was the throne
of grace, which could not have ftood on mere mercy, firmly

promised to meet Moses, and to commune with him of all things, which he would give him in commandment to them, Exod. xxv. 22.

Ant. But, Sir, was the form quite taken away, so as the ten commandments were no more the covenant of works?

Evan. Oh no, you are not so to understand it For the form of the covenant of works *, as well as the matter, on God's part † came immediatly from God himself; and so consequently, is eternal like himself; whence it is that our Saviour saith, Matth. v. 18. " Till heaven and earth pass, one jot, or one tittle, shall in no ways pass from the law, till all be fulfilled." So that either man himself, or some other for him, must perform or fulfil the condition of the law, as it is the covenant of works; or else he remains still under it, in a damnable condition: but now Christ hath fulfilled it for all believers; and therefore I said, the form of the covenant of works was covered or taken away, as touching the believing Jews; but yet was it neither taken away in itself, nor yet as touching the unbelieving Jews.

Nom. Was the law then still of use to them, as it was the covenant of works?

Evan. Yea indeed.

Ant. I pray you, Sir, shew of what use it was to them.

---

established in Jesus Christ; according to Psal. lxxxix. 14. " Justice and judgment are the habitation (Marg. Establishment) of thy throne." The word properly signifies a base, supporter, stay, or foundation, on which a thing stands firm, Ezra ii. 68. and iii. 3. Psal. civ. 5. The sense is, O God and Father of our Lord Jesus Christ (Psal. lxxxix. 19.) justice satisfied, and judgment fully execute, in the person of the Mediator, are the foundation and base which thy throne of grace stands upon.

* Namely, the promissory, and penal, sanction, of eternal life, and death, in which God's truths was engaged.

† Man's part was, his consenting to the terms set before him by his Creator.

Evan. I remember * Luther faith, there be two forts
of unrighteous perfons, or unbelievers, the one to be
juftified, and the other not to be juftified: even fo was
there among the Jews. Now to them that were to
be juftified, as you have heard, it was ftill of ufe to
bring them to Chrift, as the apoftle faith, Gal. iii 24.
" The law was our fchool-mafter until Chrift †, that
we might be made righteous by faith ;" that is to fay, the
moral law ‡ did teach and fhew them what they fhould
do, and fo what they did not ; and this made them go to
the ceremonial law ‖ ; and by that they were taught that
Chrift had done it for them § ; the which they believing ¶,
were made righteous by faith in him. And to the fecond
fort it was of ufe, to fhew them what was good, and what
was evil; and to be as a bridle to them, to reftrain them
from evil ; and as a motive to move them to good, for
fear of punifhment **,††, or hope of reward in this life :
which though it was but a forced and conftrained obedience ; yet was it neceffary for the public common-wealth,
the quiet thereof being thereby the better maintained.
And though thereby they could neither efcape death, nor
yet obtain eternal life, for want of perfect obedience, yet
the more obedience they yielded thereunto, the more

---

* On Gal. p. 171.
† *i e.* To bring us unto Chrift, as we read it with the
fupplement.
‡ As the covenant of works, fo the author ufeth that term
here; as 'tis ufed, Larg. Cat. Queft. 93. above cited.

‖ Broken under the fenfe of guilt, the curfe of the law, and
their utter inability to help themfelves by doing or fuffering.

§ Chrift's fatisfying the law for finners, by his obedience
and death, being the great leffon taught by the ceremonial law,
which was the gofpel written in plain characters, to thofe whofe
eyes were opened.
¶ Appropriating and applying to themfelves, by faith,
Chrift's fatisfaction, held forth and exhibited to them in thefe
divine ordinances.

** Both in time and eternity. †† Calv. inftit. p. 167.

they were freed from temporal calamities, and poffeffed with temporal bleffings; according as the Lord promifed and threatned, Deut xxviii.

Ant. But, Sir, in that place the Lord feemeth to fpeak to his own people, and yet to fpeak according to the tenor of the covenant of works; which hath made me think, that believers in the Old Teftament, were partly under the covenant of works.

Evan. Do you not remember how I told you before, that the Lord did manifeft fo much love to the body of that nation, that the whole pofterity of Abraham * were brought under a ftate-covenant or national church; fo that for the believers fakes he infolded unbelievers in the compact; whereupon the Lord was pleafed, to call them all, by the name of his people, as well unbelievers as believers; and to be called their God. And though the Lord did there fpeak according to the tenor of the covenant of works; yet I fee no reafon, why he might not direct and intend his fpeech to believers alfo, and yet they remain, only under the covenant of grace.

Ant. Why Sir? you faid that the Lord did fpeak to them out of the tabernacle, and from the mercy-feat: and that doubtlefs was according to the tenor of the covenant of grace, and not according to the tenor of the covenant of words.

Evan. I pray you take notice, that after the Lord had pronounced all thofe bleffings and curfes, Deut. xxviii. in the beginning of the 29th chapter, it is faid, " Thefe are the words of the covenant, which the Lord commanded Mofes to make with the children of Ifrael in the land of Moab, befide the covenant, which he made with them in Horeb." Whereby it doth appear to me, that this was not the covenant of works, which was delievered

---

* Which were of that nation; according to Gen. xxi. 12.: " In Ifaac fhall thy feed be called." And chap. xxviii. 13. " I am the Lord God of Abraham thy father, and the God of Ifaac; the land whereon thou lieft, to thee will I give it, and to thy feed."

to them on mount Sinai * ; for the form of that covenant was eternal bleffings and curfes † : But the form of this covenant was temporal bleffings and curfes ‡. So that this rather feems to be the pedagogy of the law, than the covenant of works : for at that time thefe people feemed to be carried by temporal promifes, into the way of obedience, and deterred by temporal threatenings, from the ways of difobedience, God dealing with them as in their infancy and under age, and fo leads them on, and allures them, and fears them, by fuch refpects as thefe, becaufe they had but a fmall meafure of the fpirit.

Nom. But, Sir, was not the matter of that covenant, and this all one ?

Evan Yea indeed ; the ten commandments, were the matter of both covenants, only they differed in the forms.

Ant. Then, Sir, it feems that the promifes and

---

* The author does not make the covenant at Horeb, diftinct from that at Sinai ; for he takes Horeb and Sinai for one and the fame mountain, according to the holy fcripture, Exod. xix. 20. compared with Deut. v. 2. And therefore, becaufe the text fpeaks of this covenant in the land of Moab, as another covenant, befide that in Horeb; he infers that it was not the fame, not the covenant of works delivered on mount Sinai, otherwife called Horeb. And howbeit there are but two covenants, containing the only two ways to happinefs ; the author cannot, on that account, be juftly blamed for diftinguifhing this covenant, from them both ; unlefs temporal bleffings do make men happy; the which bleffings, with curfes of the fame kind, he takes to be the form of this covenant.

† Deut. xxvii. 26. " Curfed be he that confirmeth not all the words of this law to do them." Compare Gal. iii. 10. " For as many as are of the works of the law, are under the curfe ; for it is written, Curfed is every one that continueth not in all things written in the book of the law to do them."

‡ See Deuteronomy xxviii. throughout. Chap. xxix. 1. ver. 9. " Keep therefore the words of this covenant, and do them, that ye may profper in all that ye do." And here ends a great fection of the law.

threatnings, contained in the Old Teftament, were but temporary and terreftrial ; only, concerning the good and evil things of this life.

Evan. This we are to know, that like as the Lord by his prophets, gave the people in the Old Teftament, many exhortations to be obedient to his commandments, and many dehortations from difobedience thereunto : even fo did he back them, with many promifes and threatnings concerning things temporal ; as thefe and the like fcriptures do witnefs. Ifa. i 10 " Hear the word of the Lord, ye rulers of Sodom ; give ear unto the law of our God, ye people of Gomorrah."— Ver. 19, 20 " If ye be willing and obedient, ye fhall eat the good things of the land ; but if you refufe, and rebel, ye fhall be devoured with the fword; for the mouth of the Lord hath fpoken it." And Jer. vii. 3. " Amend your ways and your doings. and I will caufe you to dwell in this place : but ye fteal, murder, commit adultery, and fwear falfly by my name ; therefore thus faith the Lord God, behold mine anger and my fury fhall be poured out upon this place," ver. 20. And furely there be two reafons why the Lord did fo : 1ft, Becaufe all men are born under the covenant of works, they are naturally prone to conceive, that the favour of God, and all good things, do depend and follow upon their obedience to the law * ; and that the wrath of God, and all evil things. do depend upon, and follow their difobedience to it † : and that man's chief happinefs is to be had and found in terreftrial paradife, even in the good things of this life; fo the people of the Old Tefta. ment, being neareft to Adam's covenant and paradife, were moft prone to fuch conceits. And 2dly, Becaufe the covenant of grace, and celeftial paradife, were but

---

* Not on a faving intereft in the Lord Jefus Chrift, by faith.

† Not confidering the great fin of unbelief; and that the wrath of God, due to them for difobedience, may be averted by their fleeing to Chrift for refuge.

little mentioned in the Old Testament, they, for the most part *, had but a glimmering knowledge of them; and so could not yield obedience freely, as sons †. Therefore the Lord saw it meet to move them to yield obedience to his laws, by their own motives ‡, and as servants or children under age ||.

Ant. And were both believers and unbelievers, that is, such as were under the covenant of grace, and such as were under the covenant of works, equally and alike subject, as well to have the calamities of this life inflicted upon them for their disobedience, as the blessings of this life conferred upon them for their obedience.

Evan. Surely the words of the preacher do take place here, Eccl ix. 2. when he saith, " All things come alike to all; there is one event to the righteous, and to the wicked." Were not Moses and Aaron, for their disobedience, hindred from entring into the land of Canaan, as well as others? Numb. xx. 12. And was not Josiah, for his disobedience to God's command, slain in the valley of Megiddo? 2 Chron. xxxv. 21, 22. Therefore assure yourself, that when believers in the Old Testament did transgress God's commandments,

---

* Nor the more eminent saints, in the Old Testament times, are to be excepted; such as David and others.

† Having but a small measure of knowledge of the celestial paradise, the eternal inheritance, and of the covenant of grace, the divine disposition containing their right to it; they could not yield obedience freely, in the measure that sons (b), who are come to age, and know well their own privileges; but only as little children, who in some measure yield obedience freely, namely in proportion to their knowledge of these things, (but that measure being very small) must be drawn also to obedience by motives of a lower kind. And this the apostle plainly teacheth, Gal. iv. 1, 2, 4, 5. compare Westm. Conf. Chap. 20. Art. 1 " The liberty of Christians is further inlarged—in fuller communications of the free Spirit of God, than believers under the law did ordinarily partake of."

‡ Promises and threatening concerning things temporal.

|| By fear of punishment, and hope of reward.

God's temporal wrath * went out against them, and was manifest in temporal calamities that befel them, as well as others, Numb. xvi. 46. Only here was the difference, the believers temporal calamities had no eternal calamities included in them, nor following of them ; and their temporal blessings had eternal blessings included in them, and following of them † : and the unbelievers temporal blessings had no eternal blessings included in them ; and their temporal calamities had eternal calamities included in them, and following of them ‡.

Ant. Then, Sir, it seemeth that all obedience, that any of the Jews did yield to God's commandments, was for fear of temporal punishment, and in hope of temporal reward.

Evan. Surely the scripture seems to hold forth, that there were three several forts of people amongst the Jews, who endeavoured to keep the law of God; and they did all of them differ in their ends.

The first of them, were true believers, who, according to the measure of their faith, did believe the resurrection of their bodies after death, and eternal life in glory ; and that it was to be obtained, not by the works of the law, but by faith in the Messiah, or promised seed : and answerably as they believed this, answerably they yielded obedience to the law freely, without fear of punishment or hope of reward : but alas! the spirit of faith was very weak in the most of them, and the spirit of bondage very strong ; and therefore they stood in need to be induced and constrained to obedience for fear of punishment, and hope of reward ‖.

---

* *i. e* God's fatherly anger, whereby temporal judgments fall on his own people.

† By virtue of the covenant of grace, which they were under.

‡ By virtue of the covenant of works, which they were under.

‖ The Author doth not say, of believers under the Old Testament, simply and without any qualification, that they yielded

The second sort of them, were the Sadducees and their sect : and these did not believe that there was any resurrection, Matth. xxii. 23. nor any life, but the life of this world : and yet they endeavoured to keep the law, that God might bless them here, and that it might go well with them in this present life *.

The third sort, and indeed the greatest number of them in the future ages after Moses, were the Scribes and Pharisees, and their sects : and they held and maintained, that there was a resurrection to be looked for, and an eternal life after death ; and therefore they endeavoured to keep the law, not only to obtain temporal

---

obedience to the law, without fear of punishment, or hope of reward ; as if he minded to affert, that they were not at all moved to their obedience, by these : the scope of these words is to teach just the contrary. Compare page 86. But on good grounds he affirms, " that ANSWERABLY to their faith, their obedience ___ ___ ___ yielded freely, without fear of punishment, or hope of reward." And thus, the freeness of their obedience always bearing proportion to the measure of their faith; the greater measure of faith any Old Testament saint had attained unto. his obedience was the less influenced by fear of punishment, or hope of reward ; and the smaller his measure of faith was. his obedience was the more influenced by these : accordingly, such as had no saving faith at all, were moved to obedience, only by fear of punishment, or hope of reward : and the ___ ___ ___ faith, being once perfected in the beatific vision, in heaven, these ceased altogether to be motives of obedience to him, tho' he ceaseth not to obey from the strongest and most powerful motives. And thus the apostle John teacheth concerning love, which flows from faith; 1 John iv. 18. " Perfect love casteth out fear; because fear hath torment : he that feareth is not made perfect in love." The more there is of the one, there is still the less of the other. In the mean time, according to our author, the measure of faith in the most part of believers under the Old Testament, was very small, (and the strongest faith was imperfect) and the servile and childish disposition, which moves to obedience from fear of punishment and hope of reward, was very strong in them, Gal. iv. 1—5. And therefore as they stood in need of such inducement and constraint, there could not fail to be a great mixture of the influence of fear of punishment, and hope of reward, in their obedience.

* Bolton's true bounds, p. 259.

happiness, but eternal also. For though it had pleased the Lord to make known unto his people, by the ministry of Moses *, that the law was given, not to retain men in the confidence of their own works ; but to drive them out of themselves, and to lead them to Christ the promised seed : yet after that time, the priests and the levites, who were the expounders of the law, and whom the scribes and pharisees did succeed †, did so conceive and teach of God's intention in giving the law, as though it had been, that they, by their obedience to it, should obtain righteousness and eternal life : and this opinion was so confidently maintained, and so generally embraced amongst them, that in their book Mechilta, they say and affirm ‡, that there is no other covenant but the law : and so, in very deed they conceived, that there was no other way to eternal life, than the covenant of works.

Ant. Surely then it seems they did not understand and consider, that the law, as it is the covenant of works, doth not only bind the outward man, but also the inward man, even the soul and spirit ; and requires all holy thoughts, motions, and dispositions of the heart and soul.

Evan. Oh no, they neither taught it, nor understood it, so spirtually ; neither could they be persuaded that the law doth require so much at man's hands. For they first laid this down for a certain truth, that God gave the law for man to be justified and saved by his obedience to it ; and that therefore there must needs be a power in man to do all that it requireth, or else God would never have required it : and therefore, whereas they should have first considered, what a straight rule the law of God is, and then have brought man's heart, and have laid it, to it ; they, contrariwise, first considered what a crooked rule

---

* Ball on the covenant, p. 114.
† Perkins on Christ's sermon on the mount.
‡ Muscul. Com. Pla. p. 188.

man's heart is, and then fought to make the law like
unto it : and fo indeed they expounded the law literally,
teaching and holding, that the righteoufnefs, which the
law required, was but an external righteoufnefs, confift-
ing in the outward obfervation of the law; as you may
fee by the teftimony of our Saviour, Matth. v. fo that,
according to their expofition, it was poffible for a man
to fulfil the law pefectly; and fo to be juftified and
faved by his obedience to it *.

Ant. But, Sir, do you think the fcribes and pharifees,
and their fect, did yield perfect obedience to the law,
according to their own expofiton?

Evan. No indeed, I think very few of them; i fany
at all.

Ant. Why, what hopes could they then have to be
juftified and faved, when they tranfgreffed any of the
commandments?

Evan. Peter Martyr † tells us, that when they chanced
to tranfgrefs any of the ten commandments ‡, they had
their facrifices to make fatisfaction (as they conceived): for
they looked upon their facrifices without their fignificati-
ons ‖; and fo had a falfe faith in them; thinking that
the bare work was a facrifice acceptable to God; in a word,
they conceived, that the blood of bulls and goats would
take away fin: and fo what they wanted of fulfilling the
moral law, they thought to make up in the ceremonial
law §. And thus they feparated Chrift from their
facrifices, thinking they had difcharged their duty very
well, when they had facrificed and offered their offerings;
not confidering, that the imperfection of the typical law,
which (as the apoftle faith) made nothing perfect, fhould

---

* Gray in his ferm. of the perfection of a Chriftian.

† In his preface to the Rom.

‡ To wit, according to their own expofition.

‖ Tindal on Mark. § Bolton's true bounds, p. 161.

have led them to find prefection in Christ ; Heb. vii. 19.
But they generally rest in the work done in the ceremonial law, even as they had done in the moral law, though
they themselves were unable to do the one *, and the
other was as insufficient to help them.

And thus, " Israel which followed the law of righteousness, did not attain to the law of righteousness, because they sought it not by faith, but as it were by the
works of the law. For they being ignorant of the righteousness of God, and going about to establish their own
righteousness, did not submit themselves to the righteousness of God," Rom. ix. 31. and x. 3.

Ant. Then, Sir, it seemeth there were but very few
of them †, that had a clear sight and knowledge of
Christ.

Evan. It is very true indeed, for generally there was
such a vail of ignorance over their hearts, or such a vail
of blindness over their minds, that it made their spiritual
eye-sight so weak and dim, that they were no more able
to see Christ, the Sun of righteousness, to the end of the
law, Mal. iv. 2. ‡ than the weak eye of man is able to
behold the bright sun, when it shineth in its full strength.
And therefore we read, Exod. xxxiv. 30. that when
Moses face did shine, by reason of the Lord's talking with
him, and telling him of the glorious riches of his free
grace in Jesus Christ, and giving unto him the ten commandments, written in tables of stone, as the covenant
of works ‖ ; to drive the people out of confidence in

---

* To do any work of the moral law aright.
† To wit, of the Jews in general.
‡ *i. e.* Having in himself, a fulness of righteousness, an-
swering the law, to the utmost extent of its demands ; as the
sun hath a fulness of light.
‖ Therefore they are called, by the apostle, " the ministration of death, written and engraven on stones," 2 Cor. iii. 7.
Now, 'tis evident, the ten commandments are not the ministration of death, but as they are the covenant of works.——
And, as such, they were given to Moses, to be laid up in

K

themselves, and their own legal righteousness, unto Jesus Christ and his righteousness; the people were not able to behold his face. That is to say *, by reason of the weaknefs and dimnefs of their spiritual eye-fight, they were not able to fee and understand the spiritual sense of the law; to wit, that the Lord's end or intent in giving them the law, as a covenant of works, and as the apostle calls it, " the ministration of condemnation and death," 2 Cor. iii. 7, 9. was to drive them out of themselves to Christ, and that then † it was to be abolished to them, as it was the covenant of works, ver. 13. And therefore Moses put the cloudy vail of shadowing ceremonies over his face, Exod. xxxiv. 35. that they might be the better able to behold it: that is to say, that they might be the better able to fee through them, and understand, that " Christ is the end of the law for righteousnefs, to every one that believeth", Rom. x. 4 For Moses's face, faith godly Tindal, " is the law rightly understood." And yet alas, by reason that the priests and levites in former times, and the scribes and pharisees in after times, were " the blind leaders of the blind, Mat. xv. 14. the generality of them were so addicted to the letter of the law (and that both moral ‡ and ceremonial) that they used it not as a pedagogy to Christ, but terminated their eye in the letter and shadow; and did not fee through them to the spiritual substance, which is after Moses: for at the time of Christ's coming in the Jesus Christ; 2 Cor. iii. 13. especially in the future ages flesh, I remember but two, to wit, Simeon and Anna,

---

the ark, to fignify the fulfilling of them by Jefus Chrift alone, and the removing of that covenant-form trom them, as to believers: and so they ferved to drive finners out of themfelves to Chrift.

* i. e. This is the myftery of that typical event.

† When they fhould be driven out of themfelves to Jefus Chrift, by it.

‡ viz. As the covenant of works.

hat defired him, or looked for him, as a fpiritual Saviour
o fave them from fin and wrath. For though all of
hem had in their mouths the Meffiah (faith Calvin *)
nd the bleffed eftate of the kingdom of David; yet
hey dreamed that this Meffiah fhould be fome great
monarch, that fhould come in outward pomp and power,
and fave and deliver them from that bondage, which
they were in, under the Romans, of which bondage they
were fenfible and weary : but as for their fpiritual bondage under the law, fin and wrath, they were not at all
fenfible; and all becaufe their blind guides had turned
the whole law into a covenant of works, to be done for
juftification and falvation † ; yea, and fuch a covenant as
they were able to keep and fulfil, if not by the doing of
the moral law, yet by their offering facrifices in the
ceremonial law And for this caufe, our Saviour, in his
fermon upon the mount, took occafion to expound the
moral law truly and fpiritually, removing that falfe literal glofs, which the fcribes and pharifees had put upon
it, that men may fee how impoffible it is for any mere
man to fulfil it, and fo confequently to have juftification
and falvation by it. And at the death of Chrift, the vail
of the temple was rent in twain from the top to the bottom, to fhew, faith Tindal, "That the fhadows of Mofes
law fhould now vanifh away at the flourifhing light of the
gofpel, Matt. xxvii. 51 ‡" And after the death of Chrift,
his apoftles did both by their preaching and writing,
labour to make men underftand, that all the facrifices
and ceremonies, were but types of Chrift; and therefore he being now come, they were of no further ufe ;
witnefs that divine and fpiritual epiftle written to the
Hebrews. Yet notwithftanding we may fay of the Jews
at this day, as the apoftle did in his time, "Even until
this day remaineth the fame vail untaken away in the

---

* Harmo. p. 87.
† And fo they quite perverted the great end of the giving
of the law to them
‡ Marbeck Com. Pla. p. 112.

reading of Mofes." The Lord in mercy remove it in his due time *.

---

* The Hiftory of the vail on Mofes face is famous in the Old Teftament, and the myftery of it in the New. The former, as I gather it from the words of the infpired penman, Exod xxxiv. ftands thus briefly. There was a fhining glory on the face of Mofes, in the mount: but he himfelf knew it not, while God fpake with him there, ver. 29. and that by reafon of the excelling divine glory, 2 Cor. iii. 10. Gr. Even as the light of a candle is darkned before the fhining fun. But when Mofes, being come forth from the excelling glory, was coming down from the mount, with the tables in his hand, his face fhone fo, as to fend forth rays like horns, Exod. xxxiv 29, 30. fo that he could not but be confcious of it. Aaron and all the people, perceiving Mofes returning to them, went to meet him; but feeing an aftonifhing glory in his countenance, which they were not able to look at, they were afraid and retired, ver. 30, 31. But Mofes called to them to return, and goes into the tabernacle; whereupon the multitude not daring to return for all this, Aaron and the princes alone return to him, being now in the tabernacle, ver. 31. the middle part of which, I think, is to be read thus, " And Aaron and all the princes returned unto him in the teftimony," i. e. in the tabernacle of teftimony, as it is called, Chap. xxxviii. 21 Rev. xv. 5. From out of the tabernacle Mofes fpeaks to them, ordering (it would feem) the people to be gathered together unto that place, ver. 31, 32. The people being conveened at the tabernacle, he preached to them all, what he had received of the Lord on the mount, ver. 32 But, in the mean time, none of them faw his face; forafmuch as the tabernacle, within which he was, ferved inftead of a vail to it. Having done fpeaking, he puts a vail on his face, and comes out to them, ver. 33. Marg. Heb. " And Mofes ceafed from fpeaking with them, and put a vail on his face." Compare ver. 34. "But when Mofes went in before the Lord, to fpeak with him, he took the vail off, until he came out."

The myftery of this typical event, the apoftle treats of, 2 Cor. iii. -- The fhining glory of Mofes's face, did not prefigure nor fignify the glory of Chrift: for the glory of the Lord Chrift, ver. 18. is evidently oppofed to the glory of Mofes's countenance, ver. 7. And the open (or uncovered) face of the former, ver. 18. (as Vatablus feems to me rightly to underftand it) to the vailed face of the latter, ver. 13. The glory of the one is beheld as in a glafs, ver. 18. the fight of the face itfelf, being referved for heaven: but the glory of the other was not to be beheld at all, being vailed. But that glory fignified the glory of the law given

§ 6: *Ant.* Well, Sir, I had thought that God's covenant with the Jews had been a mixt covenant, and that they had been partly under the covenant of works; but now I perceive there was little difference betwixt their covenant of grace and ours.

Evan. Truly the oppofition between the Jews covenant of grace and ours, was chiefly of their own making: they fhould have been driven to Chrift by the law; but they expected life in obedience to it, and this was their great error and miftake *.

Ant. And furely, Sir, it is no great marvel, though they, in this point, did fo much err and miftake, who had the covenant of grace made known to them fo darkly; when many amongft us, who have it more clearly manifeft, do the like.

---

to the Ifraelites, as the covenant of works, the glory of the miniftration of death, ver. 7. agreeable to what the author tells us from Tindal, namely, that Mofes's face is the law rightly underftood. This Mofaic glory, while it was moft frefh, was darkened by the excelling glory of the Son of God, the Lord Jefus Chrift, ver. 18 compared with Exod. xxxiv 29. Howbeit the difcovery of it to finners, makes their hearts to tremble, they are not able to bear it. That glorious form of the law muft be had in Chrift the true tabernacle, and from thence only muft the law come to them; or elfe they are not able to receive it; though, before that difcovery is made to them, they are ready to embrace the law under that form; as the people were to receive Mofes with the tables in his hand, till they found themfelves unable to bear the fhining glory of his face. The vail, which Mofes put on his face, keeping the Ifraelites from beholding the glory of it, fignifies, that their minds were blinded, ver. 14. not perceiving the glory of the law given them as a covenant of works. And hence it was, that the children of Ifrael faftened not their eyes (Luke iv. 20. Acts iii. 4.) " on (Chrift) the end of that which is abolifhed, 2 Cor. iii. 13. Gr. For, had they feen that glory to purpofe, they would have faftened their eyes on him; as a malefactor at the ftake would fix his eyes on the face of one bringing a remiffion. And that is the vail, that is upon Mofes's face, and their hearts, unto this day, ver. 14, 15. which neverthelefs, in the Lord's appointed time, " fhall be taken away," ver. 16.

* Bolton's true bounds, p. 160.

Evan. And truly, it is no marvel, though all men naturally do so : for man naturally doth apprehend God to be the great master of heaven, and himself to be his servant; and that therefore he must do his work, before he can have his wages ; and, the more work he doth, the better wages he shall have. And hence it was, that when Aristotle came to speak of blessedness, and to pitch upon the next means to that end, he said, it was operation and working ; with whom also agreeth Pythagoras, when he saith, It is man's felicity to be like unto God, (as how?) by becoming righteous and holy *. And let us not marvel, that these men did so err, who never heard of Christ, nor of the covenant of grace ; when those to whom it was made known by the apostles of Christ, did the like ; witness those to whom the apostle Paul wrote his epistles, and especially the Galatians : for although he had by his preaching, when he was present with them, made known unto them the doctrine of the covenant of grace, yet after his departure, through the seducement of false teachers, they were soon turned to the covenant of works, and sought to be justified, either in whole, or in part, by it ; as you may see, if you do seriously consider that epistle. Nay, what saith Luther ? It is, saith he, the general opinion of man's reason thro'out the whole world, that righteousness is gotten by the works of the law; and the reason is, because the covenant of works was ingendered in the minds of men, in the very creation †, so that man naturally can judge no otherwise of the law, than as of a covenant of works, which was given to make righeous, and to give life and

---

* Trueness of Christian religion.

† This is not to be understood strictly, of the very moment of man's creation; in which the natural law was impressed on his heart; but with some latitude; the covenant of works being made with man newly created. And so divines call it the covenant of nature. See Dickson's Therap. Sacr. Book 1. Chap. 5. p. 116.

falvation. This pernicious opinion of the law, that it juftifieth and maketh righteous before God, (faith * Luther again) is fo deeply rooted in man's reafon, and all mankind fo wrapped in it †, that they can hardly get out : yea, I myfelf, faith he, have now preached the gofpel almoft twenty years, and have been exercifed in the fame daily, by reading and writing, fo that I may well feem to be rid of this wicked opinion ; yet notwithflaning, I now and than feel this old filth cleave to my heart, whereby it cometh to pafs, that I would willingly fo have to do with God, that I would bring fomething with myfelf, becaufe of which he fhould give me his grace. Nay it is to be feared, that (as you faid) many amongft us (who have more means of light ordinarily, than ever Luther, or any before him, had ‡, yet notwithftanding) do either wholly, or in part, expect juftification and acceptation by the works of the law.

Ant. Sir, I am verily perfuaded, that there be very many in the city of London, that are carried with a blind prepofterous zeal after their own good works and well doings ; fecretly feeking to become holy, juft and righteous before God, by their diligent keeping, and careful walking in all God's commandments ‖ ; and yet no man can perfuade them that they do fo: and truly, Sir, I am verily

---

* On Gal. p. 113.　　† Choice ferm. 108.

‡ This is not to infinuate, that Luther had arrived but to a fmall meafure of the knowledge of the doctrine of juftification and acceptation of a finner before God, in comparifon with thefe of latter times: I make no queftion but he underftood that doctrine as well as any man has done fince ; and doubt not but our author was of the fame mind anent him. But it is to fhew, that that great man of God, and others who went before him, found their way out of the mid-night darknefs of popery, in that point, with lefs means of light by far, than men now have, who notwithftanding cannot hold off from it.

‖ By which means, they put their own works in the room of Chrift, "who of God is made unto us—righteoufnefs and fanction, 1 Cor. i. 30. According to the fcripture-plan of

perfuaded that this our neighbour and friend Nomifta, is one of them.

Evan. Alas! there are a thoufand in the world, that make a Chrift of their works; and here is their undoing,. &c.* They look for righteoufnefs and acceptation more in the precept than in the promife, in the law than in the gofpel, in working than in believing; and fo mifcarry †. Many poor ignorant fouls amongft us, when we bid them obey and do duties, they can think of nothing, but work- ing themfelves to life; when they are troubled, they muft lick themfelves whole; when wounded, they muft run to the falve of duties, and ftream of performances, and neglect Chrift. Nay it is to be feared, that there be divers, who in words are able to diftinguifh between the law and gofpel, and in their judgments hold and maintain, that man is juftified by faith without the works of the law; and yet in effect and practice, that is to fay, in heart and confcience, do otherwife ‡. And there is fome touch of this in us all; otherwife we fhould not be fo up and down in our comforts, and believing, as we are ftill, and caft down with every weaknefs as we are ‖. But what fay

---

juftification and fanctification, a finner is juftified by his blood, Rom. v. 9. fanctified in Chrift Jefus, 1 Cor. i. 2. through fanctification of the Spirit, 2 Theff. ii. 13. fanctified by faith, Acts xxvi. 18.

* Bolton's true bounds, p. 97.

† Ibid. p. 162.

‡ It is indeed the practice of every unregenerate man, what- ever be his knowledge or profeffed principles; for the contrary practice, is the practice of the faints, and of them only, Matth. v. 3. " Bleffed are the poor in fpirit." Philip. iii. 3. " We are the circumcifion, which worfhip God in the fpirit, and rejoice in Chrift Jefus, and have no confidence in the flefh."

‖ For thefe flow from our building fo much on fomething in ourfelves, which is always very variable; and fo little on " the grace that is in Chrift Jefus," (2 Tim. ii. 1.) which is an immoveable foundation.

you neighbour Nomifta, are you guilty of thefe things, think you * ?

Nom. Truly, Sir, I muft needs confefs, I begin to be fomewhat jealous of myfelf, that I am fo : and becaufe I defire your judgment, touching my condition, I would intreat you to give me leave to relate it unto you.

Evan. With a very good will.

Nom. Sir, I having been born and brought up in a country, where there was very little preaching, the Lord knoweth, I lived a great while in ignorance and blindnefs ; and yet, becaufe I did often repeat the Lord's prayer, the apoftles creed, and the ten commandments ; and in that I came fometimes to divine fervice, (as they call it) and at Eafter received the communion ; I thought my condition to be good. But at laft, by means of hearing a zealous and godly minifter in this city, not long after my coming hither, I was convinced that my prefent condition was not good ; and therefore I went to the fame minifter, and told him what I thought of myfelf : fo he told me, that I muft frequent the hearing of fermons, and keep the fabbath very ftrictly, and leave off fwearing by my faith and troth, and fuch like oaths, and beware of lying, and all idle words and communication ; yea, and faid he, you muft get good books to read on, as Mr Dod on the commandments, Mr Bolton's directions for comfortable walking with God, Mr Brinfly's true watch, and fuch like ; and many fuch like exhortations and directions he gave me ; the which I liked very well, and therefore endeavoured myfelf to follow them. So I fell to the hearing of the moft godly, zealous, and powerful preachers that were in this city, and wrote their fermons after them ; and when God gave me a family, I did pray with them, and inftructed them, and repeated fermons to them, and fpent the Lord's day, in

---

* Bolton's true bounds, p. 97, 98.

public and private exercifes; and left off my fwearing and lying, and idle talking: and (according to exhortation) in few words, I did fo reform myfelf, and my life, that whereas before I had been only careful to perform the duties of the fecond table of the law, and that to the end I might gain favour and refpect from civil honeft men, and to avoid the penalties of man's law, or temporal punifhment; now I was alfo careful to perform the duties required in the firft table of the law, and that to gain favour and refpect from religious honeft men, and to avoid the penalty of God's law, even eternal torments in hell. Now, when profeffors of religion obferved this change in me, they came to my houfe, and gave unto me the right hand of fellowfhip, and counted me one of that number: and then I invited godly minifters to my table, and made much of them; and then, with that fame Micah mentioned in the book of Judges, I was perfuaded the Lord would be merciful unto me, becaufe I had gotten "a levite to be my prieft," Judg. xvii. 13. In a word, I did now yield fuch an outward obedience and conformity to both tables of the law, that all godly minifters and religious honeft men that knew me, did think very well of me, counting me to be a very honeft man, and a good Chriftian: and indeed I thought fo of myfelf, efpecially becaufe I had their approbation. And thus I went on bravely a great while, even until I read in Mr. Bolton's works, that the outward righteoufnefs of the fcribes and pharifees was famous in thofe times *; for befides their forbearing and protefting againft grofs fins, as murder, theft, adultery, idolatry, and the like, they were frequent and conftant in prayer, fafting, and almsdeeds; fo that, without queftion, many of them were perfuaded, that their doing would purchafe heaven and happinefs. Whereupon I concluded, that I had as yet

---

* Difcourfe on true happinefs, p. 64.

done no more than they ; and withal I confidered that our Saviour faith, " Except your righteoufnefs exceed the righteoufnefs of the fcribes and pharifees, you cannot enter into the kingdom of God * :" yea, and I alfo confidered that the apoftle faith, " He is not a Jew that is one outwardly, but he that is one within, whofe praife is not of men, but of God † " Then did I conclude, that I was not yet a true Chriftian : for, faid I in my heart, I have contented myfelf with the praife of men, and fo have loft all my labour and pains in performing duties ; for they have been no better than out-fide performances, and therefore they muft all fall down in a moment. I have not ferved God with all my heart ; and therefore I fee I muft either go further, or elfe I fhall never be happy. Whereupon, I fet about the keeping of the law in good earneft, and laboured to perform duties, not only outwardly, but alfo inwardly from my heart : I heard, and read, and prayed ; and laboured to bring my heart, and forced my foul to every duty : I called upon the Lord in good earneft ; and told him, that whatfoever he would have me to do, I would do it with all my heart, if he would but fave my foul. And then, I alfo took notice of the inward corruptions of my heart, the which I had not formerly done ; and was careful to govern my thoughts, to moderate my paffions, and to fupprefs the motions and rifings of lufts, to banifh privy pride and fpeculative wantonnefs, and all vain and finful defires of my heart : and then I thought myfelf not only an out-fide Chriftian, but alfo an in-fide Chriftian; and therefore a true Chriftian indeed. And fo I went on comfortably a good while, till I confidered that the law of God requires paffive obedience, as well as active ; and therefore I muft •: a fufferer, as well as a doer, or elfe I could not be a Chriftian indeed : whereupon I began

---

* Mattb. v. 10.   † Rom. ii. 28. 29.

to be troubled at my impatience under God's correcting hand, and at those inward murmurings and discontents, which I found in my spirit in time of any outward calamity that befel me. And then I laboured to bridle my passions, and to submit myself quietly to the will of God, in every condition; and then did I also, as it were, begin to take penance upon myself, by abstinence, fasting, and afflicting my soul; and made pitiful lamentations in my prayers, which were sometimes also accompanied with tears, the which I was perfuaded the Lord did take notice of, and would reward me for it: and then I was perfuaded that I did keep the law, in yielding obedience both actively and passively. And then was I confident I was a true Christian, until I confidered, that those Jews, of whom the Lord complains, Isaiah lviii. did as much as I: and that caused me to fear, that all was not right with me as yet. Whereupon I went to another minister, and told him, that tho' I had done thus and thus, and suffered thus and thus, yet I was perfuaded, that I was in no better a condition than those Jews: O yes, said he, you are in a better condition than they, for they were hypocrites, and served not God with all their hearts, as you do. Then I went home contentedly, and so went on in my wonted courfe of doing and suffering, and thought all was well with me; until I bethought myself, that before the time of my conversion, I had been a transgressor from the womb; yea, in the womb, in that I was guilty of Adam's transgression: so that I considered, that altho' I kept even with God for the time present, and to come; yet that would not free me from the guiltiness of that which was done before; whereupon I was much troubled and difquieted in my mind. Then I went to a third minister of God's holy word, and told him how the case stood with me, and what I thought of my state and condition. He cheered me up, bidding me be of good comfort; for however my obedience since my conversion would not satisfy for my former sins; yet, in as much as, at my conversion, I had

confeffed, lamented, deplored, bewailed, and forfaken
them, God, according to his rich mercy, and gracious
promife, had mercifully pardoned and forgiven them.
Then I returned home to my own houfe again, and went
to God by earneft prayer and fupplication, and befought
him to give me affurance of the pardon and forgivenefs
of my guiltinefs of Adam's fin, and all my actual tranfgreffions, before my converfion; and as I had endeavoured
my felf to be a good fervant before, fo I would ftill continue
in doing my duty moft exactly: and fo being affured that
the Lord had granted this my requeft, I fell to my bufinefs according to my promife; I heard I read, I prayed,
I fafted, I mourned, I fighed, and groaned; and watched
over my heart, my tongue and ways, in all my doings,
actions and dealings, both with God and man. But after
a while, I growing better acquainted with the fpiritual-
nefs of the law, and the inward corruptions of mine own
heart; I perceived that I had deceived my felf, in thinking that I had kept the law perfectly; for, do what I
could, I found many imperfections in my obedience: for
I had been, and was ftill fubject to fleepinefs, droufinefs,
and heavinefs in prayers, and hearing, and fo in other
duties: I failed in the manner of performance of them,
and in the end why I performed them, feeking my felf in
every thing I did: and my confcience told me I failed in
my duty to God in this, and in my duty to my neighbour
in that. And then I was much troubled again; for I
confidered that the law of God requireth, and is not fatisfied, without an exact and perfect obedience. And then
I went to the fame minifter again, and told him how I
had purpofed, promifed, ftriven, and endeavoured, as
much as poffibly I could, to keep the law of God perfectly;
and yet by woful experience I had found, that I had, and
did ftill tranfgrefs it many ways: and therefore I feared
hell and damnation. Oh! But, faid he, do not fear,
for the beft of Chriftians have their failings, and no
man keepeth the law of God perfectly; and therefore go
on, and do as you have done, in ftriving to keep the law

perfectly; and in what you cannot do, God will accept the will for the deed, and wherein you come short, Christ will help you out. And this satisfied and contented me very much. So I returned home again, and fell to prayer, and told the Lord, that now, I saw I could not yield perfect obedience to his law, and yet I would not difpair; becaufe I did believe, that what I could not do, Christ had done for me: and then I did certainly conclude, that I was now a Christian indeed, though I was not fo before. And fo have I been perfuaded ever fince. And thus, Sir, you fee I have declared unto you, both how it hath been with me formerly, and how it is with me for the prefent: wherefore I would intreat you to tell me plainly and truly what you think of my condition *.

Evan. Why truly I muft tell you, it appears to me by this relation, that you have gone as far in the way of the

---

* It is not neceffary, for faving this account of Nomifta's cafe from the odious charge of forgery, that the particulars therein mentioned fhould have been real facts; more than (not to fpeak of fcripture parables) it is neceffary to fave the whole book from the fame imputation, that the fpeeches therein contained fhould have paffed, at a certain time, in a real conference of four men, called Evangelifta, Nomifta, Antinomifta, and Neophitus. Yet I make no queftion but it is grounded on matters of fact, falling out by fome cafuifts their inadvertency, excefs of charity to, or fhifting converfe with the afflicted; as to their foul-exercife, or by means of corrupt principles, and as the former are incident to good men of found principles, at any time; which calls minifters on fuch occafions, to take heed to the frame of their own fpirits, and to be much in the exercife of dependence on the Lord; left they do hurt to fouls, inftead of doing them good; fo the latter is at no time to be thought ftrange; fince there were found, even in the primitive apoftolical churches, fome who were reputed godly zealous gofpel-minifters, efpecially by fuch as had little favour of Chrift on their own fouls; who neverthelefs, in their zeal for the law, perverted the gofpel of Chrift, Gal. i. 6, 7. and iv. 17 — Whether Nomifta was of opinion, that the covenant of works was ftill in force, or not; our Lord Jefus Chrift taught it was, Luke x. 25.—28. and fo doth the apoftle, Gal. iii. 10. and

covenant of works, as the apostle Paul did before his conversion: but yet, for ought I see, you have not gone the
right way to the truth of the gospel; and therefore I
question whether ye be as yet truly come to Christ.

Neoph. Good Sir, give me leave to speak a few words.
By the hearing of your discourse concerning the covenant
of works, and the covenant of grace, I was moved to fear
that I was out of the right way : but now having heard
my neighbour Nomista make such an excellent relation,
and yet you to queston whether he be come truly to
Christ or no, makes me to conclude absolutely that I am
far from Christ. Surely if he, upon whom the Lord hath
bestowed such excellent gifts and graces, and who hath
lived such a godly life, as I am sure he hath done, be not
right; then wo be unto me.

Evan. Truly, for ought I know, you may be in Christ
before him.

Nom. But I pray you, Sir, consider, that though I am
now thoroughly convinced, that till of late I went on in
the way of the covenant of works; yet seeing that at last
I came to see my need of Christ, and have verily believed
that in what I came short of fulfilling the law, he will
help me out; methinks I should be come truly to Christ.

Evan. Verily I do conceive that this gives you no surer
evidence of your being come truly to Christ, than some

---

unbelievers will find it so, to their everlasting ruin. For, our
Lord Jesus, who now offers to be Mediator for them who
believe on him, shall at the last day come armed with flaming
fire, to judge, condemn, and destroy all them, who have not
believed God, have not received the offer of grace made in the
gospel, nor obeyed the doctrine thereof, but remain in their
natural state, under the law or covenant of works." Practical
use of saving knowledge, Tit. For convincing a man of judgment by the law, par. 2.

of your strict Papists have. For it is the doctrine of the church of Rome, that, if a man exercise all his power, and do his best to fulfil the law, then God, for Christ's sake, will pardon all his infirmities, and save his soul. And therefore you shall see many of your Papists, very strict and zealous in the performance of duties morning and evening, so many ave-maries, and so many pater-nosters; yea, and many of them do great deeds of charity, and great works of hospitality; and all upon such grounds, and to such ends, as these. The Papists (saith Calvin) * cannot abide this saying, By faith alone; for they think that their own works are in part a cause of their salvation, and so they make a hotch potch and mingle-mangle, that is neither fish nor flesh, as men use to say.

Nom. But stay, Sir, I pray, you are mistaken in me: for though I hold that God doth accept of my doing my best to fulfil the law, yet I do not hold with the Papists, that my doings are meritorious; for I believe that God accepts not what I do, either for the work, or worker's sake, but only for Christ's sake.

Evan. Yet do you but still go hand in hand with the Papists; for though they do hold that their works are meritorious, yet they say it is by the merit of Christ that they become meritorious †; or as some of the moderate sort of them say, Our works sprinkled with the blood of Christ become meritorious. But this you are to know, that as the justice of God requires a perfect obedience, so doth it require that this perfect obedience, be a personal obedience; *viz.* It must be the obedience of one person only; the obedience of two must not be put together,

* Propos. on Gal. 2. in octav. p. 45.

† Dr Downham on justific. p, 149.

to make up a perfect obedience *: fo that, if you defire
to be juftified before God, you muft either bring to him
a perfect righteoufnefs of your own, and wholly renounce
Chrift; or elfe you muft bring the perfect righteoufnefs
of Chrift, and wholly renounce your own.

Ant. But believe me, Sir, I would advife him to bring
Chrift's, and wholly renounce his own; as, I thank the
Lord, I have done.

Evan. You fay very well, for indeed the covenant of
grace terminates itfelf only on Chrift and his righetouf-
nefs; God will have none to have a hand in the juftification and falvation of a finner, but Chrift only. And to
fay as the thing is, neighbour Nomifta, Chrift Jefus
will either be a whole Saviour, or no Saviour; he will
either fave you alone, or not fave you at all, Acts iv. 12.
"For among men there is given no other name under
heaven, whereby we muft be faved," faith the apoftle
Peter. And Jefus Chrift himfelf faith, John xiv. 6.
"I am the way, the truth, and the life; and no man
cometh to the Father but by me:" fo that, as † Luther
truly faith. befides this way Chrift. there is no way, but
wandring; no verity, but hypocrify; no life, but eternal
death. And verily, faith another godly writer ‡, we can
neither come to God the Father, be reconciled unto him,
nor have any thing to do with him, by any other way or
means, but only by Jefus Chrift; for we fhall not any-
where find the favour of God, true innocency, righteoufnefs, fatisfaction for fin, help, comfort, life or falvation,
any-where but only in Jefus Chrift; he is the fum and
center of all divine and evengelical truths; and therefore

---

* For, in that cafe, the obedience, both of the one, and of
the other, is imperfect; and fo is not conform to the law:
therefore it cin in no wife be accepted for righteoufnefs; but,
according to juftice proceeding upon it, the foul that hath it,
muft die, becaufe a finful foul; Ezek. xviii. 4.
† On Gal. p. 17.
‡ Dr Urb. Reg. in his Expof. of Chrift's ferm. going to
Emmaus.

as there is no knowledge or wifdom fo excellent, necefſary, or heavenly, as the knowledge of Chriſt, as the apoſtle plainly gives us to underſtand, when he tells the Corinthians, 1 Cor. ii. 2. That he determined to know nothing amongſt them, but only Jeſus Chriſt and him crucified ;" fo there is nothing to be preached unto men, as an object of their faith, or neceſſary element of their ſalvation, which doth not ſome way or other, either meet in Chriſt, or refere unto Chriſt * †.

§ 7. *Ant.* O, Sir, you do pleaſe me wondrous well, in thus attributing all to Chriſt : and ſurely, Sir, though of late you have not been fo evangelical in your teaching, as ſome others in this city, (which hath cauſed me to leave off hearing you, to hear them) yet have I formerly perceived, and now alſo perceive, that you have more knowledge of the doctrine of free grace, than many other miniſters in this city have : and to tell you the truth, Sir, it was by your means that I was firſt brought to renounce mine own righeouſneſs, and to cleave only to the righteouſneſs of Jeſus Chriſt ‡.   And thus it was.   After that

---

* Eph. iv. 20. " But ye have not ſo learned Chriſt. 21. If ſo be that ye have heard him, and have been taught by him, as the truth is in Jeſus."

† Reynolds on Pſal. cx. p. 16.

‡ What this is, in the ſenſe of the ſpeaker, he himſelf immediately explains, at large. In a word, in his ſenſe, it is to be an Antinomian indeed. The ſum of his compliment made to Evangeliſta, or the author, which you pleaſe, lies here : namely, that, He had left hearing of him, becauſe he did not preach the goſpel, fo purely as ſome others in the place; yet, in his opinion, he underſtood it better than many others: and (to carry the compliment to the higheſt pitch) it was by his means, he turned downright Antinomian. One would think, that, whatever was the meaſure of our author's pride or humility, ſelf-denial or ſelf-ſeeking, he had as much common ſenſe, as would render this addreſs not very taking with him ; or at leaſt would teach him, that the publiſhing of it, was none of the moſt proper means for commending of himſelf. So that the publiſhing of it may rather be imputed to the author's ſelf-denial, than to the want thereof; though I preſume, the

I had been a good while a legal profeſſor, juſt like my friend Nomiſta; and heard none but your legal-preachers, who built me up in works and doings, as they did him, and as their manner is: at laſt a familiar acquaintance of mine, who had ſome knowledge of the doctrine of free grace, did commend you for an excellent preacher; and at laſt prevailed with me to go with him, and hear you. And your text that day I well remember, was, Tit. iii. 5. " Not by the works of righteouſneſs that we had done, but according to his own mercy, he ſaved us:" Whence you obſerved, and plainly proved, That man's own righteouſneſs had no hand in his juſtification and ſalvation: whereupon you dehorted us from putting any confidence, in our own works and doings; and exhorted us, by faith to lay hold upon the righteouſneſs of Jeſus Chriſt only: at the hearing whereof, it pleaſed the Lord ſo to work upon me, that I plainly perceived that there was no need at all of my works and doings, nor nothing elſe, but only to believe in Jeſus Chriſt *. And indeed my heart

---

.conſidering reader will neither impute it to the one, nor to the other.

* The preacher taught, according to his text, " That man's own righteouſneſs had no hand in his juſtification and ſalvation." He dehorted from putting confidence in good works; and exhorted, by faith to lay hold on Chriſt's righteouſneſs only. And this hearer thence inferred, that there was no need at all, of good works; as if one ſhould conclude, that, becauſe 'tis the eye only that ſeeth; therefore there's no need at all, of the hand or foot. So the apoſtle Paul's doctrine was miſconſtrued, Rom. iii. 8. " Some affirm that we ſay, let us do evil that good may come." Yea, in the apoſtle's days, the doctrine of free grace was actually thus abuſed to Antinomianiſm by ſome turning the grace of God to laſciviouſneſs," Jude 4. The apoſtle was aware of the danger on that ſide, through the corruption of the hearts of men, Gal. v. 13. " Brethren, ye have been called unto liberty; only uſe not your liberty for an occaſion to the fleſh." And miniſters of Chriſt, (who himſelf was accounted a friend of publicans and ſinners, Matth. xi. 19.) followers of Paul's doctrine, which, in the eyes of carnal men, had a ſhew and ſemblance of favouring ſinful liberty; ought to

did affent unto it immediately ; fo that I went home with
abundance of peace and joy in believing, and gave thanks
to the Lord, for that he had fet my foul at liberty from
fuch a fore bondage as I have been under. And I told all
my aquaintance, what a flavifh life I had lived in, being
under the law ; for if I did commit any fin, I was prefently
troubled and difquieted in my confcience, and could
have no peace, till I had made humble confeffion thereof
unto God ; craved pardon and forgivenefs, and promifed
amendment.   But now I told them, that whatfoever fins
I did commit, I was no whit troubled at them, nor indeed am not at this day ; for I do verily believe, that
God for Chrift's fake hath freely and fully pardoned all
my fins, both paft, prefent, and to come : fo that I am
confident, that what fin, or fins, foever I commit, they
fhail never be laid to my charge ; being very well affured,
that I am fo perfectly clothed with the robes of Chrift's
righteoufnefs, that God can fee no fin in me at all. And
therefore now I can rejoice evermore in Chrift, as the
apoftle exhorts me ; and live merrily, though I be never
fo vile, or finful a creature : and indeed I pity them that
are in the fame flavifh condition I was in ; and would
have them to believe, as I have done, that fo they may
rejoice with me in Chrift *.   And thus, Sir, you fee I

---

fet the apoftle's example, in this matter, before them, in a
fpecial manner :—With fear and trembling keeping a jealous
eye on the danger from that part ; efpecially in this day,
wherein the Lord's indignation is vifibly going out in fpiritual
ftrokes, for a defpifed gofpel ; knowing that the gofpel of Curift
is to fome " the favour of death unto death," 2 Cor. ii. 16. and
that there are, " who wreft the fcriptures themfelves, unto
their own deftruction," 2 Pet. iii. 16.

* How eafy is the paffage from Legalifm to Antinomianifm ;
had this poor man, under his trouble and difquiet of confcience,
fled to Jefus Chrift, for the purging of his confcience from
guilt, by his blood, and the fanctifying of his nature, by his
Spirit ; and not put his own confeffions of fin, prayers for
pardon, and promifes of amendment, in the room of Chrift's

have declared unto you my condition; and therefore I intreat you to tell me, what you think of me.

Evan. There is in this city, at this day, much talk, about Antinomians; and though I hope there be but few that do juftly deferve that title, yet (I pray) give me leave to tell you, that I fear, I may fay unto you in this cafe, as it was once faid unto Peter in another cafe, " Surely thou art one of them, for thy fpeech bewrayeth thee." Matth. xxvi. 73. And therefore to tell you truly, I make fome queftion whether you have truly believed in Chrift, for all your confidence : and indeed I am the rather moved to queftion it, by calling to mind, that, as I have heard, your converfation is not fuch " as becometh the gofpel of Chrift," Phil. i. 27.

Ant. Why, Sir, do you think it is poffible for a man to have fuch peace and joy in Chrift, as I have had, and, I thank the Lord, have ftill, and not to have truly believed in Chrift?

Evan. Yea, indeed, I think it is poffible : for doth not our Saviour tell us, That thofe hearers, whom he refembles to the " ftony ground, immediately received the word with joy, and yet had no root in themfelves," Mark iv. 16, 17. and fo indeed were not true believers? And doth not the apoftle give us to underftand, that as there is a form of godlinefs, without the power of godlinefs, 2 Tim. iii. 5. fo there is a form of faith, without the power of faith? and therefore he prays that God would grant unto the Theffalonians, " the work of faith with power," 2 Theff i. 11. And as the fame apoftle gives us to underftand, " there is a faith that is not feigned," 1 Tim. i. 5. fo doubtlefs there is a faith that is feigned. And furely, when our Saviour faith,

---

attoning blood, and his blind and faithlefs refolutions to amend, in the room of the fanctifying Spirit of Chrift ; he had efcaped this fnare of the devil, Heb. ix. 14. Rom. vii. 4, 5, 6.

Mark iv. 26, 27, 28. ". The kingdom of God is as if a man ſhould caſt ſeed into the ground, and ſhould ſleep, and riſe night and day, and the ſeed ſhould ſpring up and grow, he knoweth not how, firſt the blade, then the ear, after that the full corn in the ear :" He giveth us to underſtand, that true faith is produced by the ſecret power of God, by little and little * ; ſo that ſometimes a true believer himſelf, neither knows the time when, nor the manner how, it was wrought. So that we may perceive, that true faith is not ordinarily begun, increaſed, and finiſhed all in a moment, as it ſeems yours was ; but groweth by degrees, according to that of the apoſtle, Rom. i. 17. " The righteouſneſs of God is revealed from faith to faith :" that is, from one degree of faith to another † ‡ ; from a weak faith, to a ſtrong faith ; and from faith beginning, to faith increaſing towards per-fection ; or from faith of adherence, to faith of evidence : but ſo was not yours. And again, true faith, according to the meaſure of it, produceth holineſs of life ; but it ſeems yours doth not ſo : and therefore, though you have had, and have ſtill, much peace and joy, yet that is no infallible ſign that your faith is true ‖ ; for a man may have great raptures, yea he may have great joy, as if he were lift up into the third heaven, and have a great and ſtrong perſuaſion that his ſtate is good, and yet be but a hypocrite for all that. And therefore, I beſeech you, in the words of the apoſtle, " Examine yourſelf whether you be in the faith, prove your own ſelf, know you not your own ſelf, how that Jeſus Chriſt is in you, except you be a reprobate ?" 2 Cor. xiii. 5. " And if Chriſt is in you, the body is dead, becauſe of ſin ; but

---

* Diodate on the text. † See the note ‡ page 53.

‡ Wilſon on the Rom. p. 17.

‖ Dr Preſton of faith, p. 86.

the Spirit is life, becaufe of righteoufnefs *," Rom. viii. 10.

Ant. But, Sir, if my friend Nomifta went wrong, in feeking to be juftified by the works of the law : then methinks I fhould have gone right, in feeking to be juftified by faith : and yet you fpeak as if we had both gone wrong.

Evan. I remember Luther † faith, that in his time, if they taught in a fermon, that falvation confifted not in our works or life, but in the gift of God ; fome men took occafion thence to be flow to good works, and to live a difhoneft life. And if they preached of a godly and honeft life, others did by and by furioufly attempt to build ladders to heaven ‡. And moreover he faith, that in the year 1525, there were fome fantaftical fpirits that ftirred up the ruftical people to fedition, faying, that the freedom of the gofpel giveth liberty to all men from all manner of laws ; and there were others that did attribute the force of juftification to the law ‖. Now, faith he, both thefe forts offend againft the law ; the one on the right hand, who would be juftified by the law ; and the other on the left hand, who would be clean delivered from the law. Now I fuppofe this faying of Luther's may be fitly applied to you two ; for it appears to me, friend Antinomifta, that you have offended on the left hand in not walking according to the matter of the law ; and it is evident to me, neighbour Nomifta, that you have offended on the right hand in feeking to be juftified by your obedience to it §.

---

* This doctrine of our author's, is far from cherifhing of prefumption, or opening of a gap to licentioufnefs.

† Choice ferm. p 65.

‡ *i. e.* To fcale it, and get into it, by their own good works.

‖ Luther on Gal. p. 170.

§ The offences of thefe men, here taxed, were both againft the law (or covenant) of works ; for they muft needs have been againft that law, which they were under, and not another ; and

§ 8 *Nom.* But, Sir, if feeking of juftification by the works of the law, be an error; yet it feemeth, that, by Luther's own confeffion, it is but an error on the right hand.

Evan. But, yet I tell you, it is fuch an error, that, by the apoftle Paul's own confeffion, fo far forth as any man is guilty of it, " He makes his fervices his faviours, and rejects the grace of God, and makes the death of Chrift of none effect, and perverteth the Lord's intention, both in giving the law, and in giving the gofpel; and keeps himfelf under the curfe of the law; and maketh himfelf the fon of a bond woman, a fervant; yea, and a flave; and hinders himfelf in the courfe of well-doing;" Gal. v. 4. iii. 19. i. 7. iii. 10. iv. 25. v. 7. and ii. 11. and in fhort he goeth about an impoffible thing, and fo lofeth all his labour.

Nom Why then, Sir, it fhould feem that all my feeking to pleafe God, by my good works, all my ftrict walking according to the law, and all my honeft courfe of life, hath rather done me hurt than good.

Evan. The apoftle faith, that " without faith it is impoffible to pleafe God," Heb. xi. 6. that is, faith Calvin *, " Whatfoever a man thinketh, purpofeth, or doth, before

---

both of them were as yet under the law (or covenant) of works, as being both unbelievers; the which was told Antinomifta, pag. 109. as it was to Nomifta, pag. 103. Wherefore it is manifeft, that by the matter of the law here, is not meant the law of Chrift; but the matter of the law of works, that is, the ten commandments, as they ftand in the covenant of works; which Antinomifta had no regard to in his converfation, though they had all the authority, and binding force upon him, found in that covenant. And as he offended againft the matter of it, fo did Nomifta againft the form, in feeking to be juftified by his obedience: for the covenant of works never bound a finner to feek to be juftified by his obedience to it; but, on the contrary, always condemned that, as prefumption, ftaking down the guilty under the curfe, without remedy, till fatisfaction be made by another hand.

* Inft. p. 370.

he be reconciled to God by faith in Chrift, is accurfed; and not only of no value to righteoufnefs, but of certain deferving to damnation." So that, faith Luther *, whofoever goeth about to pleafe God with works, going before faith, goeth about to pleafe God with fin; which is nothing elfe but to heap fin upon fin, to mock God, and to provoke him to wrath: nay, faith the fame ╪ Luther, in another place, if thou beeft without Chrift, thy wifdom is double foolifhnefs, thy righteoufnefs is double fin and iniquity. And therefore, though you have walked very ftrictly according to the law, and led an honeft life, yet if you have refted, and put confidence therein, and and fo come fhort of Chrift, then hath it indeed rather done you hurt than good. For, faith a godly writer ‡, vertuous life, according to the light of nature, turneth a man further off from God, if he add not thereto the effectual working of his Spirit. And faith Luther‖, " they which have refpect only to an honeft life, it were better for them to be adulterers, and adultereffes, and to wallow in the mire §. And furely for this caufe it is, that our Saviour tells the ftrict fcribes and Pharifees, who fought juftification by works, and rejected Chrift, that " publicans and harlots fhould enter into the kingdom of God before them," Matt. xxi. 31. And for this caufe it was, that I faid, for ought I know, my neighbour Neophytus might be in Chrift before you.

---

* On Gal. p. 63.   † On Gal. p. 23.

‡ Ball on the cov. p. 338.   ‖ Choice Serm. p. 65.

§ This comparifon is not ftated betwixt thefe two, confidered fimply, as to their different manner of life; but in point of pliablenefs to receive conviction, wherein the latter have the advantage of the former; which the fcripture oftener than once takes notice of, Matth. xxi. 31. quoted in the following fentence, Rev. iii. 15. " I would thou wert cold or hot." The paffage is to be found in his fermon upon the hymn of Zacharias, pag. (*mihi*) 50.

Nom. But how can·that be, when, as you know, he hath confeſſed that he is ignorant and full of corruption, and comes far ſhort of me in the gifts and graces.

Evan. Becauſe, as the phariſee had more to do before he could come at Chriſt than the publican had; ſo I conceive, you have more to do than he hath.

Nom. Why, Sir, I pray you, what have I to do, or what would you adviſe me to do? for truely I would be contented to be ruled by you.

Evan. Why, that which you have to do, before you can come to Chriſt, is to undo all that ever you have done already : that is to ſay, whereas you have endeavoured to travel towards heaven, by the way of the covenant of works, and ſo have gone a wrong way; you muſt go quite back again all the way you have gone, before you can tread one ſtep in the right way. · And whereas you have attempted to build up the ruins of old Adam, and that upon yourſelf; and ſo, like a fooliſh builder, to build a tottering houſe upon the ſands, you muſt throw down and utterly demoliſh all that building, and not leave a ſtone upon a ſtone; before you can begin to build anew. And whereas you have conceived that there is ſome ſufficiency in yourſelf, to help to juſtify and ſave yourſelf; you muſt conclude, that in that caſe there is not only in you an inſufficiency, but alſo a non-ſufficency* ; yea, and that ſufficiency that ſeemed to be in you, to be your loſs; in plain terms, you muſt deny yourſelf, as our Saviour ſaith, Matth. xvi 24. that is, you muſt utterly renounce all that ever you are, and all that ever you have done; all your knowledge and gifts ; all your hearing, reading, praying. faſting; weeping and mourning; all your wandering in the way of works, and ſtrict walking, muſt fall to the ground in a moment; briefly,

---

* *i. e.* That you are not only not able to do enough, but alſo that you are not able to do any thing, 2 Cor. iii. 5.— "Not that we are ſufficient of ourſelves to think any thing as of ourſelves."

whatfoever you have counted gain to you in the cafe of juftification, you muft now, with the apoftle Paul, Phil. iii. 7, 8, 9. " Count lofs for Chrift, and judge it to be dung, that you may win Chrift, and be found in him, not having your own righteoufnefs, which is of the law, but that which is through the faith of Chrift, the righteoufnefs which is of God by faith.

SECTION III.

Of the Performance of the Promife.

§ 1. *Chrift's fulfilling of the law, in the room of the elect.*
§ 2. *Believres dead to the law, as the covenant of works.*
§ 3. *The warrant to believe in Chrift.* § 4. *Evangelical repentance a-confequent of faith.* § 5. *The fpiritual marriage with Jefus Chrift.* § 6. *Juftification before faith refuted.* § 7. *Believers freed from the commanding and condemning power of the covenant of works.*

Neo. O But, Sir, what would you advife me to do?

Evan. Why, man, what aileth you?

Neo. Why, Sir, as you have been pleafed to hear them two, to declare their condition unto you, fo I befeech you, to give me leave to do the fame; and then you will perceive how it is with me. Sir, not long fince, it pleafed the Lord to vifit me with a great fit of ficknefs; fo that indeed, both in mine own judgment, and in the judgment of all that came to vifit me, I was fick unto death. Whereupon I began to confider, whither my foul was to go, after its departure out of my body: and I thought with myfelf that there was but two places, heaven and hell; and therefore it muft needs go to one of them. Then my wicked and finful life, which indeed I had lived, came into my mind, which caufed me to conclude, that hell was the place provided for it; which caufed me to be very fearful, and to be very ſorry that I had ſo lived ; and I deſired of the Lord that he would let me live a little longer, and I would not fail to reform my life, and amend my ways ; and the Lord was pleaſed to grant me my deſire. Since which time, tho' indeed it is true I have not lived ſo wickedly as formerly I had done ; yet alas, I have come far ſhort of that godly and religious life which I ſee other men live, and eſpecially my neighbour Nomiſta ; and yet you ſeem to conceive, that he is not in a good condition ; and therefore ſurely I muſt be in a miſerable condition. Alas ! Sir, what do you think will become of me ?

§ 1. *Evan.* I do now perceive, that it is time for me to ſhew how God, in the fulneſs of time, performed that which he purpoſed before all time, and promiſed in time, concerning the helping and delivering of fallen mankind. And touching this point, the ſcripture teſtifieth, that God " did, in the fulneſs of time, ſend forth his Son, made of a woman, made under the law, to redeem them that were under the law," &c. Gal. iv. 4. That is to ſay, look how mankind by nature are under the law, as it is the covenant of works * ; ſo was Chriſt, as man's ſurety, contented to be : ſo that now, according to that eternal and mutual agreement, that was betwext God the Father and him, he put himſelf in the room and place of all the faithful †, Iſa. liii. 6. " And the Lord hath laid on him the iniquity of us all.

Then came the law, as it is the covenant of works, and ſaid ‡, I find him a ſinner ||, yea, ſuch a one as hath

---

* Hooker's ſoul's juſt. p. 173.

† That is, all thoſe who have, or ſhall believe ; or, all the elect, which is one and the ſame, in reality, and in the judgment of our author, expreſsly declared in the firſt ſentence of his preface.

‡ Luther on Gal. p. 137.

|| By imputation and law-reckoning ; no otherways, as a ſinner believing in him, is righteous before God. (Thus, Iſaac Ambroſe, ſpeaking of juſtification, ſaith, " This righte-

oufnefs makes a finner finlefs." Media, chap. 1. fect. 2.— Marg. QUOAD REATUM. i. e. as to guilt.) This muft be owned, to be the meaning of this expreffion, unlefs one will fhut one's eyes to the immediately foregoing and following words; I find him a finner, faid the law; fuch a one as hath taken fin upon h'm. They are the words of Luther, and he was not the firft who fpoke fo. "He made him who was righteous to be a finner, that he might make finners righteous," faith Chryfoftom on 2 Cor. v. Hom. 11. cit. Owen of juftification, page 29. Famous proteftant divines have alfo ufed the expreffion after him: when our divines (faith Rutherford) fay, "Chrift took our place, and we have his condition; Chrift was made us, and made the finner, it is true, only in a legal fenfe." Trial and triumph of faith Serm. 19. Edit. Edinb. 1721. pag 257. "He (Chrift) was DEBITOR FACTUS a finner, a debitor by imputation, a debitor by law, by place, by office, ibid. pag. 245. Charnock argues the point thus: "How could he die, if he were not a reputed finner? Had he not firft had a relation to our fin, he could not in juftice have undergone our punifhment. He muft, in the order of juftice, be fuppofed a finner really, or by imputation; really he was not, by imputation then he was." Vol. 2. Edit. 2. pag. 547. Serm. on 1 Cor. v. 7. Though perfonally he was no finner, yet by imputation he was, faith the Contin. of Pool's annot. on 2 Cor. v. 21. What Illyricus wrote, fa th Rivet, That Chrift might moft truly be called a finner, Bellarmine calls blafphemy and curfed impudence. Now Bellarmine (himfelf) contends, That Chrift might attribute our fins to himfelf, —— therefore he might alfo truly call himfelf a finner, while in himfelf innocent, he did reprefent our perfon. What blafphemy, what impiety is here? Comment. in Pfal. xxii. 1. The fcripture-phrafe to this purpofe, is more forcible, 2 Cor. v. 21. "For he hath made him to be fin for us, who knew no fin; that we might be made the righteoufnefs of God in him." For as it is more to fay, We are made righteoufnefs than to fay, we are made righteous, fince the former plainly imports a perfection of righteoufnefs, if I may be allowed the phrafe, righteoufnefs not being properly capable of degrees: fo it is more to fay, Chrift was made fin for the elect world, than to fay, He was made a SINNER; fince the firft of thefe doth, accordingly, point at the univerfality and complete tale of the elect's fins, from the firft to the laft of them, laid on our footlefs Redeemer. Compare Lev. xvi. 21, 22. "And Aaron fhall—confefs over him (viz. the Scapegoat, which the apoftle hath an eye to here) all the iniquities of the children of Ifrael, and all their tranfgreffions in all their fins, putting them upon the head of the goat —And the goat fhall bear upon him all their iniquities." Ifa. liii. 6. "And

taken upon him the ſins of all men * ; therefore let him die upon the croſs. Then ſaid Chriſt, " Sacrifice and offering thou wouldeſt not. but a body haſt thou prepared me : in burnt offerings and ſacrifices for ſin thou haſt no pleaſure. Than ſaid I, Lo, I come to do thy will, **O Lord**," Heb. x. 5, 6, 7. And ſo the law proceeding in full ſcope againſt him, ſet upon him, and killed him ; and by this means was the juſtice of God fully ſatisfied, his wrath appeaſed, and all true believers acquitted † from

---

the Lord (marg.) hath made the iniquities of us all to meet on (Heb. in) him." Theſe two texts give the juſt notion of the true import of that phraſe, " He was made ſin for us."

* See the following note:

† Our Lord Jeſus Chriſt died not for, nor took upon him the ſins of all and every individual man ; but, he died for, and took upon him, the ſins of all the elect, John x. 15. and xv. 13. Acts xx. 28. Eph. v. 25. Tit. ii. 14. And no other doctrine is here taught by our author, touching the extent of the Death of Chriſt. In the preceeding paragraph, where was the proper place for giving his judgment on that head, he purpoſedly declares it. He had before taught, that Jeſus Chriſt did from eternity become man's ſurety, in the covenant that paſt betwixt him and the Father, page 27, 28, 29. A ſurety puts himſelf in the place of theſe, for whom he becomes ſurety (Gen. xliv. 32, 33.) to pay their debt, Prov. xxii. 26, 27. And our author tells us, that now, when the prefixed time of Chriſt's fulfilling the eternal covenant, paying the debt he had taken on him, and purchaſing man's redemption, by his ſufferings, was come ; he did, according to the tenor of that covenant, which ſtated the extent of his ſuretyſhip, put himſelf in the room and place (he ſaith not, of all men, but) of all the faithful, or elect of God. See note †, p. 136. Jeſus Chriſt thus ſtanding in their room and place, actually to take on the burthen, " the Lord laid on him the iniquities of us all." The which ſcripture-text can bear no other ſenſe in the connection of it here, than what is the genuine ſenſe of it, as it ſtands in the holy ſcripture ; namely, that the Father laid on Chriſt, the iniquities of all the ſpiritual Iſrael of God, of all nations, ranks and conditions : for no iniquities could be laid on him, but theirs, in whoſe room and place he lifted himſelf to receive the burthen, according to the eternal and mutual agreement. Theſe iniquities being thus laid on the

Mediator, the law came and said, I find him fuch a one, as hath taken on him the fins of all men. This is but an incident expreffion, on the head of the extent of Chrift's death; and it is a fcriptural one too. 1 Tim. ii. 6. "Who gave himfelf a ranfom for all;" *i. e.* for all forts of men; not, for all of every fort. Heb. ii. 9. "That he by the grace of God fhould tafte death for every man;" *i. e.* for every man of thofe whom the apoftle is there treaking of, namely, Sons brought, or to be brought unto glory, ver. 10. "Thefe who are fanctified," Chrift's brethren, ver. 11. given to him, ver. 13. and the fenfe of the phrafe, as ufed here by the author, can be no other: for the fins which the law found, that He had taken on him, could be no other but the fins that the Lord had laid on him; and the fins the Lord had laid on him, were the fins of all the faithful, or elect, according to the author; wherefore, in the author's fenfe, the fins of all men which the law found on Chrift, were the fins of all the elect, according to the genuine fenfe of the fcripture-phrafeology on that head. And an incident expreffion, in words which the Holy Ghoft teacheth, and determined, in its connection, to the orthodox fcriptural meaning, can never import any prejudice to his fentiments, upon that point, purpofedly declared before in its proper place. 'Tis true, the author, when fpeaking of thofe in whofe room Chrift put himfelf, ufeth not the word alone: and in the holy fcripture it is not ufed neither, on that fubject. And it may be obferved, that the Spirit of God in the word, doth not open the doctrine of election and reprobation, but upon men's rejecting or imbracing the gofpel-offer; the which different events, are then feafonably accounted for, from the depths of the eternal counfel of God. See Luke x. 17.—21, 22. Matth. xxii. 1.—14. Rom. ix. throughout. Eph. i. 3, 4, 5. to every thing there is a feafon. The author hitherto hath been dealing with the parties, to bring them to Chrift; and particularly here, he is fpeaking for the inftruction and direction of a convinced trembling finner, to wit, Neophytus: and therefore, like a wife and tender man in fuch a cafe, he ufeth a manner of fpeaking, which being warranted by the word, was fitted to evite the awakening of the ordinary fcruples in that cafe, namely, "It may be I am not elected, it may be Chrift died not for me;" and which pointed at the duty of all, and the encouragement that all have, to come to Chrift. And all this, after he had, in his very firft words to the reader, fufficiently provided for his ufing fuch a manner of expreffion, without prejudice to the truth. Further, the law adds, therefore let him die upon the crofs. Wherefore? for their fins, of the laying of which upon him, there is no mention made; or, for the fins of thefe, in whofe room he is exprefsly faid to have put himfelf, according to the eternal agreement betwixt the

all their fins, both paft, prefent, and to come *.

Father and him? Then faid Chrift, Lo, I come, viz actually to pay the debt for which I have become furety in the eternal compact; the which, whofe it was, according to our author, is already fufficien'ly declared. The law then fet upon him, and killed him: for whom, according to our author? for thefe furely, in whofe room and place he put himfelf, and fo ftood. If one confiders his account of the effect of all this, one doth not find it to be, as Arminians fay, that Chrift by the merit of his death, hath fo far forth reconciled God the Father to all mankind, that the Father, by reafon of his Son's merit, both could, and would, and did enter and eftablifh a new and gracious covenant with finful man, liable to condemnation. Examination of Tilenus pag. 164 Art 2. Sect. 2. And obtained for all and every man, a reftoration into a ftate of grace and falvation; fo that none will be condemned, nor are liable to condemnation for original fin; but all are free from the guilt of that fin. Tefte Turret. loc. 14 Queft. 14. Th. 5. neither doth he tell us, that Chrift died, to render fin remiffible to all perfons, and them falvable, as the continuator of Pool's annot. on Heb. ii 9. faith, with other Univerfalifts. But, by this means, faith our author, was the juftice of God fully fatisfied, his wrath appeafed, and all true believers acquitted. Compare Weftm. Confeff. chap. viii art. 4. this office (namely, of a furety, art. 3.) the Lord Jefus did moft willingly undertake, which that he might difcharge, he was made under the law, and did perfectly fulfil it, endured moft grievous torments, &c. art 5 the Lord Jefus, by his perfect obedience and facrifice of himfelf—hath fully fatisfied the juftice of his Father; and purchafed not only reconciliation, but an everlafting inheritance in the kingdom of heaven for all thofe whom the Father hath given unto him, chap. 11. art. 3. Chrift, by his obedience and death, did fully difcharge the debt of all thofe that are thus juftified. Wherefore, the author doth not here teach an univerfal redemption or atonement. Of this more afterward.

* Pardon is the removing of the guilt of fin. Guilt is two-fold, (1.) The guilt of eternal wrath, by which the finner is bound over to the eternal revenging wrath of God: and this, by orthodox divines, is called the guilt of fin, by way of eminency. (2.) The guilt of fatherly anger, whereby the finner is bound over to God's fatherly anger and chaftifements for fin. Accordingly, there is a twofold pardon; the one is the removal of the guilt of eternal wrath, and is called legal pardon; the other, the removal of the guilt of fatherly anger,

and is called gospel pardon. As to the latter, the believer is daily to sue out his pardon, since he is daily contracting new guilt of that kind: and this the author plainly teaches afterward in its proper place. As to the former, of which only he speaks here; all the sins of a believer, past, present, and to come, are pardoned together, and at once, in the first instance of his believing. That is to say, the guilt of eternal wrath, for sin then past and present, is actually and formally done away; the obligation to that wrath, which he was lying under for these sins, is dissolved. And the guilt of eternal wrath for sins then to come, is effectually prevented, from that moment for ever; so that he can never come under that kind of guilt any more: and this pardon, as it relates to these sins, is but a pardon improperly so called; being rather a not imputing of them, than a formal remission: forasmuch as a formal remission, being 'a dissolution of guilt actually contracted, agrees only to sins already committed. Therefore our author here useth the word acquitted, which is of a more extensive signification. All pardon of sin is an acquittance; but all acquittance of sin is not a formal pardon of it; for, at the resurrection, believers; being raised up in glory, shall be openly acknowledged and acquitted in the day of judgment. Short. Catech. But they will not then be formally pardoned. Now, this is the doctrine of the holy scriptures, Rom. iv. 6, 7, 8. " Even as David also describeth the blessedness of the man, unto whom God imputeth righteousness without works, saying, Blessed are they whose iniquities are forgiven, and whose sins are covered. Blessed is the man, to whom the Lord WILL NOT IMPUTE sin." Chap. viii. 1. " There is therefore now no condemnation to them which are in Christ Jesus." That is, not only, they shall never be actually damned, *i. e.* sent to Hell, as that phrase is ordinarily taken; for that is the privilege of all the elect, even before they believe, while yet, they are under condemnation, according to the scripture. But, there's no binding over, of them that are in Christ, to eternal wrath; no guilt of that kind to them. Compare John iii. 18. " He that believeth on him, is not condemned; but he that believeth not, is condemned already." " The one (viz. justification) doth equally free all believers from the revenging wrath of God, and that perfectly in this life, that they never fall into condemnation." Larger Catech. Quest. 77. " Albeit sin remain, and continually abide in thir our mortal bodies, yet it is not imputed unto us, but is remitted. and covered with Christ's justice," (*i. e.* righteousness) Old Confess. art. 25. Quest. What then is our only joy in life and death? Ans. That all our sins, bypast, present, and to come are buried; and Christ only is made our wisdom, justification, sanctification and redemption, 1 Cor. i. 30. Craig's Catech. Quest. 43. The liberty which Christ hath purchased for believers under the

So that the law, as it is the covenant of works, hath not any thing to ſay to any true believer * : for indeed they are dead to it, and it is dead to them.

Nom. But, Sir, how could the ſufferings of Chriſt, which in reſpect of time were but finite, make full ſatiſfaction to the juſtice of God, which is infinite.

Evan. Though the ſufferings of Chriſt in reſpect of time, were but finite, yet in reſpect of the perſon that ſuffered, his ſufferings came to be of infinite value; for Chriſt was God and man in one perſon, and therefore his ſufferings were a ſufficient and full ranſom for man's ſoul, being of more value than the death and deſtruction of all creatures.

Nom. But, Sir, you know that the covenant of works requires man's own obedience or puniſhment, when it ſaith, " He that doth theſe things ſhall live in them; and, curſed is every one that continueth not in all things which are written in the book of the law to do them: "

---

goſpel, conſiſts in their freedom from the guilt of ſin, the condemning wrath of God, the curſe of the moral law." Weſtm. Confeſſ. chap. xx. art. 1. See chap. xi. art. 5. chap. xvii. art. 3. They (the Arminians) do utterly deny that no ſins of the faithful, how great and grievous ſoever they be, are imputed unto them; or that all their ſins preſent and future are forgiven them. Exam. of Tilen. Pag. 226. art. 5. ſect. 5.

* " What things ſoever it ſaith, it ſaith to them who are under it " Rom. iii. 19. But believers are not under it, not under the law, as the covenant of works, chap. vi. 14. Therefore it ſaith nothing to them. As ſuch, it ſaid all to Chriſt in their room and place; and without the Mediator's diſhonour, it cannot repeat its demands on them, which it made upon him, as their ſurety. Meanwhile, the law, as a rule of life to believers, ſaith to them all, in the name and authority of God the Creator and Redeemer, Matth. v. 48. " Be ye therefore perfect, even as your Father which is in heaven is perfect " Howbeit, they are under a covenant, under which, though no leſs is required; yet leſs is accepted, for the ſake of Chriſt their covenant head.

How then could believers be acquitted from their fins by the death of Chrift?

Evan. For anfwer hereunto, I pray you confider, that though the covenant of works requires man's own obedience or punifhment, yet it no where difalloweth or excludeth that which is done or fuffered, by another in his behalf; neither is it repugnant to the juftice of God *: for fo there be a fatisfaction performed by man, thro' a fufficent punifhment for the difobedience of man, the law is fatisfied, and the juftice of God permitteth that the offending party be received into favour † : and God acknowledgeth him, after fuch fatisfaction made, as a juft man, and no tranfgreffor of the law ; and tho' the fatisfaction be made by a furety, yet when it is done, the principal is by the law acquitted. But yet, for the further proof and confirmation of this point, we are to confider, that as Jefus Chrift the fecond Adam entered into the fame covenant that the firft Adam did ‡ ; fo by him was done whatfoever the firft Adam had undone. So the cafe ftands thus, that like as whatfoever the firft Adam did, or befel him, was reckoned as done by all mankind, and to have befallen them : even fo, whatfoever Chrift did, or befel him, is to be reckoned as to have been done by all believers, and to have befallen them. So that as fin cometh from Adam alone to all mankind, as he in whom all have finned ; fo from Jefus Chrift alone cometh righteoufnefs unto all that are in him, as he in whom they all have fatisfied the juftice of God ‖. For as by being in Adam, and one with him, all did in him, and with him, tranfgrefs the commandment of God ; even fo, in refpect of faith, whereby believers are ingrafted into Chrift, and fpiritually made one with him, they did all in him, and with him, fatisfy the juftice of God, in his death and

---

* Urfin. Cat. † Pemb. Vind. Fid.

‡ See page 55. note ‡.

‖ Forbes on juft. p. 89.

fufferings *: And whofoever reckons thus, reckons

---

* Namely, in the fenfe of the law: for in the law-reckoning, as to the payment of a debt, and fulfilling of a covenant, or any the like purpofes, the furety and original debitor, the federal head or reprefentative, and the reprefented, are but one perfon. And thus the fcripture, determining Adam to be the figure (or type) of Chrift, Rom. v. 14. teacheth upon the one hand, that all mankind finned in Adam, ver. 12. and die in him, 1 Cor. xv. 22. And on the other hand, that believers were crucified with Chrift, Gal. ii. 20. and raifed up in him, Eph. ii. 6. The covenant (of works) being made with Adam, as a public perfon—all mankind—finned in him, Larg. Catech. Queft. 22. The covenant of grace was made with Chrift, as the fecond Adam, Queft. 31. He—fatisfied divine juftice—the which he did as a public perfon, the head of his church, Queft. 52. " That the righteoufnefs of the law, faith the apoftle, might be fulfilled in us," Rom. viii. 4. So believers fatisfied in him, as they finned in Adam. " The threatning of Death (Gen. ii. 17.) is fulfilled in the elect, fo that they die, and yet their lives are fpared; they die, and yet they live; for they are reckoned in the law to have died, when Chrift their furety died for them. Ferguffon on Gal. ii. 20. Although thou, faith Beza, haft fatisfied for the pain of thy fins in the perfon of Jefus Chrift. Beza's Confeff. Point 4. art. 12. What challenges Satan or confcience can make againft the believer,—hear an anfuer: I was condemned, I was judged, I was crucified for fin, when my furety Chrift was condemned, judged and crucified for my fins.—I have paid all, becaufe my furety hath paid all. Rutherford's trial and triumph of faith. Serm. xix. pag. 258. As in Chrift we fatisfied, fo likewife in Adam we finned." Flint Examin. pag. 144. This doctrine, and the doc-trine of the formal imputation of Chrift's righteoufnefs to believers, ftand and fall together. For if believers be reckoned in law, to have fatisfied in Chrift; then his righteoufnefs, which is the refult of his fatisfaction, muft needs be accounted theirs: but if there be no fuch law-reckoning, Chrift's righteoufnefs cannot be imputed to them, otherways than as to the effects of it; for the judgment of God is always according to truth, Rom. ii. 2. This the Neonomians are aware of, and deny both; reckoning them Antinomian principles, as they do, many other Proteftant doctrines. Hear Mr Gibbons. They (viz. the Antenomians(are dangeroufly miftaken, in thinking, that a believer is righteous in the fight of God, with the felf fame active and paffive righteoufnefs, wherewith Chrift was righteous, as tho' believers fuffered in Chrift, and obeyed in Chrift. Morn.

according to fcripture. For in Rom. v. 12. all are faid to have finned in Adam's fin ; in whom all have finned, faith the text, namely in Adam as in a public perfon * : all men's acts were included in his, becaufe their perfons were included in his. So likewife in the fame chapter it is faid, that death paffed upon all men ; namely for this, that Adam's fin was reckoned for theirs. Even fo, Rom. vi. 10. The apoftle, fpeaking of Chrift, faith, "in that he died, he died unto fin ; but in that he liveth, he liveth unto God :" fo likewife, faith he in the next verfe, "reckon ye yourfelves to be dead into fin, but alive unto God, thro' Jefus Chrift our Lord." And fo, as touching the refurrection of Chrift, the apoftle argues, 1 Cor. xv. 20. That all believers muft and fhall arife, becaufe " Chrift is rifen, and is become the firft fruits of them that fleep." Chrift as the firft fruits arifeth, and that in the name and ftead of all believers ; and fo they rife in him, and with him : for Chrift did not rife as a private perfon, but he arofe as the public head of the church ; fo that in his arifing all believers did virtually arife. And as Chrift, at his refurrection, was juftified and acquitted from all the fins of all believers, by God his Father †, as having now fully fatisfied for them ; even fo were they ‡.

Exerc. Method. Serm. 19. pag. 423. On the other hand, the Weftminfter divines teach both as found and orthodox principles, affirming Chrift's righteoufnefs, obedience, and fatisfaction, themfelves, to be imputed to believers, or reckoned their righteoufnefs, obedience, and fatisfaction. " Juftification is an act of God's free grace, wherein he pardoneth all our fins, and accepteth us as righteous in his fight, only for the righteoufnefs of Chrift imputed to us. Short. Catech. —only for the perfect obedience and full fatisfaction of Chrift, by God imputed to them. Larg. Catech. Queft. 70. —By imputing the obedience and fatisfaction of Chrift unto them." Weftm. Confeff. chap. xi. art. 1.

* Tho. Goodwin Chrift fet forth, p. 87. Rom. vi. 10, 11.
† Smith on the Creed.
‡ Virtually juftified, not actually, in his juftification ; even

N

And thus you ſee, the obedience of Chriſt being imputed unto believers, by God, for their righteouſneſs, it doth put them into the ſame eſtate and caſe, touching righteouſneſs unto life * before God, wherein they ſhould have been, if they had perfectly performed the perfect obedience of the covenant of works, Do this, and thou ſhalt live †.

---

as in his reſurrection, they did virtually ariſe. That this is the author's meaning, is evident from his own words, pag. 148. where, ſpeaking of Neophytus, he ſaith expreſsly; " He was juſtified meritoriouſly in the death and reſurrection of Chriſt ; but yet he was not juſtified actually, till he did actually believe in Chriſt."

  * So called to diſtinguiſh it from inherent righteouſneſs, which is righteouſneſs from life.

  † This is a weighty point, the plain and native reſult of what is ſaid; namely, That ſince Jeſus Chriſt hath fully accompliſhed what was to have been done, by man himſelf, for life, according to the covenant of works; and that the ſame is imputed to believers; therefore believers are in the ſame ſtate, as to righteouſneſs unto life, that they would have been in, if man himſelf had ſtood the whole time appointed for his trial. And here is the true ground, in law, of the infallible perſeverance of the ſaints: their time of trial for life is over, in their head, the ſecond Adam; the prize is won. Hence, the juſt by faith are intitled to the ſame benefit, which Adam by his perfect obedience would have been intitled to: compare Rom. x. 5. ' The man which doth theſe things ſhall live," with Hab. ii. 4. " The juſt by his faith ſhall live:" the which is the true reading, according to the original. And here, for clearing of the following purpoſe, of the believer's freedom from the law, as it is the covenant of works, let it be conſidered; that, if Adam had ſtood, till the time of his trial had been expired, the covenant of works would indeed, from that time have remained his everlaſting ſecurity for eternal life, like a contract held fulfilled by the one party : but, as in the ſame caſe, it could have no longer remained to be the rule of his obedience ; namely, in the ſtate of confirmation. The reaſon is obvious, viz. that the ſubjecting of him ſtill to the covenant of works, as the rule of his obedience, would have been a reducing him to the ſtate of trial, he was in before, and a ſetting him anew to work for what was already his own, in virtue of his (ſuppoſed) fulfilling of that covenant. Nevertheleſs, 'tis abſolutely impoſſible, but the creature, in any ſtate whatſo-

§ 2. *Nom.* But, Sir, are all believers dead to the law, and the law dead to them, fay you?

Evan. Believe it man, as the law is the covenant of works, all true believers are dead unto it, and it is dead unto them * : for they being incorporated into Chrift, what the law or covenant of works did to him, it did the fame to them ; fo that when Chrift hanged on the crofs, all believers, after a fort, hanged there with him. And therefore, the apoftle Paul having faid, Gal. ii. 19. " I thro' the law, am dead to the law ;" adds in the next verfe, " I am crucified with Chrift :" which words the apoftle brings as an argument, to prove that he was dead to the law; for the law had crucified him with Chrift. Upon which text, Luther faith, " I likewife am crucified and dead to the law, forafmuch as I am crucified and dead with Chrift †." And again, " I believing in Chrift, am alfo crucified with Chrift." In like manner, the

---

ever, muft be bound to, and own obedience unto the Creator ; and being ftill bound to obedience, of neceffi'y, he behoved to have had a rule of that obedience ; as to which rule, fince the covenant of works could not be, what remains, but that the rule of obedience, in the ftate of confirmation, would have been the law of nature, fui.ted to man's ftate of immutability improperly fo called, and fo divefted of the form of the covenant of works, namely, its promife of eternal life, and threatening of eternal death, as it is, and will be, in heaven for ever? The application is eafy, making always, as to the rule of believers obedience, fuitable referves for the imperfection of their ftate, in refpect of inherent righteoufnefs : the which imperfection, as it leaves room for promifes of fatherly fmiles, and threatenings of fatherly chaft'fements, fo it makes them neceffary ; but thefe alfo fhall be done away in heaven, when their real eftate fhall be perfect, as their relative ftate is now.

* Rom. vii 4. " Wherefore, my brethren, ye alfo are become dead to the law." Gal. ii 19 " I thro' the law am dead to the law." And this, according to the nature of co-rela'es, concludes the law, as it is the covenant of works, to be dead alfo to believers. Col. ii. 14. " Nailing it to his crofs."

† On Gal. p. 81.

apoftle faith to the believing Romans, " So ye, my brethren, are dead alfo to the law, by the body of Chrift," Rom. vii. 4. Now by the body of Chrift, is meant the paffion of Chrift upon the crofs *, or, which is all one, the fufferings of Chrift in his human nature. And therefore, certainly we may conclude with godly Tindal, that all fuch are dead concerning the law, as are by faith crucified with Chrift †.

Nom. But I pray you, Sir, how do you prove that the law is dead to a believer?

Evan. Why, as I conceive, the apofte affirmeth it, Rom. vii. 1, 6.

Nom. Surely, Sir, you do miftake ; for I remember the words of the firft verfe are, " how that the law hath dominion over a man as long as he liveth ;" and the words of the fixth verfe are, " but now we are delivered from the law, that being dead wherein we were holden," &c.

Evan. I know right well, that in our laft tranflation the words are fo rendered ; but godly and learned Tindal renders it thus, Remember ye not, brethren, that the law hath dominion over a man as long as it endureth? and Bifhop Hall paraphrafeth upon it thus, Know ye not, brethren, that the Mofaical law hath dominion over a man that is fubject unto it, fo long as the faid law is in force? fo likewife Origen ‡, Ambrofe, and Erafinus, do all agree, that by thefe words, while (he) or (it) liveth, we are to underftand, as long as the law remaineth. And Peter Martyr is of opinion, that thefe words, while (he) or (it) liveth, are differently referred, either to the law, or to the man ; for, faith he, " the man is faid to be dead," ver. 4. " and the law is faid to be dead," ver. 6. Even fo, becaufe the word (he) or (it) ‖, mentioned verfe 1. do fignify both fexes in

---

* Dr Willet on the text.   Elton on the text.
† On the text.
‡ Alledged by Dr Willet on Rom.
‖ See Dr Willet again.

the Greek, Chryfoftom thinketh that the death both of
the law and the man, is infinuated. And Theophylact,
Erafmus. Bucer, and Calvin, do all underftand the fixth
verfe, of the law being dead. And as the death of a
believer to the law, was accomplished by the death of
Chrift, even fo alfo was the law's death to him: even
as Mr Fox *, in his fermon of Chrift crucified, teftifieth,
faying, here have we upon one crofs, two crucifixes,
two the moft exellent potentates, that ever were, the
Son of God, and the law of God, wreftling together about
man's falvation, both caft down, and both flain upon
one crofs ; howbeit, not after a like fort. Firft, the
Son of God was caft down, and took the fall, not for
any weaknefs in himfelf, but was content to take it for
our victory ; by this fall, the law of God, in cafting him
down, was caught in his own trap, and fo was faft nailed
hand and foot to the crofs, according as we read in
Saint Paul's words, Col. ii. 14. And fo Luther †,
fpeaking to the fame point, faith, " This was a wonderful combat, where the law, being a creature, giveth fuch
an affault to his Creator, in practifing his whole tyranny
upon the Son of God. Now therefore, becaufe the law
did fo horribly and curfedly fin againft his God, it is
accufed and arraigned. And as a thief and curfed
murderer of the Son of God, lofeth all his right, and
deferveth to be condemned. The law therefore is
bound, dead, and crucified to me ‡. It is not only overcome, condemned, and flain unto Chrift, but alfo to me,
believing in him, unto whom he hath freely given this
victory ||. Now then, although according to the apoftle's

---

* Fox, that wrote the book of martyrs.

† On Gal. p. 184. ‡ Ibid. page 185.

|| This is cited from Luther on the epiftle to the Galatians,
according to the English tranflation, and is to be found there,
Fol. 184. p 1, 2. Fol. 185. p. 1. Fol. 82. p. 1. His own words
from the Latin original, after he had lectured that epiftle a

N 3

second time, as I find them in my copy printed at Franckfort, 1563, are here subjoined. " Hoc profecto mirabile duellum est, ubi lex creatura, cum Creatore sic congreditur, et præter omne jus, omnem tyrannidem suam in Filio Dei exercet, quam in nobis filiis iræ exercuit." Luth. Comment. in Gal. iv. 4, 5. p. (mihi) 598. " Ideo lex tanquam latro et sacrilegus homicida Filii Dei, amittit jus et meretur damnari." Ibid. p. 600. " Ergo lex est mihi surda, ligata, mortua et crucifixa." Ibid. Cap. ii. 20 Pag. 280. " Conscientia apprehendens hoc apostoli verbum, Christus a lege nos redemit—— sancta quadam superbia insultat legi, dicens·· — nunc in posterum non solum Christo victa & strangulata es, sed etiam mihi credenti in eum, cui donavit hanc victoriam." Pag. 600. That great man of God, a third Elias, and a second Paul (if I may venture the expression) tho' he was no inspired teacher, was endued with a great measure of the spirit of them both; being raised up of God for the extraordinary work of the reformation of religion from Popery, while all the world wondered after the beast. The lively savour he had of the truths of the gospel, in his own soul, and the fervour of his spirit in delivering them, did indeed carry him as far from the modern politeness of expression, as the admiration and affectation of this last, is like to carry us off from the former. What he designed, by all this triumph of faith, is summed up in a few words immediately following these last cited: " this, saith he, the law, (viz. as it is the covenant of works) is gone for ever as to us, providing we abide in Christ. This he chose to express in such figurative terms, that that great gospel truth, might be the more imprest on his own heart, and the hearts of his scholars; being prompted thereto by his experience of the necessity, and withal of the difficulty, of applying it by faith to his own case, in his frequent deep soul-exercises and conflicts of conscience. Therefore, faith he, feeling thy terrors and threatenings, O law, I dip my conscience over head and ears, into the wounds, blood, death, resurrection and victory of Christ; besides him, I will see and hear nothing at all. This faith is our victory, whereby we overcome the terrors of the law, sin, death, and all evils, but not without a great conflict. Ibid. pag. (mihi) 597. And speaking on the same subject elsewhere, he has these remarkable words, " It is easy to speak these things, but happy he that could know them aright in the conflict of conscience." Comment. in Gal. ii. 19. p. 259. Now, to turn outward the wrong side of the picture of his discourse; to make it false, horrid, prophane, and blasphemous, is hard. At this rate, many scripture-texts must suffer, not to speak of approven human writers. I instance only in that of Elias, (1 Kings xviii. 27.) " He (to wit, Baal) is a God; either he is talking, or he is pursuing, or he is in a journey, or peradventure, he fleepeth, and muft be awaked." Yet I compare not Luther's commentary to the infpired writing; only, where the holy fcripture goes before, one would think, he might be allowed to follow. Here is an irony, a rhetorical figure: there is a profopopeia, or feigning of a perfon, another rhetorical figure; and the learned and holy man tells us withal, That Paul ufed it before him, on the fame fubject, reprefenting the law, as a moft potent perfonage, who condemned and killed Chrift; whom he, having overcome death, did in like manner conquer, condemn and kill. For which he cites Eph: ii. and chap. iv. Epiftles to the Rom. Cor. Col. p. 599. Now, albeit the law (as it is the covenant of works) not being a perfon indeed, but a moft holy law of God, was incapable of real arraignment, fin, theft, or murder: yet one being allowed to fpeak figuratively of it, as fuch a perfon before-mentioned; and finding the Spirit of God to teach, that it was crucified, Jefus Chrift nailing it to his crofs, Col. ii. 14. What impiety, what blafphemy is there, in affigning crimes to it, for which it was crucified; crimes of the fame nature with its crucifixion, that is, not really and literally fo, but figuratively only? And the crucifying of a perfon, as it purpofeth his arraignment, accufation, and condemnation; fo it implies his binding and death: all which, the decency of the parable requires. And the fame decency requiring the rhetorical feigning of crimes, as the caufe of that crucifixion; they could be no other, but thefe that are affigned: forafmuch as Jefus Chrift is here confidered, not as a finner by imputation, but as abfolutely without guilt; though in the mean time, the fins of all the elect, were readily imputed to him, the which, in reality, juftified the holy law's procedure againft him. Moreover, upon the crucifixion, it may be remembered how the apoftle proves Chrift to have been made a curfe for us; for, faith he, "it is written, curfed is every one that hangeth on a tree," Gal. iii. 13. The which, if any fhould apply to the law, as the covenant of works, in a figurative manner, as its crucifixion muft be underftood, it could import no more (by reafon of the nature of the thing) than an utter abolition of it, with refpect to believers, which is a great gofpel-truth. And here alfo, one may call to mind the fcripture-phrafes, Rom. vii. 5. "The motions of fins, which were by the law." Chap. viii. 2. "The law of fin and death"——— "The covenant of works called the law of fin and death." Pract. Ufe of Sav. Knowl. Confeff. pag. 382. Edit. 5. Fig. 3. 1 Cor. xv. 56. "The ftrength of fin is the law."

After all, for my own part, I would neither ufe fome of thefe expreffions of Luther's, nor dare I, fo much as in my heart, condemn them in him: the reafon is one; becaufe of the want

intimation, Rom. vii. at the beginning. The covenant of works, and man by nature, be mutually engaged each to other, so long as they both live ; yet if, when the wife be dead, the husband be free, then much more, when he is dead also.

Nom. But, I pray, Sir, what are we to understand by this double death, or wherein doth this freedom from the law consist?

Evan. Death is nothing else but a dissolution, or untying of a compound, or a separation between matter and form ; and therefore, when the soul and body of man is separated, we say he is dead : so that, by this double death, we are to understand nothing else, but that the bargain, or covenant, which was made between God and man at the first, is dissolved, or untyed : or that the matter and form of the covenant of works is separated to a believer. So that the law of the ten commandments, doth neither promise eternal life, nor threaten eternal death to a believer, upon condition of his obedience, or disobedience to it * : neither doth a believer, as he is a

---

of that measure of the influences of grace, which I conceive he had, when he uttered these words. And the same I would say of the several expressions of the great Rutherford's, and of many eminent ministers, in their day signally countenanced of God, in their administrations. Hear Luther himself, in his preface to that book, pag. (mihi) 10. These our thoughts, saith he, on this epistle do come forth, not so much against those, (viz. the church's enemies) as for the sake of our own, (viz. her friends) who will either thank me for my diligence, or will pardon my weakness, and rashness. 'Tis pity the just expectation of one, whose name will be in honour in the church of Christ, while the memory of the reformation from Popery is kept up, should be frustrated.

* The law of the ten commandments given to Adam, as the covenant of works, promised eternal life, upon condition of obedience ; and threatned eternal death, in case of disobedience ; and this was it, that made it the covenant of works. Now, this covenant-frame of the law of the ten commands being dissolved as to believers, it can no more promise nor threaten them at

believer, either hope for eternal life, or fear eternal death, upon any such terms *. No, "we may assure ourselves, that whatsoever the law saith, on any such

---

that rate The scripture indeed testifies, that "Godliness hath the promise, not only of the life that now is, but also of that which is to come," 1 Tim. iv. 8. There being an infallible connection between godliness and the glorious life in heaven, established by promise, in the covenant of grace: but in the mean time, 'tis the obedience and satisfaction of Christ, apprehended by faith; and not our godliness, that is the condition upon which that life is promised, and upon which a real Christian, in a dying hour, will venture to plead for a share in that life. It is likewise certain, that not only are unbelievers, in virtue of the covenant of works, which they remain under, liable to eternal death as the just reward of sin: but there is, by that covenant, a twofold connection established; the one 'twixt a state of unbelief, irregeneracy, impenitency and unholiness, and eternal death: the other, 'twixt acts of disobedience, and eternal death. The former is absolutely indissoluble, and cannot but eternally remain: so that whosoever are in that state of sin, while they are in it, they must needs be in a state of death, bound over to the wrath of God, by virtue of the threatening of the law. But then, it is impossible that believers in Christ can be in that state of sin. So these, and the like sentences, "He that believeth not shall be damned," Mark xvi. 16. "Except ye repent, ye shall all likewise perish," Luke xiii. 3. "If ye live after the flesh, ye shall die," Rom. viii. 13. do indeed bind over unbelievers to eternal death: but they do not otherwise concern believers, than as they set before them a certain connection of two events, neither of which, can ever be found in their case. And yet the serious consideration of them, is of great and manifold use to believers, as a serious view of every part of the covenant of works is; particularly to move them to grow up more and more into Christ, and to make their calling and election sure. As to the latter connection, viz. betwixt acts of disobedience and eternal death, it is dissoluble; and in the case of the believer, actually dissolved: so that none have warrant to say to a believer, "If thou sin, thou shalt die eternally;" Forasmuch as the threatening of eternal death, as to a believer, being already satisfied, in the satisfaction of Christ, by faith apprehended, and imputed of God to him; it cannot be renewed on him, more than one debt can be twice charged, namely, for double payment.

* But on the having, or wanting of a saving interest in Christ.

terms, it faith to them who are under the law," Rom.
iii. 19. But believers " are not under the law, but
under grace," Rom. vi. 14. and so have escaped eternal
death, and obtained eternal life, only by faith in Jesus
Christ * : " For by him all that believe are justified
from all things, from which they could not be justified
by the law of Moses," Acts xiii. 39. " For God so
loved the world, that he gave his only begotten Son,
that whosoever believeth in him, should not perish, but
have everlasting life," John iii. 16.

And this is that covenant of grace, which as I told
you, was made with the fathers by way of promise, and
so but darkly ; but now the fulness of time being come,
it was more fully opened and promulgated.

Ant. Well, Sir, you have made it evident and plain,
that Christ hath delivered all believers from the law, as
it is the covenant of works ; and that therefore they
have nothing at all to do with it

Evan. No indeed, none of Christ's are to have any
thing to do with the covenant of works, but Christ only.
For although in the making of the covenant of works, at
first, God was one party, and man another ; yet in making

---

* This is a full proof of the whole matter. For how can the
law of the ten commands, promise eternal life, or threaten
eternal death, upon condition of obedience or disobedience, to
those who have already escaped eternal death, and obtained
eternal life by faith in Christ? The words which the Holy Ghost
teacheth, are so far from restraining the notion of eternal life to
glorification ; and of eternal death to the misery of the damned
in hell; that they declare the soul upon its union with Christ, to
be as really possessed of eternal life, as the saints in heaven are;
and without that state of union, to be as really under death, and
the wrath of God, as the damned in hell are; though not in that
measure. (The term eternal death is not, as far as I remember,
used in scripture.) And this agreeable to the nature of the
things; for as there is no mids betwixt life and death, in a
subject capable of either ; so 'tis evident, the life communicated
to the soul, in its union with Christ, the quickening Head, can
never be extinguished for the ages of eternity, John xiv. 19.
And the sinner's death under the guilt and power of sin, is, in

it the second time *, God was on both sides; God simply considerd in his essence, was the party opposite to man; and God the second person, having taken upon him to be incarnate, and to work man's redemption, was on man's side, and takes part with man, that he may reconcile him to God, by bearing man's sins, and satisfying God's justice for them, (and Christ paid God †, till he said he had enough, he was fully satisfied, fully contented, Matth. iii. 17. " This is my beloved Son, in whom I am well pleased:" Yea, God the Father was well pleased, and fully satisfied from all eternity, by virtue of that covenant that was made betwixt them.)   And thereupon all Christ's people were given to him in their election, Eph. i. 4. ‡. " Thine they were, saith Christ, and thou gavest them me,"

---

its own nature, eternal; and can never end, but by a work of almighty power, which raiseth the dead, and calleth things that are not, to be, as if they were. 1 Theff. i. 10. " Jefus which delivered us from the wrath to come." 1 john iii. 14. " We know that we have passed from death unto life." John iii. 36. " He that believeth on the Son, hath everlasting life;' and he that believeth not on the Son, shall not see life, but the wrath of God abideth on him." Chap. v. 24. " He that believeth— hath everlasting life, and shall not come into condemnation, but is passed from death unto life." Chap. vi. 47. " He that believeth on me, hath everlasting life." Ver. 54. " Whofo eateth my flesh, and drinketh my blood, hath eternal life."—— 1 John v. 12, 13. " He that hath the Son, hath life: and he that hath not the Son of God, hath not life. These things have I written unto you, that believe on the name of the Son of God, that ye may know that ye have eternal life." See Rom. viii. 1. John iii. 16, 18. and xvii. 3.

* See the note † page 55.
† All the demands of the covenant of works, on the elect world.
‡ That he, taking on their nature, might answer the demands of the covenant of works for them. Eph. i. 4. " According as he hath chosen us in him." We are said to be chosen in Christ, not that Christ is the cause of election; but that electing love, flowing immediately from God, to all the objects of it, the Father, did in one and the same decree of election, chuse the head and members of the happy body; yet Christ the head, first,

John xvii. 6. And again, faith he, " the Father loveth the Son, and hath given all things into his hands," John iii. 35. That is, he hath intrusted him with the œconomic*, and actual administration of that power in the church, which originally belonged unto himself. And hence it is, that Christ also faith, " the Father judgeth no man, but hath committed all judgment to his Son,"-John v. 22.

(in the order of nature) then all these who make up his body, who were thereby given to him, to be redeemed and saved, by his obedience and death : the which, being by him accepted, He, as elect-Mediator and head of elect men, had full power, and furniture for the work, made over to him. And thus may we conceive, the second covenant to have been concluded ; agreeable to the scripture-account of that mystery. This, the author says, was done thereupon : Not upon the Father's being well pleased, and fully satisfied, by virtue of the covenant made; the which, is the effect of the covenant, whereas, this is one of the transactions or parts of the covenant, as all the following words, brought to illustrate it, do plainly carry it : but, upon God the Son, his being on the other side, in making of the second covenant; the which, is the principal purpose in this paragraph, the explication whereof, was interrupted by the adding of a sentence concerning the execution and effect of the glorious contrivance. In making of the second covenant, the second person of the ever.blessed Trinity, considered simply as such, is one of the parties. Thereupon, in the decree of election, designing, as is said, both head and members, He is chosen Mediator and Head of the election, to be their incarnate Redeemer: the which headship accepted, He, as Mediator and Head of the election, took upon him to be incarnate, and in their nature, to satisfy the demands of the covenant of works, for them. Isa. xlii. 1. Eph. i. 4. Psal. xl. 6, 7, 8. Westminster Confession, chap. viii. art. 1. " It pleased God, in his eternal purpose, to chuse and ordain the Lord Jesus, his only begotten Son, to be the Mediator between God and man—the Head and Saviour of his church ;—Unto whom he did, from all eternity, give a people to be his seed, and to be by him in time redeemed," &c. Chap iii. art. 5. These of mankind, that are predestinated unto life, God—hath chosen in Christ, unto everlasting glory, out of his meer free grace and love." Compare what the author writes on this subject, p. 26.—29.

* Reynolds on Psal. cx. p. 7.

So that all the covenant that believers are to have regard unto, for life and salvation, is the free and gracious covenant that is betwixt Christ, or God in Christ, and them *. And in this covenant there is not any condition, or law to be performed on man's part, by himself †: no, there is no more for him to do, but only to know and believe that Christ hath done all for him ‡.

---

* *i. e.* The covenant of grace only, not the covenant of works.

† To wit, for life and salvation; the same being already performed by Jesus Christ. He having, in the second covenant, undertaken to satisfy all the demands of the covenant of works, did do all that was to be done or wrought for our life and salvation. And if it had not been so, life and salvation had remained eternally without our reach; for how is it possible, we should perform, do, or work, until we get life and salvation? what condition or law are we fit for performing of, while we are dead, and not saved from, but lying under, sin, the wrath and curse of God? see the following note.

‡ Namely, all that was to be done, for life and salvation. And neither repentance, nor sincere (imperfect) obedience, nay, nor yet believing itself, is of that sort; tho' all of these are indispensibly necessary in subjects capable of them. This expression bears a kind of MIMESIS or imitation, usual in conversation, and used by our blessed Saviour on this subject, John vi. 28, 29. "Then said they unto him, what shall we do, that we might WORK the works of God? Jesus answered and said unto them, this is the WORK of God, that ye believe." The design of it plainly is, to confront the humour, that is naturally in all men, for doing and working for life and salvation, when once they begin to lay these things to heart; there is no more, says the author, for him to do, but only to know and believe that Christ hath DONE all for him: and therefore the expression is not to be strained besides its scope. However this is true faith, according to the scripture, whether all saving faith be such a knowledge and believing, or not: and that knowledge and believing are capable of degrees of certainty, and may be mixt with doubting, without overturning of the reality of them, Isa. liii. 11. "By his knowledge shall my righteous servant justify many." John xvii. 3. "This is life eternal, that they might know thee the only true God, and Jesus Christ whom thou hast sent." Gal. ii. 20. "I live by the faith of the Son of God, who loved me, and gave himself for me." Rom. x. 9. "If

O

Wherefore, my dear neighbour Neophytus, to turn my speech particularly to you, becaufe I fee you are in heavineſs : I befeech you to be perfuaded, that here you are to work nothing, here you are to do nothing, here you are to render nothing unto God, but only to receive the treafure *, which is Jefus Chrift, and

---

thou—fhalt believe in thine heart, that God hath raifed him from the dead, thou fhalt be faved." To believe that God hath raifed him from the dead, is to believe that he has perfected the work, and done all that was to be done for life and falvation to finners : but is this enough to conftitute faving faith ? furely it is not ; for devils may believe that : therefore it muft be believed with particular application to one's felf, intimated in the phrafe, believing in thine heart ; and this is what devils and reprobates never reach unto, howbeit thefe laft may pretend to know and believe, that Chrift is raifed from the dead for them, and fo hath done all for them ; even as they alfo may pretend to receive and reft on him alone for falvation. But in all this, one who truely believes, may yet have ground to fay with tears, " Lord, I believe, help thou mine unbelief," Mark ix. 24.

Neverthelefs, under this covenant, there is much to do ; a law to be performed and obeyed, tho' not for life and falvation, but from life and falvation received ; even the law of the ten commandments, in the full extent thereof, as the author doth, at large, exprefsly teach, in its proper place, in this and the fecond volume.

This is the good old way (according to the fcriptures, Acts xvi. 30, 31. Matth. xi. 28, 29. Tit. ii. 11, 12.) if the famous Mr John Davidfon underftood the Proteftant doctrine.—— " Q. Then the falvation of man, faith he, is fo fully wrought and perfectly accomplifhed by Chrift in his awin perfon, that nothing is left to be done or wrought by us in our perfons, to be onie caufe of the leaft part thereof? A. That is moft certaine." Mr J. Davidfon's Catechifm, Edit. Edinb. 1708 pag 15. " Sa we are perfitely fayed by the warkes, whilk Chrift did for us in his awin perfon, and nawayes by the gude warkes, whilk he workes in us, with and after faith. Marg. 'Here is the maine point and ground of our difagreement with the Papifts. Ibid. Pag. 46. Refts then any thing for us to doe, after that we are perfitely juftified in God's fight, by faith in Chrift? Difciple. Yes, very meikle, albeit na wayes to merite falvation ; but only to witnefs, by the effects of thankfulnefs, that we ARE truly SAVED." Ibid. pag. 48, 49.

* Luther on Gal. p. 19. 194.

apprehended him in your heart by faith, although you
be never so great a sinner *. And so shall you obtain
forgiveness of sins, righteousness, and eternal happiness;
not as an agent, but as a patient; not by doing, but
by receiving †. Nothing here cometh betwixt, but
faith only, apprehending Christ in the promise ‡.——
" This then is perfect righteousness, to hear nothing, to
know nothing, to do nothing of the law of works, but
only to know and believe that Jesus Christ is now gone
to the Father, and sitteth at his right hand, not as a judge,
but is made unto you of God, wisdom, righteousness,
sanctification and redemption ‖. Wherefore, as Paul and

---

* See the two foregoing notes. And hear another passage
from the same book, whence this is taken, namely, the English
translation of Luther's commentary on the epist. to the Galat.
f. 75. " Good works ought to be done—the example of Christ
is to be followed—: well, all these things will I gladly do.
What then followeth? Thou shalt then be saved, and obtain
everlasting life. Nay, not so. I grant indeed that I ought to
do good works, patiently to suffer troubles and afflictions, and
to shed my blood also, if need be, for Christ's cause: but yet am
I not justified, neither do I OBTAIN SALVATION THEREBY."
† This is the stile of the same Luther, who useth to distinguish betwixt active and passive righteousness, *i. e.* the righteousness of the law, and the righteousness of faith; agreeable to
Rom. iv. 5. " But to him that worketh not, but believeth on
him that justifieth the ungodly, his faith is counted for
righteousness."
‡ The passage at more length is this: " The marriage is
made up without all pomp and solemnity: that is to say, nothing at all cometh between, no law, nor work is here required.
Here is nothing else but the Father promising—and I receiving—
but these things, without experience and practice, cannot be
understood." Luther ubi sup. f. 194.
‖ These words also are Luther's, in his argument of the
epistle to the Galatians, p. 24. of the Latin copy; and f. 7. of
the translation: but what our author reads, nothing of the law
of works, is, in Luther's own words, nothing of the law, or of
works; the sense is the same. What concerns the assurance in
the nature of faith, which these words seem to bear, we'll meet
with anon.

Silas said to the jailor, so say I unto you, " Believe on
the Lord Jesus Christ, and thou shalt be saved;" that is,
be verily persuaded in your heart, that Jesus Christ is
yours, and that you shall have life and salvation by him ;
that whatsoever Christ did for the redemption of mankind, he did it for you * †.

---

* Definition of faith.

† In this definition of saving faith, there is the general nature
or kind of it, *viz.* A real persuasion, agreeing to all forts of faith
divine and human, be verily persuaded : the more special nature
of it; an appropriating persuasion, or special application to one's
self, agreeing to a convinced sinner's faith or belief of the law's
curse, Gal. iii. 10. as well as to it, be verily persuaded in your
heart; thus Rom. x. 9. " If thou shalt believe in thine heart,
that God, &c. thou shalt be saved." And finally, the most
special nature of it, whereby 'tis distinguished from all other,
namely, an appropriating persuasion of Christ's being yours,
and, &c. And as one's believing in one's heart, or appropriating persuasion of, the dreadful tidings of the law, imports not
only an assent to them as true, but an horror of them as evil ;
so believing in the heart, or an appropriating persuasion of, the
glad tidings of the gospel, bears not only an assent to them as
true, but a relish of them as good.

The parts of this appropriating persuasion, according to our
author, are,

1. That Jesus Christ is yours, viz. By the deed of gift and
grant made to mankind lost, or (which is the same thing in
other words) by the authentic gospel-offer, in the Lord's own
word : the which offer is the foundation of faith; and the
ground and warrant of the ministerial offer, with ut which it
could avail nothing. That this is the meaning, appears from
the answer to the question immediately following, touching the
warrant to believe. By this offer, or dead of gift and grant,
Christ is ours before we believe ; not that we have a saving
interest in him, or are in a state of grace : but that we have a
common interest in him, and the common salvation, Jude 3.
which fallen angels have not; so that it is lawful and warrantable
for us; not for them, to take possession of Christ and his salvation. Even as when one presents a piece of gold, to a poor
man, saying, take it, 'tis yours ; the offer makes the piece
really his, in the sense, and to the effect before declared; nevertheless, while the poor man does not accept, nor receive it ;

whether apprehending the offer too great to be real, or that he has no liking of the neceſſary conſequents of the accepting: it is not his in poſſ ſſion, nor hath he the benefit of it ; but on the contrary muſt ſtarve for all it, and that ſo much the more miſerably, that he hath ſlighted the offer, and refuſed the gift. So this act of faith is nothing elſe, but to believe God, 1 John v. 10. to believe the Son, John iii. 36. to believe the report concerning Chriſt, Iſa. liii. 1. or, to believe the goſpel, Mark i 15. not as devils believe the ſame, knowing Chriſt to be Jeſus, a Saviour, but not their Saviour, ver. 24. Chap. iii. 11, 12. but with an appropriating perſuaſion, or ſpecial application, believing him to be our Saviour. Now what this goſpel report, record, or teſtimony of God to be believed by all, is, the inſpired penman expreſsly declares, 1 John v 11. '' This is the record, that God hath given to us eternal life; and this life is in his Son.'' The giving, here mentioned, is not giving in poſſeſſion in greater or leſſer meaſure ; but giving by way of grant, wereupon one may take poſſeſſion. And the party to whom, is not the elect, on only, but mankind loſt. For this record is the goſpel, the foundation of faith, and warrant to all, to believe in the Son of God, and lay hold on eternal life in him : but, that God hath given eternal life to the elect, can be no ſuch foundation nor warrant ; for, that a gift is made to certain ſelect men, can never be a foundation or warrant, for all men to accept and take it. The great ſin of unbelief lies in not believing this record or teſtimony, and ſo making God a liar ; '' He that believeth not God, hath made him a liar, becauſe he believeth not the record that God gave of his Son. And this is the record,'' &c. 1 John v. 10, 11. on the other hand, '' He that hath received his teſtimony, hath ſet to his ſeal that God is is true,'' John iii. 33. But the great ſin of unbelief, lies not in not believing, that God hath given eternal life to the elect. For the moſt deſperate unbelievers, ſuch as Judas and Spira, believe that ; and the belief of it adds to their anguiſh and torment of ſpirit : yet do they not ſet to their ſeal, that God is true ; but on the contrary, they make God a liar, in not believing, that, to loſt mankind, and to themſelves in particular, God hath given eternal life, in way of grant, ſo as they, as well as others, are warranted and welcome, to take poſſeſſion of it ; ſo fleeing in the face of God's record and teſtimony in the goſpel, Iſa. ix. 6. John iii. 16. Acts iv. 12. Prov. viii. 4. Rev. xxii. 17. In believing of this, not in believing of the former, lies the difficulty, in the agonies of conſcience ; the which neverthelſſ, till one do, in greater or leſſer meaſure ſurmount ; one can never believe on Chriſt, receive and reſt upon him for ſalvation The truth is, the receiving of Christ, doth necessarily presuppose this giving of him. There may indeed be a giving where there is no receiving, for a gift may be refused; and there may be a taking where there is no giving; the which is a presumptuous action, without warrant; but there can be no place for receiving of Christ, where there is not a giving of him before. In the matter of faith, saith Rollock, there are two things, first there is a giver, and next there is a receiver. God gives, and the soul receives. Lecture 10 on 2 Thess. page 126. The scripture is express to this purpose, John iii. 27. "A man can receive nothing except it be given him from heaven."

2. And that you shall have life and salvation by him; namely, a life of holiness, as well as of happiness; salvation from sin, as well as from wrath; not in heaven only, but begun here, and compleated hereafter. That this is the author's notion of life and salvation, agreeable to the scripture, we have had sufficient evidence already: and will find more, in our progress. Wherefore, this persuasion of faith is inconsistent with an unwillingness to part with sin, a bent or PURPOSE of heart to continue in sin; even as receiving and resting on Christ for salvation, is. One finds it exprest, almost in so many words, Acts xv. 11. "We believe that thro' the grace of the Lord Jesus Christ, we shall be saved." It is fitly placed after the former, for it cannot go before it, but follows upon it. The former is a believing of God, or believing the Son; this is a believing on the Son; and so is the same with receiving of Christ, as that receiving is explained, John i. 12. "But as many as received him, to them gave he power to become the sons of God, even to them that BELIEVE ON his name." It doth also evidently bear the soul's resting on Christ for salvation; for it is not possible to conceive a soul resting on Christ for salvation without a persuasion that it shall have life and salvation by him; namely, a persuasion which is of the same measure and degree as the resting is. And thus it appears, that there can be no saving faith, without this persuasion, in greater or lesser measure. But withal it is to be remembered, as to what concerns the habit, actings, exercise, strength, weakness, and intermitting of the exercise, of saving faith; the same is to be said of this persuasion, in all points.

3. That whatsoever Christ did for the redemption of mankind, he did it for you, Gal. ii. 20. "I live by the faith of the Son of God, who loved me, and gave himself for me." This comes in the last place: and I think none will question, but whosoever believes, in the manner before explained, may and ought to believe this, in this order. And it is believed, if not explicitly, yet virtually, by all who receive and rest on Christ for salvation.

From what is said, it appears that this definition of faith is the fame, for fubftance and matter, though in different words, with that of the fhorter catechifm, which defines it by receiving and refting upon Chrift alone for falvation, as he is offered to us in the gofpel. In which, though the offer to us is mentioned laft: yet it is evident, it is to be believed firft.

Object. But the author's definition makes affurance to be of the effence of faith.

Anf. Be it fo: however he ufeth not the word affurance or affured in his definition, nor will any thing contained in it, amount to the idea now commonly affixed to that word, or to what is now, in our days, commonly underftood by affurance. And (1.) he doth here teach that affurance of faith, whereby believers are certainly affured that they are in the ftate of grace, the which is founded upon the evidence of grace, of which kind of affurance, the Weftminfter confeffion exprefsly treats, chap. 18. art. 1, 2, 3. But an affurance, which is in faith, in the direct acts thereof, founded upon the word allenarly, Mark xvi 15.16. John iii. 16. and this is nothing elfe, but a fiducial appropriating perfuafion. (2.) He doth not determine this affurance or perfuafion to be full, or to exclude doubting: he faith not, be FULLY perfuaded; but, be VERILY perfuaded; which fpeaks only the reality of the perfuafion, and doth not at all concern the degree of it. And it is manifeft, from his diftinguifhing between faith of adherence, and faith of evidence, page 101. that, according to him, faving faith may be without evidence. And fo one may have this affurance or perfuafion, and yet not know affuredly that he hath it, but need marks to difcover it by: for though a man cannot but be confcious of an act of his own foul, as to the fubftance of the act; yet he may be in the dark, as to the fpecifical nature of it; than which nothing is more ordinary among ferious Chriftians. And thus, as a real faint is confcious of his own heart's moving in affection towards God; yet fometimes, doth not affuredly know it to be the true love of God in him, but fears it be an hypocritical flafh of affection: fo he may be confcious of his perfuafion; and yet doubt, if it is the true perfuafion of faith, and not that of the hypocrite.

This notion of affurance or perfuafion in faith, is fo agreeable to the nature of the thing called believing, and to the ftile of the holy fcripture, that fometimes where the original text reads faith or believing, we read affurance, according to the genuine fenfe of the original phrafe, Acts xvii. 31. whereof he hath given affurance; Orig. Faith, as is noted in the margent of our Bibles. Deut. xxviii. 66. Thou fhalt have none affurance of thy life; Orig. Thou fhalt not believe in thy life. This obfer-vation fhews, that to believe, in the ftile of the holy fcripture,

a. well as in the common usage of mankind in all other matters, is to be assured or persuaded, namely according to the measure of one's believing.

And the doctrine of assurance, or an appropriating persuasion, in saving faith, as it is the doctrine of the holy scriptures. Rom. x. 9. Acts xv. 11. Gal. ii. 20. So it is a Protestant doctrine, taught by Protestant divines against the Papists, sealed with the blood of martyrs in Popish flames; 'tis the doctrine of reformed churches abroad, and the doctrine of the church of Scotland.

The nature of this work will not allow multiplying of testimonies, on all these heads

Upon the first, it shall suffice to adduce the testimony of Essenius in his Compendium Theologiæ, the system of divinity, taught the students in the college of Edinburgh by professor Campbell: "There is therefore, saith he, in saving faith, a special application of gospel benefits. This is proved against the Papists; (1.) From the profession of believers, Gal. ii. 20. I live by that faith of the Son of God, who loved me, and gave himself for me. Psal. xxiii. 1.—The Lord is my shepherd: I shall not want. In cotes of budding grass, he maketh me to lie down, &c. Though I walk through the valley of the shadow of death, I will not fear evil; for thou art with me:" &c. And Job xix. 25. Phil. i. 21, 23. Rom. viii. 33.—39. x. 9, 10. 2 Cor. v. 1, 2, 6 with 2 Cor. iv. 13. &c. Essen. Compend. Theol. chap. 1. S. 12. And speaking of the method of faith, he saith it is, " 4. That according to the promises of the gospel, out of that spiritual desire, the Holy Spirit also bearing witness in us, We acknowledge Christ to be OUR Saviour; and so receive and apply him, every one to OURSELVES; apprehending him again, who first apprehended us. 2 Cor. iv. 13. Rom. viii. 16. John i. 12. 2 Tim. i. 12. Gal. ii. 20. Phil. iii. 12. The which is the FORMAL ACT of saving faith. 5. Furthermore, that we acknowledge ourselves to be in communion with Christ, partakers of all and every one of his benefits.—6. The which is the latter act of saving faith, yet also a proper and elicit act of it.—7. That we observe all these acts above-mentioned, and the sincerity of them in us: and THENCE gather, that we are true believers, brought into the state of grace," &c. Ibid. S 21. Observe here the two kinds of assurance before distinguished.

Peter Brulie, burnt at Tourney, anno 1545, when he was sent for out of prison to be examined, the friars interrogating him before the magistrate, he answered——" How it is faith that bringeth unto us salvation; that is, when we trust unto God's promises, and believe stedfastly, that for Christ his Son's sake our sins are forgiven us." Sleid. comment. in English, Book 16. Fol. 217.

Mr Patrick Hamilton, burnt at Saint Andrews about the year 1527. " Faith, says he, is a sureness; faith is a sure confidence of things which are hoped for, and a certainty of things which are not seen. The faith of Chrift is, to believe in him, that is, to believe in his word, and to believe that he will help THEE in all thy need, and deliver THEE from all evil." Mr Patrick's Articles, Knox's Hiftory in 4to, p. 9.

For the doctrine of foreign churches, in this point, I shall inftance only in that of the church of Holland, and the reformed church of France.

Queft. " What is a fincere faith ? Anf. It is a fure know-ledge of God and his promifes revealed to us in the gofpel, and a hearty confidence that all my fins are forgiven ME, for Chrift's fake." Dutch brief compend. of Chriftian religion, Vra. 19. bound up with the Dutch Bible.

Minifter. " Since we have the foundation, upon which the faith is grounded, can we rightly from thence conclude, what the true faith is? Child. Yes : namely, a certain and fteady knowledge of the love of God towards us, according as by his gofpel he declares himfelf to be OUR Father and Saviour, by the means of Jefus Chrift." The Catechifm of the refo med church of France; bound up with the French Bible, Dimanche 18. To obviate a common prejudice, whereby this is taken for an eafy effort of fancy and imagination, it will not be amifs to fubjoin the queftion immediately following there. M. " Can we have it of ourfelves, or cometh it from God ? C. The fcripture teacheth us, that it is a fingular gift of the holy Spirit, and experience alfo fheweth it." Ibid. Follows the doctrine of the church of Scotland on this head.

" Regeneratioun is wrocht be the power of the Holy Goft, working in the hartes of the elect of God ane affured faith in the promife of God reveild to us in his word, be quhi'k faith we apprehend Chrift Jefus, with the graces and benefites promifed in him." Old Confeff. Art 3.

" This our faith, and the affurance of the fame, proceeds not frà flefh and blude, that is to fay, frà na natural power is within us, bot is the infpiration of the Holy Goft." Ibid. art. 12.

For the better underftanding of this, take the words of that eminent fervant of Chrift, Mr John Davidfon minifter of Salt-Prefton alias Prefton-Pans, (of whom fee the Fulfilling of the Scripture, pag. mibi 361.) in his Catechifm, pag. 20. as follows. And certain it is, that both the enlightning of the minde to acknawledge the trueth of the promife of falvation to us in Chrift; and the fealing up of the certainty thairof in our hearts and mynds (of the whilk twa parts, as it were, faith confifts) are the works and effects of the Spirite of God, and neither of nature, nor arte.

. The old confession above-mentioned is, the confession of faith professed and believ'd by the Protestants, within the realm of Scotland, published by them in parliament, and by the estates thereof, ratified and approved, as wholesom and found doctrine, grounded upon the infallible truth of God. Knox's history, lib. 3. p. 263. It was ratified at Edinburgh, July 17. 1560. Ibid. p. 279. And this is the confession of our faith, mentioned and sworn to, in the national covenant, framed about twenty years after it.

In the same national covenant, with relation to this particular head of doctrine, we have these words following, viz. " We detest and refuse the usurped authority of that Roman antichrist, his general and doubtsom faith." However the general and doubtsom faith of the Papists may be clouded, one may, without much ado, draw these two plain conclusions from these words. (1.) That since the Popish faith abjured is a doubtsom faith, the Protestant faith, sworn to be maintain'd, is an assured faith; as we heard before from the old confession, to which the covenant refers. (2.) That since the Popish faith is a general one; the Protestant faith must needs be an appropriating persuasion, or a faith of special application; which, we heard already from Essenius, the Papists do deny. As for a belief and persuasion of the mercy of God in Christ, and of Christ's ability and willingness to save all that come unto him; as it is altogether general, and hath nothing of appropriation or special application in it: so I doubt if the Papists will refuse it. Sure, the council of Trent, which fixed and established the abominations of Popery, affirms, that no pious man ought to doubt of the mercy of God, of the merit of Christ, nor of the virtue and efficacy of the sacraments. Council Trid. Cap. 9. (I hope, none will think, the council allows impious men to doubt of these.) But withal they tell us, " It is not to be affirmed, that no man is absolved from sin, and justified, but he who assuredly believes, that he himself is absolved and justified." Here they overturn the assurance and appropriation, or special application of saving faith, maintain'd by the Protestants. And they thunder their anathema's against them, who hold these, in opposition to their general and doubtsom faith. " If any shall say, that justifying faith is nothing else, but a confidence of the mercy of God, pardoning sins for Christ's sake; or that, that confidence is it alone, by which they are justified, Let him be accursed." Ibid. cap. 13 can. 12. " If any shall say, that a man is absolved from sin, and justified by that, that he assuredly believes himself to be absolved and justified; —— let him be accursed." Ibid. can. 14.

. Moreover, in the national covenant, as it was renewed in the year 1638, and 1639, mention is made of public catechisms, in which the true religion, as expressed in the confession of faith (there) above written, (*i.e.* the national covenant; otherwise called the confession of faith) and former larger confession (viz. the old confession) is said to be set down. The doctrine on this head, contained in these catechisms, is here subjoined.

M. " Which is the first point ? C. To put our whole confidence in God. M. How may that be? C. When we have an assured knowledge that he is almighty, and perfectly good. M. And is that sufficient ? C. No.—M. What is then further required? C. That every one of us be fully assured in his conscience, that he is beloved of God, and that he will be both his Father and Saviour." Calvin's Catech. used by the kirk of Scotland, and approved by the first book of discipline, Quest. 8, 9, 10, 11. This is the catechism of the reformed church of France, mentioned before. M. " Since we have the foundation, whereupon our faith is builded, we may well gather hereof, what is the right faith? C. Yea verily; that is to say, it is a sure persuasion and stedfast knowledge of God's tender love towards us, according as he hath plainly uttered in his gospel, that he will be both a Father and a Saviour unto us, through the means of Jesus Christ." Ibid. Quest. 111.

M. " By what means may we atteyne unto him there? C. By faith, which God's Spirit worketh in our hearts assuring us of God's promises, made to us in his holy gospel." The manner to examine children before. they be admitted to the Supper of the Lord. Quest. 16. This is called the little catechism, Assembly, 1592. Sess. 10. Q. " What is true faith ? A. It is not only a knowledge, by which I do stedfastly assent to all things, which God hath revealed unto us in his word; but also an assured affiance, kindled in my heart by the Holy Ghost, by which I rest upon God, making sure account, that forgiveness of sins, everlasting righteousness and life, is bestowed not only upon others, but also upon ME, and that freely by the mercy of God, for the merit and desert of Christ alone."—— The Palatine catechism, printed by public authority for the use of Scotland. This famous catechism is used in most of the reformed churches and schools; particularly in the reformed churches of the Netherlands, and is bound up with the Dutch Bible. As for the church of Scotland, the Palatine catechism, says Mr Wodrow, in the dedication of his history, was adopted by us, till we had the happiness to join with the venerable Assembly at Westminster. Then indeed it gave place to the larger and shorter catechisms in the church: nevertheless it continued to be taught in grammar-schools.

Q. " What thing is faith in Christ? A. A sure persuasion that he is the only Saviour of the world; but OURS in special, who believe in him." Craig's Catech. approven by the general Afsembly 1592.

To thefe may be added, the three following teftimonies. Q. "What is faith? A. When I am perfuaded, that God loves me and all his faints, and freely giveth us Chrift, with all his benefits." Summula Catechifmi, ftill annexed to the rudiments of the Latin tongue, and taught in grammar fchools to this day, fince the reformation.

"What is thy faith? My fure belief that God baith may and will fave ME in the bloud of Jefus Chrift, becaufe he is almighty, and has promifed fa to do." Mr James Melvil's catechifm, in his propine of a paftor to his people, page 44. publifhed in the year 1598.

Teacher. "What is this faith, that is the only inftrument of this ftrait conjunction between Chrift crucified and us?—— Difciple. It is the fure perfuafion of the heart, that Chrift by his death and refurrection hath taken away our fins, and clothing us with his awin righteoufnefs, has throughly reftored us to the favour of God." Mr John Davidfon's Catech. pag. 46. printed anno 1602. reprinted 1708.

In the fame national covenant, as it was renewed 1638. and 1639. is exprefsed an agreement and refolution, to labour to recover the purity of the gofpel, as it was eftablifhed and profefsed before the (there) forefaid novations; the which, in the time of prelacy, then caft out, had been corrupted by a fet of men in Scoland, addicted to the faction of Laud, archbifhop of Canterbury. In the year 1640. Mr Robert Baily, then minifter of Kilwinning, afterwards one of the commiffioners from Scotland to the Weftminfter Afsembly, wrote againft that faction, proving them guilty of Popery, Arminianifm, &c. And on the head of Popery, thus reprefents their doctrine concerning the nature of faith, viz "That faith is only a bare afsent, and requires no application, no perfonal confidence; and that that perfonal application is mere prefumption, and the fiction of a crazy brain." Hift Motuum in Regno Scotiæ, pag. 517.

Thus, as above declared, ftood the doctrine of the church of Scotland, in this point, in her confeffions, and in public catechifms, confirmed by the renewing of the national covenant, when, in the year 1643. it was anew confirmed by the firft article of the folemn league and covenant, binding to (not the reformation, but) the prefervation of the reformed religion in the church of Scotland, in doctrine, &c. And that before the Weftminfter confeffion, larger & fhorter catechifms, were in being.

When the Weftminfter confeffion was received, anno 1647; and the larger and fhorter catechifms, anno 1648, the general Afsembly did, in their three acts refpectively approving them, exprefsly declare them to be in NOTHING contrary to the received doctrine in this kirk. And put the cafe they were contrary thereto in any point; they could not, in that point, be reckoned the judgment of the church of Scotland; since they were received by her, as in nothing contrary to previous standards of doctrine, to which she stands bound by the covenants aforesaid. But the truth is, the doctrine is the same in them all.

" This faith is different in degrees, weak or strong;—growing in many to the attainment of a full assurance." Westminster Confes. chap. 14. art. 3. Now, how faith can grow in any to a full assurance, if there be no assurance in the nature of it, I cannot comprehend.

" Faith justifies a sinner—only as it is an instrument, by which he receiveth and applieth Christ and his righteousness." Larg. Catech. Q 73. " By faith they receive and apply unto themselves Christ crucified, and all the benefits of his death." Ibid. Q. 170. " When do we by faith receive and apply to ourselves the body of Christ, crucified? A. While we are persuaded that the death and crucifixion of Christ, do no less belong to us, than if we ourselves had been crucified for our own sins : now this persuasion is that of true faith." Sum. Catech. " Faith in Jesus Christ is a saving grace, whereby we receive and rest upon him alone for salvation, as he is offered to us in the gospel." Short Catech.

Now to perceive the entire harmony, betwixt this and the old definitions of faith, compare with it, as to the receiving therein mentioned, the definition above cited from the Old Confes. art. 3. Viz. " An assured faith in the promise—by which they apprehend Christ," &c. Mr John Davidson joins them thus. Q " What is faith? A. It is an hearty assurance, that our sins are freely forgiven us in Christ. Or after this manner : it is the harty receiving of Christ offered in the preaching of the word and sacraments, by the working of the Haly Spirit, for the remission of sins, whereby he becummes ane with us, and we ane with him, He our head, and we his members." Mr John Davidson's Catechism, page 24. As to the resting mentioned in the Westminster definition, compare the definition above-cited from the Palatine Catechism, Viz " A sure confidence—whereby I rest in God, assuredly concluding, that—to me—is given forgiveness," &c. Quest. 21. See also Larg. Catech. Quest. last. " We by faith are emboldened to plead with him that he would, and quietly to rely upon him that he will fulfil our requests; and to testify this our desire and assurance, we say, Amen." In which words 'tis manifest, that quietly to rely upon him that he will, &c. (the same with resting on him for, &c.) is assurance in the sense of the Westminster divines.

P

§ 3. *Neo.* But, Sir, hath such an one as I, any warrant to believe in Christ?

Evan. I beseech you consider *, that God the Father, as he is in his Son Jesus Christ, moved with nothing, but with his free love to mankind lost, hath made a deed of gift and grant unto them all, that whosoever of them all, shall believe in this his Son, shall not perish, but have eternal life †. And hence it was, that Jesus Christ himself said

---

* Culverwell of faith, p. 15.

. † Mr Culverwell's words, here cited, stand thus at large.—The matter to be believed unto salvation, is this: that God the Father, moved by nothing, but his free love to mankind lost, hath made a deed of gift and grant of his Son Christ Jesus unto mankind, that whosoever of all mankind shall receive this gift, by a true and lively faith, he shall not perish, but have everlasting life. Doctor Gouge, in his preface to this treatise of that author's, hath these remarkable words concerning him, Never any took such pains to so good purpose, in and about the FOUNDATION of FAITH, as he hath done.

This deed of gift and grant, or authentic gospel offer, (of which see the preceeding note *) is expressed in so many words, John iii. 16. " For God so loved the world, that he gave his only begotten Son, that WHOSOEVER believeth in him should not perish, but have everlasting life." Where the gospel comes, this grant is published, and the ministerial offer made: and there is no exception of any of all mankind in the grant. If there was, no ministerial offer of Christ could be warrantably made to the party excepted, more than to the fallen angels; and without question, the publishing and proclaiming of heaven's grant, unto any, by way of ministerial offer, presupposeth the grant in the first place, to be made to them: otherwise it would be of no more value, than a cryer's offering of the king's pardon, to one who is not comprehended in it. This is the good old way, of discovering to sinners, their warrant to believe in Christ: and it doth indeed bear the sufficiency of the sacrifice of Christ, for all: and that Christ crucified is, the ordinance of God for salvation, unto all mankind, in the use-making of which only they can be saved; but not an universal atonement or redemption. " What is thy faith? My sure belief that God baith may and will save me, &c. Tell me the promise whereon thou leans assuredly? Whasoever (says God) will believe in the death of my Sonne, Jesus, sall not perish, but get eternal life." Mr James Melvil's Catech. ubi sup. " He freely OFFERETH unto SINNERS life

unto his disciples, Mark xvi. 14. " Go and preach the gospel to every creature under heaven * : that is, Go and tell every man † without exception, that here is good news for him, Christ is dead for him ; and if he will take him, and accept of his righteousness, he shall have him ‡. There-

---

and salvation by Jesus Christ, requiring of them faith in him, that they may be saved, Mark xvi. 15, 16. John iii 16 Westm. Conf. chap. 7. art. 3. " The visible church hath the privilege—of enjoying OFFERS of grace by Christ to all the members of it, in the ministry of the gospel, testifying, that, WHOSOEVER believes in him shall be saved." Larg. Catech. Quest. 63. " This general offer in substance is equivalent to a special offer made to every one in particular, as appeareth by the apostle's making use of it, Acts xvi. 31. The reason of which offer is given John iii. 16." Pract. use of saving knowledge. Confes. Pag. 380. The Synod of Dort may be heard without prejudice on this head. " It is the promise of the gospel, say they, that whosoever believeth in Christ crucified, should not perish, but have life everlasting : which promise, together with the injunction of repentance and faith, ought promiscuously, and without distinction to be declared and published to all men and people, to whom God in his good pleasure sends the gospel." Chap. 2. art. 5. " But forasmuch as many being called by the gospel, do not repent nor believe in Christ, but perish in their infidelity, this comes not to pass for want of, or by any insufficiency of the sacrifice of Christ offered upon the cross, but by their own default." Art. 6.

* *i. e.* From this deed of gift and grant, it was, that the ministerial offer was appointed to be made in the most extensive terms.

† Dr Preston of faith, p. 8.

‡ That the reader may have a more clear view of this passage, which is taken from Dr Preston's treatise of faith, I shall transcribe the whole paragraph, in which it is found. That eminent divine, speaking of that righteousness by which alone we can be saved, and having shown that it is communicated by gift, faith, " But when you hear this righteousness is given, the next question will be, to whom it is given ? If it be only given to some, what comfort is this to me ? But (which is the ground of all comfort) it is given to every man, there is not a man excepted ; for which we have the sure word of God, which will not fail. When you have the charter of a king, well confirmed, you

reckon it a matter of great moment : what is it then, when you have the charter of God himself? which you shall evidently see in these two places, Mark ult. 15. " Go and preach the gospel to every creature under heaven." What is that? Go and tell every man without exception, that here is good news for him; Christ is dead for him ; and if he will take him, and accept of his righteousness, he shall have it: restraint is not. but go and tell every man under heaven. The other text is Rev. ult. " Whosoever will, let him come, and take of the water of life freely." There is a QUICUNQUE VULT, whosoever will come, (none excepted) may have life, and it shall cost him nothing. Many other places of scripture there be. to prove the generality of the offer ; and having a sure word for it, consider it." Pag. 7, 8. The words UNDER HEAVEN, are taken from Col. i. 23. The scope here, is the same with that of our author, not to determine concerning the extent of Christ's death ; but to discover the warrant sinners have to believe in Christ : namely, that the offer of Christ is general, the deed of gift or grant is to every man. This necessarily supposeth, Christ crucified to be the ordinance of God for salvation, to which lost mankind is allowed access, and not fallen angels, for whom there is none provided : even as the city of refuge, was the ordinance of God, for the safety of the manslayer, who had killed any person unawares, Numb. xxxv. 16. and the brazen serpent, for the cure of these bitten by a serpent, chap. xxi. 8. Therefore he saith not, " Tell every man, Christ died for him ; but," tell every man Christ is dead for him ; that is, for him to come to, and believe on: a Saviour is provided for him ; there is a crucified Christ for him, the ordinance of heaven for salvation, for lost mankind, in the use-making of which he may be saved : even as if one had said of old, tell every man that hath slain any person unawares, that the city of refuge is prepared for him, namely, to flee to; that he may be safe : and every one bitten with a serpent, that the brazen serpent is set up on a pole for him, namely, to look unto, that he may be healed. Both these were eminent types of Christ ; and upon the latter the scripture is full and clear, in this very point, " Numb. xxi. 8. And the Lord said unto Moses, make thee a fiery serpent ; and set it upon a pole : and it shall come to pass, that EVERY ONE that is bitten, when he looketh upon it, shall live." John iii. 14, 15, 16. " And as Moses lifted up the serpent in the wilderness ; even so must the Son of man be lifted up: that whosoever believeth on him, should not perish, but have eternal life. For God so loved the world, that he gave his only begotten Son, that whosoever," &c.

Thus, what, according to Dr Preston and our author, is to be told every man, is no more than what ministers of the gospel have in commission from their great Master, Matth. xxii. 4.

" Tell them which are bidden, Behold, I have prepared my dinner; my oxen and my fatlings are killed, and all things are ready; come unto the marriage." There's a crucified Saviour, with all saving benefits, for them, to come to, feed upon, and partake of freely. See also Luke ii. 30, 31. Prov. ix. 2, 3, 4. Isa. xxv. 6.

To confirm this to be the true and defigned fenfe of the phrafe in queftion, compare the following three paffages of the fame treatife, giving the import of the fame text, Mark xvi. " Chrift hath provided a righteoufnefs and falvation, that is his work, that he hath done already. Now if ye will believe, and take him upon thefe terms that he is offered, you fhall be faved. This, I fay, belongs to all men. This you have thus expreffed, in the gofpel, in many places: if you believe, you fhall be faved; as it is Mark xvi. Go and preach the gofpel to every creature under heaven ; he that will believe fhall be faved." Prefton of faith, page 32. " You muft firft have Chrift himfelf, before you can partake of thofe benefits by him: and that I take to be the meaning of that in Mark xvi. Go preach the gofpel to every creature under heaven ; he that believeth, and is baptized, fhall be faved ; that is, he that will believe, that Jefus Chrift is come in the flefh, and that he is offered to mankind for a Saviour, and will be baptized ; that will give up himfelf to him, that will take his mark upon him—fhall be faved " Ibid. page 46.— " Go and preach the gofpel to every creature ; go and tell every man, under heaven, that Chrift is offered to him, he is freely given to him, by God the Father ; and there is nothing required of you, but that you marry him, nothing but to accept of him." Ibid. p. 75.

Thus it appears that univerfal atonement or redemption is not taught here, neither, by our author. But that the candid reader may be fatisfied as to his fentiments touching the queftion, For whom Chrift died? let him weigh thefe two things.

1. Our author puts a man's being perfuaded that Chrift died for him in particular, in the definition of faving faith, and that as the laft and higheft ftep of it. But Arminians and other univerfalifts, might as good put there a man's being perfuaded that he was created, or is preferved by Jefus Chrift ; fince, in being perfuaded that Chrift died for him, he applies no more to himfelf, than what, according to their principles, is common to all mankind, as in the cafe of creation and prefervation. Hear Grotius upon this head. " Some, faith he, have here interpreted faith to be a perfuafion, whereby a man believes that Jefus died for him in particular, and to purchafe falvation, all manner of ways for him, or (what with them is the fame thing) that he is elected; when, on the contrary, Paul in many

P 3

places teacheth, that Chrift died for all men; and fuch a faith, as they talk of, has not in it any thing true or profitable." Grotius apud pol. fynop. crit proleg. in epift. ad Rom.—— Thefe, whom this learned adverfary here taxeth, are Proteftant Anti-Arminian divines. Thefe were they who defined faith by fuch a perfuafion, and not the univerfalifts. On the contrary, he argues againft that definition of faith, from the doctrine of univerfal atonement or redemption. He rejects that definition of it, as in his opinion having nothing in it true; namely, according to the principles of thofe that gave it, to wit, that Chrift died not for all and every man in particular, but for the elect only: and as having nothing in it profitable; that being, according to his principles, the common priviledge of all mankind.

2. He teacheth plainly throughout the book, that they were the elect, the chofen, or believers, whom Chrift reprefented, and obeyed and fuffered for. See, among others, pag. 27, 29, 66, 113, 147 I fhall repeat only two paffages; the one, p. 108. "According to that eternal and mutual agreement, that was betwixt God the Father and Him, he put himfelf in the room and place of all the faithful." The other, in the firft fentence of his own preface, *viz.* "Jefus Chrift, the fecond Adam, did, as a common perfon, enter into a covenant with God his Father, for all the elect, (that is to fay, all thofe, that have, or fhall believe, on his name) and for them kept it." What can be more plain, than that, in the judgment of our author, they were the elect, whom Jefus Chrift the fecond Adam entered into covenant with God for; that it was in the elect's room, he put himfelf, when he came actually to obey and fuffer; and that it was for the elect, he kept that covenant, by doing and fuffering what was required of him as our Redeemer? As for the defcription, or character, he gives of the elect, Viz. That by the elect he underftands, all that have or fhall believe; in it, he follows our Lord himfelf, John xvii. 20. "Neither pray I for thefe alone, but for them alfo which fhall believe on me." And fo doing, he is accompanied with orthodox divines.—— "Thus did the fins of all God's elect, or all true believers, (for of fuch, and only fueh, he there, Viz. Ifa. liii. 6. fpeaks) meet together upon the head of their common furety, the Lord Chrift" Brinfley's Mefites, page 64 "The Father is well fatisfied with the undertakings of the Son, entred Redeemer and furety to pay the ranfom of believers." Pract.-Ufe of Sav. Knowledge, Tit. 4. Warrant to believe. "The invifible church is the whole number of the elect, that have been, are or fhall be gathered into one, under Chrift the head." Larg. Cat. Quft. 64. "Chrift's church, wherein ftandeth only remiffion of fins, purchafed by Chrift's blood to all them that believe." The

fore faith a godly * writer, forasmuch as the holy scripture speaketh to all in general, none of us ought to distrust himself, but believe that it doth belong particularly to himself †. And to the end, that this point, wherein lieth and consisteth the whole mystery of our holy faith, may be understood the better ; let us put the case, that some good and holy king should cause a proclamation to be made thro' his whole kingdom, by the sound of a trumpet, that all rebels and banished men, shall safely

---

confes. of faith used in Geneva, approved by the church of Scotland. Sect. 4. § ult. But Arminians neither will nor can, in consistency with their principles, touching election and the falling away of believers, admit that description or character of the elect ; else they are widely mistaken by one of their own, who tells us, that " Upon the consideration of his (Viz Christ's) blood, as shed ; He (to wit, God) decreed that all these who should believe in that Redeemer, and persevere in that faith, should through mercy and grace by him, be made partakers of salvation. Exam. of Tilenus, p. 131. Brought unto faith, and persevere therein ; this being the condition required in every one, that is to be elected, unto eternal life. Ibid page 139. Behold the Arminian election ! they do utterly deny, that God did destine, by an absolute decree, to give Christ a Mediator only to the elect, and to give faith to them ALONE." Ibid p 149. As for Universalists, not Arminians, they contend, that the decree of the death of Christ, did go before the decree of election ; and that God, in sending of Christ, had no respect unto some, more than to others, but destin'd Christ for a Saviour to all men alike. This account of their principles is given us by Turretin, Loc 14 Quest. 14 Th. 6. I leave it to the impartial reader, to judge of the evident contrariety betwixt this and our author's words above repeated.

* In a little book called the Benefit of Christ's death

† Namely, the deed of gift and grant, or the offer of Christ in the word, of which our author is all along speaking : And if there be any man, to whom it doth not belong particularly, that man hath no warrant to believe on Jesus Christ : and whosoever pretends to believe on him, without believing that the grant or offer belongs to himself particularly : does but act presumptuously, as seeing no warrant he has to believe on Christ, whatever others may have

return home to their houses; becaufe that at the fuit
and defert of fome dear friend of theirs, it hath pleafed
the king to pardon them : certainly, none of thefe rebels
ought to doubt, but that he fhall obtain true pardon for
his rebellion : and fo return home, and live under the
fhadow of that gracious king   Even fo our good king,
the Lord of heaven and earth, hath, for the obedience
and defert of our good brother Jefus Chrift, pardoned all
our fins* ; and made a proclamation throughout the whole

---

* So far as he hath made the deed of gift and grant, or
authentic gofpel offer of the pardon of all our fins, as of all
other faving-benefits, in Chrift, fuch a thing, among men, is
called the king's pardon; though in the mean time, none have
the benefit of it, but fuch as come in, upon its being proclaimed,
and accept of it: and why may not it be called the king of
heaven's pardon? The holy fcripture warrants this manner of
expreffion : " And this is the record that God hath given to us
eternal life," (1 John v 11) In which life, without queftion,
the pardon of all our fins is included ; " through this man is
preached unto you the forgivenefs of fins," Acts xiii 38 The
preaching of the gofpel, is the proclaiming of pardon to condemned finners   But pardon of fin cannot be preached or proclaimed, unlefs, in the firft place, it be granted ; even as the
king's pardon muft be, before one can proclaim it to the rebels

That this is all that is meant by pardon here, and not a
formal perfonal pardon, is evident from the whole ftrain of the
author's difcourfe upon it   In the propofal of the Simile whereof
this paffage is the application, he tells us, that after it hath
pleafed the king (thus) to pardon the rebels; they ought not to
doubt, but they fhall obtain pardon: and in the following
paragraph he brings in Neophytus objecting, that in fuch a cafe,
an earthly king doth indeed intend to pardon all ; but the King
of heaven doth not fo, the which Evangelifta in his anfwer
grants   So that, for all this general pardon, the formal perfonal
pardon remains to be obtained by the finner, namely by his
accepting of the pardon offered   And in the forefaid anfwer, he
expounds the pardon in queftion, of the Lord's offering pardon
generally to all . This, one would think, may well be admitted
as a fruit of Chrift's obedience and defert without fuppofing an
univerfal atonement or redemption   And to reftrain it to any
fet of men whatfoever under heaven, is to reftrain the authentic
gofpel-offer, of which before

world *, that every one of us may fafely return to God in Jefus Chrift: wherefore, I befeech you, make no doubt of it, but, " draw near with a true heart, in full affurance of faith," Heb. x. 22. †

Neo. O! But, Sir, in this fimilitude the cafe is not alike. For when the earthly king fendeth forth fuch a proclamation, it may be thought, that he doth indeed intend to pardon all: but it cannot be thought that the King of heaven doth fo: for doth not the fcripture fay, that " fome men are ordained before, to condemnation ?" Jude v. 4. and doth not Chrift himfelf fay, that " many are called, but few are chofen," Matth xxii. 14. And therefore it may be, I am one of them that are ordained to condemnation; and therefore, though I be called, I fhall never be chofen, and fo fhall not be faved.

---

* Col i 23 " The gofpel which ye have heard, and which was preached to every creature, which is under heaven".

† Make no doubt of the pardon offered, or of the proclamation, bearing, That every one of us may fafely return to God in Chrift; but thereupon draw near to him, in full affurance of faith That there can be no faving faith, no acceptance with God, where there is any doubting, is, what can hardly enter into the head of any fober Chriftian, if it is not under a grievous temptation, in his own foul's cafe; nor is it in the leaft infinuated here Neverthelefs, the doubting mixt with faith, is fin; and difhonoureth God; and believers have ground to be humbled for it, and afhamed of it, before the Lord; and therefore, the full affurance of faith is duty The Papifts indeed contend earneftly for doubting; and they know very well, wherefore they fo do; for doubting being removed, and the affurance of faith in the promife of the gofpel brought into its room; their market is marr'd, their gain by indulgences, mafses, pilgrimages, &c is gone, and the fire of purgatory extinguifhed But) as Proteftant divines prove againft them, the holy fcripture condemns it Matth xiv 31 " O thou of little faith, wherefore didft thou doubt?" Luke xii 29 " Neither be ye of doubtful mind;" 1 Tim ii 8 " Lifting up holy hands, without wrath and doubting"

Evan. I befeech you to confider, that although fome men be ordained to condemnation; yet fo long as the Lord hath concealed their names, and not fet a mark of reprobatatin upon any man in particular; but offers the pardon generally to all, without having any refpect either to election, or reprobation : it may be I am not elected, and therefore fhall not have benefit by it ; and therefore I will not accept of it, nor come in *. For it fhould rather move every man to give diligence, " to make his calling and election fure," (2 Pet. i 10.) by believing it ; for fear we come fhort of it †, according to that of the Apoftle, " Let us therefore fear, left a promife being left us of entring into his reft, any of us fhould feem to come fhort of it," Heb. iv. 1. Wherefore I befeech you, do not you fay, it may be I am not elected, and therefore I will not believe in Chrift : but rather fay ‡, I do believe in Chrift, and therefore I am fure I am elected. And check your own heart ||, for meddling with God's fecrets, and prying into his hidden counfel; and go no more beyond your bounds, as you have done in this point: for election and reprobation is a fecret; and the fcripture tells us, " That fecret things belong unto God, but thofe things that are revealed belong unto us," Deut. xxix. 29. Now this is God's revealed will ; for indeed it is his exprefs command, " that you fhould believe on the name of his Son," 1 John iii. 23. And it is his promife, " That if you believe, you fhall not perifh

---

* Had the author once dreamed of an univerfal pardon, otherwife, than that God offers the pardon generally to all; all this had been needlefs; it would have furnifhed him a fhort anfwer, viz. That God hath pardoned all already.

† By believing the offered pardon, with particular application to himfelf; without which, one can never accept of it, but will undoubtedly come fhort of it.

‡ Like that man, mentioned Mark ix. 24. who at once did and faid.

|| Poor doubting Chriftian, p. 69.

but have everlasting life *. Wherefore you having so good a warrant as God's command, and so good an encouragement as his promise, do your duty † : and by the doing thereof, you may put it ‡ out of question, and be sure that you are also one of God's elect ‖. Say then, I beseech you, with a firm faith, the righteousness of Jesus Christ belongs to all that believe; but I believe §, and therefore it belongs to me. Yea, and say with Paul, " I live by the faith of the Son of God, who loved me, and gave himself for me," Gal. ii. 20. He saw in me (saith Luther on the text) nothing but wickedness, going astray, and flying from him. Yet this good Lord had mercy on me, and of his mere mercy he loved me, yea so loved me, that he gave himself for me ¶. Who is this me? Even I wretched and damnable sinner was so dearly beloved of the Son of God, that he gave himself for me.

** O print this word (me) in your heart, and apply it to your own self, not doubting but that you are one of those, to whom this (me) belongeth ††.

Neo. But may such a vile and sinful wretch as I am, be persuaded, that God commands me to believe, and

---

* John iii. 16.
† Believe on the name of Christ.
‡ Viz. Your believing.
‖ Dr Sibb's Soul's conflict, p. 981.

§ This is what is commonly called the reflex act of faith, which presupposeth, and here includeth the direct act, namely, a man's doing of his duty, in obedience to the command to believe on Christ; by reflecting on which he may put it out of question, that he is a believer, one of God's elect, and one of these for whom Christ died; the which he insists upon in the following words. See the foregoing note ‡. p. 178. This passage is taken out of Dr Preston's treatise of faith, page 8.

¶ Luther on Gal. English, Fol. 86. § 4.
** Ibid. Fol. 87. § 2.

†† Ibid. Fol. 88. § 5. This manner of applying, saith the same Luther, is the very true force and power of faith. Ibid. Fol. 88. line 1.

that he hath made a promise to me * ?

Evan. Why do you make a question, where there is none to be made? " Go, faith Chrift, and preach the gofpel to every creature under heaven," that is, go tell every man without exception, whatfoever his fins be, whatfoever his rebellions be, go and tell him thefe glad tidings, that if he will come in, I will accept of him, his fins fhall be forgiven him, and he fhall be faved; if he will come in, and take me, and receive me, I will be his loving hufband, and he fhall be mine own dear fpoufe †. Let me therefore fay unto you, in the words of the Apoftle, " Now then, I as an Ambaffador for Chrift, " as tho' God did befeech you by me, I pray you in " Chrift's Stead, be ye reconciled unto God; for he " hath made him to be fin for you, who knew no fin, " that you might be made the righteoufnefs of God

Neo. But do ye fay, Sir, that if I believe, I fhall be efpoufed unto Chrift?

Evan. Yea, indeed fhall you ‡; for faith coupleth the foul with Chrift, even as the fpoufe with her hufband; by which means Chrift and the foul are made one: for as in corporal marriage, man and wife are made one flefh; even fo is this fpiritual and myftical marriage, Chrift and his fpoufe are made one fpirit ‖. And this marriage, of all others, is moft perfect, and abfolutely accomplifhed, between them: for the marriage between man and wife, is but a flender figure of this union. Wherefore, I befeech you to believe it; and then you fhall be fure to enjoy it §.

---

* He had told him, That for his warrant to believe on Chrift, he had God's command, 1 John iii 23. And for his encouragement, God's promife, John iii 16. Thereupon this queftion is moved; the particular application to one's felf, being a matter of no fmall difficulty, in the experience of many who lay falvation to heart.

† Dr Prefton of love, p. 146.

‡ Roufe myftical marriage, p. 10.

‖ Luther's Chriftian liberty, p. 21.

§ Believe the word of promife; the offer of the fpiritual

Neo. But, Sir, if David said, "Seemeth it to you a light thing to be an earthly king's son-in-law, seeing that I am a poor man, and lightly esteemed?" 1 Sam. xviii. 23. then surely I have much more cause to say, seemeth it a light thing to be a heavenly King's daughter-in-law, seeing that I am such a poor sinful wretch? surely, Sir, I cannot be persuaded to believe it.

Evan. Alas, man, how much are you mistaken! for you look upon God, and upon yourself, with the eye of reason; and so as standing in relation to each other, according to the tenor of the covenant of works: whereas you being now in the case of justification and reconciliation, you are to look both upon God and upon yourself, with the eye of faith; and so standing in relation to each other, according to the tenor of the covenant of grace. For saith the apostle, "God was in Christ reconciling the world unto himself, not imputing their sins unto them." 2 Cor. v. 19. As if he had said, because as God stands in relation to man, according to the tenor of the covenant of works, and so out of Christ; he could not, without prejudice to his justice, be reconciled unto them, nor have any thing to do with them, otherwise than in wrath and in indignation: therefore, to the intent that justice and mercy might meet together, and righteousness and peace might embrace each other, and so God stand in relation to man according to the tenor of the covenant

---

marriage, which is Christ's declared consent to be yours. Believe that it is made to you in particular, and that it shall be made out to you; the which is, to embrace the offer, to receive Christ, as the evangelist teacheth, john i. 12. of which before; so shall you be, indeed, married or espoused to Christ. Thus the holy scripture proposeth this matter, Isa. lv. 3. "Hear and your soul shall live, and I will make an everlasting covenant with you." To persuade us of the reality of the covenant betwixt God and the believer of this word, the Father hath made a four-fold gift, &c. Practical Use of Sav. Knowl. Tit. Warrants to believe. Fig. 7. Compare Isa. liii. 1. Heb. iv. 1, 2.

Q

of grace; he put himself into his Son Jesus Christ, and
shrowded himself there, that so he might speak peace
to his people *. Sweetly, saith Luther †, because the
nature of God was otherwise higher, than that we are
able to attain unto it; therefore hath he humbled himself
to us, and taken our nature upon him, and so put himself
into Christ. Here he looketh for us, here he will receive
us; and he that seeketh him here, shall find him ‡.
This, saith God the Father, " Is my beloved Son, in
whom I am well pleased," Matth. iii 17. Whereupon
the same Luther says in another place, We must not
think and persuade ourselves, that this voice came from
heaven for Christ's own sake ‖, but for our sakes; even
as Christ himself saith, John xii. 30. This voice came
not because of me, but for your sakes. The truth is,
Christ had no need that it should be said unto him, This is
my well-beloved Son: he knew that from all eternity,
and that he should still so remain; tho' these words had
not been spoken from heaven; therefore by these words,
God the Father, in Christ his Son, cheareth the hearts of
poor sinners, and greatly delighteth them with singular
comfort and heavenly sweetness; assuring them, that
whosoever is married unto Christ, and so in him by faith,
he is as acceptable to God the Father, as Christ himself §;
according to that of the apostle, " he hath made us

---

* Psal. lxxxiii. 8, 10.   † Choice serm. p 199.

‡ An eminent type of this glorious mystery was, that tabernacle, so often mentioned in the Old Testament, under the
name of the tabernacle of the congregation, or rather the
tabernacle of meeting, as the original word bears; and the
Lord himself seems to give the reason of the name, Exod. xxx. 36.
" In the tabernacle of the congregation, where I will meet
with thee. Or in the tabernacle of meeting, where I will be
met with by thee. Chap. xxxiii. 7. " And it came to pass, that
every one, which sought the Lord, went out unto the tabernacle
of (the congregation, or) meeting.

‖ Luther's choice serm. p. 13. 32, 33.
§ See the following note.

acceptable in his beloved." .Eph i. 6. Wherefore, if you would be·acceptable to God, and be made·his dear child; then by faith cleave unto his beloved Son Chriſt, and hang about his neck, yea, and creep into his boſom : and ſo ſhall the love and favour of God be as deeply in-ſinuated into you, as it is into Chriſt himſelf * : and ſo ſhall God the Father, together with his beloved Son, wholly poſſeſs you, and be poſſeſſed of you : and ſo God and Chriſt, and you ſhall become one entire thing; accord-ing to Chriſt's prayer, " that. they may be .one in us, as thou and I are one," John xvii. 21, 22. †

---

* The accepta·ion, love and favour of God, here treated·of, do not refer to the real ſtate of believers; but to their relative ſtate, to their juſtifiⅽation, reconciliation and adoption: and ſo they have no reſpect to any qualities inherent in them, good nor evils to be increaſed by the one, or diminiſhed by the other : but they proceed purely upon the righteouſneſs of Chriſt, which is is theirs, in virtue of their union with him, and is imputed to them; the which righteouſneſs is the ſelf-ſame righteouſneſs, wherewith Chriſt as Mediator, and ſurety for elect ſinners, pleaſed the Father. And therefore faith one, whom no body ſuſpects of Antinomianiſm. " We are as perfectly righteous, as Chriſt the righteous, as Chriſt the righteous," citing 1 John iii. 7. " He that doth righteouſneſs, is righteous, even as he is righte-ous," Iſaac Ambroſe, Media, chap. 1. ſect. 2. p. (mihi) 4. This I take to be the true meaning of theſe paſſages of our author, and Iſaac Ambroſe, expreſt in terms ſtronger than I would deſire to uſe. There is a danger in expreſſing concerning God, even what is true.

. † The original word, here rendered One, doth indeed ſignify one thing. And it is evident from the text, that believers are united to God, as well as to Chriſt. " Faith is that grace, by which we are united to, and made one with God and Chriſt," ſays the author of the ſupplement to Pool's annot. on the place. See 1 John iv. 16. 2 Cor. vi 16. compared with Eph. iii. 17. And whoſoever do own Jeſus Chriſt to be one with the Father, muſt needs grant this, or elſe deny believers to be united to Chriſt. This derogates nothing from the prerogative of our Lord Jeſus, who is one with the Father: for, He is one with Him, as the Holy Ghoſt alſo is, by the adorable ſubſtantial union; but believers are ſo, only by a myſtical union. Neither

And by this means, you may have sufficient ground and warrant to say, (in the matter of reconciliation with God at any time, whensoever you are disputing with yourself *, how God is to be found, that justifieth and saveth sinners) I know no other God, neither will I know any other God, besides this God, that came down from heaven, and clothed himself with my flesh †,

---

doth it intrench upon GOD's supremacy, more than their (confess'd) union with Christ doth; who, notwithstanding of believers union with him remains to be, with the Father and Holy Spirit, the only supreme, most high God. See p. 247.

" Whosoever therefore cleaveth to Christ through faith, he abideth in the favour of God, he also shall be made beloved and acceptable as Christ is, and shall have fellowship with the Father and the Son." Luth. chosen sermons, sermon of the appearing of Christ, p (mihi) 23. " Here I will abide in the arms of Christ, cleaving unseparably about his neck, and creeping into his bosom, whatsoever the law shall say, and my heart shall feel. Ibid. sermon of the lost sheep, p. (mihi) 81." Seeing therefore that Christ the beloved Son, being in so great favour with God in all things that he doth, is thine,—without doubt, thou art in the same favour and love of God, that Christ himself is in. And again, the favour and love of God, are insinuated to thee, as deeply as to Christ, that now, God together with his beloved Son, doth wholly possess thee, and thou hast him again wholly; that so God, Christ, and thou, do become as one certain thing— that they may be one in us, as thou and I are one."—John xvii. Ibid. Sermon of the appearing of Christ, p. (mihi) 25.

* Luther on Gal. p. 17.

† Luther, from whom this is taken, in the place quoted by our author confirms it thus. For he that is a searcher of God's majesty, shall be overwhelmed of his glory. I know (adds he) by experience, what I say. But these vain spirits, which so deal with God, that they exclude the Mediator, do not believe me. And on Psal. cxxx he hath these remarkable words, Ego sæpe, & libenter hoc inculco, ut extra Christum oculos, & aures claudatis, & dicatis nullum vos scire deum nisi qui fuit in gremio mariæ, & suxit ubera ejus: That is, " Often and willingly do I inculcate this, that you should shut your eyes and your ears, and say, you know no God out of Christ, none but he that was in the lap of Mary, and suck'd her breasts." He means none out of him. Burroughs on Hos. iii. 5. p. 729.

unto whom all power is given, both in heaven and in earth, who is my Judge; " for the Father judgeth no man, but hath committed all judgment to the Son," John v 22. So that Chriſt may do with me whatſoever him liketh, and determine of me according to his own mind ; and I am ſure he hath ſaid, " he came not to judge the world, but to ſave the world," John xii. 47. And therefore I do believe that he will ſave me *.

Neo. Indeed, Sir, if I were ſo holy and ſo righteous as ſome men are ; and had ſuch power over my ſins and corruptions as ſome men have, then I could eaſily believe it : but (alas) I am ſo ſinful and ſo unworthy a wretch, that I dare not preſume to believe that Chriſt will accept of me, ſo as to juſtify and ſave me.

Evan Alas ! man, in thus ſaying, you do ſeem to con-tradict and gainſay, both the apoſtle Paul, and our Lord Jeſus Chriſt himſelf ; and that againſt your own ſoul : for whereas the apoſtle Paul ſaith, " That Chriſt Jeſus came into the world to ſave ſinners," 1 Tim. i. 15. and doth juſtify the ungodly, Rom. iv. 5. Why, you ſeem to hold, and do in effect ſay, that Chriſt Jeſus came into the world, to ſave the righteous, and to juſtify the godly : And whereas our Saviour ſaith, " The whole need not the phyſician, but the ſick ; and that he came not to call the righteous, but ſinners to repentance," Matth. ix. 12. Why, you ſeem to hold, and do in effect ſay, that the ſick need not the phyſician, but the whole ; and he that came not to call ſinners, but the righteous to repentance. And

---

* This is the concluſion of that, which one, by faith cleaving unto Chriſt, and hanging about his neck, hath by that means warrant to ſay according to our author. Whether or not there is ſufficient warrant for it, according to the ſcripture, let the reader judge : what ſhadow of the doctrine of univerſal atone-ment, or univerſal pardon, is in it, I ſee not.

Q 3

indeed, in so saying, you seem to conceive that Chrift's spoufe muft be purified, wafhed, and cleanfed from all her filthinefs, and adorned with a rich robe of righteoufnefs ; before he will accept of her : whereas he himfelf faid unto her, Ezek. xvi. 4. " As for thy nativity; in the day that thou waft born, thy navle was not cut, neither waft thou wafhed with water to fupple thee ; thou waft not fwaddled at all, nor falted at all." Verfe 5. " No eye pitied thee, to do any of thefe things unto thee ; but when I paffed by thee, and looked upon thee, behold thy time was a time of love. Verfe 8. And I fpread my fkirt over thee, and covered thy nakednefs ; yea, and I fwear unto thee, and entered into covenant with thee, and thou becameft mine." Hof. ii. 19. " And I will marry thee unto me for ever ; yea, I will marry thee unto me in righteoufnefs, and in judgment, and in mercy, and compaffion.

Wherefore, I befeech you, revoke this your erroneous opinion, and contradict the word of truth no longer ; but conclude for a certainty, that it is not the righteous and godly man, but the finful and ungodly man *, that Chrift came to call, juftify and fave ; fo that if you were a righteous and godly man, you were neither capable of calling, juftifying, or faving by Chrift; but being a finful and ungodly man, I will be bold to fay unto you, as the people faid unto blind Bartimeus, Mark x. 49. " Be of good comfort, arife, he calleth thee, and will juftify and fave thee." † Go then unto him, I befeech you ; and if he come and meet you, (as his

---

* *i. e.* Such as are really fo, and not in their own opinion only refpectively.

† As the people, obferving Chrift's call to Bartimeus, bid him be of good comfort (or be confident) and arife; intimating that upon his going fo unto Chrift, he would cure him: fo one, obferving the gofpel call, may, with all boldnefs, bid a finner comp'y with it confidently ; affuring him, that thereupon Chrift will juftify and fave him.

manner is) then do not you unadvifedly lay with Peter,
" Depart from me, for I am a finful man, O Lord;"
Luke v. 8. But fay in plain terms, O come unto me,
for I am a finful man, O Lord ! Yea, go on further,
and fay, as Luther * bids you, Moft gracious Jefus,
and fweet Chrift, I am a miferable poor finner, and
therefore do judge myfelf unworthy of thy grace ;
but yet I have learned from thy word, that thy falvation
belongeth to fuch a one, therefore do I come unto thee to
claim that right, which through thy gracious promife
belongeth unto me. Affure yourfelf, man, that Jefus
Chrift requires no portion with his fpoufe; no verily, he
requires nothing with her but mere poverty. " the rich he
fends empty away," Luke i. 53. but the poor are by him
enriched. And indeed, faith Luther †, the more miferable
and diftrefs'd a man doth feel himfelf, and judge himfelf to
be ; the more willing is Chrift to receive him, and relieve
him. So that, faith he, in judging thyfelf unworthy, thou
doft thereby become truly worthy ; and fo indeed haft
gotten a greater occafion of coming to him. Wherefore then, in the words of the apoftle, I do exhort and
befeech you, to " Come boldly unto the throne of grace,
that you may obtain mercy, and find grace to help in
time of need," Heb. iv. 16.

Neo. But truly, Sir, my heart doth, as it were, tremble within me, to think of coming to Chrift after fuch a
bold manner ; and furely, Sir, if I fhould fo come unto
him, it would argue much pride and prefumption in me.

Evan. Indeed, if you fhould be encouraged to come
unto Chrift, and to fpeak thus unto him, becaufe of any
godlinefs, righteoufnefs, or worthinefs that you do
conceive to be in you ; that, I confefs, were proud pre-

---

* Coice ferm. P. 87.
† Choice ferm. P. 85.

,fumption in you.' But to come to Chrift by believing
that he will accept of you, juftify and fave you freely by
his grace, according to his gracious promife, this is neither
pride nor prefumption.* : for Chrift having tendered and
offered it to you freely, believe it, man, it is true humility
of heart, to take what Chrift offereth you †.

Nom. But by your favour, Sir, I pray you give me
leave to fpeak a word by the way. I know my neighbour
Neophytus, it may be, better than you do ; yet I do not
intend to charge him with any fin, otherwife than by
way of fuppofition (as thus). fuppofe he hath been guilty
of the committing of grofs and grievous fins, will Chrift
accept of him, and juftify and fave him for all that ?

Evan. Yea indeed ; for there is no limitation of God's
grace in Jefus Chrift, except the fin againft the Holy
Ghoft ‡. " Chrift ftands at the door, and knocks,"

---

* It is to believe the offer of the gofpel, with particular application; to embrace it, and therein to receive Chrift. And
no man can ever receive and reft on Chrift for falvation, without
believing, in greater or leffer meafure, that Chrift will accept of
him to juftification and falvation. Remove that gofpel-truth,
that Chrift will accept of him, and his faith has no ground left
to ftand upon. See note * P. 131. and note * p. 134.

† Poor doubting Chriftian, P. 18.

‡ I doubt if the fin againft the holy Ghoft, can juftly be faid
to be a limitation of God's grace in Jefus Chrift. For in the
original, authentic, gofpel-offer, in which is the proper place for
fuch a limitation, (if there was any) that grace is fo laid open to
all men, without exception. that no man is excluded ; but
there's free accefs to it, for every man, in the way of believing.
John iii. 15. 16. Rev. xxii. 17. and this offer is fometime intimated to thefe reprobates, who fall into that fin ; elfe they
fhould not be capable of it. 'Tis true, that fin is a bar in
the way of the guilty ; fo as they can never partake of the grace
of God in Chrift : for it fhall never be forgiven. Matth. xii. 31.
Mark iii. 29. And any further minifterial application of the
offer to them, feems to ceafe to be lawful or warranted, 1 John
v. 16. But all this arifeth from their own wilful, obftinate,

Rev. iii. 20. And if any murdering Manaſſes, or any perſecuting and blaſpheming Saul, (1 Tim. i. 13.) or any adulterous Mary Magdalene, will open unto him, he will come in and bring comfort with him, and will ſup with him. Seek from the one end of the heavens to the other, ſaith Evangelical Hooker *, turn all the Bible over, and ſee if the words of Chriſt be not true, " Him that cometh unto me, I will in no wiſe caſt out," John vi. 37.

Nom. Why then, Sir, it ſeems you hold that the vileſt ſinner in the world ought not to be diſcouraged from coming unto Chriſt, and believing in him, by reaſon of his ſins.

Evan. Surely, if Chriſt came into the world, to ſeek, and call, and ſave ſinners, and to juſtify the ungodly, as you have heard ; and if the more ſinful, miſerable, and diſtreſſed, a man doth judge himſelf to be, the more willing Chriſt is to receive him and relieve him : then I ſee no reaſon, why the vileſt ſinner ſhould be diſcouraged from believing on the name of Jeſus Chriſt, by reaſon of his ſins. Nay, let me ſay more ; the greater any man's ſins are, either in number or nature, the more haſte he ſhould make to come unto Chriſt, and to ſay with David, " For thy name's ſake, O Lord, pardon mine iniquity, for it is great," Pſal. xxv. 11.

hindring his coming to Chrift, that they fhould further his coming : then I know not what fhould hinder him.

Evan. You fpeak very truly indeed. And therefore, I befeech you, neighbour Neophytus, confider ferioufly of it ; and neither let your own accufing confcience, nor Satan, the accufer of the brethren, hinder you any longer from Chrift. For what though they fhould accufe you of pride, infidelity, covetoufnefs, luft, anger, envy, and hypocrify ? yea, what though they fhould accufe you of whoredom, theft, drunkennefs, and many the like ? yet, do what they can, they can make no worfe a man of you than a finner, or the chief of finners, or an ungodly perfon ; and fo confequently fuch a one as Chrift came to juftify and fave. So that, in very deed, if you do rightly confider of it, they do you more good than hurt, by their accufations *. And therefore I be-feech you, in all fuch cafes or conflicts, take the counfel of Luther, who faith †, when thy confcience is throughly afraid with the remembrance of thy fins paft, and the devil affaileth thee with great violence, going about to overwhelm thee, with heaps, floods, and whole feas of fins, to terrify thee, and to draw thee from Chrift : then arm thyfelf with fuch fentences as thefe ; Chrift the Son of God was given, not for the holy, righteous, worthy, and fuch as were his friends, but for the wicked finners, for the unworthy, and for his enemies. Wherefore, if the devil fay, thou art a finner, and therefore muft be damned ; then anfwer thou and fay, Becaufe thou fayeft I am a finner, therefore will I be righteous and faved.

---

* Which may put you in mind, that you are one of that fort, which Chrift Jefus came into the world to fave, 1 Tim. i. 15. And, in pleading for mercy, may furnifh you fuch an argument, as David ufed, Pfal. xxv. 11. and the woman of Canaan, Matth. xv. 27. "Yet the dogs eat of the crumbs," &c.

† On Gal. p. 20.

And if he reply, Nay, finners muſt be damned :· then anſwer thou and ſay, No ; for I flee to Chriſt, who hath given himſelf for my fins. And therefore, Satan, in that thou ſayeſt I am a finner, thou giveſt me armour and weapons againſt thyſelf, that with thine own ſword I may cut thy throat, and tread thee under my feet *. And thus you ſee it is the counſel of Luther, that your fins ſhould rather drive you to Chriſt, than keep you from him.

Nom But, Sir, Suppoſe he hath not as yet truly repented for his many and great fins, hath he any warrant to come unto Chriſt by believing, till he hath done ſo ?

Evan. I tell you truly, that whatſoever a man is, or whatſoever he hath done, or not done, he hath warrant enough to come unto Chriſt by believing, if he can † :

---

* He adds in the place quoted, theſe weighty words; "I ſay not this for nought, for I have often-times proved by exprience, and I daily find what an hard matter it is to believe (eſpecially in the conflict of conſcience) that Chriſt was given, not for the holy, righteous, worthy, and ſuch as were his friends, but for wicked finners, for the unworthy, and for his enemies."

† It is not in vain added, if he can. : for there is, in this matter, a great differance, betwixt what a finner may do, in point of warrant ; and what he will or can do, in point of the event. "If we ſay to a man, the phyſician is ready to heal you ; before you will be healed, you muſt have a ſenſe of your ſickneſs : this ſenſe is not required by the phyſician, (for the phyſician is ready to heal him :) but if he be not ſick, and have a ſenſe of it, he will not come to the phyſician." Preſton of faith, p. 12. I make no queſtion but, before a finner will come to Chriſt, by believing, he muſt be an awakened, convinced, ſenſible finner ; pricked in his heart with a ſenſe of his fin and miſery ; made to groan under his burden, to deſpair of relief from the law, himſelf, or any other creature, and to deſire and thirſt after Chriſt and his righteouſneſs ; and this our author teacheth afterward, on this ſubject. (Theſe things alſo are required of the finner in point of duty.) And therefore the law muſt be preached by all theſe, who would preach Chriſt aright. But that theſe, or any other, things in the finner, are required to

for Chrift makes a general proclamation, faying, " Ho,
every one that thirfteth, come ye to the waters ; and he
that hath no money, come, buy and eat, yea, come buy
wine and milk, without money, and without price."
This, you fee, is the condition, Buy wine and milk (that is,
grace and falvation) without money: that is, without any
fufficiency of your own* ; only incline your ear, and hear,

warrant him, that he may come to Chrift by believing; is
what, I conceive, the fcripture teacheth not : but the general
offer of the gofpel, of which before, warrants every man, that
he may come. And in practice, it will be found, that requiring
of fuch and fuch qualifications in finners, to warrant them to
believe in Chrift ; is no great help to them, in their way towards him : forafmuch as, it engageth them in a doubtful dif-
putation, as to the being, kind, meafure and degree of their
qualifications for coming to Chrift; the time fpent in which,
might be better improven, in their going forward to Chrift, for
all, by believing. And fince no man can ever believe in Chrift,
without knowing, that he has a warrant for believing in him ;
otherwife he can but act prefumptuoufly; to tell finners, that
none may come to Chrift, or have warrant to believe, but fuch
as have true repentance ; muft needs, in a fpecial manner, in-
tangle diftreffed confciences, fo as they dare not believe, until
they know their repentance to be true repentance ; this muft
inevitably be the iffue in that cafe ; unlefs they do either reject
that principle, or elfe venture to believe without feeing their
warrant. For, howbeit they hear of Chrift and his falvation,
offered in the gofpel ; thefe will be, to them, as forbidden fruit,
which they are not allowed to touch ; till once they are perfuaded, that they have true repentance. And before they can
attain to this, it muft be made out to their confciences, that
their repentance is not legal, but evangelical, having fuch characters, as diftinguifh it from the repentance of the Ninevites,
Judas, and many reprobates. So that, one would think, the
fuggefting of this principle, is but a bad office done to a foul,
brought to the place of the breaking forth of children. Let no
man fay, that, arguing at this rate, one muft know alfo the truth
of his faith, before he can come to Chrift ; for faith is not a
qualification for coming to Chrift, but the coming itfelf, which
will have its faving effects on the finner, whether he knows the
truth of it, or not.

  * Take them freely, and poffefs them ; which every one fees
to be no proper condition.

and your souls shall live ; yea, live by hearing that
"Christ will make an everlasting covenant with you,
even the sure mercies of David *."

§ 4. *Nom.* But yet, Sir, you see that Christ requires
a thirsting before a man come unto him ; the which, I
conceive, cannot be without true repentance.

Evan. In the last chapter of the Revelation, verse 17.
Christ makes the same general proclamation, saying, "Let
him that is athirst come :" and as if the Holy Ghost had,
so long since, answered the same objection that yours is,
it followeth in the next words, " And whosoever will,
let him take of the water of life freely," even without
thirsting if he will ; for " him that cometh unto me, I
will in no ways cast out, John vi. 37. † But because it

---

* Hooker's poor doubting Christian, p. 151.   Cornwell on
gospel repent. p. 21.

† That gospel offer, Isa. lv. 1. is the most solemn one, to be
found in all the Old Testament : and that recorded Rev. xxii. 17.
is the parting offer, made to sinners, by Jesus Christ, at the
closing of the canon of the scripture, and manifestly looks to
the former : in the which, I can see no ground to think, that
the thirsting, therein mentioned, doth any way restrict the offer ;
or that the thirsty, there invited, are convinced, sensible sinners,
who are thirsting after Christ and his righteousness ; the which,
would leave without the compass of this solemn invitation, not
only the far greater part of mankind, but even, of the visible
church. The context seems decisive in this point, for the
thirsting ones invited, are such, as are " spending money for
that which is not bread, and their labour for that which satisfieth not," ver. 1, 2.   But convinced, sensible sinners, who are
thirsting after Christ and his righteousness, are not spending their
money and labour, at that rate ; but on the contrary, for that
which is bread and satisfieth, namely, for Christ.   Wherefore,
the thirsting, there mentioned, must be more extensive ; comprehending, yea, and principally aiming at, that thirst after happiness
and satisfaction, which being natural, is common to all mankind.
Men pained with this thirst (or hunger) are naturally running,
for quenching thereof, to the empty creation ; and their fulsome
lusts : so spending money for that which is not bread, and their
labour for that which satisfieth not ; their hungry souls find no

R

seems you conceive, he ought to repent before he believe; I pray tell me, what you do conceive repentance to be, or wherein doth it confist?

Nom. Why, I do conceive that repentance consists in a man's humbling of himself before God, and forrowing and grieving for offending him by his fins, and in turning from them all to the Lord.

Evan. And would you have a man to do all this truly * before he come to Christ by believing?

Nom. Yea indeed, I think it is very meet he should.

Evan. Why then, I tell you truly, you would have him to do that which is impossible † ‡.

------

food, but what is meagre and lean, bad and unwholefome, and cannot fatisfy that their appetite. Compare Luke xv. 16. In this wretched cafe, Adam left all mankind, and Christ finds them. Whereupon, the gospel-proclamation is issued forth, inviting them to come away from the broken cifterns, the filthy puddles, to the waters of life, even to Jefus Christ, where they may have bread, fatnefs, what is good, and will fatisfy that their painful thirst, John iv. 14. and vi. 35.

* *i. e.* In fuch a manner, as it shall be true evangelical repentance, and gracious humiliation, forrow, and turning, acceptable in the fight of God. This queftion (grounded on Nomifta's pretending, that Neophytus had no warrant to believe, unlefs he had truly repented) fuppofeth that there is a kind of repentance, humiliation, forrow for fin, and turning from it, which goes before faith; but that they are not after a godly fort, as the apostle's phrafe is, 2 Cor. vii. 11.

† Dyke of Repent. p. 38.

‡ I think it nothing ftrange, to find the author fo very peremptory in this point, which is of greater weight than many are aware of. True repentance, is a turning unto unto God, a coming back to him again; a returning even unto the Lord, according to an ufual Old Teftament phrafe, found, Hof. xiv. 1. and rightly fo tranflated, Ifa. xix. 22. But no man can come unto God, but by Christ, Heb. vii. 25. " He is able alfo to fave them to the uttermoft, that come unto God by him." John xiv. 6. " No man cometh unto the Father, but by me." We muft take Christ, in our way to the Father, elfe it is impoffible that we guilty creatures can reach unto him. And no man can come unto Christ, but by believing in him, John vi. 35. therefore 'tis impoffible, that a man can truly repent, before he believe in

For first of all, godly humiliation, in true penitentiaries, proceeds from the love of God their good Father, and so from the hatred of that sin which hath displeased him, and this cannot be without faith *.

2*dly*, Sorrow and grief for displeasing God by sin, necessarily argue the love of God †; and it is impossible we should ever love God, till by faith we know ourselves loved of God ‡.

Chrift. "Him hath God exalted with his right hand, to be a Prince (or Leader) and a Saviour, for to give repentance to Ifrael, and forgivenefs of fins," Acts v. 31. One would think this to be a fufficient-intimation, that finners not only may, but ought to go to him, for true repentance; and not ftand off from him, until they get it to bring along with them; efpecially, fince repentance, as well as remiffion of fin, is a part of that falvation, which he as a Saviour is exalted to give, and confequently, which finners are to receive and reft upon him for; and likewife that it is that, by which he, as a Leader, doth lead back finners even unto God, from whom they were led away, by Adam, the head of the apoftacy. And if one inquires anent the way of his giving repentance unto Ifrael, the prophet Zechariah fhewed it before, to be by faith, Zech. xii. 10. "And they fhall look upon me whom they have pierced, and they fhall mourn."

* This the fcripture teacheth, determining in the general, that without faith one can do nothing acceptable in the fight of God, John xv. 5. "Without me (*i. e.* feparate from me) ye can do nothing." Heb. xi. 6. "Without faith, it is impoffible to pleafe him:" and particularly, with refpect to this cafe, Luke vii. 37, 38. "And behold, a woman in the city, which was a finner, when fhe knew that Jefus fat at meat—ftood at his feet behind him weeping, and began to wafh his feet with tears, and did wipe them with the hairs of her head, and kiffed his feet." Ver. 44. "And he turned to the woman, and faid unto Simon —Ver. 47. Her fins, which are many, are forgiven, for fhe loved much: but to whom little is forgiven, the fame loveth little." "It is an argument gathered of the effect following, whereby any thing is proved by figns enfuing." Calv. inftit. lib. 3. cap. 4. § 37.

†.Dyke on Repent. p. 8, 9.

‡ There is a knowledge in faith, as our divines teach againft the Papifts; and the fcripture maketh manifeft, Ifa. liii. 11. "By his knowledge, fhall my righteous fervant juftify many." Heb. xi. 3. "Through faith we underftand, that the worlds

3*dly*, No man can turn to God, except he be first turned of God; and after he is turned, he repents: so

---

were framed by the word of God." Now, saving faith, being a persuasion, that we shall have life and salvation by Christ, or, a receiving and resting on him for salvation, includes in it, a knowledge of our being loved of God: the former cannot be, without the latter. In the mean time, such as the strength or weakness of that persuasion is; the steadiness or unsteadiness of that receiving and resting; just so is this knowledge, clear or unclear; free of, or accompanied with doubtings. They are still of the same measure and degree. So that this is no more, in effect, but that faith in Christ is the spring of true love to God: the which, how it is attained by a guilty soul, men will the better know, if they consider well what it is. The true love of God is not a love to him, only for his benefits, and for our own sake; but a love to him for himself, for his own sake, a liking of, and complacency in, his glorious attributes and perfections, his infinite, eternal, and unchangeable, being, wisdom, power, holiness, justice, goodness, and truth. If a convinced sinner is void of any the least measure of persuasion, of life and salvation by Christ, and of the love of this God to him; but apprehends, as he cannot miss to do in this case, that he hates him, is his enemy, and will prove so at last; this cannot fail of filling his whole soul with slavish fear of God; and how then shall this love of God spring up in one's heart, in such a case? for slavish fear and true love, are so opposite the one to the other, that, according to the measure in which the one prevails, the other cannot have access. 2 Tim. i. 7. "God hath not given us the spirit of fear, but of power, of love, and of a sound mind." 1 John iv. 18. "There is no fear in love, but perfect love casteth out fear; because fear hath torment." But when once life and salvation, and remission of sin, is with application believed, by the convinced sinner, and thereby the love of God towards him is known, then, according to the measure of that faith and knowledge, slavish fear of God is expelled; and the heart is kindly drawn to love him, not only for his benefits, but for himself, having a complacency in his glorious perfections. "We love him, because he first loved us," 1 John iv. 19. The love of God to us, is the inducement of our love to him; but love utterly unknown to the party beloved, can never be an inducement to him, to love again. Now, in consequence hereof, the sinner's bands are loosed, and his heart, which before was still hard as a stone, tho' broken in pieces by legal terrors, is broken in another manner, softned, and kindly melted, in sorrow for displeasing this gracious God.

Ephraim faith, " After I was converted, I repented," Jer. xxxi 19. * †. The truth is, a repentant finner firft believes that God will do that which he promifeth, namely, pardon his fin, and take away his iniquity ; then he refteth in the hope, of it : and from that, and for it, he leaves fin ; and will forfake his old courfe ‡ ‖, becaufe it is difpleafing to God ; and will do that which is pleafing and acceptable to him §. So that, firft of all, God's favour is apprehended, and remiffion of fins believed ¶ ; then upon that cometh alteration of life and converfation **.

---

* Stock of repent. p. 20.

† God's turning of a finner, firft brings him to Chrift, John vi. 44. " No man can come unto me, except the Father, which hath fent me, draw him." See ver. 45 And then he comes to God, by Chrift, john xiv. 26. " No man cometh unto the Father, but by me."

‡ Ibid. p. 21.

‖ In a right manner, in the manner immediately after-mentioned

§ " Faith cometh of the word of God ; hope cometh of faith ; and charity fpringeth of them both. Faith believes the word ; hope trufteth after that which is promifed by the word ; and charity doth good unto her neighbour." Mr Patrick Hamilton's articles in Knox's hiftory, p. (mihi) 11.

¶ Not as that they are pardoned already : but that one muft fo apprehend the favour of God, as to believe, that God will—pardon his fin, as the author fpeaks exprefsly in the premiffes, from whence this conclufion is drawn ; or, that God doth pardon his fin, in the prefent time. See on page 177, note (†.) Now, remiffion of fin, is a part of that falvation, which faith receives aad refts on Chrift for. See the note on the definition of faith, p. 27. As for the phrafe the author ufeth to exprefs this ; it is moft agreeable to the fcripture-phrafe, remiffion of fins preached, Luke xxiv. 47. Acts xiii. 38.

** Namely, fuch an alteration, as is pleafing and acceptable in the fight of God, the which he has defcribed in the preceeding fentence. Otherwife, he has already taught us, that there are notable alterations of life and converfation, which do not proceed from faith ; and therefore, are not accepted of God. And of thefe we fhall hear more anon.

†† Twill not be amifs here to obferve, how our author, in his

account of the relation betwixt faith and repentance, treads in the ancient paths, according to his manner.

" It ought to be out of question, faith Calvin, that repentance doth not only immediately follow faith, but also spring out of it.—As for them that think that repentance doth rather go before faith, than flow or spring forth of it, as a fruit out of a tree, they never knew the force thereof, and are moved with too weak an argument, to think so. Christ (say they) and john, in their preachings, do first exhort the people to repentance, &c. —A man cannot earneftly apply himself to repentance, unlefs he know himfelf to be of God, but no man is truly perfuaded, that he is of God, but he that hath firft received his grace—no man fhall ever revrently fear God, but he that trufteth, that God is merciful to him: no man will willingly prepare himfelf to the keeping of the law, but he that is perfuaded, that his fervices pleafe him." Inftit book 3. cap. 3. §. 1, 2.

" How foon that ever the Spirit of the Lord Jefus, quhilk God's elect children receive, be trew faith, tak's poffeffion in the heart of ony man, fo foon dois he regenerate, and renew the fame man So that he beginnis to hait that quhilk before he loved, and beginnis to love that whilk befoir he hated, and fra thence commis that continuall battell whilk is betwixt the flefh and the fpirit." Old Confeffion, art. 13.

" Being in Chrift, we muft be new creatures—fo that we muft hate and flee that whilk before-we loved and embraced, and we muft love and follow that whilk before we hated and abhorred—all whilk is impoffible to them that have no faith, and have but a dead faith." Mr John Davidfon's catech. page 29.

" Queft. When I fall afke you then, what is craved of us, after that we are joined to Chrift, by faith, and made truely righteous in him? Ye fhall anfwere, A. We muft repent, and becum newe perfons, that we may fhew forth the virtues of him that hath called us." Ibid. p. 35.

" What is thy repentance? The effect of this faith, working a forrow for my fins bypaft, and purpofe to amend in time to come." Mr James Melvil's catech. in his propine, &c. page 44.

" Repentance unto life, is a faving grace, whereby a finner, out of the true fenfe of his fin, and apprehenfion of the mercy of God in Chrift ; doth, with grief and hatred of his fin, turn from it unto God." Short catech.

" M. This is then thy faying, that unto the time that God hath received us to mercy, and regenerate us by his Spirit, we can do NOTHING but fin ; even as an evil tree can bring forth no frute, but that that is evil Matth. vii. 17. C. Even fo it is." Calvin's Catech. Queft. 117. " He doth receive us into his favour, of his bountiful mercy, through the merits of our

Nom. But Sir, as I conceive, the scripture holds forth, that the Lord hath appointed repentance to go before faith: for is it not faid, Mark i. 15. "Repent and believe the gofpel?"

Evan. To the intent that you may have a true and fatisfactory anfwer to this your objection, I would pray you to confider two things.

Firft, That the word repent in the original, fignifies a change of our minds from falfe ways to the right, and of our hearts from evil to good * † ; as that fon in the gofpel faid, "He would not go to work in his father's vineyard; yet afterwards," faith the text, "He repented and went," Matth xxi. 29. That is, he changed his mind and went.

Secondly, That in thofe days, when John the Baptift and our Saviour preached, their hearers were moft of them erroneous in their minds and judgments. For they being leavened with the doctrine of the Pharifees and Sadducees, of the which our Saviour bade his

---

Saviour Chrift, accounting his righteoufnefs to be ours, and for his fa e imputeth not our faults unto us." Ibid. Queft. 118.

" Queft. What is the FIRST fruit of this union?" (namely, of union with Chrift by faith.) " Anf. A REMISSION of our fins, and IMPUTATION of JUSTICE. Q. Which is the NEXT fruit of our union with him? A. Our SANCTIFICATION and REGENERATION to the image of God." Craig's Catech. Q. 24, 25.

" Q. What is fanctification? A. Sanctification is a work of God's grace, whereby they—are—renewed in their whole man, after the image of God, having the feeds of REPENTANCE unto life, and of all other faving graces, put into their hearts." Larg. Catech. Q. 75.

" We would beware of Mr Baxter's order of fetting repentance and works of new obedience before juftification, which is indeed a new covenant of works." Rutherford's Influences of the life of grace, p. 346.

* Laft Annot. on Matth.

† This is taken word for word, out of the Englifh annotations on Matth. iii. 2. which are cited, for it, by our author, under the name of the Laft Annotations: becaufe they were printed in the year 1645, about which time, this book alfo was firft publifhed. How the author applies it, will appear anon.

difciples to take heed and beware, Matth. xvi. 6. 12.
The moft of them were of, opinion that the Meffiah,
whom they looked for, fhould be fome great and mighty
monarch, who fhould deliver them from their temporal
bondage; as I fhewed before. And many of them were
of the opinion of the Pharifees, who held, that as an outward conformity to the letter of the law was fufficient, to
gain favour and eftimation from men; fo was it fufficient
for their juftification and acceptation before God, and fo
confequently to bring them to heaven and eternal happinefs. And therefore, for thefe ends, they were very
diligent in fafting and prayer, Luke xviii. 12, 14. and
very careful to pay tithes of mint, and annife and cum-
min, and yet did omit the weightier matters of the law,
as judgment, mercy, faith, and the love of God, Matth.
xxiii. 23. Luke xi. 42. And fo, as our Saviour told
them, Matth. xxiii. 25. " They made clean the outfide
of the cup, and of the platter, but within they were full
of extortion and excefs."

And diverfe of them were of the opinion of the
Sadducees, Acts xxiii. 8. who held that there was no
refurrection, neither angel nor fpirit; and fo had all
their hopes and comfort in the things of this life, not
believing any other.

Now our Saviour preaching to thefe people, faid
" The time is fulfilled, and the kingdom of God is at
hand : repent ye and believe the gofpel." As if he had
faid, the time fet by the prophets for the manifeftation of
the Meffiah is fully come ; and his kingdom, which is a
fpiritual and heavenly kingdom, is at hand: therefore
change your minds, from falfe ways to right, and your
hearts from evil to good *. And do not any longer,

---

* The word rendered repent, is to change one's mind, and
to lay afide falfe opinions, which they had drunken in, whether
from the Pharifees, concerning the rightcoufnefs of works,
tradition, worfhip, &c or from the Sadducees, concerning the
refurrection, &c. Lucas Brugenfis apud Polum Synop. Crit.
in Matth. iii. 2.

imagine that the Meffiah, you look for, fhall be one that fhall fave and deliver you from your temporal enemies; but from your fpiritual, that is, from your fins, and from the wrath of God, and from eternal damnation: and therefore put your confidence no longer in your own righteoufnefs, though you walk never fo exactly according to the letter of the law; but believe the glad tidings that is now brought unto you, to wit, that this Meffiah fhall fave you from fin, wrath, death, the devil, and hell, and bring you to eternal life and glory. Neither let any of you any longer imagine, that there is to be no refurrection of the dead, and fo have you hopes only in this life: but believe thefe glad tidings, that are now brought unto you, concerning the Meffiah; and he fhall raife you up at the laft day, and give you an eternal life. Now, with fubmiffion to better judgments, I do conceive, that if there be, in the book of God, any repentance exhorted unto, before faith in Chrift; or if any repentance go, either in order of nature or time, before faith in Chrift; it is only fuch a like repentance as this *.

Nom. But, Sir, do you think that there is fuch a like repentance, that goes before faith in Chrift, in men now-a-days?

' * That the reader may further fee, how little weight there is, in the objection raifed from Mark i. 15. I fubjoin the words of two learned commentators on that text. "Repent ye, turn from the wickednefs of your ways and believe---There is a repentance that muft go before faith, that is, the applicative of the promife of pardoning mercy to the foul, through true evangelical repentance, which is a forrow for fin, flowing from the fenfe of the love of God in Chrift, be the fruit and effect of faith." Contin. of Pool's Annot. on the place. Faith or believing, or order of the work of grace, is before repentance, that being the firft and mother-grace of all others; yet, is it here, and in other places, named the latter; firft, becaufe, though faith be firft wrought, yet repentance is firft feen and evidenced, &c." Lightfoot's Harm. 3d part in 4to, p. 164.

Evan. Yea indeed, I think there is. As for example; When a profane fenfual man (who lives as though, with the Sadducees, he did not believe any refurrection of the dead, neither hell nor heaven) is convinced in his confcience, that if he go on in making a God of his belly, and in minding only earthly things, his end fhall be damnation: fometimes fuch a man doth, thereupon, change his mind; and, of a profane man, becomes a ftrict Pharifee, or (as fome call them) a legal profeffor. But being convinced, that all his own righteoufnefs will avail him nothing, in the cafe of juftification, and that it is only the righteoufnefs of Jefus Chrift that is available in that cafe; then he changeth his mind, and with the apoftle, " DESIRES to be found in Chrift, not having his own righteoufnefs which is of the law, but that which is through the faith of Chrift, even the righteoufnefs which is of God through faith," Phil iii. 9. Now I conceive, that a man that doth thus, he changeth his mind from falfe ways to the right way, and his heart from evil to good, and fo confequently doth truly repent *.

Nom. But, Sir, do not you hold, that although repentance, according to my definition, goes not before faith in Chrift, yet it follows after ?

Evan Yea indeed, I hold, that although it go not before, as an antecedent of faith; yet it follows as a confequent. For when a man believes the love of God to him in Chrift, then he loves God, becaufe he loved him firft; and that love conftrains him to humble himfelf at the Lord's footftool, and to acknowledge himfelf to be lefs than the leaft of all his mercies; yea and then will

---

* *i. e.* His repentance is true in its kind, though not faving. There is a change of his mind and heart; in that, upon a conviction, he turns from profanity, to ftrictnefs of life, and upon further conviction, from a conceit of his own righteoufnefs, to a defire after the righteoufnefs of Chrift: neverthelefs, all this is but felfifh, and cannot pleafe God, while the man is void of faith. Heb. xi. 6.

he remember his own evil ways and doings that were not good; and will lothe himself in his own fight fo his iniquities, and for his abominations, Ezek. xxxvi. 31. Yea, and then will he also cleanse himself from all filthiness of flesh and spirit, perfecting holiness in the fear of God, having respect unto all God's commandments, 2 Cor. vii. 1. Pfal: cxix. 6. *.

Nom. Well, Sir, I am answered.

§ 5. *Neo.* And truly, Sir, you have fo declared, and fet forth Chrift's difpofition towards poor finners, and fo anfwered all my doubts and objections; that I am now verily perfuaded that Chrift is willing to entertain me; and furley I am willing to come unto him, and receive him: but alas, I want power.

Evan. But tell me truly, are you refolved to put forth all your power to believe, and fo to take Chrift? †

---

* See the note * page 140.

† His conviction of his loft and undone ftate, was before reprefented, in its proper place. After much difputing, whether fuch a vile and finful wretch, as he, had any warrant to come to Chrift? he appears, in his immediately foregoing fpeech, to be fo far enlightned in the knowledge of Chrift, that he is verily perfuaded, Chrift is willing to entertain him; and to have his heart and will fo overcome by divine grace, that he is willing to come unto Chrift: yet after all, he, through weaknefs of judgment, apprehends himfelf to want power to believe; whereas it is by thefe very means, that a foul is perfuaded and enabled too, to believe in Jefus Chrift. Hereupon the author, waving the difpute anent his power to believe, wifely afks him, if he was refolved to put forth the power he had? forafmuch as it was evident, from the account given of the prefent condition of his own foul, that it had felt a day of power, Pfal cx. 3. and that he was drawn of the Father, and therefore could come to Chrift, John vi. 44. For " effectual calling is the work of God's Spirit, whereby convincing us of our fin and mifery, inlightning our minds in the knowledge of Chrift, and renewing our wills, he doth perfuade and enable us to embrace Jefus Chrift." Short Catech.——" Savingly inlightning their minds, renewing and powerfully determining their wills, fo as they—are HEREBY made willing and able." Larg. Catech. Q. 67.

Neo. Truly, Sir, me-thinks my refolution is much like the refolution of the four lepers, which fat at the gate of Samaria : for as they faid, " If we enter into the city, the famine is in the city, and we fhall die there ; and if we fit ftill here, we die alfo : now therefore let us fall into the hoft of the Syrians ; if they fave us, we fhall live ; and if they kill us, we fhall but die," 2 Kings vii. 4. Even fo fay I in mine heart, if I go back to the covenant of works to feek juftification thereby, I fhall die there ; and if I fit ftill and feek it no way, I fhall die alfo : now therefore, though I be fomewhat fearful, yet am I refolved to go unto Chrift ; and if I perifh, I perifh *.

Evan. Why, now I tell you, the match is made, Chrift is yours †, and you are his ; this day is falvation come to your houfe (your foul I mean) for, what though you have not that power to come fo faft to Chrift, and to lay fuch firm hold on him, as you defire? yet coming with fuch a refolution to take Chrift, as you do, you need not care for power to do it, inafmuch as Chrift will enable you to do it ‡; for is it not faid, John i. 12. " But as many as

---

* See the foregoing note. This is the concluding point, in this matter. The man being drawn by efficacious grace, tho' he is not without doubts and fears, as to the event; yet is no more in doubt whether to embrace the offer, or not. And the inward motion of his heart, breaking through the remaining doubts and fears, after a long ftruggle, unto Jefus Chrift in the free promife; being in itfelf indifcernible, but to God, and one's own foul : it is agreeably enough to one's way in that cafe: difcovered in that expreffion of a conquered foul, now am I refolved to go unto Chrift, now am I determined to believe; the which cannot but reprefent to him, who deals with the exercifed perfon, the whole foul going out unto Jefus Chrift. Hence the match may juftly, thereupon, be declared to be made, as our author does in the words immediately following. Thus Job in his diftrefs expreffeth his faith, Job xiii. 15. " Though he flay me, yet will I truft in him." Compare Acts xi. 23. " That with purpofe of heart they would cleave unto the Lord."
† In poffeffion.
‡ *i. e.* You need not, holding back your hand, ftand difputing

received him, to them gave he power to become the sons of God, even to them that believe on his name?" * O therefore, I beseech you, stand no longer disputing : but be peremptory and resolute in your faith, and in casting yourself upon God in Christ for mercy ; and let the the issue be what it will.†. Yet let me tell you, to your comfort, that such a resolution shall never go to hell ‡. Nay, I will say more, if any soul have room in heaven, such a soul shall ; for God cannot find in his heart to damn such a one. I might then with as much true confidence say unto you, as faithful John Careless said to godly John Bradford ‖; hearken, O heavens, and thou O earth, give ear, and bear me witness at the great day, that I do here faithfully and truly declare the Lord's message unto his dear servant, and singularly beloved John Bradford, saying, John Bradford, thou man so specially beloved of God, " I do pronounce and testify unto thee, in the word and name of the Lord Jehovah, that all thy sins whatsoever they be, though never so many, grievous, or great, be fully and freely pardoned, released and forgiven thee, by the mercy of God in Jesus Christ, the only Lord and sweet Saviour, in whom thou dost undoubtedly believe : as truly as the Lord liveth, he will not have thee die the death ; but hath verily purposed, determined and decreed, that thou shalt live with him for ever.

---

with yourself, how you will get power : but with the power given, stretch forth the withered hand ; and Christ will strengthen it, and enable you to take a firm hold, John xii. 32. " And I, if I be lifted up from the earth, will draw all men unto me." Isa. xl. 29. " He giveth power to the faint ; and to them that have no might, he increaseth strength."

* The power, here mentioned, seems rather to denote right or privilege, (as the original word is rendered in the margent of our Bibles) than strength or ability.
† Goodwin's child of light, p. 196, 199.
‡ See the preceding note *, p. 204.
‖ In a letter to him.

Neo. O Sir, if I have as good warrant to apply this saying to myself, as sweet Mr Bradford had to himself, then I am a happy man.

Evan. I tell you from Christ, and under the hand of the Spirit, that your person is accepted, your sins are done away, and you shall be saved : and if an angel from heaven should tell you otherwise, let him be accursed *. Therefore you may (without doubt) conclude that you are a happy man ; for, by means of this your matching with Christ, you are become one with him, and one in him, you " dwell in him, and he in you," 1 John iv. 13. He is " your well-beloved, and you are his." Cant. ii. 16. So that the marriage-union betwixt Christ and you, is more than a bare notion or apprehension of your mind; for it is a special, spiritual, and real union, it is an union betwixt the nature of Christ, God and man, and you ‡ ‡; it is a knitting and closing, not only of your apprehension with a Saviour, but also of your soul with a Saviour. When it must needs follow, that ‖ you cannot be condemned, except Christ be condemned with you; neither can Christ be saved, except you be saved with him §. And

---

* Hooker's poor doubting Christian, p. 51.

† Hooker's soul-union, p. 6, 7, 9, 10.

‡ *i. e.* An union with whole Christ, God-Man. 1 Cor. vi. 17. " He that is joined to the Lord, is one spirit." Eph. v. 30. " For we are members of his body, of his flesh and of his bones.

‖ Tindal Par Wick. Mam. p. 75.

§ Jesus Christ and the believer, being one person in the eye of the law; there is no separating of them, in law, in point of life and death. John xiv. 19. " Because I live, ye shall live also." I have adventured this once, to add one syllable to the text of the author; and so to read condemned for damned. The words are of the same signification : only; the latter hath an idea of horror affixed to it, which the former has not; and which perhaps it had not neither in the days of our forefathers, when godly Tindal used the expression, as our author informs us. And I take this liberty, the rather that a like expression of

as by means of corporal marriage, all things become common betwixt man and wife; even so, by means of this spiritual marriage, all things become common betwixt Christ and you: for when Christ hath married his spouse unto himself, he passeth over all his estate unto her; so that whatsoever Christ is, or hath, you may boldly challenge as your own, " He is made unto you, of God, wisdom, righteousness, sanctification, and redemption," 1 Cor. i 30. And surely, by virtue of this near union it is, that as Christ is called, the Lord our righteousness, Jer. xxii· 6. Even so is the church called, " The Lord our righteousness," Jer. xxxiii 16. I tell you, man, you may by virtue of this union, boldly take unto yourself as your own*, Christ's watching, abstinence, travels, prayers, persecutions, and slanders; yea, his tears, his sweat, his blood, and all that ever he did and suffered in the space of three and thirty years, with his passion, death, burial, resurrection, and ascension: for they are all yours. And as Christ passeth over all his estate unto his spouse, so doth he require that she should pass over all unto him. Wherefore, you being now married unto Christ, you must give all that you have of your own unto him; and truly you have nothing of your own but sin, and therefore

---

John Careless, in a letter to William Tyms, seems to me, to run more smooth, by means of the same addition, though I doubt if the word stood so in the original copy. " Christ (saith he) is made unto us holiness, righteousness, and justification; he hath clothed us in all his merits—and taken to himself all our sin—so that if any should be now CONDEMNED for the same, it must needs be Jesus Christ, who hath taken them upon him." The sufferers mirror, p. 66. and in the old confession of faith, art. 9. according to the ancient copies, it is said, ' The clean innocent Lamb of God, was damned in the presence of an earthly judge, that we uld be absolved befoir the tribunal seat of our God." But in the copy standing in Knox's history, reprinted at Edinburgh, anno 1644. 'tis read condemned."

* Bernardine Ochinis serm.

S 2

you muft give him that. I befeech you then * fay unto
Chrift with bold confidence, I give to thee my dear hufband, my unbelief, my miftruft, my pride, my arrogancy,
my ambition, my wrath and anger, my envy, my covetoufnefs, my evil thoughts, affections and defires: I make
one bundle of thefe, and all my other offences, and give
them unto thee †. And thus was Chrift " made fin for

---

* Ibid. in his ferm. how a Chriftian muft make his laft will.
† This gift would indeed be a very unfuitable return, for all
the benefits received from Chrift, by virtue of the fpiritual
marriage : if he did not deal with us in the way of free grace;
like unto a phyfician, who defires nothing of a poor man full of
fores, but that he will employ him in the cure of them. But
this gift, fuch as it is; as it is all we have of our own to give;
fo one needs make no queftion, but it will be very acceptable.
Pfal. lv. 22. " Caft thy burden upon the Lord, and he fhall
fuftain thee;" not only thy burden of duty, fuffering and fuccefs,
but of fin too, wherewith thou art heavy laden, Matth. xi 28.
We are allowed not only to give him our burden, but to caft
it upon him. He knows very well, that all thefe evils mentioned,
and many more, are in the heart of the beft: yet doth he fay,
Prov. xxiii. 26. " My fon, give me thine heart;" notwithftanding of the wretched ftuff, he knows to be in it. In the language
of the Holy Ghoft, thefe things, as black as they are, are a gift,
by divine appointment to be given. Lev. xvi. 21. fpeaking of
the fcape goat, an eminent type of Chrift, he faith, " And Aaron
fhall—confefs over him, all the iniquities of the children of
Ifrael, and all their tranfgreffions, in all their fins: and he fhall
'GIVE them upon the head of the goat.' Thus the original
exprefleth what we read, " putting them," &c. view again
page 59. and note ‡.
  Now, the end, for which the finner is to give thefe to Chrift,
is two-fold, (1.) For removing of the guilt of them. (2) For
the mortifying of them. And tho' this is not an eafy way of
mortification, fince the way of believing is not eafy, but more
difficult than all the popifh aufterities; forafmuch as thefe laft
are more agreeable to nature : yet it is indeed the fhort way to
mortification, becaufe the only way ; without which, the practice of all other directions, will be but as fo many cyphers,
without a figure ftanding on their head, fignifying nothing, for
true Chriftian mortification, Acts xv. 9. " Purifying their hearts
by faith." Rom. vi. 6. " Knowing this, that our old man is
crucified with him." And viii. 13. " If ye through the Spirit,

us, that knew no sin, that we might be made the righteousness of God in him," 2 Cor. v. 21 * Now then, saith
Luther †, let us compare these things together, and we
shall find inestimable treasure. Christ is full of grace,
life, and saving health; and the soul is freight-full of all
sin, death, and damnation: but let faith come betwixt
these two, and it shall come to pass that Christ shall be
laden with sin, death and hell; and unto the soul shall be
imputed grace, life, and salvation. Who then (saith he)
is able to value the royalty of this marriage accordingly?
Who is able to comprehend the glorious riches of his
grace, where this rich and righteous husband, Christ, doth
take unto wife, this poor and wicked harlot, redeemed her
from all devils, and garnishing her with all his own
jewels ‡. So that you (as the same Luther saith) through
the assuredness of your faith in Christ your husband, are
delivered from all sins, made safe from death, guarded
from hell, and endowed with everlasting righteousness,
life, and saving health of this your husband Christ. And
therefore you are under the covenant of grace, and freed
from the law, as it is the covenant of works; for (as
Mr Ball truly saith) at one and the same time, a man
cannot be under the covenant of works, and the covenant
of grace ‖.

---

do mortify the deeds of the body, ye shall live." Gal. v. 24.
" And they that are Christ's, have crucified the flesh, with the
affections and lusts;" namely, nailing them to the cross of
Christ, by faith.

* THUS, namely, by the giving of our sins to him; not by
believers, but by his Father, as saith the text, He (not we)
" made him to be sin for us." Nevertheless, the Lord's laying
our iniquities upon Christ, is good warrant for every believer,
to give his sins, in particular, upon him; the latter being a
cordial falling-in with, a practical approbation, and taking the
benefit of the former.

† Christ. Lib. p. 21, 22.

‡ Ibid. p. 24.   ‖ On the cov. p. 15.

Neo. Sir, I do not yet well know how to conceive of this freedom from the law, as it is the covenant of works; and therefore I pray you make it as plain to me as you can.

Evan. For the true and clear underſtanding of this point, you are to conſider, that when Jeſus Chriſt, the ſecond Adam, had, in the behalf of his choſen, perfectly fulfilled the law, as it is the covenant of works *; divine juſtice delivered that bond in to Chriſt, who " utterly cancelled that hand-writing," Col. ii. 14. So that none of his choſen were to have any more to do with it, nor it with them. And now, you, by your believing in Chriſt, having manifeſted, that you are one, who was choſen in him before the foundation of the world, Eph. i. 4. his fulfilling of that covenant, and cancelling that hand-writing, is imputed unto you: and ſo you are acquitted and abſolved from all your tranſgreſſions againſt that covenant, either paſt, preſent, or to come †; and ſo you are juſtified, as the apoſtle ſaith,

---

* Namely, by doing perfectly, what is demanded to be done, by virtue of its commanding power; and ſuffering completely, what it demanded to be borne by virtue of its condemning power.

† Although believers, in the firſt moment of their union with Chriſt by faith, are delivered from the law, as it is the covenant of works; and therefore their after-ſins, neither are, nor can be, formally, tranſgreſſions of that covenant: yet they are interpretatively ſo; giving a plain proof of what they would have done againſt that covenant, had they been under it ſtill. And foraſmuch as they could never have been freed from it; had not the glorious Mediator wrought their deliverance, by fulfilling it in their room and ſtead: all their ſins whatſoever, from their birth to their death, after, as well as before, their union with Chriſt, were charged upon him, as tranſgreſſions againſt that covenant; and as ſuch are pardoned to them, in their juſtification. Even as, who redeems a ſlave, muſt pay in proportion to the ſervice, which, 'tis ſuppoſed, he would have done his maſter, during life: and the ſlave is looſed, from all obligation to theſe ſeveral pieces of ſervice unto that maſter, upon the ranſom paid, in compenſation of all and every one of them. And thus our

" Freely by his grace, through the redemption that is in Jesus Christ," Rom. iii. 24.

§ 6. *Ant.* I pray you, Sir, give me leave to speak a word by the way; was not he justified before this time?

Evan. If he did not believe in Christ before this time, as I conceive he did. not; then certainly he was not justified before this time

Ant. But, Sir, you know, as the apostle saith, " It is God that justifieth ;" and God is eternal : and as you have shewed, Christ may. may be said to have fulfilled the covenant of works from all eternity : and if he be Christ's now, then was he Christ's from all eternity. And therefore, as I conceive, he was justified from all eternity.

Evan. Indeed God is from all eternity : and in respect of God's accepting of Christ's undertaking to fulfil the covenant of works, he fulfilled it from all eternity : and in respect of God's electing of him, he was Christ's from

---

author saith, that a believer, in his justification, is acquitted from all his transgressions against the covenant of works, not only past and present, but to come. So that he leaves no ground to question, but to come. So that he leaves no ground to question, but Christ satisfied for all the sins of believers whatsoever, whether in their state of regeneracy, or irregeneracy. Nor does he make the least insinuation, that the sins of believers, after their union with Christ, are not properly transgressions of that law, which was (yea, and to unbelievers still is) in the covenant of works ; but, on the contrary, expressly teaches, that it is the very same law of the ten commands, which is the law of Christ, and which the believer transgresseth, that was, and is in the covenant of works. And although the revenging wrath of God, and eternal death, are not threatened against the sins of believers, after their union with Christ ; and that for this one reason, that that wrath, and that death (the eternity whereof rose not from the nature of the thing, but the infirmity of the sufferer, and therefore could have no place in the Son of God) were not only threatened before, but executed too upon their surety, Jesus Christ, to whom they are united : it is manifest there was great need of Christ's being made a curse, for those sins of believers, as well as for these preceeding their union with him.

all eternity *. And therefore it is true, in respect of God's decree, he was justified from all eternity † ; and he was justified meritoriously in the death and resurection of Christ ‡ : but yet he was not justified actually, till he did actually believe in Christ; for, saith the apostle, Acts xiii 39. " By him, all that believe are justified" ‖. So that in the act of justifying, faith and Christ must have a mutual

---

*, Bolton's true bounds, p. 289.

† " The sentence of justification, was as it were conceived in the mind of God, by the decree of justifying. Gal. iii. 8. " The scripture foreseeing that God would justify the heathen through faith." Ames. Med. cap. xxxvii. § 9. " In which sense, grace is said to be given us in Christ, before the world began, 2 Tim. i. 9. Turret. Loc. 16. Q. 9. Th. 11. " Sins were pardoned from eternity in the mind of God " Rutherford's Exerc. Apolog. Ex. 1. C. 2. § 21 p. 53. The same Rutherford adds, " 'Tis one thing for a man to be justified in Christ, and that from eternity; and another, for a man to be justified in Christ in time, according to the gospel-covenant.—Faith is not so much as the instrument of the eternal and immanent justification and remission of sins." Ibid. p 55.

‡ " Justification may be considered, as to the execution of it in time: and that again, either as to the purchase of it, which was made by the death of Christ on the cross, concerning which it is said, Rom. v. 9. 10. That we are justified and reconciled to God, by the blood of Christ; and that Christ reconciled all things unto God, by the blood of the cross, Col. i. 20. And elsewhere, Christ is said to be raised again for our justification, Rom. iv. 25. Because, as in him dying, we died; so in him raised again and justified, we are justified ; that is, we have a certain and undoubted pledge and foundation of our justification —Or as to the application of it, &c. Turret. ubi sup. The sentence of justification was pronounced in Christ, our head, risen from the dead, 2 Cor v. 19. Ames. ubi sup. We were virtually justified, especially when Christ, having finished the purchase of our salvation, was justified, and we in him, as our head. 1 Tim. iii. 16. 2 Cor. v. 19. Esen. Comp. Cap xv. § 25.

‖ " Actual justification is done in time, and follows faith. Turret. Loc 16 Q 9. Th. 3. " Justification is done formally when an elect man, effectually called, and so apprehended of Christ, apprehends Christ again." Rom. viii. 39. Essen. ubi. sup.

relation; and muſt always concur and meet together; faith as the action which apprehendeth; and Chriſt the object, which is apprehended : for neither doth Chriſt juſtify without faith, neither doth faith, except it be in Chriſt *.

Ant. Truly, Sir, you have indifferently well ſatisfied me in this point : and ſurely, I like it marvelous well, that you conclude no faith juſtifieth, but that, whoſe object is Chriſt.

Evan. The very truth is, though a man believe that God is merciful and true of his promiſe, and that he hath his elect number from the beginning; and that he himſelf is one of that number : yet if this faith do not eye Chriſt, if it be not in God as he is in Chriſt, it will not ſerve the turn : for God cannot be comfortably thought upon out of Chriſt our Mediator † : for if we find not God in Chriſt, ſaith Calvin ‡, ſalvation cannot be known. Wherefore, neighbour Neophytus, I will ſay unto you, as ſweet Mr. Bradford ſaid unto a gentlewoman in your caſe, thus then, if you would be quiet and certain in conſcience, then let your faith burſt forth thro' all things;

" The ſentence of juſtification is pronounced virtually, from that firſt relation, which ariſeth from faith. - Rom. viii. 1. Ameſ. ubi ſup.

Upon the whole, 'its evident, our author keeps the path troden by orthodox divines on the ſubject. And though, in order to anſwer the objections of his adverſary, he uſeth the ſchool-terms, of being juſtified in reſpect of God's decree, meritoriouſly, and actually; agreeable to the practice of other ſound divines : yet, otherwiſe he begins and ends his deciſion of this controverſy, by aſſerting in plain and ſimple terms, without any diſtinction at all, that a man is not juſtified, before he believe, or without faith. So his anſwer amounts juſt to this, that " God did, from all eternity, decree to juſtify all the elect; and Chriſt did, in the fulneſs of time, die for their ſins, and riſe again for their juſtification : nevertheleſs, they are not juſtified, until the holy Spirit doth in due time actually apply Chriſt unto them." Weſtm. Confeſſ. Chap. 11. art. 4.

* Mr John Fox upon election.
† Dr Sibbs ſoul's conflict, p. 55.   § Inſt. p. 155.

not only that you have within you, but also whatsoever is
in heaven, earth and hell ; and never rest until it come
to Christ crucified, and the eternal sweet mercy and
goodness of God in Christ.

§ 7. *Neo.* But, Sir, I am not satisfied concerning the
point you touched before ; and therefore, I pray you,
proceed to shew me how far forth I am delivered from
the law, as it is the covenant of works.

Evan. Truly as it is the covenant of works, you are
wholly and altogether delivered and set free from it ;
you are dead to it, and it is dead to you ; and if it be
dead to you, then it can do you neither good nor hurt ;
and if you be dead to it, you can expect neither good
nor hurt from it *. Consider, man, I pray you, that,

---

* Concerning the deliverance from the law, which, according
to the scripture, is the privilege of believers, purchased unto
them by Jesus Christ ; there are two opinions equally contrary
to the word of God, and to one another. The one, of the
legalist, that believers are under the law, even as it is the covenant of works : the other of the Antinomian, that believers are
not at all under the law, no, not as it is a rule of life. Betwixt
these extremes, both of them destructive of true holiness and
gospel-obedience, our author, with orthodox divines, holds the
middle path ; asserting (and in the proper place proving) that
believers are under the law, as a rule of life, but free from it, as
it is the covenant of works. To be delivered from the law, as
it is the covenant of works, is no more, but to be delivered
from the covenant of works ; and the asserting, that believers
are delivered from the law, as it is the covenant of works, doth
necessarily import, that they are under the law, in some other
respect thereto contradistinguished : and forasmuch as the
author teaches, that believers are under the law, as it is the
law of Christ, and a rule of life to them, 'tis reasonable to
conclude, that to be it. He must needs, under the term, the
covenant of works, understand and comprehend, the law of the
ten commands : because no man, understanding what the covenant of works is, can speak of it, but he must, under that term,
understand and comprehend the ten commands, even as none
can speak of a man, with knowledge of the sense of that word,
but under that term, must understand and comprehend an
organic body, as well as a soul. But 'tis manifest, that the law

as I faid before, you are now under another covenant, to wit, the còvenant of grace ; and you cannot be under

---

of the ten commands, without the form of the covenant of works upon it, is not the thing he understands by that term, the covenant of works. Neither is the form of the covenant of works (which is no more the covenant itself, than the foul without the body is the man) effential to the ten commands, fo that they cannot be without it. See p. 5. note. If it be faid, that the author, by the covenant of works, underftands the moral law, as it is defined Larg. Catech. Q. 92. it is granted; but then, it amounts to no more, but, that by the covenant of works, he underftands the covenant of works; for by the moral law there, is underftood the covenant of works, as has been already evinced, page 7. note.

The doctrine of believers freedom from the covenant of works, or from the law as that covenant, is of greateft importance, and is exprefsly taught. Larg. Catech. Q. 97. " They that are regenerate, and believe in Chrift, be delivered from the moral law, as a covenant of works. Rom. vi. 14. Rom. vii. 4, 6. Gal. iv. 4, 5. Weftm. Confeff. chap 19 art 6. " True believers be not under the law, as a covenant of works." To thefe I fubjoin one teftimony, from the Pract. Ufe of fav. knowledge, Tit. for ftrengthening the man's faith, &c. Rom. viii. " Albeit the apoftle himfelf, (brought in here for example's caufe) and all other true believers in Chrift, be, by nature, under the law of fin and death, or under the covenant of works, (called the law of fin and death, becaufe it bindeth fin and death upon us, till Chrift fet us free) yet the law of the fpirit of life in Chrift Jefus, or the covenant of grace (fo called becaufe it doth enable and quicken a man to a fpiritual life through Chrift) doth fet the apoftle, and all true believers free from the covenant of works, or the law of fin and death." See more Tit, for convincing a man of judgment by the law. Para. 2. and laft. and Tit Evidences of true faith.

Now, delivering from a covenant, being the diffolution of a relation, which admits not of degrees; believers being delivered from the covenant of works, muft be wholly and altogether fet free from it.

This appears alfo from the believer's being dead to it, and it dead to him, of which before, at large.

There is a twofold death competent to a believer, with refpect to the law, as it is the covenant of works; and fo to the law as fuch, with refpect to the believer. (1.) The believer is dead to

two covenants at once, neither wholly, nor partly:
and therefore, as, before you believed, you were
wholly under the covenant of works, as Adam left
both you, and all his posterity after his fall; so now,
since you have believed. you are wholly under the
covenant of grace. Assure yourself then, that no minister
or preacher of God's word, hath any warrant to say
unto you hereafter, either do this and this duty, contained in the law ; and avoid this and this sin, forbidden.
in the law ; and God will justify thee, and save thy
soul : or do it not, and he will condemn thee, and damn
thee.* : No, no, you are now set free, both from the

---

it really, and in point of duty, while he carries himself as one
who is dead to it. And this I take to be comprehended in that
saying of the apostle, Gal. ii 19. " I through the law, am dead
to the law." - In the best of the children of God here, there are
such remains of the legal disposition, and inclination of heart,
to the way of the covenant of works; that as they are never
quite free of it in their best duties, so at some times their services
smell so rank of it, as if they were alive to the law, and still dead
to Christ. And sometimes the Lord, for their correction, trial
and exercise of faith, suffers the ghost of the dead husband, the
law, as a covenant of works, to come in upon their souls, and
make demands on them, command, threaten, and afright them,
as if they were alive to it, and it to them. And 'tis one of the
hardest pieces of practical religion, to be dead to the law in
such cases. This death to it, admits of degrees, is not alike in
all believers, and is perfect in none, till the death of the body.
But of this kind of death to the law, the question proceeds not
here. 2. The believer is dead to it relatively, and in point of
privilege: the relation betwixt him and it is desolved, even as
the relation between a husband and wife is desolved by death,
Rom. vii. 4. " Wherefore, my brethren, ye also are become
dead to the law, by the body of Christ, that ye should be
married to another." This can admit of no degrees, but is
perfect in all believers: so that they are wholly and altogether
set free from it, in point of privilege, upon which the question
here proceeds ; and in this respect, they cannot expect neither
good nor hurt from it.

* See pag. 116 note. " Believers be not under the law, as a
covenant of works, to be thereby justified or condemned."
Westm. Confess. Chap. 19 Art. 6.

commanding and condemning power of the covenant of works *. So that I will fay unto you, as the apoſtle

---

* From the general concluſion already laid down and proven, namely, that believers are wholly and altogether ſet free from the covenant of works, or from the law as it is that covenant, this neceſſarily follows. But to conſider particulars, for further clearing of this weighty point, (1.) That the covenant of work's hath no power to juſtify a ſinner, in regard of his utter inability to pay the penalty, and to fulfil the condition of it, is clear from the apoſtle's teſtimony, Rom. viii. 3. " Whit the law could not do, in that it was weak through the fleſh, God ſending his own Son," &c. (2.) That the believer is not under the condemning power of it, appears from Gal. iii. 13. " Chriſt hath redeemed us from the curſe of the law, being made a curſe for us." Rom. viii. 1. " There is therefore now no condemnation to them which are in Chriſt Jeſus." Ver. 33, 34. " It is God that juſtifieth: who is he that condemneth?" (3.) As to its commanding power, believers are not under it neither. For, 1. Its commanding, and condemning power, in caſe of tranſgreſſion, are inſeparable. For, by the ſentence of that covenant, every breaker of its commands, is bound over to death, Gal. iii. 10. " Curſed is every one that continueth not in all things, which are written in the book of the law, to do them." And whatſoever it ſaith, it ſaith to them who are under it, Rom. iii. 19. Therefore, if believers be under its commanding power, they muſt needs be under its condemning power, yea, and actually bound over to death ; foraſmuch as they are, without queſtion, breakers of its commands, if they be indeed under its commanding power.

2. If, as to any ſet of men, the juſtifying and condemning power be removed from that law, which God gave to Adam, as a covenant of works, and to all mankind in him : Then the covenant-form of that law is done away, as to them ; ſo that there is not a covenant of works in being unto them, to have a commanding power over them. But ſuch is the caſe of believers, that law can neither juſtify them, nor condemn them: therefore there is no covenant of works in being betwixt God and them, to have a commanding power over them ; our Lord Jeſus " blotted out the hand-writing, took it out of the way, nailing it to his croſs," Col. ii. 14.

3. Believers are dead to the law, as it is the covenant of works, and married to another, Rom. vii. 4. Therefore they

T

faith unto the believing Hebrews, Heb. xii. 18, 22, 24.
" You are not come to Mount Sinai, that might be touched, and that burned with fire, nor unto' blackness and
darkness, and tempest;, but you are come unto' Mount
Zion, the city of the living God; and to Jesus the
Mediator of 'the new covenant " So that (to speak
with holy reverence) God cannot, by virtue of the covenant of works, either require of you any obedience, or
punish you for any disobedience;: no, he cannot, by virtue

----

are set free from the commanding power of the first husband,
the covenant of works.

4. They are not under it, Rom. vi. 14. " Ye are not under
the law, but under grace:" How then can it have a commanding power over them.

5. The consideration of the nature of the commands of the
covenant of works, may sufficiently clear this point. Its commands bind to perfect obedience, under the pain of the curse,
which, on every slip, is bound upon the transgressor, Gal. iii. 10;
" Cursed is every one 'that continueth not in all things," &c.
But Christ hath redeemed believers from the curse, ver. 13. and
the law they are under speaks in softer terms, Psal. lxxxix. 31, 32.
" If they break my statutes—then will I visit their transgression
with the rod," &c. Moreover, it commands obedience, upon
the ground of the strength to perform, given to mankind in
Adam, which is now gone; and affords no new strength; for
there's no promise of strength for duty, belonging to the covenant of works. And to state believers under the covenant of
works, to receive commands for their duty, and under the
covenant of grace, for the promise of strength to perform; looks
very unlike to the beautiful order of the dispensation of grace,
held forth to us in the word, Rom. vi. 14. " Ye are NOT under
the law, BUT under grace."

Lastly, Our Lord Jesus put himself under the commanding
power of the covenant of works, and gave it perfect obedience,
to deliver his people from under it, Gal. iv. 4. 5. " God sent
forth his Son, made of a woman, made under the law, to
redeem them that were under the law." That they, then,
should put their necks under that yoke again, cannot but be
highly dishonouring to this crucified Christ, who disarmed the
law of its thunders, defaced the obligation of it, as a covenant,
and, as it were, ground the stones upon which it was wrote, to
powder, Charnock, vol. 2. p 531.

of that covenant, so much as threaten you, or give you an angry word, or shew you an angry look : for indeed he can see no sin in you, as a transgression of that covenant; for saith the apostle, " where there is no law, there is no transgression," Rom. iv. 15.* And therefore, tho' here-after you do, through frailty, transgress any of all the ten commandments † ; yet do you not thereby transgress the covenant of works ; there is no such covenant, now, betwixt God and you ‡.

And therefore, tho' hereafter you shall hear such a voice as this, If thou wilt be saved, keep the commandments ; or, " Cursed is every one that continueth not in all things which are written in the book of the law, to do them;" nay, though you hear the voice of thunder, and a fearful noise ; nay, though you see blackness and darkness, and feel a great tempest ; that is to say, though you hear us that are preachers, according to our commission Isa. lviii. 1. " Lift up your voice like a trumpet." in threatening hell and damnation to sinners, and, transgressors of the law :

---

* And therefore, since there is no covenant of works (or law of works, as 'tis called, Rom. iii. 27.) betwixt God and the believer; it is manifest there can be no transgressing of it, in their case. God requires obedience of believers ; and not only threatens them, gives them angry words and looks, but brings heavy judgments on them, for their disobedience; but the promise of strength, and penalty of fatherly wrath only, annexed to the commands requiring obedience of them, and the anger of God against them, purged of the curse; do evidently discover, that none of these come to them, in the channel of the covenant of works.

† And though all the sins of believers are not sins of daily infirmity ; yet they are all, sins of frailty, Gal. v. 17. " For the flesh lusteth against the spirit, and the spirit against the flesh— So that you cannot do the things that ye would." Rom. vii. 19. " The evil which I would not, that I do." See ver. 15, 17. and vi. 12.

‡ Thus far of the believer's complete deliverance from the covenant of works, or from the law, namely, as it is the covenant of works. Follows the practical use to be made of it, by the believer. And, I. in hearing of the word.

T 2

though these be the words of God, yet are you not to think that they are spoken to you *. No, no, the apostle assures you, that "there is no condemnation to them, that are in Christ Jesus," Rom. viii. 1. Believe it, man, God never threatens eternal death, after he hath given to a man eternal life †. Nay, the truth is, God never speaks to a believer out of Christ; and in Christ he speaks not a word in the terms of the covenant of works ‡. And if the law, of itself, should presume to come into your conscience, and say, herein, and herein, thou hast transgressed, and broken me; and therefore thou owest so much, and so much to divine justice, which must be satisfied, or else I will take hold on thee: then answer you and say, O law, be it known unto thee, that I am now married unto Christ, and so I am under covert ||; and therefore if you charge me with any debt, thou must enter thine action against my husband Christ, for the wife is not sueable at the law, but the husband: but the truth is, I through him am dead to thee, O law, and thou art dead to me; and therefore justice hath nothing to do with me, for it judgeth according to the law. § ¶

---

* Though they are God's own sayings, found in his written word; and spoken by his servants, as having commission from him for that effect: yet, forasmuch as they are the language of the law, as it is his covenant of works; they are directed only to those, who are under that covenant, Rom. iii. 19. and not to believers, who are not under it.

† And to believers he hath given eternal life already, according to the scripture. See p. 116. note.

‡ Follows II. The use of it, in conflicts of conscience, with the law, in its demands; sin in its guilt; Satan in his accusations; death in its terrors.

|| Greenham's afflicted conscience, p. 70.

§ Bern. Ochin, in his serm. how to answer before the judgment seat.

¶ He begins with the conflict with the law: for as the apostle teacheth, "The sting of death is sin, and the strength of sin is the law," 1 Cor. xv. 56. While the law retains its power over a man, death hath its sting, and sin its strength, against him: but

And if it yet reply and fay, I, but "Good works muſt be done, and the commandments muſt be kept, if thou wilt obtain falvation * :" then anſwer you, and

---

if once he is dead to the law, wholly and altogether ſet free from it, as it is the covenant of works; then ſin, hath loſt its ſtrength, death its ſting, and Satan his plea againſt him. That the author ſtill ſpeaks of the law, as it is the covenant of works, from the commanding and condemning power of which believers are delivered; and no otherways; cannot reaſonably be queſtioned; ſince he is ſtill purſuing the practical uſe of the doctrine, and not it as ſuch: and having before ſpoken of it, as acting by commiſſion from God, he treats of it, here, as acting (as it were) of its own proper motion, and not by any ſuch commiſſion. To theſe who are under the law, the law ſpeaks its demands and terrors, as ſent from God; but to believers, who are not under it, it cannot ſo ſpeak, but of itſelf. Rom. viii. 15. "For ye have not received the ſpirit of bondage again to fear."

Now, in the conflict, the believer hath with the law or covenant of works, the author puts two caſes; in the which the conſcience needs to be ſoundly directed, as in caſes of the utmoſt weight.

The firſt caſe is this, The law, attempting to exerciſe its condemning power over him, accuſeth him of tranſgreſſion, demands of him ſatisfaction to the juſtice of God for his ſin, and threatens to hale him to execution. In this caſe, the author dare not adviſe the afflicted to ſay, with the ſervant in the parable, Matth. xviii. 26. "Have patience with me, and I will pay thee all:" but he teacheth him to devolve his burden wholly upon his Surety. He bids him plead, that ſince he is married to Chriſt, whatever action the law may pretend to be competent to it, for the ſatisfaction of juſtice, upon the account of his ſin, it muſt ly betwixt the law and Chriſt, the buſband: but that, in very deed, there remains no place for ſuch action; foraſmuch as, thro' Jeſus Chriſt's ſuffering and ſatisfying to the full, he is ſet free from the law, and owes nothing to juſtice, nor to the law, upon that ſcore. If any man will adventure to deal in other terms, with the law in this caſe, his experience will at length ſufficiently diſcover his miſtake. Now, 'tis manifeſt, that this relates to the caſe of juſtification.

* Here is the ſecond caſe, namely, the law attempting to exerciſe its commanding power over the believer, requires him to do good works, and to keep the commandments, if he will obtain ſalvation. This comes in natively, in the ſecond place. The author could not, reaſonably, reſt ſatisfied, with the believer's being delivered from the curſe of the covenant of works, from the debt owing to divine juſtice, according to its

T 3

penal fanction; if he had, he would have left the afflicted still in the lurch, in the point of juftification, and of inheriting eternal life; he would have propofed Chrift to him, only as a half-faviour, and left as much of the law's plea behind, without an anfwer. as would have concluded him incapable of being juftified before God, and made an heir of eternal life: for the law, as it is the covenant of works, being broken, hath a twofold demand on the finner, each of which muft be anfwered, before he can be juftified. The one is a demand of fatisfaction for fin, arifing from, and according to its penal fanction: this demand was made in the preceeding cafe, and folidly anfwered. But there remains yet another, namely, the demand of perfect obedience, arifing from, and according to, the fettled condition of that covenant: and the afflicted muft have wherewith to anfwer it alfo: otherwife he fhall ftill fink in deep mire, where there is no ftanding. For as no judge can abfolve a man, meerly on his having paid the penalty of a broken contract, to which he was obliged by, and attour the fulfilling of the condition: fo no man can be juftified before God, nor have a right to life. till this demand of the law be alfo fatisfied in his cafe. Then, and not till then, is the law's mouth ftopt, in point of his juftification. Thus Adam, before his fall, was free from the curfe; yet neither was, nor could be juftified, and entitled to life, until he had run the courfe of his obedience, prefcribed him, by the law as the covenant of works. Accordingly, we are taught, that God juftifieth finners, not only by imputing the fatisfaction, but alfo the OBEDIENCE of Chrift unto them. Weftm. Confeff. Chap. 11 Art. 1 And that juftification is an act of God's free grace, wherein we (not only) pardoneth all our fins, (but accepteth us as righteous in his fight. Short. Catech.

Here then is the fecond demand of the law, namely, the demand of perfect obedience, refpecting the cafe of juftification, no lefs than the demand of fatisfaction for fin. And it is propofed in fuch terms, as the fcripture ufeth to exprefs the felf-fame thing by. Luke x 28. " This do, and thou fhalt live." Matth. xix. 17 " If thou wilt enter into life, keep the commandments." In both which paffages, our Lord propofeth this demand of the covenant of works, for the conviction of the proud Legalifts with whom he there had to do And the truth is, that the terms, in which this demand ftands here conceived, are fo very agreeable to the ftile and language of the covenant of works, expreffed in thefe texts and elfewhere, that the law, without receding in the leaft from the propriety of expreffion, might have addreffed innocent Adam, in the very fame terms; changing only the word falvation into life, becaufe he was not yet miferable; and fo faying to him, good works muft be done, and the commandments muft be kept, if thou wilt obtain life. What impropriety there could have been in this faying, while as yet, there was no covenant known in the world, but the covenant of works, I see not. Even innocent Adam was not, by his works, to obtain life, in the way of proper merit; but in virtue of compact only.

Now, this being the case, one may plainly perceive, that in the true answer to it, there can be no place for bringing in any holiness, righteousness, good works, and keeping of the commandments, but Christ's only : for nothing else can satisfy this demand of the law. And if a believer should acknowledge the necessity of his own holiness and good works, in this point; and so set about them, in order to answer this demand : then he should grosly and abominably pervert the end, for which the Lord requires them of him; putting his own holiness and obedience, in the room of Christ's imputed obedience. And so should he fix himself in the mire, out of which he could never escape, until he gave over that way, and betook himself again to what Christ alone has done, for satisfying this demand of the law. But that the excluding of our holiness, good works, and keeping of the commandments, from any part in this matter, militates nothing against the absolute necessity of holiness in its proper place, (without which, in mens own persons, no man shall see the Lord) is a point too clear among sound Protestant divines, to be here insisted upon.

And hence our author could not instruct Neophytus to say, in this conflict with the law or covenant of works, it is my sincere resolution, in the strength of grace, to follow peace with all men, and holiness. Neither would any sound Protestant divine, have put such an answer into the mouth of the afflicted in this case : knowing that our evangelical holiness and good works, (suppose we could attain unto them before justification) would be rejected by the law, as filthy rags : forasmuch as the law acknowledgeth no holiness, no good works, no keeping of the commandments, but what is every way perfect ; and will never be satisfied with sincere resolutions, to do, in the strength of grace to be given; but requires doing in perfection, in the strength of grace given already, Gal. iii. 10. Therefore our author sends the afflicted unto Jesus Christ, the surety, for all that's demanded of him by the law or covenant of works ; and teaches him, in this case, to plead Christ's works and keeping of the commands: and this is the only safe way, which all true Christians will find themselves obliged to take, at long-run, in this conflict.

The difficulty raised on this head, is owing to that antiscriptural principle, that believers are under the commanding power of the covenant of works, which is overthrown before.

The case itself, and the answer to it at large, is taken from

say, I am already faved *, before thou cameft; there-

Luther, fermon of the loft fheep, page (mihi) 77, 78. and fermon
upon the hymn of Zacharias, p. (mihi) 50.

* Saved, to wit, really, though not perfectly; even as a drown-
ing man is faved, when his head is got above the water, and he,
leaning on his deliverer, is making towards the fhore: in this
cafe, the believer hath no more need of the law, or covenant
of works, than fuch a man hath, of one, who, to fave him,
would lay a weight up on him, that would make him fink again
beneath the ftream. Obferve the manner of fpeaking and reafoning, ufed upon this head, Tit. iii. 5. "Not by works of
righteoufnefs, which we have DONE, but according to his
mercy he SAVED us, by the wafhing of REGENERATION, and
RENEWING of the Holy Ghoft." Eph. ii. 8 9, 10. "For by
grace ARE ye SAVED, through faith—not of WORKS, leaft any
man fhould boaft. FOR we are his workmanfhip, created in
Chrift Jefus, UNTO good works." Here, (1.) 'Tis undeniable,
efpecially according to the original words, that the apoftle afferts
believers to be faved already. (2.) Denying that we are faved
by works, which we have done, be plainly enough intimates,
that we are faved by the works, which Chrift hath done.
(3.) He argues againft falvation by our works, upon this very
ground, that our good works are the fruit following our being
faved, and the end for which we are faved. Thus he, at once,
overthroweth the doctrine of falvation by our good works, and
eftablifheth the neceffity of them, as of breathing, and other
actions of life, to a man faved from death. (4.) He fheweth
that inherent holinefs is an effential part of falvation, without
which, it can no more confift, than a man, without a reafonable
foul: for, according to the apoftle, we are faved by our being
regenerated, renewed, created in Chrift Jefus, unto good works.
And fo is our juftification alfo, with all the privileges depending thereupon. In one word, the falvation beftowed on be-
livers, comprehends both holinefs and happinefs. Thus the
apoftle Peter difapproves that principle (Acts xv. 1. "Except ye
be circumcifed after the manner of Mofes, ye cannot be faved,")
from his own obfervation of the contrary, namely, that God
purified the hearts of the Gentiles by faith, ver 9. Adding for
the part of the jews, who were circumcifed, ver. 11. "We
believe that through the grace of the Lord Jefus Chrift, we
fhall be faved even as they," i e. Even as they were laved, to
wit, by faith without the works of the law. And the apoftle
Paul encountering the fame error, carries on the difpute in
thefe terms, that a man is not juftified by works, Gal. chap. ii.
and iii. From whence one may conclude, that juftification

fore I have no need of thy presence *, for in Christ

---

doth no further differ from salvation, in the scripture-sense, than an essential part from the whole.

This is the doctrine of holy Luther, and of our author after him, upon this head, here and elsewhere. And the disuse of this manner of speaking, and in setting of salvation so far from justification, as heaven is from earth, are not without danger, as leaving room for works to obtain salvation by.

" They that believe have already everlasting life, and there-fore undoubtedly are justified and holy, without all their own labour." Luther chof. serm. sermon 10 p. (mihi) 113. How hes God then remeided thy miserie ? He hes forg'ven all my sinnes, and freed me fra the reward thereof, and made me righteous, halie, and happy, to live for ever, and that of his free grace allenerly, be the merites of Jesus Christ, and working of the Haly Ghaist." Mr James Melvil's Catech. propine of a pastor, page. 44 " Now, being made truly and really partakers of Christ, and his righteousness by faith only; and so justified, saved, and counted truly righteous—we are to fee, what God craveth of us in our awin part, to witness our thankfulness." Mr John Davidson's Catech. p. 27. see Palat. Catech. Q. 86. " God de-livereth his elect out of it, (viz. the estate of sin and misery) and bringeth them unto an estate of salvation by the second cove-nant." Larg. Catech. Q. 30. And surely one cannot be in a state of salvation, who is not really saved; more than one can be in a state of health and liberty, who is not really saved from sickness and slavery " Those whom God hath predestinated unto life, and those only, he is pleased, in his appointed and accepted time, effectually to call, by his word and Spirit, out of that state of sin and death, in which they are by nature, to grace and salvation—Effectually drawing them to Jesus Christ." Westm. Confess. Chap. 10. Art. 1. Whence one may easily perceive, that a sinner, drawn to Jesus Christ, is saved; tho' not yet carried to heaven.

* A good reason, why a soul united to Jesus Christ, and already saved by him, really tho' not perfectly, hath no need of the presence of her first husband the law, or covenant of works: namely, because she hath, in Christ her head and present husband, all things necessary to save her perfectly, that is, to make her compleatly holy and happy. If it were not so, be-lievers might yet despair of attaining to it : since Christ shareth his office of Saviour with none ; neither is there salvation in any

I have all things at once: neither need I any thing more than is neceſſary * to ſalvation †. He is my righteouſ-

---

other, whether in whole or in part, Acts iv. 12. But ſurely believers have all that is neceſſary to complete their ſalvation in Jeſus Chriſt: foraſmuch as he of God is made unto us wiſdom, and righteouſneſs, and ſanctification, and redemption; in the compaſs of which, there is ſufficient proviſion for all the wants of all his people. It is the great ground of their comfort, that it " pleaſed the Father, that in Him ſhould all fulneſs dwell," Col. i. 1. And it becomes them, with their whole hearts to approve of the deſign and end of that glorious and happy conſtitution; to wit, that " he that glorieth, glory in the Lord," 1 Cor. i. 31. 'Tis true, that fulneſs is ſo far from being actually conveyed, in the meaſure of every part, into the perſons of believers, at once; that the ſtream of conveyance will run thro' all the ages of eternity, in heaven, as well as on earth. Nevertheleſs, whole Chriſt, with all his fulneſs, is given to them, at once: and therefore they have all neceſſary for them, at once, in him as their head. 1 Cor. iii. 21. " All things are yours." Philip. iv. 18. " I have all, and abound." 2 Cor. vi. 10. " As having nothing, yet poſſeſſing all things." Col. ii. 10. " And ye are complete in Him, which is the Head."

* Luther choice ſerm. p. 99, 100, 101.

† But are not perſonal holineſs, and godlineſs, good works, and perſeverence in holy obedience, juſtled out, at this rate, as unneceſſary? no, by no means. For Chriſt is the only fountain of holineſs, and the cauſe of good works, in theſe who are united to him: ſo that, where union with Chriſt is, there is perſonal holineſs infallibly; there they do good works, (if capable of them) and perſevere therein: and where it is not, all pretences to theſe things are utterly vain. Therefore are miniſters directed, to proſecute ſuch doctrines, and make choice of ſuch uſes, eſpecially, " As may moſt draw ſouls to Chriſt, the fountain of light, holineſs, and comfort." Directory, Tit. Of the preaching of the word. " As we willingly ſpoyle ourſelves of all honour and gloir of our awin creation and redemption, ſo do we alſo of our regeneration and ſanctification; for of ourſelves we are not ſufficient to think one gude thocht; bot he quha hes begun the wark in us, is only he that continewis us in the ſame, to the praiſe and glory of his undeſerved grace. Sa that the cauſe of gude warkis, we confeſs to be not our free-will, bot the Spirit of the Lord Jeſus, who dwelling in our heartes be trewe faith, bringis furth ſik warkis, as God hes prepared for us to walke in.

For this we maifte boldelie affirme, that blafphemy,. is to fay,
that Chrift abydes in the heartes of fik, as in whome there is no
fpirite of fanctification." Old Conf.ff 'Art. 12, 13. '' M. What
is the effect of thy faith? C. ——That Jefus Chrift his Son came
doun into this' world, ,and acc ·mplifhed ALL things, which
were neceffarie for our SALVATION." The manner to examine
children, &c. Queft. 3. " Whether we look to our juftification
or fanctification, they are wholly wrought and perfited by Chrift,
in 'whom we are compleit, howbeit 'after a diverfe fort.''
Mr John Davidfon's Catechifm, p. 34. ' The truth is, perfonal
holinefs, godlinefs, and,perfeverance, are parts of the falvation
already beftowed on the believer ; and- good works begun, the
neceffary fruit thereof. See the preceeding note, and p. 116. note.
And he hath, in Chrift his head, what infallibly fecures, the
confervation of his perf nal holinefs and godlinefs ; his bringing
forth of good works ftill,. and perfeverance in holy obedience;
and the bringing of the whole to perfection in another life, and
fo compleating the begun falvation. If men will, . without
warrant from the word, reftrain the term falvation to happinefs
in heaven ; then all thefe, according to the doctrine here taught,
are neceffary to falvation, as what of neceffity muft go before it,
in fubjects capable: fince, in a falvation carried on by degrees,
what is, by the unalterable order of the covenant, firft conferred
on a man, muft neceffarily go before that, which by the fame
unalterab'e order is conferred on him in the laft place. But, in
the fenfe of Luther and our author, all thefe are comprehended
in the falvation itfelf. For juftifying of which, one may obferve,
that when the falvation is compleated, they are perfected; and
the faints in glory work perfectly good works, without inter-
ruption, throughout all eternity: for they were the great end,
God defigned to bring about by the means of falvation. To the
fcripture texts adduced, in the preceeding note, adds 2 Tim.
ii. 10. " I endure all things for the elect's fake, that they may
alfo obtain the falvation, which is in Chrift Jefus, with eternal
glory." Here is a fpiritual falvation, plainly diftinguifhed from
eternal glory. Compare 1 Pet. i. 8, 9. " Believing, ye rejoice—
receiving the end of your faith, even the falvation of your fouls ''
This receiving of falvation, in the prefent time, is but the
accomplifhment of that promife, in part, Acts xvi, 31. " Believe
on the Lord Jefus Chrift, and thou fhalt be faved," which, I
make no queftion, bears a great deal of falvation, communicated .
on this fide death, as well as beyond it, Matth. i. 21. " He fhall
fave his people from their fins." Thus falvation comprehends
perfonal holinefs and godlinefs. And the fcripture holds out
good works, as things that accompany falvation, Heb. vi. 9. And
as the fruit f it, Luke i. 71, 74, 75. " That we fhould be faved
from our enemies——being delivered out of the hands of our

nefs, my treafure and my work*; I confefs, O law, that I am neither godly, nor righteous †; but yet this I am fure of, that he is godly and righteous for me ‡. And to tell the truth, O law, I am now with him in the

---

enemies. might ferve him without fear, in holinefs and righteoufnefs before him, all the days of our life." For it is an everlafting falvation, Ifa. xlv 17. importing a perfeverance in holy obedience to the end.

* My righteoufnefs, upon which I am juftified; my treafure, out of which all my debt to the law, or covenant of works, is paid; and my work, whence my righteoufnefs arifeth, and which I can, with fafety and comfort, oppofe to the law-demand of work. " The law of God we confeffe and acknowledge maift juft, maift equall, maift halie, and maift perfite, commanding thir thingis, quhilk being wrocht in perfectioun, were abill to give life, and abill to bring man to eternal felicitie. But our nature is fa corrupt, fa weake, and fa unperfite, that we are never abill to fulfill the warkis of the law in perfection.—And therefore it behovis us to apprehend Chrift Jefus with his juftice (i e righteoufnefs) and fatisfaction, wha is the end and accomplifhment of the law." Old Confeff. Art. 15.

† Namely, in the eye of the law, which acknowledgeth no godlinefs, nor righteoufnefs, but what is every way perfect, Rom. iv. 5. —Believeth on him that juftifieth the ungodly. And to plead any other fort of godlinefs or righteoufnefs, in the conflict of confcience with the law, is vain, Gal. iii. 10.

‡ i e. Chrift hath perfect purity of nature and life, which is all that the law can demand in point of conformity and obedience to its commandments: he was born holy, and he lived holy in perfection. Now, both thefe are imputed to believers not in point of fanctification, but of juftification : for without the imputation of them both, no flefh could be juftified before God, becaufe the law demands of every man, purity of nature, as well as purity of life, and both of them in perfection; and and fince we have neither the one nor the other in ourfelves, we muft have both by imputation, elfe we muft remain under the condemnation of the law. So the Palatine Catechifm. " Q. How art thou righteous before God?" A —The perfect fatisfaction, righteoufnefs, and holinefs of Chrift, is imputed and given unto me, as if I had neither committed any fin, neither were there any blot or corruption cleaving unto me,"

bride-chamber, where it maketh no matter * what I am, or what I have done; but what Chrift my fweet hufband is, hath done, and doth for me † : and therefore leave off, law, to difpute with me, for by faith I apprehend him, who hath apprehended me, and put me into his bofom. Wherefore I will be bold to bid Mofes with his tables, and all lawyers with their books, and all men with their works, hold their peace and give place ‡ : fo

---

" Q. 60. The ufe—if Satan yet lay to my charge, although in Chrift Jefus, thou haft fatisfied the punifhment, which thy fins deferved, and haft put on his righteoufnefs by faith; yet thou canft not deny, but that thy nature is corrupt, fo that thou art prone to all ill, and thou haft in thee, the feed of all vices. Againft this temptation, this anfwer is fufficient, that by the goodnefs of God, not only perfect righteoufnefs, but even the holinefs of Chrift alfo, is imputed and given unto me, &c. Ibid." The fatisfaction, righteoufnefs, and holinefs of Chrift alone, is my righteoufnefs in the fight of God. Ibid. Queft. 61.

* Viz. To the law or covenant of works, which hath no power over me, who am now married to another.

† Luther expreffeth it thus, " What I am, or what I ought to do, and what not to do; but what Chrift himfelf is, ought to do, and doth."

‡ Mofes with his tables, here, is no more, in the fenfe of Luther and our author, but the law, as it is the covenant of works: the which, whofo in the conflict of confcience with it, can treat at this rate; he is ftrong in faith, and happy is he. Confider the fcripture-phrafe, John v. 45. " There is one that accufeth you, even MOSES, in whom ye TRUST." Compare Rom. ii. 17. " Behold, thou art called a Jew, and refteft in the law." By Mofes here, is not meant the perfon of Mofes, but Mofes's law, which the carnal Jews trufted to be faved and juftified by, that is plainly, by the law, as it is the covenant of works. And, in our author's judgment, the law was given on Mount Sinai, as the covenant of works, p. 40. And he fhews, that although Luther and Calvin (too) do thus exempt a believer from the law, in the cafe of Juftification, and as it is the covenant of works; yet do they not fo out of the cafe of juftification, and as it is the law of Chrift, p. 163, 165, 166. And fo, at once, clears them and himfelf, from that odious charge, which fome might find in their hearts to fix upon them, from fuch expreffions.

U

that I fay unto thee, O law, be gone ; and if it will not be gone, then thruft it out by force, faith Luther * †.

And if fin offer to take hold of you, as David faid his did on him, Pfal. xl. 12. then fay you unto it, thy ftrength, O fin, is the law, 1 Cor xv. 56. and the law is dead to me. So that, O fin, thy ftrength is gone ; and therefore, be fure thou fhalt never be able to prevail againft me, nor do me any hurt at all ||.

---

* Choice ferm. p. 42, 99.

† Luther's words are, Then is it time to fend it (the law) away, and if it will not give place, &c. See the preceeding note.

‡ Here is the ufe to be made of the fame former doctrine, in the conflict of confcience with fin. Guilt, even the guilt of revenging of wrath, is the handle, by which, in this conflict, fin offers to take hold of the believer, as it did, of David, Pfal. xl. 12. who, in that pfalm, fpeaks as a type of Chrift, on whom the guilt of the elects fin was laid. Now, in refpect of that guilt, the ftrength of fin is the law, or covenant of works, with its curfing and condemning power: from which, fince believers are delivered, that ftrength of fin is gone, as to them ; they are free from the GUILT of SIN, the condemning wrath of God. Weftm. Confeff. Chap. 20. Art. 1., The revenging wrath of God, and that PERFECTLY IN THIS LIFE. Larg. Catech. Q. 77. Whence it neceffary follows, that fin, in this attack, can never prevail, nor really hurt them, in this point ; fince there neither is, nor can be, any fuch guilt remaining upon them, How fin may otherways prevail againft a believer, and what hurt it may do him in other refpects, the author exprefsly teaches, page 210 and elfewhere. In the manner of expreffion, he follows famous divines, whofe names are in honour in the church of Chrift. " God faith unto me, I will forgive thee thy fin, neither fhall thy fins hurt thee." Luther chof. ferm. p. (mihi) 40. "Forafmuch as Jefus Chrift hath, by one infinite obedience, made fatisfaction to the infinite Majefty of God, it followeth that my iniquities can no more fray nor trouble me, my accounts being affuredly razed by the precious blood of Chrift." Beza, Confeff. point. 4. Art. 19. Even as the viper that was upon Paul's hand, though the nature of it was to kill prefently, yet, when God had charmed it, you fee it hurt him not: fo it is with fin, though it be in us, and though it hang upon us, yet, the venom of it is taken away, it hurts us not, it condemns us not." Dr Prefton, of faith, p. 51. Hear the

And if Satan take you by the throat, and by violence draw you before God's judgment-feat; then call to your hufband Chrift, and fay, Lord I fuffer violence, make anfwer for me, and help me. And by his help you fhall be eabled to plead for yourfelf after this manner: O God the Father, I am thy Son Chrift's, thou gaveft me unto him, and thou haft given unto him all power both in heaven and in earth, and haft committed all judgment to him: and therefore I will ftand to his judgment, who faith, He came not to judge the world, but to fave it; and therefore he will fave me, according to his office. And if the jury * fhould † bring in their verdict, that they have found you guilty: then fpeak to the Judge, and fay ‡, in cafe any muft be condemned for my tranf-greffions, it muft needs be Chrift, and not I ||; for albeit I have committed them, yet he hath undertaken and bound himfelf to anfwer for them, and that by the confent and good-will of God his Father: and indeed he hath fully fatisfied for them. And if all this will not ferve the turn, to acquit you; then add moreover, and fay, as a woman, that is conceived with child, muft not fuffer death, becaufe of the child, that is within her: no more muft I, becaufe I have conceived Chrift in my heart: though I have committed all the fins in the world §.

And if death creep upon you, and attempt to devour you: then fay, thy fting, O death, is fin; and Chrift my

---

language of the Spirit of God, Luke x. 19. " And NOTHING fhall by ANY means hurt you." Nothing fhall hurt their fouls, as to the favour of God, and their eternal happinefs, faith the author of the Suppl. to Pool's Annot. on the text.

* The ten commandments.
† By your own confcience.
‡ Ber. Ochin. ferm. of predeft.
|| See page 149. note ||.
§ Gal. iv. 19. " My little children, of whom I travel in birth again, until Chrift be formed in you." Col. i. 27. " Chrift, in you, the hope of glory."

U 2

hufband hath fully vanquifhed fin, and fo deprived thee of thy fting : and therefore do I not fear any hurt, that thou, O death, canft do unto me. And thus you may triumph with the apoftle, faying, " Thanks be unto God, who hath given me victory, through our Lord Jefus Chrift," 1 Cor. xv. 56, 57.

And thus have I alfo declared unto you, how Chrift, in the fulnefs of time, performed that, which God before all time purpofed, and in time promifed, touching the helping and delivering of fallen mankind.

And fo have I alfo done with the law of faith.

CHAP. III.

Of the Law of Christ.

§ 1. *The nature of the law of Chrift.* § 2. *The law of the ten commandments, a rule of life to believers.* § 3. *Antinomian objections anfwered.* § 4. *The necefity of marks and figns of grace.* § 5. *Antinomian objections anfwered.* § 6. *Holinefs and good works attained to only by faith.* § 7. *Slavifh fear, and fervile hope, not the fprings of true obedience.* § 8. *The efficacy of faith for holinefs of heart and life.* § 9. *Ufe of means for ftrengthening of faith.* § 10. *The diftinction of the law of works, and law of Chrift applyed to fix paradoxes.* § 11. *The ufe of that diftinction in practice* § 12. *That diftinction a mean betwixt Legalifm and Antinomianifm.* § 13. *How to attain to affurance.* § 14. *Marks and evidences of true faith.* § 15. *How to recover loft evidences.* § 16. *Marks and figns of union with Chrift.*

§ 1. *Nom.* THen, Sir, I pray you, proceed to fpeak of the law of Chrift ; and firft, let us hear, what the law of Chrift is?

Evan. The law of Chriſt, in regard of ſubſtance and matter, is all one with the law of works, or covenant of works. Which matter is ſcattered through the whole Bible, and ſummed up in the decalogue, or ten commandments, commonly called * the moral law, containing ſuch things as are agreeable to the mind and will of God, to wit, piety towards God, charity towards our neighbour, and ſobriety towards ourſelves. And therefore was it given of God, to be a true and eternal rule of righteouſneſs, for all men of all nations, and at all times †. So that evangelical grace directs a man to no other obedience, than that, whereof the law of the ten commandments is to be the rule ‡ ||.

---

* Bolton's true bounds, p. 73. p. 47.
† Baſtin Cat p. 10.
‡ Reynold's uſe of the law, p. 388.
|| The author here teacheth, that the matter of the law of works, and of the law of Chriſt, is one, to wit, the ten commandments, commonly called the moral law. See p. 27. note *. And that this law of the ten commandments, was given of God, and ſo of divine authority; to be a rule of righteouſneſs, for men to walk by; a true rule, agreeable in all things, to the divine nature and will; an eternal rule, indiſpenſible, ever to continue, without interruption for any one moment : and that for ALL men, good and bad, ſaints and ſinners; of ALL nations, Jews and Gentiles; and at ALL times, in all ages, from the moment of man's creation, before the fall, and after the fall, before the covenant of works, under the covenant of works, and under the covenant of grace, in its ſeveral periods. Thus he aſſerts this great truth, in terms uſed by orthodox divines ; but with a greater variety of expreſſion, than is generally uſed upon this head; the which ſerves to inculcate it the more. And ſpeaking of the ten commandments, he declares in theſe expreſs words, page 167, that neither hath Chriſt delivered believers ANY otherwiſe from them, than as they are the covenant of works. The ſcope of this part of the book, is to ſhew, that believers ought to receive them, as the law of Chriſt, whom we believe to be, with the Father, and the Holy Ghoſt, the eternal JEHOVAH, the ſupreme, the moſt high God. And conſequently, as a law, having a commanding power, and binding force upon

Nom. But yet, Sir, I conceive, that though (as you say) the law of Christ, in regard of substance and matter, be all one with the law of works, yet their forms do differ.

Evan. True indeed, for (as you have heard) the law of works speaketh on this wise, " Do this, and thou shalt live ; and if thou do it not, then thou shalt die the death :" but the law of Christ speaketh on this wise, Ezek. xvi. 6.

---

the believer, from the authority of God ; and not as a simple passive rule, like a workman's rule, that hath no authority over him, to command and bind him to follow its direction. Nay. our author owns the ten commandments to be a law to believers, as well as others, again and again, commanding, requiring, forbidding, reproving, condemning sin, p. 161, 162. to which believers must yield obedience, p. 160. and fenced with a penalty, which transgressing believers are to fear, p. 206. As being under the law to Christ, page 164, &c. These things are so manifest, that 'tis quite beyond my reach to conceive, how, from the author's doctrine on this head, and especially from the passage we are now upon, it can be inferred, that he teacheth, that the believer is not under the law as a rule of life ; or can be affirmed, that he doth not acknowledge the law's commanding power, and binding force upon the believer, but makes it a simple passive rule to him : unless the meaning by, that the author teacheth, " That the believer is not under the covenant of works, as a rule of life ; or, that the law, as it is the covenant of works, is not a rule of life to the believer ; and that he doth not acknowledge the commanding power, and binding force of the covenant of works, upon the believer ; nor that obedience is commanded him, upon the pain of the curse, and bound upon him with the cords of the threatning of eternal death in hell ;" for otherwise, it is evident, that he teacheth the law of the ten commandments to be a rule of life to a believer, and to have a commanding and binding power over him. Now if these be errors, the author is undoubtedly guilty ; and if his sentiments, on these heads, were proposed in those terms, as the thing itself doth require, no wrong would be done him therein ; but that these are gospel-truths, appears from what is already said ; and the contrary doctrines do all issue out of the womb of that dangerous position, that the believer is not set free, both from the commanding and condemning power of the covenant of works ; of which before, see more p. 27. note * ; and p. 31. note †.

" And when I paſſed by thee, and ſaw thee polluted in
thine own blood; I ſaid unto thee, when thou waſt in
thy blood, live." John xi. 26. " And whoſoever liveth,
and believeth in me, ſhall never die *." Eph. v. 1, 2.
" Be ye therefore followers of God as dear children: and
walk in love, as Chriſt hath loved us. And if ye love me,
keep my commandments," John xiv. 15. And, " If they
break my ſtatutes, and keep not my commandments, then
will I viſit their tranſgreſſions with a rod, and their iniquity with ſtripes: nevertheleſs my loving-kindneſs
will I not utterly take away from him, nor ſuffer my
fathfulneſs to fail," Pſal. lxxxix. 31, 32, 33. Thus you
ſee, that both theſe laws agree, in ſaying, do this, but
here is the difference; the one ſaith, do this, and live;
and the other ſaith, live, and do this: the one ſaith, do
this, for life; the other ſaith, do this from life: the one
ſaith, If thou do it not, thou ſhalt die; the other ſaith,
If thou do it not, I will chaſtiſe thee with the rod †.
The one is, to be delivered by God, as he is Creator out
of Chriſt, only to ſuch as are out of Chriſt; the other is
to be delivered by God, as he is a Redeemer in Chriſt,

---

*. Theſe texts are adduced to ſhew, that they, to whom the
law of the ten commandments is given, as the law of Chriſt, are
thoſe, who have already received life, even life that ſhall never
end; and that of God's free gift, before they were capable of
doing good works; who therefore need not to work for life,
but from life. " The preface to the ten commandments teacheth us, that becauſe God is the Lord, and our God, and
Redeemer, therefore we are bound to keep all his commandments." Luke i. 74. " That we being delivered out of the
hands of our enemies, might ſerve him without fear."—
1 Pet. i. 15. " As he that hath called you, is holy, ſo be ye holy.
Becauſe it is written, be ye holy, for I am holy. Foraſmuch
as ye know, that ye were not redeemed with corruptible things,
—But with the precious blood of Chriſt." Short. Catech. with
the ſcriptures at large.

† See p. 127. note *; and p. 116. note ‡. Of this penalty
of the law of Chriſt, the author treats afterwards.

only to such as are in Christ *. Wherefore, neighbour

---

* To direct the believer, how to receive the law of the ten commandments, with application to himself he assigns this difference betwixt the law of works and the law of Christ. The one, to wit, the law of works, is the law of the ten commandments, but supposed to be delivered by God, as he is Creator out of Christ; and so standing in relation to man, only as Creator, not as Redeemer; the other, to wit, the law of Christ, is the same law of the ten commandments, but supposed to be delivered by God, as he is not only Creator, but Redeemer in Christ And although the notion of Creator doth not imply that of Redeemer, yet the latter implies the former; as he is Redeemer, he is sovereign Lord Creator, else we are yet in our sins; for none of inferior dignity could remove our offence or guilt; but the word of truth secures this foundation of believers safety and comfort. Isa. xliv. 6. " Thus saith the Lord the King of Israel, and his Redeemer, the Lord of hosts, I am the first, and I am the last, and besides me there is no God. Ver. 24. Thus saith the Lord thy Redeemer, and he that formed thee from the womb, I am the Lord that maketh all things, that stretcheth forth the heavens alone, that spreadeth abroad the earth by myself. Chap. liv. 5. Thy Maker is thine husband."

Now, the law of the ten commandments is given, the former way, only to unbelievers, or such as are out of Christ, the latter way, only to believers, or such as are in Christ. And to prove, whether this be a vain distinction, or not? One needs but to consult the conscience, when throughly awakened, whether it is all a case to it, to receive the law of the ten commandments, in the thunders from Mount Sinai, or in the still small voice, out of the tabernacle; that is from an absolute God, or from a God in Christ.

'Tis true, unbelievers are not under the law, as it is the law of Christ: and that is their misery; even as it is the misery of the slaves, that the commands of the master of the family, tho' the matter of them be the very same to them, and to the children, yet they are not fatherly commands to them, as they are to the children, but purely masterly. And they are not hereby freed from any duty, within the compass of the perfect law, of the ten commandments: for these commands are the matter of the law of works, as well as of the law of Christ. Neither are they thereby exempted from Christ's authority and jurisdiction; since the law of works is his law, as he is, with the Father and Holy Ghost, the sovereign Lord Creator; yea, and even as Mediator, he rules in the midst of his enemies, and over them with a rod of iron.

Neophytus, ſith that you are now in Chriſt, beware that you receive not the ten commandments at the hands of God out of Chriſt; nor yet at the hands of Moſes: but only at the hands of Chriſt; and ſo ſhall you be ſure to receive them, as the law of Chriſt *.

Nom. But, Sir, may not God, out of Chriſt, deliver the ten commandments, as the law of Chriſt?

Evan. O no! for God out of Chriſt, ſtands in relation to man, according to the tenor of the law, as it is the co-venant of works; and therefore can ſpeak to man, upon no other terms, than the terms of that covenant †.

---

* The receiving of the ten commandments at the hands of Chriſt, is here oppoſed, 1. To the receiving of them, at the hands of God out of Chriſt. 2. To the receiving of them at the hands of Moſes, namely, as our law-giver. The firſt is a re-ceiving of them immediately from God, without a Mediator: and ſo receiving of them as the law of works. The ſecond is a receiving of them from Chriſt, the true Mediator, yet imme-diately, by the intervention of a typical one; and ſo is a receiving of them, as the law of Moſes, the typical mediator, who delivered them from the ark or tabernacle. To this it is, and not to the delivering of them from Mount Sinai, that the author doth here look, as is evident from his own words, p. 160. The former manner of receiving them, is not agreeable to the ſtate of real believers; ſince they never were, nor are, given in that manner, to believers in Chriſt, but only to unbelievers; whether under the Old or New Teſtament. The latter is not agreeable to the ſtate of New Teſtament believers; ſince the true Mediator is come, and is ſealed of the Father, as the great Prophet, to whom Moſes muſt give place. Matth. xvii. 5. Acts iii. 22. See p. 160. Alſo ſee Turret. Loc. 11. Queſt. 24. Th. 15. However the not receiving of Moſes as the law-giver of the Chriſtian church, carries no prejudice to the honour of that faithful ſervant; nor to the receiving of his writings as the word of God; they being of divine inſpiration, yea, and the fundamental divine revelation.

† This plainly concludes, that to receive the law of the ten commandments, from God, as Creator out of Chriſt, is to re-ceive them as the law (or covenant) of works; unleſs men will fancy, that after God hath made two covenants, the one of works, the other of grace; he will yet deal with them, neither in the way of the one, nor of the other.

§ 2. But, Sir, why may not believers, amongst the Gentiles, receive the ten commandments, as a rule of life, at the hands of Mofes, as well as the believers amongst the Jews did?

Evan. For anfwer hereunto, I pray you confider *, that the ten commandments, being the fubftance of the law of nature † engraven in the heart of man in innocency; and the exprefs idea ‡, or reprefentation of God's own image, even a beam of his own holinefs, they were to have been a rule of life both to Adam and to his pofterity, though they had never been the covenant of works ‖ : but being become the covenant of work, they

---

* Bolton's true bounds, p. 77.

† Calling the ten commandments but the fubftance of the law of nature, he plainly intimates, that they were not the whole of that law; but that the law of nature had a penal fanction. Compare his fpeaking of the fame ten commands, ftill as the fubftance of the law of works, and of the law of Chrift, page 155, 156. Indeed he is not of that opinion, that a penal fanction is infeparable from the law of nature. That would put the glorified faints, and confirmed angels, in heaven (to fay nothing more) under a penal fanction too: for, without queftion, they are, and will remain for ever, under the law of nature. The truth is, the law of nature is fuited both to the nature of God, and to the nature of the creature: and there's no place for a penal fanction, where there is no poffibility of tranfgreffion.

‡ Perk. on Gal. 4, 5. alledged by D. Tay, Reg. v. t. p. 211.

‖ The ten commandments, being the fubftance of the law of nature, a reprefentation of God's image, and a beam of his holinefs, behoved, for ever, unalterably to be a rule of life to mankind, in all poffible ftates, conditions, and circumftances: nothing but the utter deftruction of human nature, and its ceafing to be, could diveft them of that office; fince God is unchangeable in his image and holinefs. Hence there being a rule of life, to Adam and his pofterity, had no dependance on their becoming the covenant of works: But they would have been that rule, tho' there never had been any fuch covenant: yea, whatever covenant was introduced, whether of works or of grace; whatever form might be put upon them; they behoved ftill to remain the rule of life. No covenant, no form whatfoever, could ever prejudice this their royal dignity. Now, whether this ftate of the matter, or their being the covenant of

were to have been a rule of life to them, as 'a covenant of works *. And then, being as it were razed out of man's heart, by his· fall, they were made known to Adam, and the reſt of the believing fathers, by viſions and revelations, and ſo were a rule of life to him †; yet not as the covenant of works, as they were before his ʻfall, and ſo continued until the time of Moſes. And as they were delivered by Moſes unto the believing Jews from the ark, and ſo as from Chriſt, they were a rule

---

works, which was merely acceſſory to them, and might never have been at all; is the firmer foundation, to build their being a rule of life, upon? is no hard queſtion to determine.

* And would have been ſo always to them all, till they had perfectly fulfilled that covenant: had they not been diveſted of that form, unto believers, through Jeſus Chriſt their ſurety. To them they remain to be a rule of life, but not under the form of the covenant of works; but to unbelievers, they are, and ſtill will be a rule of life under that form.

† And to them. One will not think ſtrange to hear, that the ten commands were, as it were razed, out of man's heart, by the fall; If one conſiders the ſpirituality and vaſt extent of them, and that they were, in their perfection, engraven on the heart of man, in his creation ; and doth withal take notice of the ruin brought on man, by the fall. Hereby, he indeed loſt the very knowledge of the law of nature ; if the ten commandments are to be reckoned, as certainly they are, the ſubſtance and matter of that law; although he loſt it not totally, but ſome remains thereof were left with him. Concerning theſe the apoſtle ſpeaks, Rom. i. 19, 20. and ii. 14, 15. And our author teacheth expreſsly, that the law is PARTLY known by the nature, to wit, in its corrupt ſtate, page 268. And here he ſaith not ſimply, that the ten commandments were razed; tho' in another caſe, p 239. he ſpeaks after that manner, where yet 'tis evident he means not a razing quite: but he ſays, they were, as it were razed. But what are theſe remains of them, in compariſon with that body of natural laws, fairly written, and deeply engraven, on the heart of innocent Adam ? If they were not as it were razed, what need is there of writing a new copy of them in the hearts of the elect, according to the promiſe of the new covenant, " I will put my laws into their hearts, and in their minds will I WRITE them," Heb. x. 16 and viii. 10. Jer. xxxi. 33. What need was there of writing them in the book of the Lord, the Bible, in which they are made known

of life to them, until the time of Chrift's coming in the fleſh *. And ſince Chrift's coming in the fleſh, they have been, and are to be, a rule of life, both to believing Jews and believing Gentiles, unto the end of the world; not as they are delivered by Moſes, but as they are delivered by Chrift : for when Chrift the Son comes and ſpeaks, himſelf, then Moſes the ſervant muſt keep ſilence ; according as Moſes himſelf foretold, Acts iii 22. ſaying, " A prophet ſhall the Lord your God raiſe up unto you of your brethren, like unto me ; him ſhall you hear in all things, which he ſhall ſay unto you †." And therefore, when the diſciples ſeemed to deſire to hear Moſes and Elias ‡ to ſpeak, on the mountain Tabor, they were preſently taken away ; and a voice came out of the cloud, ſaying, " This is my beloved Son, in whom I am well pleaſed, hear him," Matth. xvii. 4, 5. As if the Lord had ſaid, You are not now to hear either Moſes or Elias, but my well-beloved Son; and therefore I ſay unto you, hear Him ‖. And is it not ſaid,

---

again to us ; as they were, to Adam and the believing fathers, the author ſpeaks of, by viſions and revelations? The latter being as neceſſary to them, as the former is to us, for that end ; ſince theſe ſupplied to them, the want of the ſcriptures. As for thoſe, who neither had theſe viſions and revelations given to themſelves, nor the doctrine thereby taught, communicated to them by others; it is manifeft, that they could have no more knowledge of thoſe laws, than was to be found among the ruins of mankind in the fall.

* As to the delivering of the ten commandments from the ark, or the tabernacle ; ſee the ſenſe of it, and the ſcripture-ground for it, p. 85, 86. note †, and page 91. note *.

† See upon this point, p. 170. note †.

‡ The former, tne giver of the law ; the latter, the reſtorer of it.

‖ " Which words eſtabliſh Chrift as the only doctor and teacher of his church ; the only one, whom he had betruſted, to deliver his truths and will to his people; the only one, to whom Chriſtians are to hearken. Sup to Pool's Annot. on Matth. xvii. 5.

Heb. i. 2. That " in thefe laft days, God hath fpoken to us by his Son ?" and doth not the apoftle fay, " Let the word of Chrift dwell in you richly ; and whatfoever you do, in word or deed, do all in the name of our Lord Jefus Chrift," Col. iii. 16, 17.? The wife muft be fubject unto the hufband, as unto Chrift, ver. 18. *. The child muft yield obedience to his parents as unto Chrift, ver. 20. And the believing fervant muft do his mafter's bufinefs as Chrift's bufinefs : for, faith the apoftle, " ye ferve the Lord Chrift;" ver. 24. yea, faith he to the Galatians, " Bear ye one anothers burthens, and fo fulfil the law of Chrift," Gal. vi. 2.

Ant. Sir, I like you very well, that you fay, Chrift fhould be a Chriftian's teacher, and not Mofes : but yet I queftion, whether the ten commandments may be called the law of Chrift; for where can you find them repeated, either by our Saviour, or his apoftles, in the whole New Teftament ?

Evan. Though we find not that they are repeated in fuch a method, as they are fet down in Exod. and Deut. Yet fo long as we find, that Chrift and his apoftles did require and command thefe things, that are therein commanded ; and reprove and condemn thofe things, that are therein forbidden ; and that both by their lives and doctrines ; it is fufficient to prove them to be the law of Chrift †.

---

* " Wives, fubmit yourfelves unto your own hufbands, as unto the Lord," Eph. v. 22.

† Whether or not this be fufficient to prove them to be the law of Chrift, having a divine, authoritative, binding power on mens confciences, notwithftanding of the term, doctrines, here ufed by the author? one may judge from thefe texts, Matth. vii. 28, 29. " The people were aftonifhed at his doctrine. For he taught them as one having authority, and not as the Scribes. John vii. 16. My doctrine is not mine, but his that fent me. Heb. i. 1, 2, 3. God, who at fundry times, and in divers manner, fpake in time paft unto the fathers, by the prophets, hath in thefe laft days, fpoken unto us by his Son, whom he hath

X

Ant. I think indeed, they have done so, touching some of the commandments, but not touching all.

Evan. Because you say so, I intreat you to consider,

First, Whether the true knowledge of God, required, John iii. 19. and the want of it condemned, 2 Thess i. 8. and the true love of God, required, Matth. xxii. 37. and the want of it reproved, John v. 42. and the true fear of God required, 1 Pet ii. 17. Heb. xii. 28. and the want of it condemned, Rom. iii. 18. and the true trusting in God required, and the trusting in the creature forbidden, 2 Cor. 1. 9. 1 Tim vi. 17. be not the substance of the first commandment?

And consider *2dly,* Whether the hearing and reading of God's word, commanded. John v. 39 Rev. i. 3. and prayer, required, Rom xii. 12. 1 Thess v. 17 and singing of Psalms required, Col iii. 16. James v 13. and whether idolatry forbidden, 1 Cor x 14. 1 John v. 21. be not the substance of the second commandment?

And consider *3dly,* Whether worshipping of God in vain, condemned. Matth. xv. 9 and using vain repetitions in prayer, forbidden, Matth. vi. 7 and hearing of the word only. and not doing, forbidden, James i 22. whether worshipping God in Spirit and truth, commanded, John iv 24 and praying with the Spirit and with understanding also, and singing with the Spirit, and with understanding also, commanded, 1 Cor. xiv. 15 and taking

---

appointed heir of all things, by whom also he made the worlds; who being the brightness of his glory, and the express image of his person, &c. Matth. xxviii 18, 19, 20. All power is given unto me in heaven and earth: go ye therefore and teach all nations—to observe all things whatsoever I have commanded you.". The original word, in the Old Testament, rendered law, doth properly signify a doctrine. Hence, Matth. xv. 9. "Teaching for doctrines the commandments of men," *i. e.* the laws and commands of men, for the laws and commands of God. Compare ver. 4, 5, 6.

heed what we hear, Mark iv. 24. be not the fubftance of the third commandment?

Confider, 4*thly*, Whether Chrift's rifing from the dead, the firft day of the week, Mark xvi 2, 9. the difciples affembling, and Chrift's appearing unto them, two feveral firft days of the week, John xx. 19, 26 and the difciples coming together and breaking bread, and preaching afterwards on that day, Acts xx. 7. 1 Cor. xvi. 2 and John's being in the fpirit on the Lord's day, Rev. 1. 10. I fay, confider, whether thefe things do not prove, that the firft day of the week is to be kept as the Chriftian fabbath.

Confider, 5*thly*, Whether the apoftle's faying, " Children, obey your parents in the Lord, for this is right; honour thy father and thy mother, which is the firft commandment with promife," Eph. vi. 1, 2. And all thefe other exhortations, given by him, and the apoftle, Peter, both to inferiors and fuperiors, to do their duty, either to other, Eph. v. 22, 25. Eph. vi. 4. 5. 9. Colof. iii. 18, 19, 20, 21, 22. Tit. iii. 1. 1 Pet iii. 1. 1 Pet. ii. 18. I fay, confider, whether all thefe places, do not prove, that the duties of the fifth commandment, are required in the New Teftament?

Here you fee are five of the ten commandments : and as for the other five, the apoftle reckons them up altogether, faying, " Thou fhalt not commit adultery, thou fhalt not kill, thou fhalt not fteal, thou fhalt not bear falfe witnefs, thou fhalt not covet," Rom. xiii. 9 Now judge you whether the ten commandments be not repeated in the New Teftament; and fo confequently, whether they be not the law of Chrift ; and whether a believer be not under the law to Chrift, or in the law through Chrift ; as the apoftle's phrafe is, 1 Cor. ix 21.

§ 3 *Ant.* But yet, Sir, as I remember, both Luther and Calvin do fpeak, as though a believer were fo quite freed from the law, by Chrift, as that he need not make any confcience at all of yielding obedience to it.

Evan. I know right well that Luther * faith, the conscience hath nothing to do with the law of works: and
that Calvin † faith, the consciences of the faithful, when
the affiance of their justification before God is to be
fought, must raise and advance themselves above the
law, and forget the whole righteousness of the law, and
lay aside all thinking upon works. Now, for the true
understanding of these two worthy servants of Christ,
two things are to be considered and concluded First,
That when they speak thus of the law, it is evident they
mean only, in the case of justification. Secondly, That
when the conscience hath to do with the law in the case
of justification, it hath to do with it only as it is the
covenant of works: for as the law is the law of Christ, it
neither justifies nor condemns ‡. And so if you understand it, of the law as it is the covenant of works, according to their meaning; then it it most true that they say:

---

* On Gal. p. 59.   † Inst. p. 4:3.

‡ *i. e.* The law of the ten commandments, commonly called
the moral law, as it is the law of Christ, neither justifies nor
condemns, mens persons, in the sight of God. How can it do
either the one, or the other, as such? Since to be under it, as it
is the law of Christ, is the peculiar privilege of believers, already
justified by grace, and set beyond the reach of condemnation;
according to that of the apostle, Rom. viii 1. " There is therefore now, no condemnation to them which are in Christ Jesus."
But to say, that this makes the law of Christ despicable, is to
forget the sovereign authority of God in him; his matchless love,
in dying for sinners; the endearing relations, wherein he stands
to his people; and upon the one hand, the enjoyment of actual
communion and fellowship with God, and the many precious
tokens of his love, to be conferred on them, in the way of close
walking with God: and upon the other hand, the want of that
communion and fellowship, and the many fearful tokens of his
anger against them, for their fins. See pag. 217, 218. note *.
All these belong to the law of Christ, and will never be despicable, in the eyes of any gracious soul: though I doubt if ever
hell and damnation were more despised in the eyes of others,
than they are at this day, wherein believers and unbelievers, are
set so much upon a level, with respect to these awful things.

for why fhould a man let the law come unto his confcience? that is, why fhould a man make any confcience,

---

As to the point of condemnation, 'tis evident from fcripture,
that no law can condemn thefe, who are in Chrift Jefus,
Rom. viii. 1, 33. 34. And the law as it is the covenant of
works, condemns all thofe, who are not in Chrift, but under
the law, Gal. iii. 10. Rom. iii. 19. And particularly, it condemns every unbeliever; whofe condemnation will be fearfully
aggravated, by his rejection of the gofpel-offer: the which rejected offer will be a witnefs againft him, in the judgment; in
refpect whereof our Lord faith, John xii. 48. " The word that
I have fpoken, the fame fhall judge him in the laft day."
Compare chap. xv. 22. " If I had not come and fpoken unto
them, they had not had fin; but now they have no cloke for
their fin." Therefore the law, which unbelievers ftill remain under, as a covenant of works, will condemn them with
a double condemnation, John iii. 18. " He that believeth not,
is condemned already, becaufe he hath not believed in the
name of the only-begotten Son of God." And hence it appears,
that there is as little need of, as there is warrant for, a condem-
ning-gofpel. The holy fcripture ftates it as the difference, betwixt
the law and the gofpel, that the former is the miniftration of
condemnation and death; the latter, the miniftration of righteoufnefs and life, 2 Cor. iii. 6, 7, 8, 9. Compare John xii. 47.
" If any man hear my words, and believe not, I judge him
not; for I came not to judge the world, but to fave the
world."
     As to the point of juftification; no man is, nor can be
juftified by the law. 'Tis true, the Neonomians or Baxterians,
to wind in a righteoufnefs of our own, into the cafe of juftification, do turn the gofpel into a law, properly fo called; and do
tell us, that the gofpel juftifieth as a law; and roundly own what
is the neceffary confequent of that doctrine, to wit, that faith
juftifieth, as it is our evangelical righteoufnefs, or our keeping
the gofpel-law, which runs thus, He that believeth fhall not
perifh. Gibbon's Serm. morning exercife method. p. 421, 428.
But the holy fcripture teacheth, that we are juftified by grace,
and by no law, nor deed, or work of a law properly fo called,
call it the law of Chrift, or the gofpel-law, or what law one
pleafeth: and thereby faith itfelf, confidered as a deed or work
of a law, is excluded from the juftification of a finner, and hath
place therein, only as an inftrument, Gal. ii. 11. " That no
man is juftified by a law in the fight of God, it is evident."

of doing the law, to be juftified thereby, confidering
it is a thing impoffible ? nay, what. need hath a man to
make confcience of doing the law, to be juftified thereby,
when he knows he is already juftified another way ?
nay, what need hath a man to make confcience, of doing
that law, that is dead to him, and he dead to it? hath a
woman any need to make any confcience of doing her
duty to her hufband, when he is dead, nay, when fhe
herfelf is dead alfo ? or hath a debtor any need to make
any confcience of paying that debt, which is already fully
difcharged by his furety? will any man be afraid of that

Chap. v. 4. " Whofoever of you are juftified by a law ; ye are
fallen from grace." Rom. iii. 28. " Therefore we conclude,
that a man is juftified by faith, without deeds of a law."
Gal. ii. 16. " Knowing that a man is not juftified by works of
a law" I read, a law, deeds, works, fimply ; becaufe fo the
original words, ufed in thefe texts, do undeniably fignify.

To this agrees Weftm. Confeff Chap. 11. Art. 1. " Thefe
whom G-d effectually calleth, he alfo freely juftifieth—not for
any thing wrought in them, or done by them, but for Chrift's
fake alone ; nor by imputing faith itfelf, the act of believing, or
any other evangelical obedience, to them, as their righteoufnefs ; but, &c."—Larg Catech. Q. 73. " Faith juftifies a finner
in the fight of God, not—as if the grace of faith, or any act
thereof, were imputed to him for his juftification ; but ONLY
as it is an inftrument, by which he receiveth, and applieth Chrift
and his righteoufnefs" Weftm. Confeff. Chap. 19. Art. 6.
" Although true believers be not under the law, as a covenant
of works, to be thereby juftified or condemned ; yet is it of
great ufe to them, as well as to others, in that, as a rule of life,
informing them of the will of God and their duty, it directs and
binds them to walk accordingly." From this laft paffage of
the confeffion, two important points plainly offer themfelves.
(1.) That the law is a rule of life to believers, directing and
binding them to duty, tho' they are neither juftified nor condemned by it. (2.) That neither juftifying nor condemning
belong unto the law, as a rule of life fimply, but as a covenant
of works. And thefe are the very points here taught, by our
author.

obligation which is made void *, the feal torn off, the writing defaced, nay, not only cancelled and croft, but torn in pieces † ? I remember the apoftle faith, Heb. x. 1, 2. " That if the facrifices which were offered in the Old Teftament, could have made the comers thereunto perfect, and have purged the worfhippers, then fhould they have had no more confcience of fins;" that is, their confcience would not have accufed them of being guilty of fins. Now the blood of Chrift hath purged the confcience of a believer, from all his fins, (Chap. ix. 14.) as they are tranfgreffions againft the covenant of works : and therefore what needs his confcience be troubled about that covenant? but, now, I pray you, obferve, and take notice, that although Luther and Calvin do thus exempt a believer from the law, in the cafe of juftification, and as it is the law or covenant of works; yet do they not fo, out of the cafe of juftification, and as it is the law of Chrift.

For thus faith Luther ‡, out of the matter of juftification, we ought with-Paul, Rom. vii. 12, 14. " To think reverently of the law, to commend it highly, to call it holy, righteous, juft, good, fpiritual, and divine." Yea, out of the cafe of juftification, we ought to make a god of it ‖ And in another place, faith he §, There is a civil righteoufnefs, and a ceremonial righteoufnefs : Yea, and befides thefe, there is another righteoufnefs, which is the righteoufnefs of the law, or of the ten commandments which Mofes teacheth ; this alfo we teach after the

---

* Bolton's true bounds, p. 31.

† Col. ii. 14. " Blotting out the hand-writing—nailing it to his crofs."

‡ On Gal. p. 182.

‖ *i e.* Raife our efteem of it, to the higheft pitch : and give it illimited obedience. Compare this, with what is cited from the fame Luther, concerning the law, page 115.

§ On Gal. p. 5.

doctrine of faith And in another place *, he, having shewed that believers, through Christ, are far above the law, adds howbeit I will not deny but Moses sheweth to them their duties, in which respect they are to be admonished and urged: wherefore such doctrines and admonitions ought to be among Christians. as it is certain there was among the apostles; whereby every man may be admonished of his estate and office

And Calvin, having said (as I told you before) that Christians, in the case of justification, must raise and advance themselves above the law, adds; neither can any man thereby gather, that the law is superfluous to the faithful, whom notwithstanding it doth not cease to teach, exhort, and prick forward to goodness, although before God's judgment seat it hath no place in their conscience.

Ant. But, Sir, if I forget not, Musculus saith, that the law is utterly abrogated †.

Evan. Indeed, Musculus speaking of the ten commandments, saith, If they be weak, if they be the letter, if they do work transgression, anger, curse and death; and if Christ, by the law of the spirit of life, delivered them that believed in him from the law of the letter, which was weak to justify, and strong to condemn, and from the curse, being made a curse for us; surely they be abrogated. Now this is most certain, that the ten commandments do no way work transgression, anger, curse and death, but only as they are the covenant of works ‡. Neither hath Christ delivered believers any otherwise

---

* Choice serm. p. 103.

† Com. Pla. Fol. English. 119, 120.

‡ According to the holy scripture, it is certain, that the law of the ten commandments, hath an irritating effect, whereby they increase sin; and a condemning and killing effect, so that they work curse, death and wrath, called anger (it would seem)

from them, than as they are the covenant of works.
And therefore we may affuredly conclude, that they are
no otherwife abrogated, than as they are the covenant of
works *. Neither did Mufculus intend any otherwife :
for, faith he, in the words following, it muft not be un-

---

in the language of our forefathers, when Mufculus common
places were Engl.fhed : and it is no lefs certain, tnat Jefus Chrift
hath delivered believers from the law, as it hath thefe effects,
Rom. xiv. 15. " For if they which are of the law be heirs, faith
is made void, and the promife made of none effect, becaufe the
law worketh wrath." Chap. vii. 5, 6. " For when we were in
the flefh, the motions of fins, which were by the law, did work
in our members, to bring forth fruit unto death. But now we
are delivered from the law—that we fhould ferve in newnefs of
fpirit," &c. Chap. viii. 2 " For the law of the fpirit of life, in
Chrift jefus, hath made me free from the law of fin and death."
Gal iii. 13. " Chrift hath redeemed us from the curfe of the law,
being made a curfe for us." If then the ten commandments have
thefe effects, not only as they are the covenant of work° ; but
as they are the law of Chrift, or, a rule of life ; then believers
are altogether delivered from them, which is abfurd and abominable doctrine. Therefore it evidently follows, that the ten
commandments have thefe effects, only as they are the covenant
of works. The truth is, unto a gracious foul, the ftrongeft
poffible temptation to Antinomianifm, or cafting off the ten
commandments, for good and all, would be to labour to perfuade him, that they have thefe effects, not only as they are the
covenant of works, but as they are the law of Chrift : fo that,
take them what way he will, he fhall find they have not only a
curfing, condemning and killing power, but alfo an irritating
effect, increafing fin in him. Neverthelefs a Chriftian man's
doing againft them, (which is the reverend Mufculus his phrafe,
as cited by the author in the following page) may be a tranfgreffion : for a man may tranfgrefs the law, tho' the motions of
his fins be not by the law. And how fuch a man's finning is
more outragious, than an ungodly man's, will convincingly
appear, if one meafures the outragioufnefs of finning, by the
obligations to duty lying on the finner, and not by his perfonal
hazard, which is a meafure, more becoming a flave than a fon.

 * Thus our author hath proven, That the law of the ten
commandments, is a rule of life to believers ; and hath vindicated Luther and Calvin from the oppofite Antinomian error,

derstood, that the points of the substance of Moses covenant, are utterly brought to nothing,* : God forbid.
For a Christian man is not at liberty, to do those things
that are ungodly and wicked : and if the doing of those
things the law forbids, do not displease Christ; if they be
not much different †, yea, contrary, if they be not repugnant, to the righteousness which we received of him, let

———————————————————————

as he doth Musculus also, in the following words; and that
from their express declarations, in their own words. And
here is the conclusion of the whole matter. To shew the judgment of other orthodox Protestant divines, on this head against
the Antinomians; it will not be amiss to aduce a passage out of
a system of divinity, commonly put into the hands of students, not
very many years ago, I am sure. "It is one thing (saith Turretin,
disputing against the Antinomians) to be under the law as a
covenant; another thing, not to be under the law as a rule of
life. In the former sense, Paul saith, "That we are not under
the law, but under grace," Rom. vi. 14. as to its covenant-
relation, curse and rigor; but in the latter sense, we always
remain bound unto it, though for a different end: for in the
first covenant, man was to do this, to the end that he might
live; but in the other, he is bound to perform the same thing,
not that he may live, but because he lives." Turret. Loc. 11.
Quest. 24. Thes. 7. view again Westminst. Confess. Chap. 19.
Art. 6. The words whereof, are cited p. 163. note. Hereunto
agreeth our author's conclusion, viz. That believers are no
otherwise, not any otherwise delivered from the law of the ten
commandments, but as they are the covenant of works. Now,
how can those, who oppose Antinomianism, on this head,
contradict the author thereupon, but by asserting, that believers
are not delivered from the law, as it is the covenant of works;
but that they are still under the power of the covenant of works?
the which are principles as opposite to the received doctrine of
orthodox Protestant divines, and to the confession of faith, as
they are to the doctrine of our author.

* *i. e.* That the particular precepts of the law of the
ten commandments, called by Musculus, the substance of the
law-covenant (compare page 155. line penult.) are disanulled,
and no more to be regarded.

† *i. e.* Very unsuitable.

it be lawful·for a Chriſtian man to do them ; or elſe not *.
But a Chriſtian man doing againſt thoſe things, which be
commanded in the decalogue, doth ſin more outragiouſly,
than he that ſhould ſo do, being under the law † So
far off is he from being free from thoſe things that be
there commanded.

§ 4. Wherefore, friend Antinomiſta, if either you,

---

* *i. e.* Or if they be as certainly they are, diſpleaſing to
Chriſt ; moſt unſuitable, contrary and repugnant to the righteouſneſs, which the believer hath received from Chriſt ; then
they are by no means to be done.

† Theſe are the words of Muſculus ſtill, adduced by the
author to ſhew, that that famous divine was no Antinomian :
and if they will not ſerve to clear him, but he ſtill be on that
ſide, I apprehend, orthodox Proteſtants will be ſorry for their
loſs of that great man. But though it be obſerved, that he
ſpeaks of doing againſt the things commanded in the law, but
not againſt the law itſelf : there is no hazard : for 'tis evident,
that, by the law, Muſculus underſtands the covenant of works,
or, in his ſtile, Moſes covenant ; and ſince he was not of the
opinion, that believers are under the covenant of works, no, not
under the commanding power of that covenant, he could not
ſay, that they ſinned againſt it : however, he ſtill looks on the
ten commandments, the ſubſtance of that covenant, to be alſo
the law of Chriſt, binding the Chriſtian man to obedience.
From his ſaying that a Chriſtian doing againſt theſe things, ſins
more outragiouſly, than one who is under the law : it doth
indeed follow, that a Chriſtian's ſin is more diſpleaſing to God,
and deſerves a heavier curſe, in itſelf ; though, in the mean
time the law of Chriſt hath no curſe annexed unto the tranſgreſſions of it For, ſins deſerving of a curſe, ariſeth not from
the threatening, but from its contrariety to the precept, and
conſequently, to the holy nature of God : ſince 'tis manifeſt,
that ſin doth not therefore deſerve a curſe, becauſe a curſe is
threatened ; but a curſe is threatened, becauſe ſin deſerves it.
And the ſins of believers do in themſelves, deſerve a heavier
curſe, than the ſins of others. Yet the law of Chriſt hath not a
curſe annexed to the tranſgreſſions of it, becauſe the heavy curſe,
deſerves by the ſins of believers, was already laid on Chriſt, to
whom they are united : and he bare it for them, and bore it
away from them ; ſo that they cannot be threatened with it,
over again, after their union with him.

or any man elſe, ſhall, under a pretence of your being in
Chriſt, exempt yourſelves from being under the law of the
ten commandments, as they are the law of Chriſt, I tell
you truly, it is a ſhrewd ſign you are not yet in Chriſt:
for if you were, then Chriſt were in you; and if Chriſt
were in you, then would he govern you, and you would
be ſubject unto him. I am ſure the prophet Iſaiah tells
us, that the ſame Lord, who is our Saviour, is alſo our
King and law-giver, Iſa. xxxiii 22. and truly, he will
not be Jeſus, a Saviour, to any, but only to thoſe, unto
whom he is Chriſt a Lord: for the very truth is, where-
ſoever he is Jeſus a Saviour, he is alſo Chriſt a Lord:
and therefore I beſeech you, examine yourſelf, whether
he be ſo to you, or no?

Ant. Why then, Sir, it ſeemeth that you ſtand upon
marks and ſigns.

Evan. Yea, indeed, I ſtand ſo much upon marks and
ſigns, that I ſay unto you in the words of the apoſtle
John, 1 John iii. 10. " In this the children of God
are manifeſt, and the children of the devil: whoſoever doth not righteouſneſs, is not of God." For
ſaith Luther *, He that is truly baptiſed, is become a
new man, and hath a new nature, and is endowed with
new diſpoſitions: and loveth, liveth, ſpeaketh, and
doth far otherwiſe then he has wont, or could before.
For ſaith godly Tindal †, God worketh with his word,
and in his word; and bringeth faith into the hearts of
his elect, and looſeth the heart from ſin, and knitteth it
to God, and giveth a man power to do that, which was
before impoſſible for him to do, and turneth him into a
new nature ‡. And therefore, ſaith Luther ‖ in another
place, Herein works are to be extolled and commended,
in that they are fruits and ſigns of faith; and therefore

---

* Choice ſerm. p. 122.
† Tindal Par. Wick. Mam. p. 65, 66.
‡ *i. e.* Makes him a new man.   ‖ Choice ſerm. p. 197.

he that hath no regard how he leadeth his life, that he may ſtop the mouths of all blamers and accuſers, and clear himſelf before all, and teſtify that he hath lived, ſpoken, and done well, is not yet a Chriſtian. How then, ſaith * Tindal again, dare any man think that God's favour is on him, and God's Spirit within him ; when he feeleth not the working of his Spirit, nor himſelf diſpoſed to any good thing † ?

Ant. But by your favour, Sir, I am perſuaded that many a man deceives his own ſoul, by theſe marks and ſigns.

Evan. Indeed I muſt needs confeſs with Mr Bolton and Mr Dyke, that in theſe times of Chriſtianity ‡, a reprobate may make a glorious profeſſion of the goſpel, and perform all duties and exerciſes of religion ; and that in outward appearance, with as great ſpirit and zeal, as a true believer : yea, he may be made partaker of ſome meaſure of inward illumination ‖, and have a ſhadow of true regeneration ; there being no grace effectually wrought in the faithful, a reſemblance whereof may not be found in the unregenerate. And therefore, I ſay, if any man pitch upon the ſign, without the thing ſignified by the ſign §, that is, if he pitch upon his graces (or gifts rather) and duties, and conclude aſſurance from them, as they are in him; and come from him, without having reference to Jeſus Chriſt, as the root and fountain of them ; then they are deceitful marks and ſigns ¶ : but if he look upon them with reference to Jeſus Chriſt, then

---

* Para. Wick. Mam. p. 68.
† viz. Habitually.
‡ Diſcourſe of true happineſs, p. 35.
‖ On the heart, p. 111.
§ To wit, Chriſt in the heart.
¶ Becauſe all true grace and acceptable duty, flow from Jeſus Chriſt, dwelling in one's heart, by his Spirit; and whatſoever comes not that way, is but a ſhew and ſemblance of theſe things. Rom. viii. 9. "If any man have not the Spirit of Chriſt,

are they not deceitful, but true evidences and demonſtra-
tions of faith in Chriſt. And this a man doth, when he
looks upon his outward, actions: as flowing from the inward actions of his mind; and upon the inward actions of
his mind, as flowing from the habits of grace within him;
and upon the habits of grace within him, as flowing from
his juſtification; and upon his juſtification as flowing from
his faith; and upon his faith, as given by, and embracing
Jeſus Chriſt. Thus, I ſay, if he reſts not till he comes
to Chriſt, his marks and ſigns are not deceitful, but
true *.

---

he is none of his." John xv. 5. " Without me ye can do nothing." Chap. i. 16. " And of his fulneſs have we all received,
and grace for grace." Gal. ii. 20. " I live, yet not I, but Chriſt
liveth in me." " The cauſe of good works, we confeſs to be,
not our free-will, but the Spirit of our Lord Jeſus, who dwelling in our hearts, by true faith, bringeth forth ſuch works, as
God hath prepared for us to walk in." Old Confeſſ. Art. 13:
" Sa gude warkis follow as effects of Chriſt in us, poſſeſſed by
faith." Mr John Davidſon's Catech. page 30.

* Here is a chain, ſerving to lead a child of God unto aſſurance, that he is in the ſtate of grace; wherein duties and graces,
being run up unto their true ſpring, do ſo ſhine after trial of
them, as one may conclude aſſurance from them, as the author
phraſeth it. And here it is to be obſerved, that theſe words;
outward actions, actions of the mind, habits of grace, juſtification, faith, embracing of Chriſt, are, in the progreſs of the trial,
to be taken in their general notion, agreeing both to what is
true, and what is falſe, in each particular; as faith feigned and
unfeigned, juſtification real and imaginary, grace common and
ſaving, &c. For the ſpecial nature of theſe, is ſtill ſuppoſed to
be undetermined, to the perſon under trial, until he come to
the end of the trial. This is evident from the nature of the
thing; and from the author's words too, in the ſentence immediately preceeding, where he ſaith, if he pitch upon his
graces, or gifts rather. The which correction he makes, becauſe the former word is ordinarly reſtricted to ſaving grace;
the latter not ſo. And hence it appears, that the author was
far from imagining, that a man muſt have the aſſurance he ſpeaks
of, before he can conclude it from his graces or duties.

Ant. But, Sir, if an unbeliever may have a resemblance of every grace that is wrought in a believer, then it

---

The links of this chain are five. The first, outward actions, or works materially good, flowing from the inward actions of the mind. Otherwise they are but pieces of gross dissimulation; as was the respect and honour put upon Christ by the Herodians and others, when they asked him, " If it was lawful to give tribute unto Cæsar?" Matth xxii. 16, 17, 18. The second, These actions of the mind, flowing from the habits of grace within the man. Otherwise, they are but fair flowers, which, " Because they have no root, wither away," Matth. xiii. 6, like the " Israelites their seeking, returning, enquiring after, and remembring God, when he flew them," Psal. lxxviii. 34, 35, 36, 37. The third, These habits of grace within the man, flowing from his justification. Otherwise, they are but the habits of common grace, or of meer moral virtues, to be found in hypocritical professors, and sober Heathens. The fourth, The man's justification, flowing from his faith. Otherwise, it is but as the imaginary justification of Pharisees, Papists and Legalists, who are they which justify themselves, Luke xvi. 15, The fifth, His faith given by Christ, and embracing Christ. Otherwise, it is but feigned faith, which never knits the soul to Christ, but leaves the man in the case of the fruitless branch, which is to be taken away, John xv. 2.

This chain is not of our author's framing, but is a scriptural one, 1 Tim. i. 5. Now, (1.) the end of the commandment is charity. (2.) out of a pure heart, (3.) and of a good conscience, (4.) and of faith; (5) unfeigned. " Wherein the apostle teacheth, that the obedience of the law must flow from love, and love from a pure heart, and a pure heart from a good conscience, and a good conscience from faith unfeigned: thus he maketh the only right channel of good works." Pract. Use of saving knowledge, Tit. The third thing requisite to evidence true faith, is, that obedience to the law, run in the right channel, that is, through faith in Christ.

If one examines himself by this infallible rule, he cannot safely take his obedience for a mark, or evidence of his being in the state of grace; until he run it up unto his faith, embracing Christ. But then finding that his faith made him a good conscience, and his good conscience, a pure heart, and his pure heart produced love, from whence his obedience flowed; in that case, his obedience is a true mark of the unfeignedness of

muſt needs be an hard matter to find out the difference; and therefore, I conceive, it is beſt for a man not to trouble himſelf at all about marks and ſigns.

---

his faith, from whence he may aſſuredly conclude, that he is in a ſtate of grace. Our author's method being a copy of this, the objections againſt it muſt affect both.

   Let us ſuppoſe two men to put themſelves on a trial of their ſtate, according to this method; and to pitch upon ſome external duties of theirs, or ſome graces, which they ſeem to diſcern in themſelves, as to the ſubſtance thereof, though, as yet, they know not the ſpecific nature of the ſame; namely, whether they be true or falſe.

   The one finds, that his external duties proceeded not from the inward actions of his mind; or if they did, that yet theſe actions of his mind, did not proceed from habits of grace in him; or if they did proceed from theſe, yet, theſe flowed not from his juſtification, or, which is the ſame, followed not upon the purging of his conſcience; or, if they did; that yet his juſtification, or good conſcience, ſuch as they are, proceeded not from his faith; or, if they did proceed from it, that yet that faith of his, did not embrace Chriſt, and conſequently, was not of the ſpecial operation of God, or, given him by Chriſt in him, by his Spirit. In all, or any of theſe caſes, 'tis plain, that the external duties, or the (ſo called) graces, which he pitched upon, can be no true marks, from which he may conclude himſelf to be in a ſtate of grace.

   The other finds, that his external duties did, indeed, flow from the inward actions of his mind, and theſe from habits of grace in him, and theſe again, from his juſtification, or good conſcience, and that from his faith; and that his faith embraced Chriſt. Here two things are obſervable. (1.) That neither the duties nor graces pitched upon, could be ſure marks to him, before he came to the laſt point; in regard of the flaw that poſſibly might ſtill be found in the immediate, or mediate ſprings of them. And therefore the looking, mentioned by the author, is indeed, a progreſſive knowledge and diſcovery; but ſtill unclear and uncertain, till one comes to the end, and the whole evidence is put together: even as it is in ſearching out ſome abſtruſe point, by obſervation of the dependance and connection things have, one with another. Wherefore our author doth by no means, ſuppoſe, that I muſt know certainly, that I am in Chriſt, and juſtified, and that my faith is given me by Chriſt, before theſe external duties or graces can be true marks and

Evan. Give me leave to to deal plainly with you in telling you, that although we cannot say. every one that hath a form of godliness, hath also the power of godliness; yet we may truly say, that he, who hath not the form of godliness, hath not the power of godliness, for though all be not gold that glistereth,. yet all gold doth glister. And therefore, I tell you truly, if you have no regared to make the law of Christ your rule, by endeavouring to do what is required in the ten commandments, and to avoid what is there forbidden, it is a very evil sign : and and therefore, I pray you consider of it. . .

§ 5. *Ant.* But, Sir, you know, the Lord hath promised, to write his law in a believer's heart ; and to give him his Spirit to lead him into all truth : and therefore he hath no need of the law, written with paper and ink, to be a rule of life to him; neither hath he any need to endeavour to be obedient thereunto, as you say.

Evan. Indeed saith Luther *, the matter would even so fare, as you say; if we were perfectly and altogether

---

evidences to me. (2.) That the man perceiving his embracing of Christ, as to the substance of the action, is assured of the saving nature of it, (namely, that it is a faith uniting him to Christ, and given him by Christ in him) by the train of effects, he sees to have followed it, according to the established order in the covenant of grace, 1 Tim. i. 5. From which effect of his faith embracing Christ, that which might have deceived him, was all along gradually removed in the progress. Thus he is indeed sent back to the fruits of his frith, for true marks and evidences of it: But he is sent back to them, as standing clear now in his regress; though they were not so in his progress. And at this rate he is not left to run in a circle, but hath a comfortable end of his self-examination, being assured by his duties and graces, the fruits of his faith, that his faith is unfeigned, and himself in the state of grace.

Of the placing of faith before the habits of grace, see on p 189. note.

* Christ. lib. p. 39.

Y 3

the inward and fpiritual men; which cannot be in any
wife before the laft day, at the rifing again of the dead.*:
fo long as we be cloathed with this mortal fleth, we do
but begin and proceed onwards, on our courfe towards
perfection, which will be confummated in the life to
come : and for this caufe, the apoftle, Rom. viii. doth,
call this the firft fruits of the Spirit, which we do enjoy in
this life; the truth and fulnefs of which we fhall receive
in the life to come. And therefore (faith he in another
place †) it is neceffary fo to preach to them, that have
received the doctrine of faith, that they might be ftirred
up to go on in good life, which they have embraced; and
that they fuffer not thmfelves to be overcome by the
affaults of the raging flefh: for we will not fo prefume
of the doctrine of faith, as if, that being had, every man
might do what he lifted ‡ ; no, we muft earneftly endeavour ourfelves, that we may be without blame ; and
when we cannot attain thereunto, we muft flee to prayer,
and fay before God and man, forgive us our trefpaffes.
And faith Calvin ‖, one proper ufe and end of the law,
concerning the faithful §, in whofe hearts liveth and
reigneth the Spirit of God, is this; to wit, although they
have the law written and engraven in their hearts by
the finger of God, yet is the ¶ law to them a very good
means, whereby they may daily; better and more affuredly learn what is the will of the Lord: and let none of us
exempt himfelf from this need, for no man hath hitherto

---

* We would have no need of the law written without us, if,
as we are fpiritual in part, in refpect of fanctification begun in
us, we were perfectly and altogether, fpiritual, both in body
and foul. But that is not to be expected, till the refurrection;
when that, which is now fown a natural body, is raifed a fpiritual
body, (1 Cor. xv. 44.) being reunited to the fpirit, or foul made
perfect at death; Heb. xii. 23.) the which doth therefore no more
from the moment of death, need the law written without it.

† Choice ferm. p. 246.
‡ Ibid. p. 297.   ‖ Inftit. p. 162.
§ *i. e.* refpecting believers.   ¶ Written.

attained to ſo great wiſdom, but that he hath need to be daily inſtructed by the law. And herein Chriſt differeth from us, that, the Father hath powered out upon him the infinite abundance of his Spirit *; but whatſoever we do receive, it is ſo, by meaſure, that we have need one of another.

Now mind it, I pray you, if believers have the Spirit but in meaſure, and know but in part; then have they the law written in their hearts, but in meaſure and in part †, 1 Cor. xiii. 9. And if they have the law written in their hearts, but in meaſure and in part; then have they not a perfect rule within them; and if they have not a perfect rule within them, then they have need to have a rule without them. And therefore doubtleſs the ſtrongeſt believer of us all, had need to hearken to the advice of godly Tindal ‡, who ſaith, ſeek the word of God in all things, and without the word of God do nothing. And ſaith another godly and evangelical writer, My brethren, let us do our whole endeavour to do the will of God, as it becometh good children; and beware that we ſin not, as near as we can ‖.

Ant. Well, Sir, I cannot tell what to ſay, but (methinks) when a man is perfectly juſtified by faith; it is a very needleſs thing, for him to eneavour to keep the law, and to do good works §.

---

* Calv. on John iv. 34.

† They have not the law written completely and perfectly in their hearts

‡ In his works, p. 86.

‖ Author of the benefit of Chriſt's death, p. 85.

§ This Antinomian principle, that it is needleſs for a man, perfectly juſtified by faith, to endeavour to keep the law, and do good works, is a glaring evidence, that legality is ſo ingrained in man's corrupt nature, that, until a man truly come to Chriſt, by faith, the legal diſpoſition will ſtill be reigning in him; let

Evan. I remember Luther * faith, that in his time there were some, that did reason after the like manner ; If faith, say they, do accomplish all things, and if faith be only and alone sufficient unto righteousness, to what end are we commanded to do good deeds? we may go play then, and work no working at all. To whom he makes an answer, saying, not so, ye ungodly, not so. And there were others that said, † if the law do not justify, then it is in vain, and of none effect : yet it is not therefore true, (saith he) for like as this consequence is nothing worth ; money doth not justify or make a man righteous, therefore it is unprofitable : the eyes do not justify ; therefore they must be plucked out : the hands make not a man righteous, therefore they must be cut off : so is this naught also; the law doth not justify, therefore it is unprofitable. We do not therefore destroy and condemn the law, because we say it doth not justify : but we say with Paul, (1 Tim i. 8.) "The law is good, if a man do rightly use it." And that " this is a faithful saying, that they which have believed in God, might be careful to maintain good works : these things are good and profitable unto men, Titus iii. 8.

§ 6. *Neo.* Truly, Sir, for mine own part, I do much marvel, that this my friend Antinomista, should be so confident of his faith in Christ ; and yet so little regard

---

him turn himself into what shape, or be of what principles he will, in religion : though he run into Antinomianism, he'll carry along, with him, his legal spirit, which will always be a slavish and unholy spirit. He is constrained, as the author observed, page 179. To do all, that he doth, for fear of punishment, and hope of reward : and if it is once fixed in his mind, that these are ceased in his case, he stands still like a clock, when the weights that made her go, are removed, or like a slave, when he is in no hazard of the whip ; than which there cannot be a greater evidence of lothsom legality.

* Chrift. lib. p. 39.　　† On Gal. p. 156.

holineſs of life, and keeping of Chriſt's commandments, as it ſeems he doth. For I give the Lord thanks, I do now, in ſome ſmall meaſure, believe, that I am, by Chriſt, freely and fully juſtified, and acquitted from all my ſins: and therefore have no need, either to eſchew evil, or to do good, for fear of puniſhment, or hope of reward : and yet (methinks) I find my heart more willing and deſir-ous to do what the Lord commands, and to avoid what he forbids, than ever it was before I did thus believe *.

---

* It is not the ſcope or deſign of Neophytus, here, to ſhew wherein the eſſence of faith conſiſts, or to give a definition of it. But ſuppoſe it was ſo; his definition falls conſiderably ſhort of ſome, given by famous, orthodox, Proteſtant divines, yea, and churches too. See the note on the definition of faith—— I repeat here, Mr John Davidſon's definition only, viz. Faith is an HEARTY ASSURANCE, that our ſins are freely forgiven us in Chriſt. From whence one may clearly ſee, that ſome time-a-day, it was reckoned no abſurdity, that one's juſtification was made the object of one's belief. For the underſtanding of which ancient Proteſtant doctrine, grown almoſt quite out of ken, with unlearned readers, I ſhall adduce a paſſage out of Wendelin's Chriſt. Theol. Lib. 1. Cap. 24. pag. 542, 543. He propoſeth the Popiſh objection thus, Juſtifying faith muſt go before juſti-fication: but the faith of ſpecial mercy doth not go before juſtification; if it did, it were falſe; for at that rate, a man ſhould believe, that his ſins are forgiven, which as yet are not forgiven; ſince they are not forgiven but by juſtification: therefore the faith of SPECIAL MERCY is not juſtifying faith. In anſwer to which, he denies the ſecond of theſe propoſitions, with the proofs thereof; and concludes in theſe words, juſtify-ing faith therefore, hath for the ſpecial object of it, forgiveneſs of ſins, FUTURE, PRESENT, and PAST. He explains it thus, by the faith of ſpecial mercy, as it goeth before juſtification, a man doth not believe, that his ſins are forgiven him already, before the act of believing. (This, by the by, is the Antino-mian faith, juſtifying only declaratively; follows the true doctrine of faith.) But that he ſhall have forgiveneſs of ſins: IN the VERY ACT of juſtification, he believes his ſins are for-given him, and ſo receives forgiveneſs: AFTER juſtification, he believes the paſt application, to wit, of forgiveneſs, that is, that his ſins are now already forgiven him.

But the defign of Neophytus is, to make a profeffion of his faith, and, by an argument drawn from Chriftian experience, to refute the Antinomian pretended faith, whereby a finner, at firft brufh, believes his fins to be already forgiven him, before the act of believing; and thereafter hath no regard to holinefs of life: a plain evidence, that that perfuafion is not of God. And in oppofition to it, is this profeffion made, which confifts of three parts.

(1.) He profeffeth; that he believes himfelf to be juftified and acquitted from all his fins: and this is the belief of the paft application, AFTER juftification, which we heard before from Wendeline. For we have already found Neophytus brought unto faith in Chrift, and the match betwixt Chrift and him declared to be made, tho' his faith was accompanied with fears, p. 142. And now, he finds his faith grown up in fome fmall meafure, unto the hight, which Antinomifta pretended his faith to be at, namely, unto believing himfelf to be already juftified; but withal, he intimates, that his faith had not come to this pitch, all of a fudden, as Antinomifta's had done, page 97,---101. but that it was fometime after he believed, ere he did THUS believe. And now indeed, his believing THUS, only in fome fmall meafure, was his fin, and argued the weaknefs of his faith: but fuch a man's believing in any meafure, great or fmall, that he was juftified and acquitted from all his fins, muft be commended and approven; unlefs we will bring back the Popifh doctrine of doubting.

(2.) He profeffeth, that therefore, namely, fince he was juftified, and believed himfelf to be fo, he had no need to efchew evil, or to do good, for fear of punifhment, or hope of reward: the which; Antinomifta, pretending to likewife, had caft off all care of keeping the law, or doing good works; having no other principle of obedience within him. This doth not at all look to punifhments and rewards, improperly fo called, to wit, fa herly chaftifments and favours, of which the author afterwards treats exprefsly: but, 'tis plainly meant of rewards and punifhments, taken in a proper fenfe, as flowing from the juftice of God, remunerative and vindictive, and proceeding upon our works, good and evil; and particularly 'tis meant of heaven and hell. This is the fenfe, in which that phrafe is commonly ufed by divines: and that it is fo to be taken here, is evident from its being inferred from his juftification, which indeed leaves no place for fear of punifhment, and hope of reward, in the latter fenfe; but not fo in the former fenfe. And thus, it appears, Nomifta underftood it p. 181. where this point is purpofedly handled.

(3.) He profeffeth, that he was fo far from being the lefs inclined to duty, that he believed himfelf to be fully juftified; and that the fear of punifhment and hope of reward were

Surely, Sir, I do perceive that faith in Chrift * is no hindrance to holinefs of life, as I once thought it was.

Evan. Neighbour Neophytus, if our friend Antinomifta, do content himfelf with a meer gofpel knowledge, in a notionary way; and have run out, to fetch in notions from Chrift, and yet is not fetched in by the power of Chrift; let us pity him, and pray for him. And in the mean time I pray you, know that true faith in Chrift † is fo far from being a hindrance from holinefs of life and good works, that it is the only furtherance; for only by faith in Chrift, a man is enabled to exercife all Chriftian graces aright, and to perform all Chriftian duties aright, which before he could not. As for example, before a man believe God's love to him in Chrift ‡; though he may have a kind of love to God, as he is Creator and Preferver, and gives him many good things for this prefent life: yet if God do but open his eyes, to fee what condition his foul is in; that is, if he do but let him fee that relation, that is betwixt God and him, according to the tenor of the covenant of works; then he conceives of him as an angry Judge, armed with juftice againft him, and muft be pacified by the works of the law, whereunto he finds his nature oppofite and contrary: and therefore he hates both God and his law; and doth fecretly wifh and defire, there were neither God nor law.

---

ceafed in his cafe: that, on the contrary, he found, as his faith grew, his love to, and readinefs for, holinefs of life, grew; he was more willing and more defirous, to do the Lord's commandments, than he had been, before his faith was advanced to that pitch. And herein, I conceive the experience of the faints, will not contradict him. Thus he gives a plain teftimony againft the Antinomian faith.

* Namely, the faith of fpecial mercy, or a faith of particular application, without which, in greater or leffer meafure, it is not faving faith.

† See the preceeding note. ‡ See on page 136, note.

And though God fhould now give unto him never fo many temporal bleffings, yet could he not love: for what malefactor could love that judge or his law, from whom he expected the fentence of condemnation, though he fhould feaft him at his table, with never fo many dainties? "But after that the kindnefs and love of God his Saviour hath appeared, not by works of righteoufnefs that he hath done, but according to his mercy he faved him," Titus iii. 4, 5. That is, when as, by the eye of faith, he fees himfelf to ftand in relation to God, according to the tenor of the covenant of grace * ; then he conceives of God, as a moft merciful and loving Father to him in Chrift, that hath freely pardoned and forgiven him all his fins, and quite releafed him from the covenant of works † : and by this means " the love of God is fhed abroad in his heart through the Holy Ghoft, which is given to him ;" and then " he loves God, becaufe he firft loved him," Rom v. 5. 1 John iv. 19. For as a man feeth and feeleth by faith, the love and favour of God towards him, in Chrift his Son ; fo doth he love again both God and his law : and indeeed it is impoffible for any man to love God, till by faith he know himfelf beloved of God ‡.

Secondly, Though a man, before he believe God's love to him in Chrift, may have a great meafure of legal humiliation, compunction, forrow, and grief ‖ ; and be brought down (as it were) to the very gate of hell ; and feel the very flafhings of hell-fire in his confcience for his fins : yet it is not, becaufe he hath thereby offended God ; but rather becaufe he hath thereby offended himfelf ; that is, becaufe he hath thereby brought himfelf

---

* His foul refting on Chrift, whom he hath received for falvation.

† Thus he conceives of God, according to the meafure of his faith, or of his foul's refting on Chrift, which admits of various degrees.

‡ See on p. 136. note.　‖ Dyke on rep. p. 9.

into the danger of eternal death and condemnation *. But when once he believes the love of God to him in Chrift, in pardoning his iniquity, and paffing by his tranf- greffions † ; then he forrows and grieves for the offence of God by the fin, reafoning thus with himfelf, and is it fo indeed ? Hath the Lord given his own Son, to death, for me, who have been fuch a vile finful wretch ? And hath Chrift born all my fins, and was he wounded for my tranfgreffions ? ‡ O, then, the working of his bowels ! the ftirring of his affections, the melting and relenting of his repenting heart! " Then he remembers his own evil ways, and his doings, that were not good, and lothes himfelf in his own eyes for all his abominations ; looking upon Chrift, whom he hath pierced, he mourns bitterly for him, as one mourneth for his only Son," Ezek. xxxvi. 31 Zech. xii. 10. Thus, when faith hath bathed a man's heart in the blood of Chrift, it is fo molified, that it quickly diffolves into tears of godly forrow : fo that if Chrift do but turn and look upon him, O, then, with Peter, he goes out and weeps bitterly ! and this is true gofpel-mourning ; and this is right evangelical repenting‖.

Thirdly, Though before a man do truly believe in Chrift, he may fo reform his life and amend his ways,

---

* A man's believing God's love to him, is woven into the very nature of faving faith, as hath been already fhown. Wherefore, whatfoever humiliation, compunction, forrow, and grief, for fin, go before it, they muft needs be but legal, being before faith, " Without which, it is impoffible to pleafe God," Heb. xi 6.

† The belief of which, in fome meafure, is included in the nature of faith. See the note on the definition of faith, and on p. 177. note †.

‡ Dyke on Repent. p. 21.

‖ This is the fpringing up of the feeds of repentance put into

Z

that as touching the righteousness, which is of the law, he may be with the apostle (Phil. iii. 6.) blameless : yet being under the covenant of works ; all the obedience that he yields to the law, all his leaving of sin and performance of duties, all his avoiding of what the law forbids, and all his doing of what the law commands, is begotten by the law of works, of Hagar the bond-woman, by the force of self-love : and so indeed they are the fruit and works, of a bond-servant, that is moved and constrained to do all that he doth, for fear of punishment and hope of reward *. For, saith Luther,

----

the heart, in sanctification. Larg. Catech. Q. 75. a work of sanctifying grace, acceptable to God ; the curse being taken off the sinner, and his person accepted in the beloved : and like to the mourning and repenting of that woman, Luke vii. who, having much forgiven her, loved much; ver. 47. Betwixt which repentance and pardon of sin, there is an inseparable connection ; so that it is of such necessity to all sinners, that none may expect pardon, without it. Westm. Confess. Chap. 15. Art. 3.

* This can have no reference at all to the motives of a believer's obedience ; unless believers, as well as unbelievers, are to be reckoned to be under the covenant of works : for, 'tis manifest, that the author speaks here, of such only, as are under that covenant. But, on the contrary ; if a man is under the covenant of works, (called the law, in the stile of the Holy Ghost) he is not a believer; but an unbeliever. Rom. vi. 14. " Sin shall not have dominion over you : for ye are not under the law, but under grace." This reasoning proceeds upon this principle, viz. These, who are under the covenant of works, and they only, are under the dominion, or reigning power of sin. And if men, being under the covenant of works, are under the dominion of sin ; 'tis evident, that they are not believers ; that they are but bond-servants : that the love of God dwelleth not in them ; but corrupt self-love reigns in them ; and therefore, unto the good they do, they are constrained; by fear of punishment, and hope of reward, agreeable to the threatening and promise of the broken covenant of works, they are under : that their obedience conform to their state and condition, is but servile; no better than it is here described to be; having only the letter, but not the spirit of true obedience, the which, before any man can attain unto, he must be set free from the covenant

* the law given on Mount Sinai, which the Arabians call 'Agar, begetteth none but servants. And so indeed all that such a man doth is but hypocrisy; for he pretends the serving of God, whereas indeed he intends the serving of himself. And how can he do otherwise? for whilst he wants faith, he wants all things: he is an empty vine, and therefore must needs " bring forth fruit unto himself," Hof. x. 1. Till a man be served himself, he will not serve the Lord Christ †. Nay, whilst he wants faith, he wants the love of Christ; and therefore he lives not to Christ; but to himself, because he loveth himself. And hence, surely we may conceive, it is, that Doctor Preston saith. All that a man doth, and not out of love, is out of hypocrisy ‡. Wheresoever love is not, there is nothing but hypocrisy in such a man's heart ‖.

But when a man, through the hearing of faith, receives the Spirit of Christ, Gal. iii. 2. That Spirit,

---

of works, as the apostle teacheth, Rom. vii. 6. " But now, we are delivered from the law, that being dead wherein we were held, that we should serve in newness of spirit, and not in the oldness of the letter." And finally, that as is the condition, and the obedience of these under the covenant of works; so shall their end be, Gal. iv. 30. " Cast out the bond-woman and her son: for the son of the bond-woman shall not be heir with the son of the free-woman.

* On Gal. p. 218.

† *i. e.* Till the empty vine be filled, with the Spirit, from Jesus Christ, it will never bring forth fruit unto him. Till a man do once eat, by faith; he'll never work aright. The conscience must be purged from dead works; else one is not in case to serve the living God, Heb. ix. 14. The covenant of works faith to the sinner, who is yet without strength, work, and then thou shalt be filled: but the covenant of grace faith to him, be filled, and then thou must work. And until the yoke of the covenant of works be taken off a man's jaws, and meat be laid unto him; he'll never take on and bear, the yoke of Christ acceptably.

‡ Of Love, p. 19.   ‖ Ibid. p. 18.

according to the meaſure of faith, writes the lively law of love in his heart, (as Tindal ſweetly ſaith) whereby he is enabled to work freely, and of his own accord, without the co-action or compulſion of the law *. For

---

* The words co-action and compulſion, ſignify one and the ſame thing, to wit, forcing: ſo that to work without the co-action or compulſion of the law, is to work without being forced thereto by the law.

One would think it ſo very plain and obvious, that the way how the law forceth men to work, is by the terror of the dreadful puniſhment, which it threatens, in caſe of not working ; that it doth but darken the matter, to ſay, the co-action or compulſion of the law conſiſts in its commanding and binding power or force. The which muſt needs be meant, of the commanding and binding power of the covenant of works, or of the law ; as it is the covenant of works. For it cannot be meant (as theſe words ſeem to bear) of that power, which the law of the ten commands, as a rule of life, hath over men, to bind them to obedience ; under which, I think, the impartial reader is, by this time, convinced, that the author denies not believers ſtill to be : for to call that co-action, or compulſion, is contrary to the common underſtanding and uſage of theſe words in ſociety At this rate, one muſt ſay, that the glorified ſaints and angels (to aſcend no higher) being, as creatures of God, under the commanding and binding power of the eternal rule of righteouſneſs, are compelled and forced to their obedience too: and that when we pray, Thy will be done on earth, as it is in heaven; we pray to be enabled to obey the will of God, as the angels do in heaven, by co-action and compulſion in the height thereof ; for ſurely the angels have the ſenſe of the commanding and binding power of the eternal rule of righteouſneſs, upon them, in a degree far beyond what any believer on earth has. Wherefore that expoſition of the co-action or compulſion of the law, and ſo putting believers under the law's co-action or compulſion, amount juſt to what we met with before, namely, that believers are under the commanding power (at leaſt) of the covenant of works, having obedience bound upon them, with the cords of hell, or under the pain of the curſe. Accordingly, the compulſion of the law, is more plainly deſcribed to be, its binding power and moral force, which it derives from the awful authority of the ſovereign Law-giver, commanding obedience to his law, and threatening diſobedience with wrath, or with death, or hell. And ſo our author is blamed for not ſubjecting believers to this compulſion of the law.

that love wherewith Chrift, or God in Chrift, hath loved him, and which by faith is apprehended of him, will conftrain him to do fo ; according to that of the apoftle, 2 Cor. v. 14. " The love of Chrift conftraineth us."

In the preceeding paragraph, he had fhown, that the obedience of unbelievers to the law of the ten commandments, is produced by the influence of the law (or covenant) of works upon them, forcing or conftraining them thereto, by the fear of the punifhment which it threatens. Thus they work by the co-action or compulfion of the law, or covenant of works; being deftitute of the love of God. Here he affirms, That when once a man is brought unto Chrift, he having the fanctifying Spirit of Chrift dwelling in him, and being endowed with faith that purifies the heart, and with love, that is ftrong as death, is enabled to work freely, and of his own accord, without that co-action or compulfion.

This is the doctrine of the holy fcripture, Pfal. li. 12. " Uphold me with thy free Spirit. Compare Gal. v. 18. But if ye be led by the Spirit, ye are not under the law. So Pfal. cx 3. Thy people fhall be willing in the day of thy power. Compare 1 Pet. v. 1. Not by conftraint, but willingly. And believers are declared to be, not under the law, Rom. vi. 14. to be made free from the law of death, chap. viii. 2. Not to have received the fpirit of bondage again to fear, but the fpirit of adoption," ver. 15. How then can they be ftill under the co active and compulfive power of the law, frighting and forcing them to obedience, by its threatenings of the fecond death, or eternal wrath.

And 'tis notour, that this is the received doctrine of orthodox divines ; which might be attefted by a cloud of witneffes, if the nature of this work did permit. " Not to be under the law (faith Luther) is to do good things, and abftain from wicked things, not through compulfion of the law, but by free love and with pleafure." Chof. Ser. 20 p. (mihi) 235.

" The fecond part (viz. of Chriftian liberty) is, faith Calvin, That confciences obey the law, not as compelled by the neceffity of the law : but being free from the yoke of the law itfelf, of their own accord, they obey the will of God." Inftit. Book 3. Chap. 19 § 4.

" We would diftinguifh betwixt this law, confidered as a law, and as a covenant ; a law doth neceffarily imply no more than, 1. To direct. 2. To command, inforcing that obedience by authority. A covenant doth further neceffarily imply, pro-that is *, it will make him to do so, whether he will or no, he cannot chuse but do it †.　I tell you truly,

---

mifes made upon some condition, or threatenings added, if such a condition be not performed: the firft two are effential to the law, the laft two, to believers, are made void through Chrift; in which fenfe it is faid, that by him, we are freed from the law as a covenant; fo that believers life depends not on the promifes annexed to the law, nor are they in danger by the threatenings adjoined to it." Durham on the commands, p. 4.

" What a new creature doth, in obfervance of the law, is from natural freedom, choice and judgment, and not by the force of any threatnings annexed to it." Charnock, vol. 2 p. 59.

See Weftminfter Confeffion, Chap. 20. Art. 1. Of which afterwards.

And thus is that text, 1 Tim i. 9. " The law is not made for a righteous man," generally underftood by divines, critics and commentators. " The law, threatening, compelling, condemning, is not made for a righteous man, becaufe he is puſh'd forward to duty of his own accord, and is no more led by the fpirit of bondage and fear of punifhment." Turret Loc. 2. Q. 24. Th 8. " By the law is to be underftood, the moral law, as 'tis armed in ftings and terrors, to reftrain rebellious finners. By the righteous man, is meant, one in whom a principle of divine grace is planted, and who, from the knowledge and love of God, choofes the things that are pleafing to him. As the law has annexed fo many fevere threatnings to the tranfgreffors of it; 'tis evident that 'tis directed to the wicked, who will only be compelled by fear from the outragious breaking of it." Continuat. Pool's Annot. on the text. " The law is not for him, as a mafter to command him, to conftrain him, as a bondman." Lo Joric. de Dieu. " The law doth not compel, prefs on, fright, lie heavy upon, and punifh a righteous man." Strigelius " It lies not on him as a heavy burden, compelling a man againft his will, violently preffing him on, and pufhing him forward; it doth not draw him to obedience, but leads him, being willing." Scultetus. " For of his own accord, he doth right." Caftalio. apud. Pol. Synop. in Loc.

* Dr Prefton of Love, p. 28.

† " It is a metonymy from the effect, that is, love makes me to do it, in that manner, as a man that is compelled; that is the meaning of it. So it hath the fame effect, that compulfion hath, though there be nothing more different from compulfion than love." Dr Prefton, ibid. p. 29.

anſwerably as the love of Chriſt is ſhed abroad in the heart of any man, it is ſuch a ſtrong impulſion, that it carries him on, to ſerve and pleaſe the Lord in all things: according to the ſaying of an evangelical man * †. The will and affections of a believer, according to the meaſure of faith and the Spirit received, ſweetly quickens and bends, to chuſe, affect, and delight in, whatever is good and acceptable, to God, or a good man; the Spirit freely and cheerfully moving and inclining him to keep the law, without fear of hell, or hope of heaven ‡. For a Chriſtian man, ſaith ſweet Tindal ‖, worketh only becauſe 'tis the will of his Father: for after that he is overcome with love and kindneſs, he ſeeks to do the will of God, which indeed is a Chriſtian man's nature, and what he doth, he doth it freely, after the example of Chriſt. As a natural ſon; aſk

---

* Towne's Aſſertion of Grace, p. 131, 138.

† If one conſiders, that the drift and ſcope of this whole diſcourſe, from p. 175. is to diſcover the naughtineſs of Antinomiſta's faith, obſerved by Neophytus, Ibid. One may perceive, that by the author's quoting Towne the Antinomian, upon that head, he gives no more ground to ſuſpect himſelf of Antinomianiſm, though he calls him an evangelical man; than a Proteſtant gives in point of Popery, by quoting cardinal Bellarmine againſt a Papiſt, though withal, he call him a Catholic: and the epithet given to Towne, is ſo far from being a high commendation, that really it is none at all. For though both theſe epithets, the latter as well as the former, are in themſelves honourable; yet, in theſe caſes, a man ſpeaking in the language of his adverſary, they are nothing ſo. Evangeliſta could not but remember, that Antinomiſta had told him roundly, p 96. That he had not been ſo evangelical, as ſome others in the city, which cauſed him to leave hearing of him, to hear them, viz thoſe evangelical men: and why might not he give him a ſound note from one of theſe evangelical men, even under that character, ſo acceptable to him, without ranking himſelf with them?

‡ See the preceeding note * p. 268. and on p. 181. note †.

‖ Pathway to Script. p. 139.

him why he doth such and such a thing; why, faith he,
It is the will of my Father, and I do it that I may please
him : for indeed love desireth no wages, it is wages
enough to itself, it hath sweetness enough in itself, it
desires no addition, it pays its own wages *. And
therefore it is the true child-like obedience, being begotten by faith, of Sarah the free woman, by the force of
God's love. And so it is indeed the only true and sincere
obedience : for, faith Dr Preston †, To do a thing in
love, is to do it in sincerity; and indeed there is no other
definition of sincerity, that is the best way to know it by.

§ 7. *Nom:* But stay, Sir, I pray you, would you not
have believers to eschew evil, and do good, for fear of
hell, or for hope of heaven?

Evan. No indeed, I would not have any believer to do
either the one or the other ; for so far forth as they do
so, their obedience is but slavish ‡. And therefore,

---

* Dr Preston of Love, p. 27.   † Ibid p. 198.
§ As for what concerns the hope of heaven, the author pur-
posedly explains that matter, p. 183. That he would not have
any believer, to eschew evil and do good, for fear of hell ; the
meaning thereof plainly is this, you, being a believer in Christ,
ought not to eschew evil and do good, for fear you be condemned, and cast into hell. So far as a believer doth so, the author
justly reckons his obedience accordingly slavish. This is the
common understanding and sense of such a phrase, as when we
say, The slave works, for fear of the whip : some men abstain
from stealing, robbing, and the like, for fear of the gallows;
they eschew evil, not from love of virtue, but for fear of punishment, as the Heathen Poet faith of his pretender to virtue,

Oderunt peccare boni virtutis amore,
Tu nihil admittes in te formidine pœnæ.
                                          Horat. Epist. 16.
Which may be thus Englished,

Hatred of vice, in gen'rous souls,
   From love of virtue flows :
While nothing vicious minds controuls,
   But servile fear of blows.

though, when they were first awaked, and convinced of their misery, and set foot forward, to go on in the way

---

This is a quite other thing, than to say, that a believer, in doing good, or eschewing evil, ought not to regard threatenings, nor be influenced by the threatening of death. For though believers ought never to fear, that they shall be condemned, and cast into hell; yet they both may, and ought, awfully to regard the threatenings, of the holy law. And how they ought to regard them, one may learn from the Westminster Confession, Chap 19. Art. 6. in these words, " The threatenings of it (viz. the law) serve to shew, what even their sins deserve; and, what afflictions, in this life, they may expect for them, although freed from the curse thereof, threatened in the law." Thus they are to regard them, not as denunciations of their doom, in the case of sinning; but as a looking-glass, wherein to behold, the fearful demerit of their sins; the unspeakable love of God, in freeing them from bearing it; his fatherly displeasure against his own, for their sin; and the tokens of his anger, to be expected by them, in that case. So will they be influenced to eschew evil and do good, being thereby filled with hatred and horror of sin, thankfulness to God, and fear of the displeasure and frowns of their Father; though not with a fear, that he'll condemn them, and destroy them in hell; this glass represents no such thing.

Such fear, in a believer, is groundless. For, 1. He is not under the threatening of hell, or liable to the curse. See p. 116. notes. If he were, he behoved, that moment he sinneth, to fall under the curse. For, since the curse is the sentence of the law, passing on the sinner, according to the threatening, adjudging, and binding him over to the punishment threatened; if the law say to a man, before he sinneth, in the day thou eatest thereof, thou shalt surely die; it saith to him in the moment he sinneth, Cursed is every one that continueth not in all things written in the law, to do them. And forasmuch as, believers sin, in every thing they do; their very believing and repenting being always attended with sinful imperfections; it is not possible, at this rate, that they can be one moment from under the curse; but it must be continually wreathed about their necks. To distinguish, in this case, betwixt gross sins, and lesser sins, is vain. For as every sin, (even the least) deserves God's wrath and curse, Short. Catech. So, against whomsoever the curse takes place, (and by virtue of God's truth, it takes place against all those who are threatened with hell, or eternal death) they

of life ; they, with the prodigal, would be hired servants: yet when, by the eye of faith, they see the mercy and

---

are cursed for all sins, smaller or greater, Cursed is every one that continueth not in all things ; though still there is a diffe-rence made betwixt greater and lesser sins, in respect of the degree of punishment; yet there is none, in respect of the kind of punishment. But now, believers are set free from the curse, Gal. iii. 13. " Christ hath redeemed us from the curse of the law, being made a curse for us." 2 By the redemption of Christ already applied to the believer, and by the oath of God, he is perfectly secured from the return of the curse upon him, Gal. iii. 13. (see before) compared with Isa. liii. and liv. 9. " For this is as the waters of Noah unto me ; For as I have sworn, that the waters of Noah should no more go over the earth; so have I sworn that I would not be wroth with thee, nor rebuke thee." Therefore he is perfectly secured, from be-ing made liable, any more, to hell, or eternal death. For a man being under the curse, is so made liable to the pains of hell for ever. Short. Cat. 3. He is justified by faith, and so adjudged to live eternally in heaven. This is unalterable; for the gifts and calling of God are without repentance, Rom. xi. 29. And a man can never stand adjudged to eternal life, and to eternal death, at one and the same time. 4. One great difference be-twixt believers and unbelievers, lies here, that the latter are bound over to hell and wrath, the former are not. John iii. 18. " He that believeth, is not condemned; but he that believeth not, is condemned already;" not, that he is in hell already, but bound over to it. Now, a believer is still a believer, from the first moment of his believing: and therefore it remains true concerning him, from that moment, for ever, that he is not condemned, or bound over to hell and wrath. He is expresly secured against it, for all time to come, from that moment, John v 24. " He shall not come into condemnation." And the apostle cuts off all evasion by distinctions of condemnation, here, while he tells us in express terms, " There is no condem-nation to them which are in Christ Jesus," Rom. viii. 1. 5. The believer's union with Christ, is never dissolved, Hos ii. 19. " I will betrothe thee unto me for ever." And being in Christ, he is set beyond the reach of condemnation, Rom. viii. 1. Yea, and being in Christ, he is perfectly righteous for ever; for he is never again stript of the white raiment of Christ's imputed righteousness: while the union remains, it cannot be lost: but tobe perfectly righteous, and yet liable to condemnation, before a just judge, is inconsistent.

indulgence of their heavenly Father in Chrift, running to meet them, and embrace them ; I would have them.

Neither is fuch a fear, in a believer, acceptable to God. For, (1.) 'Tis not from the Spirit of God, but from one's own fpirit, or a worfe. Rom. viii. 15. " Ye have not received the fpirit of bondage again to fear:" namely, to fear death or hell. Heb. ii. 15. " Who, through fear of death, were all their life-time fubject to bondage." (2.) It was the defign of the fending of Chrift, that believers, in him, might ferve God without that fear, Luke i. 74. " That we, being delivered out of the hands of our enemies, might ferve him without fear." Compare 1 Cor. xv. 26. " The laft enemy that fhall be deftroyed is death." And for this very caufe, Jefus Chrift came, " That through death, he might deftroy him that had the power of death, that is the devil ; and deliver them, who, through fear of death, were all their life-time (namely, before their deliverance by Chrift) fubject to bondage." Heb. ii. 14, 15. (3.) Though it is indeed confiftent with, yet it is contrary to faith, Matth. viii. 26. " Why are ye fearful, O ye of little faith?" And to love too, 1 John iv. 18. " Perfect love cafteth out fear ; becaufe fear hath torment." 2 Tim. i. 7. " God hath not given us the fpirit of fear, but of power, of love, and of a found mind."

(4.) As it is not agreeable to the character of a father who is not a revenging judge to his own family, to threaten to kill his own children, though he threaten to chaftife them : fo fuch a fear is no more agreeable to the Spirit of adoption, nor becoming the ftate of fonfhip to God, than for a child to fear, that his father, being fuch a one, will kill him. And therefore the fpirit of bondage to fear, is oppofed to the Spirit of adoption, whereby we cry, Abba Father, Rom. viii. 15.

" Adoption is an act of the free grace of God ;—whereby all thofe, that are juftified, are received unto the number of his children, have his name put upon them, the Spirit of his Son given to them, (receive the Spirit of adoption. Weft. Confeff. Chap. 12.) are under his fatherly care and difpenfations, admitted to all the liberties and privileges of the fons of God, made heirs of all the promifes, and fellow-heirs with Chrift in glory." Larg. Catech. Q. 74.

" The liberty, which Chrift has purchafed for believers under the gofpel, confifts in their freedom from the guilt of fin, the condemning wrath of God, the curfe of the moral law—as alfo in their free accefs to God, and their yielding obedience unto him ; not out of flavifh fear, but a child-like love, and willing (with him) to talk no more of being hired ſervants *. I would have them ſo to wreſtle againſt doubting, and ſo to exerciſe their faith ; as to believe, that they are by Chriſt delievered from the hands of all their enemies, both the law, ſin, wrath, death, the devil, and hell ; " That they may ſerve the Lord without fear, in holineſs and righteouſneſs all the days of their lives, Luke i. 74, 75. I would have them ſo to believe God's love to them in Chriſt; as that thereby they may be conſtrained to obedience †.

Nom. But, Sir, you know that our Saviour ſaith, " Fear him that is able to deſtroy both ſoul and body in hell," Matth. x. 28. And the apoſtle ſaith, " We ſhall receive of the Lord, the reward of the inheritance," Col. iii. 24. And is it not ſaid, that Moſes had reſpect, unto the recompenſe of reward, Heb. xi. 26.

Evan. Surely the intent of our bleſſed Saviour, in that ſcripture, is to teach all believers, that when God com-

---

mind. All which were common alſo to believers under the law." Weſtm. Confeſſ. chap. 20. Art. 1. By the guilt of ſin, here, muſt needs be underſtood, obligation to eternal wrath, See page 108. note.

" The end of Chriſtian liberty is, that being delivered out of the hands of our enemies, we might ſerve the Lord without fear." Ibid. Art. 3.

" The one (viz. Juſtification) doth equally free all believers from the revenging wrath of God, and that perfectly in this life, that they never fall into condemnation." Larg. Catech. Q. 77.

" Though a ſoul be juſtified, and freed from the guilt of eternal puniſhment; and ſo the ſpirit is no more to be afraid and diſquieted for eternal wrath and hell." Rutherfoord's trial and triumph, &c. Serm. 19. p. 265.

" The believer hath no conſcience of ſins: that is, he in conſcience is not to fear everlaſting condemnation, that is moſt true." Ibid. p. 266.

See more to this purpoſe, page 112. note. page 116. note. page 180 note.

* Compare Luke xv. 19, 21.

† And no marvel one would have them do ſo; ſince that is what all the children of God, with one mouth, do daily pray for, ſaying, " Thy will be done in earth, as it is in heaven."

mands one thing, and man another, they fhould obey God, and not man ; rather than to exhort them, to efchew evil for fear of hell *. And as for thofe other fcriptures by you alledged, if you mean reward, and the means to ob-

---

* There is a great difference betwixt a believer's efchewing evil, for fear of hell ; and h's efchewing it from the fear of God, as able to deftroy both foul and body in. hell. The former refpects the event, as to his eternal ftate; the latter doth not: to this purpofe, the variation of the phrafe in the text, is obfervable: " Fear not them which kill the body;" this notes the event, as to temporal death, by the hands of men, which our Lord would have his people to lay their accounts with: but with refpect to eternal death, he faith not, Fear him which deftroys; but, " which is able to deftroy both foul and body in hell." Moreover, the former is a flavifh fear of God, as a revenging Judge; the believer efchewing fin, for fear be be damned ; the latter is a reverential fear of God, as of a Father, with whom, is awful dominion and power. The former carries in it, a doubtfulnefs and uncertainty, as to the event, plainly contrary to the remedy prefcribed, in this fame cafe, Prov. xxix. 25. " The fear of man bringeth a fnare; but whofo putteth his truft in the Lord, fhall be fafe." The latter is confiftent with the moft full affurance of one's being put beyond all hazard of hell. Heb. xii. 28, 29. " Wherefore we receiving a kingdom, which cannot be moved, let us have grace, whereby we may ferve God acceptably, with reverence, and godly fear. For our God is a confuming fire." A believer, by fixing his eyes on God, as able to deftroy both foul and body in hell, may be fo filled with the reverential fear of God, his dreadful power and wrath againft fin ; as to be fenced againft the flavifh fear, of the moft cruel tyrants, tempting him to fin; though in the mean time, he moft firmly believe, that he is paft that gulf, can never fall into it, nor be bound over unto it. For, fo he hath a lively reprefentation of the juft deferving of fin, even of that fin in particular, unto which he is tempted ; and fo muft tremble at the thought of it, as an. evil, greater than death. And as a child, when he feeth his father lafhing his flaves, cannot but tremble, and fear to offend him ; fo a believer's turning his eyes on the miferies of the damned, muft raife in him an awful apprehenfion of the feverity of his Father, againft fin, even in his own ; and caufe him to fay in his heart, " My flefh trembleth for fear of thee ; and I am afraid of thy judgments," Pfal. cxix. 120. Thus alfo he hath a view of the frightful danger

A a

tain that reward, in the scripture sense ; then it is another matter : but I had thought you had meant in our common sense, and not in scripture sense.

Nom. Why Sir, I pray you, what difference is there, betwixt reward, and the means to obtain the reward, in our common sense, and in the scripture sense?

Evan. Why, reward in our common sense, is that, which is conceived to come from God, or to be given by God ; which is, a fancying of heaven under carnal notions, beholding it as a place, where there is freedom from all misery ; and fulness of all pleasures and happiness, and to be obtained by our own works and doings *. But reward, in the scripture sense, is not so much that which comes from God, or is given by God : as that which

---

he has escaped; the looking back to which, must make one's heart shiver, and conceive a horror of sin; as on the case of a pardoned criminal, looking back to a dreadful precipice, from which, he was to have been thrown headlong, had not a pardon seasonably prevented his ruin, Eph. ii. 3. "We were, by nature, the children of wrath, even as others."

* Thus, to eschew evil, and do good, for hope of heaven, is to do so in hope of obtaining heaven, by our own works. And certainly, that hope shall be cut off, and be a spider's web, Job viii. 24. For a sinner shall never obtain heaven, but in the way of free grace ; but if it be of works, then it is no more grace, Rom. xi. 6. But that a believer may be animated to obedience, by viewing the reward already obtained for him, by the works of Christ, our author no where denies. So indeed the apostle exhorts believers to run their Christian race, looking unto Jesus, who for the joy that was set before him, (to be obtained by his own works, in the way of most proper merit) endured the cross, Heb. xii. 1, 2.

" Papists (saith Doctor Preston) tell of escaping damnation, and of getting into heaven. But scripture gives other motives. (viz. to good works) Thou art in Christ, and Christ is thine : consider what he hath done for thee, what thou hast by him, what thou hadst been without him, and thus stir up thyself to do for him, what he requireth." Abridg. of his works, p. 394.

lies in God; even the full fruition of God himfelf in Chrift. " I am (faith God to Abraham) thy fhield, and thy exceeding great reward,"Gen.xv.1. And, " Whom have I in heaven but thee?" faith David; " And there is none upon earth, that I defire befides thee, Pf lxxiii.25. And, " I fhall be fatisfied when I awake with thy likenefs," Pfal. xvii. 15. * And the means to obtain this reward, is not by doing, but by believing; even by drawing near with a true heart, in the full affurance of faith, Heb. x. 22. And fo indeed it is given freely †. And therefore, you are not to conceive of that reward, which the fcripture fpeaks of, as if it were the wages of a fervant; but as it is the inheritance of fons ‡. And

---

* Man's chief end, is to glorify God, and to enjoy him for ever " Short. Catech. " Believers—fhall be—made perfectly bleffed in full enjoying of God, to all eternity." Ibid.

† Rom. iv. 16. " Therefore it is of faith, that it might be be by grace; to the end the promife (viz. of the inheritacce, ver. 13, 14.) might be fure to all the feed. Otherwife, it is not given freely; for, to him that worketh is the reward not reckoned of grace, but of debt," ver. 4.

‡ The apoftle's decifion, in this cafe, feems to be pretty clear, Rom. vi. 23. " For the wages of fin is death; but the gift of God is eternal life;" he will not have us to look upon it, as the wages of a fervant, too. The joining together of both thefe notions of the reward, was, it feems, the doctrine of the Pharifees, Mark x 17. " Good mafter, what fhall I do, that I may inherit eternal life?" And how unacceptable it was to our bleffed Saviour, may be learned from his anfwer to that queftion. " The Papifts confefs, that life is merited by Chrift, and is made ours by the right of inheritance; fo far we go with them; yea touching works, they hold many things with us, (1.) That no works of themfelves can merit life everlafting. (2.) That works done before converfion, can merit nothing at God's hand. (3.) That there is no merit at God's hand, without his mercy, no exact merit, as often there is amongft men. The point, whereabout we diffent, is, That with the merit of Chrift, and free promife, they will have the merit of works joined, as done by them, who are adopted children." Bayne on Eph. ii. 8.

when the scripture seemeth to induce believers to obedience, by promising this reward ; you are to conceive,
that the Lord speaketh to believers, as a father doth to
his young son, Do this or that, and then I will love
thee ; whereas we know, that the father loveth the
son first, and so doth God * : and therefore this is the
voice of believers, "We love him, because he first loved us," 1 John iv. 19. The Lord doth pay them, or at
least giveth them a sure earnest of their wages, before
he bid them work †.: and therefore the contest of a
believer (according to the measure of his faith) is not,
What will God give me ? but, What shall I give God ?
"What shall I render unto the Lord for all his goodness ?
for thy loving kindness is before mine eyes, and I have
walked in thy truth," Psal. cxvi. 12. xxvi. 3.

Nom. Then, Sir, it seems that holiness of life, and good
works, are not the cause, of eternal happiness, but only
the way thither.

Evan. Do you not remember that our Lord Jesus
himself, saith, " I am the way, the truth and the life?"
John xiv. 6. and doth not the apostle say to the believing
Colossians, " As ye have received Jesus Christ the Lord,
so walk in him?" Col. ii. 6. ‡ That is, as ye have
received him by faith, so go on in your faith, and by
his power walk in his commandments. So that good
works (as I conceive) may rather be called a believer's
walking in the way of eternal happiness, than the way
itself : but however, this we may assuredly conclude, that
the sum and substance, both of the way, and walking in
the way, consists in the receiving of Jesus Christ by faith,
and in yielding obedience to his law, according to the
measure of that receiving ‖.

---

* Tindal Par. Wick. Mam. p. 88.
† Namely in the way of the covenant of grace. See p. 179.
note.
‡ Elton on the text.
‖ Our author, remembering Nomista's bias, toward good

§ 8. Sir, I am perfuaded, that through my neighbour, Nomifta's afking you thefe queftions, you have been in-

---

works, as feparated from Chrift, puts him in mind, that Chrift, is the way, and that the foul's motion heavenward, is in Chrift; that if a man, being once united to Chrift by faith, moveth heavenward, making progrefs in believing, and by influences derived from Jefus Chrift, walking in his holy commandments. The fcripture acknowledgeth no other holinefs of life, or good works; and concerning the neceffity of thefe, the author moves no debate. But, as to propriety of expreffion, fince good works are the keeping of the commandments, in the way of which we are to go, he conceives, they may, with greater propriety, be called the walking in the way, than the way itfelf. 'Tis certain, that the fcripture fpeaks of walking in Chrift, Col ii. 6. " Walking in his commandments," 2 Chron. xvii. 4. and walking in good works, Eph. ii. 10. And that as thefe terms fignify but one and the fame thing, fo they are all metaphorical. But one would think, the calling of good works, the way to be walked in, is farther removed from the propriety of expreffion, than the calling them, the walking in the way. But the author waving this, as a matter of phrafeology, or manner of fpeaking only, tells us, that affuredly the fum and fubftance, both of the way to eternal happinefs, and of the walking in the way to it, confifts in the receiving of Jefus Chrift by faith, and in yielding obedience to his law, according to the meafure of that receiving. Herein is comprehended, Chrift and holinefs, faith and obedience; which are infeparable. And no narrower is the compafs of the way and walking mentioned, Ifa. xxxv 8, 9. " It fhall be called the way of holinefs—the redeemed fhall walk there." The way of holinefs, or, the holy way, (according to an ufual Hebraifm) as it is generally underftood by interpreters, is, the way leading to heaven, faith Pifcator; to wit, Chrift, faith,—and the doctrine of a holy life. Fererius apud Pol. Synop in Loc. And now, that our author, though he conceives good works are not fo properly called the way, as the walking; yet doth not fay, that in no fenfe, they may be called the way, but doth exprefsly affert them, to be the foul's walking in the way of eternal happinefs: he cannot juftly be charged here (more than any where elfe in his book) with teaching, that holinefs is not neceffary to falvation; unlefs one will in the firft place, fay, that though the way itfelf, to eternal happinefs, is neceffary to falvation, yet the walking in the way is not neceffary to it; which would be Antinomianifm with a witnefs.

A a 3

terrupted in your difcourfe, in fhewing how faith doth enable a man to exercife his Chriftian graces, and perform his Chriftian duties aright: and therefore I pray you go on.

Evan. What fhould I fay more? for the time would fail me to tell, how that according to the meafure of any man's faith. is his true peace of confcience ; for faith the apoftle, " Being juftified by faith, we have peace with God,,' Rom. v. 1.   Yea, faith the prophet Ifaiah, " Thou wilt keep him in perfect peace, whofe mind is ftaid on thee, becaufe he trufteth in thee," Ifa. xxvi. 3. Here there is a fure and true grounded peace : therefore it is of faith, faith the apoftle, " That it might be by grace, and that the promife might be fure to all the feed," Rom. iv. 16.   And anfwerable to a man's believing, that he is, juftified freely by God's grace, through that redemption that is in Jefus Chrift*, Rom iv. 3, 24: is his true humility of fpirit.   So that, although he be endowed with excellent gifts and graces, and though he perform never fo many duties, he denies himfelf in all: he doth not make them as ladders, for him to afcend up into heaven by; but defires to " be found in Chrift, not having his own righteoufnefs, which is of the law, but that which is thro' the faith of Chrift," Phil. iii. 9.   He doth not think himfelf to be one ftep nearer to heaven, for all his works and performances.   And if he hear any man praife him for his gifts and graces, he will not conceit that he hath obtained the fame by his own induftry and pains-taking, as fome men have proudly thought : neither will he fpeak it out, as fome have done, faying thefe gifts and graces have coft me fomething, I have taken much pains to obtain them ; but he faith, "By the grace of God I am what I am; and not I, but the grace of God that was

---

* And not for any thing wrought in himfelf, or done by himfelf. See more, p. 177. note †.

with me," 1 Cor. xv. 10. And if he behold an ignorant man, or a wicked liver, he will not call him carnal wretch, or prophane fellow ; nor fay, " Stand by thyfelf, come not near to me, for I am holier than thou," Ifa. lxv. 5. (as fome have faid :) but he pitieth fuch a man, and prays for him ; and in his heart he faith concerning himfelf, " Who maketh thee to differ ? and what haft thou, that thou haft not received ?" 1 Cor. iv. 7.

And thus I might go on, and fhew you, how according to any man's faith, is his true joy in God, and his true thankfulnefs to God, and his patience in all troubles and, afflictions, and his contentednefs in any condition, and his willingnefs to fuffer ; and his cheerfulnefs in fuffering, and his contentednefs to part with any earthly thing. Yea, according to any man's faith, is his ability to pray aright, Rom x. 14. to hear or read the word of God aright, to receive the facrament with profit and comfort ; and to do any duty, either to God, or man, after a right manner, and to a right end, Heb. iv. 2. Yea, according to the meafure of any man's faith, is his love to Chrift, and fo to man for Chrift's fake ; and fo confequently his readinefs and willingnefs to forgive an injury, yea, to forgive an enemy, and to do good to them that hate him : and the more faith any man hath, the lefs love he hath to the world, or the things that are in the world. To conclude, the greater any man's faith is, the more fit he is to die, and the more willing he is to die.

Neo. Well, Sir, now I do perceive that faith is a moft excellent grace, and happy is that man, that hath a great meafure of it.

Evan. The truth is, faith is the chief grace that Chriftians are to be exhorted to get, and excercife ; and therefore, when the people afked our Lord Chrift, what they fhould do to work the works of God ? he anfwered and faid, " This is the work of God, that ye believe on him, whom he hath fent," John vi. 29. Speaking, as if there no other duty at all required; but only believing: for indeed, to fay as the thing is, believing includeth all other duties in it, and they fpring all from it; and therefore, faith one, preach faith, and preach all. Whilft I bid man believe, faith learned Rollock *, I bid him do all good things; for faith Dr Prefton †, truth of belief will bring forth truth of holinefs: if a man believe, works of fanctification will follow; for faith draws after it inherent righteoufnefs and fanctification. Wherefore (faith he) if a man will go about this great work, to change his life to get victory over any fin, that it may not have dominion over him, to have his confcience purged from dead works, and to be made partaker of the divine nature, let him not go about it as a moral man; that is, let him not confider what commandments there are, what the rectitude is which the law requires, and how to bring his heart to it; but let him go about it as a Chriftian, that, is, let him believe the promife of pardon, in the blood of Chrift; and the very believing the promife, will be able to cleanfe his heart from dead works. ‡

Neo. But I pray you, Sir, whence hath faith its power and virtue to do all this?

Evan. Even from our Lord Jefus Chrift: for faith doth ingraft a man, who is by nature a wild olive branch, into Chrift, as into the natural olive; and fetcheth fap from the root Chrift, and thereby makes the tree bring forth fruit in its kind ‖: Yea, faith fetcheth a fupernatural efficacy from the death and life of Chrift; by virtue where-

---

* Rollock on John.   † Pag. 330, 340, 344, 346.

‡ The fum hereof, is, That no confiderations, no endeavours, whatfoever, will truly fanctify a man, without faith. Howbeit, fuch confiderations and endeavours are neceffary, to promote and advance the fanctification of the foul by faith.

‖ Ward's life of faith, p. 6, 7, 8, 74, 75.

of it metamorphofeth * the heart of a believer, and cre-
ates and infufeth into him new principles of actions †. So

------

* Transformeth or changeth, Rom. xii. 2. " Be ye tranf-
formed by the renewing of your mind."

† Viz. Inftrumentally. It cannot be denied, that our author
placeth faith before the new principles of actions, in this paffage;
and before the habits of grace, p. 170. And yet it will not
follow, that, in his opinion, there can be no gracious change in
the foul before faith. What he doth indeed teach, in this
matter, is warranted by the plain teftimony of the apoftle,
Eph. i. 13. " After that ye believed, ye were fealed with that
Holy Spirit of promife." And what this fealing is, at leaft,
as to the chief part of it, may be learned from John i, 16. " And
of his fulnefs have all we received, and grace for grace." For
as fealing is the impreffion of the image of the feal on the wax,
fo that it thereby receives, upon it, point for point on the feal;
fo believers, being fealed with the Spirit of Chrift, receive grace
for grace in Chrift, whereby they are made like him, and bear
his image. And as it is warranted by the word; fo it is agreeable to the old Proteftant doctrine, That we are regenerate by
faith; which is the title of the third chapter of the third book
of Calvin's inftitutions; and is taught in the old confeffion,
Art. 3. in thefe words, Regeneration is wrought by the power
of the Holy Ghoft, working in the hearts of the elect of God,
an affured faith; and Art. 13. in thefe words, So foon as the
Spirit of the Lord Jefus (which God's elect children receive by
true faith) taketh poffeffion in the heart of any man, fo foon
doth he regenerate and renew the fame man.

' Neverthelefs, I am not of the mind, that, either in truth, or
in the judgment of our reformers, or of our author, the firft act
of faith, is an act of an irregenerate, that is to fay, a dead foul.
But to underftand this matter aright, I conceive, one muft
diftinguifh, betwixt regeneration taken ftrictly, and taken largely; and betwixt new powers, and new habits or principles, of
action. Regeneration, ftrictly fo called, is the quickning of the
dead foul, by the Spirit of Chrift paffively received; and goes
before faith, according to John i. 12, 13. " But as many as
received him, to them gave he power to become the fons of
God, even to them that believe on his name; which were born,
not of blood—but of God." This is called, by Ameftus, the
firft regeneration, Medul. Lib. 1. Chap. 29. §. 6. See Cap. 26.
§. 19. And it belongs to, or is the fame with, effectual calling;
in the defcription of which, in the Shorter Catechifm, one finds

that, what a treasure of all graces Christ hath stored up in him, faith draineth, and draweth them out to the use

---

a RENEWING mentioned, whereby sinners are enabled to embrace Jesus Christ: and faith the Larg Catech. on the same subject, they, although in themselves dead in sin, are hereby made able to answer the call. Regeneration, largely taken, presupposing the former, is the same with sanctification, wrought in the soul by the Spirit of Christ, actively received by faith; and so follows faith, Acts xxvi. 18. " Among them which are sanctified by faith, that is in me:" the subjects (of which) are the redeemed, called, and justified. Essen. Comp. Cap. 16. § 3. And accordingly, in the description thereof, in the Shorter Catech. Mention is made of a second renewing, namely, whereby we are renewed in the whole man after the image of God, and are enabled more and more to die unto sin, and live unto righteousness. And thus I conceive regeneration to be taken in the above passages of the Old Confession. The which is confirmed by the following testimonies : being in Christ, we must be new creatures, not in substance, but in qualities and disposition of our minds, and change of the actions of our lives—all which is impossible to them that have no faith. Mr John Davidson's Catech. p. 29. " Sa gude warkes follow as effects of Christ in us, possessed by faith, who—beginneth to work in us regeneration, and renewing of the hail parts and powers of saul and body. Whilk begun sanctification and holiness, he never ceaseth to accomplish, &c." Ibid. p 30. " The effect (viz. of justification) inherent in us, as in a subject, is that new qualitie, which is called inherent righteousness or regeneration." Grounds of Christian Religion, (by the renowned Beza, and Faius, 1586) Chap. 29. § 11. " That new qualitie, then, called inherent righteousness, and regeneration, testified by good works, is a necessary effect of true faith." Ibid. Chap. 31. § 13.

Now, in regeneration taken in the former sense, new powers are put into the soul, whereby the sinner, who was dead in sin, is enabled to discern Christ in his glory, and to embrace him, by faith. But, it is in regeneration taken in the latter sense, that new habits of grace, or immediate principles of actions are given; namely, upon the soul's uniting with Christ, by faith. So Estenius having defined, regeneration, to be, the putting of spiritual life in a man spiritually dead. Comp. Cap. 14. § 11. Afterwards faith, as by regeneration, new powers were put into the man, so by sanctification are given new spiritual habits, theological virtues. Ibid. Cap. 16. § 5. And as the scriptures

of a believer; being as a conduit-cock that watereth all the herbs in the garden. Yea, faith doth apply the blood of Chri∫t to a believer's heart : and the blood of Chri∫t hath in it, not only a power to wa∫h from the guilt of ∫in ; but to clean∫e and purge likewi∫e, from the power and ∫tain of ∫in. And therefore, ∫aith godly Hooker *, If you would have grace, you mu∫t fir∫t of all get faith, and that will bring all the re∫t : let faith go to Chri∫t, and there is meekne∫s, patience, humility, and wi∫dom, and faith will fetch all them to the ∫oul : therefore ∫aith he, You mu∫t not look for ∫anctification †, till you come to Chri∫t in vocation.

Nom. Truly, Sir, I do now plainly ∫ee that I have been deceived, and have gone a wrong way to work : for I verily thought that holine∫s of life mu∫t go before faith, and ∫o be the ground of it, and produce and bring it forth ; wherea∫ I do now plainly ∫ee, that faith mu∫t go before, and ∫o produce and bring forth holine∫s of life.

Evan. I remember a man, who was much enlightened in the knowledge of the go∫pel ‡, who ∫aith,

---

are expre∫s, in that men are ∫anctified by faith, Acts xxvi. 18: So is the Larger Catech. in that, it is in ∫anctification they are " Renewed in their whole man, having the ∫eeds of repentance unto life, and of all other ∫aving graces put into their hearts." Que∫t. 75.

* Poor doubting Chri∫tian, p. 159. † Ibid. p. 154.

‡ This man, Bernardine Ochine, an infamous apo∫tate, was at fir∫t a monk : but as our author ∫aith, being much enlightened in the knowledge of the go∫pel, he not only made profe∫∫ion of the Prote∫tant religion, but, together with the renowned Peter Martyr, was e∫teemed a mo∫t famous preacher of the go∫pel, throughout Italy. Being in danger, on the account of religion, he left Italy, by Martyr's advice : and being much a∫∫i∫ted by the Dutche∫s of Ferrara in his e∫cape, he went fir∫t to Geneva, and then to Zurich, and was admitted a mini∫ter in that city. But di∫covering him∫elf there, as Simon Magus did, after he had joined him∫elf to the church at Samaria, he was bani∫hed : and as ju∫tly reckoned among the fore-runners of the

There be many that think, that, as a man choofeth to ferve a prince, fo men choofe to ferve God. So likewife they think, that as thofe who do beft fervice *, do obtain moft favour of their lord; and as thofe that have loft it, the more they humble themfelves, the fooner they recover it: even fo they think the cafe ftands betwixt God and them; whereas, faith he, it is not fo, but clean contrary, for he himfelf faith, " Ye have not chofen me, but I have chofen you ;" John xv. 16. And not, for that we repent, and humble ourfelves, and do good works; he giveth us his grace: but we repent, humble ourfelves, do good works, and become holy, becaufe he giveth us his grace. The good thief on the crofs was not illuminated becaufe he did confefs Chrift; but he did confefs Chrift becaufe he was illuminated. For, faith Luther†, The tree muft firft be, and then the fruit. For the apples make not the tree, but the tree maketh the apples. So faith firft maketh the perfon, which afterwards bringeth forth works. Therefore to do the law without faith, is to make the apples of wood and earth without the tree : which is not to make apples, but meer fantafies. Wherefore, neighbour Nomifta, let me intreat you, that whereas before, you have reformed your life that you might believe; why now believe, that you may reform your life : and do not any longer work

---

execrable Socinus. See Hornbeck, Apar. ad Controv. Soc. p. 47. Hence one may plainly fee, how there are fermons of his, which might fafely, and to good purpofe, be quoted. And as for the character given him by the author here; if one is in hazard of reckoning it an applaufe. One muft remember, that it is no greater than what the apoftle gives to the guilty of the fin againft the Holy Ghoft, Heb. vi. 6. " Thofe who were once enlightened, and have tafted of the heavenly gift," &c. Which I make no queftion, but our author had his eye upon, in giving this man his character very pertinently.

* Bernard. Ochine's ferm. of Predeft.

† On Gal. page 124.

to get an interest in Christ; but believe your interest in Christ, that so you may work *. And then you will not make the change of your life the ground of your faith, as you have done; and, as Mr † Culverwell saith, many do, who being asked, what caused them to believe? They answer, because they have truly repented, and changed their course of life ‡.

Ant. Sir, what think you of a preacher, that in my hearing said, he durst not exhort nor persuade sinners to believe their sins were pardoned, before he saw their lives reformed; for fear they should take more liberty to sin?

Evan. Why, what should I say, but that I think that preacher was ignorant of the mystery of faith ‖ § ?

---

* *i. e.* By believing, get a saving interest in Christ; whereas before, you have set yourself, as it were, to work it. See the note on the definition of faith.

† In his treatise of faith.

‡ Which, adds he, if it proceed not from faith, is not so much as a sound proof of faith, much less can it be any cause to draw them to believe, p. 20. " The only firm ground of saving faith, is God's truth, revealed in his word; as is plainly taught, Rom. x. 17." Ibid. pag. p. 21.

‖ Ward's life of faith, p. 56.

§ This censure, as it natively follows upon the overthrowing of that doctrine, viz. That holiness of life must go before faith, and so be the ground of it, and produce and bring it forth. p. 190. so it is founded on these two ancient Protestant principles, (1.) That the belief of the remission of sin, is comprehended in saving, justifying faith; of which, see page 175. note; and the note on the definition of faith. (2) That true repentance, and acceptable reformation of life, do necessarily flow from, but go not before saving faith; of which, see page 136. note; and page 137. note. Hence it necessarily follows, that remission of sin must be believed, before there can be any acceptable reformation of life; and, that that preacher's fear was groundless, reformation of life, being so caused by the faith of remission of sin, that it is inseparable from it; as our author teacheth in the following passages. Calvin's censure, in this case, is fully as

B b

For it * is of the nature of fovereign waters, which fo wafh off the corruption of the ulcer ; that they cool the heat, and ftay the fpreading of the infection ; and fo by degrees heal the fame. Neither did he know, that it is of the nature of cordials, which fo comfort the heart and eafe it ; that they alfo expel the noxious humours, and ftrengthens nature againft them †.

Ant. And I am acquainted with a profeffor, though, God knows ‡, a very weak one, that faith, if he fhould believe before his life be reformed, then he might believe, and yet walk on in his fins: I pray you, Sir, what would you fay to fuch a man ?

Evan. Why I could fay with Dr ‖ Prefton, let him, if he can, believe truly, and do this ; but it is impoffible : let him believe, and the other will follow ; truth of belief will bring forth truth of holinefs ; for, who, if he ponder it well, can fear a flefhly licentioufnefs, where the believing foul is united and married to Chrift § ? the law, as it is the covenant of works, and Chrift, are fet in oppofiti-

---

fevere: as for them (faith he) that think that repentance doth rather go before faith, than flow or fpring forth of it, as a fruit out of a tree, they never knew the force thereof. Inftit. book 3. chap. 3. § 1. Yet when we refer the beginning of repentance to faith, we do not dream, a certain mean fpace of time, wherein it bringeth it out: but we mean to fhew that a man cannot earneftly apply himfelf to repentance, unlefs he know himfelf to be of God. Ibid. § 2.

* Viz. faith.
† Even fo, faith not only juftifies a finner, but fanctifies him in heart and life.
‡ I think this expreffion might very well have been fpared here.
‖ New. Cov. p. 361.
§ " Q. Doth not this doctrine (viz. of juftification by faith without works) make men fecure and prophane ? A. No, for it cannot be, but they, who are ingrafted into Chrift by faith, fhould bring forth fruits of thankfulnefs. Palat. Catech. Q 64.

on * : as two hufbands to one wife fucceffively † : whilft the law was alive in the confcience, all the fruits were deadly, Rom. vii 5., but Chrift taking the fame fpoufe to himfelf, (the law being dead) by his quickning Spirit doth make her fruitful to God ‡, and fo raifeth up feed to the former hufband ; for materially thefe are the works of the law, though produced by the Spirit of Chrift in the gofpel ||.

Ant. And yet, Sir, I am verily perfuaded, that there be many, both preachers and profeffors, in this city, of the very fame opinion, that thefe two are of.

Evan. The truth is §, many preachers ftand upon the praife of fome moral virtue, and do inveigh againft fome vice of the times, more than upon preffing men to believe : but faith a learned writer ¶, It will be our condemnation, if we love darknefs rather than light, and defire ftill to be groping in the twilight of morality, the precepts of moral men, than to walk in the true light of divinity, which is the doctrine of Jefus Chrift ** : and I pity the prepofterous care and unhappy travel of many

---

* Towne's affertion of grace, p. 143.
† Rom. vii. 4. ‡ Rom. vii. 4, 6.
|| As a woman married to a fecond hufband, after the death of the firft, doth the fame work for fubftance, in the family, that was required of her by the firft hufband ; yet does it not to, nor as under the authority of the dead hufband, but the living one : fo the good works of believers are materially, and but materially, the works of the law (as a covenant) the firft hufband now dead to the believer. In this fenfe only, the law is here treated of : and to make the good works of believers, formally the works of the law, as a covenant and hufband, is to contradict the apoftle, Rom. vii. 4, 5. 6 to make them deadly fruits, difhonourable to Chrift the fecond hufband, and unacceptable to God.
§ Ward's life of faith, p. 19.
¶ William's feven golden candlefticks, p. 39.
** Ward's life of faith, p. 6, 7.

well affected, who study the practice of this and that
virtue, neglecting this cardinal and radical virtue : as if
a man should water all the tree, and not the root : fain
would they shine in patience, meekness and zeal, and yet
are not careful to establish and root themselves in faith,
which should maintain all the rest; and therefore all their
labour hath been in vain and to no purpose.

Nom. Indeed, Sir, this, which ye have now said, I
have found true by my own experience: for I have *
laboured and endeavoured, to get victory over such corruptions, as to overcome my dulness, and to perform
duities with chearfulness ; and all in vain.

Evan. And no marvel ; for, to pray, to meditate, to
keep sabbath cheerfully, to have your conversation in
heaven, is as possible for you yourself to do, as for iron to
swim. †, or for stones to ascend upwards : but yet nothing
is impossible to faith, it can naturalize these things unto
you ; it can make a mole of the earth, a soul of heaven;
wherefore, tho' you have tried all moral conclusions of
purposing, promising, resolving, vowing, falling, watching, and self-revenge : yet get you to Christ, and with the
finger of faith, touch but the hem of his garment ; and
you shall feel virtue come from him, for the curing of all
your diseases. Wherefore I beseech you, come out of
yourself unto Jesus Christ, and apprehend him by faith,
as (blessed be God) you see your neighbour Neophytus
hath done ; and then shall you find the like lothing of
sin, and love to the law of Christ, as he now doth ; yea,
then shall you find your corruptions dying and decaying
daily, more and more, as I am confident he shall.

Neo I but, Sir, shall I not have power, quite to overcome all my corruptions, and to yield perfect obedience

---

* After that manner.
† Ward's life of faith, p. 68, 69, 70.

to the law of Chriſt, as the Lord knows I much deſire?

Evan. If you could believe perfectly, then ſhould it be even according to your deſire : according to that of Luther *, If we could perfectly apprehend Chriſt, then ſhould we be free from ſin : but (alas) whilſt we are here, we know but in part, and ſo believe but in part, and ſo receive Chriſt but in part, 1 Cor. xiii. 9 and ſo, conſequently, are holy but in part : witneſs James the juſt, including himſelf, when he ſaith, " In many things we ſin all," James iii. 2. John the faithful and loving diſciple, when he ſaith, " If we ſay we have no ſin, we deceive ourſelves, and the truth is not in us," 1 John i. 8. Yea, and witneſs Luther †, when he ſaith, a Chriſtian man hath a body, in whoſe members, as Paul ſaith, " Sin dwelleth and warreth," Rom vii. 15. And albeit he fall not into outward and groſs ſins, as murder, adultery, theft and ſuch like, yet is he not free from impatience, and murmuring againſt God ; yea, ſaith he, I feel in myſelf covetouſneſs, luſt, anger, pride and arrogancy, alſo the fear of death, heavineſs, hatred, murmurings, impatience ‡. So that you muſt not look to be quite without ſin, whilſt you remain in this life : yet this I dare promiſe you, that as you grow from faith to faith, ſo ſhall you grow from ſtrength to ſtrength in all other graces. Wherefore ſaith godly Hooker ||, ſtrengthen this grace of faith, and ſtrengthen all : nouriſh this, and nouriſh all. So that if you can attain to a great meaſure of faith, you ſhall be ſure to attain to a great meaſure of holineſs; according to the ſaying of Dr Preſton §, He that hath the ſtrongeſt faith, he that believeth in the greateſt degree the promiſe of pardon and remiſſion of

---

* On Gal. p. 173. † On Gal. p. 144.

‡ Ward's life of faith, p. 149.

|| Soul's effectual calling, p 610. § New Cov. p. 144.

fins; I dare boldly fay, he hath the holieft heart, and the holieft life.   And therefore I befeech you, labour to grow ftrong in the faith of the gofpel, Phil. i. 27.

§ 9. *Neo.* O, Sir, I defire it with all my heart; and therefore I pray you tell me, what you would have me to do, that I may grow more ftrong?

Evan. Why, furely the beft advice and counfel that I can give you, is to exercife that faith which you have: and wreftle againft doubtings; and be earneft with God in prayer for the increafe of it; Forafmuch, faith Luther*, as this gift is in the hands of God only, who beftoweth it when, and on whom he pleafeth; thou muft refort unto him, by prayer, and fay with the apoftles, "Lord increafe our faith," Luke xvii. 5.   And you muft alfo be diligent in hearing the word preached; for as faith cometh by hearing, Rom. x. 17.   fo it is alfo increafed by hearing.   And you muft alfo read the word, and meditate upon the free and gracious promifes of God: for the promifes is the immortal feed, whereby the Spirit of Chrift begets and increafeth faith, in the hearts of all his. And laftly, you muft frequent the facrament of the Lord's fupper, and receive it as often as conveniently you can †.

Ant. But, by your favour, Sir, if faith be the gift of God, and he give it when, and to whom he pleafeth: then I conceive that man's ufing fuch means will not procure any greater meafure of it, than God is pleafed to give.

Evan. I confefs it is not the means, that will either beget or increafe faith; but it is the Spirit of God in the ufe of means that doth it: fo that as the means will not do it without the Spirit, neither will the Spirit do it without the means, where the means may be had. Wherefore, I pray you, do not you hinder him from ufing the means.

---

* Choice fermon, p. 27.   † Poor doubt. Chrift. p. 148.

Neo. Sir, for mine own part, let him say what he will, I am resolved, by the assistance of God, to be careful and diligent in the use of these means, which you have now prescribed: that so, by the increasing of my faith, I may be the better enabled to subject to the will of the Lord, and so walk, as that I may please him.

§ 10. But forasmuch as heretofore, he hath endeavoured to persuade me to believe diverse points, which then I could not see to be true, and therefore could not assent unto them; methinks I do now begin to see some shew of truth in them: therefore, Sir, if you please to give me leave, I will tell you what points they are, to the intent I may have your judgment and direction therein.

Evan. Do so, I pray you.

1. *Neo.* Why? first of all, he hath endeavoured to persuade me that a believer is not under the law, but is altogether delivered from it.

2. That a believer doth not commit sin.

3. That the Lord can see no sin in a believer.

4. That the Lord is not angry with a believer for his sins.

5. That the Lord doth not chastise a believer for his sins.

6. *Lastly,* That a believer hath no cause, neither to confess his sins, nor to crave pardon at the hands of God for them, neither yet to fast, nor mourn, nor humble hemself before the Lord for them.

Evan. These points, which you have now mentioned, have occasioned many needless and fruitless disputes; and that because men have either not understood what they have said, or else not declared whereof they have affirmed: for in one sense they may all of them be truly affirmed; and in another sense they may all of them be truly denied: wherefore, if we would clearly understand

the truth, we muſt deſtinguiſh betwixt the law, as it is
the law of works, and as it is the law of Chriſt *.

* The Antinomian ſenſe of all theſe poſitions, is, no doubt,
erroneous and deteſtable, and is oppoſed and diſproven by our
author. The poſitions themſelves are paradoxes, bearing a
precious goſpel-truth, which he maintains againſt the legaliſt :
but, I doubt, it is too much to call them all Antinomian paradoxes. But to call them ſimply, and by the lump, Antinomian
errors, is ſhocking ; one might as good ſay, it is a Popiſh, or
Lutheran error, that the bread in the ſacrament, is Chriſt's
body : and that it is a Socinian, Arminian or Baxterian error,
that a ſinner is juſtified by faith : for the firſt four of the paradoxes, are as directly ſcriptural, as theſe are ; though the
Antinomian ſenſe of the former is antiſcriptural, as is the Popiſh,
Lutheran, Socinian, Arminian, and Baxterian-ſenſe of the latter,
reſpectively. At this rate, one might ſubvert the very founda-
tions of Chriſtianity, as might eaſily be inſtructed, if there were
ſufficient cauſe to exemplify it here. How few doctrines of the
Bible are there, that have not been wreſted to an erroneous
ſenſe, by ſome corrupt men or other ? Yet will not their corrupt
gloſſes warrant the condemning of the ſcriptural poſitions themſelves, as erroneous.

The firſt four of theſe paradoxes, are found in the following
texts of ſcripture, viz. the

1ſt, Rom. vi. 14. " Ye are not under the law, but under
grace." Chap vii. 6. " Now we are delivered from the law."

2d, 1 John iii 6. " Whoſoever abideth in him, ſinneth not."
Ver. 9. " Whoſoever is born of God, doth not commit ſin,—
and he cannot ſin."

3d, Numb. xxiii. 21. " He hath not beheld iniquity in Jacob,
neither hath he ſeen perverſeneſs in Iſrael." Cant. iv. 7. " Thou
art all fair, my love, there is no ſpot in thee."

4th, Iſa. liv 9. " So have I ſworn, that I would not be wroth
with thee, nor rebuke thee."

The caſe ſtanding thus, theſe paradoxes muſt needs be ſenſed,
one way or other, agreeable to the analogy of faith, and ſo defended, by all who own the divine authority of the holy ſcripture. And as an orthodox divine would not condemn the two
propoſitions, above mentioned, brought in for illuſtration of this
matter, but clear the ſame, by giving a ſound ſenſe of them, and
rejecting the unſound ſenſe, as, that 'tis true that the bread, is
Chriſt's body ſacramentally ; falſe, that it is ſo by tranſubſtan-
tiation, or conſubſtantiation ; that 'tis true, ſinners are juſtified
by faith, as an inſtrument, apprehending and applying Chriſt's

Now as it is the law of works, it may be truly ſaid, that a believer is not under the law, but is delivered from it *, according to that of the apoſtle, Rom. vi 14. " Ye are not under the law, but under grace ;" and Rom. vii. 6. " But now we are delivered from the law." And if believers be not under the law, but are delivered from the law, as it is the law of works ; then, though they ſin, yet do they not tranſgreſs the law of works; for, " Where no law is, there is no tranſgreſſion," Rom. iv. 15. And therefore ſaith the apoſtle John, " Whoſoever abideth in him, ſinneth not," 1 John iii. 6. that is, (as I conceive) whoſoever abideth in Chriſt by

─────────────────

righteouſneſs; falſe, that they are juſtified by it, as a work, fulfilling the pretended new proper goſpel-law : ſo our author gives a ſafe and ſound ſenſe of theſe ſcriptural paradoxes, and rejects the unſound ſenſe, put upon them by Antinomians ; and this he doth, by applying to them, the diſtinction of the law, as it is the law of works, *i. e.* the covenant of works, and as it is the law of Chriſt, *i e.* a rule of life, in the hand of a Mediator to believers. Now, if this diſtinction be not admitted here, neither in theſe, nor equivalent terms ; but the law of Chriſt, and the law of works, muſt be reckoned one and the ſame thing : then believers in Chriſt, whom none but Antinomians will deny to be under the law, as it is the law of Chriſt, or a rule of life, are evidently ſtaked down under the covenant of works ſtill ; foraſmuch as, in the ſenſe of the holy ſcripture, as well as in the ſenſe of our author, the law of works is the covenant of works. And ſince 'tis plain from the holy ſcripture, and from the Weſtminſter Confeſſion, that believers are not under the law, as a covenant of works : a way, which, by this diſtinction, our author had blocked up, is, by rejecting of it, and confounding the law of works, and law of Chriſt, opened for Antinomians to caſt off the law for good and all.

The two laſt of theſe paradoxes are conſequentially ſcriptural, as neceſſarily following upon the former, being underſtood in the ſame ſenſe as they are, and as our author explains them.

* " True believers be not under the law, as a covenant of works. Weſtm. Confeſſ. Chap. 19. § 6. The law of works, ſaith our author, p. 6. is as much to ſay, as the covenant of works.

faith, finneth not againft the law of works *. And if a
believer fin not againft the law of works; then can God
fee no fin in a believer, as a tranfgreffion of that law †.
And therefore it is faid, Numb. xxiii. 21; " He hath
not beheld iniquity in Jacob, neither hath he feen per-
verfenefs in Ifrael." And again, it is faid, Jer. l. 20.
" At that time the iniquity of Ifrael fhall be fought for,
and there fhall be none ; and the fins of Judah, and they
fhall not be found." And in Cant iv. 7. Chrift faith
concerning his fpoufe, " Behold, thou art all fair, my
love, and there is no fpot in thee." And if God can
fee no fin in a believer, then affuredly he is neither
angry, nor doth chaftife a believer for his fins, as a
tranfgreffion of that law ‡ : and hence it is that the Lord
faith concerning his own people that were believers,
Ifa xxvii. 4 " Anger is not in me." And again, Ifa liv 9.
The Lord, fpeaking comfortably to his fpoufe the church,

---

* " As the warld is altogether fet upon finne, and can do
nathing but finne: fo they that are borne of God finne not: not
that their fiones of themfelves are not deadly, but becaufe their
perfoos are fo lively in Chrift, that the deadlinefs of finne cannot
prevail againft them." Mr John Davidfon's Catechifm, p. 32.
What he means by the deadlinefs of fin, appears from thefe
words a little after. " Howbeit the condemnation of finne be
removed from the faithful altogidder, &c." The penalty, which
the law of works threatneth, fays our author to Neophytus, p. 204.
" is condemnation, and death eternal; and this you have no caufe
at all to fear."

† Mr James Melvil, to the fame purpofe expreffeth it thus,

But God unto his daughter dear fees nane iniquitie,
Nor in his chofen Ifrael will fpy enormitie:
Not luking in her bowk, whilk is with ferntickles repleit,
But ever into Chrift her face, whilk pleafand is and fweet.
          Morning Vifion, dedicated to King James VI p. 85.

‡ Such anger is revenging wrath; and fuch chaftifement is
proper punifhment, inflicted for fatisfying offended juftice; in
which fenfe, it is faid, Ifa. liii. 5 " The chaftifement of our
peace was upon him:" to wit, on Jefus Chrift; and therefore it
cannot be on believers themfelves.

faith, " As I have ſworn that the waters of Noah ſhall
no more go over the earth, ſo have I ſworn that I will
no more be wroth with thee, nor rebuke thee "
Now, if the Lord be not angry with a believer, neither
doth chaſtiſe him for his ſins, as they are any tranſgreſſion of the law of works; then hath a believer neither
need to confeſs his ſins unto God, nor crave pardon for
them; nor yet to faſt, nor mourn, nor humble himſelf
for them, as conceiving them to be any tranſgreſſion of
the law, as it is the law of works *. Thus you ſee,
that if you conſider the law in this ſenſe, then all theſe
points follow; according as you ſay our friend Antinomiſta
hath endeavoured to perſuade you.

---

* Our author doth not indeed here refute the Antinomian
error, that the believer ought not to mourn for his ſins: he doth
that effectually in the next paragraph. But here he refutes the
legaliſt, who will needs have the believer ſtill to be under the
law, as it is the covenant of works; and therefore to confeſs
and mourn, &c. for his ſins, as ſtill committed againſt the covenant of works. But, it is evident as the light, that believers are
not under the covenant of works, or in other terms, under the
law, as, that covenant; and that principle being once fixed, the
whole chain of conſequences, which our author hath here made,
does neceſſarily follow thereupon. It is ſtrange that nothing
can be allowed, in believers, to be mourning for ſin: unleſs
they mourn for it, as unbelievers, as perſons under the covenant
of works, who doubtleſs are under the curſe and condemnation,
for their ſin, Gal. iii. 10. But, As our obedience, now, is not
the performance, ſo our ſinning is not the violation, of the condition of the old covenant. Believers—their ſins now, though
tranſgreſſions of the law, are not counted violations of the conditions of the covenant of works, under which they are not."
Brown on juſtification, Chap. xv. p. 224. " If ſenſe of ſin be
taken for the unbelieving feeling of, and judging myſelf caſt out
of his ſight, and condemned; whereas yet I am in Chriſt, and
it is God that juſtifies me; who is he that ſhall condemn?
Rom. viii. 33, 34. we ſhall agree with Antinomians. This is
indeed the haſty ſenſe of unbelief, Pſal. xxxi. 22. John ii. 4.
" Hence let them be rebuked, who ſay not that Chriſt in the
goſpel hath taken away this ſenſe of ſin." Rutherfoord on the
covenants, p. 222.

But if you do confider the law, as it is the law of
Chrift; then they do not fo, but quite contrary. For
as the law is the law of Chrift, it may be truly faid,
that a believer is under the law, and not delivered
from it : according to that of the apoftle, 1 Cor. ix. 21.
" Being not without law to God, but under the law
to Chrift:" and according to that of the fame apoftle,
Rom. iii. 31. " Do we then make void the law through
faith? God forbid; yea, (by faith) we eftablifh the
law." And if a believer be under the law, and not
delivered from it, as it is the law of Chrift; then if he
fin, he doth thereby tranfgrefs the law of Chrift : and
hence I do conceive it is, that the apoftle John faith,
both concerning himfelf and other believers, 1 John i: 8.
" If we fay we have no fin, we deceive ourfelves, and
the truth is not in us." And fo faith the apoftle
James, chap. iii. 2. " In many things we offend all."
And if a believer tranfgrefs the law of Chrift, then
doubtlefs, he feeth it : for it is faid, Prov. v. 21.
" That the ways of men are before the eyes of the Lord,
and he pondereth all his goings." And in Heb. iv. 13.
it is faid, " All things are naked and open unto the eyes
of him, with whom we have to do." And if the Lord
doth fee the fins that a believer doth commit againft the
law, as it is the law of Chrift ; then doubtlefs he is angry
with them : for it is faid, Pfal. cvi. 40. That, becaufe
the people, " went a whoring after their own inventions,
therefore was the wrath of the Lord kindled againft his
people, infomuch that he abhorred his own inheritance:"
and in Deut. i. 37. Mofes faith concerning himfelf,
the Lord was angry with him. And if the Lord be
angry with a believer for his tranfgreffing the law of
Chrift, then affuredly (if need be) he will chaftife him for
it : for it is faid * concerning the feed and children of
Jefus Chrift †, " If they forfake my law, and walk not in
my judgments, then will I vifit their tranfgreffions with

---

* Pfal. lxxxix. 30, 31, 32.　　† Ball on the Cov. p. 41.

the rod, and their iniqu'ties with ſtripes." And in 1 Cor.
xi. 30. it is ſaid concerning believers, "for this cauſe (namely, their unworthy receiving of the ſacrament) many are
weak and ſickly among you, and many ſleep." And if the
Lord be angry with believers, and do chaſtiſe them for
their ſins, as they are a tranſgreſſion of the law of Chriſt;
then hath a believer cauſe to confeſs his ſins unto the
Lord, and to crave pardon for them, yea, and to faſt,
and mourn, and humble himſelf for them, as conceiving
them to be a tranſgreſſion of the law of Chriſt *.

§ 11. And now my loving neighbour Neophytus, I
pray you to conſider ſeriouſly of theſe things: and learn
to diſtinguiſh aright betwixt the law, as it is the law of
works, and as it is the law of Chriſt; and that in effect
and practice, I mean, in heart and conſcience.

Neo. Sir, it is the unfeigned deſire of my heart, ſo to
do; and therefore I pray you give me ſome direction
therein †.

Evan. Surely the beſt direction that I can give you,
is, to labour truly to know, and firmly to believe, that
you are not under the law, as it is the law of works;
and that you are now under the law, as it is the law of
Chriſt: and that therefore you muſt neither hope for
what the law of works promiſeth, in caſe of your moſt
exact obedience; nor fear what it threateneth, in caſe of

---

* Thus our author hath ſolidly refuted, in this paragraph,
the Antinomian ſenſe of all the ſix poſitions above mentioned.

† Namely, how to improve theſe points of doctrine, in my
practice. There lies the great difficulty: and according as unbelief or faith, has the aſcendant; ſo will the ſoul, in practice,
carry itſelf; confeſſing, begging pardon, faſting, mourning, and
humbling itſelf, either as a condemned malefactor, or as an
offending child.

your moſt imperfect and defective obedience. And yet you may both hope for what the law of Chriſt promiſeth, in caſe of your obedience; and are to fear what it threateneth, in caſe of your diſobedience.

Neo. But, Sir, what be theſe promiſes and threatenings? and, firſt, I pray you tell me, what it is, that the law of works promiſeth?

Evan. The law of works, or which is all one (as I have told you) the covenant of works promiſeth juſtification and eternal life, to all that yield perfect obedience thereto: and this you are not to hope for, becauſe of your obedience. And indeed, to ſay as the thing is, you being dead to the law of works, can yield no obedience at all unto it; for, how can a dead wife yield any obedience to her huſband? and if you can yield no obedience at all unto it, what hope can you have of any reward for your obedience? Nay, let me tell you more. Jeſus Chriſt, the Son of God, hath purchaſed both juſtification, and eternal life, by his perfect obedience to the law of works; and hath freely, given it to you, as it is written, Acts xiii. 39. "By him, all that believe are juſtified from all things, from which ye could not be juſtified by the law of Moſes:" and, verily, verily, ſaith our Saviour, "He that believeth in me, hath everlaſting life," John vi. 47.

Neo. And I pray you, Sir, what doth the law of works threaten, in caſe of man's diſobedience unto it?

Evan. Why, the penalty, which the law of works, in that caſe, threatneth, is condemnation, and death eternal: and this you have no cauſe at all to fear, in caſe of your moſt defective obedience; for no man hath any cauſe to fear the penalty of that law, which he lives not under. Surely a man, that liveth under the laws of England, hath no cauſe to fear the penalties of the laws of Spain or France: even ſo you, that now live under the law of faith, have no cauſe to fear the penalty of the law of works *. Nay, the law of works is dead to you ; and therefore you have no more caufe to fear the threats thereof, than a living wife hath to fear the threats of her dead hufband ; nay, than a dead wife hath to fear the threats of a dead hufband †. Nay, let me fay yet more, Jefus Chrift, by his condemnation, and death upon the crofs, hath delivered you, and fet you free from condemnation, and eternal death; as it is written, Rom. viii. 1. " There is therefore now no condemnation to them that are in Chrift Jefus :" and faith Chrift himfelf, John xi. 26. " Whofoever liveth, and believeth in me, fhall never " die."

And thus you fee your freedom and liberty from the law, as it is the law of works. And that you may be the better enabled to ftand faft in this liberty, where-with Chrift hath made you free ; beware of conceiving that the Lord now ftands in any relation towards you, or will any way deal with you, as a man under that law. So that if the Lord fhall be pleafed, hereafter to beftow upon you a great meafure of faith, whereby you fhall be enabled to yield an exact and perfect obedience to the mind and will of God ‡ : then beware of conceiving that the Lord looks upon it as obedience to the law of works ; or will in any meafure reward you for it, according to

---

* See page 116. notes. " The law as it condemneth and curfeth, is, to the believer, a mere paffive, and a naked ftander by, and hath no activity, nor can it act in that power, upon any f Spain is merely paffive in condemning a free-born man dwelling in Scotland." Rutherfoord's Spirit. Antichrift. p. 87. " The law being fully fatisfied by Chrift, it neither condemneth, nor can it condemn to eternal fufferings, for that is removed from the law to all that are in Chrift." Ibid.

† For, according to the fcripture, the believer is dead to the law, and the law is dead to the believer; namely, as it is the law (or covenant) of works.

‡ Exact and perfect comparatively, not abfolutely.

C c 2

the promifes of that law.   And if in cafe, at any time hereafter, you be, by reafon of the weaknefs of your faith, and ftrength of temptation, drawn afide, and prevailed with, to fwerve from the mind and will of the Lord; then beware of conceiving, that the Lord fees it as any tranfgreffion of the law of works. For if you cannot tranfgrefs that law; then it is impoffible the Lord fhould fee that which is not: and if the Lord can fee no fin in you, as a tranfgreffion of the law of works; then it is impoffible that he fhould either be angry with you, or correct you for any fin, as it is a tranfgreffion of that law. No, to fpeak with holy reverence, (as I faid before) the Lord cannot, by virtue of the covenant of works, either require any obedience of you, or give you an angry look, or an angry word; much lefs threaten and afflict you for any difobedience to that covenant. And therefore, whenfoever your confcience fhall tell you, that you have broken any of the ten commandments; do not conceive that the Lord looks upon you as an angry judge, armed with juftice againft you: much lefs do you fear, that he will execute his juftice upon you, according to the penalty of that covenant; in unjuftifying of you, or depriving you of your heavenly inheritance, and giving you your portion in hell fire. No, affure yourfelf, that your God in Chrift will never unfon you, nor unfpoufe you: no, nor yet, as touching your juftification and eternal falvation, will he love you ever a whit the lefs; though you commit never fo many, or great fins; for this is a certain truth, that as no good, either, in you, or done by you, did move him to juftify you, and give you eternal life; fo no evil in you, or done by you, can move him to take it away from you, being once given *.   And

---

* The author fpeaks exprefsly of the love of God, touching believers juftification and eternal falvation, which, according to the fcripture, he reckons to be given them already. And he afferts, that as no good in them, or done by them, did move

therefore believe it, man, whilſt you live, that as .the
Lord firſt loved you freely, ſo will he hereafter heal your

---

him to love them, ſo as to juſtify them, and give them eternal
life; ſo no evil in them, or done by them, ſhall leſſen that love,
as to their juſtification, and eternal ſalvation; that is, as himſelf
explains it, move him to take eternal life (which includes juſtification) away from them, being once given. This is moſt firm
truth: howbeit the more and the greater the ſins of a believer
are, he may lay his accounts with the more and the greater
effects of God's fatherly indignation againſt him; and the corruption of human nature makes the adding of ſuch a clauſe, in
ſuch a caſe, very neceſſary. What our author here advanceth,
is evident from the holy ſcripture, Pſal. lxxxix. 30, 31, 32. 33, 34.
" If his children forſake my law, and walk not in my judgments,
if they break my ſtatutes and keep not my commandments: then
will I viſit their tranſgreſſion with the rod, and their iniquities
with ſtripes. Nevertheleſs my loving-kindneſs will I not utterly
take from him, nor ſuffer my faithfulneſs to fail; my covenant
will I not break, nor alter the thing that is gone out of my
lips " And to deny it, is, in effect, to affirm, That God loves
believers, as touching their juſtification and eternal ſalvation,
for their holineſs; contrary to Titus iii. 5. " Not by works of
righteouſneſs, which we have done, but according to his mercy
he ſaved us." Rom. vi. 23. " The wages of ſin is death, but
the gift of God is eternal life, through Jeſus Chriſt our Lord."
And, that that love of his to them, changeth according to the
variations of their frame and walk; contrary to Rom. xi. 29.
" The gifts and calling of God are without repentance " But
while the doctrine of the perſeverance of the ſaints, ſtands,
namely, that true believers can neither fall away totally, nor
finally, neither from relative grace, nor from inherent grace;
our author's doctrine in this point, muſt ſtand alſo: and the ſins
of believers, how great or many ſoever they be, can never be of
that kind, which is inconſiſtent with a ſtate of grace; nor of
another, than that of infirmities. See p. 151. note. And how
low ſoever grace is brought in the ſoul of a believer at any time,
through the prevalency of temptation; yet can he never altogether loſe his inherent holineſs, nor can he at any time live
after the fleſh. For, according to the ſcripture, that is not the
ſpot of God's children: but he, who ſo lives, neither is, nor
ever was one of them. Rom. vi. 2. " How ſhall we that are
dead to ſin, live any longer therein? Ver. 14. " Sin ſhall not
have dominion over you: for ye are not under the law, but

backſlidings, and ſtill love you freely, Hoſ. xiv 4: Yea, " He will love you unto the end," John xiii. 1. And although the Lord doth expreſs the fruits of his anger towards you, in chaſtiſing and afflicting of you : yet do not you imagine that your afflictions are penal, proceeding from hatred and vindictive juſtice ; and ſo as payments and ſatisfactions for ſins ; and ſo as the beginning of eternal torments in hell : for you, being (as you have heard) freed from the law of works, and ſo conſequently from ſinning againſt it ; muſt needs likewiſe be freed from all wrath, anger, miſeries, calamities, afflictions, yea and from death itſelf, as * fruits and effects of any tranſ-greſſion againſt that covenant.

---

under grace: Chap. viii. 1. Them which are in Chriſt Jeſus, who walk not after the fleſh, but after the Spirit. See ver. 4. 1 John iii. 9. " Whoſoever is born of God, doth not commit ſin : for his ſeed remaineth in him, and he cannot ſin ; becauſe he is born of God.

" God foreſaw what infirmities, thou wouldſt have, before he gave Chriſt this commiſſion ; and Chriſt foreſaw them, before his acceptance of the charge. If their preſcience could not ſtop God in his gift, nor cool Chriſt in his acceptance, why ſhould it now ?— -" While they do continue, the love of God to thee is not hindred by them." Charnock, vol. 2. Edit. 2. p. 749.

" Obſerve a two-fold diſtinction, 1. Between God's love in itſelf, and the manifeſtation of it to us. That is perpetual and one—without change, increaſe or leſſening :—But the manifeſtation of this love—is variable, according to—our more or leſs careful exerciſe of piety—2. Between God's love to our perſons, and God's love to our qualities and actions. A diſtinction which God well knows how to make.—Parents, I am ſure, are well ſkilled in putting this difference between the vices and perſons of their children ; thoſe they hate, theſe they love.—The caſe is alike between God and the elect : his love to their perſons is from everlaſting the ſame ; nor doth their ſinfulneſs leſſen it, nor their ſanctity increaſe it; becauſe God, in loving their perſons, never conſidered them otherwiſe, than as moſt perfectly holy and unblameable in Chriſt." Pemble his works, page 23.

* They are.

And therefore you are never to confeſs your ſins unto the Lord, as though you conceived them to have been committed againſt the law of works; and ſo making you liable to God's everlaſting wrath, and hell-fire : neither muſt you crave pardon and forgiveneſs, for them, that thereupon you may eſcape that penalty : neither do you either faſt, or weep, or mourn, or humble yourſelf, out of any conceit that you ſhall thereby ſatisfy the juſtice of God, and appeaſe his wrath, either in whole or in part ; and ſo eſcape his everlaſting vengeance. For if you be not under the law of works ; and if the Lord ſee no ſin in you, as a tranſgreſſion of that law ; and be neither angry with you, nor doth afflict you, for any ſin, as it is a tranſgreſſion of that law ; then conſequently, you have no need either to confeſs your ſins, or crave pardon for them, or faſt, or weep, or mourn, or humble yourſelf for your ſins, as conceiving them to be any tranſgreſſion of the law of works *.

Neo. Well, Sir, you have fully ſatisfied me in this point : and therefore I pray you proceed to ſhew, what is that reward, which the law of Chriſt promiſeth; which you ſaid I might hope for, in caſe of my obedience thereunto ?

Evan. Why, the reward, which (I conceive) the law of Chriſt promiſeth to believers, and which they may hope for, anſwerably to their obedience to it †, is, " a comfortably being, in the enjoyment of ſweet communion with God in Chriſt, even in the time of this life; and a freedom from afflictions, both ſpiritual and corporal, ſo far forth as they are fruits and effects of ſin, as it is any tranſgreſſion of the law of Chriſt ‡" For you know, that

---

* See page 201. note.

† Though not for their obedience, but for Chriſt's obedience.

‡ I read the laſt word of this ſentence, Chriſt, not works,

fo long as a child doth yield obedience to his father's commands, and doth nothing that is difpleafing to him, if he love his child, he will carry himfelf lovingly and kindly towards him, and fuffer him to be familiar with him, and will not whip, nor fcourge him for his difobedience : even fo, if you unfeignedly defire, and endeavour to be obedient unto the mind and will of your loving Father in Chrift ; in doing that which he commands, and in avoiding that which he forbids, both in your general and particular calling ; and that to the end that you may pleafe him ; then, anfwerably as you do fo, your Father will fmile-upon you, when you fhall draw near to him in prayer, or any other of his own ordinances ; and manifeft his fweet prefence, and loving favour towards you ; and exempt you from all outward calamities, except in cafe of trial of your faith and patience, or the like ; as it is written, 2 Chron. xv. 2. " The Lord is with you, while ye are with him ; and if you feek, him he will be found of you." And fo the apoftle James faith, James iv. 8. " Draw nigh to God, and he will draw nigh to you " And O faith the Lord, " That my people had hearkned unto me, and Ifrael had walked in my ways ! he fhould have fed them with the fineft of the wheat, and with honey out of the rock fhould I have fatisfied thee," Pfal. lxxxi. 13, 16. And this may fuffice to have fhewed you what you may hope for, anfwerable to your obedience to the law of Chrift.

Neo. Then, Sir, I pray you proceed to fhew, what is the penalty which the law of Chrift threatneth, and which I am to fear, if I tranfgrefs that law ?

Evan. The penalty which the law of Chrift threatneth, to you, if you tranfgrefs the law of Chrift, and which you are to fear, is the want of near and fweet com-

---

judging it plain, that the latter is a prefs-error. See the laft claufe of page 207, and the reafon here immediately following, with the third paragraph, p. 310.

munion with God in Chriſt, even in the time of this life ;
and a liableneſs to all temporal afflictions, as fruits and
effects of the tranſgreſſing of that law *.

---

* An awful penalty, if rightly underſtood! as comprehending
all manner of ſtrokes and afflictions on the outward and inner
man, called by our author temporal and ſpiritual afflictions,
page 211. on the outward man; not to ſpeak of the reproach,
diſgrace, and contempt, ſucceſsleſs labour and toil, poverty,
miſery and want, and the like, which the believer is liable to,
for his diſ.bedience, as well as others : his ſins lay him open to
the whole train of maladies, pains, torments, ſores, diſeaſes,
and plagues, incident to ſinful fleſh ; by which he may become
a burden to himſelf, and a burden to others. And theſe máy be
inflicted on him, not only by the hand of God, but by the hand
of the devil; as it appears in the caſe of Job. Yea, and the
Lord may, in virtue of this penalty annexed to his law, purſue
the controverſy with the offending believer, even to death: ſo
that his natural life may go in the cauſe of his tranſgreſſion,
1 Cor. xi. 30, 32. To this may be added the marks of God's
indignation againſt his ſin, ſet upon his relations; witneſs the
diſorders, miſchiefs, and ſtrokes, on David's family, for his ſin
in the matter of Uriah, more bitter than death, 2 Sam. xii.
10 11, 12, 14. Chap. xiii. and xv. In the inner man, by virtue
of the ſame penalty, he is liable, for his tranſgreſſion, to be
deprived of the comfort, ſenſe, exerciſe, and ſome meaſure, of
his graces; of his ſenſe of God's love, his peace, joy, actual
communion with God, and acceſs to him in duties; to be
brought under deſertion, hiding of God's face, withdrawing of
the light of the Lord's countenance ; and left to walk in darkneſs, to go mourning without the ſun, and to cry and ſhout
while the Lord ſhutteth out his prayer: to be thrown into
agonies of conſcience, pierced with the arrows of the Almighty
in his ſpirit, compaſſed about and diſtracted with the terrors of
God, ſeized with the fearful apprehenſions of God's revenging
wrath againſt him, and thereby brought unto the brink of abſolute deſpair. Beſides all this, he is liable to the buffetings of
Satan, and horrid temptations, and, for the puniſhment of one
ſin, to be ſuffered to fall into another. And all theſe may, in
virtue of the penalty annexed to the law in the hand of Chriſt,
meet in the caſe of the offending believer, together and at once.
Thus, howbeit God no where threatens to caſt believers in
Chriſt into hell ; yet, he both threatens, and often executes, the
caſting of a hell into them, for their provocations.

· Wherefore, whenſoever you ſhall hereafter tranſgreſs
any óf the ten commandments, you are to know, that you
have thereby tranſgreſſed the law óf Chriſt ; and that the
Lord ſees it, and is angry with it, with a fatherly anger;
and (if need be) will chaſtiſe you, 1 Pet. i. 6. either
with temporal or ſpiritual afflictions, or both.   And this
your heavenly Father will do in love to you ; either
to bring your ſins to remembrance, as he did the ſins
of Joſeph's brethren, Gen xlii. 21.   And as the widow
of Zarephath confeſſeth concerning herſelf, 1 Kings
xvii. 18. or elſe to purge and take away your ſins,
according to that which the Lord ſaith, Iſa. xxvii. 9.
" By this therefore ſhall the iniquity of Jacob be purged,
and this is all the fruit, even the taking away of ſin."
For indeed, ſaith Mr Culverwell *, afflictions, through
God's bleſſing, are made ſpecial means to purge out
that ſinful corruption, which is ſtill in the nature of

Only, the (revenging) wrath and curſe of God, are no part
of the penalty to believers in Chriſt, according to the truth and
our author.   But, whether or not this penalty, as it is without
theſe, leaves the moſt holy and awful law of the great God, and
our Saviour JESUS CHRIST, moſt baſe and deſpicable ? the
ſober-minded reader will eaſily judge for himſelf.
   " The one" viz. (juſtification) " doth equally free all believers
from the revenging wrath of God, and that perfectly in this life."
Larg. Catech. Queſt. 77. " They can never fall from the ſtate
of juſtification ; yet they may, by their ſins, fall under God's
fatherly diſpleaſure, and not have the light of his countenance
reſtored unto them, until they humble themſelves, confeſs their
ſins, beg pardon, and renew their faith and repentance."—
Weſtm. Confeſſ. Chap. 11. Art. 5. " They may—fall into
grievous ſins, and for a time continue therein ; whereby they
incur God's diſpleaſure, and grieve his holy Spirit, come to be
deprived of ſome meaſure of their graces and comforts, have
their hearts hardned, and their conſciences wounded ; hurt and
ſcandalize others, and bring temporal judgments upon themſelves." Ibid. chap. 17. Art. 3. " The threatnings of it ſerve
to ſhew, what even their ſins deſerve ; and what afflictions, in
this life, they may expect for them, although freed from the
curſe thereof, threatned in the law." Ibid. Chap. 19. Art. 6.
   * Of faith, p. 426.

of believers ; and therefore are they in ſcripture moſt
aptly compared to medicines, for ſo they are indeed to
all God's children, moſt ſovereign medicines to cure all
their ſpiritual diſeaſes. And indeed we have all of us
great need thereof ; for as Luther * truly ſaith, we are
not yet perfectly righteous ; for whilſt we remain in this
life, ſin dwelleth ſtill in the fleſh, and this remnant of ſin,
God purgeth. Wherefore, ſaith the ſame Luther in
another place †, When God hath remitted ſins, and
received a man into the boſom of grace, then doth he
lay on him all kind of afflictions ; and doth ſcour and
renew him from day to day. And to the ſame purpoſe
Tindal truly ſaith, If we look on the fleſh, and into the
law ; there is no man ſo perfect, that is not found a ſinner ; nor no man ſo pure, that hath not need to be
purged. And thus doth the Lord chaſtiſe believers, to
heal their natures, and purging out that corruption that
remains therein.

And therefore, whenſoever you ſhall hereafter feel
the Lord's chaſtiſing hand upon you ; let it move you to
take the prophet Jeremiah's counſel, that is, " To ſearch
and try your ways, and turn unto the Lord," Lam. iii. 40.
And confeſs your ſins unto him, ſaying with the prodigal,
Luke xv. 21. " Father, I have ſinned againſt heaven,
and in thy ſight, and am no more worthy to be called
they ſon." And beg pardon and forgiveneſs at his
hands, as you are taught in the fifth petition of the Lord's
prayer, Matth. vi. 12. Yet do not you crave pardon
and forgiveneſs at the hands of the Lord, as a malefactor
doth at the hands of a judge, that feareth condemnation
and death ; as though you had ſinned againſt the law of
works, and therefore feared hell and damnation : but
do you beg pardon and forgiveneſs as a child doth at the
hands of his loving father ; as feeling the fruits of his

---

* On Gal. p. 66.

† Chof. ſermons, ſcrm. of the kingdom of God, p. (mihi) 120.

fatherly anger, in his chaſtiſing hand upon you ; and as fearing the continuance and augmentation of the ſame, if your ſin be not both pardoned and ſubued * : and therefore do you alſo beſeech your loving Father to ſubdue your iniquities, according to his promiſe, Micah vii. 19. And if you find not that the Lord hath heard your prayers, by your feeling your iniquities ſubdued † : then join with your prayers, faſting and weeping, if you can : that ſo you may be the more ſeriouſly humbled before the Lord, and more fervent in prayer. And this, I hope, may be ſufficient to have ſhewed you, what is the penalty, which the law of Chriſt threateneth.

Neo. O but, Sir, I ſhould think myſelf a happy man, if I could be ſo obedient to the law of Chriſt, that he might have no need to inflict this penalty upon me.

Evan. You ſay very well ; but yet, whilſt you carry this body of ſin about you, do the beſt you can, there will be need that the Lord ſhould, now and then, give you ſome fatherly corrections : but yet, this let me tell you, the more perfect your obedience is, the fewer laſhes you ſhall have ; " For the Lord doth not afflict willingly, nor grieve the children of men," Lam. iii. 33. And therefore, according to my former exhortation, and your reſolution, be careful to exerciſe your faith ; and uſe all means to increaſe it ; that ſo it may become effectual ‡, working by love, 1 Theſ. i. 3. Gal. v. 6. For, according to the meaſure of your faith, will be your

---

* Matth. vi. 9, 12. " After this manner therefore pray ye : Our Father which art in heaven—forgive us our debts, as we forgive our debtors."

† The ſubduing of ſin, is the mark of God's hearing prayer for the pardon of it ; if one feels not his iniquity ſubdued, he cannot find that God hath heard his prayers for pardon.

‡ To the producing of holy obedience, according to the meaſure and degree of it.

true love to Chriſt, and to his commandments; and according to your love to them, will be your delight in them, and your aptneſs and readineſs to do them: And hence it is, that Chriſt himſelf ſaith, John xiv. 15. " If ye love me, keep my commandments. And this is the love of God," ſaith that loving diſciple, " That we keep his commandments, and his commandments are not grievous;" 1 John v. 3. Nav, the truth is, if you have this love in your hearts, it will be grievous unto you, that you cannot keep them as you would. O! if this love do abound in your heart, it will cauſe you to ſay with godly Joſeph, in caſe you be tempted as he was, " How can I do this great wickedneſs, and ſo ſin againſt God?" How can I do that, which I know will diſpleaſe ſo gracious a Father, and ſo merciful a Saviour? No, I will not do it; no, I cannot do it: no, you will rather ſay with the Pſalmiſt, " I delight to do thy will, O my God; yea, thy law is within my heart," Pſal. xl. 8.

Nay, let me tell you more, if this love of God in Chriſt be truly, and in any good meaſure, rooted in your heart: then, tho' the chaſtning hand of the Lord be not upon you; nay, tho' the Lord do no way expreſs any anger towards you: yet if you but conſider the Lord's ways towards you, and your ways towards him; you will mourn with a goſpel-mourning, reaſoning with yourſelf after this manner: and was I under the law of works, by nature; and ſo, for every tranſgreſſion againſt any of the ten commandments, made liable to everlaſting damnation? and am I now, through the free mercy and love of God in Chriſt, brought under the law of Chriſt; and ſo ſubject to no other penalty for my tranſgreſſions, but fatherly and loving chaſtiſements, which tend to the purging out of that ſinful corruption that is in me? O! what a loving Father is this! O what a gracious Saviour is this! O what a wretched man am I, to tranſgreſs the laws of ſuch a good God, as he hath been to me! O! the due conſideration of this, will even, as it were,

D d

melt your heart, and cause your eyes to drop with
the tears of godly forrow ; yea, the due confideration
of thefe things will caufe you to lothe yourfelf in your
own fight for your tranfgreffions. Ezek. xxxvi 31. yea,
not only to lothe yourfelf for them, but alfo to leave
them, faying with Ephraim, " What have I to do any
more with idols ?" Hof. xiv. 8. And to caft them away
as a menftruous cloth, faying unto them, get ye hence :
Ifa. xxx. 22. And truly you will defire nothing more,
than that you might fo live, as that you might never fin
againft the Lord any more.   And this is that goodnefs
of God, which, as the apoftle faith, leadeth to repentance :
yea, this is that goodnefs of God, which will lead you to
a free obedience.   So that if you do but apply the goodnefs of God in Chrift to your foul, in any good meafure,
then will you anfwerably yield obedience to the law of
Chrift ; not only without having refpect to what the law
of works either promifeth or threatneth ; but alfo without having refpect to what the law of Chrift either
promifeth or threatneth : you will do that, which the
Lord commandeth, only becaufe he commandeth it,
and to the end that you may pleafe him : and you will
forbear what he forbids, only becaufe he forbids it, to
the end you may not difpleafe him *.   And this obedi-

---

* The author doth here no otherwife exhort a believer, to
yield free obedience, without refpect to what either the law of
works, or law of Chrift, promifeth or threatneth ; than he exhorts him to perfection of obedience, which, in the beginning
of this anfwer he told him, not to be attainable in this life : and
the truth is, neither the one nor the other is the defign of thefe
words. But he had exhorted him before, to ufe all means to
encreafe his faith : and, for his encouragement, he tells him
here, that if he by faith applied the goodnefs of God in Chrift
to his own foul. in any good meafure ; then he would anfwerably, yield obedience. without refpect to what either the law
of works, or law of Chrift promifeth or threatneth, and only
becaufe God commands or forbids. The freenefs of obedience
is of very different degrees ; and believers obedience is never
abfolutely free, till it be abfolutely perfect in heaven : but the
freenefs of their obedience, will always bear proportion to the

ence is like unto that, which our Saviour exhorteth his
diſciples unto, Matth x 8. ſaying, " Freely you have

---

meaſure of their faith, which is never perfect in this life : thus
the more faith, the more freeneſs of obedience ; and the leſs
faith, the leſs of that freeneſs.

" The believer obeys with an angel-like obedience : then
the Spirit ſeems to exhauſt all the commanding aweſomeneſs of
the law, and ſupplies the law's imperious power, with the
ſtrength and power of love." Rutherford, Spirit. Antichriſt,
page 318. " The more of the Spirit, (becauſe the Spirit is eſ-
ſentially free, Pſal. li. 11. 2 Cor. iii. 17) the more freeneſs :
and the more-freeneſs, the more renewed will in the obed ence ;
and the more renewed will, the leſs conſtraint, becauſe freeneſs
exhauſteth conſtraint." Ibid.

" When Chriſt's blood is ſeen by faith, to quiet juſtice, then
the conſcience becometh quiet alſo, and will not ſuff r the heart
to entertain the love of ſin, but ſets the man on work to fear
God for his mercy, and obey all his commandments, out of
love to God for his free gift of juſtification, by grace beſtowed
upon him : for this is the end of the law indeed, whereby it
obtaineth of a man more obedience than any other way."—
Pract. Uſe of ſav. Knowledge, Tit. the third thing requiſite, &c.

Promiſes and threatnings are not, by this doctrine, annexed
to the holy law in vain, even with reſpect to believers : for the
law of God is, in his infinite wiſdom, ſuited to the ſtate of the
creature, to whom it is given ; and therefore, howbeit the
believer's eternal happineſs is unalterably ſecured, from the
moment of his union with Chriſt by faith ; yet, ſince ſin dwells
in him ſtill, while in this world, the promiſes of fatherly ſmiles,
and threatnings of fatherly chaſtiſements, are ſtill neceſſary.
But it is evident, that this neceſſity is intirely founded on the
believer's imperfection ; as in the caſe of a child under age.
And therefore, although his being influenced to obedience, by
the promiſes and threatnings of the law of Chriſt, is not indeed
ſlaviſh, yet it is plainly childiſh, not agreeing to the ſtate of a
perfect man, of one come unto the meaſure of the ſtature of the
fulneſs of Chriſt. And, in the ſtate of perfection, he ſhall yield
ſuch free obedience, as the angels do in heaven ; without being
moved thereto by any promiſes or threatnings at all : and the
nearer he comes, in his progreſs to that ſtate of perfection, the
more will his obedience be of that nature. So by the doctrine
here advanced, the author doth no more diſown the neceſſity of

received, freely give." And this is to ſerve the Lord without fear of any penalty, which either the law of works, or the law of Chriſt threatneth, in holineſs and. righteouſneſs all the days of your life, according to that ſaying of Zacharias, Luke i. 74, 75 * And this is to paſs the time of your ſojourning here in fear to offend the Lord, by ſinning againſt him; as the apoſtle Peter exhorts, 1 Pet i. 17. Yea, and this is to ſerve God acceptably, with reverence and godly fear; as the author to the Hebrews exhorts, Heb. xii. 28. And thus, my dear friend Neophytus, I have endeavoured, according to your deſire, to give you my judgment and direction in theſe points.

N∘o. And truly. Sir, you have done it very effectually: the Lord enable me to practiſe according to your direction.

§ 12. *Nom* Sir, in this your anſwer to his queſtion, you have alſo anſwered me; and given me full ſatisfaction in diverſe points, about which my friend Antinomiſta and I, have had many a wrangling fit. For I uſed to affirm with tooth and nail (as men uſe to ſay) that believers are under the law, and not delivered from it; and that they do ſin; and that God ſees it, and is angry with them; and doth afflict them for it; and that therefore they ought to humble themſelves, and mourn for their ſins, and confeſs them, and crave pardon for them: and yet truly, I muſt confeſs, I did not underſtand what I ſaid, nor whereof I affirmed; and the

_____

promiſes to influence and encourage the believers obedience; or ſay, that he ought not to have regard to promiſes and threatnings; than one is to be reckoned to ſay, that a lame man hath no need of, and ſhould not have regard unto, the crutches provided for him; when he only ſaith, that the ſtronger his limbs grow, he'll have the leſs need of them, and will lean the leſs to them.

* See the preceeding note.

reason was, because I did not know the difference betwixt the law, as it is the law of works, and as it is the law of Chrift.

Ant. And believe me, Sir, I ufed to affirm, as earneftly as he, that believers are delivered from the law; and therefore do not fin; and therefore God can fee no fin in them; and therefore is neither angry with them, nor doth afflict them for fin; and therefore they have no need either to humble themfelves, or mourn, or confefs their fins, or beg pardon for them: the which I believing to be true, could not conceive how the contrary could be true alfo. But now I plainly fee, that by means of your diftinguifhing betwixt the law, as it is the law of works, and as it is the law of Chrift; there is a truth in both. And therefore, friend Nomifta, whenfoever either you, or any man elfe, fhall hereafter affirm, that believers are under the law; and do fin; and God fees it, and is angry with them; and doth chaftife them for it; and that they ought to humble themfelves, mourn, weep, and confefs their fins, and beg pardon for them: if you mean only, as they are under the law of Chrift; I will agree with you and never contradict you again.

Nom. And truly, friend Antinomifta, if either you, or any man elfe, fhall hereafter affirm, that believers are delivered from the law; and do not fin; God fees no fin in them; nor is angry with them; nor afflicts them for their fins; and that they have no need either to humble themfelves, mourn, confefs or crave pardon for their fins: If you mean it only as they are not under the law of works; I will agree with you, and never contradict you again.

Evan. I rejoice to hear you fpeak thefe words each to other; and truly, now I am in hope, that you two will come back from both your extremes; and meet my neighbour Neophytus in the golden mean; having, as the apoftle, faith, " The fame love, being of one accord, and of one mind."

Nom: Sir, for my part, I thank the Lord, I. do now plainly see that I have erred exceedingly, in seeking to be justified, as it were by the works of the law *. And yet could I never be persuaded to it, before this day ; nor indeed should not have been persuaded to it now, had not you so plainly and fully handled this threefold law. And truly, Sir, I do now unfeignedly desire to renounce myself, and all that ever I have done; and by faith to adhere only to Jesus Christ ; for now I see that he is all in all. O that the Lord would enable me so to do! and I beseech you, Sir, pray for me.

Ant And truly, Sir, I must needs confess, that I have erred as much upon the other hand : for I have been so far from seeking to be justified by the works of the law, that I have neither regarded law nor works. But now I see mine error; I purpose (God willing) to reform it.

Evan. The Lord grant that you may.

§ 13. But how do you, neighbour Neophytus? for methinks you look very heavily.

Neo. Truly, Sir, I was thinking of that place of scripture, where the apostle exhorts us, " To examine ourselves, whether we be in the faith or no," 2 Cor. xiii. 5. Whereby it seems to me, that a man may think he is in the faith, when he is not Therefore, Sir, I would gladly hear, how I may be sure that I am in the faith.

Evan. I would not have you to make any question of it ; since you have grounded your faith upon such a firm

---

* The scriptural phrase is here aptly used, to intimate, how men deceive themselves, thinking they are far from seeking to be justified by the works of the law, because they are convinced they cannot do good works, in the perfection which the law requires : mean-while, since God is merciful, and Christ hath died, they look for the pardon of their sins, and acceptance with God, upon the account of their own works, though attended with some imperfections; that is, " As it were, by the works of the law," Rom. ix. 32.

foundation, as will never fail you; for the promife of God in Chrift, is a tried truth, and never yet failed any man, nor ever will *. Therefore, I would have you to clofe with Chrift in the promife, without making any queftion, whether you are in the faith or no: for there is an affurance which arifeth from the exercife of faith by a direct act; and that is, when a man by faith directly lays hold upon Chrift, and concludes affurance from thence †.

---

* This anfwer proceeds, upon taking Neophytus to fpeak, not of the grace, but of the doctrine of faith; namely, the foundation of faith, or ground of believing; as if he had defired to know, whether the foundation of his faith, was the true foundation of his faith, or not; this is plain from the two following paragraphs. And upon the fuppofition, that he had grounded his faith on the promife of the gofpel, the tried foundation of faith; the author tells him, he would not have him to make a queftion of that; having handled that queftion already at great length, and anfwered all his, and Nomifta's objections, on the head, from p 119 to p 141. Where Neophytus declared himfelf fatisfied. And there's no inconfiftency betwixt the author's advice, in this cafe, given to Neophytus; and the advice given, in the text laft cited, unto the Corinthians, unreafonably and peevifhly demanding a proof of Chrift fpeaking in the apoftle : whether, with feveral judicious Critics and Commentators, we underftand that text, concerning the doctrine of faith, as if the apoftle put them to try, whether they retained the true doctrine, or not; or, which is the common, and (I think) the true underftanding of it, concerning the grace of faith. I fee nothing here determining our author's opinion, as to the fenfe of it: but whether he feems here to be againft felfexamination, efpecially after he had urged that duty on Antinomifta, and anfwered his objections againft it, from p. 167. to p. 171. let the candid reader judge.

† See the note on the definition of faith.
" The affurance of Chrift's righteoufnefs, is a direct act of faith, apprehending imputed righteoufnefs: the evidence of our juftification, we now fpeak of is the reflect light, not by which we are juftified, but by which we know that we are juftified." Rutherfoord's Chrift dying and drawing, p. 111.
" We had never a queftion with Antinomians, touching the firft affurance of juftification, fuch as is proper to the light of faith. He might have fpared all his arguments to prove, That we are

Neo. Sir, I know that the foundation, whereon I am to ground my faith, remaineth sure; and I think I have already built thereon: but yet because, I conceive a man may think he hath done so, when he hath not; therefore would I fain know, how I may be assured that I have done so *.

Evan. Well, now I understand you, what you mean : it seems you do not want a ground for your believing that you have believed †.

Neo. Yea, indeed, that is the thing I want.

Evan. Why, the next way to find out and know this, is to look back and reflect upon your own heart; and consider what actions have passed thro'. there : for indeed this is the benefit that a reasonable soul hath, that it is able to return upon itself, to see what it hath done ; which the soul of a beast cannot do. Consider then, I pray you, that you have been convinced in your spirit that you are a sinful man; and therefore have feared the Lord's wrath and eternal damnation in hell : and you have been convinced that there is no help for you at all, in yourself, by any thing that you can do: and you heard it plainly proved, that Jesus Christ alone is an all-sufficient help. And the free and full promise of God in Christ, hath been made so plain and clear to you; that you had nothing to object, why Christ did not belong to you in particular ‡ : and you have perceived a

---

first assured of our justification by faith, not by good works ; for we grant the arguments of one sort of assurance, which is proper to faith; and they prove nothing against another sort of assurance, by signs and effects, which is also divine." Ib.d. p. 110.

* A good reason, why this assurance, in, or by the direct act of faith, is to be tried by marks and signs. There is certainly a persuasion, that cometh not of him that called us; which obligeth men to examine their persuasion, whether it be of the right sort, or not.

† This is called assurance by a reflex act.

‡ In virtue of the deed of gift and grant.

willingnefs in Chrift to receive you, and to embrace you
as his beloved fpoufe : and you have thereupon confented
and refolved to take Chrift, and to give yourfelf unto him,
whatfoever betides you: and I am perfuaded, you have
thereupon felt a fecret perfuafion in your heart, that
God in Chrift doth bear a love to you * ; and anfwerably,
your heart hath been inflamed towards him in love again,
manifefting itfelf, in an unfeigned defire, to be obedient,
and fubject to his will in all things, and never to difpleafe him in any thing.   Now tell me I pray you (and
that truly) whether you have not found thefe things
in you, as I have faid?

  Neo. Yea, indeed, I hope I have in fome meafure.

Evan. Then I tell you truly, you have a fure ground,
to lay your believing, that you have believed, upon ;
and as the apoftle John faith, "Hereby you may know
that you are of the truth, and may affure your heart,
thereof, before God," 1 John iii. 19.

  Neo. Surely, Sir, this I can truly fay, that heretofore,
when I have thought upon my fins, I have conceived of
God and Chrift, as of a wrathful judge, that would condemn
all unrighteous men to eternal death : and therefore,
when I have thought upon the day of judgment, and
hell-torments ; I have even trembled for fear, and have
as it were even hated God.   And though I have laboured to become righteous, that I might efcape his wrath ;
yet all that I did, I did it unwillingly.   But fince I have
heard you make it fo plain, that a finner, that fees and
feels his fins, is to conceive of God, as of a merciful, loving and forgiving Father in Chrift; that hath committed all judgment to his Son, who came not to condemn
men, but to fave them : methinks I do not now fear his
wrath, but do rather apprehend his love towards me :
whereupon my heart is inflamed towards him with fuch
love, that, methinks, I would willingly do or fuffer any
thing that I knew would pleafe him ; and would rather.

  * See page 136. note.

choofe to fuffer any mifery, than I would do any thing, that I knew were difpleafing to him.

Evan. We read in the feventh chapter of St Luke's gofpel, that when that finful, yet believing woman, did manifeft her faith, in Chrift, by her love to him, " in washing his feet with her tears, and wiping them with the hairs of her head," ver. 38. He faid unto Simon the Pharifee, ver 47. " I fay unto thee, her fins which are many are forgiven her, for fhe loved much :" even fo may I fay unto you, Nomifta, in the fame words, concerning our neighbour Neophytus. And to you yourfelf, Neophytus, I fay, as Chrift faid unto the woman, ver. 48. 50. " Thy fins are forgiven thee, thy faith hath faved thee, go in peace."

Ant. But, I pray you, Sir, is not this his reflecting upon himfelf, to find out a ground to lay his believing, that he hath believed, upon, a turning back from the covenant of grace to the covenant of works, and from Chrift to himfelf.

Evan. Indeeed, if he fhould look upon thefe things in himfelf, and thereupon conclude, that becaufe he hath done thus, God hath accepted of him, and juftified him, and will fave him ; and fo make them the ground of his believing : this were to turn back from the covenant of grace to the covenant of works ; and from Chrift to himfelf. But if he look upon thefe things in himfelf, and thereupon conclude, that becaufe thefe things are in his heart, Chrift dwells there by faith ; and therefore he is accepted of God, and juftified, and fhall certainly be faved ; and fo make them an evidence of his believing, or the ground of his believing that he hath believed : this is neither to turn back from the covenant of grace to the covenant of works ; nor from Chrift to himfelf. So that thefe things in his heart being the daughters of faith, and the off-pring of Chrift ; tho' they cannot at firft produce, or bring forth their mother, yet may they in time of need nourifh her *.

* Goodwin's Chrift fet forth, p. 23.

§. 14. *Nom.* But I pray you, 'Sir,' are there not other things beſide theſe, that he ſaith, he finds in himſelf; that a man may look upon. as evidences of his believing, or (as you call them) as grounds to believe that he hath believed ?

Evan. Yea indeed, there are diverſe other effects of faith ; which if a man have in him truly, he may look upon them as evidences that he hath truly believed : and I will name three of them unto you.

Whereof the firſt is when a man truly loves the word of God, and makes a right uſe of it : and this a man doth, firſt, when he hungers and thirſts after the word, as after the food of his ſoul, deſiring it at all times, even as he doth his appointed † food, Job xxiii. 12.

Secondly, When he deſires and delights to exerciſe himſelf therein, day and night, that is, conſtantly, Pſal. i. 2.

Thirdly, When he receives the word of God, 'as the word of God, and not as the word of man ‡ ; ſetting his heart, in the time of hearing or reading it, as in God's preſence; and being affected with it, as if the Lord himſelf ſhould ſpeak unto him ; being moſt affected with that miniſtry, or that portion of God's word, which ſheweth him his ſins, and ſearcheth out his moſt ſecret corruptions ; denying his own reaſon and affections ; yea, and his profits and pleaſures, in any thing, when the Lord ſhall require it of him.

Fourthly, This a man doth, when he makes the word of God to be his chief comfort, in the time of his afflictions; finding it, at that time, to be the main ſtay and ſolace of his heart ‖.

The ſecond evidence is, when a man truly loves the children of God, (1 John v. 1. that is, all godly and religious perſons) above all other ſorts of men ; and that is, when he loves them not for carnal reſpects, but for the

---

* Sɴ the margent reads it. † 1 Theſſ. ii. 13.
‡ Pſal. cxix. 49, 50.

graces of God, which he feeth in them, 2 John i. 2. 3 John i And when he delights in their fociety and company, and makes them his only companions, Pfal cxix·63. and when his well-doing (to his power) extends itfelf to them, Pfal. xvi. 3. In being pitiful and tenderhearted towards them, and in gladly receiving of them, and communicating to their neceffities with a ready mind, Philem. 7. 1 John iii. 17. And when he hath not the glorious faith of Chrift, in refpect of perfons, Jam. ii. 1, 2. But can make himfelf equal to them of the lower fort, Rom xii. 16. And when he loves them at all times; even when they are in adverfity, as poverty, difgrace, ficknefs, or otherwife in mifery.

The third evidence is, when a man can truly love his enemies, Matth. vi. 14. And that he doth, when he can pray heartily for them: and forgive them, their particular trefpaffes againft him; being more grieved for that they have finned againft God, than for that they have wronged him: and when he can forbear them; and yet could be revenged of them, either by bringing fhame or mifery upon them, 1 Pet. iii. 9. Rom. xii 14. And when he ftrives to overcome their evil with goodnefs, being willing to help them, and relieve them in their mifery, and to do them any good in foul or body: and laftly, When he can freely and willingly acknowledge his enemy's juft praife, even as if he were his deareft friend.

§ 15. *Neo* But, Sir, I pray you, let me afk you one queftion more, touching this point; and that is, fuppofe, that hereafter I fhould fee no outward evidences, and queftion, whether I had ever any true inward evidences, and fo whether, ever I did truly believe or no: what muft I do then?

Evan. Indeed it is poffible you may come to fuch a condition, and therefore you do well, to provide aforehand for it. Now then, if ever it fhall pleafe the Lord to give you over to fuch a condition; firft, let me warn you to take heed of forcing, and conftraining yourfelf to yield obedience to God's commandments, to the end, you may so get an evidence of faith again, or a ground to lay your believing, that you have believed, upon; and so forcibly to haften your affurance before the time * : for although this be not to turn quite back to the cove-nant of works, (for that you fhall never do) yet it is to turn afide towards that covenant, as Abraham did ; who, after that he had long waited for the promifed feed, though he was before juftified by believing the free promife; yet, for the more fpeedy fatisfying of his faith †, he turned afide to go in unto Hagar, who was (as you have heard) a type of the covenant of works. So that, you fee, this is not the right way. . But the right way for you, in this cafe, to get you affurance again, is, when all other things fail, to look to Chrift ‡ : that is, go to the word and promife ; and leave off, and ceafe a while to reafon about the truth of your faith ; and fet your heart on work to believe, as if you had never yet done it ; faying in your heart, Well Satan ‖, fuppofe my faith hath not been true hitherto, yet now will I begin to endeavour after true faith ; and therefore, O Lord, here I caft myfelf upon thy mercy afrefh, for " in thee the father-lefs find mercy," Hof. xiv. 3. Thus I fay, hold to the

---

* This forcing one's felf to yield obedience, which the author warns Chriftians againft, when they have loft fight of their evidences, and would fain recover them : is, by preffing to yield obedience, without believing, till once by their obedi-ence, they have recovered the evidence of their having faith. To advife a Chriftian to beware of taking this courfe, in this cafe, is not to favour laxnefs ; but to guard him againft begin-ning his work at the wrong end, and fo labouring in vain : for obeying, indeed, muft ftill fpring from believing ; fince without faith, it is impoffible to pleafe God, Heb. xi. 6. And whatfo-ever is not of faith is fin, Rom. xiv. 23. The following advice fets the matter in full light.

† Mr Cotton of New England, in his thirteenth queft.

‡ Poor doubting Chriftian, p. 37.

‖ Goodwin's child of light, p. 194.

E e

word; go not away, but keep you here; and you shall bring forth fruit with patience, Luke viii. 15. *-

§ 16. *Neo.* Well, Sir, you have fully fatisfied me concerning that point: but as I remember, it followeth in the fame verfe, "Know ye not your ownfelves, how that Chrift is in you, except ye be reprobates," 2 Cor. xiii. 5. Wherefore I defire to hear, how a man may know, that Jefus Chrift is in him.

Evan. Why, if Chrift be in a man, he lives in him, as faith the apoftle, "I live not, but Chrift liveth in me."

Neo. But, how then fhall a man know, that Chrift lives in him.

Evan. Why, in what man foever Chrift lives; according to the meafure of his faith, he executes his threefold office in him, *viz* his prophetical, prieftly, and kingly office.

Neo. I defire to hear more of this threefold office of Chrift: and therefore I pray you, Sir, tell me, firft, how a man may know that Chrift executes his prophetical office in him?

Evan. Why, fo far forth as any man hears, and knows, that there was a covenant made betwixt God and all mankind in Adam; and that it was an equal covenant †; and that God's juftice muft needs enter ‡ upon the breach of it; and that all makind, for that caufe, were liable to eternal death and damnation; fo that if God had condemned all mankind, yet had it been but the fentence of an equal and juft judge, feeking rather the execution of his juftice, than man's ruin and deftruction: and thereupon takes it home, and applies it particularly to himfelf, Job v. 27. and fo is convinced, that he is a miferable, loft and helplefs man: I fay, fo far forth as a man doth this, Chrift executes his prophetical office in him; in

---

* Namely, obedience, whereby you fhall recover your evidence.

† See p. 13. note.　　‡ Demanding fatisfaction.

teaching him, and revealing unto him the covenant of
works. And so far-forth as any man hears and knows,
that God made a covenant with Abraham, and all his
believing seed, in Jesus Christ; offering him freely to all,
to whom the sound of the gospel comes; and giving him
freely to all that receive him by faith; and so justifies
them, and saves them eternally: and thereupon hath his
heart opened to receive this truth; not as a man taketh
an object, or a theological point, into his head, whereby
he is only made able to discourse; but as an habitual and
practical point, receiving it into his heart by the faith of
the gospel, Phil. i. 27. and applying it to himself, and laying
his eternal state upon it, and so setting to his seal, that
God is true; I say, so far forth as a man doth this, Christ
executes his prophetical office in him; in teaching him,
and revealing to him the covenant of grace. And so
far forth as any man hears and knows, that this is the
will of God, even his sanctification, 1 Thess. iv. 3. and
thereupon concludes, that it is his duty to endeavour
after it; I say, so far forth as a man doth this, Christ
executes his prophetical office in him; in teaching and
revealing his law to him. And this I hope is sufficient
for answer to your first question

Neo. I pray you, Sir, in the second place, tell me,
how a man may know, that Christ executes his priestly
office in him?

Evan. Why so far forth as any man hears and
knows, that Christ hath given himself, as that only, absolute and perfect sacrifice, for the sins of believers,
Heb. ix. 26. and joined them unto himself by faith, and
himself unto them by his Spirit, and so made them one
with him: and is now entred into heaven itself, to
appear in the presence of God for them, Heb. ix. 24.
and hereupon is emboldened to go, immediately to * God
in prayer, as to a father, and meet him in Christ, and

* *i. e.* Even unto. See p. 136. note.

preſent him with Chriſt himſelf, as with a ſacrifice with. out ſpot or blemiſh : I ſay, ſo far forth as any man doth this, Chriſt executes his prieſtly office in him.

Neo. But, Sir, would you have a believer to go im. mediately unto God ? how then doth Chriſt make inter. ceſſion for us at God's right hand, as the apoſtle ſaith he doth, Rom. viii. 34.?

Evan. It is true indeed, Chriſt as a public perſon, repreſenting all believers, appears before God his Father * ; and willeth according to both his natures, and deſireth, as he is man, that God would, for his ſatiſ. faction's ſake. grant unto them, whatſoever they aſk according to his will. But yet you muſt go immediatly to God in prayer, for all that †.

You muſt not pitch your prayers upon Chriſt, and terminate them there, as if he were to take them, and preſent them to his Father ‡ ; but the very preſenting place of your prayers muſt be God himſelf in Chriſt. Neither muſt you conceive, as though Chriſt the Son were more willing, to grant your requeſt ; than God the Father : for whatſoever Chriſt willeth, the ſame alſo the Father (being well pleaſed with him) willeth In Chriſt, therefore, I ſay, and no where elſe, muſt you expect to have your petitions granted. And as in Chriſt, and no place elſe ; ſo for Chriſt's ſake, and nothing elſe. And therefore I beſeech you to beware you forget not Chriſt, when you go unto the Father to beg any thing you deſire, either for yourſelf or others ; eſpecially when you deſire to have any pardon for ſin, you are not to think, that when you join with your prayers, faſting, weeping, and afflicting of yourſelf, that for ſo doing you ſhall prevail with God to hear you, and grant your peti- tions; no, no, you muſt meet God in Chriſt, and preſent

---

* Perkins on the creed, p. 356.
† That is to ſay.
‡ But you, yourſelf, were not to come near unto him ; nay, we muſt come unto God by Chriſt, Heb vii. 25.

him with his ſufferings; your eye, your mind, and all your confidence, muſt be therein; and in that be as confident as poſſible you can: yea, expoſtulate the matter, as it were, with God the Father, and ſay, Lo! here is the perſon, that hath well deſerved it.; here is the perſon, that wills and deſires it; in whom, thou haſt ſaid, thou art well pleaſed; yea, here is the perſon, that hath paid the debt, and diſcharged the bond for all my ſins; and therefore, O Lord! now it ſtandeth with thy juſtice to forgive me. And thus if you do, why then you may be aſſured, that Chriſt executes his prieſtly office to you.

Neo. I pray you, Sir, in the third place, ſhew me, how a man may know that Chriſt executes his kingly office in him?

Evan. Why, ſo far forth as any man hears and knows, " That all power is given unto Chriſt, both in heaven and in earth." Matth. xxviii. 18. both to vanquiſh and overcome all the luſts and corruptions of believers, and to write his law in their hearts; and hereupon takes occaſion to go unto Chriſt, for the doing of both in him: I ſay, ſo far forth as he doth this; why, Chriſt executes his kingly office in him.

Neo. Why then, Sir, it ſeems, that the place, where Chriſt executes his kingly office, is in the hearts of believers?

Evan. It is true indeed; for Chriſt's kingdom is not temporal or ſecular, over the natural lives*, or civil negotiations of men: but his kingdom is ſpiritual and heavenly, over the ſouls of men, to awe and over-rule the hearts, to captivate the affections, and to bring into the obedience the thoughts, and ſubdue and pull down ſtrong holds: For when our father Adam tranſgreſſed, he, and we, all of us, forſook God, and chooſe the devil for our lord and king; ſo that every mothers child of us are by nature under the government of Satan; and he rules over us, till

* Reynolds on Pſal. cx. p. 9.

Chrift come into our hearts, and difpoffeffeth him; according to the faying of Chrift himfelf, Luke xi. 21, 22. " When a ftrong man armed keepeth his palace, his goods are in peace :" that is, faith * Calvin, Satan holdeth them that are in fubjection to him in fuch bonds and quiet poffeffion, that he rules over them without refiftance. But when Chrift comes to dwell in any man's heart by faith ; according to the meafure of faith, he difpoffeffeth him, and feats himfelf in the heart, and roots out, and pulls down all that withftands his government there : and as a valiant eaptain, he ftands upon his guard ; and enables the foul to gather together all its forces and powers, to refift and withftand all its, and his enemies ; and fo fet itfelf in good earneft againft them, when they at any. time offer to return again. And he doth efpecially enable the foul to refift, and fet itfelf againft the principal; enemy ; even that which doth moft oppofe Chrift in his government : fo that whatfoever luft or corruption is in a believer's heart or foul, as moft predominant, Chrift doth enable him to take that into his mind, and to have moft revengeful thoughts againft it ; and to make complants to him againft it ; and to defire power and ftrength, from him againft it ; and all, becaufe it moft withftands the government of Chrift ; and is the rankeft traitor to Chrift. So that he ufeth all the means he can, to bring it before the judgment feat of Chrift; and there he calls for juftice againft it ; faying, O Lord Jefus Chrift, here is a rebel and a traitor, that doth withftand thy government in me : wherefore, I pray thee, come, and execute the King's office in me, and fubdue it, yea vanquifh and overcome it. Whereupon Chrift gives the fame anfwer, that he did to the centurion, " Go thy way, and as thou haft believed, fo be it done unto thee," Matth viii. 13. †

---

* Harmony, p 329.
† Umely, believed the promife of fanctification, Ezck. xxxvi. 27. Micah vii. 19. which belief brings always along with it, the ufe of the means, that are of devine inftituiton, for that end.

And as Chrift doth thus fupprefs all other governors but himfelf, in the heart of a believer, : fo doth he raze out and deface all other laws, and writes his own there, according to his promife, Jer.xxxi.33. And makes them pliable and willing to do and fuffer his will ; and that becaufe it is his will. So that the mind and will of Chrift, laid down in his word, and manifefted in his works, is not only the rule of a believer's obedience, but alfo the reafon of it : as I once heard a godly minifter fay in the pulpit : So that he doth not only do that which is Chrift's will, but he doth it becaufe it is his will *.

O that man which hath the law of Chrift written in his heart! according to the meafure of it, he reads, he hears, he prays, he receives the facrament, he keeps the Lord's day holy, he exhorts, he inftructs, he confers, and doth all the duties that belong to him in his general calling, becaufe he knows it is the mind and will of Chrift he fhould do fo : yea, he patiently fuffers, and willingly undergoes afflictions, for the caufe of Chrift, becaufe he knows it is the will of Chrift. Yea, fuch a man doth not only yield obedience, and perform the duties of the firft table of the law, by virtue of Chrift's command ; but, of the fecond alfo. O that hufband, parent, mafter, or magiftrate, that hath the law of Chrift written in his heart ! he doth his duty to his wife, child, fervant, or fubject, willingly and uprightly, becaufe Chrift requires it, and commands it. And fo that wife, child, fervant, or fubject, that hath the law of Chrift written in his or her heart; they do their duties to hufband, parent, mafter, or governor freely and cheerfully, becaufe their Lord Chrift commands it. Now then, if you find thefe things in your heart, you may conclude that Chrift rules and reigns there, as Lord and King.

* Mr Caryl at Black friars.

CHAP. IV.

Of the Heart's Happiness, or Soul's Rest.

§ 1. *No rest for the soul, till it come to God.* § 2. *How the soul is kept from rest in God.* § 3. *God in Christ, the only true rest for the soul.*

§ 1 *Neo.* SIR, be pleased to give me leave, to tell you some part of my mind; and then will I cease to trouble you any more at this time. The truth is, I have, ever since I could remember, felt a kind of restless discontentedness in my spirit: and for many years together, I fed myself with hopes of finding rest and content, in persons and things here below; scarce thinking of the state and condition of my soul, or of any condition beyond this life, until (as I told you before) the Lord was pleased to visit me with a fit of sickness. And then I began to bethink myself of death, judgment, hell and heaven; and to take care and seek rest for my soul, as well as for my body: but alas, I could never find rest for it, before this day; because indeed I sought it not by faith, but as it were by the works of the law; or in plain terms, because I sought it not in Christ, but in myself. But now, I bless God, I see that Christ is all in all: and therefore, by the grace of God, I am resolved, no longer to seek rest and content, neither in any earthly thing, nor in mine own righteousness; but only in the free love and favour of God, as he is in his Son Jesus Christ: and God willing, there shall be my soul's rest. And I beseech you, Sir, pray for me, that it may be so; and I have done.

Evan. This point, concerning the heart's happiness, or soul's rest, is a point very needful for us to know; and indeed it is a point, that I have formerly thought upon: and therefore tho' my occasions do now begin

to

to call me away from you; yet neverthelefs, fince you have begun to fpeak of it, I fhall, if you pleafe, proceed on, if you fhall, any of you, give occafion, and as the Lord fhall enable me.

Ant. With a very good will, Sir; for indeed it is a point that I much defire to hear of.

Evan. Firft, then I would intreat you to confider with me, that when God at firft gavē man an elementifh body *; he did alfo infufe into him an immortal foul, of a fpiritual fubftance : and though he gave his foul a local being in his body, yet he gave it a fpiritual being in himfelf; fo that the foul was in the body by location, and at reft in God by union and communication : and this being of the foul in God at firft, was man's true being, and his true happinefs. Now, man falling from God, God in his juftice left man; fo that the actual union and communion, that the foul of man had with God at firft, is broken off; God and man's foul, are parted; and it is in a reftlefs condition. Howbeit, the Lord, having feated in man's foul, a certain character of himfelf, the foul is thereby made to re-afpire towards, that *fummum Bonum,* that chief good, even God himfelf, and can find no reft no where, till it come to him †.

---

* *i. e.* An elementary body, made up (as it were) of the four elements, as they are called, viz. Fire, air, water, and earth.

† The foul of man hath a natural defire of happinefs : nothing can make it happy, but what is commenfurable to its defires, or capable of affording it a full fatisfaction : nothing lefs than an infinite good, is fuch; and God himfelf only is an infinite good, in the enjoyment of which, the foul can reft, as fully fatisfied, defiring no more. Now, fince, by reafon of the vaft capacity of the foul, nothing but God himfelf, can indeed fatisfy this its defire of happinefs, the which is fo woven into the very nature of the foul, that nothing but the deftruction of the very being of the foul can remove it; it is evident, that it is impoffible the foul of man can ever find true reft, until it return to God, and take up its reft with him; but muft ftill be in queft of, or defiring its chief good and happinefs, wherein it

Nom. But ſtay, Sir, I pray you; how can it be ſaid, that man's ſoul doth re-aſpire towards God the Creator, when as it is evident, that every man's ſoul naturally is bent towards the creature, to ſeek a reſt there?

Evan. For anſwer hereunto, I pray you conſider, that naturally man's underſtanding is dark and blind: and therefore is ignorant, what his own ſoul doth deſire, and ſtrongly aſpire unto: it knoweth indeed that there is a want in the ſoul; but till it be enlightened, it knoweth not what it is, which the ſoul wanteth. For indeed the caſe ſtandeth with the ſoul, as with a child new born, which child, by natural inſtinct, doth gape and cry for nutriment; yea, for ſuch nutriment, as may agree with its tender condition: and if the the nurſe, through negligence or ignorance, either give it no meat at all; or elſe ſuch as it is not capable of receiving; the child refuſeth it, and ſtill crieth in ſtrength of deſire after the dug: yet doth not the child, in this eſtate, know by any intellectual power and underſtanding, what itſelf deſireth. Even ſo man's poor ſoul doth cry to God, as for its proper nouriſhment*: but his underſtanding, like a blind

---

may reſt; and this, in reality, is God himſelf only; though the practical underſtanding, being blinded, knows not that, and the perverſe will and affections carry away the ſoul from him, ſeeking the deſired good and happineſs in other things. This is what the author calls the ſoul's re-aſpiring towards the chief good, even God himſelf; and it is ſo conſiſtent with the total depravation of man's nature, that it will remain for ever, in the damned, in hell; a chief part of whoſe miſery, will ly in that this deſire ſhall ever be rampant in them, but never in the leaſt ſatisfied; they ſhall never be freed from this ſcorching thirſt there, nor yet get a drop of water to cool the tongue.

* Man's poor ſoul, before it is enlightned, naturally cries to God, as the young ravens cry to him, Job xxxviii. 41. not knowing to whom; and it cries for him, as its proper nouriſhment; as the new-born infant for the breaſt, not knowing for what. Only it feels a want, deſires ſupply proper for filling it up, and can never get kindly reſt, till it be ſuppiied accordingly; that is, till it come to the enjoyment of God; then it

ignorant nurfe, not knowing what it crieth for, doth offer to the heart, a creature inftead of a Creator ; thus, by reafon of the blindnefs of the underftanding, together with the corruption of the will, and diforder of the affections, man's foul is kept by violence * from its proper center, even God himfelf.

§ 2. O how many fouls are there in the world, that are hindred, if not quite kept, from reft in God ; by reafon that their blind underftanding, doth prefent unto their fenfual appetite, varieties of fenfual objects !

Is their not many a luxurious perfou's foul hindred, if not quite kept, from true reft in God, by that beauty which nature hath placed in feminine faces † ; efpecially when Satan doth fecertly fuggeft, into fuch feminine hearts, a defire of an artificial dreffing, from the head to the foot : yea, and fometimes painting the face, like their mother Jezabel ?

And is there not many a voluptuous epicure's foul hindred, if not quite kept, from reft in God, by beholding the colour, and tafting the fweetnefs of dainty delicate dilhes, his wine red in the cup, and his beer of amber-colour in the glafs ? In the fcripture we read of a certain man, that fared delicioufly every day ; as if there had been no more but one fo ill difpofed ; but in our times, there are certain hundreds, both of men and women, that do not only fare delicioufly, but voluptuoufly twice every day, if not more.

And is there not many a proud perfon's foul hindred, if not quite kept from reft in God, by the harmonious found of popular praife, which like a loadftone, draweth the vain glorious heart to hunt fo much the more eagerly, to augment the echo of fuch vain windy reputation ?

reſts, as the infanf fet to the full breaſt, Ifa. lxvi. 11. " That ye may fuck, and be fatisfied with the breaſts of her confolations."

* Namely, violence done to its natural make and conftitution (if I may fo exprefs it) by the blindnefs, corruption and diforder, that have feized its faculties.

† *i. e.* Womens faces.

And is there not many a covetous perſon's ſoul hindred, if not quite kept, .from reſt in God, by the cry of
great abundance, the words of wealth, and the glory
of gain?

And is there not many a muſical mind hindred: if not
quite kept, from ſweet comfort in God, by the harmony
of artificial concord, upon muſical inſtruments?

And how many perfumed fools are there in the world,
who, by ſmelling their ſweet apparel, and their ſweet
noſe-gays, are kept from ſoul-ſweetneſs in Chriſt?

And thus doth Satan, like a cunning fiſher, bait his
hook with a ſenſual object, to catch men with: and
having gotten it into their jaws, he draweth them up and
down in ſenſual contentments; till he hath ſo drowned
them therein, that the peace and reſt of their ſouls in
God is almoſt forgotten. And hence it is, that the
greateſt part of man's life, and in many their whole life,
is ſpent in ſeeking ſatisfaction, to the ſenſual appetite.

Nom. Indeed, Sir, this which you have ſaid, we may
ſee, truly, verified in many men, who ſpend their days
about theſe vanities, and will afford no time for religious
exerciſes; no, not upon the Lord's day; by their
good will.

Evan. You ſay the truth: and yet let me tell you
withal, that a man, by the power of natural conſcience,
may be forced to confeſs, that his hopes of happineſs
are in God alone, and not in theſe things; yea, and to
forſake profits, and pleaſures, and all ſenſual objects, as
unable to give his ſoul any true contentment; and fall to
the performance of religious exerciſes, and yet reſt there;
and never come to God for reſt. And if we conſider it,
either in the rude multitude of ſenſual livers; or in the
more ſeemingly religious; we ſhall perceive that the
religious exerciſes of men do ſtrongly deceive, and
ſtrangely delude many men of their hearts happineſs
in God.

' ' For the first fort *, though they be such as make their
belly their beft God, and do no facrifice but to Bacchus,
Apollo or Venus † ; though their confcience do accufe
them, that thefe things are naught : yet in that they
have the name of Chriftians put upon them in their
baptifm ; and forafmuch as they do often repeat the
Lord's prayer, the apoftles creed, and the ten commandments ; and in that, it may be, they have lately accuftom-
ed themfelves to go to church, to hear divine fervice,
and a preaching now and then ; and in that they have
divers times, received the facrament ; they will not be
perfuaded, but that God is well pleafed with them : and
a man may as well perfuade them, that they are not
men and women, as that they are not in a good condition.

And for the fecond fort ‡, that ordinarily have more
human wifdom, and human learning than the former fort;
and feem to be more holy and devout, than the former
fort of fenfual ignorant people : yet how many are there
of this fort, that never pafs further, than the outward
court of bodily performances : feeding and feafting themfelves, as men in a dream ? fuppofing themfelves to have
all things, and yet indeed have nothing, but only a blad-
der full, or rather a brain full, of wind and worldly
conceptions ?

Are there not fome, who give themfelves to more
efpecial fearching, and feeking out for knowledge in the
fcripture-learnednefs, and clerk-like fkill, in this art, and
that language, till they come to be able to repeat all the
hiftorical places in the Bible ; yea, and all thofe texts of
fcripture, that they conceive do make for fome private

---

* Namely, fenfual livers, who yet perform religious exercifes.

† i. e. Give up themfelves to drunkennefs, mufic and
lafcivioufnefs.

‡ Namely, the more feeming religious.

F f

opinion of theirs, concerning ceremonies, church-govern-
ment, or other such circumstantial points of religion,
touching which points they are very able to reason and
dispute, and to put forth such curious questions, as are
not easily answered?

Are not some of these men *. called sect-makers, and
begetters or devisers of new opinions in religion; especially in the matter of worshipping God, as they use to call
it, wherein they find a beginning, but hardly an end? for
this religious knowledge, is so variable, through the multi-
plicity of curious wits and contentious spirits, that the life of
man may seem too short to take a full view of this variety:
for though all sects say, they will be guided by the word
of truth, and all seem to bring scripture, which indeed is
but one, as God is but one; yet, by reason of their several
constructions and interpretations of scripture, and conceits
of their own human wisdom, they are many.

And are there not others of this sort of men, that are
ready to embrace any new way of worship; especially, if
it come under the cloke of scripture-learning, and have
a shew of truth founded upon the letter of the Bible, and
seem to be more zealous and devout, than their former
way: especially, if the teacher of that new way, can but
frame a sad and demure countenance; and, with a grace,
lift up his head and his eyes towards heaven, with some
strong groan; in declaring of his newly conceived
opinion; and that he frequently use this phrase of the
glory of God; O then, these men are, by and by, of
another opinion; supposing to themselves, that God
hath made known some further truth to them: for, by
reason of the blindness of their understanding, they are
not able to reach any supernatural truth: although they
do, by literal learning, and clerk-like cunning, dive never

---

* Viz: Of these spoken of in the paragraph immediatly preceeding, whom he begins to distribute here into three classes
or sorts; all belonging to the second sort, to wit, the more
seemingly religious.

Evan. I pray you, do not miftake me : I do not contemn
nor defpife the ufe of reafon; only I would not have you
to eftablifh it to * the chief good ; but I would have you
to keep it under ; fo that if, with Hagar, it attempt, to
bear rule, and lord it over your faith, then would I have
you in the wifdom of God, like Sarah, to caft it out from
having dominion. In few words, I would have you more
ftrong in defire, than curious in fpeculation ; and to long
more to feel communion with God, than to be able to
difpute of the genius or fpecies of any queftion, either
human or divine ; and prefs hard to know God by
powerful experience. And though your knowledge be
great, and your obedience furpaffing many ; yet would
I have you to be truly nulified, annihilated, and made
nothing, and become fools in all flefhly wifdom, and
glory in nothing, but only in the Lord.† And I would
have you, with the eye of faith, fweetly to behold all
things extracted out of one thing; and in one to fee all ‡.
In a word, I would have in you a moft profound filence,
contemning all curious queftions and difcourfes ; and to
ponder much in your heart, but, prat little with your
tongue ; " Be fwift to hear, but flow to fpeak, and flow
to wrath," as the apoftle James advifeth you James i. 19.
And by this means will your reafon be fubdued, and
become one with your faith ; for then is reafon one
with faith, when it is fubjugated unto faith ; and then
will reafon keep its true lifts and limits ; and you will
become ten times more reafonable, than you were before.
So that I hope you now fee, that the heart's farewel
from the fenfual and rational life, is not to be confidered
abfolutely, but refpectively ; it doth not confift in a
going out of either, but in a right ufe of both.

---

* *i. e.* For, or to be.
† 2 Cor. xii. 11. " Though I be nothing." 1 Cor. iii. 18.
" Let him become a fool, that he may be wife." Chap. i. 31.
" He that glorieth, let him glory in the Lord."
‡ According to that faying of our Lord, Matth. xix. 17.
" There is none good, but one, that is God."

§ 3. *Nom.* Then, Sir, it feemeth to me, that God in Chrift, apprehended by faith, is the only true reft for man's foul.

Evan. There is the true reft indeed; there is the reft which David invites his foul unto, when he faith, " Return unto thy reft, my foul: for the Lord hath dealt bountifully with thee," Pfal. cxvi. 7. " For we which have believed," faith the author to the Hebrews, " have entered into his reft *," Heb iv. 3. And, " Come unto me, faith Chrift, all ye that labour, and are " heavy laden, and I will give you reft," Matth. xi. 28. †

---

§ * Do enter into reft, or that reft, viz. his reft, ver. 1. He means, that we even now enter into that reft, by faith.— Compare ver. 10.

† This is one of the moft folemn gofpel-offers, to be found in all the New Teftament; and our author feems here to point at, what I conceive to be, the true and genuine fenfe of it. The words, labouring and heavy laden, do not reftrict the invitation and offer, to fuch as are fenfible of their fins, and long- ing to be rid of them; though indeed none but fuch will really accept; but they denote the reftlefnefs of the finful foul of man; a qualification (if it is fo called) to be found in all that are out of Chrift, whether they have, or have not, any notable law-work on their confciences.

I fay notable; to diftinguifh it from that which is common to all men, even to Heathens, Rom ii. 15. Our father Adam led his whole family away, out of their reft in God; and fo left them with a confcience full of guilt, and a heart full of un- fatisfied defires. Hence his children foon find themfelves, like the horfe-leech, having two daughters, crying, Give, give; namely, a reftlefs confcience, and a reftlefs heart: and to each of thefe, the poor foul muft needs fay, as Naomi faid to Ruth, My daughter, fhall I not feek reft for thee? So the blinded foul falls a labouring, for reft to them. And it labours in the barren region of the fiery law, for a reft to the confcience; and in the empty creation, for a reft to the heart: but, after all, the con- fcience is ftil heavy laden with guilt, whether it has any lively feeling thereof or not; and the heart is ftill under a load of un- fatisfied defires. So neither the one, nor the other, can find reft indeed. This is the natural cafe of all men; and to fouls thus labouring, and laden, Jefus Chrift here calls, that they may come to him, and he will give them reft; namely, a reft

And truly my neighbours and friends, believe it, we ſhall never find a heart's happineſs, and true ſoul's reſt, until we find it here. For howſoever a man may think, if he had this man's wit, and that man's wealth; this man's honour, and that man's pleaſure; this wife, or that huſband; ſuch children, and ſuch ſervants; his heart would be ſatisfied, and his ſoul would be contented: yet which of us hath not, by our own experience, found the contrary? For, not long after that we have obtained the thing we did ſo much deſire; and wherein we promiſed ourſelves ſo much happineſs, reſt and content; we have found nothing but vanity and emptineſs in it. Let a man but deal plainly with his own heart; and he ſhall find, that, notwithſtanding he hath many things; yet there is ever one thing wanting: for indeed man's ſoul cannot be ſatisfied with any creature, no not with a world of creatures. And the reaſon is, becauſe the deſires of man's ſoul are infinite; according to that infinite goodneſs, which is once loſt in loſing God. Yea, and man's ſoul is a ſpirit; and therefore cannot communicate with any corporal thing: ſo that all creatures, not being that infinite and ſpiritual fulneſs, which our hearts have loſt, and towards the which they do ſtill re-aſpire; they cannot give it full contentment.

---

for their conſciences, under the covert of his blood; and a reſt to their hearts, in the enjoyment of God, through him.

This is moſt agreeable to the ſcripture-phraſeology, Eccleſ. x. 15. "The labour of the fooliſh wearieth every one of them, becauſe he knoweth not how to go to the city. Hab. ii. 13. The people ſhall labour in the very fire, and the people ſhall weary themſelves for very vanity. Iſa. lv. 2. Wherefore do ye ſpend—your labour for that which ſatisfieth not?" See p. 135 note. The prophet laments over a people, more inſenſible than the ox or the aſs, ſaying, "Ah ſinful nation, a people laden with iniquity," Iſa. i. 3, 4. And the apoſtle ſpeaks of "ſilly woman laden with ſins, led away with divers luſts, ever learning, and never able to come to the knowledge of the truth, 2 Tim. iii. 6, 7.

Nay, let me fay more; howfoever a man may, in the midft of his fenfual fulnefs, be convinced in his confcience, that he is at enmity with God, and therefore in danger of his wrath and eternal damnation; and, be thereupon moved to reform his life, and amend his ways, and endeavour to feek peace and reft to his foul * : yet this being in the way of works, it is impoffible that he fhould find it: for his confcience will ever be accufing him, that this good duty he ought to have done, and hath not done it.; and this evil he ought to have forborn, and yet he hath done it; and in the performance of this duty he was remifs, and in that duty very defective: and many fuch ways will his foul be difquieted.

But when a man once comes to believe, that all his fins, both paft, prefent, and to come, are freely and fully pardoned † : and God in Chrift gracioufly reconciled unto him: the Lord doth hereupon fo reveal his fatherly face unto him in Chrift, and fo make known that incredible union betwixt him and the believing foul; that his heart becomes quietly contented in God, who is the proper element of its being; for hereupon there comes into the foul, fuch peace flowing from the God of peace, that it fills the emptinefs of the foul with true fulnefs, in the fulnefs of God. So that now the heart ceafeth to moleft the underftanding and reafon; in feeking either variety of objects, or argumentation of degrees, in any comprehenfible thing: and that becaufe the reftlefs longing of the mind, which did before caufe unquietnefs, and diforder; both in the variety of mental projects, and alfo in the fenfual and beaftly exercifes of the corporal and external members; is fatisfied and truly quieted. For when a man's heart is at peace in God, and is become truly full, in that peace and joy, paffing underftanding; then the devil hath not that hope to prevail

---

* There.
† Namely, in refpect of the guilt of eternal wrath. See p. 108. note.

againft his foul, as he had before: he- knows right well, that it is in vain to bait his hook, with profits, pleafures, honour, or any other fuch like feeming good, to catch fuch a foul, that is thus at quiet in God; for he hath all fulnefs in God, and what can be added to fulnefs, but it runneth over? Indeed empty hearts, like empty hogf-heads, are fit to receive any matter which fhall be put into them: but the heart of the believer, being filled with joy and peace in believing, doth abhor all fuch bafe allurements; for that it hath no room in itfelf, to receive any fuch feeming contentments. So that to fpeak as the truth is, there is nothing, that doth truly and unfeignedly root wickednefs out of the heart of man; but only the true tranquillity of the mind, or the reft of the foul in God. And to fay as the thing is, this is fuch a peace, and fuch a reft to the creature in the Creator; that according to the meafure of its eftablifhment by faith, no created comprehenfible thing can either add to it, or detract from it: the increafe of a kingdom cannot augment it; the greateft loffes and croffes in worldly things cannot diminifh it: a believer's good works do all flow from it, and ought not to return to it *; neither ought human frailties to moleft it.†. However, this is moft certain, neither fin nor Satan, law nor confcience, hell nor grave, can quite extinguifh it: for it is the Lord alone, that gives and maintains it: " Whom have I in heaven but thee?" faith David: " And there is none upon earth that I defire befides thee," Pfal. lxxiii. 25.

---

* Namely, to be any part of the fountain of it, for the time to come; as the rivers return unto the fea, whence they came, making a part of the ftore for their own frefh fupply; nay, " It is the Lord alone that gives and maintains it," as our author afterwards expreffeth it.

† For, thefe we are never free from in this life. And true repentance, and gofpel-mourning for fin, are fo confiftent with it, that they flow from it, according to the meafure thereof, Pfal. lxv. 3. " Iniquities prevail againft me; as for our tranf-greffions, thou fhalt purge them away. Zech. xii. 10. They

It is the pleaſant face of God in Chriſt, that puts gladneſs into his heart, Pſal. iv. 7. And when that face is hid, then he is troubled, Pſal. xxx. 7. But to ſpeak more plainly; though the peace and joy of true believers may be extenuated or diminiſhed; yet doth the teſtimony of their being in nature * remain ſo ſtrong, that they could ſkill to ſay, yea, even when they have felt God to be withdrawing himſelf from them, " My God, my God, why haſt thou forſaken me?" Pſal. xxii 1. Yea, and in the night of abſence to remain confident; that though ſorrow be over night, yet joy will come in the morning, Pſal. xxx. 5. Nay, though the Lord ſhould ſeem to kill them with unkindneſs, " Yet will they put their truſt in him;" Job viii. 15. knowing that, for all this, their Redeemer liveth; Job. xix. 25. So ſtrong is the joy of their Lord, Neh. viii. 10. Theſe are the people, that are kept in perfect peace, becauſe their minds are ſtaid in the Lord, Iſa. xxvi. 3.

Wherefore, my dear friends and loving neighbours, I beſeech you, take heed of deeming any eſtate happy; until you come to find this true peace and reſt to your ſouls in God. O, beware leſt any of you do content yourſelves with a peace rather of ſpeculation, than of power! O, be not ſatisfied with ſuch a peace, as conſiſt-eth either in the act of oblivion, or neglect of examina-tion! nor yet, in any brain-ſick ſuppoſition of knowledge, theological or divine; and ſo frame rational concluſions, to protract time, and ſtill the cries of an accuſing conſci-ence. But let your hearts take their laſt farewel of falſe felicities; wherewith they have been, all of them, more or leſs detained, and kept from their true reſt. O be ſtrong in in reſolution! and bid them all farewel : for what

---

ſhall look upon me, whom they have pierced, and they ſhall mourn."

* *i. e* The evidence that they, (viz. the peace and joy of believers) are ſtill in being (in rerum Naturæ) and not quite extinct.

have your ſouls to do any longer, among theſe groſs, thick, and bodily things here below ; that you ſhould ſet your love upon them, or ſeek happineſs in them ? your ſouls are of a higher and purer nature ; and therefore their well-being muſt be ſought, in ſomething that is higher and purer than they, even in God himſelf.

True it is, that we are all of us, indeed, too unclean to touch God in any immediate unity : but yet there is a pure counter-part of our natures *, and that pure huma-nity is immediately † knit to the pureſt Deity: and by that immediate union, you may come to a mediate union ; for the Deity, and that humanity being united, make one Saviour, Head, and Huſband of ſouls. And ſo you being married to Him, that is God ; in him; you come alſo to be one with God; he one by perſonal union, and you one by a myſtical. Clear up then your eye, and fix it on Him; as on the faireſt of men, the perfection of a ſpiritual beau-ty, the treaſure of heavenly joy, the true object of moſt fervent love. Let your ſpirits look, and long, and ſeek, after this Lord ; let your ſouls cleave to Him, let them hang about Him, and never leave him, till he be brought into the chambers of your ſouls : yea, tell him reſolutely, you will not leave him, till you hear his voice in your ſouls, ſaying, My well-beloved is mine, and I am his; yea, and tell him, you are ſick of love. Let your ſouls go, as it were, out of your bodies, and out of the world, by heavenly contemplations ; and treading upon the earth, with the bottom of your feet, ſtretch your ſouls up, to look over the world, into that upper world, where her ‡ treaſures is, and where her beloved dwelleth.

And when any of your ſouls ſhall thus forget her own people, and her father's houſe ; Chriſt her King ſhall ſo deſire her beauty, Pſal. xlv, 10, 11. and be ſo much in love with her ; that, like a load-ſtone, this love of his ſhall

---

* Viz. The pure and ſpotleſs human nature of Chriſt.
† Rouſe myſtical marriage, p. 8, 9.
‡ Your ſoul's.

draw the ſoul in pure deſire to him again : and then,
" As the hart panteth after the rivers of water, ſo will
your ſoul pant after God," Pſal. xlii. 1.

. And then according to the meaſure of your faith, your
ſouls ſhall come to have a real reſt in God ; and be filled
with joy unſpeakable and glorious·

· Wherefore, I beſeech you, ſet your mouths to this
fountain Chriſt : and ſo ſhall your ſouls be filled with
the water of life, with the oil of gladneſs, and with the
new wine of the kingdom of God ; from him you ſhall have
weighty joys, ſweet embracements, and raviſhing conſo-
lations. And how can it be otherwiſe, when your ſouls
ſhall really communicate with God ; and by faith have a
true taſte, and by the Spirit have a ſure earneſt, of all
heavenly· preferments ; having, as it were, one foot in
heaven, whilſt you live upon earth ? O then, what an
euchariſtical love * will ariſe from your thankful heart's
extending itſelf firſt towards God, and then towards man
for God's ſake ? And then, according to the measure of
your faith, will be your willing obedience to God, and
alſo to man. for God's ſake : for obedience being the
kindly fruit of love, a loving ſoul bringeth forth this
fruit, as kindly, as a good tree bringeth forth her fruit.
For the ſoul having· taſted Chriſt in an heavenly communion, ſo loves him, that to pleaſe him is a pleaſure
and delight to herſelf ; and the more Chriſt Jeſus comes
into the ſoul by his Spirit, the more ſpiritual he makes
her ; and turns her will into his will, making her of one
heart, mind, and will, with him.·

So that, for a concluſion, this I ſay, That if the everlaſting love of God in Jeſus Chriſt be truly made known to
your ſouls ÷ according to the meaſure thereof, you ſhall
have no need to frame, and force yourſelves, to love and
do good works ÷ for your ſoul will ever ſtand bound † to
love God, and to keep his commandments ; and it will
be your meat and drink to do his will. And truly this
love of God will cut down ſelf-love, and love of the

---

* A love of thankſgiving ; bearing thankfulneſs in its nature.
† Or conſtrained, by the force of that love.

world ; for the fweetnefs of Chrift's Spirit, will turn the
fweetnefs of the flefh into bitternefs, and the fweetnefs.
of the world into contempt. And 'if you can behold
Chrift with open face, you fhall fee and feel things un-
utterable ; and be changed from beauty to beauty, from
glory to glory, by the Spirit of this Lord ; and fo be
happy in this life, in your union with happinefs, and
happy hereafter, in the full fruition, of happinefs * :
whither the Lord Jefus Chrift bring us all in his due
time. *Amen.*

The CONCLUSION.

AND now, brethren, I commend you to God, and
to the word of his grace, which is able to build
you up, and to give you an inheritance amongft all them
which are fanctified, Acts xx 32.

Neo. Well, Sir, at this time I will fay no more ; but
that it was a happy hour, wherein I came to you, and a
happy conference that we have had together : furely,
Sir, I never knew Chrift before this day. O what caufe
have I to thank the Lord for my coming hither, and my
two friends as a means of it! And, Sir, for the pains
that you have taken with me, I pray the Lord to requit
you ; and fo, befeeching you to pray the Lord to increafe
my faith, and to help my unbelief, I humbly take my
leave of you, praying the God of love and peace to be
with you.

Nom. And truly, Sir, I do believe that I have caufe
to fpeak as much in that cafe as he hath ; for though I
have outftript him in knowledge, and it may be alfo in
ftrict walking ; yet do I now fee, that my actions were
neither from a right principle, nor to a right end ; and
therefore have I been in no better a condition than he.
And truly, Sir, I muft needs confefs, I never have heard
fo much of Chrift and the covenant of grace, as I have

* *i. e.* Of God himfelf in Chrift.

done this day *. The Lord make it profitable to me ; and I beseech you, Sir, pray for me.

Ant. And truly, Sir, I am now fully convinced, that I have gone out of the right way ; in that I have not had regard to the law, and the works thereof, as I should : but, God willing, I shall hereafter (if the Lord prolong my days) be more careful how I lead my life ; seeing the ten commandments are the law of Christ ; and I beseech you, Sir, remember me in your prayers. And so, with many thanks to you for your pains, I take my leave of you, beseeching the grace of our Lord Jesus Christ to be with your spirit. *Amen.*

Evan. " Now the very God of peace, that brought again from the dead our Lord Jesus, that great Shepherd of the sheep, through the blood of the everlasting covenant ; make you perfect in every good work, to do his will, working in you that which is well-pleasing in his sight, through Jesus Christ ; to whom be glory for ever and ever, *Amen.* Heb. xiii. 20, 21. John viii. 36. If the Son make you free, you shall be free indeed. Gal v. i. Stand fast therefore in the liberty wherewith Christ hath made us free. Verse 13 Only use not your liberty for an occasion to the flesh, but by love serve one another. Chap vi 16. And as many as walk according to this rule, peace be upon them, and mercy, and upon the Israel of God. Matth xi. 15. I thank thee, O Father, Lord of heaven and earth, because thou hast hid these things from the wise and prudent, and hast revealed them to babes. i Cor. xvi. 10 I laboured more abundantly than they all ; yet not I, but the grace of God that was with me. Psal. xxxvi. 11. Let not the foot of pride come against me."

---

* This is here fitly put into the mouth of Nomista, the prevailing of legal principles and practices among legal professors, being much owing to legal preaching ; the success whereof, is not to be wondered at, since it is a rowing with the stream of nature.

F I N I S.

THE
MARROW
OF
MODERN DIVINITY.

PART SECOND.

TOUCHING

The moſt plain, pithy, and ſpiritual EXPOSITION of the
TEN COMMANDMENTS, the examination of the heart
and life by them, the reaſon why the Lord gave them,
and the uſe that both unbelievers and believers are to
make of them.

Profitable for any man, who either deſires to be driven
out of himſelf to Chriſt, or ſo to walk as that he may
pleaſe Chriſt.

In a DIALOGUE betwixt

EVANGELISTA, a Miniſter of the Goſpel.
NOMOLOGISTA, a Pratler about the Law. And,
NEOPHITUS, a young Chriſtian.

By EDWARD FISHER,
AUTHOR of the FIRST PART.

To which is added,

An APPENDIX, containing the difference betwixt the
LAW and the GOSPEL, by the ſame Author.

ALSO,

The TWELVE QUERIES which were propoſed to the
Twelve Marrow-men, by the Commiſſion of the General
Aſſembly of the CHURCH of SCOTLAND, 1721. With the
Marrow-men's ANSWERS to ſaid QUERIES.

1 Tim. i. 8. *We know that the Law is good, if a man uſe
it lawfully.*

FALKIRK:
Printed and ſold by PATRICK MAIR.
M.DCC.LXXXIX.

THE Marrow of the fecond bone, is like that of the firft, fweet and good. The commandments of God are marrow to the faints, as well as the promifes; and they fhall never tafte the marrow of the promife, who diftafte the commandments. This little treatife breaketh the bone, the hard part of the commandments, by a plain expofition, that fo all, even babes in Chrift, yea, fuch as are yet out of Chrift, may fuck out and feed upon the marrow, by profitable meditation.

Sept. 6. 1648.

JOSEPH CARYL.

To the Right Honourable J O H N W A R N E R,
Lord Mayor, of the moft renowned city of London,
E. F. wifheth a moft plentiful increafe of fpiritual
wifdom, and all neceffary graces for the difcharge of
his duty, to the glory of God, and the good of his
people.

Right Honourable,

THE rod of God's judgments hath been now long
upon us, which we by our manifold fins have
procured, according as it is faid concerning Jerufalem,
Jer. iv. 18. "Thy way and thy doings have procured
thefe things unto thee" And have we any juft ground
to hope, that till the caufe be taken away, the effect will
ceafe? Can we expect that the Lord will turn away his
judgments, till we turn away from our fins? And can
we turn away from our fins, before we know them? And
can we come to know our fins any otherwife than by the
law? Doth not one apoftle fay, that " Sin is the tranfgreffion of the law"? 1 John iii. 4 And doth not another
apoftle therefore fay, that " By the law is the knowledge
of fin?" Rom. iii. 20. Surely then, a treatife wherein
is fhewn, what is required, and what is forbidden in every
commandment of the law, and fo confequently what
is fin, muft needs be for this caufe very feafonable.
But yet alas! fuch is the power of fin, and the dominion
of Satan in many mens hearts, that although there be
never fo many treatifes written, nor never fo many fermons preached upon this fubject, yet do they either remain wilfully ignorant of their fins, or elfe tho' they know
them, yet will they not forego them, but rather chufe
wilfully to wallow on in the mire of iniquity, fo fweet
and dear are their fins unto them. But what then,
muft they be fuffered fo to go on without reftraint?
No, God forbid. Such perfons as the law and love of
God will not conftrain, fuch muft the execution of juftice
reftrain, upon fuch muft the penalty of the laws of the
land,

land, (being grounded upon God's laws) be by the civil magistrate inflicted. And for this cause is it that the king is required, "When he sitteth upon the throne of his kingdom, to write him a copy of the law of God in a book," Deut. xvii. 18. And for this cause it is that the civil magistrate is called, The keeper of both tables; for saith Luther, * God hath ordained magistrates, and other superiors, and appointed laws, bounds, and all civil ordinances, that if they can do no more, yet at least they may bind the divil's hands, that he rage not in his bond-slaves after his own lust. And hence it is, that the apostle speaking of the civil magistrate, saith, " If thou do that which is evil, be afraid, for he beareth not the sword in vain," Rom. xiii. 14. Wherefore, right honourable, God having called you to wield the sword of authoity. in the most famous city of this kingdom, I, a poor, inhabitant thereof, the author of this ensuing dialogue, have, through the advice and persuasion of some godly ministers, and through the consideration of the suitableness of the subject with your place, been moved to take the boldness to offer this work to your worthy name and patronage, (not for that I do conceive your honour is ignorant of your duty, nor yet for that I see you to neglect your duty; for your Christian integrity in your place, and your zealous forwardness to reform things amiss by punishing of evil-doers, doth to me witness the contrary, but rather) to encurage your honour to continue your godly course in the ways of well doing, and to advance forward in paths of piety, being more swift in your motion now towards the end of your race (your year, I mean) that so your master Christ, may have cause to say concerning you, as he once did concerning the church at Thyatira, " I know thy works, and charity, and service, and faith, and thy works: and the last to be more than the first," Rev. ii. 19. Yea, and that it also may be said concerning you, " Well done, thou good and faithful servant, thou hast been faithful over a few things, I will

* Luther on Gal. p 151.

will make thee ruler over many things, enter thou into the joy of thy Lord," Matth. xxv. 21.

And so most humbly begging of your Honour, that these my poor labours may be accepted, and that under your Honour's name, they may go forth into the world, and praying the Lord of power, and the God of all grace, to multiply his Spirit upon your Honour, with all the blessed fruits of the same, I take my leave, and rest,

Your Honour's most

humble Servant to

be commanded,

E. F.

++ ++ ++ ++ ++ ++ ++ ++ ++ ++ ++ ++ ++ ++ ++ ++ ++ ++ ++ ++

The Author to the well-affected Reader.

Good Reader,

I Do confess, there are so many both godly and learned expositions upon the ten commandments already extant, that it may seem needless to add any more unto that number. Nevertheless, I pray thee, do not think it impossible, but that God may by such a weak instrument, as I myself am, shew his power in doing something more, touching this subject, than hath yet been done. I do confess, I have had good helps from the labours of others, and have made much use thereof, especially for matter, yet have I not confined my discourse within the compass of what I have found in other books, but have from the warrant of the word of God, taken the boldness

to

to enlarge it, both as touching the matter and manner, and especially touching the application, wherein I have endeavoured to give both believers and unbelievers their distinct portion, by distinguishing betwixt the ten commandments, as they are the law of works, having the promise of eternal life, and the threatning of eternal death annexed to them, and so applying them to the unbeliever; and as they are the law of Christ, having the promise of eternal life, and the threatning of eternal death seperated from them, and so applying them to the believer. I have not denied, but acknowledged, yea, and proved, that the law of the ten commandments, truly expounded, are to be a perpetual rule of life to all mankind, yea, to believers themselves; for though the Spirit of Jesus Christ, do, according to his promise, write this law in their hearts, as their inward rule, yet, in regard that whilst they live in this world, it is done but in part, they have need of the ten commandments to be unto them as an outward rule: for though the Spirit have begotten in them a love to this law, and wrought in them a willing disposition to yield obedience thereunto, yet have they need of the law to be unto them as a glass, wherein they may see what the will of God is, and as a rule to direct them how to actuate their love and willingness, so that as a precious godly minister of Jesus Christ truly saith, the Spirit within, and the law without, " Is a lamp unto their feet, and, a light unto their paths," Psal. cxix. 105.

　But yet I do conceive, that expositors on the commandments should not only endeavour to drive on their designs to that end, and there terminate their endeavours, as if there were no further use to be made of the law, neither in believers, nor in unbelievers, but they should aim at a further end, an end beyond this, especially in unbelievers, and that is to discover to them how far short they come of doing that which the law requireth, that so they may not take up their rest in themselves, but hasten out of
them-

themſelves, to Jeſus Chriſt; and that believers, by beholding their own imperfections, ſhould take occaſion to humble themſelves, and cleave the more cloſe unto him
by faith.

For when by way of expoſition, it is only declared
what is required, and what is forbidden, in every commandment, with exhortations, motives, and means to do
thereafter, it hath been obſerved that divers both profane
and mere civil honeſt people; upon the hearing or reading of the ſame, have concluded with themſelves, that
they muſt either alter their courſe of life, and ſtrive and
endeavour to do more than they have done, and better
than they have done, or elſe they ſhall never be ſaved;
and hereupon they have taken up a form of godlineſs, in
hearing, reading, and praying, and the like, and ſo have
become formal profeſſors, and therein have reſted, coming far ſhort of Jeſus Chriſt; yea, and believers themſelves have ſometimes taken occaſion thereby, to conceit
that they muſt do ſomething towards their own juſtification
and ſalvation.

Wherefore I. yet not I, by any power of mine own, but
by the grace of God that is with me, have endeavoured
not only to ſhew what is required, and what is forbidden
in every commandment, but alſo, that it is impoſſible for
any man, whether he be an unbeliever or a believer, to
keep any one commandment perfectly: yea, or to do any
one action or duty perfectly; that ſo by the working of
God's Spirit in the reading of the ſame, men my be moved, not only to turn from being profane, or mere civil
honeſt men, to be formal profeſſors, but that they may
be driven out of all their own works and performances
unto Jeſus Chriſt, and ſo become Chriſtians indeed; and
that thoſe who are Chriſtians indeed, may thereby be
moved to prize Jeſus Chriſt the more: and if the Lord
ſhall be pleaſed to enable either myſelf, or any other
man or woman, to make this uſe of this enſuing
dialogue, then ſhall not my labour be in vain: but my
heart's deſire and prayer to God ſhall be, that many may

in

receive as much good by the marrow which is contained in this fecond bone, as they fay they have done by that which is contained in the firft, that fo God may be glorified, and their fouls edified, and then I have my reward; only let me beg of thee, that (for what good thou receiveft thereby) thou wilt beg at the throne of grace for me, that my faith may be increafed, and fo my love inflamed towards God, and towards man for God's fake, and then I am fure I fhall keep the law more perfectly than I have yet done The which that we may all do, the grace of our Lord Jefus Chrift be with all your fpirits. *Amen.*

Thine in the Lord Jefus Chrift,

This 21ft of September, 1648.

E. F.

❋❋❋

To the Ingenious Reader.

ART thou a freind or an enemy? whether the one or the other, fure I am thou art much concerned in this treatife. Should I particularize the ufefulnefs of what is herein delivered, would it not fwell to a book of bulk?

There is that fcattereth and lofeth nothing, as the wife man fpeaketh. "It is knowledge and love," the more they fpread and dilate themfelves, the greater is their growth.

A fea is a congregation of waters, all graces in Chrift are as a confluence and congregation of fhining favours from the Father of fpirits; for he is the ocean of reft and fulnefs; from this fountain comes all riyers, ftreams and beams of light and life; and effects are more copioufly in

their

their-caufes than in themfelves, as water is more emi-
nently in the element and fountain than in the ftreams.

Try, and thou fhalt find this author hath been
at the well-head, and having received wherewithal
to draw, hath thence made *occults occulars,* dark
things clear, and maffy things light; perufe him
well, and thou wilt be a gainer; for the expounder
of fecrets hath taught him. There are two grand
teftimonial difcoveries of God in fcripture, the one
legal, the other evangelical, law and gofpel; the
one lets us know what God is in himlelf, the
other what he is in his Son to us. I find them both
united in the xxth. of Exodus, where the laft named
hath the firft place, as a preface to what fhould follow; fweet is that faying, " I am the Lord thy
God." And ver. 3. " Thou fhalt have none before me." What! that fuch a faying fhould be
heard on mount Sinai, a mount, that burnt with
fire! That God fhould fpeak out, himfelf as their
own Lord, in thunderings and lightnings, with
founds of terrible trumpets; that there fhould be the
face of a Sion on that mount, words of terror, and
words of delight; words of pleafure and difpleafure
at once; a people of God's delight, and a God
the delight of his people. Is not this the law evan-
gelized? And will not this, O mortal wight! let
thee fee that his commandments are not grievous?
Quo levius mandatum eo gravius peccatum. The
more grievous then is the breach of them; is not
this a tempering of frowns with fmiles, weigh it
wifely and well: will you hear God the Lord fpeak
out to a people, I am thine once more? Then read
Hof. iii. 2, 3. where you have a piece of gofpel, like
to this.

Captive woman bought for " fifteen pieces of
filver, and an homer of barley, and an half homer of
barley, thou fhalt abide for me, thou fhalt not be for
another." So I will be for thee; as if God fhould

fay,

fay, " I confent : fay *Amen* to the contract or bargain, that I will be thy hufband, and thou fhalt be my fpoufe." So at the giving out of the law, God begins firft with the relation that is between him and his people, *viz.* I am God, I made you, therefore think not much that I command you : I am your God, I ferve you, will you not then ferve me ? I have faid, you fhall command me, Ifa. xlv. 11. " Concerning the works of mine hands, command you me."

O' that you would fuffer me to command you, and you yourfelves yield obedience ! God is the hufband, his people the fpoufe, the wife of his youth, his firft and only one, his firft and laft wife ; and, as the author tells thee, hufbands and wives fhould do for each other. I am thy God, faith the Lord, that hath done for thee; done great things for thee ; I am he that brought thee out of Egypt, and bought thee out of bondage ; thou haft been a flave, but ferve me, and I will make thee a king: thou haft been a vaffal to an earthly prince, a wicked nation and generation, but I will " reprove kings for thy fake," 1 Chron. xvi. 21. And thou fhalt rule nations with a rod of iron, Rev. ii. 26, 27. All this have I done for thee, and made fure to thee : now hear what thou muft do for me, thou fhalt keep clofe to me, " Have none other Gods befides me." Notwithftanding all this, *Is dat qui mandat, qui jubet, ille juvat.*

He gives who commands, and helps to perform what he commands. O bleffed Mafter ! woe to the man that ferves an earthly mammon inftead of thee. This, even this, made the father breathe out fweetly, *Da Domine quod jubes, & jube quid vis.* Lord give me; what thou requireft from me, and then command what thou wilt. Mofes may preach law and a curfe to the ftiff-necked Jews ; and Chrift may preach gofpel to the hard-hearted Pharifees ; yet are they not

not drawn or driven. Sounds and syllables of a thousand hills, and as many heavens, are alike fruitless and useless, if there be not a gospel-spirit to give an omnipotent pull, and translate the man out of his element.

Art thou a believer, and sayest thou art free from the law? Art thou not under the law in a sense? Consider first the gospel-love of Jesus Christ, frees thee from the law as a curser, but not from the law as a pedagogue. For, after a soul is brought home to Christ, though love be the immediate Lord that commands and constrains into the obedience of Christ, yet law is the mediate Lord, and love works by law, as the will of the loveliest Lord. Will not this consideration sweeten the sourest precept?

Christ's love shed abroad in a soul, works upwards, and facilitates law; and though corrupt will, before Christ came, was a wicked tyrant, and lust a lawless landlord, which brought the man under the law-curse; yet Christ being come, brings the soul and whole man under the law's command, having first taken the law-road into his own hand, and broken and spent it on his own back

Hence the law which was forced by power, becomes fettering by love, Christ's own silken cord. Add to this, that the law leaves not off to be a rule of righteousness, because it gives not grace to obey; for then the gospel should be no rule of faith, because it gives no grace to believe, and God requires no more than he gives, in the one or in the other.

Take a hint of the differences that is betwixt the law and the gospel thus: Under the law, the covenant of works, one slip from the way of life bolteth the paradise-door against the offender; and into it again he cannot enter: the law knows no such thing as repentance, Gal iii 10. Deut xxvii. 26.

But the covenant of grace, being made with a poor undone sinner, a slip, an act of unbelief, doth not

fore-

forefeit the mercy of the covenant; the covenant ſtands firm, that there may be a repetition of grace ſtill : and though a gracious child ſhould ſin againſt a gracious father, yet can he not ſin the unpardonable ſin, and ſin away an eternal prieſt and covenant out of heaven.

Secondly, The law ſtints the meaſure of thy obedience, even to the higheſt degree: thy whole ſoul, might and ſtrength, any leſs is the forefeiting of the life that is laſting, everlaſting, but the covenant of grace ſtints no weak ſoul ; Chriſt's racks not crying out, " The ſtrongeſt faith, or none at all." Many who were poor bruiſed reeds on earth, are now mighty cedars, high, tall, green, growing on the banks of the river of life.

What then if Adam be the firſt in heaven, and David be but as he deſired, the keeper of the door, yet his ſeeing the throne, and the Lamb that ſits thereon, is enough to him.

In a word, the theme or ſubject of this treatiſe is (as Paul ſpeaks) holy and ſpiritual, the manner and method of handling of it, very ſavoury, familiar and plain. Reader bleſs thou the Lord, that thou liveſt in a land of light and life, and bleſs God for this author, who hath like the bee, painfully fetched this honey out of various flowers, and at laſt brought it into this hive, farewel in the Lord.

Thine if thou be Chriſt's,

From my ſtudy in
  Bride's church-
  yard, Septem-
  ber 22, 1648.

S. MOOR.

To the READER.

IT is reported of Linacrus, reading a sermon of Christ's in the mount, and considering the conversation of men in the world *, said, "Either this is not God's gospel, or we are not God's people." Look abroad into the world, and, (if thine eye be not carnal) thou wilt find that most men live without God in the world, many having conscience of divine power, yet few knowing God in Christ; some ignorant for want of teaching, others ignorant for want of will to be taught; a price they have (as Solomon saith) in the hand to get wisdom, but they have no heart to it, despising knowledge †, and hating it, casting it at their heels, Psal 1. 17. Some knowing, but not doing; others knowing, and doing something materially good, theologically evil, yet reposing the weight of their souls upon the crazy bottom of their duties; ignorance of the spiritual sense of the law, and of the right use of it, appertaining unto unbelievers and believers, is a main ground of the latter.

This treatise will help thee to understand both; and as in Ezekiel's vision, *Rota erit in rota;* thou hast gospel in the law, and law in the gospel.

Art thou in thy sins, and out of Christ? Here thou mayest see the exorbitancies of each wheel, both of soul and body, and that all thy doings are a ladder too short to reach heaven. O happy thou, did thy soul fathom her own misery! Wert thou more out of love with thyself, thou wouldst be more in love with Christ? Were thy self-confidences levelled, thy breathings after Christ would be more earnest; thy leanings upon Christ with greater confidence.

Art thou in Christ? Here thou mayest see what use thou art to make of the law; lawless profane liberty

* Eph. ii. 12. † Prov. xvii. 7.

liberty ought not to be by thee pleaded for, or practif- ed. *Tace lingua loquere vitæ.* Indeed many a man's life fpeaks what he is, though his tongue be filent; like Erafmus's ruffian, that carried by the one fide a gay gilded Teftament, and by the other fide a good bottle of fack. Many that hear much, and talk more, having God's law in their mouths, yet hating to be reformed. Chriftian, it is thy duty to endeavour to keep the whole law of God. The gofpel requires obedience as well as the law : yea, the gofpel wills no lefs inward or outward holinefs than the law : and if thy nature be fpiritualized, though thou be not able, yet thou wilt be willing to obey the law of God in the higheft degree, and thy coming fhort of gofpel- fervice, will call for thy laying cut of gofpel-forrow. Whoever thou art, take heed of being wedded to thine own blindnefs ; if thou be'eft blind, thou art blind at noon-day ; thou and I have caufe to blefs God for his affifting grace vouchfafed unto this author, who (I dare fay) knows much of God, and therefore not a little of himfelf. The blefling of heaven go along with his labours; this is, and fhall be the earneft prayer of,

Thine affectionate Servant

in the gofpel,

JOHN CRADOCOT.

+++

Reader,

EVery thing is, and is to be judged[*], not according to its out-fide and appearance, but according to its more hidden and inward being. Therefore the Stoics call the foul, *To pan homnis*, the all of man, or all the man : and Solomon, fpeaking of the evil-eyed,

or

[*] John vii. 2.

or envious man, fays of him, Prov. xxiii. 7. " As he
thinketh in his heart, fo is he." And the lawyers fay
of the law, *Mens legis eft lex,* the mind or meaning of
of the law, is the law: They then which acquaint thee
with things in this kind, fhould be moft acceptable and
welcome to thee, among which thou mayeft reckon
this author for one ; who hath fifhed out the meaning and ufe of the law, in which, as in a glafs, thou
mayeft fee (if thou forget not) what manner of man
thou oughteft to be, in thy converfatation, towards
God, toward thyfelf, and towards others. The * ten
commandments, or ten words, (which Chrift contracted
into two, Matth. xxii. 40. and which are wrapt up in
this one word, Love) tho' for the letter of them, they
take up but a little room, yet they are, in their meaning, exceeding broad and comprehenfive ; and though
the letter be the word of God, it is the fpirit, or inward meaning, which is the will and mind of God ;
not as if there were any thing in the letter, which was
not in the meaning, but that the meaning is of far
larger extent than the words do exprefs ; now the
meaning being expreft fo briefly, and in fo few words,
became obfcure † ; and hence it was, that the Scribes,
Pharifees and lawyers, were fo much in the dark, as to
the meaning of the law, fuppofing that there had not
been any *jub intelligitur* at all. Now, left thou,
reader, fhouldft ftumble at the fame ftone, here's
a light to guide thee. I fhall fay no more, for the
wine is fo good, that it needs no bufh, only to tell
thee, that 'tis here to be fold.

RALPH VENNING.

* Decalogue.

† Qui brevis erit, obfcuris erit,

THE
MARROW
OF
MODERN DIVINITY.
PART II.

+++++++++++++++++++++++++++===+++++++++++++++++++++++

INTERLOCUTORS.

EVANGELISTA, a Minifter of the gofpel.
NOMOLOGISTA, a Pratler of the law. And,
NEOPHITUS, a young Chriftian.

++++++++++++++++++++++++++===+++++++++++++++++++++++++

Neo. SIR, here is our neighbour Nomologifta, who
as I fuppofe, is much miftaken, as touching
a point that he and I have had fome conference about;
and becaufe I found you fo ready and willing to inform
and inftruct me, when I came to you with my neighbour Nomifta and Antinomifta, I have prefumed to
intreat him to come along with me to you; affuring
both myfelf and him, that we fhall be welcome to you,
and that you will make it appear he is deceived.

Evan. You are both of you very kindly welcome
to me, and as I have been willing to give you the
beft inftruction, when you were formerly with me;
even fo, God willing, fhall I be now: wherefore I
pray you let me underftand what the point is, wherein you do conceive he is miftaken.

Neo. Why Sir, this is the thing. He tells me he is
perfuaded that he goes very near the perfect fulfilling
the law of God; but I cannot be perfuaded to it.

Evan. What fay you, neighbour Nomologifta, are
you perfuaded?

Nom. Yea, indeed Sir, I am fo perfuaded, for
whereas you know the firft commandment is, " I am
the Lord thy God, thou fhalt have none other Gods
be-

before my face." I am confident I have the only true God for my God; and none others.

And whereas the second commandment is, " Thou ſhalt not make to thyſelf any graven image," &c. I tell you truly, I do defy all graven images; and do count it a great folly in any man, either to make them, or worſhip them.

And whereas the third commandment is, " Thou ſhalt not take the name of the Lord thy God in vain." It is well known that I am no ſwearer; neither can I abide to-hear others to ſwear by the name of God.

And whereas the fourth commandment is, " Remember that thou keep holy the ſabbath day." I am ſure I do very ſeldom either work or travel on that day; but do go to the church both forenoon and afternoon; and do both read, and hear the word of God read, when I come home.

And whereas the fifth commandment is, " Honour thy father and thy mother," &c. I thank God, I was very careful to do my duty to my parents when I was a child.

And whereas the ſixth commandment is, " Thou ſhalt not kill." I thank God I never yet murdered either man, woman, or child; and I hope, I never ſhall.

And whereas the ſeventh commandment is, " Thou ſhalt not commit adultery." I thank God, I was never given to women; God hath hitherto kept me from committing that ſin, and ſo I hope he will do, whilſt I live.

And whereas the eighth commandment is, " Thou ſhalt not ſteal." I do not remember that ever I took the worth of twelve-pence of any man's goods in all my life.

And whereas the ninth commandment is, " Thou ſhalt not bear falſe witneſs againſt thy neighbour." I thank God, I do abhor that ſin, and was never guilty of it in all my life.

And

And whereas the tenth commandment is, "Thou shalt not covet." I thank God, I never coveted nothing but what was mine own in all my life.

Evan. Alas! neighbour Nomologista, the commandments of God have a larger extent than it seems you are aware of; for it seems you do imagine that the whole moral law is confined within the compass of what you have now repeated; as though there were no more required or forbidden, than what is expressed in the words of the ten commandments; as though the Lord required no more but the bare external, or actual performance of a duty; and as though he did forbid no more than the bare abstinence and gross acting of sin. The very same conceit of the law of God the Scribes and Pharisees had: and therefore it is no marvel though you imagine you keep all the commandments even as they did.

Nom. Well, Sir, if I have been deceived, you may do well to instruct me better.

Evan. I shall endeavour to do it with all my heart, as the Lord shall be pleased to enable me. And because I begin to fear that it is not your case alone to be thus ignorant of the large extent, and the true sense and meaning of the law of God; I also begin to blame myself, for that I have not taken occasion to expound the commandments in my public ministry, since I came amongst you; and therefore I do now resolve, by the help of God, very speedily to fall about that work; and I hope I shall then make it appear unto you, that the * ten commandments are but an epitomy or an abridgment of the law of God, and that the full exposition thereof is to be found in the books of the prophets and apostles, called the Old and New Testament.

Neo. Indeed, Sir, I have told him that we must not stick upon the bare words of any of the ten commandments, nor rest satisfied with the bare literal sense,

* Exod. xxxiv. 27.

fenfe, but labour to find out the full expofition and true fpiritual meaning of every one of them, according to other places of holy fcripture.

Evan. If you told him fo, you told him that which is moft true; for he that would truly underftand and expound the commandments, muft do it according to thefe fix rules.

First, He muft confider that every commandment * hath both a negative and an affirmative part contained in it; that is to fay, where any evil is forbidden, the contrary good is commanded; and where any good is commanded; the contrary evil is forbidden; for faith Urfinus's catechifm, † "The law-giver doth in an affirmative commandment comprehend the negative; and contrariwife, in a negative he comprehendeth the affirmative."

Secondly, He muft confider that under one good action commanded, or one evil action forbidden, ‡ all of the fame kind or nature are comprehended; yea, all occafions, and means leading thereunto; according to the faying of judicious Virell, "The Lord minding to forbid divers evils of the fame kind, he compre-hendeth them under the name of the greateft."

Thirdly, He muft confider that the law of God is fpiritual, reaching to the very heart or foul, and all the powers thereof, ‖ for it chargeth the underftand-ing to know the will of God; § it chargeth the memory to retain, and the will to chufe the better, and to leave the worfe; it chargeth the affections to love the things that are to be loved, and to hate the things that are to be hated, and fo bindeth all the

---

* Pfal. xxxiv. 14.   † Page 529.
‡ Grounds of religion, page 207.
‖ Rom. vii. 14   Matth. v. 27.
§ Dod on the Com. page 24.

powers of the foul to obedience, as well as the words, thoughts and geftures.

Fourthly, He muft confider, that the law of God muft not only be the rule of our obedience, but it muft alfo be the reafon of it ; we muft not only do that which is there commanded, and avoid that which is there forbidden, but we muft alfo do the good, becaufe the Lord requireth it, and avoid the evil, becaufe the Lord forbiddeth it ; * yea, and we muft do all that is delivered and prefcribed in the law, for the love we bear to God ; the love of God muft be the fountain, the impulfive and efficient caufe of all our obedience to the law.

Fifthly, He muft confider, that as our obedience to the law muft arife from a right fountain, fo muft it be directed to a right end, and that is, that God alone may be glorified by us ; for otherwife it is not the worfhip of God, but hypocrify, faith Urfinus's catechifm † ; fo that according to the faying of another godly writer ‡, the final caufe, or end of all our obedience, muft be God's glory ; || or which is all one, that we may pleafe him : for in feeking to pleafe God, we glorify him, and thefe two things are always co-incident.

Sixthly, He muft confider that the Lord doth not only take notice what we do in obedience to his law, but alfo after what manner we do it : and therefore we muft be careful to do all our actions after a right manner, *viz.* humbly, reverently, willingly and zealoufly.

Neo. I befeech you, Sir, if you can fpare fo much time, let us have fome brief expofition of fome, if not of all the commandments, before we go hence, according to thefe rules.

Evan. What fay you, neighbour Nomologifta, do you defire the fame ?

* Urfin. Cat. p. 37.
† Page 518. ‡ Mr Whateley God's hufb. p. 120.
|| 1 Cor. x. 31.

Nom. Yea, Sir, with all my heart, if you pleafe.

Evan. Well then, although my occafions at this time might juftly plead excufe for me : yet, feeing that you do both of you defire it, I will for the prefent difpenfe with all my other bufinefs, and endeavour to accomplifh your defires, according as the Lord fhall be pleafed to enable me : and therefore I pray you underftand and confider, That in the firft commandment there is a negative part exprefled in thefe words, " Thou fhalt have none other Gods before my face." And an affirmative part included in thefe words, " But thou fhalt have me only for thy God." For if we moft have none other for our God, it implies ftrongly, that we muft have the Lord for our God.

Neo. I pray you, Sir, begin with the affirmative part; and firft tell us, what the Lord requireth of us in this commandment?

COMMANDMENT I.

Evan. In this firft commandment, the Lord requireth the duty of our hearts or fouls, Prov. xxiii. 26. That is to fay, of our underftandings, wills, and affections, and the effects of them.

Neo. And what is the duty of our underftandings?

Evan. The duty of our our underftandings is to know God *, 1 Chron. xxviii. 9. Now, the end of knowledge is but the fulnefs of perfuafion, even a fettled belief, which is called faith, fo that the duty of our underftandings is, fo to know God, as to believe him to be according as he hath revealed himfelf to us in his word and works, Heb. xi. 6.

Neo. And how hath the Lord revealed himfelf to us in his word?

Evan. Why, he hath revealed himfelf to be moft
wife,

* Andr. on the Com. p. 125.

I i

wife, Rom. xvi 27. Moſt mighty, Deut. vii. 21.
Moſt true, Deut. xxxii. 4. Moſt juſt, Neh. ix. 33.
And moſt-merciful, Pſal. cxlv. 8.

Neo. And how hath he revealed himſelf to us in
his works?

Evan. He hath revealed himſelf in his works
to be the Creator of all things, Exod. xx. 11. And
the preſerver of all things, Pſal. xxxvi. 6. And the
governor of all things, Pſal. cxxxv. 6. And the
giver of every good gift, James i. 17.

Neo. And how muſt our knowledge of God, and
our belief in him, be expreſſed by their effects?

Evan. We muſt expreſs, that we know and believe God to be according as he hath revealed himſelf
in his word and works, by our remembering and acknowledging him whenſoever there is occaſion for us
ſo to do.

As for example. When we read or hear thoſe
judgments that the Lord in his word hath threatned
to bring upon us for our ſins *, we are to expreſs,
that we do remember and acknowledge him to be
moſt mighty, true and juſt, by our fearing and trembling thereat, Pſal. cxix. 120. Hab. iii. 16. And when
we read or hear of bleſſings, that the Lord in his word
hath promiſed to beſtow upon us for our obedience †,
then we are to expreſs, that we do remember
and acknowledge him to be moſt true, and merciful,
by our obedience unto him, and by our truſting in him,
and relying upon him, Gen. xxxii. 9. And when we
behold the excellent frame of heaven and earth, and
the creatures contained therein, then we are to expreſs,
that we do remember and acknowledge the Lord to
be the Creator and Maker of them all, by our praiſing
and magnifying his name, Pſal. cvi 5. and cxxxix. 14.
And when the Lord doth actually inflict any judgment
upon us, then we are to expreſs that we do remember
and acknowledge him to be the governor of all things,
and

---

* Deut. xxviii. 16. † Deut. xxvii. 2.

and most mighty, wife, and juft, by humbling our-felves under his mighty hand, 1 Pet. v. 6 And by judging ourfelves worthy to be deftroyed for our ini-quities, Ezek xxxvi 31. And by bearing the pu-nifhment thereof, Lev xxvi. 41. with willing, patient, contented fubmiffion to his will and pleafure, Pfal. xxxix. 9. And when the Lord doth actually beftow any bleffing upon us, then we are to exprefs, that we do remember and acknowledge him to be the moft merciful Giver of every good gift, by our humbly ac-knowledging that we are unworthy of the leaft of his mercies Gen. xxxii. 10. and in giving him thanks for all things, 1 Theff. v. 18. And thus have I fhewed unto you, what is the duty of our underftandings.

Neo. I pray you, Sir, let us in the next place hear what is the duty of our wills.

Evan. The duty of our wills is to chufe the Lord alone for our portion, Pfal. xvi. 5. and cxix. 57.

Neo. And how muft we exprefs that we have chofen the Lord for our portion ?

Evan. By our loving him with all our hearts, with all our fouls, and with all our might, Deut. v. 6.

Neo. And how muft we exprefs, that we do thus love the Lord ?

Evan. We muft exprefs that we do thus love the Lord, by the acting of our other affections, as by our defire of moft near communion with him, Phil. i. 23. and by our delighting moft in him, Pfal. xxxvii. 4. and by our rejoicing moft in him, Phil. iv. 4. and by our fearing moft to offend him, Matth. x. 28. and by our forrowing moft for offending him, Luke xxii. 62. and by being moft zealous againft fin, and for the glory of God, Rev. iii. 19. And thus have I fhewed you what the Lord requireth in the affirmative part of this commandment.

Neo. I pray you, Sir, proceed to the negative part, and fhew us what the Lord forbiddeth in this com-mandment.

Evan.

Evan. In this firſt commandment is forbidden ignor-ance of God, Jer. iv. 22. and ſo alſo is unbelief, or doubting of the truth of God's word, Iſa. vii. 9. And ſo alſo, is the want of fearing the threatnings of. God, Deut. xxviii. 58. And the fearing the threat-nings of men, either more, or as much as the threat-nings of God, Iſa. li. 12, 13. And ſo alſo is the want of truſting unto, or relying upon the promiſes of God; Luke xi. 29. And the truſting or relying upon our-ſelves, mens promiſes, or any other thing either more, or as much as we do upon God, Jer. xvii. 5. Luke xii. 20. And ſo alſo is the want of acknowledging the hand of God in the time of affliction, Iſa. xxvi. 11. And acknowledging that the road can ſmite without the hand of God, John xix. 11. And ſo alſo is the the want of humbling ourſelves before the Lord; Dan. v. 22. and pride of heart, Prov. xvi 5. And ſo alſo is impatience, and diſcontentedneſs under the chaſtning hand of God, Exod. xvii. 2 And not re-turning unto him that ſmitteth us, Iſa. ix. 13. And ſo alſo is our forgetfulneſs of God, in not acknow-ledging his merciful and bountiful hand in reaching forth all good things unto us in the time of proſperity, Pſal. lxxviii. 11. Deut xxxii. 18. And ſo alſo is our ſacrificing to our own nets, Hab. i. 16. In aſcribing the coming in of our riches to our own care, pains, and diligence in our callings, Deut. viii. 17 And ſo alſo is unthankfulneſs to the Lord for his mercies, Rom. i. 21. And ſo alſo is our want of love to God, 1Cor. xvi. 22. And our loving any creature either more than God, or equal with God, Matth x 37. And ſo alſo is our want of deſiring his preſence, Job xxi. 14. And our deſiring the preſence of any creature either more or ſo much as God, Prov. vi. 25. And ſo alſo is our want of rejoicing in God, Deut. xxviii. 47. And our rejoicing either more, or as much in any thing as in God; Luke x. 20. And ſo alſo is our want of fearing to offend God, Jer. v. 22. And our fearing to offend any

any mortal man, either more, or as much as to offend
God, Prov. xxix. 25. And fo alfo is our want of
forrow and grief for offending God, 1 Cor. v. 2. And
our forrowing more, or as much for any worldly lofs,
or crofs, as for our finning againft God, 1 Theff. iv. 15.
And fo alfo is our want of zeal, or our luke-warmnefs
in the caufe of God and his truth, Rev. iii. 16. And
our corrupt, blind, and undifcreet zeal, Luke ix. 55.
And thus have I fhewed unto you, what the Lord
requireth, and what he forbiddeth in this commandment: And now neighbour Nomologifta, I pray you
tell me whether you keep it perfectly or no?

Nom. Sir, before I tell you that, I pray you tell
me how you prove that the Lord in this commandment
doth require all thefe duties, and forbid all thefe fins?

Evan. Firft, I know that the Lord in this commandment doth require all thefe duties, becaufe no
man can truly have the Lord for his God, except he
hath chofen him for his portion; and no man can
truly chufe the Lord for his portion, before he truly
know him; and he that doth truly know God, doth
truly believe both his threatenings and his promifes:
and he that doth truly believe the Lord's threatenings,
muft needs needs fear and tremble at them: and he
that doth truly believe the Lord's promifes, muft
needs truly love him, for faith doth always produce
and bring forth love; and whofoever doth truly
love God, muft needs defire near communion with
him; yea, and fear to offend him; yea, and forrow
for offending him; yea, and be zealous for his glory.

Secondly, I know that all thefe fins are forbidden
in this commandment, becaufe that whatfoever the
mind, will, and affections of men, are fet upon, or
carried after, either more, or as much, as after God,
that is another god unto them: and therefore if a man

I i 3   ftand

stand in fear of any creature, or fear the lofs of any creature, either more than God, or equal with God, he makes that creature his god; and if he truft unto, and put confidence in any creature, either more than in God, or equal with God, that creature is his god: and hence it is, that the covetous man is called an idolater, Eph. v 5. for that he maketh gold his hope, and faith to the fine gold, "Thou art my confidence," Job xxxi. 24. And if any man be proud of any good thing he hath, and do not acknowledge God to be the free Giver and Beftower of the fame; or if he be impatient and difcontented under the Lord's correcting hand, he makes himfelf a god; and if a man fo love any creature, as that he defires it being abfent, or delights in its being prefent, either more than God, or equal with God, that creature is another god unto him. And hence it is, that voluptuous men are faid to make their belly their god, Phil. iii 19. In a word, whatfoever the mind of man is carried after, or his heart and affections fet upon, either more, or as much as upon God, that he makes his god. And therefore, we may undoubtedly conclude, that all the fins before mentioned, are forbidden in this commandment.

Nom. Then believe me, Sir, I muft confefs that I come far fhort of keeping this commandment perfectly.

Evan. Yea, and fo we do all of us, am I confident; for have not every one of us fometimes queftioned in our hearts, whether there be a God or no? And as touching the knowledge of God, may not we all three of us truly fay with the apoftle, 1 Cor. xiii. 9. "We know in part." And which of us hath fo feared and trembled at the threatenings of God, and at the fhaking of his rod, as we ought? Nay, have we not feared the frowns, threats, and power of fome mortal man, more than the frowns, threats, and power of God? It is well, if it have not appeared by our chufing to obey man rather than God: and which of us both

fo

fo trufted unto, and relied upon the promifes of God, in time of need, as he ought. Nay, have we not rather trufted unto, and relied upon men and means, than upon God? Hath it not been manifefted by our fearing of poverty, and want of outward things, when friends, trading, and means begin to fail us, though God hath faid, " I will not fail thee, nor forfake thee," Heb. xiii. 5. And which of us hath fo humbled ourfelves under the chaftifing and correcting hand of God, as we ought: nay, have we not rather expreffed abundance of pride, by our impatience and difcontentednefs, and want of fubmitting to the will of God ; and by our quarrelling and contending with his rod. And which of us hath fo acknowledged God in the time of profperity, and been fo thankful unto him for his bleffings, as we ought? Nay, have we not rather at fuch times forgotten God, and facrificed to our own nets, faying in our hearts, if not alfo with our mouths, " I may thank mine own diligence, care, and pains-taking, or elfe it had not been with me as it is?" And which of us hath fo manifefted our love to God, by our defire of near communion with him in his ordinances, and by our defire to be diffolved and to be with him, as we ought?. Nay, have we not rather expreffed our great want of love to him, by our backwardnefs to prayer, reading, hearing his word, and receiving the facrament, and by our little delight therein, and by our unwillingnefs to die? Nay, have we not manifefted our greater love to the world, by our greater defires after the profits, plea-fures, and honours of the world, and by our greater delight therein than in God? Or, which of us have fo manifefted our love to God, by our forrow and grief for offending him as we ought? Nay, have we not rather manifefted our greater love to the world, by our forrowing and grieving more for fome worldly lofs or crofs, than for offending God by our fins? Or which of us have fo manifefted our love to God, by

being

being so zealous for his glory as we ought? Nay, have we not rather expressed greater love to ourselves, in being more hot and fiery in our own cause than in God's cause? And thus have I endeavoured to satisfy your desires concerning the first commandment.

Neo. I beseech you, Sir proceed to do the like concerning the second commandment, and first tell us how the first and second commandment differ, the one from the other.

COMMANDMENT II.

Evan. Why as the first commandment teacheth us to have the true God for our God, and none other; so the second commandment requireth that we worship this true God alone, with true worship: and in this commandment likewise there is a negative part expressed in these words, " Thou shalt not make to thyself any graven image," &c. And an affirmative part included in these words, " But thou shalt worship " me only and purely, according to my will revealed " in my word."

Neo. I pray you then, Sir, begin with the affirmative part, and tell us what be the means of God's worship prescribed in his word.

Evan. If we look into the word of God, we shall find that the ordinary means and parts of God's worship, are invocation upon the name of God, ministry and hearing of the word of God, administration and receiving the sacraments, with all helps and furtherances to the right performance of the same.

But to declare this more particularly *, First of all, Prayer both public and private is required in God's word, as you may see, 1 Tim. ii. 8. Acts ii. 21, 22. Dan. vi. 10. *Secondly,* Reading the word, or hearing it read, both publickly and privately is required in God's

* Elton and Downham on the second Com.

God's word, as you may fee, Rev. i. 3. Deut. v. 6. *Thirdly*, Preaching, and hearing of the word preached, is required in the word of God, as you may fee, 2 Kings iv. 1. 1 Theff ii. 13. *Fourthly*, The adminiftration and receiving the facrament, is required in the word of God, as you may fee, Matth. iii. 6. Matth. xxvi. 26. 1 Cor. x. 16. *Fifthly*, Praifing of God, in finging of pfalms, both publickly and privately, is required in the word of God, as you may fee, Col. iii. 16. James v. 13 *Sixthly*, Meditation in the word of God, is required in the word of God, as you may fee, Pfal i. 2 Acts xvii. 11. *Seventhly*, Conference about the word of God, is required in the word of God, as you may fee, Mal. iii. 16. And *Laftly*, For the better fitting and ftirring us up to the right performance of thefe duties, religious fafting *, both in public and in private, is required in the word of God, as you may fee, Joel i. 14. Joel ii. 15. And fo also is a religious vow, or free promife made to God, to perform fome outward work, or bodily exercife for fome end, as you may fee, Eccl. v. 3, 4. And thus have I fhewed you what be the means of God's worfhip which he hath prefcribed in his word.

Neo. I pray you, Sir, then proceed to the negative part, and tell us what the Lord forbiddeth in this commandment?

Evan. Well then, I pray you underftand, that in this commandment is forbidden neglecting of prayer, as you may fee, Pfal. xiv. 4. And fo also is abfenting ourfelves from the hearing of the word preached, or any other ordinance of God, when the Lord calls us thereunto, as you may fee, Luke xiv 18, 19, 20. And fo also is our rejecting the facrament of baptifm, as you may fee, Luke vii. 30. And fo also is our flighting the facrament of the Lord's fupper, as you may fee, 2 Chron. xxx. 10. And fo also is the flighting and omitting any of the other fore-named duties, as you

may

* Elton on the Com. Page 43.

may fee, Pfal x. 4. John iii 31. Ifa. xxii. 12, 13, 14. And fo alfo is praying to faints and angels, as you may fee, Ifa lxiii. 16. Rev. xix 10. And fo alfo is the making of images for religious ufes, as you may fee, Lev. xix 4. And fo alfo is the reprefenting God by an image, as you may fee, Exod. xxxii. 8, 9. And fo alfo is all carnal imaginations of God in his worfhip, as you may fee, Acts xvii. 29. And fo alfo is all will worfhip, or the worfhipping of God according to our own fantafy, as you may fee, 1 Sam. ix. 10, 13. Col. ii. 23. And thus have I fhewed unto you both what the Lord requireth, and what he forbiddeth in this commandment: and now, neighbour Nomologifta, I pray you tell me whether you keep it perfectly or no.

Nom. Yea, Sir, I am pefuaded that I go very near it. But I pray you, Sir, tell me how you do prove that all thefe duties are required, and all thefe fins forbidden in this commandment.

Evan. For the proof of this, I pray you confider, that the worfhipping of falfe gods is flatly forbidden in the negative part of this commandment, in thefe words, "Thou fhalt not bow down thyfelf to them, nor ferve, nor worfhip them," Exod. xx. 5. And the worfhipping of the true God, is implied and expreffed in thefe words, Matth iv. 10· "Thou fhalt worfhip the Lord thy God, and him only fhalt thou ferve."

Nom. But Sir, how do you prove that thefe duties which you have named, are parts of God's worfhip?

Evan For anfwer hereunto, I pray you confider, * that to worfhip God is to tender up that homage and refpect that is due from a creature to a Creator; now, in prayer we are faid to tender up this homage unto him, and to manifeft our profeffion of dependance upon him for all the good we have, and acknowedge him

* Borrough's Gofpel-worfhip, page 27.

him to be author of all good ; and indeed prayer is
fuch a great part of God's worfhip, that fometimes
in fcripture it is put for the whole worfhip of God :
" He that calls upon the name of the Lord, fhall be
faved," Rom. x. 13.   That is, * he that worfhips God
aright. Jer. x. 25. " Pour out thy wrath upon the
heathen that know thee not, and on the families that
call not upon thy name :" that do not pray, that do
not worfhip God.

  And that hearing the word is a part of God's worfhip, is manifeft, becaufe that in hearing, we do manifeft our dependancy upon God, for knowing his mind,
and the way to eternal life : every time we come to
hear the word of God, † if we know what to do, we
do this much, we profefs that we depend upon the
Lord God for the knowing of his mind, and the way
and rule to eternal life : and befides, herein alfo we
come to wait upon God in the way of ordinance, to
have that good conveyed unto us by way of an ordinance, beyond what the thing itfelf is able to do, therefore this is worfhip. And that the receiving the facrament is a part of God's worfhip, it is manifeft, in that
when we come to receive thefe holy figns and feals,
we come to prefent ourfelves before God, and come
to God for a bleffing in communicating unto us fome
higher good, than poffibly thofe creatures that we
have to deal with, ‡ are able of themfelves to convey
to us ; we come to God to have communion with him,
and that we might have the bleffing of the covenant
of grace conveyed unto us through thefe things; and
therefore when we come to be exercifed in them, we
come to worfhip God.   The like we might fay of the
reft of the duties before-mentioned, but I hope this
may fuffice to fatisfy you, that they are parts of God's
worfhip.

---

* Borrough's Gofpel-Worfhip, Page 272.
† Ibid. Page 163.   ‡ Ibid. Page 127.

Nom. But Sir, you know that in this commandment, there is nothing exprefsly forbidden, but the making and worfhipping of images, and therefore I queftion whether all thofe other fins that you have named be likewife forbidden.

Evan. But you muft know, that when the Lord condemneth the chief or greateft and moft evident kind of falfe worfhip, namely, the worfhip of God at, or by images, it is manifeft that he forbiddeth alfo the other kinds of falfe worfhip, feeing this is the head and fountain of all the reft : wherefore, whatfoever worfhips are inftituted by men, * or do any way hinder God's true worfhip, they are contrary to this commandment.

Nom. Well, Sir, though that thefe things be fo, yet, for all that, I am perfuaded I go very near the keeping of this commandment ; for I do conftantly perform the moft of thefe duties, and am not guilty of doing the contary.

Evan. But you muft know, that for the worfhipping of God aright, it is not only required that we do the good which he commandeth, and avoid the evil that he forbiddeth ; but alfo that we do it in obidience to God, to fhew that we acknowledge him alone to be the true God, who hath willed this worfhip to be thus done unto him : fo that, as I told you before, the word of God muft not only be the rule of our actions, but alfo the reafon of them; we muft do all things which are delivered and prefcribed in the commandments, † even for the love we bear to God, and for the defire we have to worfhip him ; for except we fo do them, we do them, not according to the fentence and prefcript of the law, neither do we pleafe God therein. Where-fore, though you have prayed and heard the word of God, and received the facrament, and done all the reft of the fore-named duties, yea, and tho' you have not done the contrary, yet if all this hath been either be-

cauſe

Uſin. Cat. Page 540.   † Ibid. p 528.

caufe the laws of the kingdom require it, or in more
obedience to any fuperior, or to gain the praife or
efteem of men, or if you have any way made yourfelf your higheft end, you have not obeyed nor worfhipped God therein : for, faith a judicious writer, * " If
any man fhall obferve thefe things in mere obedience
to the king's laws, or thereby to pleafe holy men, and
not through an immediate reverence of that heavenly
Majefty who hath commanded them, that man's obedience is non-obedience : his keeping of thefe laws, is
no keeping of them." Becaufe the main thing here
intended, is neglected, which is the fetting up God in
his heart ; and that which is moft of all abhorred, is
practifed, viz. The " fear of God taught by the precepts of men," Ifa. xxix. 13. And to this purpofe,
that worthy man of God, hath this faying, † " Take
heed, faith he, that the praifes of men be not thy higheft end that thou aimeft at ; for if it be, thou worfhip-
peft men, thou doft make the praife of men to be thy
god ; for whatfoever thou doft lift up in the higheft
place, that is thy god, whatfoever it be : wherefore,
if thou lifteft up the praife of men, and makeft that
thy end, thou makeft that thy god ; and fo thou art
a worfhipper of men, but not a worfhipper of God.

Again, faith he, Take heed of making feif thy end.
That is, take heed of aiming at thine own peace, and
fatisfying thine own confcience in the performance of
duties. It is true, faith he, when we perform duties
of God's worfhip, we may be encouraged thereunto
by the expectations of good to ourfelves, yet we muft
look higher, we muft look at the honour and praife of
God ; it is not enough to do it merely to fatisfy confcience ; thy main end muft be that thou mayeft by the
performance of the duty be fitted to honour the name
of God, otherwife we do them not for God, but for

---

* Dr Mayer in his Cat. page 193.
† Mr Borrough's Gofpel Worfhip, page 72.

ourſelves, which the Lord condemneth, Zech. vii. 5, 6. And now, neighbour Nomologiſta, I pray you let me aſk you once again, whether you think you keep this commandment perfectly or no.

Nom No, believe me Sir, I do now begin to fear I do not.

Evan. If you make any queſtion of it, I would intreat you to conſider with yourſelf, whether you have not gone to the church on the Lord's day to hear the word of God, and to receive the ſacrament, and do other duties, becauſe the laws of the kingdom require it ; or, becauſe your parents, or maſters have required it; or becauſe it is a cuſtom to do ſo; or becauſe you conceive it to be a credit for you to do ſo. And I pray you alſo conſider, whether you have not abſtained from worſhipping of images, and other ſuch idolatrous and ſuperſtitious actions, which the Papiſts uſe, merely becauſe the laws of the land, wherein you live, do condemn ſuch things. And I pray you, alſo, conſider whether you have not been ſometimes zealous in prayer, in the preſence and company of others, to gain their praiſe and approbation; have you not deſired that they ſhould think you to be a man of good gifts and parts? And have you not in that regard endeavoured to enlarge yourſelf? And have you not ſometimes performed duties, merely becauſe otherwiſe conſcience would not let you be quiet? And have you not ſometimes faſted and prayed, and humbled yourſelf, merely or chiefly, in hope the Lord would, for your ſo doing, prevent or remove ſome judgment from you, or grant you ſome good thing which you deſire. Now, I beſeech you, anſwer
do not think you have done ſo.

Nom. Yea, believe me, Sir, I think I have.

Evan. Then have you in all theſe things honoured and worſhipped your parents, your maſters, your magiſtrates, your neighbours, your friends, and yourſelf, as ſo many falſe Gods, inſtead of the true
God;

God; and therein have been guilty of breach of the second commandment.

Neo. I pray you, Sir, proceed to speak of the third commandment, as you have done of the first and second: and first tell us how the second and third commandment differ.

COMMANDMENT III.

Evan. Why, as the Lord, in the second commandment, doth require that we worship him alone by true means, so doth he, in the third commandment, require that we use the means of his worship after a right manner, that so they may not be used in vain, Matth. xv 9. And in this commandment likewise there is a negative part expressed in these words, "Thou shalt "not take the name of the Lord thy God in vain." And that is, Thou shalt not profane it, by using my titles, attributes, ordinances, or works ignorantly, irreverently, or after a formal superstitious manner. And an affirmative part included in these words, "But thou shalt sanctify my name," Isa. viii. 13. By using my titles, attributes, ordinances, works, and religion, with knowledge, reverence, and after a spiritual manner, John iv 24.

Neo. I pray you, Sir, begin with the affirmative part, and first tell us what the Lord requireth in this commandment.

Evan. The Lord in this commandment doth require, that we sanctify his name in our hearts, with our tongues, and in our lives, by thinking, conceiving, speaking, writing, and walking so as becomes the excellency of his titles, attributes, ordinances, works, and religion.

Neo. And how are we to sanctify the name of the Lord in regard of his titles?

Evan. By thinking, conceiving, speaking, and writing holily, reverently, and spiritually of his titles;

Lord

Lord and God, Deut. xxviii. 58. And this we do when we meditate on them, and use them in our speeches and writings with an inward spiritual fear and trembling, to the glory of God, and the good of men, Jer. v. 22.

Neo. And how are we to sanctify the name of the Lord, in regard of his attributes?

Evan. By thinking, conceiving, speaking, and writing holily, reverently, and spiritually of his power, wisdom, justice, mercy, and patience, Psal. civ. 1 and ciii. 6, 8. And this we do, when we think, speak, and write of them, after a careful, reverent, and spiritual manner, and apply them to such good uses for which the Lord hath made them known, Psal. xxxvii. 30.

Neo. And in which of God's ordinances are we to sanctify his name?

Evan. In every one of his ordinances, prayer, preaching, and hearing the word, administring and receiving the sacraments.

Neo. And how are we to sanctify the name of the Lord in prayer?

Evan. In prayer we are to sanctify the name of the Lord in our hearts, and with our tongues, in calling upon his name, after a holy, reverent, and spiritual manner: and this we do when our prayers are the speech of our souls, and not of our mouths only, and that is when in prayer we lift up our hearts unto God, Psal. xxv. 1. And pour them out unto him Psal. lxii. 8. And when we pray with the Spirit, and with the understanding also, 1 Cor. xiv. 15 and with humility, Gen. xviii. 27. and Gen. xxxii. 10. Luke xviii 13. and with fervency of spirit, James v. 16. and out of a sense of our own wants, James i. 5. and with a special faith in the promises of God, Matth. xxi. 22.

Neo. And how are you ministers to sanctify the name of the Lord in preaching his word?

Evan. We are to sanctify the name of the Lord in our hearts, and with our tongues, in preaching after a holy, re-

reverent, and spiritual manner : * and this we do when the word is preached, not only outwardly by the body, but also inwardly with the heart and soul ; when the heart and soul preacheth, then is the ministry of the word on the ministers part used after an holy, and spiritual manner, † and that is, when we preach the demonstration of the Spirit, 1 Cor. ii. 4. and in sincerity, 2 Cor. ii. 17. and faithfully without respect of persons, Deut. xxxiii. 9. and with judgment and discretion, Matth. xxiv. 49. and with authority and power, Matth. vii. 29. and with zeal to God's glory, John vii. 18 and with a desire of the peoples salvation, 2 Cor. xi. 2.

Neo. And how are we hearers to sanctify the name of the Lord in hearing his word?

Evan. In hearing it after an holy, reverent, and spiritual manner : and this you do when your heart and soul heareth the word of God ; and that is, when you set yourselves in the presence of God, Acts x. 33. And when you look upon the minister as God's messenger or ambassador, 2 Cor. v. 20. And so hear the word as the word of God, and not as the word of man, 1 Thess. ii. 13. With reverence and fear, Isa. lxvi 2. And with a ready desire to learn, Acts xvii. 11. And with attention, Acts viii. 6. And with alacrity without wearisomness or sleepiness, Acts xx. 9

Neo. And how are you ministers to sanctify the name of the Lord ‡, in administring the sacraments?

Evan. By administring them after an holy, reverent and spiritual manner : and that is when we administer them with our hearts or souls, according to Christ's institution, Matth. xxvi. 26. To the faithful in profession at least, 1 Cor. x. 10. And with a hearty desire that they may become profitable to the receivers,

---

* Elton on the Com. p. 40. † Downham on the Com.
‡ Elton on the Com. p 41.

Neo. And how are we to sanctify the name of the Lord in receiving the sacraments?

Evan. This we do, when we rightly and seriously examine ourselves aforehand, 1 Cor. xi. And rightly and seriously mind and consider of the sacramental union of the sign, and the thing signified, and do in our hearts perform those inward actions, which are signified by the outward actions, Acts viii. 37, 38. 1 Cor. x. 6.

Neo. And how are we to sanctify the name of the Lord in regard of his works?

Evan. In thinking and speaking of them after a wise, reverent, and spiritual manner; and this we do, when we meditate and make mention in our speeches and writings of the inward works of God's eternal election and reprobation with wonderful admiration of the unsearchable depths thereof, Rom. xi. 33, 34. And when we meditate in our hearts of the works of God's creation and administration, and make mention of them in our words and writings, so as that we acknowledge therein his wisdom, power, and goodness, Rom. i. 19, 20. Psal. xix. 1. And acknowledging the workmanship of God therein, do speak honourably of the same, Psal. cxxxix. 14 Gen. i 31.

Neo. And how are we to sanctify the name of the Lord in regard of his religion?

Evan. By a holy profession of his true religion, and a conversation answerable thereunto, to the glory of God, the good of ourselves, and others, Matth. v. 16 1 Pet. ii 12

Neo. And, Sir, are we not also to sanctify the name of God in swearing thereby?

Evan. Yea, indeed, that was well remembered, we are to sanctify the name of the Lord in our hearts, and with our tongues in swearing thereby after a holy, religious and spiritual manner; and this we do when the magistrate requires an oath of us, by the order of justice, that is not against piety or charity, Gen. xliii. 3.

1 Sam.

ır Sam. xxiv. 21, 22. And when we fwear in truth *;
that is, when we are perfuaded in our confcience
the thing we fwear is truth, and fwear fimply and
plainly, without fraud or deceit, Pfal xv. 4, and xxiv 4.
And when we fwear in judgment ; that is, when we
fwear with deliberation, well confidering both the
nature and greatnefs of an oath, *viz.* That God is
thereby called to witnefs the truth, and judge and
punifh us, if we fwear falfely, Gal. i. 20. 2 Cor. i 23.
And when we fwear in righteoufnefs ; that is, when
the thing we fwear, is lawful and juft, and when our
fwearing is that God may be glorified, Jofh. vii. 19.
Our neighbour fatisfied, controverfies ended, Heb.
vi 16. Our own innocency cleared, Exod xxii. 11.
and our duty difcharged, 1 Kings viii. 31.

Neo. Well, Sir, now I pray you proceed to the
negative part, and tell us what the Lord forbiddeth
in this commandment.

Evan. As the Lord, in the affirmative part of this
commandment, doth require that we fanctify his name
in our hearts, with our tongues, and in our lives, by
thinking, conceiving, fpeaking, writing, and walking
fo as becomes the excellency of his titles, attributes,
ordinances, and religion; fo doth he in the negative
part thereof forbid the profanation of his name by
doing the contrary.

Neo Well then, Sir, I pray you, firft, tell us how
the titles of God are profanely abufed.

Evan. They are profanely abufed divers ways, as
firft, by thinking irreverently of them, or ufing them
in our common talk, or in our writings, after a rafh,
carelefs, and irreverent manner, Pfal. l. 22. Rom. i. 21.
As when in foolifh admiration we fay, " Good God,
good Lord ! Lord have mercy on us, what a thing
is this!" and the like ; or when by way of idle wifhes,
or imprecations, we fay, " The Lord be my judge,"
Gen. xvi. 5. Or, " I pray God, I may never ftir,
if

* Jer. iv. 2.

if fuch a thing be not fo," and the like; or when by
way of vain fwearing, we mingle our fpeeches, and
fill up our fentences with needlefs oaths, as, Not fo, by
my faith, and the like, Matth. v. 34. James v. 12.
Or when by way of jefting, or after a formal manner,
we fay, God be thanked, God fpeed you, God's name
be praifed, and the like, 2 Sam. xxiii. 21.

Neo. And I pray you Sir, how are the attributes of
God profanely abufed?

Evan. The attribute of God's power is profanely
abufed, either by calling it in queftion, 2 Kings vii. 2.
Or by thinking, fpeaking, or writing of it carnally,
carelefly, or contemptuoufly, Pfal. xii 4. Exod. v. 2.
And the attribute of God's providence is abufed,
either by murmuring thereat in our hearts, Deut xv. 9
Or by fpeaking grudgingly againft it, under the name
of fortune or chance, in faying, " What a misfortune
was this? what a mifchance was that?" and the like,
Deut i. 27. 1 Sam vi 9   And the attribute of
God's juftice is profanely abufed, either by thinking,
or faying, that God likes of fin, or wicked finners,
Pfal. l 21. Mal. iii 15   And the attribute of God's
mercy is profanely abufed, either in prefuming
to fin, upon hopes that God will be merciful, or by
fpeaking bafely and contemptuoufly thereof, as when
we fay, fpeaking of fome trifling thing, " It is not
worth god-a-mercy. And the attribute of God's
patience is profanely abufed by thinking or faying
upon occafion of his forbearance to punifh for a time,
that he will neither call us to an account, nor punifh
us for our fins, Rom ii 4

Neo. Now, Sir, I pray you proceed to fhew how
God's name is profanely abufed in his ordinances;
and firft of all, begin with prayer.

Evan. God's name is profanely abufed in prayer,
either by praying ignorantly, without the true knowledge of God and his will, Acts xvii. 23. Matth. xx. 22.
Or when we pray with the mouth only, and not with
the

the defires of our hearts agreeing with our words, Hof. iii. 14. Pfal lxxviii. 36 And when we pray drowfily and heavily, without fervency of fpirit, Matth. xxiv. 41. and when we pray with wandering worldly thoughts, Rom. xii. 12. and when we pray with any. conceit of our own worthinefs; Luke xviii. 9, 11. and and when we pray without faith in the promifes of God, James i 6.

Nec. And how is God's name profanely abufed in hearing or reading his word?

Evan. God's name is hereby abufed, when we hear it or read it, and do not underftand it, Acts viii. 30. And when we hear it only with the outward ears of our bodies, and not alfo with the inward ears of the heart and foul; and this we do, when we read it, or hear it with hearts full of worldly and wandering thoughts, Ezek. xxxiii. 30. And when we read it, or hear it with dull, drowfy, and fleepy fpirits; and when in hearing of it, we rather conceive it to be the word of a mortal man that delivereth it, than the word of the great God of heaven and earth, 1 Theff. ii. 13. And when we do not with our hearts believe every part and portion of that word which we read or hear, Heb iv. 2. And when we do not humbly and heartily fubject ourfelves to what we read or hear, 2 Kings xxii. 19. Ifa. lxii. 2.

Neo. And how is the Lord's name profanely abufed in receiving the facrament of the Lord's fupper?

Evan. This we do, when we either through want of knowledge cannot examine ourfelves, or thro' our own negligence do not examine ourfelves, before we eat of that bread, and drink of that cup, 1 Cor. xi. 28. And when we in the act of receiving, do not mind the fpiritual fignification of the facrament, but do either terminate our thoughts in the elements themfelves, or elfe fuffer them to rove and run out to fome other object, Luke xxii. 19 And when after receiving, we do not examine ourfelves what communion we have

had

had with Chrift in that ordinance, nor what virtue we have found flowing out from Chrift, into our own fouls, by means of that ordinance, 2 Cor. xiii. 5.

Neo. And how is the name of the Lord profanely abufed in taking of an oath?

Evan. This we do, when we call the Lord to be a witnefs of vain and frivolous things, by our ufual fwearing in our common talk, Hof iv 2. Jer. xxiii. 10. And when we call God to be a witnefs of our furious anger, and wicked purpofe, as when we fwear we will be revenged on fuch a man, and the like, 1 Sam. xiv. 39. and xxv. 34. And when we call God to be a witnefs to our fwearing falfely, Lev. xix. 12. Zech. v. 4. And when we fwear by the mafs, or by our faith, or troth, or by the rood, or by any thing elfe that is not God, Jer. v. 7. Matth. v. 34, 35, 36, 37.

Neo. And how is the name of God profanely abufed, as touching his works?

Evan. When we either take no notice of his works at all, or when we think and fpeak otherwife of them, than we have warrant from his word to do, as when we do not fpeak of the inward works of God's election and reprobation, and are called thereunto, or when we murmur and cavil thereat, Rom. ix. 20. And when we either do not at all mind the works of his creation and adminiftration, or do not take occafion thereby to glorify the name of God, Pfal. xix. 1. Rom i 21.

Neo. And how is the name of God profanely abufed, in refpect of his religion?

Evan. When our converfation is not agreeable to our profeffion, 2 Tim. iii 5. And that either when in refpect of God it is but hypocrify, or when in refpect of men we walk offenfively; for if we live fcandaloufly in the profeffion of religion, we caufe the name of God to be profaned by them that are without, Rom. ii. 24. And become ftumbling blocks to our weak brethren, Rom. xiv. 13

And

And now, neighbour Nomologiſta, I pray you tell me, whether you think you keep this commandment perfectly or no?

Nom. Sir, to tell you the truth, I had not thought that the name of God had ſignified any more than his titles, Lord and God.

Evan. Ay, but you are to know that the name of God in ſcripture, ſignifieth all thoſe things *, that are affirmed of God, or any thing whatſoever it is † whereby the Lord makes himſelf known to men.

Nom. Then believe me, Sir, I have come far ſhort of keeping this commandment perfectly, and ſo doth every man elſe, I am perſuaded.

Evan. I am of your mind, for where is the man that hath and doth ſo meditate on God's titles, and uſe them in his ſpeeches and writings, with ſuch reverence, fear and trembling as he ought? Or what man is he that can truly ſay, he never in all his life thought on them, nor uſed them in his common talk, either raſhly, careleſly, or irreverently. I am ſure, for mine own part, I cannot ſay ſo, for alas! in the time of mine ignorance, I uſed many times to ſay, by way of fooliſh admiration, "Good Lord, good God, Lord have mercy on us! What a thing is this?" Yea, and I alſo many times uſed to ſay, "I pray God I may never ſtir, if ſuch a thing be not ſo." Yea, and I have divers times ſaid, "The Lord be with you and ſpeed you; and the Lord's name be praiſed," after a formal curſory manner, my thoughts being exerciſed about ſomething elſe all the while.

And where is the man that hath always thought, conceived, ſpoken, and written ſo holily, reverently, and ſpiritually, of the Lord's power, wiſdom, juſtice, mercy, and patience, as he ought? Nay, what a man is he that can truly ſay, he never in all his life called the attribute of the Lord's power into queſtion, nor

---

* Urſin. Cat. page 556.
† Elton on the Com. page 54.

never murmured at any act or paſſage of God's provi‑
dence, nor never preſumed to ſin, upon hopes, that
God would be merciful unto him? I am ſure I cannot
truly ſay ſo.

And where can we find the man that can truly ſay,
he hath always read and heard the word of God, after
a holy, reverent, and ſpiritual manner? Nay, where
is the man that hath not ſometimes both heard it, and
read it, after a formal curſory and unprofitable manner?
Is there any man that can truly ſay, he hath always
perfectly underſtood, whatſoever he hath read and
heard?- and that hath not ſometimes heard more with
the outward ears of his body, than with the inward
ears of his heart and ſoul? and that was never dull
and drowſy, if not ſleepy, in the time of hearing and
reading? and that had never worldly, nor wandering
thought came in at that time? and that never had the
leaſt doubting or queſtioning the truth of what he hath
read or heard? I am ſure, for mine own part, I have
been faulty many of theſe ways.

And is it poſſible to find a man that can truly ſay,
he hath always called upon the name of the Lord
after a holy, reverent, and ſpiritual manner? or hath
not rather many times prayed after a carnal, unholy,
or ſinful manner? Where is the man that hath always
had a perfect knowledge of God, and of his will, in
prayer? and whoſe heart hath always gone along
with his word in prayer? and that never was drowſy
nor heavy, nor never had wandering thoughts in
prayer? and that never had the leaſt conceit that God
would grant him any thing for his prayer's ſake? and
that never had the leaſt doubting or queſtioning in
his heart, whether God would grant him the thing he
aſked in prayer? I am ſure, for mine own part, I can
ſcarce clear myſelf from any of theſe.

And can any man truly ſay, he hath always receiv‑
ed the ſacrament, after a holy, reverent, and ſpiritual
manner? Nay, hath not every man rather cauſe to
ac-

acknowledge the contrary? Is there a man to be found, that hath always serioufly and rightly examined himfelf before hand; and that hath always rightly, with his heart, performed all thofe inward actions, that are fignified by the outward: or hath not every man and woman rather caufe to confefs, that either for want of knowledge, or through their own negligence, they have not fo examined themfelves as they ought? nor fo actuated their faith, nor minded the fpiritual fignification of the outward elements, in the time of receiving the facrament, as they ought? nor fo examined themfelves, after receiving, what benefit they have got to their fouls thereby? I am fure, I have caufe to confefs all this.

And where fhall we find a man that hath always fanctified the name of the Lord in his heart, and with his tongue, by fwearing after a holy, religious, and fpiritual manner? or rather have not moft men that have been called to take an oath profaned the name of the Lord, either by fwearing ignorantly, falfely, malicioufly, or for fome bafe and wicked end? And I think it is fomewhat hard to find a man that never in all his life did fwear, either by his faith, or by his troth, by the mafs, or by the rood; I am fure I am not the man: and he is a rare man that can truly fay, he hath always fanctified the name of God in his heart, and with his tongue, by admiring and acknowledging the wifdom, power, and goodnefs of God, manifefted in his works; for it is to be feared, that moft men do either take no notice at all of the works of God, or elfe do think and fpeak of them otherwife than the word of God warrants them to do. I am fure I am one of thefe moft.

And he is a precious man that hath always fo fanctified the name of the Lord, by a holy and unblameable converfation, as he ought! for alas! many profeffors of religion, by their fruitlefs and offenfive walking, do

L l

either

either caufe the enemies of God to fpeak evil of the ways of God, or elfe do thereby caufe their weak brother to ftumble : it is well if I never did fo, and thus have I alfo endeavoured to fatisfy your defires concerning the third commandment.

Neo. I befeech you, Sir, proceed to fpeak to the fourth commandment, as you have done of the other three.

COMMANDMENT IV.

Evan. Well then, I pray you confider, that, as the Lord, in the third commandment, doth prefcribe the right manner how he will be worfhipped, fo doth he in the fourth commandment, fet down the time when he will be moft folemnly worfhipped, after the right manner, and in this commandment there is an affirmative part expreffed in thefe words, " Remember the fabbath day, to keep it holy," &c. That is, " Remember that a feventh-day," * in every week, be fet apart from wordly things and bufineffes, † and be confecrated to God, by holy and heavenly employments: and a negative part expreffed alfo in thefe words, " In it thou fhall not do any work," &c. That is, thou fhalt not on that day do any fuch thing or work as doth any way hinder thee from keeping an holy reft unto God.

Neo. I pray you, Sir, begin with the affirmative part, and firft tell us what the Lord requireth of us in this commandment.

Evan. In this fourth commandment the Lord requireth that we finifh all our works in the fpace of fix days, Deut v. 13. and think on the feventh day before it come, and prepare for it, Luke xxiii. 54. and rife early on that day in the morning, Pfal. xcii. 2.

---

* Exod. xxiii. 12.
† Elton on the Com. page 87.

Mark i. 35, 38, 39. Yea, and the Lord requireth that we fit ourſelves for the public exerciſes, by prayer, reading and meditation, Eccl v. 1. Iſa. vii. 10. and that we join with the miniſter and people publicly aſſembled, with aſſent of mind, and fervency of affection in prayer, Acts ii 42 in hearing the word read and preached, Acts xiii. 14, 15, 44. in ſinging of Pſalms, 1 Cor. xiv 15 Col iii. 16. and iii. 16. in the ſacrament of baptiſm. Luke i. 58, 59 and in the ſacrament of the Lord's ſupper, ſo often as it ſhall be adminiſtred in that congregation whereof we are members, 1 Cor. xi 26.

Then afterwards, when we come home, the Lord requireth that we ſeriouſly meditate on that portion of the word of which we have heard, Acts xvii. 11. and repeat it to our families, Deut vi 7. and confer of it with others, if there be occaſion, Luke xxiv. 14, 17. and that we crave his bleſſing, when we have done all this, John xvii 17.

Neo And is this all that the Lord requireth us to do on that day.

Evan. No, the Lord doth alſo require that we do works of mercy on that day, as to viſit the ſick, and do them what good we can, Neh. viii 12. Mark iii. 3, 4, 5. and relieve the poor and the needy, and ſuch as be in priſon, Luke xiii. 16. and labour to reconcile thoſe that be at variance and diſcord, Matth. v. 9.

Alſo the Lord doth permit us to do works of inſtant neceſſity on that day, as to travel to the places of God's worſhip, 2 Kings iv 23. to heal the diſeaſed, Hoſ. vi. 6. Matth xii. 7, 12. to dreſs food for the neceſſary preſervation of our temporal lives, Exod. i. 1. to tend and feed cattle, Matth. xii. 11. and ſuch like.

Neo. I pray you Sir, proceed to the negative part, and tell us what the Lord forbiddeth in this commandment?

Evan.

Evan. In this commandment the Lord forbiddeth idleness, or sleeping more on the Lord's day in the morning, than is of necessity, Matth. xx. 6. And he also forbiddeth us to labour in our particular callings; Exod. xvi 28, 29, 30. and he also forbiddeth us to talk about our worldly affairs, and business on that day, Amos viii. 5 Isa. lviii. 13. And he also forbiddeth us to travel any journey about our worldly business on that day, Matth. xxiv 20. or to keep any fairs or markets on that day, Neh. xiii. 16, 17. or to labour in seed time and harvest on that day. In a word, the Lord on that day forbiddeth all worldly works and labours, except works of mercy and instant necessity, which were mentioned before. And thus have I also declared, both what the Lord requireth, and what he forbiddeth in the fourth commandment. And now neighbour Nomologista, I pray you tell me, whether you think you keep it perfectly or no.

Nom. Indeed, Sir, I must confess, there is more both required and forbidden in this commandment than I was aware of; but yet I hope I go very near the observing and doing all.

Neo. But Sir, is the bare observing and doing of these things sufficient for keeping of this commandment perfectly?

Evan O no! the first commandment must be understood in all the rest, that is, the obedience to the first commandment, must be the motive and final cause of our obedience to the rest of the commandments *, otherwise it is not the worship of God, but hypocrisy, as I touched before : wherefore, neighbour Nomologista, though you have done all the duties that the Lord requireth in this commandment, and avoided all the sins which he forbiddeth ; yet if all this hath been from such grounds, and to such ends as I told you in
the

* Ursin. Cat p. 48.

the conclusion of the second commandment, and not for the love you bear to God, and the desire you have to please him you come short of keeping this commandment perfectly.

Neo. Sir, whatsoever he doth, I am sure I come far short not only in this point, but in divers others; for though, it is true indeed, I am careful to finish all my worldly business in the space of six days, yet alas! I do not seriously think on and prepare for the seventh day as I ought; neither do I many times rise so early on that day as I ought; neither do I so thoroughly fit and prepare myself by prayer and other excercises before-hand as I ought; neither do I so heartily join with the minister and people when I come to the assembly, as I ought; but am subject to many wandering wordly thoughts and cares, even at that time. And when I come home, if I do either meditate, repeat, pray, or confer? yet, alas! I do none of these with such delight and comfort as I ought; neither have I been so mindful nor careful to visit the sick, and relieve the poor, as I ought; neither can I clear myself from being guilty of doing more worldly works and labours on that day, than the works of mercy and instant necessity, the Lord be merciful unto me. But I pray you, Sir, proceed to speak of the fifth commandment, as you have done of the rest. But first of all, I pray you tell us what is meant by father and mother.

COMMANDMENT V.

Evan. By father and mother, is meant not only natural parents, but others also that are our superiors, either in age, in place, or in gifts, 2 Kings v. 13. and vi. 21. and xiii. 14,

Neo. And why did the Lord use the name of father and mother to signify and comprehend all other superiors?

Evan.

Evan. Becaufe the government of the fathers is the firft and moft ancient of all other ; and becaufe the fociety of father and mother, is that from whom all others focieties do come.

Neo. And are the duties of inferiors towards their fuperiors only here intended ?

Evan. No, but alfo of fuperiors towards their inferiors, and of equals amongft themfelves: fo that the general duty required in the affirmative part of this fifth commandment, " Honour thy father and mother," *&c.* is, that every man, woman, and child, be careful to carry themfelves as becometh them in regard of that order God hath appointed amongft men, and that relation they have to others, either as inferior, fuperior, or equal.

Neo. I pray you, Sir, proceed to the particular handling of thefe things ; and firft tell us, what is the duty of children to their parents.

Evan. Why the Lord in this commandment doth require, that children do reverence their parents, by thinking and efteeming highly of them, Gen. xxxi. 35. and by loving them dearly, Gen. xvi. 29. and by fearing them in regard of their authority over them, Lev. xix. 3 And this inward reverent efteem of them is to be expreffed by their outward reverent behaviour towards them, Gen. xlviii 12. And this outward reverent behaviour, is to be expreffed in giving them reverent titles, Gen. xxxi. 35. and by bowing their bodies before them, 1 Kings ii. 19. and by embracing their inftruction, Prov. i 8. and by fubduing patiently to their corrections, Heb xii 9 and by their fuccouring and relieving of them, in cafe of want and neceffity, Gen. xlvii. 12. and by making their prayers unto God for them, 1 Tim ii. 12.

Neo. And, Sir, what be the duties of parents towards their children ?

Evan. Why the Lord in this commandment doth require that parents be careful to bring their children

with

with all convenient fpeed, and in due order, to be admitted into the vifible church of God by baptifm, Luke i 59. and that they, according to their ability, do yield and give unto their children fuch competent food, cloathing, and other neceffaries, as are fit for them, Matth. vii 9, 12. 1 Tim. v. 8.

And that they train them up in learning, inftruct them in religion, and endeavour to fow the feeds of godlinefs in their hearts, fo foon as they be able to fpeak, and have the ufe of reafon and underftanding, Deut. iv. 10. and vi. 7, 20. 21. And that they be careful to check and rebuke them, when they do amifs, Prov. xxxi. 2. and that they be careful feafonably to correct their faults, Prov. xiii. 24 and xix. 18. and that they be careful in time. to train them up in fome honeft calling, Gen. iv. 2. and that they be careful to beftow them in marriage in due time, Jer. xxix. 6: 1 Cor. vii 36, 38. and that they be careful to lay up fomething for them, as their ability will fuffer, Prov. xix. 14. 2 Cor. xii. 14 and that they be earneft with God in prayer, for a bleffing upon their childrens fouls and bodies, Gen. xlvii. 15, 16.

Neo. And what be the duties of fervants towards their mafters?

Evan. Why, the Lord, in this commandment, doth require that fervants have an inward, high, and reverent efteem of their mafters, Eph. vi 5 6, 7. yea, and that they have in their hearts a reverent awe and fear of them, 1 Pet. ii. 18. and this reverence and fear they are to exprefs by their outward reverent behaviour towards them, both in word and deed, as by giving them reverent titles, 2 Kings v. 23, 25 and by an humble, fubmiffive countenance and carriage, either when their mafters fpeak to them, or they fpeak to their mafters, Gen xxiv. 9. Acts x 7. and by yielding of fincere, faithful, willing, painful, and fingle-hearted fervice to their mafters in all they go about, Col. iii. 22. Tit. ii. 10.

and

and by a meek and patient bearing of those checks, rebukes and corrections which are given to them, or laid upon them by their masters, without grudging, stomach, or sullen countenance, tho' the master do it without just cause, or exceed in the measure, 1 Pet. ii. 18, 20. and by being careful to maintain their masters good name, in keeping secret those honest intents, which he would not have disclosed; and as much as may be to hide and cover their masters wants and infirmities, not blazing them abroad, 2 Sam. xv. 23. 2 Kings vi. 11.

Neo. And what is the duty of masters towards their servants?

Evan. Why, the Lord in this commandment doth require that masters be careful to chuse unto themselves religious servants. Psal. ci. 6. and that they do instruct them in religion and the ways of godliness, Gen xviii. 19 and that they be careful to bring them to the public exercises, Josh. xxiv. 15. and that they do daily pray with them and for them, Jer. x 25. and that they do yield and give unto them meat, drink, and apparel, fitting for them, Deut. xxiv 14, 15. and that they see to them that they follow the works of their callings with diligence, Prov. xxxi 27. and that they be careful to instruct them, and give them direction therein, Exod. xxxv. 34. and that they be careful to give them just reproof and correction for their faults, Prov xxix 19 and xix. 26. and that they look carefully unto them, when they are sick, Matth. viii. 5, 6.

Neo. And what is the duty of wives towards their husbands?

Evan. Why, the Lord, in this commandment, doth require, that wives do carry in their hearts an inward opinion, and their esteem of their husbands, Eph. v. 33. the which they are to express in their speeches, by giving them reverend titles and terms, 1 Pet. iii. 6. and in their countenance and behaviour, by their

mo-

modefty, fhamefacednefs, and fobriety, 1 Tim. ii 9.
and in being willing to yield themfelves to be commanded, governed and directed by their hufbands in
all things honeft and lawful, Gen. xxxi. 4, 16, 17.
2 Kings iv. 22. and they are alfo required to love
their hufbands, Tit ii. 4. and to exprefs their love by
their chaftity and faithfulnefs to their hufbands, both
in body and mind, Tit. ii 5. 1 Tim iii. 11. and by
their ufing the beft means they can to keep their
hufbands bodies in health, Cen xxvii 9. they are alfo
required to be helpful to them in the government of
the family, and to be provident for their eftate, by
exercifing themfelves in fome profitable employment,
Prov. xxxi 13, 15, 19. and they are alfo required to
ftir up their hufbands to good duties, and join with
them in the performance of them, 2 Kings iv. 9, 10.
and to pray for them, 1 Tim ii. 12.

Neo. And what is the duty of hufbands towards
their wives?

Evan. Why the Lord in this commandment requireth, that hufbands be careful to chufe religious
wives, 2 Cor. vi. 14. and that they dwell with them
as men of knowledge, 1 Pet. iii 7. and that they
cleave unto them with true love and affection of heart,
Col. iii. 19. yea, and that they content themfelves
only with the love of their own wives, and keep themfelves to them both in mind and body, Prov. v. 19, 20.
they are alfo to be careful to maintain their authority
over them, Eph v 23. and to live cheerfully and
familiarly with them, Prov. v. 19. and to be careful
to provide all things needful and fitting for their
maintainance, 1 Tim v. 8 and to teach, inftruct and
admonifh them, as touching the beft things, 1 Sam i. 8.
and to pray with them and for them, 1 Pet. iii. 7. and
to endeavour to reform and amend what they fee amifs
in them, by feafonable and loving admonition and
reproof, Gen xxx. 2. and wifely and patiently to bear
with their natural infirmities, Gal. vi. 2.

Neo.

Neo. And what is the duty of subjects towards their magistrates?

Evan. Why, the Lord in this commandment, doth require that subjects do think and esteem reverently of their magistrates, 2 Sam. x. 16, 17. and that they carry in their hearts a reverent awe and fear of them, Prov xxiv. 21 the which they are to express by their outward reverent behaviour towards them, both in word and deed, 2 Sam. ix. 6, 8 and by an humble, ready, and willing submitting of themselves to their commands, either to do, or to suffer, 1 Pet. ii 13 and by yielding a loyal and found hearted love to them, in not shrinking from them when they have need, but defending them with their goods, bodies, and lives, if occasion require, 2 Sam. xviii 3. and xxi. 27. also they are required to make their prayers unto God for them, 1 Tim. ii 12.

Neo. And what is the duty of magistrates towards their subjects?

Evan. Why, the Lord, in this commandment, doth require, that magistrates be careful to establish good laws in their kingdoms, and good orders amongst their subjects, 2 Kings xviii 4 Rom xii. 17. and that they be careful to see them duly and impartially executed, Jer xxxviii. 4. 6. Rom xiii. 3, 4. and that they be careful to provide for the peace, safety, quietness and outward welfare of their subjects, Rom. xiii 4 1 Tim. ii 2. and not to oppress them with taxations and grievances, 1 Kings xii. 14.

Neo. And what duties are people to perform towards their minister?

Evan. Why, the Lord, in this commandment doth require that people have their minister in reverent account and estimation, 1 Cor iv 1. and that they humbly and willingly yield themselves to be taught and directed in their spiritual affairs by him, Heb xii. 17. and that they pray for him, that the Lord would enable him to do his duty, Rom. xv. 30, 31. and that they

they do their beſt to defend him againſt the wrongs of wicked men, Rom. xvi 4 and that they yie!d unto him double honour *, that is, both ſingular love for his work's ſake, and ſufficient maintainance, both in regard of his perſon and calling, 1 Tim. v. 17, 18. Gal. iv. 15.

Neo. And what is the duty of a miniſter towards the people ?

Evan. Why, the Lord, in this commandment, doth require that miniſters do diligently and faithfully preach the pure word of God unto their people, both in ſeaſon and out of ſeaſon, 1 Cor. ix. 16. 2 Kings iv. 2. and that they do ſo truly and plainly expound the ſame, that the people may underſtand it, and that they pour out their ſouls to God in prayer, for the ſpiritual good of the people, 1 Theſſ. i. 2. and that they go before the people, as a pattern of imitation to them, in all holineſs of converſation, Phil. iv. 9.

Neo. And what is the duty of equals ?

Evan. Why, the Lord, in this commandment, doth require, that equals regard the dignity and worth of each other, and carry themſelves modeſtly one towards another, and in giving honour, go one before another, Eph. v. 21. Rom xii. 20. And thus having ſhewed you the duties required in this commandment, I pray you, neighbour Nomologiſta, tell me whether you think you have kept it perfectly or no.

Nom. Sir, though I have not kept it perfectly, yet I am perſuaded I have gone very near it ; for when I was a child I loved and reverenced my parents, and was obedient unto them: and when I was a ſervant, I reverenced and feared my maſter, and did him faithful ſervice ; and ſince I became a man, I have. I hope, carried myſelf well towards my wife, and toward my ſervants ; yea, and done my duty both to magiſtrates and miniſters.

Evan.

* E'ton on the Com. Page 161.

Evan. Ay, but I muſt ſtill tell you, the Lord doth require, that you do them in obedience unto him; that is, in conſcience to God's commandment, or for his ſake, even becauſe he requireth it. Therefore, although you did your duty to your parents when you were a child, and to your maſter, when you were a ſervant; yet, if you did it either for the praiſe of men, or for fear of their corrections, or to procure a greater portion, or greater wages, and not becauſe the Lord ſaith, Eph. vi. 4. "Children, obey your parents in the Lord." And becauſe he ſaith to ſervants, Col. iii. 2. "Whatſoever ye do, do it heartily, as to the Lord, and not unto men;" you have not, in ſo doing, kept this commandment: and though you have loved your wife, and every way carried yourſelf well towards her, yet, if it hath been either becauſe ſhe is come of rich parents, or or becauſe ſhe is beautiful, or becauſe ſhe brought you a good portion, or becauſe ſhe ſome way ſerveth and pleaſeth you after the fleſh: and not becauſe the Lord ſaith, "Huſbands love your wives," Eph. v. 25. You have not therein kept this commandment: and tho' you have carried yourſelf never ſo well towards your ſervants; yet, if it have been, that they might praiſe you, or to make them follow your buſineſs more diligently and faithfully; and not becauſe the Lord ſaith, "Maſters give unto your ſervants that which is juſt and equal," you have not therein kept this commandment. And though you have done your duty never ſo well towards your magiſtrate; yet, if it have been for fear of his wrath, and not for conſcience-ſake, *viz.* becauſe the Lord ſaith, "Let every ſoul be ſubject unto the higher powers," you have not therein kept this commandment: and though you have given your miniſter his due maintainance, and invited him oft to your table and carried yourſelf never ſo well towards him; yet, if it have been, that he or others might think you a good Chriſtian, and a kind man,

man, and not becaufe the Lord faith, Gal. vi. 6.
" Let him that is taught in the word comunicate unto
him that teacheth in all good things," you have not
therein kept this commandment.

Neo. Well Sir, I cannot tell what my neighbour
Nomologifta hath done, but for mine own part, I am
fure, I have come far fhort of doing my duty in any
relation I have had to others; for when I was a child,
I remember that I was many times ftubborn and difobedient to my parents, and vexed if I might not have
my will, and flighted their admonitions, and was impatient at their corrections, and fometimes defpifed and
contemned them in my heart, becaufe of fome infirmity, efpecally when they grew old ; neither did I pray
for them, as it feemeth I ought to have done : and
the truth is, if I did yield any obedience to them at all,
it was for fear of their corrections, or fome fuch by-
refpects, and not for confcience towards God. And
when I was a fervant, I did not think fo reverently,
nor efteem fo highly of my mafter and miftrefs, as I
fhould have done, but was fubject to flight and defpife
them, and did not yield fuch humble, reverent, and
cheerful obedience to them, as I fhould have done ;
neither did I patiently and contentedly bear their
checks and rebukes, but had divers times rifings and
fwellings in my heart againft them.; neither was I fo
careful to maintain their good name and credit, as I
ought to have been ; neither did I pray unto the
Lord for them as I ought to have done ; and the
very truth is, all the fubjection which I yielded unto
them, was for fear of their reproofs and corrections,
or for the praife of men, rather than in confcience
to the Lord's commandment.

And when I entered into the married eftate, I was
not careful to chufe a religious wife : no, I aimed at
beauty more than piety ; and I have not dwelt with
my wife as a man of knowledge ; ro, I have expreffed

much ignorance and folly in my carriage towards her; neither have I loved her so as a husband ought to love his wife; for though it is true, I have had much fond affection for her, yet have I had little true affection towards her, as hath been evident, in that I have been easily provoked to anger and wrath against her; and have not carried myself patiently towards her; neither have I been careful to maintain mine authority over her, but have lost it by my childish and undiscreet carriage towards her; neither have I lived so cheerfully and delightfully with her as I ought to have done, but very heavily, discontentedly, and uncomfortably have I carried myself towards her; neither have I been so careful to instruct and admonish her as I ought; and though I have now and then reproved her, yet for the most part it hath been in a passion, and not with the spirit of meekness, pity, and compassion; neither have I prayed for her, either so often, or so fervently as I ought; and whatsoever I have done, that hath been well, I have been moved thereunto (in former times especially) rather by something in her, or done by her, than by the commandment of God. And since I became a father and a master, I have neither done my duty to my children nor servants as I ought; for I have not had such care, nor taken such pains for their eternal good, as I have done for their temporal. I have had more care, and taken more pains to provide food and raiment for them, than I have to admonish, instruct, teach, and catachize them; and if I have reproved or corrected them, it hath been rather because they have offended myself, than because they have offended God: and truly I have neither prayed for them so often, nor so fervently as I ought. In a word, whatsoever I have done by way of discharging my duty to them, I fear me it hath been rather out of natural affection, or to void the blame, and gain the good opinion of men, than out of conscience to the Lord's will and commandment.

And

And if I have at any time carried myself well, or done my duty either to magistrate or minister, it hath rather been for fear, or praise of men, than for conscience sake towards God; so far have I been from keeping this commandment perfectly, the Lord be merciful unto me.

Evan. Assure yourself neighbour Neophytus, this is not your case alone, but the case of every man that hath stood in all these relations to others, as it seems you have done, as I am confident any man that doth truly know his heart will confess; yea, and any woman that is well acquainted with her own heart, I am persuaded will confess, that she hath not had such a reverent esteem and opinion of her husband as she ought, nor so willingly yielded herself to be commanded, governed, and directed by him as she ought, nor loved him so truly as she ought, nor been so helpful to him no way as she ought, nor prayed, neither so oft nor so fervently for him as she ought; and I fear me most women do all that they do rather for fear of their husbands frowns, or to gain his favour, than for conscience to the Lord's will and command.

And where is the magistrate that is so careful to establish in his dominions such good and wholesome laws as he ought, or to see them executed and put in practice as he ought? or that is so careful to uphold and maintain the truth of religion as he ought? or that is so careful to provide for the peace, safety, and welfare of his people, as he ought? or where is the magistrate that doth not do what he doth for some other cause, or to some other end, rather than because God commands them, or to the end he may please him?

And where is the minister that doth his duty so in his place as he ought? I am sure for mine own part, I have neither so diligently nor faithfully preached the pure word of God as I ought, nor so fully nor truly expounded it, and applied it to my hearers as I ought;

nor so poured out my soul to God for them in prayer as I ought; neither have I gone before them as a pattern of imitation in holiness of life and conversation as I ought; the Lord be merciful to me.

Neo. Well, Sir, now I intreat you to proceed to speak of the sixth commandment as you have done of the rest.

COMMANDMENT VI.

Evan. Well then, I pray you consider, that in the sixth commandment there is a negative part expressed in these words, " Thou shalt do no murder." That is, thou shalt neither in heart, tongue, nor hand, impeach or hurt either the life of thine own soul or body, or the life of any other man's soul or body. And an affirmative part included in these words, " But thou shalt every way, by all good means, seek to preserve them both."

Neo. I pray you, Sir, speak of these things in order, and first tell us what is forbidden in this commandment, as tending to the murdering of our own souls.

Evon. That we may not be guilty of murdering the souls of others, in this commandment, is forbidden, all giving occasion to others to sin against God, either by provoking of them, 1 Kings xxi. or by counselling of them, 2 Sam. xvi. 21. or by evil example, Rom xiv. 15.

Neo. And what is forbidden in this commandment, as tending to the murdering of our own bodies?

Evan. That we may not be guilty of murdering our own bodies, in this commandment is forbidden, excessive worldly sorrow, 1 Cor. vii. 10. Prov. xviii. 22. and so also is the neglect of meat, drink, apparel,
re-

creation, phyſic, or any ſuch refreſhments, Eccl. v. 19. and vi. 1. and ſo alſo is exceſſive eating and drinking, Prov. xxiii 29, 30 Hoſ vii. 5. and ſo alſo is laying violent hands upon ourſelves, 1Sam.iii 14 Acts xvi.28.

Neo. Well, Sir, now I pray you tell us what is forbidden in this commandment as tending to the murdering of others bodies : and firſt, what is forbidden in reſpect of the heart?

Evan. That we may not be guilty of murdering others in our hearts, in this commandment is forbidden all haſty, raſh, and unjuſt anger, Matth. v 22 and ſo alſo is malice, or hatred, Lev xix. 19. John iii. 15. and ſo alſo is envy, Pſal. xxxvii. 1 Prov xxiv. 1. and ſo alſo is deſire of revenge, Lev. xix 18.

Neo. And what is forbidden in reſpect of the tongue?

Evan. That we may not be guilty of murdering others with our tongues, in this commandment is forbidden, all bitter and provoking terms, Eph iv. 31. and ſo alſo are all wrangling and contentious ſpeeches, Prov. xv. 1 and ſo alſo is crying and unſeemly lifting up of the voice, Eph. iv. 31. and ſo alſo is railing or ſcolding, Prov. xvii. 19. 1 Pet. iii. 19. and ſo alſo are all reviling and threatening ſpeeches, Matth. v 22. and ſo alſo are all mocking, ſcoffing, and deriding ſpeeches, 2 Kings ii. 23 John xix. 3.

Neo. And what is forbiddin in reſpect of the whole body, and more eſpecially of the hand?

Evan. That we may not be guilty of murdering others with our hands, in reſpect of the other parts of the body, in this commandment is forbidden all diſdainful, proud, and ſcornful carriage, Gen. iv. 5. Prov. vi 17 and ſo alſo is all provoking geſtures, as nodding of the head, gnaſhing with the teeth, and the like, Matth. xxvii. 39. Acts vii. 45. and ſo alſo

is

is all froward and churlish behaviour, 1 Sam. xxv. 17. and so also is brawling and quarreling. Tit. iii. 2. And more especially in respect of the hand is forbidden striking and wounding, Exod xxi. 18. 22. and so also is all taking away of life, otherwise than in case of Public justice, just war, and necessary defence, Exod. xxi. 12. Gen. ix. 6.

Neo. I pray you, Sir, proceed to the affirmative part of this commandment, and first tell us what is required of us in respect of the life of our own souls?

Evan. In respect of the preservation of the life of our own souls is required, a careful avoiding of all sorts of sin, Prov. xi. 19. and so also is a careful use of all means of grace, and spiritual life in our souls, 1 Pet. ii. 2.

Neo. And what is required of us in respect of the preservation of the life of others souls?

Evan. In respect to the preservation of the life of the souls of others, is required, that according to our place, and calling, and as present occasion is offered, we teach and instruct others to know God and his will, Gen. xviii. 19. Deut. vi. 7. and also that we do our best to comfort others that are in distress of conscience, 1 Thess. v. 14 and that we pray for the, welfare and comfort of others souls, Gen. xliii. 29. and that we give others good examples by our Christian-like walking, Matth. v. 16.

Neo And what is required of us in respect of the preservation of the life of our own bodies?

Evan. In respect of the preservation of the life of our own bodies, is required in this commandment, that we be careful to procure unto ourselves the use of wholesome food. cloathing, and lodging, and physic when there is occasion, 1 Tim. v 23. Eccl. x. 17. 2 Kings xx 7. And also that we use honest and lawful mirth, rejoicing in an holy manner, Prov. xvii. 22. Eccl. iii. 4.

Neo.

Neo. And what is required of us, in refpect of the prefervation of the life of the bodies of others?

Evan. In refpect of the prefervation of the life of the bodies of others, in this commandment is required a kind and loving difpofition, with tendernefs of heart towards them, Eph. iv. 31, 32. and fo alfo is a patient bearing of wrongs and injuries, Col. iii. 12, 13. and fo alfo is the taking of all things in the beft fenfe, 1 Cor. xiii. 5, 7. and fo alfo is the avoiding of all occafions of ftrife, and parting with our own right, fometimes for peace fake. Gen. xiii. 8, 9 and fo alfo is all fuch looks and geftures of the body, as do exprefs meeknefs and kindnefs, Gen. xxxiii. 10. and fo alfo is relieving the poor and needy, Job xxxi. 16. and fo alfo is the vifiting of the fick, Matth xxv. 36. And now, neighbour Nomologifta, I pray you tell me, whether you think you keep this commandment perfectly or no?

Nom. No indeed, Sir, I do not think I keep it perfectly, nor no man elfe, as you have expounded it.

Evan. Affure yourfelf neighbour Nomologifta, that I have expounded it according to the mind and will of God, revealed in his word, for you fee I have proved all by fcripture.: I told you at the beginning, that the law is fpiritual, and bindeth the very heart and foul to obedience ; and that under one vice exprefsly forbidden, all of the fame kind, with all occafions and means leading thereunto, are likewife forbidden ; and according to thefe rules have I expounded it. Wherefore, I pray you confider, that fo many fins as you have committed, and fo many times as you have carelefsly neglected, and wilfully rejected the means of falvation, fo many wounds you have given your own foul.

And fo many times as you have given occafion to others to fin, fo many wounds you have given to their fouls.

And

And fo many fits of worldly forrow as you have had, and fo many times as you have neglected the moderate ufe either of meat, drink, apparel, recreation or phyfic, when need hath required, fo many wounds you have given to your own body.

And fo many times as you have been either unad-vifedly angry with any, or have born any malice and hatred towards any, or have fecretly in your heart wifhed evil unto any, or borne envy in your heart towards any, or defired to be revenged upon any, then have you been guilty of murdering them in your heart. And if you have given any wrangling and contentious fpeeches, or have carried yourfelf fro-wardly and churlifhly towards others, then have you been guilty of murdering them with your tongue. And if you have quarreled with any man, or ftricken or wounded any man, then have you murdered them with your hand, though you have not taken away their lives. And thus have I endeavoured to fatisfy your defires concerning the fixth commandment.

Neo. I befeech you, Sir, proceed to fpeak of the feventh commandment as you have done of the reft.

COMMANDMENT VII.

Evan. Well then, I pray you confider, that in the feventh commandment there is a negative part ex-preffed in thefe words, " Thou fhalt not commit adultery." That is, thou fhalt not think, will, fpeak, or do any thing whereby thine own chaftity, or the chaftity of others may be hurt or hindered. And an affirmative part included in thefe words, " But thou fhalt every way, and by all good means, preferve and keep the fame."

Neo. I pray you, Sir, begin with the negative part, and firft tell us what is that inward uncleannefs that is forbidden in this commandment?

Evan.

Evan. That we may not be guilty of the inward uncleannefs of the heart, in this commandment is forbidden, all filthy imaginations, unchafte thoughts and inward defires and motions of the heart to uncleannefs, Matth. v. 28. Col. iii. 5. with all the caufes and occafions of ftirring up and nourifhing of thefe in the heart.

Neo. And what be the caufes and occafions of ftirring up and nourifhing thefe things in the heart which we are to avoid ?

Evan. That we may not ftir up nor nourifh inward uncleannefs in our hearts, is forbidden in this commandment, gluttony, or exceffivenefs in eating and pampering of the belly with meats, Jer v 8. and fo alfo is drunkennefs, or excefs in drinking, Prov. xxii. 30, 31, 33. and fo alfo is idlenefs, 2 Sam. xi. 12 and fo alfo is the wearing of lafcivious garnifh and new-fangled attire, Prov. vii 10 1 Tim ii 9 and fo alfo is keeping company with lafcivious, wanton, and flefhly perfons, Gen. xxxix. 10. and fo alfo is immodeft, unchafte, and filthy fpeaking, Eph. iv. 29. And fo alfo is idle and curious looking of men on women, or women on men, Gen vi. 2. and xxxix 7. and fo alfo is the beholding of love-matters, and light behaviour of men and women, reprefented on ftage-plays, Ezek xxiii. 14 Eph v. 3, 4. and fo alfo is immoderate and wanton dancing of men and women together, Job xxi. 11, 12. Mark vi. 21, 22. and fo alfo is wanton kiffing and embracing, with all unchafte touching and daliance, Prov. vii. 13.

Neo. And what is that outward actual uncleannefs which is forbidden in this commandment.

Evan. The actual uncleannefs forbidden in this commandment, is fornication, with a flefhly defilement of the body, committed between man and woman, being both of them fingle and unmarried perfons, 1 Cor x 8. and fo alfo is adultery, which is a defilement of the body, committed between man and woman, being

being either one or both of them married perfons, or at leaft contracted, 1 Cor. vi 9, 18. Hof. xiii. 4.

Neo. I pray you Sir, proceed to the affirmative part, and tell us what the Lord requireth in this commandment.

Evan. The Lord in this commandment doth require purity of heart, 1 Theff iv 5 and he alfo requireth fpeeches favouring of fobriety and chaftity, Col iv. 6. Gen iv. 1. and he alfo requireth that we keep our eyes from beholding vanity and luftful objects, Pfal. cxix. 37. Job xxxi. 1 and he alfo requireth that we be temperate in our diet, in our fleep, and in our recreations, Luke xxiii. 34. and he alfo requireth that we poffefs our veffels in holinefs and honour, 1 Theff. iv. 9. and if we have not the gift of chaftity, he requireth that we take the benefit of holy marriage, 1 Cor. vii. 29. and that the man and wife do in that eftate render due benevolence each towards other, 1 Cor. vii. 5. Thus have I alfo endeavoured to fatisfy your defires concerning the feventh commandment; and now neighbour Nomologifta, I pray you tell me, whether you think you keep it perfectly or no?

Nom. Sir, I thank the Lord I am free from all actual uncleannefs, fo that I am neither fornicator nor adulterer.

Evan. Well, but though you be free from the outward act, yet if you have had in your heart filthy imaginations, unchafte thoughts, or inward defires, or motions of the heart to uncleannefs, you have notwithftanding tranfgreffed this commandment; or if you have been guilty of gluttony, or drunkennefs, or idlenefs, or delighted to keep company with lafcivious and wanton perfons, or have with your tongue uttered any unchafte, or corrupt communication, or have been a frequenter of ftage-plays, or have ufed immoderate dancing with women, or have ufed wanton dalliance with kiffing and embracing, then have you broke this commandment.

Neo.

Neo. I befeech you, Sir, proceed to fpeak of the eighth commandment, as you have done of the reft.

COMMANDMENT VIII.

Evan. Well then, I pray you confider, that in the eighth commandment there is a negative part exprefled in thefe words, " Thou fhalt not fteal," that is, thou fhalt by no unlawful way or means, hurt or hinder the wealth and outward eftate either of thyfelf or others ; and an affirmative part included in thefe words, " But thou fhalt by all good means preferve and further them both."

Neo. I pray you, Sir, begin with the negative part, and firft, tell us what is forbidden in this commandment, as a hurt or hinderance of our own outward eftate?

Evan. That we may not hurt or hinder our own outward eftate, in this commandment is forbidden idlenefs, floth, and inordinate walking, Prov. xviii. 9. 2 Theff. iii. 11. and fo alfo is unthriftinefs, and careleffnefs, either in fpending our goods, or in ordering our affairs and bufineffes, Prov. xxi. 17. 1 Tim. v. 8. and fo alfo is unadvifed furetifhip, Prov. xi. 15.

Neo And what is forbidden in this commandment, as tending to the hurt or hinderance of our neighbour's eftate?

Evan. That we may not hurt or hinder our neighbour's outward eftate, in this commandment is forbidden, covetoufnefs and difcontentednefs with our own eftate, Heb. xiii 5. and fo alfo is envioufnefs at the profperity of others, Prov. xxiv. 1. and fo alfo is refolutions or hafting to be rich, as it were whether the Lord afford means or not, 1 Tim. vi. 9. Prov. xxviii 20. and fo alfo is borrowing, and not paying again, we being able, Pfal. xxxvii. 21. and fo alfo is

lend-

lending upon ufury, Exod. xxii. 25. and fo alfo is the not reftoring of things borrowed, Pfal. xxxvii. 21. and fo alfo is cruelty, in requiring all our debts, without compaffion or mercy, Ifa. lviii. 3. and fo alfo is the praifing of any commodity we fell, contrary to our own knowledge, or the debafing of any thing we buy, againft our own confciene, Ifa. v. 20. Prov xx. 14. and fo alfo is the hoarding up, or withholding the felling of corn, and other neceffary commodities, when we may fpare them, and others have need of them, Prov. xi. 26 and fo alfo is the retaining of hirelings wages, James v. 4. and fo alfo is uncharitable inclofure, Ifa. v. 8. and fo alfo is the felling of any commodity by falfe weights, or falfe meafures, Lev. xix. 35. and fo alfo is the concealing of things found, and withholding them from the right owners, when they are known. And fo alfo is robbery, or the laying of violent and ftrong hands on any part of the wealth that belongs unto another, Zech. iv. 3, 4. and fo alfo is the pilfering and and fecret carrying away of the wealth that belongs unto another, Jofh. vii. 21. and fo alfo is the confenting to the taking away of the goods of another, Pfal. xc. 18. and fo alfo is the receiving or harbouring of ftolen goods, Prov. xxix 24.

Neo. Well, now, Sir I pray you proceed to the affirmative part of this commandment, and tell us what the Lord therein requireth.

Evan. In this commandment is required contentednefs of mind, with that part and portion of wealth and outward good things which God in his providence hath alotted unto us, Heb. xiii. 1. 1 Tim. vi. 6, 7, 8. and fo alfo in refting by faith upon the promife of God, and depending upon his providence, without diftruftful care, Matth. vi 20, 26. and fo alfo is a moderate defire of fuch things as are convenient and neceffary for us, Matth. vi. 21. Prov. xxx 8. and fo alfo is a moderate care to provide thofe things which are needful for us, Gen. xxx. 30. 1 Tim. v 8. and fo also

alfo is an honeft calling, Gen iv. 2. and fo alfo is diligence, painfulnefs, and faithful labouring therein, Gen.
iii. 19. and fo alfo is frugality or thriftinefs, Prov. xxvii.
23, 24. John vi. 12. and fo alfo is borrowing for need
and good ends, what we are able to repay, and making
payment with thanks and chearfulnefs, Exod xxii. 14.
and fo alfo is lending freely, without compounding for
gain, Deut xv 8. Luke vi. 35. and fo alfo is giving,
or communicating outward things unto others, according to our ability and their neceffity, Luke xi 41.
So alfo is the ufing of truth, fimplicity, and plainnefs in
buying and felling, in hiring and letting, Lev. xxv 14.
Deut. xxv. 13, 14, 15. and fo alfo is the reftoring of
things found, Deut. xxii. 2, 3. and fo alfo is the reftoring of things committed to our truft, Ezek. xviii 7.
And thus have I endeavoured to fatisfy your defire
concerning the eighth commandment; and now,
neighbour Nomologifta, I pray you tell me whether
you think you keep it perfectly or no.

Nom. I can fay this truly, that I never in all my
life took away, nor confented to the taking away of fo
much as a penny-worth of any other man's goods.

Evan. Tho' you did not, yet, if there ever have
been in your heart any difcontentednefs with your
own eftate ? or any envious thoughts towards others
in regard of their profperity in the world ? or any
refolution to be rich otherwife than by the moderate
ufe of lawful means ? or if ever you borrowed and
payed not again, to the utmoft of your ability, or if
ever you lent upon ufury? or if ever you did cruelly
require any debt above the ability of your debtor?
or if ever you praifed any thing you had to fell above
the known worth of it? or if ever you did undervalue
any thing you were to buy, contrary to your own
thoughts of it? or if ever you hoarded up corn in the
time of dearth? or if ever you retained the hireling's
wages in your hands, to his lofs or hinderance ? or if

N n   ever

ever you did fell any commodity by falfe weights or meafures? or if ever you did conceal any thing found, from the right owner, when you knew him? then have you been guilty of theft, and fo have been a tranfgreffor of this commandment.

And though you never have done any of thefe things (as it it is ftrange if you have not) yet if ever you were guilty of idlenefs, floth, or any way un-warrantably neglected your calling? or if ever you did unthriftily mifpend any of your own goods, or ever were negligent and carelefs in ordering your own affairs and bufinefs, or if ever you fuftained any lofs by your unadvifed furetifhip, or if ever you borrowed upon ufury, except in cafe of extreme neceffity, then have you been guilty of robbing yourfelf, and fo have been a tranfgreffor of this commandment.

Neo. Now, I pray you, Sir, proceed to fpeak of the ninth commandment, as you have done of the reft.

COMMANDMENT IX

Evan. Well then, I pray you confider, that in the ninth commandment there is a negative part exprefs-ed in thefe words. "Thou fhalt not bear falfe witnefs againft thy neighbour." That is, thou fhalt not think or fpeak any thing contrary to the truth, or that may tend to the hurt or hinderance either of thine own or thy neighbour's good name. And an affirmative part included in thefe words, " But thou fhalt by all good means, feek to preferve them both, according to truth and a good confcience."

Neo. Well, Sir, I pray you begin with the negative part, and firft tell us what is forbidden in this com-mandment, in refpect of our own good name.

Evan.

Evan. That we may not be guilty of bearing false witness againſt ourſelves either by overvaluing or undervaluing ourſelves, in this commandment is forbidden too high a conceit or eſteem of ourſelves, Luke xviii. 9, 10, 11 and ſo alſo is too mean a conceit, in underweeing the good things that be in ourſelves, Exod iv. 10, 13. and ſo alſo is the procuring of ourſelves an evil name, by walking indiſcreetly and offenſively, Rom ii 24. and ſo alſo is the unjuſt accuſing of ourſelves, when we, in a way of proud humility, ſay, " We have no grace, no wit, no wealth," &c Prov xiii. 7. and ſo alſo is the excuſing of our faults, by way of lying, Lev. xix. 11.

Neo. And what is forbidden in this commandment, in reſpect of our neighbour's good name ?

Evan. That we may not be guilty of bearing falſe witneſs againſt any other man, in this commandment is forbidden, contemning or thinking baſely of others, 2 Sam. vi. 16 and ſo alſo is wrongful ſuſpicion, or evil ſurmiſings, 2 Sam. x. 3. and ſo alſo is raſh, uncharitable, unjuſt judging, and contemning of others, Matth. vii. 1 and ſo alſo is fooliſh admiring of others, Acts xii. 22. and ſo alſo is the unjuſt reviving the memory of our neighbour's crimes, which were in tract of time forgotten, Prov. xvii. 9. and ſo alſo is the forbearing to ſpeak in the cauſe, and for the credit of our neighbours, Prov xxxi. 8, 9. and ſo alſo is all flattering ſpeeches, Job xxxii. 21, 22. and and ſo alſo is tale-bearing, back-biting, and ſlanderous ſpeeches, Lev. xix. 16. Prov. xx. 19, and ſo alſo is liſtening to tale-bearers, Prov. xxvi. 20. and xxv. 23. and ſo alſo is falſely charging ſome ill upon another, before ſome magiſtrate, or in ſome open court, Amos vii 10. Acts xxv. 2.

Neo. I pray you, Sir, proceed to the affirmative part in this commandment, and firſt tell us what the Lord requireth of us, for the maintenance of our own good name ?

Evan.

Evan. For the maintenance of our own good name, the Lord in this commandment requireth a right judgment of ourselves, 2 Cor. xiii 5 with a love to, and a care of our good name, Pov. xxii. 1.

Neo. And what doth the Lord in this commandment require of us for the maintenance of our neighbour's good name?

Evan. For the maintenance of our neighbour's good name, in this commandment is required a charitable opinion and estimation of others, 1 Cor. xiii. 7. and so also is a desire of and rejoicing in, the good name of others, Rom. i. 8. Gal. i. 24. and so also is sorrowing and grieving for their infirmities, Psal. cxix. 136. and so also, is the covering of others infirmities in love, Prov. xvii 9. 1 Pet. iv. 8. and so also is the hoping and judging the best of others, 1 Cor. xii 5, 6, 7. and so also is the admonishing of others before we bewray their faults, Prov. xxv. 9. and so also is speaking of the truth from our hearts simply and plainly, upon any just occasion, Psal. xv. 2. Zech. viii. 16. and so also is the giving of sound and seasonable reproofs for known faults, in love and with wisdom, Lev. xix. 17. and so also is the praising and commending of those that do well, Rev. ii. 23. and so also is the defending of the good name of others, if need so require. And thus have I also endeavoured to satisfy your desires concerning the ninth commandment: and now neighbour Nomologista, I pray you tell me, whether you think you keep it perfectly or not?

Nom. The truth is, Sir, I did conceive that there was nothing tended to the breaking of this commandment, but falsely charging some ill upon another before some magistrate, or in some open court of justice; and that, I thank God, I am not guilty of.

Evan.

Evan. Though you have not been guilty of that, yet, if you have contemned or thought too basely of any person, or have had wrongful suspicions, or evil surmisings concerning them, or have rashly and unjustly judged and condemned them, or if you have foolishly admired them, or unjustly revived the memory of any forgotten crime, or have given them any flattering speeches, or have been a tale-bearer, or a back-bitter, or a slanderer, or a listener to tale-bearers, you have borne false witness against your neighbour, and so have been guilty of the breach of this commandment.

Or if you have not had a charitable opinion of others, or have not desired and rejoiced in the good name of others, or have not sorrowed and grieved for their sinful infirmities, or have not covered them in love, or have not hoped and judged the best of them, or have not admonished them before you have discovered their faults to others, or have not given to others sound and seasonable reproof, or have not praised them that do well; then have you also been guilty of false-witness-bearing against your neighbour, and so have transgressed this commandment. And though you never have done any of these things (as it is strange if you have not) yet if you have had too high a conceit of yourself, or have, after a proud humble manner unjustly accused yourself, or have procured yourself an evil name, by walking indiscreetly and offensively, or have excused any fault by way of lying, then have you borne false witness against yourself, and thereby have transgressed this commandment.

Neo. I beseech you, Sir, proceed to speak of the last commandment, as you have done of the rest.

COMMANDMENT X.

Evan. Well then, I pray you consider, that in the tenth commandment there is a negative part

ex-

expreffed in thefe words, " Thou fhalt not covet," &c. That is, thou fhalt not inwardly think on, nor long after that which belongs to another, though it be without confent of will, or purpofe of heart to feek after it. And an affirmative part included in thefe words, " But thou fhalt be well contented with thine own outward condition, and heartily defire the good of thy neighbours"

Neo. Well Sir, I pray you begin with the negative part; and firft tell us what the Lord forbiddeth in this commandment?

Evan. I pray you take notice, and confider, that this tenth commandment was given to be a rule and level, * according to the which we muft take and meafure our inward obedience to all the other commandments contained in the fecond table of God's law †. For the Law-giver having in the reft of the commandments dealt with thofe fins efpecially which ftand in deeds, and are done of purpofe, or with an advifed confent of will, (although there is no doubt but that the law of reftraining concupifcence is implied and included in all the former commandments. Now laft of all, in this laft commandment he dealeth with thofe fins which are called only concupifcences, and do contain all inward ftirring and conceit in the underftanding and affections againft every commandment of the law, and are, as it were, rivers boiling out of the fountain of that original fin: for to covet, in this place, fignifies to have a motion of the heart without any fettled confent of the will ‡. Briefly then in this commandment is forbidden not only the evil act and evil thought fettled, and with full and deliberate confent of will, as in the former commandments; but here alfo is forbidden, ‖ the very firft motions and inclinations, to every evil that is forbidden in any of

---

* Urfin. Cat p. 614.   † Bafting Cat. p. 162.
‡ Dod on the Com p 363.   ‖ Elton on the Com.

the former commandments, as it is evident, Rom. vii. 7. and xii 9. For it is not said in this commandment, Thou shalt not consent to lust, but, " Thou shalt not lust." It doth not only command the binding of lust, but it also forbiddeth the being of lust; which being so, * who seeth not that in this commandment is contained, the perfect obedience to the whole law; for how cometh it to pass, that we sin against every commandment, but because this corrupt concupiscence is in us, without which, we should of our own accord, with our whole mind and body, be apt to do the only good without any thought or desire at all to the contrary? And this is all I have to say touching the negative part of this commandment.

Neo. Well then, Sir, I pray you proceed to the affirmative, and tell us what the Lord requireth in this commandment?

Evan. Why, original justice, or righteousness, is required in this commandment, which is a disposition and an inclination and desire to perform unto God, and to our neighbour for God's sake, all the duties which are contained both in the first and second table of the law ; whence it doth evidently appear, that it is not sufficient, though we forbear the evil, and do the good which is contained in every commandment except we do it readily and willingly, and for the Lord's sake. As for example, to give you a few instances, it is not sufficient, tho' we abstain from making of images, or worshipping God by an image, no though we perform all the parts of his true worship, as, praying, reading, hearing, receiving the sacraments, and the like; if we do it unwillingly, or in obedience to any law or commandment of man, and not for the Lord's sake; neither is it sufficient, though we abstain from the works of our callings on the Lord's day, and perform

never

* Basting Cat. p. 163.

never fo many religious exercifes; yet if it be unwillingly, and for form and cuftom-fake, or in mere obedience to any fuperior, and not for the Lord's fake. Neither is it fufficient, though a child fhew never fo much honour, love, and refpect to his parents, if he do it by conftraint and unwillingly, or to gain the praife of men, and not for the Lord's fake. Neither is it fufficient, though a fervant do his duty, and carry himfelf never fo well, if it be for fear of correction, and for his own profit and gain, and not for the Lord's fake. Neither is it fufficient, though a wife carry herfelf never fo dutifully and refpectfully towards her hufband, both in word and deed, if it be unwillingly, for fear of his frowns, or to gain the applaufe of them that behold it, and not for the Lord's fake. Neither is it fufficient, though a hufband fhew much love and refpect to his wife, if it be becaufe fhe is amiable or profitable, or to gain the praife of men, and not for the Lord's fake. In a word, it is not fufficient, tho' any man or woman do all their duties, in all their relations, if they do them merely for their own fake, and not for the Lord's fake.

Neither is it fufficient, tho' a man abftain from killing, yea, and from ftriking, if it be for fear of the law, and not for the Lord's fake. Neither is it fufficient, though he bridle his anger, and abftain from expreffing any wrath, if it be becaufe he would be counted a patient man, and not for the Lord's fake. Neither is it fufficient, though a man vifit the fick, clothe the naked, feed the hungry, or never fo many ways feek to preferve the life of his neighbour, if it be for the praife of men, and not for the Lord's fake. Neither is it fufficient, though a man abftain from committing adultry, if it be for fear of the fhame or punifhment that will follow, and not for the Lord's fake. Nor though we alfo abftain from idlenefs, gluttony and drunkennefs, if it be for our own gain's fake, and not for the Lord's fake. Neither is it

fuffi-

fufficient, though we abftain from 'ftealing, and labour diligently in our callings, if it be for fear of fhame or punifhment, or for the praife of men. Neither is it fufficient, though we have abftained from falfe witnefs bearing, and have fpoken the truth, if it have been for fear or fhame, or merely to do our neighbour a courtefy, and not becaufe the Lord requireth it.

Thus I might have inftanced, in divers other particulars, wherein, though we have done that which is required, and avoided that which is forbidden, yet, if it have been for our own ends, in any of the particulars before-mentioned; yea, or if it have been merely or chiefly to efcape hell, and to obtain heaven, and not for the love we bear to God, and for the defire we have to pleafe him, we have therein tranfgreffed the Lord's commandments. And now, neighbour Nomologifta, I pray you confider, whether you have gone near to the keeping of all the commandments perfectly or no?

Nom. But, Sir, are you fure that the Lord requireth that every man fhould keep all the ten commandments according as you have now expounded them?

The Ufe of the Law.

Evan. Yea, indeed he doth, and if you make any queftion of it, I pray you, confider further, that one afking our Saviour, which is the " great commandment in the law," he anfwered, * " Thou fhalt love the Lord thy God with all thy heart, and with all thy foul, and with all thy mind. 'This," faith he, " is the firft and great commandment; and the fecond is like unto this, Thou fhalt love thy neighbour as thyfelf."

Whereupon faith a famous fpiritual expofitor †, " God will have the whole heart; and all the powers

of

* Matth. xxii. 6, 7, 8, 9.   † Urfin. Cat. p. 37, 38.

of our fouls muſt be bent towards him, he will have himſelf to be acknowledged and reckoned as our ſovereign and ſupreme good; our love to him muſt be perfeⱨ and abſolute: he requireth, that there be not found in us the leaſt thought, inclination, or appetite of any thing which may diſpleaſe him; and that we direⱨ all our aⱨions to this very end, that he alone may be glorified by us: and that for the love we bear unto God, we muſt do well unto our neighbour, according to the commandments of ·God. Conſider alſo, I pray you, that it is ſaid, Deut xxvii. 26. Gal iii 10. " Curſed is every one that continueth not in all things which are written in the book of the law, to do them " Now, if you do conſider theſe things well, you ſhall perceive that the Lord requireth that every man do keep all the ten commandments perfeⱨly, according as I have expounded them, and concludes all thoſe under the curſe that do not ſo keep them.

Nom. Surely, Sir, you did miſtake, in ſaying that the Lord requireth that every man do keep all the ten commandments perfeⱨly; for I ſuppoſe you would have ſaid, the Lord requireth that every man do endeavour to keep them perfeⱨly.

Evan. No, neighbour Nomologiſta, I did not miſtake, for I ſay it again, that the Lord requireth of every man, perfeⱨ obedience to all the ten commandments, and concludes all thoſe under the curſe, that do not yield it; for it is not ſaid, Curſed is every man that doth not endeavour to continue in all things, but, " Curſed is every man that continueth not in all things," &c.

Nom., But Sir, do you think that any man doth continue in all things, as you have expounded them?

Evan. No, no, it is impoſſible that any man ſhould.

Nom. And, Sir, what is it to be under the curſe?

Evan.

Evan. To be under the curfe, as Luther and Perkins do well agree, is to be under fin, the wrath of God, and everlafting death.

Nom. But, Sir, I pray you how can this ftand with the juftice of God, to require man to do that which is impoffible, and yet to conclude him under the curfe for not doing it.

Evan. You fhall perceive that it doth well ftand with the juftice of God to deal fo with man, if you do confider, that this law of God, or thefe ten commandments, which we have now expounded, are, as Urfinus's catechifm truly faith, " A doctrine agreeing with the eternal and immortal wifdom and juftice that is in God," wherein faith Calvin, " God hath fo painted out his own nature, that it doth in a manner exprefs the very image of God." And we read, Gen. i 27 That man at the firft was created in the image or likenefs of God; whence it muft needs follow that this law was written in his heart, (that is to fay) God did engrave in man's heart fuch wifdom and knowledge of his will and works, and fuch integrity in his foul, and fuch a fitnefs in all the powers thereof, that his mind was able to conceive, and his heart was able to defire, and his body was able to put in execution, any thing which was acceptable to God; fo that in very deed he was able to keep all the ten commandments perfectly.

And therefore though God do require of man impoffible things, yet is he not unjuft, neither doth he injure us in fo doing, becaufe he commanded them when they were poffible; and though we have now loft our ability of performance, yet it being by our voluntary falling from the ftate of innocence in which we were at firft created. God hath not loft his right of requiring that of us, which he once gave us.

Nom. But, Sir, you know it was our firft parents only that did fall away from God in eating the forbidden fruit, and none of their pofterity; how then can

it

it be truly said, that we nave lost that power through our own default?

Evan. For answer to this, I pray you consider, that Adam by God's appointment, was not to stand or fall as a single person only, but as a common public person representing all mankind which were to come of him. And therefore, as in case if he had been obedient, and not eaten the forbidden fruit, he had retained and kept that power which he had by creation, as well for all mankind as for himself; even so by his disobedience in eating that forbidden fruit, he was disrobed of God's image, and so lost that power, as well for all mankind as for himself.

Nom. Why then, Sir, it should seem that all mankind are under sin, wrath, and eternal death.

Evan. Yea, indeed, by nature they are so, " For we know, saith the apostle, that whatsoever the law saith, it saith to them who are under the law, that every mouth may be stopped, and all the world may become guilty before God." Rom. iii. 19. And again saith he, " We have proved both Jews and Gentiles, that they are all under sin." Rom. iii. 9 And in another place he saith, " We were by nature children of wrath as well as others," Eph. ii. 3. and lastly, he saith, " So death passed upon all men, for that all have sinned," Rom. v. 12.

Nom. But, Sir, I pray you tell me whether you think that any regenerate man doth keep the commandments perfectly according as you have expounded them?

Evan. No, not the most sanctified man in the world.

Nom. Why then, Sir, it should seem, that not only natural men, but regenerate men also, are under the curse of the law. For if every one that keepeth not the law perfectly be concluded under the curse; and if rege-

regenerate men do not keep the law perfectly, then they muſt alſo needs be under the curſe.

Evan. The concluſion of your argument is not true, for if by regenerate men you mean true believers, then they have fulfiled the law perfectly in Chriſt, or rather Chriſt hath perfectly fulfilled the law in them, and was made a curſe for them, and ſo hath redeemed them from the curſe of the law, as you may ſee, Gal. iii. 13.

Nom. Well, Sir, now I do underſtand you, and have ever been of your judgment in that point, for I have ever concluded thus, that either a man himſelf, or Chriſt for him, muſt keep the law perfectly, or elſe God will not accept of him, and therefore have I endeavoured to do the beſt I could to keep the law perfectly, and wherein I have failed and come ſhort, I have believed that Chriſt hath done it for me.

Evan. The apoſtle ſaith, Gal. iii. 10. " So many as are of the works of the law, are under the curſe." And truly neighbour Nomologiſta, if I may ſpeak it without offence, I fear me you are ſtill of the works of the law, and therefore ſtill under the curſe.

Nom. Why, Sir, I pray you what is it to be of the works of the law ?

Evan. To be of the works of the law, is for a man to look for, or hope to be juſtified or accepted in the ſight of God, for his own obedience to the law.

Nom But ſurely, Sir, I never did ſo ; for tho' by reaſon of my being ignorant of what is required and forbidden in every commandment, I had a conceit that I came very near the perfect fulfilling of the law, yet I never thought I did do all things that are contained therein, and therefore I never looked for, nor hoped that God would accept me for mine own obedience without Chriſt's being joined with it.

Evan.

Evan. Then it seemeth that you did conceive, that your obedience and Chrift's obedience muft be joined together, and fo God would accept you for that.

Nom. Yea, indeed, Sir, there hath been my hopes, and indeed there is ftill my hopes.

Evan. Ay but neighbour Nomologifta, as I told my neighbour Neophytus and others not long fince; fo I tell you now, that as the juftice of God requires a perfect obedience, fo doth it require that this perfect obedience be a perfonal obedience, *viz.* It muft be the obedience of one perfon only. The obedience of two muft not be put together to make up a perfect obedience : and indeed to fay as the thing is, God will have none to have a hand in the juftification and falvation of any man, but Chrift only; for, faith the apoftle Peter, Acts iv. 12. " Neither is there falvation in any other; for there is none other name under heaven given among men whereby we muft be faved." Believe it then, I befeech you, that Chrift Jefus will either be a whole Saviour, or no Saviour; he will either fave you alone, or not fave you at all.

Nom. But, Sir, if man's obedience to the law do not help to procure his juftification and acceptance with God, then why did God give the law to the Ifraelites upon mount Sinai, and why is it read and expounded by you that are minifters ? I would gladly know of what ufe it is.

Evan. The apoftle faith, Gal. iii. 19. That the law was added becaufe of tranfgreffion." That is, (as Luther expounds it) " That tranfgreffions might increafe, and be more known and feen ?" Or as Perkins expounds it, " For the revealing of fin, and the punifhment thereof; for by the law comes the knowledge of fin," as the fame apoftle faith, Rom. iii. 20. And therefore when the children of Ifrael had a conceit that they were righteous, and could keep all God's commandments perfectly as it is manifeft by

.their

their faying, Exod. xix. 8. " All that the Lord commandeth we will do, and be obedient." The Lord gave them this law to the intent they might fee how far fhort they came of yielding that obedience which is therein required, and fo confequently how finful they were. And juft fo did our Saviour deal alfo with the young expounder of the law, Matth. xix. 16. who it feems was fick of the fame difeafe, *. " Good Mafter (faith he) what fhall I do, that I may inherit eternal life?" " He doth not (faith Calvin) † fimply afk, which way, or by what means he fhould come to eternal life, but, what good he fhould do to get it." Whereby it appears, that he was a proud jufticiary, one that fwelled in flefhly opinion, that he could keep the law, and be faved by it ; therefore he is worthily fent to the law to work himfelf weary, and to fee his need, to come to Chrift for remedy.

Now then, if you would know of what ufe the law is, why firft let me tell you, it is of fpecial ufe to all fuch as have a conceit that they themfelves can do any thing for the procuring of their own juftification, and acceptation in the fight of God, to let them fee, as in a glafs, that in that cafe they can do nothing. And therefore, feeing that you yourfelf have fuch a conceit, I befeech you labour to make that ufe of it, that fo you may be hereby quite driven out of yourfelf unto Jefus Chrift.

Nom. Believe me, Sir, I fhould be glad I could make fuch a good ufe of it, and therefore I pray you, give me fome directions how I may do it.

Evan. Why firft of all, I would defire you to confider, that in regard that all mankind were at firft created in fuch an eftate as I have declared unto you : the law and juftice of God doth require that the man who undertakes by his obedience to procure his juftifi-

cation

---

* Calvin's Inftit. p. 403.   † Ibid. p. 401.

cation and acceptation in the fight of God, either in whole, or in part, be as compleatly furnished with the habit of righteousnefs and true holinefs, and as free from all corruption of nature, as Adam was in the state of innocency, that fo there may not be the least corruption mingled with any of thofe good actions which he doth, nor the least motion of heart, or inclination of will towards any of thofe evil actions which he doth not do.

Secondly, I would defire you to confider, that neither you, nor no man elfe, whilft you live upon the earth, fhall be fo furnished with perfect righteouf-nefs, and true holinefs, nor fo free from all corrupti-ons of nature, as Adam was in a state of innocency ; fo that no good action which you do, fhall be free from having fome corruption mingled with it; nor no evil action which you do not do, free from fome motion of heart, or inclination of will, towards it : and that, therefore, you can do nothing towards the procuring of your juftification and acceptation in the fight of God : the which the prophet David, well confidering, cries out, Pfal cxlii. 2. " Enter not into judgment with thy fervant, O Lord, for in thy fight fhall no man living be juftified." Yea, and this made the apoftle Paul cry out, " O wretched man that I am, who fhall deliver me from the body of this death!" Rom. vii. 24. Yea, and this made him defire to be found in Chrift, not having his own righteoufnefs, which is of the law, but that which is through the faith of Chrift," Phil. iii. 9.

Nom. But, Sir, I am perfuaded there be fome good actions which I do, that are free from having any corruption at all mixed with them ; and fome evil actions I do not do, towards the which I have no motion of heart, or inclination of will at all.

Evan. Surely, neighbour Nomologifta, you do not truly know yourfelf ; for I am confident, that any man, who truly knows himfelf, doth fee fuch fecret cor-

corruptions of heart in every duty he performeth, as causeth him unfeignedly to confess, that whatever good action he doth, it is but a polluted stream, of a more corrupt fountain. And whatsoever you or any man else do conceive of yourselves, it is most certain, that whatsoever sin is forbidden in the word *, or hath been practised in the world, that sin every man carries in his bosom, for all hath equally sinned in Adam, and therefore original lust is equally in all.

Nom. Sir, I can hardly be persuaded to this.

Evan. Well, neighbour Nomologista, I cannot so well tell how it is with you, but for mine own part, I tell you truly, I find my knowledge corrupted and defiled with ignorance and blindness, and my faith corrupted and defiled with doubting and distrust, and my love to God very much corrupted and defiled with sinful self love, and love to the world; and my joy in God much corrupted and defiled with carnal joy, and my godly sorrow very much corrupted and defiled with worldly sorrow.

And I find my prayers, my hearings, my reading, my receiving the sacrament, and such like duties, very much corrupted and defiled with dulness, drowsiness, sleepiness, wandering, worldly thoughts, and the like.

And I find my sanctifying of the Lord's name very much corrupted and defiled, by thinking and speaking lightly and irreverently of his titles; and by thinking, if not by speaking, grudgingly against some acts of his providence.

And I find my sanctifying of the Lord's day, very much corrupted and defiled by sleeping too long in the morning, and by worldly thoughts and words, if not by worldly works.

And I find that all my duties that I have performed, either towards my superiors or inferiors, have been corrupted and defiled, either with too much indul-
gency,

* Capel on Temptation, page 60. and 41.

gency, or with too much feverity, or with bafe fears, orbafe hopes, or fome felf-end and by-refpect.

And I find that all the duties which I have performed, either for the prefervation of mine own, or others life, chaftity, goods, or good name, have been very much corrupted and defiled, either with defire of mine own praife, mine own profit here, or to efcape hell, and to obtain heaven hereafter; fo that I fee no good action which I have ever done, free from having fome corruption mixed with it.

And as for motion of heart, and inclination of will, towards that evil which I have not done, it is alfo manifeft for though I have not been guilty of idolatry, either in making or worfhipping of images, yet have I not been free from carnal imaginations of God in the time of his worfhip, nor from will-worfhip.

And though I have not been fo guilty of profaning the name of the Lord, after fuch a grofs manner as fome others have been, yet have I not been free from an inclination of heart, and difpofition of will thereunto; for I have both thought and fpoken irreverently both of his titles, attributes, word, and works; yea, and many times do fo to this day.

And though I do not now fo grofsly profane the Lord's day, as it may be others, have done, and do ftill, yet have I formerly done it grofsly, yea, and do find ftill an inward difpofition of heart, and inclination of will, both to omit thofe duties which tend to the fanctifying of it, and to do thofe worldly actions which tend to the profanation of it.

And though when I was a child and young, I did not fo grofsly difhonour and difobey my parents and other fuperiors as fome others did, yet had I an inclination of heart, and difpofition of will thereunto, as it was manifeft by my ftubbornnefs, and by my not
yield-

yieding of willing obedience to their commands, nor
submitting patiently to their reproofs and corrections.

And though it may be, I have done more of my
duty to my inferiors, than some others have done,
yet. have I found an inclination of heart, and a difposition of will many times, to omit thofe duties which
I have performed, fo that I have, as it were, been fain
to conftrain myfelf to do that which I have done.

And though I have not been guilty of the grofs
act of murder, yet have I had, and have ftill, an inclination of heart and a difpofition of will thereunto,
in that I have been and am ftill many times fubject to
rafh, unadvifed, and exceffive anger, yea I have been,
and am ftill divers times wrathful and envious towards
others that offend me.

And though I never was guilty of the foul and
grofs act of fornication or adultery, yet have I had an
inclination of heart, and difpofition of will thereunto,
in that I have not been free from filthy imaginations,
unchafte thoughts, and inward motions and defires to
uncleannefs.

And though I was never guilty of the grofs act of
ftealing, yet have I had an inclination of heart, and a
difpofition of will thereunto, in that I have neither
been free from difcontentednefs with mine own eftate,
nor from covetous defires after that which belongs
to another.

And though I never did bear falfe witnefs againft
any man, yet have I had an inclination of heart, and
difpofition of will thereunto ; in that I have been free
from contemning, defpifing, and thinking too bafely
of others, neither yet have I been free from evil
furmifings, groundlefs fufpicions, and rafh judging
of others.

And now, neighbour Nomologifta, I pray you tell
me whether you do not think that fome of thefe
corruptions are in you, which you hear are in me?

Nom.

Nom. Yea, believe me, Sir, I muſt needs confeſs that ſome of them are.

Evan. Well, though you have but only one of
them in you, yet I pray you conſider, that you do
thereby tranſgreſs one of the ten commandments;
and the apoſtle James ſaith, that " Whoſoever ſhall
keep the whole law, and yet offend in one point, he
is guilty of all," James ii. 10. And call to mind, I
alſo pray you, that a curſe is denounced againſt all
thoſe that continue not in " all things which are
written in the book of the law to do them." Mind
it I pray you, " that doth not continue in all things "
So that although you could for a time do all that the
Lord requireth, and avoid all that he forbiddeth,
and that never ſo exactly; yet, if you do not continue
ſo doing, but tranſgreſs the law once in all your life,
and that only in one thought, you are thereby become
ſubject to the curſe, which, as you have heard, is
eternal damnation in hell.

Nay, let me tell you more, although you never
yet had tranſgreſſed the law in all your life hitherto,
not ſo much as in the leaſt thought, nor never ſhould
do whilſt you live, yet ſhould you thereby become
far ſhort of the perfect fulfilling of the law, and ſo
conſequently of your juſtification, and acceptation in
the ſight of God.

Nom. That is very ſtrange to me, Sir, for what can
be required more, or what can be done more, than
yielding of perfect and perpetual obedience?

Evan. That is true indeed, there is no more required, neither can there be more done, but yet you
muſt underſtand, that the law doth as well require
paſſive obedience as active, ſuffering as well as doing;
for our common bond, entered into for us all,* by
God's benefits towards the firſt man, is by his diſobedience become forfeited, both in reſpect of himſelf and
all mankind; and therefore, ever ſince the fall of man,
the

* **Trueneſs of the Chriſt. Rel. p. 534.**

the law and juſtice of God doth not only require the payment of the debt, but alſo of the forfeiture; there is not only required of him perfect doing, but alſo perfect ſuffering. " In the day that thou eateſt thereof, thou ſhalt die the death," ſaith the Lord, Gen. ii. 17.

Nay, let me tell you yet more, in order of juſtice, the forfeiture ought to be paid before the debt, perfect ſuffering ſhould go before perfect doing. becauſe all mankind, by reaſon of that firſt and great tranſgreſſion, are at odds and enmity with God, they are all of them children of his wrath, and therefore God (as we may ſpeak with holy reverence) cannot be reconciled unto any man, before a full ſatisfaction be made to his juſtice by a perfect ſuffering; Col. i. 21. perfect ſuffering then is required for the reconciling of man unto God, Eph. ii. 3. and ſetting him in the ſame condition he was in before his fall, and perfect doing is required for the keeping of him in that condition.

Nom. And, Sir, is man as unable to pay the forfeiture, as he is to pay the debt? I mean, is he as unable to ſuffer perfectly, as to do perfectly?

Evan. Yea indeed, every whit as unable; foraſmuch as man's ſin in eating of the forbidden fruit was committed againſt God, and God is infinite and eternal, and the offence is always multiplied according to the dignity of the perſon againſt whom it is committed: man's offence muſt needs be an infinite offence, and the puniſhment muſt needs be proportionable to the fault, therefore an infinite and eternal puniſhment is required at man's hands, or elſe ſuch a temporal puniſhment, as is equal, and anſwerable to eternal. Now eternal puniſhment man cannot ſuſtain, becauſe then he ſhould never be delivered, he ſhould ever be ſatisfying, and never have ſatisfied; which ſatisfaction, is ſuch as is the puniſhment of devils and damned men in hell, which never ſhall have end. And for temporal puniſhment, which ſhould be equivalent

valent to eternal, that cannot be neither, becaufe the power and vigour of no creature is fuch, that it may fuftain a finite and temporal punifhment, equivalent to infinite and eternal ; for fooner fhould the creature be wafted, confumed, and brought to nothing, than it could fatisfy the juftice of God by this means : wherefore we may certainly conclude, that no man can fatisfy the law and juftice of God, neither by active nor by paffive obedience, and fo confequently no man fhall be juftified and accepted in the fight of God by his own doings or fufferings.

Nom. Sir, I fee it clearly, and am therein fully convinced, and I hope I fhall make, that ufe of it. But, Sir, is there no other ufe to be made of the law than this ?

Evan. Yea, neighbour Nomologifta, you muft not only labour thereby to fee your own infufficiency, to procure your own juftification, and acceptation in the fight of God, (though that indeed be the chief ufe that any unjuftified perfon ought to endeavour to make of it) but you muft alfo endeavour to make it a rule of direction to you in your life and converfation.

Nom. But, Sir, if I cannot by my obedience to the law, do any thing towards the procuring of mine own juftification and acceptation in the fight of God, or (which as I do conceive is all one) if I can do nothing towards the procuring of mine own eternal falvation, then methinks all that I do fhould be in vain, for I cannot fee any good that I fhall get thereby.

Evan. No, neighbour Nomologifta, it fhall not be in vain ; for though you cannot by your obedience to the law, do any thing towards the procuring of your own juftification, or eternal falvation ; yea, and though you fhould never make fuch a ufe of it, as to be thereby driven out of yourfelf unto Jefus Chrift for juftification, and eternal falvation, but fhould be everlaftingly condemned ; yet, this let me tell you,

the

the more obedience you yield unto the law, the more
eafy fhali your condemnation be ; for although , no
man, walk he never fo exactly and ftrictly according
to the law, fhall thereby either efcape the torments of
hell, or obtain the joys of heaven, yet the more exactly and ftrictly any man walks according to the law,
the eafier fhall his torments be. Matth. xi 22. fo
although you by your obedience to the law cannot
obtain the uneafieft place in heaven, yet may you
thereby obtain the moft eafy place in hell ; and therefore your obedience fhall not be in vain. Nay, let me
tell you more, although you by your obedience to the
law, can neither efcape that hell, nor enjoy that
heaven that is in the world to come ; yet may you
thereby efcape that hell, and enjoy that heaven which
is to be had in this prefent world; for the Lord dealeth fo equally and juftly with all men, that every
man fhall be fure to receive his due at his hands : fo
that, as every man who is truly juftified in the fight
of God by faith in Chrift's blood, fhall for that blood's
fake be fure of the joys of heaven, be his life never
fo unconformable to the law, yet the more unconformable his life is thereunto, the more croffes and afflictions
he fhall be fure to meet withal in this life, Pfal.
lxxxix. 30, 31. 32. even fo, though no man, that is
not juftified by faith in Chrift's blood, fhall either efcape
the torments of hell, or attain the joys of heaven, be
his life never fo conformable to the law, yet the more
conformable his life is thereunto, the lefs of the
miferies and the more of the bleffings of this life he
fhall have ; for is it not to men unjuftified, though I
fuppofe not only to them, that the Lord fpeaketh,
Ifa. i. 19. faying, " If you be willing and obedient,
ye fhall eat the good things of the land " And doth not
the Lord in the fifth commandment promife the bleffing
of long life to all inferiors that are obedient to their
fuperiors ? And may we not obferve, and is it not
found true by experience, that thofe children who
are

are moft careful of doing their duties to their parents, are commonly more free both from their parents corrections and the Lord's corrections; and are like-wife bleffed with obedient children themfelves, and do tafte of their parents bounty and the Lord's bounty, as touching the bleffings of this life, more than others that are difobedient? And may we not obferve, and is it not found true by experience, that thofe fervants that are moft faithful and diligent in their places, are com-monly more free either from the Lord's or their mafter's corrections; and are likewife rewarded with fuch fer-vants themfelves, and with other temporal bleffings both from their mafters and from the Lord, than others that are not fo? And may we not obferve, and is it not found true by experience, that thofe wives that are obedient and fubject to their hufbands, are com-monly more free from the frowns, checks, and rebukes of their hufbands, at leaft they are more bleffed with peace of confcience, and a good name amongft men, than others that are not fo? And may we not obferve, that our mere honeft men, who for the moft part live without committing any grofs fin againft the law, are commonly more exempted from the fword of the magiftrate, and have many earthly bleffings more in abundance, than fuch as are grofs finners? And the Scribes and Pharifees, who were ftrict obfervers of the law, in regard of the outward man, were no lofers by it. " Verily, faith our Saviour, I fay unto you, they have their reward," Matth vi. 2.

So that ftill you fee, your obedience to the law fhall not be in vain; wherefore, I pray you, do your beft to keep the ten commandments as perfecly as you can. But above all, I befeech you, be careful to confider of that which hath been faid touching the fpecial ufe of the law to you that fo through the powerful working of God's Spirit, it may become an effectual means to drive you out of yourfelves unto Jefus Chrift.   O

O confider, in the firſt place, what a great number of duties are required, and what a great number of fins are forbidden in every one of the ten command-ments. And in the ſecond place, confider, how many of thoſe duties you have omitted, and how many of thoſe fins you have committed. And in the third place, confider, that there hath been much corruption mixed with every good duty which you have done, fo that you have finned in doing that which in itſelf is good ; and that you have had an inclination of heart and diſpofition of will to every fin you have not committed, and ſo have been guilty of all thoſe fins which you have not done. And in the fourth place, con-fider, that the law denounceth a curfe unto every one which continueth not in all things which are written in the book of the law to do them. And then, in the fifth place, make application of the curfe unto yourſelf, by ſaying in your heart, if every one be curfed which continueth not in all things, then ſurely I am curfed that have coutinued in nothing. And then, in the fixth place, confider, that before you can be delivered from the curfe, the law and juſtice of God re-quireth that there be a perfect ſatisfaction made, both by paying the debt and the forfeiture to the very utmoſt farthing, perfect doing and perfect fuffering are both of them required. And then, in the laſt place, confider, that you are fo far from being able to make a perfect ſatisfaction, that you can do nothing at all towards it, and that therefore, as of yourſelf you are in a moſt miferable and helpleſs condition.

Nom. Well, Sir, I do plainly fee that I have been deceived, for I verily thought, that the only reafon why the Lord gave the law, and why you that are miniſters do ſhew us what is required and forbidden in the law, had been, that all men might thereby come to fee what the mind and will of the Lord is, and be exhorted, and perfuaded to lead their lives thereafter. And I alfo verily thought, that the more

P p any

any man did ſtrive and endeavour to reform his life and do thereafter, the more he procured the love and favour of God towards him, and the more God would bleſs him and do him good, both in this world, and in the world to come; yea, and I alſo verily thought, that it had been in man's power to have come very near the perfect fulfilling of the law, for I never read nor heard any miniſter to ſhew how impoſſible it is for any man to keep the law; nor never make any mention of ſuch uſe of the law, as you have done this day.

Evan. Surely, neighbour Nomologiſta, theſe have not only been your thoughts, but alſo the thoughts of many other men: for it is natural for every man to think that he muſt and can procure God's favour, and eternal happineſs by his obedience to the law, at the leaſt to think he can do ſomething towards it; for naturally men think that the law requireth no more but the external act, and that therefore it is in man's power to keep it perfectly. Is it not an ordinary and common thing for men when they hear or read that there is more required and forbidden in the law than they were aware of, to think with themſelves, Surely I am not right, I have tranſgreſſed the law more than I had thought I had done, and therefore God is more angry with me than I had thought he had been; and therefore to pacify his anger, and procure his favour towards me, I muſt repent, amend, and do better; I muſt reform my life according to the law, and ſo by my future obedience, make amends for my former diſobedience: and if hereupon they do attain to any good meaſure of outward conformity, then they think they come near the perfect fulfilling of the law; and if it were not that the doctrine of the church of England is, that no man can fulfil the law perfectly, and that none but Papiſts do ſay the contrary, they would both think and ſay they did, or hoped they ſhould keep all the commandments perfectly. And upon

upon occasion of this their outward reformation according to the law, they think ; yea, and sometimes say, they are regenerate men and true converts, and that the beginning of this their reformation was the time of their new birth, and conversion unto God. And if these men do confess themselves to be sinners, it is rather because they hear all others confess themselves so to be, than out of any true fight and knowledge, sense or feeling, they have of any inward heart-corruption. And if they do acknowledge, that man is not to be justified by the works of the law, but by faith in Christ, it is rather because they have heard it so preached, or because they have read it in the Bible, or some other book, than because of any imperfection which they see in their own works, or any need they see of the righteousness of Jesus Christ. And if they do see any imperfection in their own works, and any need of the righteousness of Jesus Christ, then they imagine that so long as their hearts are upright and sincere, and they do desire and endeavour to do their best to fulfil the law, God will accept of what they do, and make up their imperfect obedience with Christ's perfect obedience, and so will justify them and save them ; but all this while their own works must have a hand in their justification and salvation, and so they are still of the works of the law, and therefore under the curse ; the Lord be merciful both to you and them, and bring you under the blessing of Abraham.

Nom. Sir, I thank you for your good wishes towards me, and for your great pains which you have now taken with me, and so I will for this time take my leave of you; only, Sir, I could wish, if it might not be too much trouble to you, that you would be pleased at your leisure, to give me in writing a copy of what you have this day said concerning the law.

Evan. Well, neighbour Nomologista, though I shall hardly spare so much time, yet because you do desire it, and in hope you may receive good by it, I will ere long find fome time to accomplifh your defire.

Neo. I pray you, neighbour Nomologifta, tarry a little longer, and I will go with you.

Nom. No, I muft needs be gone, I can ftay no longer.

Evan. Then fare you well, neighbour Nomologifta, and the' Lord make you to fee your fins.

Nom. The Lord be with you, Sir.

Neo. Well, Sir, now I hope you have fully convinced him that he comes far fhort of keeping all the commandments perfectly : I hope he will no longer be fo well conceited of his own righteoufnefs as he hath formerly been. But now, Sir, I pray you tell me before I depart, whether you would have me to endeavour to make the fame ufe of the law, which you have advifed him to make ?

Evan. No, neighbour Nomologifta, I look not upon you as an unbeliever, as I did upon him, but I look upon you as one who have already been by the law driven out of yourfelf to Jefus Chrift ; I look upon you as a true believer, and as a perfon already juftified in the fight of God by faith in Chrift, and fo as one who are neither to queftion your inheritance in heaven, nor fear your portion in hell. And therefore I will not perfuade you to labour to yield obedience to the law, by telling you that the more obedient you are thereunto, the eafier torments you fhall have in hell, as I did him. Neither would I have you to make application of the curfe of the law to yourfelf, as I advifed him to do ; for if you do truly and thoroughly believe (as God requires you, 1 John iii. 23) that Jefus Chrift, the Son of God, and your furety, hath by his active and paffive obedience fully difcharged and paid both the debt and the forfeiture, which the law and juftice of God obliged you to pay, then will

will not you yield obedience to the law, to pay that
which you do truly believe is fully paid and difcharged
already; and if you do not yield obedience to the law
to difcharge that, then do you not yield obedience
to the law, in hopes to be thereby made juft or
juftified in the fight of God, and if you yield not obedience to the law, in hopes to be thereby made juft,
or juftified in the fight of God, then are you not of
the works of the law; and if you are not of the works
of the law, then are you not under the curfe of the
law; and if you be not under the curfe of the law,
then muft you not make application of the curfe unto
yourfelf. And therefore, whenfoever you fhall either
hear or read thefe words, "Curfed is every one which
continueth not in all things which are written in the
book of the law to do them." And your confcience
tells you that you have not, nor do not continue in all
things, and that therefore you are accurfed; then do
you make fo much ufe of the curfe, as thereby to take
occafion by faith to cleave more clofs unto Chrift, and
fay, O law! thy curfe is not to come into my confcience, my confcience is freed from it; for tho' it is
true, I have not continued in all things which are
written in the book of the law to do them, yet this
my furety Jefus Chrift, hath continued in all things
for me, fo that although I am unable to pay either the
debt or the forfeiture, yet he hath payed them both
for me, and fo hath difcharged me from the curfe,
and therefore I fear it not.

Neo. But, Sir, though I be a believer, and fo be
fet free from the curfe of the law, yet I fuppofe I
ought to endeavour to do whatfoever is required, and
to avoid whatfoever is forbidden in the law.

Evan. Yea, neighbour Neophytus, that you ought
indeed, for mind it, I pray you, thus ftands the cafe;
fo foon as any man doth truly believe, and fo is juftified
in the fight of God, then as the Holy Ghoft, from the

teſtimony of holy writ, doth warrant us to conceive; Jeſus Chriſt, or, which is all one, God in Chriſt, doth deliver unto him whatſoever is required and forbidden in the ten-commandments, ſaying, Col. ii. 14. Eph. ii 15. This hand-writing, even this law of commandments, which was againſt thee, and contrary to thee, whilſt it was in the hands of my father, as he ſtood in relation to thee as a Judge, and was not cancelled; but had the curſe or penalty annexed unto it, Iſa: xxxviii. 14. and ſo had power to convince, Heb. vii. 22. accuſe, condemn, and bind thee over to puniſhment; I, who undertook for thee, * and become thy ſurety, have paid the principal debt, and have alſo anſwered the forfeiture which did ly againſt thee, for the breach of that bond; and my Father hath delivered it into mine hands, and I have blotted out the curſe or penalty, ſo that one letter or tittle remains not for thee to ſee; yea, I have " taken it out of thy way, and faſtened it to my croſs;" yea, and torn it in pieces with the nails of my croſs, ſo that it is altogether fruſtrate, and hath no force at all againſt thee, yet notwithſtanding the matter contained in this law, even thoſe precepts and prohibitions which I have now delivered unto thee, being the mind and will of my Father, and the eternal and unchangeable rule of righteouſneſs, and that which is in my heart, Pſal. xl. 8. Yea, and that which I have promiſed to write in the hearts of all thoſe that are mine, Jer. xxxi. 33. Yea, and that which I have promiſed to make them yield willing obedience unto, Pſal. cx. 3. I and my Father do commend it unto thee, as that rule of obedience whereby thou art to expreſs thy love and thankfulneſs unto us for what we have done for thee. And therefore I will ſay no more unto thee but this, " If thou love me, keep my commandments," John xiv. 15. And thou art my friend, " If thou do whatſoever I command thee," John xv 14.

Neo.

* Elton on Col p. 311, 312.

Neo. But, Sir, doth God in Chrift require me to yield perfect obedience to all the ten commandments, according as you have this day expounded them?

Evan. I anfwer, yea: for though God in Chrift do not require of you, or any true believer, any obedience to the law at all, by way of fatisfaction to his juftice, for that Chrift hath fully done already; yet doth he require, that every true believer do purpofe, defire, and endeavour to do their beft to keep all the ten commandments, perfectly, according as I have this day expounded them; witnefs the faying of Chrift himfelf, Matth. v. 48. " Be ye therefore perfect, as your Father which is in heaven is perfect."

Neo But, Sir, do you think it poffible, that either I, or any believer elfe, fhould keep the commandments perfectly, according as you have this day expounded them?

Evan. O no! both you and I, and every believer elfe, have, and fhall have caufe to fay with the apoftle, Phil. iii. 12. " Not as though I had already attained, or were already perfect."

Neo. But will God in Chrift accept of my obedience, if it be not perfect?

Evan. Yea, neighbour Neophytus, you being a juftified perfon, and fo it not being in the cafe of juftification, but in the cafe of child-like obedience, I may, without fear of danger, fay unto you, God will accept the will for the deed, and " will fpare you as a man fpareth his own fon that ferveth him," Mal. iii. 18. Yea, " like as a father pitieth his children, fo the Lord will pity you, for he knoweth your frame, he remembereth that you are but duft," Pfal. ciii. 13, 14. Nay, he will not only fpare you and pity you, for what you do not, but he will alfo reward you for what you do.

Neo. Say you fo, Sir, then I befeech you tell me what this reward fhall be.

Evan.

Evan. Why if there be degrees of glory in heaven, as fome both godly and learned have conceived there is, then I tell you that the more obedient you are unto the law, the more fhall be your glory in heaven; but becaufe degrees of glory are difputable, I cannot affure you of that.

Howbeit this you may affure yourfelf, that the more obedience you yield unto the ten commandments, the more you pleafe your moft gracious God and loving Father in Chrift, 1 Sam. xv. 20 And the more your confcience witneffeth that you pleafe God, the more quiet you fhall feel it to be, and the more inward peace you fhall have, according to that of the Pfalmift, " Great peace have they that love thy law, and nothing fhall offend them." For though faith in the blood of Chrift hath made your peace with God as a Judge, yet obedience muft keep your peace with him as a Father ; yea, the more your confcience witneffeth that you do that which pleafeth God, the more encouragement you will have, and the more confidently you will approach towards God in prayer. " Beloved, faith the loving apoftle, if our hearts condemn us not, then have we boldnefs towards God," 1 John iii. 21 For tho' faith in the blood of Chrift takes away that guilt which fubjecteth you to the legal curfe, yet obedience muft take away that guilt which fubjecteth you to a fatherly difpleafure. Furthermore, you are to know, that the m ∙ e obedience you yield unto the ten commandments, the more temporal bleffings, outward profperity, and comfort of this life (in the ordinary courfe of God's dealing) you fhall have : O ! faith the Lord, " That my people had hearkened unto me, and Ifrael had walked in my ways, he fhould foon have fed them with the fineft of the wheat, and with honey out of the rock, fhould I have fatisfied thee." Befides the more obedience you yield unto the ten commandments, the more glory will you bring to God, according to that of

our

our Saviour, John xv 8. "Herein is my Father glorified, that ye bear much fruit" To conclude, the more obedience you yield unto the ten command: ments, the more good you will do unto others, according to that of the apoftle, Tit. iii 8. "This is a faithful faying,. and thefe things I will that thou affirm conftantly, that they which have believed in Chrift, might be careful to maintain good works, thefe things are good and profitable unto men."

Neo. But, Sir, what if I fhould not purpofe, defire, and endeavour to yield obedience to all the ten commandments, as you fay the Lord requireth; what then?

Evan. Why then, although it is true you have no caufe to fear that God will proceed againft you as a wrathful judge proceedeth againft a malefactor; yet have you caufe to fear that he will proceed againft you as a difpleafed father doth againft an offending child; that is to fay, although you have no caufe to fear that he will unjuftify you, and unfon you, and deprive you of your heavenly inheritance, and inflict the penalty of the law of works upon you, and fo condemn you; for faith the apoftle, "There is no condemnation to them that are in Chrift Jefus," Rom. viii. 1. Yet have you caufe to fear that he will hide his fatherly face, and withdraw the light of his countenance from you; and that your confcience will be ever accufing and difquieting of you, which if it do, then will you draw back, and be afraid to afk any thing of God in prayer; for even as a child whofe confcience tells him that he hath angered and difpleafed his father, and will be unwilling to come into his father's prefence, efpecially to afk of him any thing that he wanteth, even fo it will be with you; and befides, you fhall be fure to be whipped and fcourged with many bodily and temporal chaftifements and corrections, according to that which is faid concerning Jefus Chrift and his

feed,

feed even true believers, and juſtified perſons, Pſal. lxxxix. 30, 31, 32, 33. "If his children forſake my law, and walk not in my judgments; if they break my ſtatutes, and walk not in my commandments, then will I viſit their tranſgreſſions with the rod, and their iniquities with ſtripes. Nevertheleſs, my loving kindneſs will I not utterly take from him, nor ſuffer my faithfulneſs to fail."

Wherefore, neighbour Neophytus, to apply theſe things a little more cloſely to you, and ſo to conclude, Let me exhort you when you come home, call to mind and conſider of every commandment, according as you have heard them this day expounded, and reſolve to endeavour yourſelf to do thereafter; and always take notice how and wherein you fail and come ſhort of doing what is required, and of avoiding what is forbidden; and eſpecially be careful to do this when you are called, to humble yourſelf before the Lord, in faſting and prayer, and upon occaſion of going to receive the ſacrament of the Lord's ſupper, and ſo ſhall you make a right uſe of the law.

Neo. And Sir, why would you have me more eſpecially to take notice of my ſins, when I am called to humble myſelf before the Lord in faſting and prayer?

Evan. Becauſe the more ſinful you ſee yourſelf to be, the more humble will your heart be; and the more humble your heart is, the more fit you will be to pray, and the more the Lord will regard your prayers; wherefore upon occaſion of ſome heavy and ſore affliction, either felt, or feared to come upon yourſelf, or ſome ſore judgment and calamity either felt, or feared to come upon the nation, or place where you live, the Lord calleth you to humble yourſelf, in faſting and prayer, then do you thereupon take occaſion to meditate and conſider ſeriouſly what duties are required, and what

what fins are forbidden in every one of the ten commandments, and then confider how many of thofe
duties you have omitted, and how many of thofe fins
you have committed; confider alfo the finful manner
of performing thofe duties you have performed, and
the bafe and finful felf-ends which you have had in
the performance of them; confider alfo how many
finful corruptions there are in your heart, which break
not forth in your life, and the difpofition of heart
which you have naturally to every fin which you do
not commit; and then confider that although the fins
which you do now commit, are not a tranfgreffion of
the law of works, becaufe you are not now under the
law, Rom. vi. 14. yet are they a tranfgreffion of the
law of Chrift, becaufe you are ftill under that law,
1 Cor. ix. 31. And though they be not committed
againft God, as ftanding in relation to you as a wrathful Judge, yet have they been committed againft him
as he ftands in relation to you, as a merciful and loving
Father; and though they fubject you not to the wrath
of a judge, nor to the penalty of the law of works,
yet they fubject you to the anger and difpleafure of a
loving Father, and to the penalty of the law of Chrift.

Whereupon do you draw near unto God by prayer,
faying unto him after this manner:

O Merciful and loving Father, I do acknowledge
that the fins which I did commit before I was a
believer, were a tranfgreffion of the law of works,
becaufe I was then under that law; yea, and that
they were committed againft thee, as thou ftoodeft in
relation to me as a Judge, and that therefore thou
mighteft moft juftly have inflicted the curfe or penalty
of the law of works upon me, and fo have caft me to
hell; but feeing that thou haft enabled me to believe
the gofpel, viz. That thou haft been pleafed to give
thine own Son Jefus Chrift to undertake for me, to
be,

become my surety, to take my nature upon him, and
to be made under the law, to redeem me from under
the law.*, and to be made a curse for me, to redeem
me from the curse, and to reconcile me unto thee by
his death. Now, I know it ftandeth not with thy
juftice to proceed againft me by virtue of the law of
works, and fo to caft me to hell. Neverthelefs,
Father, I know that the fins which I have committed
fince I did believe, have been a tranfgreffion of the
law of Chrift, becaufe I am ftill under that law : yea,
and I do acknowledge that they have been committed
againft thee, even againft thee, my moft gracious,
merciful and loving Father in Jefus Chrift, and that
it is therefore meet thou fhouldeft exprefs thy fatherly
anger and difpleafure towards me, for thefe fins
which thy law hath difcovered unto me, in bringing
this affliction upon me, or this judgment upon the
place or nation wherein I live : howbeit, Father, I
knowing that thy fatherly anger towards thy children
is never mixed with hatred, but always with love;
and that in afflicting of them, thou never intendeft any
fatisfaction to thine own juftice, but their amendment,
even the purging out the remainders of thofe finful
corruptions which are ftill in them, and the conform-
ing of them to thine own image ; I therefore come
unto thee this day to humble myfelf before thee, and
to call upon thy name, not for any need nor power
that I do conceive I have to fatisfy thy juftice, or to
appeafe thy eternal wrath, and to free my foul from
hell ; for that I do believe Chrift hath fully done for
me already : but I do it in hopes thereby to pacify thy
fatherly anger and difpleafure towards me, and to
obtain the removal of this affliction or judgment which
I feel or fear : wherefore I befeech thee to pardon
and forgive thefe my fins, which have been the
procuring caufe thereof ; yea, I pray thee not only to
pardon them, but alfo to purge them, that fo this may
be

* Gal. iv. 4. and vii. 13. Rom. v. 10.

be all the fruit. even the taking away of fin, and making me partaker of thy holinefs; and then, Lord, remove this affliction or judgment when thy will and pleafure is.

And thus have I fhewed you the reafon why I would have you more efpecially to take notice of your fins; when you come to humble yourfelf before the Lord in fafting and prayer.

Neo. And, Sir, why would you have me to take notice of my fins, upon occafion of my going to receive the facrament of the Lord's fupper?

Evan. Becaufe that the more finful you fee yourfelf to be, the more need you will fee yourfelf to have of Chrift; and the more need you fee yourfelf to have of Chrift, the more you will prize Chrift, and the more you prize Chrift, the more you will defire him, and the more you do defire Chrift, the more fit and worthy receiver you will be.

Wherefore when you are determined to receive the facrament, then take occafion to examine yourfelf as the apoftle doth exhort you; behold the face of your fouls in the glafs of the law, lay your heart and life to that rule, as I directed you before; then think with yourfelf, and commune with your own heart, faying in your heart after this manner, Though I do believe that all thefe my fins are for Chrift's fake freely and fully pardoned and forgiven, fo as that I fhall never be condemned for them, yet do I not fo fully and comfortably believe it as I ought, but am fometimes apt to queftion it: and befides, though my fins have not dominion over me, yet I feel them too prevalent in me, and I would fain have more power and ftrength againft them; I would fain have my graces ftronger, and my corruptions weaker; wherefore I knowing that Chrift in the facrament of the Lord's fupper doth feal up unto me the affurance of the pardon and forgivennefs of all my fins; yea,

and

and knowing that the death and bloodfhed of Jefus
Chrift which is there reprefented, hath in it both a
pardoning and a purging virtue; yea, and knowing
that the more fully I do apprehend Chrift by faith,
the more ftrength of grace, and power againft corruptions I fhall feel. Wherefore I will go to partake
cf that ordinance, in hope that I fhall there meet with
Jefus Chrift, and apprehend him more fully by faith,
and fo obtain both more affurance of the pardon of
my fins, and the more power and ftrength againft
them, which the Lord grant you for Chrift's fake.
And thus having alfo fhewed you the reafon why I
would have you more efpecially to take notice of your
fins before you come to receive the facrament of the
Lord's fupper, I will now take my leave of you:
for my other occafions do call me away.

Neo. Well, Sir, I do acknowledge, that you have
taken great pains both with my neighbour and me
this day, for the which I do give you many thanks.
And yet I muft intreat you to do the like courtefy
for me which you promifed my neighbour Nomologifta,
and that is, at your leifure, to write me out a copy of
the conference we have had this day.

Evan. Well, neighbour Neophytus, I fhall think
of it, and it may be accomplifh your defire. And fo
the God of peace be with you.

Neo. The Lord be with you, Sir.

APPENDIX.

APPENDIX.

The Difference between the LAW *and the* GOSPEL.

THere is little more in all this to be attributed unto me than the very gathering and composing of it; that which I aim at, and intend therein, is to shew unto myself, and others that shall read it, the difference betwixt the law and the gospel, a point (as I conceive) very needful for us, to be well instructed in; and that for these reasons:

First, Because, if we be ignorant thereof, we shall be very apt to mix and mingle them together, and so to confound the one with the other: which, as Luther on the Galatians, p. 31. truly faith, doth more mischief than man's reason can conceive; and therefore he doth advise all Christians (in the case of justification) to separate the law and the gospel as far asunder as heaven and earth are separated.

Secondly, Because, if we knew aright how to distinguish betwixt them, the knowledge thereof will afford us no small light towards the true understanding of the scripture, and will help us to reconcile all such places, both in the Old and New Tastament, as seem to be repugnant; yea, and it will help us to judge aright of cases of conscience, and quiet our own conscience in time of trouble and distress; yea, and we shall thereby be enabled to try the truth and falsehood of all doctrines: wherefore, for our better instruction in the point, we are first of all to consider and take notice what the law is, and what the gospel is.

Now the law is a doctrine partly known by nature, teaching us that there is a God, and what God is, and what he requireth us to do, binding all reasonable

crea-

creatures to perfect obedience, both internal and external, promising the favour of God, and everlasting life to all those who yield perfect obedience thereunto, and denouncing the curse of God and everlasting damnation to all those who are not perfectly correspondent thereunto.

But the gospel is a doctrine revealed from heaven, by the Son of God, presently after the fall of mankind into sin and death, and afterwards manifested more clearly and fully to the patriarchs and prophets, to the evangelists and apostles, and by them spread abroad to others; wherein freedom from sin, the curse of the law, the wrath of God, death and hell, is freely promised for Christ's sake unto all those who truly believe on his name.

2*dly*, We are to consider what the nature and office of the law is, and what the nature and office of the gospel is.

Now the nature and office of the law is, to shew unto us our sin, Rom. iii 20. our condemnation and death, Rom. ii. 1. and vii. 10. But the nature and office of the gospel is to shew unto us that Christ hath taken away our sin, John i. 29. and that he also is our redemption and life, Col. i. 14. and iii. 4

So that the law is a word of wrath, Rom. iv. 14.

But the gospel is a word of peace, Eph. ii. 17.

3*dly*, We are to consider where we may find the law written, and where we may find the gospel written.

Now we shall find this law and this gospel written, and recorded in the writings of the prophets, evangelists and apostles, namely, in the books called the Old and New Testaments, or the scripture. For indeed the law and the gospel are the chief general heads which comprehend all the doctrine of the scriptures; yet are we not to think that these two doctrines are to be distinguished by the books and leaves of the scriptures, but by the diversity of God's Spirit speaking

in

in them : we are not to take and underftand whatfoever is contained in the compafs of the Old Teftament
to be only and merely the word and voice of the law,
neither are we to think that whatfoever is contained
within the compafs of the books called the New Teftament is only and merely the voice of the gofpel ; for
fometimes in the Old Teftament, God doth fpeak
comfort, as he comforted Adam, with the voice of the
gofpel ; fometimes alfo in the New Teftament he
doth threaten and terrify, as when Chrift threatened
the Pharifees. In fome places again, Mofes and the
prophets do play the evangelifts ; infomuch that Hierom
doubteth whether he fhould call Ifaiah a prophet or an
evangelift In fome places likewife Chrift and the
apoftles fupply the part of Mofes : Chrift himfelf until
his death, was under the law ; which law he came not
to break but to fulfil ; fo his fermons made to the
Jews, for the moft part, run all upon the perfect
doctrine, and works of the law, fhewing and teaching
what we ought to do by the right law of juftice, and
what danger enfueth in the not-performance of the
fame. All which places, though they be contained in
the book of the New Teftament, yet are they to be
referred to the doctrine of the law, ever having included in them a privy conception of repentance, and
faith in Chrift Jefus. As for example, where Chrift
thus preacheth, " Bleffed are the pure in heart, for
they fhall fee God," Matth. v. 8. Again, " Except
ye be converted, and become as little children, ye fhall
not enter into the kingdom of heaven," Mat. xviii. 3.
And again, " He that doth the will of my Father
which is in heaven, fhall enter into the kingdom of
heaven," Matth. vii. 22. And again, the parable of
the wicked fervant caft into prifon for not forgiving
his fellow, Matth. xviii. 30. the cafting of the rich
glutton into hell, Luke xvi. 23. and again, " He that
denieth me before men, I will deny him before my
Father which is in heaven," Luke xii. 9. with divers

Qq 3

fuch

such other places; all which, I say, do appertain to the doctrine of the law.

Wherefore in the fourth place, we are to take heed when we read the scriptures, we do not take the gospel for the law, nor the law for the gospel, but labour to discern and distinguish the voice of the one from the other : and if we would know when the law speaketh, and when the gospel speaketh, let us consider, and take this for a note, That when in scripture there is any moral work commanded to be done, either for the eschewing of punishment, or upon promise of any reward, temporal or eternal; or else when any promise is made, with the condition of any work to be done, which is commanded in the law, there is to be understood the voice of the law.

Contrariwise, where the promise of life and salvation is offered unto us freely, without any condition of any law, either natural, ceremonial, or moral, or any work done by us ; all those places, whether we read them in the Old Testament, or in the New, are to be referred to the voice and doctrine of the gospel, yea, and all these promises of Christ's coming in the flesh, which we read in the Old Testament, yea, and all these promises in the New Testament, which offer Christ upon condition of our believing on his name, are properly called the voice of the gospel, because they have no condition of our mortifying annexed unto them, but only faith to apprehend and receive Jesus Christ, as it is written, Rom. iii. 22. " For the righteousness of God, which is by faith of Jesus Christ unto all, and upon all that believe," &c.

Briefly then, if we would know when the law speaketh, and when the gospel speaketh, either in reading the word, or in hearing it preached ; and if we would skilfully distinguish the voice of the one from the voice of the other, we must consider,

Law.

Law. That the law faith, Thou art a finner, and therefore thou fhalt be damned," Rom. vii. 2. 2 Theff. ii. 12.

Gofp. But the gofpel faith, No, " Chrift Jefus came into the world to fave finners ;" and therefore " believe on the Lord Jefus Chrift, and thou fhalt be faved," 1 Tim. i. 15. Acts xvj. 31.

Law. Again the law faith, " Knoweft thou not that the unrighteous fhall not inherit the kingdom of God : be not deceived," &c. 1 Cor. vi. 9. And therefore thou being a finner, and not righteous, fhalt not inherit the kingdom of God.

Gofp. But the gofpel faith, " God hath made Chrift to be fin for thee, who knew no fin ; that thou mighteft be made the righteoufnefs of God in him, who is THE LORD THY RIGHTEOUSNESS, Jer. xxiii. 6.

Law. Again the law faith, " Pay me that which thou oweft me, or elfe I will caft thee into prifon," Matth. xvii. 28, 30.

Gofp. But the gofpel faith, " Chrift gave himfelf a ranfom for thee, 1 Tim ii 6 And fo is made redemption unto thee," 1 Cor. i. 30.

Law. Again the law faith, " Thou haft not continued in all that I require of thee, and therefore art accurfed," Deut. xxvii. 6.

Gofp But the gofpel faith, " Chrift hath redeemed thee from the curfe of the law, being made a curfe for thee," Gal. iii. 13.

Law. Again the law faith, " Thou art become guilty before God, and therefore thou fhalt not efcape the judgment of God." Rom. iii 19. and ii 3.

Gofp. But the gofpel faith, " The Father judgeth no man, but hath committed all judgment to the Son," John v. 12.

And now, knowing rightly how to diftinguifh between the law and the gofpel, we muft, in the fifth place take heed that we break not the orders between
thefe

thefe two, in applying the law where the gofpel is
to be applied, either to ourfelves or to others. For
albeit the law and the gofpel, in order of doctrine,
are many times to be joined together; yet, in the-
cafe of juftification, the law muft be utterly feparated
from the gofpel.

Therefore, whenfoever, or wherefoever any doubt
or queftion arifeth of falvation, or our juftification
before God, there the law, and all good works,
muft be utterly excluded, and ftand apart, that grace
may appear free, and that the promife and faith
may ftand alone; whi.h faith alone, without law or
works, bringeth thee in particular to thy juftification
and falvation thro' the mere promife and free grace of
God in Chrift; fo that I fay, in the action and office of
juftification, both law and works are to be utterly
excluded and exempted, as things which have nothing
to do in that behalf. The reafon is this; for, feeing
that all our redemption fpringeth out from the body
of the Son of God crucified, there is there nothing
that can ftand us in ftead, but that only wherewith
the body of Chrift is apprehended. Now, forafmuch
as neither the law nor works, but faith only is the
thing which apprehendeth the body and paffion of
Jefus Chrift; therefore faith only is that matter
which juftifieth a man before God, through the
ftrength of that object Jefus Chrift, which it apprehendeth; like as the brazen ferpent was the object
only of the Ifraelites looking, and not of their hands
working; by the ftrength of which object, through the
promife of God, immediately proceeded health to the
beholders, fo the body of Chrift being the object of
our faith, ftriketh righteoufnefs to our fouls, not
through working, but through believing.

Wherefore, when any perfon, or perfons do feel
themfelves oppreffed and terrified with the burden
of their fins, and feel themfelves with the majefty of
the law and judgment of God terrified and oppreffed,

out-

outweighed and thrown down into utter difcomfort; almoft to the pit of hell, as happeneth fometimes to God's own dear fervants, who have foft and timorous confciences; when fuch fouls, I fay, do read or hear any fuch place of fcripture which appertaineth to the law, let them then think, and affure themfelves, that fuch places do not appertain or belong to them ; nay, let not fuch only who are thus deeply humbled and terrified, do this, but alfo let every one that doth but make any doubt or queftion of their own falvation, through the fight and fenfe of their fin, do the like.

And to this end and purpofe, let them confider and mark well the end why the law was given, which was not to bring us to falvation, nor to make us good, and fo to procure God's love and favour towards us ; but rather to declare and convict our wickednefs, and make us feel the danger thereof ; to this end and purpofe, that we feeing our condemnation, and being in ourfelves confounded, may be driven thereby to have our refuge in the Son of God, in whom alone is to be found our remedy. And when this is wrought in us, then the law hath accomplifhed its end in us; and therefore it is now to give place unto Jefus Chrift, who, as the apoftle faith, " is the end of the law," Rom. x 3. Let every true convicted perfon then, who fears the wrath of God, death and hell, when they hear, or read, any fuch place of fcripture, as do appertain to the law, not think the fame to belong to them, no more than a mourning-weed belongeth to a marriage-feaft ; and therefore, removing utterly out of their minds all cogitations of the law, all fear of judgment and condemnation, let them only fet be-fore their eyes the gofpel, to wit, the glad and joyful tidings of Chrift. the fweet comforts of God's promifes, free forgivennefs of fins in Chrift, grace, redemp-tion, liberty, pfalms, thanks, finging, a paradife of fpiritual jocundity, and nothing elfe : thinking thus within themfelves, the law hath now done its office

in

in me, and therefore muſt now give place to its better, that is, it muſt needs give place to Jeſus Chriſt. the Son of God, who is my Lord and Maſter, Fulfiller and Accompliſher of the law.

Laſtly, As we muſt take heed and beware that we apply not the law where the goſpel is to be applied; ſo muſt we alſo take heed and beware that we apply not the goſpel where the law is to be applied: let us not apply the goſpel inſtead of the law; for as the other before was even as much as to put on a mourning-gown at a marriage-feaſt, ſo this is but even the caſting of pearls before ſwine, wherein is great abuſe amongſt many; for commonly it is ſeen, that theſe proud ſelf-conceited and unhumbled perſons, theſe worldly Epicures and ſecure Mammoniſts, to whom the doctrine of the law doth properly appertain, do yet notwithſtanding put it away from them, and bleſs themſelves with the ſweet promiſes of the goſpel, ſaying, "They hope they have as good a ſhare in Chriſt as the beſt of them all, for God is merciful, and the like." And contrariwiſe, the other contrite and bruiſed hearts, to whom belongeth not the law, but the joyful tidings of the goſpel, for the moſt part receive and apply to themſelves the terrible voice and ſentence of the law. Whereby it cometh to paſs, that many do rejoice when they ſhould mourn; and, on the other ſide, many do fear and mourn when they ſhould rejoice. Wherefore, to conclude, in private uſe of life. let every perſon diſcreetly diſcern between the law and the goſpel, and apply to himſelf that which belongeth unto him; let the man or the woman who did never yet to any purpoſe (eſpecially in the time of health and proſperity) think of, or conſider their latter end, that did never yet fear the wrath of God, nor death, nor devil, nor hell, but hath lived, and do ſtill live a jocund and merry life; let them apply the curſe of the law to themſelves, for to them

it

it belongeth ; yea, and let all your civil honeft men and women, who it may be, do fometimes think of their latter end, and have had fome kind of fear of the wrath of God, death and hell, in their hearts, and yet have falved up the fore with a plaifter made with their own civil righteoufnefs, with a falve compounded of their outward conformity to the duties contained in the law, their freedom from grofs fins, and their upright and juft dealing with men, let thefe hearken to the voice of the law, when it faith, " Curfed is every one that continueth not in all things which are written in the book of the law to do them :" but let all felf-denying, fearful, trembling fouls, apply the gracious and fweet promifes of God in Chrift unto themfelves, and rejoice becaufe their names are written in the book of life.

THE END.

THE

TABLE.

R r

F I N I S.

TWELVE
QUERIES,

Propofed by the COMMISSION of the GENERAL ASSEMBLY of the CHURCH of SCOTLAND, 1721. to Mr JAMES HOG, and Eleven other Minifters of the Gofpel, hereunto fubfcribing, who had given in a Reprefentation to faid Affembly in favours of the *Marrow of Modern Divinity* :—With their ANSWERS to the QUERIES.

QUERY I. W*HETHER are there any precepts in the gofpel, that were not actually given before the gofpel was revealed?*

ANSWER. The paffages in our reprefentation, marked out to us, for the grounds of this query, are thefe; "The gofpel-doctrine, known only by a new revelation after the fall. Par. 2. Of the fame difmal tendency we apprehend to be the declaring of that diftinction of the law, as it is the law of works, and as it is the law of Chrift, as the author applies it, to be altogether groundlefs, Par. 5. The erroneous doctrine of juftification, for fomething wrought in, or done by the finner, as his righteouf-nefs, or keeping the new and gofpel-law. Par. penult. Now, leaving it to others to judge, if thefe paffages gave any juft occafion to this queftion, we anfwer,

1mo, In the gofpel, taken ftrictly, and as contradiftinct from the law, for a doctrine of grace, or good news from heaven, of help in God through Jefus Chrift, to loft, felf deftroying crea-tures of Adam's race; or the glad tidings of a Saviour, with life and falvation in him to the chief of finners, there are no precepts; all thefe, the command to believe, and repent. not excepted, belonging to, and flowing from the law, which faftens the new duty on us, the fame moment the gofpel reveals the new object.

That in the gofpel, taken ftrictly, there are no precepts, to us feems evident from t', holy fcriptures. In the firft revelation of it, made in thefe words, "The feed of the woman fhall bruife the head of the ferpent," Gen. iii. 15. we find no precept but a promife, containing glad tidings of a Saviour, with grace, mercy, life, and falvation in him, to loft finners of Adam's family.

And

And the gospel preached unto Abraham, namely, " In thee, (i e. in thy seed, which is Christ) shall all nations be blessed," Gal. iii. 8. compared with Gen. xii. 3. xxi. 18. Acts iii. 25. is of the same nature. The good tidings of great joy to all people, of a Saviour born in the city of David, who is Christ the Lord, brought and proclaimed from heaven by the angels, Luke i. 10, 11. we take to have been the gospel, strictly and properly so called, yet is there no precept in these tidings. We find likewise, the gospel-of peace. and glad tidings of good things, are in scripture convertible terms, Rom. x. 15. And the word of the gospel, which Peter spoke to the Gentiles, that they might believe, was no other than peace by Jesus Christ, crucified, risen. and exalted to be judge of quick and dead, with remission of sins through his name, to be received by every one believing in him, Acts xv. 7. xx. 36,—43. Much more might be added on this head, which, that we be not tedious, we pass. See Luke iv. 18. compared with Isa. xli. 1, 2. Acts xx. 24. 2 Tim. i. 10. Of the same mind, as to this point, we find the body of reformed divines; as, to instance in a few, Calvin, Chamier, Pemble, Wendelin, Alting, the professors of Leyden, Witsius, Maftrich, Marcsius, Troughton, Essenius.

That all precepts (these of faith and repentance not excepted) belong to, and are of the law. is no less evident to us : For the law of creation, or of the Ten Commandments, which was given to Adam in paradise, in the form of a covenant of works, requiring us to believe whatever God should reveal, or promise, and to obey whatever he should command ; all precepts whatsoever must be virtually and really included in it : So that there never was, nor can be an instance of duty owing by the creature to God, not commanded in the moral law, if not directly and expresly, yet indirectly and by consequence. The same first command, for instance, which requires us to take the Lord for our God, to acknowledge his essential verity, and sovereign authority ; to love, fear, and trust in JEHOVAH, after what manner soever he shall be pleased to reveal himself to us ; and likewise to grieve and mourn for his dishonour, or displeasure ; requires believing in JEHOVAH, our righteousness, as soon as ever he is revealed to us as such, and sorrowing after a godly sort for the transgression of his holy law, whether by one's self, or by others. It is true, Adam was not actually obliged to believe in a Saviour, till, being lost and undone, a Saviour was revealed. to him ; but the same command that bound him to trust and depend on, and to believe the prom. of God Creator, no doubt, obliged him to believe in God Redeemer, when revealed: Nor was Adam obliged to sorrow for sin ere it was committed : But this same law that bound him to have a sense of the evil of sin in its nature and effects, to hate, loath, and flee from sin, and

and to resolve against it, and for all holy obedience; and to have a due apprehension of the goodness of God, obliged him also to mourn for it, whenever it should fall out. And we cannot see how the contrary doctrine is consistent with the perfection of the law; for if the law be a complete rule of all moral, internal and spiritual, as well as external and ritual obedience, it must require faith and repentance, as well as it does all other good works: and that it does indeed require them, we can have no doubt of, when we consider, That without them all other religious performances are in God's account as good as nothing; and that sin being, as the scripture, 1 John iii. 4. and our own standards tell us, any want of conformity to, or transgression of the law of God, unbelief and impenitency must be so too: And if they be so, then must faith and repentance be obedience and conformity to the same law, which the former are a transgression of, or an inconformity unto; unbelief particularly, being a departing from the living God, Heb. iii. 12. is, for certain, forbidden in the first command; therefore faith must needs be required in the same command, Isa. xxvi. 4. according to a known rule. But what need we more, after our Lord has told us, That faith is one of the weightier matters of the law, Matth. xxiii. 23. And that it is not a second table duty, which is there meant, is evident to us, by comparing the parallel place in Luke, chap. xi 42. where, in place of FAITH, we have, " the love of God." As for repentance, in case of sin against God, it becomes naturally a duty; and though neither the covenant of works, or of grace admit of it, as any expiation of sin, or federal condition giving right to life, it is a duty included in every command, on the supposal of a transgression.

What moves us to be the more concerned for this point of doctrine, is, That if the law does not bind sinners to believe and repent, then we see not how faith and repentance, considered as works, are excluded from our justification before God; since in that case they are not works of the law, under which character all works are in scripture excluded from the use of justifying in the sight of God. And we call to mind, that on the contrary doctrine, Arminius laid the foundation of his rotten principles, touching sufficient grace, or rather natural power. " Adam," said he, " had not power to believe in Jesus Christ, because he needed him not; nor was he bound so to believe, because the law required it not: Therefore, since Adam by his fall did not lose it, God is bound to give every man power to believe in Jesus Christ." And Socinians, Arminians, Papists, and Baxterians, by holding the gospel to be a new, proper, preceptive law, with sanction, and thereby turning it into a real, though milder covenant of works, have confounded the law and the gospel, and brought works into the matter and cause of a sinner's

justi-

comfortable to himfelf, without the Creator's authority come
to him in that channel.

We are clear and full of the fame mind with our Confeffion,
" That the moral law of the Ten Commandments doth for ever
" bind all, as well juftified perfons as others, to the obedience
" thereof, not only in regard of the matter contained in it, but
" alfo in refpect of God the Creator, who gave it; and that
" Chrift doth not in the gofpel any way diffolve, but much
" ftrengthen this obligation." cap. 19   For, how can it lofe
any thing of its original authority, by being conveyed to the
believer in fuch a fweet and bleffed channel, as the hand of
Chrift, fince both he himfelf is the fupreme God and Creator,
and fince the authority, majefty, and fovereignty of the Father
is in his Son, he being the fame in fubftance, equal in power
and glory? " Beware of him, (fays the Lord unto Ifrael, concerning Chrift the angel of the covenant) and obey his voice,
provoke him not: For my name is in him," Exod xxiii. 21.
that is, as we underftand it, my authority, fovereignty, and
other adorable excellencies, yea, the whole fulnefs of the Godhead is in him, and in him only will I be ferved and obeyed.
And then it follows, " But if thou fhalt indeed obey his voice,
and do all that I fpeak,"- ver. 22.   The name of the Father is
fo in him, he is fo of the fame nature with his Father, that his
voice is the Father's voice; " If thou obey his voice, and do all
that I fpeak."

We defire to think and fpeak honourably of him, whofe name
is " Wonderful, Counfellor, the mighty God, the Everlafting
Father, and the Prince of Peace."   And it cannot but exceedingly grate our ears, and grieve our fpirits, to find fuch doctrines
or pofitions vented in this church, efpecially at a time when the
Arian herefy is fo prevalent in our neighbour nations, as have
an obvious tendency to darken and difparage his divine authority, as that, " If a believer ought not to receive the law of the
" Ten Commands at the hand of God, as he is Creator out of
" Chrift, then he is not under its obligation, as it was delivered
" by God the Creator, but is loofed from all obedience to it,
" as it was enacted by the authority of the Lord Creator; and
" that it is injurious to the infinite majefty of the Sovereign
" Lord Creator, and to the honour of his holy law, to reftrict
" the believer to receive the Ten Commands only at the hand
" of Chrift." What can be more injurious to the infinite
majefty of the Sovereign Lord. Redeemer, by whom all things
were created that are in heaven and in earth, vifible and invifible,
whetherthey be thrones or dominions, principalities or powers,
than to fpeak as if the Creator's authority was not in him; or,
as if the receiving the Creator's law from Chrift did loofe men
from obedience to it, as enacted by the authority of the Father.

We

Wo unto us, if this doctrine be the truth; for so should we be brought back to consuming fire indeed: For, out of Christ, "He that made us, will have no mercy on us; nor will he that "formed us, shew us any favour." We humbly conceive, the Father does not reckon himself glorified, but contemned by Christians offering obedience to him as Creator out of Christ: Nor does the offering to deal with him after this sort, or to teach others so, discover a due regard to the mystery of Christ revealed in the gospel; for it is the will of the Father, the Sovereign Lord Creator, That all men should honour the Son, even as they honour himself; and that all, or in, the name of Jesus, every knee should bow; and that every tongue should confess Jesus Christ is Lord, to the glory of God the Father, who having in these last days spoken unto us by his Son, by whom also he made the world, and with an audible voice from heaven hath said, ' This is my beloved Son in whom I am well-pleased; hear ye him." We're it not we would be thought tedious, Perkins, Durham, Owen, and others, might have been heard on this head. But we proceed to

Query III. *Doth the annexing of a promise of life, and a threatning of death to a precept, make it a covenant of works?*

We answer, as in our representation, That the promise of life and threatning of death, superadded to the law of the Creator, made it a covenant of works to our first parents, PROPOSED: And their own consent, which sinless creatures could not refuse, made it a covenant of works: ACCEPTED. " A law, saith the " judicious Durham, doth necessarily imply no more, than " 1st, To direct. 2dly, To command; enforcing that obedience " by authority. A covenant doth further necessarily imply " promises made upon some conditions or threatnings added, if " such a condition be not performed. Now, says he, this law " may be considered without the consideration of a covenant; " for it was free to God to have added, or not to have added " promises; and the threatnings, upon supposition the law had " been kept, might never have taken effect." (Treatise on the commands, page 4 quarto edit.) From whence it is plain, in the judgment of this great divine, the law of nature was turned into a covenant by the addition of a promise of life, and threatning of death. Of the same mind is Burgess, and the London ministers, Vindiciæ Legis, page 61. " There are only " two things which go to the essence of a law; and that is, " 1mo, Direction. 2do, Obligation. 1mo, Direction, therefore " a law is a rule; hence the law of God is compared to light. " 2do, Obligation; for therein lieth the essence of sin, that it
break-

" breaketh this law, which fuppofes the obligatory foree of it.
" In the next place, there are two confequents of the law, which
" are AD BENE ESSE, that the law may be the better obeyed;
" and this indeed turneth the law into a covenant. 1ft, The
" fanction of it, by way of promife, that is a mere free thing:
" God, by reafon of that dominion which he had over man,
" might have commanded his obedience, and yet never made
" a promife of eternal life unto him. And, adly, As for the
" other confequent act of the law, to curfe and punifh, this is
" but an accidental act; not neceffary to a law; for it comes
" in upon fuppofition of tranfgreffion ——— A law is a complete
" law, obliging, though it do not actually curfe; as in the
" confirmed angels, it never had any more than obligatory and
" mandatory acts upon them: For that they were under a law,
" is plain, becaufe otherwife they could not have finned; for
" where there is no law, there is no tranfgreffion."

Tho' there is no ground from our reprefentation to add more
on this head, yet we may fay, That a promife of life made to a
precept of doing, that is in confideration, or upon condition of
one's doing, (be the doing more or lefs, it is all one, the divine
will in the precept being the rule in this cafe) is a covenant of
works. And as to believers in Chrift, tho' in the gofpel,
largely taken, we own there are promifes of life, and threatnings
of death, as well as precepts; and that godlinefs hath the
promife, not only of this life, but of that which is to come,
annexed to it, in the order of the covenant; yet we are clear,
no promife of life is made to the performance of precepts, nor
eternal death threatned, in cafe of their failing whatfoever in
performing; elfe fhould their title to life be founded, not entirely
on Chrift, and his righteoufnefs imputed to them, but on fomething in, or done by themfelves: And their after fins fhould
again actually bring them under vindictive wrath, and the curfe
of the law; which upon their union with Chrift, who was made
a curfe for them, to redeem them from under it, they are, according to fcripture, Rom. vi. 14, 15. Rom. viii. 1. Gal. iii. 13,
4, 5. and our Confeffion, Chap. 20. § 2. Chap. 11. § 5. for
ever delivered from. Hence we know of no fanction the law,
ftanding in the covenant of grace, hath with refpect to believers,
befides gracious rewards, all of them freely promifed on Chrift's
account, for their encouragement in obedience; and fatherly
chaftifement and difpleafure, in cafe of their not walking in his
commandments; Pfal lxxxix. 31, 33. 1 Cor. xi. 30, 32. Luke i. 20.
which to a believer are no lefs awful, and much more powerful,
reftraints from fin, than the profpect of the curfe and hell itfelf
would be. The Reverend Commiffion will not, we hope, grudge
to hear that eminent divine Mr PERKINS, in a few words, on
this head, who having put the objection, " In the gofpel there
                                                            " are

" are promises of life upon condition of our obedience, as
" Rom. viii. 13. " If ye through the Spirit, &c." Answers,
" The promises of the gospel are not made to the work, but to
" the worker; and to the worker, not for his work, but for
" Christ's sake according to his work. *e. g.* The promise of life
" is not made to the work of mortification, but to him that
" mortifies his flesh; and that not for his mortification, but
" because he is in Christ, and his mortification is the token and
" evidence thereof." On Gal. page 236. in Fol. This, as it
is the old protestant doctrine, so we take it to be the truth.
And as to the believer's total and final freedom from the curse
of the law, upon his union with Christ, protestant divines, particularly RUTHERFORD and OWEN, throughout their writings,
are full and clear on the head.

Query IV. *If the Moral Law, antecedent to its receiving the form of a covenant of works, had a threatning of
hell annexed to it ?*

ANSW Since the law of God never was, nor will ever in this
world be the stated rule, either of man's duty towards God, or
of God's dealing with man, but as it stands in one of the two
covenants of works and grace, we are at a loss to discover the
real usefulness of this query, as well as that foundation it hath
in our representation.

As to the intrinsical demerit of sin, we are clear, whether
there had ever been any covenant of works or not, it deserves
hell, even all that an infinitely holy and just God ever has or shall
inflict for it : Yet what behoved to have been the Creator's dis-
posal of the creature, in the supposed event of sin's entring,
without a covenant being made, we incline not here to dip into :
but, we reckon, it is not possible to prove a threatning of hell to
be inseparable from the law of creation, the obligation of which,
because resulting from the nature of God, and of the creature,
is eternal and immutable: for confirmed angels, glorified saints,
yea, and the human nature of Christ, are all of them naturally,
necessarily, and eternally obliged to love, obey, depend on, and
submit unto God, and to make him their blessedness, and ultimate end; but none, we conceive, will be peremptory in saying,
They have a threatning of hell annexed to the law they are
under. And we can by no means allow, That a believer,
delivered by Christ from the curse of the covenant of works. is
still obnoxious, upon every new transgression, to the threatning
of hell, supposed to be inseparably annexed to the law of creation, or of the ten commandments; which law every reasonable
creature must for ever be under, since this would in effect, be
no other than, after he is delivered from hell in one respect,

to

to bind him over to it in another. Whatever threatn'ng one may suppose belonged to the moral law of the ten commandments, antecedently to its receiving a covenant-form, all was, for certain, included in the sanction of the covenant of works: So that Christ, in bearing the curse of it; redeemed believers from the hell, vindictive wrath and curse, their sins in any sort deserved: the hand-writing, that was against them, he cancelled, tore to pieces, and nailed to his cross. Hence the threatning of hell, and the curse, are actually separated from the law of the ten commandments, which believers are under as a rule of life: And to hold otherwise, is the leading error, yea, the very spring and fountain-head of Antinomianism; on all which, Burgess, Rutherford, and others, may be heard.

Query V. *If it be peculiar to believers, to be free of the commanding power of the law, as a covenant of works?*

Answ. Though our saying, We cannot comprehend how the covenant of works, as such, continues to have a commanding power over believers, that covenant-form of it being done away in Christ with respect to them, (Par 4.) gives no sufficient foundation to this query, since we affirm nothing concerning any but believers, whose freedom from the commanding power of that covenant, the query seems, as much as we do, to allow of; We answer affirmatively: For, since it is only to believers the Spirit of God in scripture says " Ye are not under the law, (the main import of which phrase is, subjection to the commanding power of it, as a covenant) but under grace," Rom. vi 14. Gal iv. 5, 21 and since they only are, by virtue of their union with Christ actually freed from being under the law, by Christ's being made under it (*i. e.* under its command, as above; as well as under its curse) for them; and since, according to our Confession, cap. 19 § 6. it is the peculiar privilege of believers, which therefore unbelievers have no interest in, not to be under the law as a covenant of works, to be justified or condemned thereby; we can allow no other, besides believers, to be invested with that immunity.

All unbelievers within, as well as without the pale of the visible church, since they seek righteousness only by the works of the law, and are strangers to the covenant of grace, we always took to be debtors to the whole law, in their own persons: and thus their obligation under the do, or commanding power of that covenant, we took to be inviolably firm, till such time as by faith they had recourse to him, who " is the end of the law for righteousness to every one that believeth;" else we thought, and do still think, if their obligation to the command of that covenant be dissolved, merely by their living under an external gospel-

gospel dispensation, they would be cast quite loose from being under any covenant at all; contrary to the common received doctrine of the protestant churches, namely, That every person whatsoever is under one or other of the two covenants of works and grace: Nor could they, unless they be under the commanding power of the covenant of works, be ever found transgressors of the law of that covenant, by any actual sin of their own; nor be bound over anew under the covenant-curse thereby.

The covenant of works, it is true, is by the fall, weak and ineffectual, as a covenant, to give us life, by reason of our weakness, and disability to fulfil it, being antecedently sinners, and obnoxious to its curse; which no person can be, and yet at the same time have a right unto its promise. Hence, for any to seek life and salvation by it now, is no other than to labour after an impossibility; yet does it nevertheless continue in full force, as a law, requiring of all sinners, while they continue in their natural state, without taking hold, by faith, of Christ and the grace of the new covenant; requiring of them. we say, personal, and absolutely perfect obedience. and threatning death upon every the least transgression: From the commanding power of which law, requiring universal holiness in such rigour, as that on the least failure in substance, circumstance or degree, all is rejected, and we are determined transgressors of the whole law; believers, and they only, are freed, as we said above. " But to " suppose a person, says Doctor Owen, by any means freed " from the curse due unto sin; and then to deny, that, upon " the performance of the perfect sinless obedience which " the law requires, he should have right to the promise of " life thereby, is to deny the truth of God, and to reflect " dishonour upon his justice. Our Lord himself was justified " by the law; and it is immutably true, That he who does " the things of it, shall live in them." (On justification, page 345.) " It is true," adds the same author, " That God " did never formally and absolutely renew, or give again this " law, as a covenant of works, a second time; nor was there " any need that so he should do, unless it were declaratively " only: And so it was renewed at Sinai; for the whole of it, " being an emanation of eternal right and truth, it abides, and " must abide in full force for ever. Wherefore it is only so far " broke as a covenant, that all mankind having sinned against " the command of it, and so by guilt, with the impotency to " obedience, which ensued thereupon, defeated themselves of " any interest in its promise, and possibility of attaining any such " interest, they cannot have any benefit by it. But as to its " power to oblige all mankind unto obedience, and the un- " changeable truths of its promises and threatnings, it abides " the same as it was from the beginning." (Ibid.) " The

" introducing of another covenant, adds he again on the fame
" head, inconfiftent with, and contrary to it; does not inftantly
" free men from the law, as a covenant: For though a new
" law abrogates a former law inconfiftent with it, and frees all
" from obedience, it is not fo in a covenant, which operates
" not by fovereign authority; but becomes a covenant by
" confent of them with whom it is made. So there is no free-
" dom from the old covenant, by the conftitution of the new,
" till it be actually complied with: In Adam's covenant we
" muft abide under obligation to duty and punifhment, till by
" faith we be interefted in the new." (Ibid 351)

From all which it appears to be no cogent reafoning to fay,
If the unbeliever be under the commanding power of the covenant of works, then would he be under two oppofite commands
at once, viz. to feek a perfect righteoufnefs in his own perfon,
and to feek it alfo by faith in a furety: For, though the law
requires of us now, both active and paffive righteoufnefs in our
own perfons; and likewife, upon the revelation of Jefus Chrift
in the gofpel, as Jehovah our righteoufnefs, obliges us to believe
in, and fubmit to him as fuch; yet, as it is in many other cafes
of duties, the law requires both thefe of us, not IN SENSO
COMPOSITO, as they fay, but IN SENSO DIVISO. The law
is content to fuftain, and hold for good, the payment of a re-
fponfible furety, though itfelf provides none; and wils us,
being infolvent of ourfelves, chearfully, thankfully, and without
delay, to accept of the non-fuch favour offered unto us: But till
the finner, convinced of his undonenefs otherwife, accept of,
ufe and plead that benefit in his own behalf, the law will, and
does go on in its juft demands, and diligence againft him:
Having never had pleafure in the finful creature, by reafon of
our unfaithfulnefs, it can eafily admit of the marriage to another
hufband, upon a lawful divorce, after fair count and reckoning,
and full fatisfaction and reparation made for all the invafions
upon, and violations of the firft hufband's honour; but when
the finner, unwilling to bear of any fuch motion, ftill cleaves
to the law its firft hufband, what wonder the law in that cafe,
go on to ufe the finner as he deferves? In fhort, this pretended
abfurdity, at worft, amounts to no more than this, Make full
payment yourfelf, or find me good and fufficient payment by a
furety, till which time, I will continue to proceed againft you,
without mitigation or mercy. Wherefore, the unbeliever is
juftly condemned by the law, both becaufe he did not continue
in all things written in the book of the law to do them, and
becaufe he did not believe on the name of the Son of God.

Query VI.

Query VI. *If a sinner, being justified, has all things at once, that is necessary for salvation? And if personal holiness, and progress in holy obedience, is not necessary to a justified person's possession of glory, in case of his continuing in life after his justification?*

Ans. The ground of this query, marked out to us, in these words of holy Luther, " For in Christ I have all things at once; " neither need I any thing more, that is necessary unto salva-" tion." And to us it is evident, that this is the believer's plea, viz. Christ's most perfect obedience to the law for him, in answer unto its demand of good works for obtaining salvation, according to the tenor of the first covenant ; which plea the Representation alledges to be cut off, and condemned by the act of Assembly. Par. 6, 11. But without saying any thing of the old Popish reflection on the doctrine of free justification by faith without works, as it was taught by Luther and other reformers, or the hardship of having this question put to us, as if we had given ground of being suspected for enemies to gospel-holiness, which, our consciences bear us witness, is our great desire to have advanced in ourselves and others, as being fully persuaded, that without it neither they nor we shall see the Lord. We answer to the first part of the query,

That since a justified person, being passed from death to life, translated from the power of darkness, into the kingdom of God's dear Son, and blest with all spiritual blessings in Christ, is, by virtue of his union with him, brought into, and secured in a state of salvation; and therefore, in the language of the Holy Ghost, actually, though not completely, saved already; and since, in him, he has particularly a most perfect law-biding and law-magnifying righteousness, redemption in his blood, even the forgiveness of sins, peace with God, access, acceptance, wisdom, sanctification, everlasting strength, and, in one word, an over-flowing, ever-flowing fulness, from which, according to the order of the covenant, he does, and shall receive what-ever he wants : Hence, according to the scripture, in Christ all things are his, and in him he is complete. Considering, we say, these things, we think, a justified person has in Christ at once all things necessary to salvation, though of himself he has nothing.

To the second part of the query, we answer, That personal holiness, and justification being inseparable in the believer, we are unwilling, so much as the query does, to suppose their separation. Personal holiness we reckon so necessary to the possession of glory, or to a state of perfect holiness and happiness, as in the morning light to the noon-day warmth and brightness; as is a reasonable soul to a wise, healthy, strong and full-grown

man;

man; as an antecedent is to its conf quent; as a part is to the whole (for the difference betwixt a ſtate of grace and of glory, we. take to be gradual only, according to the uſual ſaving, " Grace is glory begun, and glory is grace in perfection.") So neceſſary again, as motion is to evidence life, or, in order to walking; not only habitual, but actual holineſs and progreſs in holy obedience, one continuing in life, we are cle r are ſo neceſſary, that without the ſame none can ſee the Lord. And as it is not only the beꞏliever's intereſt, but his neceſſary and indiſpenſible duty, to be ſtill going on " from ſtrength to ſtrengꞏh, " until he appear before the Lord in Zion ;" ſo the righteous, we believe, " will hold on his way, and he who is of clean " hands will grow ſtronger and ſtronger." For tho' the believer's progreſs in holy obedience, by reaſon of the many ſtops, inter-ruptions and aſſaults he frequently meets with from Satan, the world, and indwelling corr ption, is far from being alike at all times; " yet the path of the j ſt, though he frequently fall, will be as the ſhining light that ſhineth more and more unto the perfect day :" Tho' he may at times become " weary and faint in his mind ; yet ſhall he, by waiting on the Lord, renew his ſtrength, and mount up as with eagles wings &c." But ſtill the believer has all this in and from Chriſt : For, whence can our progreſs in holineſs come, but from the ſupply of his Spirit ? Our walking in holy obedience, and every good motion of ours, muſt be in him, and from him, who is the WAY and the LIFE, who is our head of iꞏfluences, and the fountain of our ſtrength, and who " works in us both to will and to do. Abide in me, ſays he, and I in you :— For without me ye can do noꞏhing. If a man abide not in men, he is caſt forth as a branch, and is withered."

But if the meaning of the query be, of ſuch a neceſſiꞏy of holy obedience, in order to the poſſeſſion of glory, as imports any kind of cauſuality we dare not anſwer in the affirmative : For, we cannot look on perſonal holineſs, or good works, as properly federal and conditional means of obtaining the poſſeſſion of heaven, tho' we own they are neceſſary to make us meet for it.

Query VII. *Is preaching the neceſſity of a holy life, in oraer to the obtaining of eternal happineſs, of dangerous conſꞏquence to the doctrine of free grace?*

Anſw. The laſt of the two clauſes of the eighth act of Aſſembly, being complained of in the Repreſentation, is the firſt and main ground of this query. Par. 16, 15. And e're we make anſwer to it, we crave leave to explain ourſelves more fully, as to the offence we conceive to be given by that act; Namely, That in oppoſition to, and in place of the believer's plea of Chriſt's active righteouſneſs, in anſwer to the law, demanding good works,

for

for obtaining falvation according to the tenor of the firſt covenant, cut off, as we apprehend, by the fifth act ; miniſters are
ordered, in the eighth act, to preach the neceſſity of our own
perſonal holineſs, in order to the obtaining of everlaſting happineſs. As alſo, That our inherent holineſs ſeems to be put too
much upon the ſame foot, in point of neceſſity for obtaining
everlaſting happineſs, with juſtification by the Surety ; which
the frame of the words, being as follows, will well admit, viz.
" Of free juſtification through our bleſſed Surety the Lord Jeſus
Chriſt, received by faith alone; and of the neceſſity of an holy
life, in order to the obtaining of everlaſting happineſs." Moreover, That the great fundamental of juſtification is laid down in
ſuch general terms, as adverſaries will eaſily agree to, without
mention of the Surety's righteouſneſs, active or paſſive, or the
imputation of either ; eſpecially ſince a motion in open Aſſembly,
for adding the few, but momentuous words, IMPUTED RIGHTE-
OUSNESS, was ſlighted. And finally, That that act is ſo little
adapted to the end it is now given out to have been deſigned for ;
viz A teſtimony of the ſupreme Godhead of our glorious God
and Saviour Jeſus Chriſt ; and againſt Arianiſm ; eſpecially ſince
not the leaſt intimation or warning againſt that damnable hereſy
is to be found in the act itſelf; nor was made to that Aſſembly
in paſſing of it.

To the query, we anſwer, That we cordially and ſincerely
own a holy life or good works, NECESSARY, as an acknowledg-
ment of God's ſovereignty, and in obedience to his command ;
" For this is the will of God, even our ſanctification:" and, by
a ſpecial ordination, he has appointed believers to walk in them:
NECESSARY, for glorifying God before the world, and ſhewing
the virtues of him, who hath called us out of darkneſs into this
marvellous light: NECESSARY, as being the end of our election,
our redemption, effectual calling and regeneration; for, " the
Father choſe us in Chriſt, before the foundation of the world,
that we ſhould be holy : The Son gave himſelf for us, that he
might redeem us from all iniquity, and purify to himſelf a
peculiar people zealous of good works " And by the holy
Spirit we are created in Chriſt Jeſus unto them: NECESSARY,
as expreſſions of our gratitude to our great Benefactor; for,
being bought with a price, we are no more our own, but henceforth in a moſt peculiar manner bound, in our bodies, and in our
ſpirits, which are his, to glorify, and by all poſſible ways, to
teſtify our thankſgiving to our Lord Redeemer and Ranſomer;
" to him who ſpared not his own Son, but gave him up to the
death for us all; to him, who humbled himſelf, and became
obedient unto death, even the death of the croſs, for us."
NECESSARY, as being the deſign, not only of the word, but
of all ordinances and providences ; even that as " he who has

called

called is holy, fo we fhould be holy in all madner of converfation." NECESSARY again, for evidencing and confirming our
faith, good works being the breath, the native offspring and iffue
of it: NECESSARY, for making our calling and election fure;
for they are, though no plea, yet, a good evidence for heaven;
or an argument confirming our affurance and hope of falvation.
Neceffary, to the maintaining of inward peace and comfort,
tho' not as the ground or foundation, yet as effects, fruits, and
concomitants of faith: Neceffary, in order to our entertaining
communion with God, even in this life; for, "If we fay, we
have fellowfhip with him, and walk in darknefs, we lie, and do
not the truth." Neceffary, to the efcaping of judgments, and
to the enjoying of many promifed bleffings; particularly there
is a neceffity of order and method, that one be holy ere he can
be admitted to fee and enjoy God in heaven; that being a difpofing mean, preparing for the falvation of it, and the King's
high-way chalked out for the redeemed to walk in to the city.
Neceffary, to adorn the gofpel, and grace our holy calling and
profeffion. Neceffary further, for the edification, good, and
comfort of fellow-believers. Neceffary, to prevent offence,
and to ftop the mouths of the wicked; to win likewife the
unbelieving, and to commend Chrift, and his ways, to their
confciences. Neceffary finally, for the eftablifhment, fecurity,
and glory of churches and nations. Though we firmly believe
holinefs neceffary upon all thefe, and more accounts, and that
the Chriftian ought to live in the continued exercife of gofpel-
repentance, which is one main conftituent of gofpel-holinefs;
yet we dare not fay, A holy life is neceffary in order to the
obtaining of eternal happinefs. For, to fay nothing of the more
grofs fenfe of thefe words, (manifeftly injurious to the free grace
of our Lord Jefus Chrift, by faith in whofe righteoufnefs alone
we are appointed to obtain falvation, from firft to laft) which
yet is obvious enough, though we are far from imputing it to
the Affembly; we cannot, however they may be explained into
an orthodox meaning, look upon them as wholefome words,
fince they have at leaft an appearance of evil, being fuch a way
of expreffion, as Proteftant churches and divines, knowing the
ftrong natural byafs in all men towards feeking falvation, not
by faith in our Lord Jefus Chrift, but by works of righteoufnefs
done by themfelves, and the danger of fymbolizing with Papifts,
and other enemies of the grace of the gofpel, have induftrioufly
fhunned to ufe, on that head: They chufing rather to call
holinefs and good works neceffary duties of the perfons juftified
and faved, than conditions of falvation; confequents and effects
of falvation already obtained, or antecedents, difpofing and
preparing the fubject for the falvation to be obtained, than any
fort of caufes, or proper means of obtaining the poffeffion of

fal-salvation; which last honour, the scripture, for the high praise and glory of sovereign grace, seems to have reserved peculiarly unto faith: And rather to say, that holiness is necessary in them that shall be saved, than necessary to salvation: That we are saved, not by good works, but rather to them, as fruits and effects of saving grace; or that holiness is necessary unto salvation, not so much as a mean to the end, as a part of the end itself; which part of our salvation is necessary to make us meet for the other, that is yet behind

Wherefore, since this way of speaking of holiness with respect to salvation, is, we conceive, without warrant in the holy scripture, dissonant from the doctrinal standards of our own and other reformed churches, as well as from the chosen and deliberate speech of reformed divines treating on these heads; and since it, being at best but PROPOSITO MALE SONANS, may easily be mistaken, and afterwards improved, as a shade or vehicle, for conveying corrupt sentiments, anent the influence of works upon salvation: We cannot but reckon preaching the necessity of holiness in such terms, to be of some dangerous consequence to the doctrine of free grace. In which apprehension we are the more confirmed, that at this day the doctrine of Christ, and his free grace, both as to the purity and efficacy of the same, seems to be much on the wane, and popery, with other dangerous errors and heresies destructive of it, on the waxing; which certainly calls aloud to the churches of Christ, and to his ministers in particular, for the more zeal, watchfulness, and caution, with reference to the interests of truth; and that especially at such a time, " Cùm hereticis, nec nomina " habeamus communia, ne eorum errori favere videamur."

If in any case, certainly in framing acts and standards of doctrine, there is great need of delicacy in the choice of words: For the words of the Holy Ghost in scripture, under which we include such as in meaning and import are equivalent to them, being an ordinance of divine institution, for preserving the truth of the gospel, if these be once altered or varied, all the wisdom and vigilance of men will be ineffectual to that end. And it is well known, by costly experience to the churches of Christ, that their falling in with the language or phrase of corrupt teachers, instead of serving the interest of truth, which never looks so well as in its own native simplicity, does but grieve the stable and judicious, stagger the weak, betray the ignorant: and, instead of gaining, harden and open the mouths of adversaries. And that it is said in a text, " They do it to obtain a corruptible crown, but we an uncorruptible," will not warrant the manner of speech in the query: For the word, in the original, signifies only to Receive or Apprehend, being accordingly rendred in all Latin versions we have seen, and in

our

our own tranflation, in the verfe immediately preceding, viz. " On receiveth the prize;" and though the word did fignify to OBTAIN, in the moft ftrict and proper fenfe, it could not make for the purpofe, unlefs it were meant of the believer's obtaining the incorruptible crown, not by faith, but by works. And that an ill-chofen word in a ftandard may prove more dangerous to the truth, than one not fo juftly rendred in a tranflation, with feveral other things on this head, might be made very evident, were it not that we have been, we fear, tedious on it already.

Query VIII *Is knowledge, and perfuafion that Chrift died for me, and that he is mine, and whatever he did and fuffered, he did and fuffered for me, the dir. ct act of faith, whereby a finner is united to Chrift, interefted in him, inftated in God's covenant of grace? Or, is that knowledge a perfu fion included in the very effence of that juftifying act of faith?*

Anf. The query, it is evident, exceedingly narrows the import and defign of the Reprefentation in the place referred to: Par 7. For there we affert nothing pofitively concerning the paffages relating to faith, but remonftrate againft condemning them, as what to us feemed to hurt the appropriating act of faith, and to fix a blot upon the reformation, reformed churches and divines, who had generally taught concerning faith, as in the condemned paffages; all which we might fay, without determining whether the perfuafion fpoke of in the query, was the very direct and formal act of juftifying faith, yea or no. But now, fince the query is put fo clofs, and fince the matter in queftion is no other than the old proteftant doctrine on that head, as we fhall endeavour to make appear, the reverend commiffion, we humbly conceive, cannot take it amifs, we, in the Firft place, enquire into the true fenfe and meaning of this way of fpeaking of faith, that we are now queftioned about.

The main of the condemned paffages, the query refers to, runs not in the order therein fet down, but as follows: " Believe on the Lord Jefus Chrift, and thou fhalt be faved; that is, be verily perfuaded in your heart that Chrift Jefus is yours, and that you fhall have life and falvation by him; That whatever Chrift did for the redemption of mankind, he did it for you;" being in matter the fame with what has been commonly taught in the proteftant churches, and in words of the renown'd Mr. John Rogers of Dodham (a man fo noted for orthodoxy, holinefs, and the Lord's countenancing of his miniftry, that no found proteftants in Britain or Ireland, of what denomination foever, would in the age wherein he lived, have taken upon them

them to condemn as erroneous) his definition of faith, which we have as follows; "A particular persuasion of my heart, That Christ Jesus is mine, and that I shall have life and salvation by his means; That whatsoever Christ did for the redemption of mankind, he did it for me." Doctrine of Faith, page 23. Where one may see, though the difference in words be almost none at all, yet it runs rather stronger with him, than in the Marrow.

In which account of saving faith, we have, First. The general nature of it, viz. A real persuasion, agreeing to all sorts of faith whatsoever; for, it is certain, whatever one believes, he is verily persuaded of. More particularly, it is a persuasion in the heart, whereby it is distinguished from a general dead, and naked assent in the head, which one gives to things that no way affect him, because he reckons they do not concern him: " But with the heart man believes" here; " If thou believest with all thine heart," says the scripture. Acts viii. 37. Rom. x. 10. For as a man's believing in his heart the dreadful tidings of the law, or its curse, imports not only an assent to them as true, but a horror of them as evil; so here, the being persuaded in one's heart of the glad tidings of the gospel, bears not only an assent unto them as true, but a relish of them as good.

Then we have the most special nature of it, viz. An appropriating persuasion, or a persuasion, with application to a person's self, that Christ is his, &c. The particulars whereof are, First, That Christ is yours; the ground of which persuasion is the offer and grant of Christ as a Saviour in the word, to be believed in for salvation, by all to whom the gospel is made known: By which offer, and setting forth of Christ as a Saviour, though before we believe, we wanting union with him, have no actual or saving interest in him; yet he is in some sense ours, namely, so as it is lawful and warrantable for us, not for fallen angels, to take possession of him, and his salvation, by faith; without which, our common interest in him as a Saviour, by virtue of the offer and grant in the word, will avail us nothing. But though the call and offer of the gospel, being really particular, every one, both in point of duty, and in point of interest, ought to appropriate, apply, or make his own the thing offered by believing, they having good and sufficient ground and warrant in the word so to do; yet it is either neglected and despised, or the truth and sincerity of it suspected and called in question, until the Holy Spirit, by setting home the word of the gospel with such a measure of evidence and power as is effectual, satisfies the convinced sinner, that, with application to himself in particular, " it is a faithful saying, worthy of all acceptation, that Jesus Christ came to save sinners;" and enables him to believe it. Thus the persuasion of faith is begot, which is always proportioned to the measure of evidence and power from above, that sovereign grace is pleased to put forth for working of it.

The

The next branch of the persuasion is, That you shall have life and salvation by him," namely, the life of holiness, as well as of happiness; salvation from sin, as well as from wrath, not in heaven only, but begun, carried on here, and compleated hereafter: The true notion of life and salvation, according to the scriptures, and as Protestant divines are wont to explain it. Wherefore this persuasion of faith is inconsistent with an unwillingness to part with sin, a bent or purpose of heart to continue in it. There can be little question, we apprehend, whether this branch of the persuasion belongs to the nature of justifying faith: For salvation being above all things in a sensible sinner's eye, he can never believe any thing to his satisfaction, without he sees ground to believe comfortably concerning it: Few therefore will, we conceive, differ from Dr. Collin's laying it down as a conclusion on this very head, namely, " That a Christian cannot have true, saving, justifying faith, unless he doth (I, says ne, do not say, unless he think he doth, or unless he faith he doth, but unless he doth) believe, and is persuaded that God will pardon his sins " (Cordial, part I page 208.) Further, this believing on the Son for life and salvation, is the same with receiving of him (as this last is explained by the Holy Spirit himself. John i. 12.) and likewise evidently bears the soul's resting on Christ for salvation: For it is not possible to conceive a soul resting on Christ for salvation, without a persuasion that it shall have life and salvation by him; namely, a persuasion of the same measure and degree, as resting is.

The third branch of the persuasion, That whatsoever Christ did for the redemption of mankind, he did it for you; being much the same in other words, with these of the apostle, " Who loved me, and gave himself for me;" and coming in the last place, we think none will question, but whosoever believes in the manner before explained, may, and ought to believe this in the like measure, and in the same order: And, it is certain, all who receive and rest on Christ for salvation, believe it, if not explicitly, yet virtually and really.

Now, as this account of justifying faith runs in terms much less strong, than these of many eminent Protestant divines, who used to define it by a persuasion of God's love; of his special mercy to one's self; of the remission of his sins, &c. so it is the same for substance and matter, though the words be not the same, with that of our Shorter Catechism, viz A receiving and resting upon Christ alone for salvation, as he is offered to us in the gospel. Where it is evident, the offer of Christ to us, tho' mentioned in the last place, is to be believed first: For till the soul be persuaded, that Christ crucified is in the gospel set forth, offered, and exhibited to it, as it expressed by same, there can be no believing on him: And when the offer is brought home to a perſon by the Holy Ghoſt, there will be a meaſure of per-ſuaſion that Chriſt is his, as above explained: And that receiv-ing, or believing in, and reſting on him for life and ſalvation by him, was ſaid already. But more directly to the query,

We anſwer, 1mo, Since our reformers and their ſucceſſors, ſuch as Luther, Calvin, Melancton, Beza, Bullinger Bucer, Knox, Craig, Melvil, Bruce, Davidſon, Forbes, &c. Men emi-nently endued with the Spirit of truth, and who fetch their notions of it immediately from the fountain of the holy ſcripture, the moſt eminent doctors and profeſſors of theology. that have been in the Proteſtant churches, ſuch as, Urſinus, Zanchius, Junius, Piſcator, Rollock. Danæus, Wendelinus, Chamierus, Sharpius, Bodius, Pareus, Altingius, Englandii (Giſbertus and Jacobus) Arnoldus, Mareſius, the four profeſſors of Leyden, viz. Wallæus, Heidegerus, Eſſenius, Turrentinus &c. with many eminent Britiſh divines, ſuch as, Perkins, Pemble, Willet, Gouge, Roberts, Burgeſs, Owen, &c. The churches them-ſelves of Helvetia. the Palatinate, France, Holland, England, Ireland, Scotland, in their ſtandards of doctrine; all the Lutheran churches, who in point of orthodoxy and faith, are ſecond to none: the renowned ſynod of Dort, made up of eminent divines, called and commiſſionate from ſeven reformed ſtates and king-doms, beſides theſe of the ſeveral provinces of the Netherlands. Since theſe, we ſay all of them ſtand for that ſpecial fiducia, confidence, or appropriating perſuaſion of faith ſpoke of in the condemned paſſages of the Marrow, upon which this query is raiſed; the ſynod of Dort, beſides the minds of the ſeveral delegates on this head, in their ſeveral ſuffrages anent the five articles, declaring themſelves plainly both in their final deciſions concerning the ſaid articles, and in their ſolemn and ample approbation of the Palatine catechiſm, as agreeable to the word of God in all things, and as containing nothing that ought to be either altered or amended: Which catechiſm being full and plain, as to this perſuaſion of faith, has been commented up-a by many great divines, received by moſt of all the reformed churches, as a moſt excellent compend of the orthodox Chriſtian doctrine; and particularly by the church of Scotland, as the reverend Mr. Robert Wodrow, lately told his preſent majeſty King George, in the dedication of his hiſtory: And ſince we, with this whole church and nation are, by virtue of the awful tie of the oath of God in our National Covenant, bound ever to abhor and detest the Popiſh general and doubtſome faith, with all the erroneous decrees of Trent;" among which (in op-poſition to the ſpecial FIDUCIA of faith therein condemned) this is eſtabliſhed; being by Proteſtants; ſo called, mainly for their denying and oppoſing the confidence and perſuaſion of faith, with application to one's ſelf, now in queſtion; by which

renun-

renunciation our forefathers, no doubt, pointed at, and asserted
to be held and professed as God's undoubted truth and verity,
that particular and confident, or assured faith then commonly
known and maintained in this church. as standing plain and
express in her standards; t the profession and defence of which,
they in the same c venant promising and swearing by the great
name of the Lord our God, bound themselves and us: And
since the same persuasion of faith, however the way of speaking
on that head is come to be somewhat altered, was never by any
judicatory of a reformed church, until now, denied or condemned. Considering all these things. we say, and of what
dangerous, consequence such a judicial alteration may be, we
cannot, we dare not consent unto the condemnation of that
point of doctrine: For we cannot think of charging error and
delusion in a matter of such importance, upon so many Protestant divines, eminent for holiness and learning: upon the
Protestant churches; and upon our own forefathers, so signally
owned of the Lord; and also on the standards of Protestant
doctrine in this church, for nigh an hundred years after her
reformation: Else, if we shou'd thus speak, we are persuaded
we should offend against the generation of his children. Nor
can it ever en er into our minds, that the famous Assembly of
Westminster had it so much as once in their thoughts to depart
in this point from the doctrine of their own, and of this church,
which they were all of them by the strongest ties bound to
maintain: Or to go off from the synod of Dort, which had but
so lately before them settled the Protestant principles as to
doctrine; and by so doing, yield up to Socinians, Arminians,
and Papists, what all of them have a mortal aversion to, namely,
the special FIDUCIA. or appropriating persuasion of faith, which
Protestant divines before and since that time, contended for to
their utmost, as being not only a precious truth, but a point of
vast consequence to religion. And we are sure, the Assemblies
of this church understood, and received their Confessions and
Catechisms, Larger and Shorter, as intirely consistent with our
Confessions and Catechisms, before that time, as we have already made evident in our Representation, from the acts of
Assembly, receiving and approving the Westminster Confession
and Catechisms.

Answer ado, It is to be considered, that most of the words of
the Holy Ghost made use of in the Old and New Testament,
for expressing the nature of faith and believing, do import the
confidence or persuasion in question: And that confidence and
trust in the Old Testament, are expounded by faith and believing in the New; and the same things attributed to the former;
that diffidence and doubting are in their nature, acts and effects,
contrary to faith: that, peace and joy are the native effects of
believ-

believing: that the promises of the gospel, and Christ in his priestly office therein held forth, are the proper object of justifying faith: that, faithfulness in God, and faith in the believer, being relatives, and the former the ground of the latter, our faith should answer to his faithfulness, by trusting to his word of promise for the sake of it: That, it is certain, a believer in the exercise of justifying faith, does believe something with reference to his own salvation, upon the ground of God's person whatsoever, does, or can believe; which if it be not to this purpose, that now Christ is and will be a Saviour to him, that he shall have life and salvation by him, we are utterly at a loss to conceive what it can be: That, persuasion, confidence, and assurance, are so much attributed to faith in the scripture, and the saints in scripture ordinarily express themselves in their addresses to God, in words of appropriation: And finally, That according to our Larger Catechism, faith justifies a sinner in the sight of God, as an instrument, receiving and applying Christ, and his righteousness held forth in the promise of the gospel, and resteth thereupon for pardon of sin, and for the accepting and accounting one's person righteous before God for salvation; the which, how faith can do without some measure of the confidence or appropriating persuasion we are now upon, seems extreme hard to conceive. Upon these considerations, and others, too long to be here inserted, we cannot but think, that confidence, or trust in Jesus Christ, as our Saviour, and the free grace and mercy of God in him as crucified, offered to us in the gospel for salvation (including justification, sanctification, and future glory) upon the ground and security of the divine faithfulness, plighted in the gospel-promise; and upon the warrant of the divine call and command to believe in the name of the Son of God: Or, which is the same in other words, A persuasion of life and salvation, from the free love and mercy of God, in and through Jesus Christ; a crucified Saviour offered to us upon the security and warrant aforesaid, is the very direct, uniting, justifying and-appropriating act of faith, whereby the convinced sinner becomes possest of Christ, and his saving benefits, instated in God's covenant and family: Taking this always along, as supposed, that all is set home and wrought by the Holy Spirit, who brings Christ, his righteousness, salvation, and the whole fulness, nigh to us in the promise and offer of the gospel; clearing at the same time our right and warrant to intermeddle with all, without fear of vitious intromission, encouraging and enabling to a measure of confident application, and taking home of all to ourselves freely, without money, and without price.

This confidence, persuasion, or whatever other name it may be called by, we take to be the very same with what our Con-

feffion

feffion and Catechifm call accepting, receiving, and refting on Chrift offered in the gofpel for falvation; and with what pol mic and practical divines call " Fiducia fpecialis mifericordiæ, fiducial application, fiducial apprehenfion, fiducial adherence, recumbence affiance, fiducial acquiefcence, appropriating perfuafion, &c " All which, if duly explained, would iffue in a meafure of this confidence or perfuafion we have been fpeaking of. However, we are fully fatisfied, this is what our fathers, and the body of proteftant divines, fpeaking with the fcriptures, called the Affurance of Faith. That once burning and fhining light of this church, Mr John Davidfon, though in hi- catechifm he defires faith by a hearty affurance, that our fins are freely forgiven us in Chrift; or, a fure perfuafion of the heart, that Chrift by his death and refurrection hath taken away our fins, and clothing us with his own perfect righteoufnefs, has throughly reftored us to the favour of God; which he reckoned all one with a hearty receiving of Chrift offered in the gofpel for the remiffion of fins: Yet in a former part of the fame catechifm, he gives us to underftand what fort of affurance and perfuafion it was, he meant, as follows; " And certain it is, fays he, that both the inlightning of the mind to acknowledge the truth of the promife of falvation to us in Chrift: and the fealing up of the certainty thereof in our hearts and minds, (of the whilk twa parts, as it were, faith confifts) are the work and effects of the Spirit of God." In like manner, in our confeffion of Faith, Art 3. 12. it is called, " An affured faith in the promife of God, revealed to us in his word; by which faith we apprehend Chrift Jefus, with the graces and benefits promifed in him —— This faith, and the affurance of the fame proceeds not from flefh and blood " And in our firft catechifm, commonly called Calvin's catechifm, faith is defined by a fure perfuafion and ftedfaft knowledge of God's tender love towards us, according as he has plainly uttered in the gofpel, that he will be a Fa her and Saviour to us, through the means of Jefus Chrift. And again, faith which God's Spirit worketh in our hearts, affuring of God's promifes made to us in his holy gofpel. In the Summula Catechifmi, or Rudimenta Pietatis, to the Queftion, Quid eft fides? The Anfwer is, Cum mihi perfuadeo Deum me omnefque fanctos amare, nobifque Chriftum cum omnibus fuis bonis gratis donare; and in the margin, Nam in fide duplex perfuafio. 1 De amore Dei erga nos. 2. De Dei beneficus qua ex amore fluunt, Chrifto nimirum, cum omnibus fui bonis. &c. And to that Queftion, Quomodo fide percipimus, & nobis applicamus corpus Chrifti crucifixi? The Anfwer is, Dum nobis perfuademus Chrifti mortem & crucifixionem non minue ad nos pertinere quam fi ipfi nos pro peccatis noftris crucifixi effemus. Perfuafio autem hæc eft veræ fidei. From all which it is evident,

they

they held, that a belief of the promiſes of the goſpel, with appliꝛ
cation, to one's ſelf, or a confidence in a crucified Saviour, for
a man's own ſalvation, is the very eſſence of juſtifying faith :
or, that we become actually poſſeſſed of Chriſt, remiſſion of
ſins, &c. in and by the act of believing, or confidence in him,
as above explaind. And this with them was the aſſurance of
faith, which widely differs from the Antinomian ſenſe of the
aſſurance or perſuaſion of faith; which is, that Chriſt, and pardon
of ſin, are ours, no leſs before believing than after; a ſenſe which
we heartily diſclaim.

Whether theſe words in the query, viz. Or, is that knowledge
a perſuaſion included in the very eſſence of that juſtifying act of
faith? be exegetic of the query; We anſwer, That we have
already explained the perſuaſion of faith by us held, and do
think, that in the language of faith. though not in the language
of philoſophy, knowledge and perſuaſion, relating to the ſame
object, go hand in hand in the ſame meaſure and degree.

It is evident, That the confidence or perſuaſion of faith, for
which we plead, includes, or neceſſarily and infallibly infers
conſent and reſting, together with all the bleſſed fruits and
effects of faith, in proportion to the meaſure of it. And that
we have mentioned conſent, we cannot but be the more confirmed in this matter, when we conſider, That ſuch a noted
perſon as Mr. Baxter, though he had made the marriage conſent
to Chriſt, as King and Lord. the formal act of juſtifying faith,
as being an epitome of all goſpel-obedience, including and
binding to all the duties of the married ſtate, and ſo giving right
to all the privileges; and had thereby, as well as by his other
dangerous notions about juſtification and other points connec-
ted therewith, ſcattered through his works, corrupted the
fountain, and endangered the faith of many.; yet, after all,
came to be of another mind, and had the humility to tell the
world ſo much: For Mr. Croſs informs us, (Sermon on Rom.
iv. page 148.) That Mr Baxter, in his little book againſt
Dr. Criſp's error, ſays, " I formerly believed the formal nature
of faith to ly in conſent; but now I recant it: I believe (ſays he)
it lies in truſt; this makes the right to ly in the object; for it is,
I depend on Chriſt as the matter or merit of my pardon, my life,
my crown, my glory."

There are two things further, concerning this perſuaſion of
faith, that would be adverted to: One is, That it is not axio-
matical, but real. i. e. the ſinner has not always, at his firſt
cloſing with Chriſt, nor afterwards, ſuch a clear, ſteady, and
full perſuaſion that Chriſt is his, that his ſins are forgiven, and
he eventually ſhall be ſaved; as that he dare profeſs the ſame
to others, or even poſitively aſſert it within himſelf: Yet, upon
the firſt ſaving manifeſtation of Chriſt to him, ſuch a perſuaſion

and

and humble confidence is begotten, as is real and relieving, and particular as to himself, and his own salvation, and which works a proportionable hope as to the issue; though through the humbling impressions he has of himself, and his own guilt at the time, the awe of God's majesty, justice, and holiness on his spirit, and his indistinct knowledge of the doctrine of the gospel, with the grounds and warrants of believing therein contained, he fears to express it directly and particularly of himself. The Other is, That, whatever is said of the habit, actings, strength, weakness, and intermittings of the exercise of saving faith, the same is to be said of this persuasion in all points. From all which, it is evident, the doubts, fears, and darkness, so frequently to be found in true believers, can very well consist with this persuasion in the same subject: For though they may be and often are in the believer, yet they are not of his faith, which in its nature and exercise is as opposite to them, as light is to darkness, the flesh to the spirit; which though they be in the same subject, yet as contrary the one to the other, Gal. v. 17. And therefore faith wrestles against them, though with various success, it being sometimes so far overcome and brought at under by the main force, and much superior strength of prevailing unbelief, that it cannot be discerned more than the fire is, when covered with ashes, or the sun, when wrapt up in thick clouds. The confidence and persuasion of faith, being in many, at first especially, but as the grain of mustard-seed cast into the ground, or like a spark amidst the troubled sea of all manner of corruption and lusts, where the rowling waves of unbelieving doubts and fears, hellish temptations and suggestions, and the like, moving on the face of that depth, are every now and then going over it; and, were there not a divine hand and care engaged for its preservation, would effectually extinguish and bury it: what wonder that in such a case it many times cannot be discerned? Yet will it still hold so much of the exercise of justifying faith, so much persuasion. Yea, not only may a believer have this persuasion, and not know of it for the time, (as say Collins, Roberts, Amesius, and others, who distinguish the persuasion from the sense of it) but he, being under the power of temptation and confusion of mind, may resolutely deny he has any such persuasion or confidence; while it is evident to others at the same time, by its effects, that he really has it: For which, one may, among others, see the holy and learned Mr Halyburton, in his Inquiry into the nature of God's act of justification, page 27. And if one would see the consistence of faith's persuasion with doubting, well discoursed and illustrated, he may consult Downhame's Christian Warfare, Part 2. lib. 2. page 134; &c. But we

Answer

Answer 3dly, There is a full persuasion and assurance, by reflection, spiritual argumentation, or inward sensation, which we are far from holding to be of the essence of faith; but this last, being mediate, and collected by inference, as we gather the cause from such signs and effects as give evidence of it, is very different from that confidence or persuasion, by divines called the Assurance of Faith. Sanctification, says Rutherford, does not evidence justification, as faith doth evidence it, with such a sort of clearness, as light evidenceth colours, though it be no sign, or evident mark of them; but as smoke evidenceth fire, and as the morning star, in the east, evidenceth the sun will shortly rise; or as the streams prove there is a head-spring whence they issue; tho' none of these make what they evidence visible to the eye: So doth sanctification give evidence of justification, only as marks, signs, effects, give evidence of the cause. He calls it a light of arguing, and of heavenly logic, by which we know, That we know God, by the light of faith, because we keep his commandments. In effect, says he, " we know rather the person must be justified, in whom these gracious evidences are by hear-say, report, or consequence, than that we know, or see justification or faith itself in abstracto: But the light of faith, the testimony of the spirit by the operation of free grace, will cause us, as it were, with our eyes see justification and faith, not by report, but as we see the sun-light. Again, he says, We never had a question with Antinomians, touching the first assurance of justification, such as is proper to the light of faith. He (Cornwall) might have spared all his arguments, to prove that we are first assured of our justification by faith, not by good works; for we grant the arguments, of one sort of assurance, which is proper to faith; and they prove nothing against another sort of assurance by signs and effects, which is also divine " Further, as to the difference between these two kinds of assurance; the assurance of faith has its object and foundation without the man, but that of sense has them within him : The Assurance of Faith looks to Christ, the promise and covenant of God, and says, " This is all my salvation, God has spoken in his holiness, I will rejoice." But the Assurance of Sense looks inward at the works of God, such as the person's own graces, attainments, experiences, and the like. The Assurance of Faith giving an evidence to things not seen, can claim an interest in, and plead a saving relation to a hiding, withdrawing God; Zion said, " My Lord hath forgotten me " And the spouse, " I opened to my beloved; but my beloved had withdrawn himself, and was gone." So he may be a forgetting and withdrawing God to my feeling; and yet to my faith, my God, and my Lord, still, says holy Rutherford; even the wife may believe the angry and forsaking husband, is still

T t 3   her

her hufband. But, on the other hand, the affurance of fenfe is the evidence of things feen and felt. The one fays, " I take him for mine;" the other, fays, " I feel he is mine:" The one fays with the church, " My God (though he cover himfelf with a cloud, that my prayer cannot pafs through, yet) will hear me;" The other, " My God has heard me ;" The one fays, " He will bring me forth to the light, and I fhall behold his righte-oufnefs ;" The other, " He has brought me forth to the light, and I do behold his righteoufnefs:" The one fays, " Though he fhould kill me, yet will I truft in him;" The other, " He fmiles and fhines on me, therefore will I love him, and truft in him."

Upon the whole, we humbly conceive, Were the nature and grounds of faith's perfuafion, more narrowly and impartially, under the guidance of the Spirit of truth, fearch'd into, and laid open ; it would, inftead of difcouraging weak Chriftans, exceedingly tend to the ftrengthning and increafe of faith ; and confequently have a mighty influence on fpiritual comfort, and true gofpel-holinefs, which will always be found to bear pro-portion to faith, as effects do to the efficacy and influence of their caufes.

Query IX. *What is that act of faith, by which a finner appropriates Chrift, and his faving benefits to himfelf ?*

Anfw. This queftion being plainly and fully anfwered, in what is faid on the immediately foregoing, we refer thereto, and proceed to the tenth.

Query X. *Whether the revelation of the divine will, in the word, affording a warrant to offer Chrift unto all, and a warrant to all to receive him, can be faid to be the Father's making a deed of gift and grant of Chrift unto all mankind ? Is this grant made to all mankind by fovereign grace ? And, whether is it abfolute or conditional ?*

Anfw. Here we are directed to that part of our Reprefenta-tion, where we complain that the following paffage is condem-ned, viz. " The Father hath made a deed of gift or grant unto all mankind, that whofoever of them fhall believe in his Son, fhall not perifh ;" and where we fay, " That this treatment of the faid paffage feems to incroach on the warrant aforefaid, and alfo upon fovereign grace, which hath made this grant, not to devils, but to men, in terms than which none can be imagined more extenfive," Par 8. agreeable to what we have already faid in our Reprefentation. We anfwer to the firft part of the queftion, that by the deed of gift or grant unto all mankind, we underftand

ſtand no more than the revelation of the divine will in the word, affording warrant to offer Chriſt to all, and a warrant to all to receive him. For although we believe the purchaſe and application of redemption, to be peculiar to the elect, who were given by the Father to Chriſt, in the counſel of peace ; yet the warrant to receive him, is common to all : miniſters, by virtue of the commiſſion they have received from their great Lord and Maſter, are authorized and inſtructed to go to preach the goſpel to every creature, *i e.* to make a full, free and unhampered offer of him, his grace, and righteougneſs, and ſalvation, to every rational ſoul, to whom they may in providence have acceſs to ſpeak. And though we had a voice like a trumpet, that could reach all the corners of the earth, we think we would be bound, by virtue of our commiſſion, to lift it up, and ſay, ' To you, O men, do we call, and our voice is to the ſons of men. God hath ſo loved the world, that he gave his only-begotten Son, that whoſoever believes in him, ſhould not periſh, but have everlaſting life,' John iii 16. And although this deed of gift and grant, 'That whoſoever believeth in Chriſt, ſhall not periſh, &c.' is neither in our Repreſentation, nor in the paſſages of the book condemned on that head, called a " Deed of gift, and grant of Chriſt:" yet, being required to give our judgment in this point, we think, that agreeable to the holy ſcriptures, it may be ſo called, as particulary appears from the text laſt cited, John iii. 16. where, by the 'giving of Chriſt," we underſtand, not only his eternal deſtination by the Father, to be the Redeemer of an elect world, and his giving him unto the death for them, in the fulneſs of time : but more eſpecially, a giving of him in the word, unto all, to be received and believed in : The giving here, cannot be a giving in poſſeſſion, which is peculiar only unto them, who actually believe, but it muſt be ſuch a giving, granting, or offering, as warrants a man to believe or receive the gift ; and muſt therefore be anterior to actual believing; This is evident enough from the text itſelf, He gave him, " That whoſoever believeth in him, ſhould not periſh, &c." The context alſo, to us, puts it beyond controverſy ; the brazen ſerpent was given, and lifted up as a common good to the whole camp of Iſrael, that whoſoever in all the camp, being ſtung by the fiery ſerpents, looking thereunto, might not die, but live ; So here, Chriſt is given to a loſt world, in the word, that whoſoever believes in him, ſhould not periſh, &c. And in this reſpect, we think, Chriſt is a common Saviour, and his ſalvation is a common ſalvation ; and it is " glad tidings of great joy, unto all people," that unto us (not to angels that fell) this Son is given, and this Child is born, whoſe name is called Wonderful, &c." Iſa. ix. 6.

We

We have a scripture also to this purpose, John vi. 32. where Christ speaking to a promiscuous multitude, makes a comparison between himself and the manna that fell about the tents of Israel in the wilderness, says, " My Father giveth you the true bread from heaven." As the simple raining of the manna about their camp, is called a Giving of it, Verse 31. before it was tasted, or fed upon ; so the very revelation and offer of Christ is called (according to the judicious Calvin on the place) a Giving of him, e're he be received and believed on.

Of his Giving of Christ to mankind lost, we read also, 1 John v 11 ' And this is the record, that God hath given unto us eternal life ; and this life is in his son.' This Giving in the text, is not, we conceive, a giving in possession, in greater or lesser measure ; but a Giving by way of grant and offer, whereupon one may warrantably take possession ; and the party to whom, is not the election only, but lost mankind : For the record of God here, must be such a thing as warrants all to believe on the Son of God. But it can be no such warrant, to tell, That God hath given eternal life to the elect : For the making of a gift to a certain select company of persons, can never be a warrant for all men to receive or take possession of it. This will be further evident, if we consider, That the great sin of unbelief lies, in not believing this record of God ; " He that believes not, hath made God a liar, (says the apostle, Ver 10.) because he believes not the record that God gave of his Son ;" and then it followeth, Ver. 11. " And this is the record, that God hath given to us eternal life, &c." Now, are we to think, that the rejecting of the record of God, is a bare disbelieving of this proposition, That God hath given eternal life unto the elect? No surely ; for the most desperate unbelievers, such as Judas, and others, believe this ; and their belief of it adds to their anguish and torment: Or, do they by believing this, set to their seal that God is true? No, they still continue, notwithstanding of all this, to make him a liar, in not believing this record of God, That to lost mankind, and to themselves in particular, God hath given eternal life, by way of grant, so as they, as well as others, are warranted and welcome ; and every one to whom it comes, on their peril, required by faith to receive, or take possession of it. By not receiving this gifted and offered remedy, with application and appropriation. they fly in the face of God's record and testimony ; and therefore do justly and deservedly perish, seeing the righteousness, salvation, and kingdom of God, was brought so near to them, in the free offer of the gospel, and yet they would not take it. The great pinch and strait, we think, of an awakened conscience, does not lie in believing, That God hath given eternal life to the elect ; but in believing or receiving Christ, offered to us in the gospel,

with

with particular application to the man himfelf, in fcripture, called, An eating the flefh, and drinking the blood of the Son of man. And yet, till this difficulty be furmounted, in greater or leffer meafure, he can never be faid to believe in Chrift, or receive and reft upon him for falvation. The very taking or receiving, muft needs prefuppofe a giving of Chrift; and this giving may be, and is for the moft part, where there is no receiving; but there can be no receiving of Chrift for falvation, where there is not revelation of Chrift in the word of the gofpel, affording warrant to receive him, Rom. x 14 and then, by the effectual operation of the Spirit, perfuading and enabling the finner to embrace him upon this warrant and offer: " A man (fays the Spirit of God, John iii. 27.) can receive nothing, except it be given him from heaven." Hence, Mr. Rutherford, in his Chrift dying and drawing, &c. page 442 fays, " That reprobates have as fair a warrant to believe as the elect have.".

.. As to the fecond part of this queftion, to wit, " Is this grant made to all mankind by fovereign grace? And whether is it abfolute or conditional?" We anfwer, That this grant made in common to loft mankind, is from fovereign grace only; and it being minifters warrant to offer Chrift unto all, and people's warrant to receive him, it cannot fail to be abfolutely free; yet, fo as none can be poffeffed of Chrift and his benefits till by faith they receive him

Query XI. *Is the divifion of the law, as explained and applied in the Marrow, to be juftified, and which cannot be rejected without burying feveral gofpel-truths?*

Anfw. We humbly judge, the tripartite divifion of the law, if rightly underftood, may be admitted as orthodox; yet, feeing that which we are concerned with, as contained in our Reprefentation, is only the divifion of the law, into the Law of Works, and the Law of Chrift : we fay, That we are ftill of opinion, that this diftinction of the law is carefully to be maintained; in regard that by the Law of Works, we, according to the fcripture, underftand the Covenant of Works, which believers are wholly and altogether delivered from, although they are certainly under the law of the ten commands in the hand of a Mediator: And if this diftinction of the law thus applied, be overthrown and declared groundlefs, feveral fweet gofpel-truths muft unavoidably fall in the ruins of it. For inftance, if there be no difference put between the law as a covenant, and the law as a rule of life to believers in the hand of Chrift; it muft needs follow, That the law ftill retains its covenant-form with refpect to believers, and that they are ftill under the law in this formality, contrary to fcripture, Rom. vi. 14. and vii. 1, 2, 3. and to the Confeffion of Faith, chap. 19. §. 6. It would a fo

follow, That the fins of believers are ſtill to be looked upon as
breaches of the covenant of works; and conſequently, that
their ſins not only deſerve the wrath and curſe of God, (which
is a moſt certain truth) but alſo makes them actually liable to
the wrath of God, and the pains of hell for ever; which is true
only of them that are in a ſtate of black nature, Leſſer Catechiſm,
Queſt. 19. and contrary to Confeſſion of Faith, Chap. 19. § 1.
It will likewiſe follow, That believers are ſtill to eye God as a
vindictive and wrathful Judge, though his juſtice be fully
ſatisfied in the death and blood of their bleſſed Surety, apprehended by faith. Theſe and many other ſweet goſpel-truths,
we think, fall in the ruins of the foreſaid diſtinction condemned
as groundleſs.

Query XII. _Is the hope of heaven, and fear of hell, to
be excluded from the motives of the believer's obedience?
And if not, how can the Marrow be defended, that expreſly
excludes them, though it ſhould allow of other motives?_

Anſw. Here we are referred to the third particular head,
wherein we think the Marrow injured by the Aſſembly's act,
which for brevity's ſake we do not tranſcribe: But, agreeable
both to our Repreſentation and the ſcope of the Marrow,
We anſwer, That, taking heaven for a ſtate of endleſs felicity,
in the enjoyment of God in Chriſt, we are ſo far from thinking,
that this is to be excluded from being a motive of the believer's
obedience, that we think it the chief end of man, next to the
glory of God, Pſal. lxxiii. 25. " Whom have I in heaven, but
thee? &c" Heaven, inſtead of being a reward to the believer,
would be a deſolate wilderneſs to him, without the enjoyment
of a God in Chriſt; the Lord God and the Lamb are the light
of that place; God himſelf is the portion of his people; he is
their ſhield, and exceeding great reward. The very Cope ſtone
of the happineſs of heaven lies in being for ever with the Lord,
and in beholding of his glory; and this indeed the believer is to
have in his eye, as the recompence of reward; and a noble
motive of obedience: But, to form conceptions of heaven, as a
place of pleaſure and happineſs, without the former views of it,
and to fancy that this heaven is to be obtained by our own
works and doings, is unworthy of a believer, a child of God, in
regard it is ſlaviſh, legal, mercenary, and carnal.

As for the fear of hell its being a motive of the believer's
obedience, we reckon it one of the ſpecial branches of that
glorious liberty wherewith Chriſt hath made his people free,
that they yield obedience to the Lord; not out of ſlaviſh fear of
hell and wrath, but out of a child-like love and willing mind,
Confeſ. Chap. 20. §. 6. " Chriſt hath delivered us out of the
hands

hands of our enemies, that we might serve him without fear, in holiness and righteousness, all the days of our lives," Luke i. 74, 75. A filial fear of God, and of his fatherly displeasure, is worthy of the believer being a fruit of faith, and of the spirit of adoption; but a slavish fear of hell and wrath, from which he is delivered by Christ, is not a fruit of faith, but of unbelief. And in so far as a believer is not drawn with love, but driven on in his obedience with a slavish fear of hell, we think him, in so far, under a spirit of bondage. And judging this to be the Marrow's sense of rewards and punishments with respect to a believer, we think it may and ought to be defended.

And this doctrine, which we apprehend to be the truth, stands supported, not only by scripture and our Confession of Faith, but also by the suffrages of some of our soundest divines; For instance, Mr Rutherford; " Believers (says he) are to be sad for their sins, as offensive to the authority of the Lawgiver, and the love of Christ, though they be not to fear the eternal punishment of them " Christ dying and drawing, &c " p. 513. For sorrow for sin, and fear for sin, are most different to us. Again, says the same author, " Servile obedience, under apprehension of legal terror, was never commanded in the spiritual law of God to the Jews, m re than to us." Trial and triumph, old edit. page 107. Durham, (Loco Citato) " The believer (says he) being delivered from the law as a covenant, his life depends not on the promises annexed to the law, nor is he in danger by threatnings adjoined to it, both these to believers being made void through Christ ". And to conclude, We are clear of Dr. Owen's mind, anent the use of the threatnings of everlasting wrath with reference unto believers, who, tho' he owns them to be declarative of God's hatred of sin, and his will to punish it; yet, in regard the execution of them is inconsistent with the covenant, and God's faithfulness therein, says, " The use of them cannot be to beget in believers an anxious, doubting, solicitous fear about the punishment threatned, grounded on a supposition that the person fearing shall be overtaken with it, or a perplexing fear of hell-fire ; which, though it oft times be a consequence of some of God's dispensations towards us, of our own sins, or the weakness of our faith, is not any where prescribed unto us as a duty, nor is the ingenerating of it in us, the design of any of the threatnings of God " His reasons; together with the nature of that fear, which the threatnings of eternal wrath ought to beget in believers, may be viewed among the rest of the authorities.

These are some thoughts that have offered to us upon the queries. which we lay before the Reverend Commission, with all becoming deference, humbly craving, That charity, which thinketh no evil, may procure a favourable construing of our words, fo as no fenfe may be put upon, nor inference drawn from them, which we never intended. And, in regard the tenor of our doctrine, and our aims in converfation, have (tho' with a mixture of fuch finful weaknefs) been fincerely pointed at the honour of the Lord Jefus, as our King, as well as Prieft, as our fanctification, as well as our righteoufnefs: We cannot but regret our being afperfed, as turning the grace of our God into lafcivioufnefs, and cafting off the obligation of the holy law of the ten commands; being perfuaded that the damnation of fuch, as either do or teach fo, is juft and unavoidable, if mercy prevent it not. But now, if, after this plain and ingenious declaration of our principles, we muft ftill ly under the fame load of reproach, it is our comfort, that we have the teftimony of our confciences clearing us in that matter, and doubt not but the Lord will in due time " bring forth our righteoufnefs as the light, and our judgment as the noon-day." We only add, That we adhere to our Reprefentation and Petition in all points; and fo much the rather, that we have already obferved the fad fruits, and bad improvement made of the Affembly's deed, therein complained of.

Thefe anfwers, contained in this and the fixteen preceeding pages, (viz. of the manufcript given in) are fubfcribed at Edinburgh, March 12th, 1722, by us,

Mr James Hog		Carnock
Thomas Bofton		Etterick
John Williamfon		Innerafk
James Kid		Queensferry
Gabriel Wilfon	Minifter of the Gofpel at	Maxton
Ebenezer Erfkine		Portmoak
Ralph Erfkine		Dumfermline
James Warlaw		
Henry Davidfon		Galafhiels
James Bathgate		Orwel
William Hunter		Lillisleaf

N. B. Mr John Bonar, Minifter of the Gofpel at Torphichen, being detained by indifpofition, could neither attend when the Queries were given, nor the Anfwers returned.

F I N I S.

Lightning Source UK Ltd.
Milton Keynes UK
UKOW06f1855020717
304524UK00019B/575/P